THE UNI

World Politics
INTERESTS, INTERACTIONS, INSTITUTIONS

World Politics
INTERESTS, INTERACTIONS, INSTITUTIONS

Jeffry A. Frieden
HARVARD UNIVERSITY

David A. Lake
UNIVERSITY OF CALIFORNIA, SAN DIEGO

Kenneth A. Schultz
STANFORD UNIVERSITY

W. W. NORTON & COMPANY
NEW YORK LONDON

W. W. Norton & Company has been independent since its founding in 1923, when William Warder Norton and Mary D. Herter Norton first published lectures delivered at the People's Institute, the adult education division of New York City's Cooper Union. The firm soon expanded its program beyond the Institute, publishing books by celebrated academics from America and abroad. By mid-century, the two major pillars of Norton's publishing program—trade books and college texts—were firmly established. In the 1950s, the Norton family transferred control of the company to its employees, and today—with a staff of four hundred and a comparable number of trade, college, and professional titles published each year—W. W. Norton & Company stands as the largest and oldest publishing house owned wholly by its employees.

Editor: Ann Shin
Managing Editor, College: Marian Johnson
Assistant Editor: Mollie Eisenberg
Copy Editor: Alice Vigliani
Production Manager: Eric Pier-Hocking
Design Director: Rubina Yeh
Photo Editor: Stephanie Romeo
Photo Research: Susan Buschhorn
Print Ancillaries Editor: Rachel Comerford
Emedia Editor: Dan Jost
Marketing: Nicole Netherton
Maps: Mapping Specialists Ltd.
Composition: TSI Graphics, Inc.
Manufacturing: Worldcolor—Taunton division

Library of Congress Cataloging-in-Publication Data
Frieden, Jeffry A.
    World politics: interests, interactions, institutions/Jeffry A. Frieden, David A. Lake,
Kenneth A. Schultz—1st ed.
        p. cm.
    Includes bibliographical references and index.
    ISBN: 978-0-393-92709-2 (pbk.)
1. International relations. I. Lake, David A., 1965– II. Schultz, Kenneth A. III. Title.
    JZ1242.F748 2009
    327—dc22
                                                                    2009020706

W. W. Norton & Company, Inc., 500 Fifth Avenue, New York, NY 10110
wwnorton.com

W. W. Norton & Company, Ltd., Castle House, 75/76 Wells Street, London WIT3QT

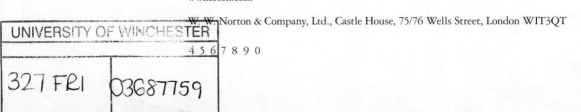

4 5 6 7 8 9 0

CONTENTS IN BRIEF

CONTENTS

Part Three   International Political Economy   214

Chapter 6   International Trade   216

Part Five   Looking Ahead   485

Chapter 13   The Future of International Politics   486

PREFACE

While the process of writing a textbook is a long and winding road, we have been guided throughout by two principles that spurred our enthusiasm for the project and that, we believe, make this textbook special. First, this text is organized around substantive puzzles that draw scholars and students alike to the study of world politics. This is a field that grapples with some of the most interesting and important questions in political science: Why are there wars? Why do countries have a hard time cooperating to prevent genocides or global environmental problems? Why are some countries rich while others are poor? This book gives students the tools they need to start thinking analytically about the answers to such questions. Second, we have sought to bridge the gap between how scholars of international relations conduct their research and how they teach their students. The text draws from the insights and findings of contemporary international relations scholarship and presents them in a way that is accessible to undergraduates who are just starting out in this field. Our ambition is to provide students with a "toolbox" of analytic concepts common to many theories of world politics that can be applied to a wide variety of topics. We hope to lay a solid foundation on which students can build their own understanding of the continually evolving world of international politics.

The core concepts in this toolbox are interests, interactions, and institutions. Chapter 2 presents the framework, and the remaining chapters apply it. The book is organized around the principle that problems in world politics can be analyzed using these key concepts.

- Who are the relevant actors and what are their interests?
- What is the nature of their interactions? What strategies can they be expected to pursue? When are their choices likely to bring about cooperation or conflict?
- How do institutions constrain and affect interactions? How might they impede or facilitate cooperation? When and how do institutions favor different actors and their interests?

Different problems and issues will emphasize interests, interactions, or institutions to varying degrees. There is no single model of world politics that applies equally to war, trade and international financial relations, and the struggles for improved human rights and a cleaner global environment. Nonetheless, any complete understanding must include all three concepts. Although we do not refer extensively to the traditional paradigms based on realism, liberalism, and constructivism in the rest of the book, we show briefly in the Introduction how each of the major "-isms" of international relations theory can be understood as a different set of assumptions about interests, interactions, and institutions in world politics.

Pedagogical Features

Our approach to the study of international relations is problem-oriented. Each chapter begins with a puzzle about world politics: a question or set of questions that lack obvious answers. We then use the concepts of interests, interactions, and institutions—along with known empirical regularities, current research results, and illustrative cases—to "solve" the puzzle and lead students to a deeper understanding of world politics. Each chapter includes three kinds of "boxes" that supplement the main text, as well as other pedagogical features intended to facilitate student learning.

- **"Controversy"** boxes probe ethical issues to stimulate classroom discussion and show how interests, interactions, and institutions can help us understand—if not necessarily resolve—the difficult normative tradeoffs involved.
- **"What Shaped Our World?"** boxes explain historical events that continue to shape contemporary world politics and illustrate the analytic theme of the chapter.
- **"What Do We Know?"** boxes describe empirical facts or regularities that are important for understanding the larger puzzle discussed in the chapter.
- **"Core of the Analysis"** overviews at the start of each chapter preview the key analytic points to be covered in the chapter.
- **"Reviewing Interests, Interactions, and Institutions"** tables at the end of each chapter summarize specific analytic insights.
- **Chapter outlines, marginal definitions of key terms, Further Readings sections, and a glossary** also aid study and review.

An extensive set of ancillary materials for instructors and students supports this book's goal of making an analytical approach to world politics accessible to introductory-level students. Students will find an array of study and review materials on the accompanying Web site (**wwnorton.com/studyspace**), as well as simulations and other exercises that encourage them to apply what they have learned in the text. For instructors, Norton offers a test bank, an instructor's manual, and an expanded PowerPoint set, all of which have been developed specifically to accompany *World Politics*.

Acknowledgments

We owe many debts in preparing this text. Roby Harrington of Norton brought us together and encouraged us to write this book. His vision, judgment, and steady editorial hand are reflected throughout. Ann Shin of Norton expertly guided the project from first draft to finished product and educated us in the art of writing a textbook. The final form and content of this book reflect her efforts to keep three sometimes over-committed academics on track, on theme, and on time. We are grateful also to the rest of the Norton team, including Marian Johnson, for her work as project editor, and Alice Vigliani for her thorough copyediting. Assistant editor Mollie Eisenberg helped keep the many pieces of the manuscript moving throughout the process, and production manager Eric Pier-Hocking kept a close eye on the quality of the printed book as all those pieces came together. Rachel Comerford ably managed the editing of the print ancillaries, and Dan Jost brought creativity and order to the development of the student website and other online resources. We owe thanks to all of them.

We are enormously grateful to the many reviewers and class-testers who provided guidance and helpful comments at many different stages of this project. In particular, we would like to thank

Rodwan Abouharb, *Louisiana State University*
Karen Adams, *University of Montana*
Todd Allee, *University of Illinois, Urbana-Champaign*
Juliann Allison, *University of California, Riverside*
Claire Apodaca, *Florida International University*
Alan Arwine, *Texas Tech University*
Robert Brown, *Temple University*
Renato Corbetta, *University of Alabama, Birmingham*
Andrew Cortell, *Lewis & Clark College*
Benjamin Fordham, *Binghamton University*
Giovanna Gismondi, *Ohio University*
Darren Hawkins, *Brigham Young University*
Paul Hensel, *Florida State University*
Uk Heo, *University of Wisconsin, Marathon*
Tobias Hofmann, *College of William & Mary*
Elizabeth Hurd, *Northwestern University*
Michael Kanner, *University of Colorado, Boulder*
Scott Kastner, *University of Maryland*
Jonathan Keller, *James Madison University*
Alan Kessler, *University of Texas*
Andy Konitzer, *Samford University*
David Leblang, *University of Virginia*
Ashley Leeds, *Rice University*
Lisa Martin, *University of Wisconsin*
Ronald Mitchell, *University of Oregon*
Layna Mosely, *University of North Carolina*
Will H. Moore, *Florida State University*

Robert Packer, *Pennsylvania State University*
Robert Pahre, *University of Illinois, Urbana-Champaign*
Glenn Palmer, *Pennsylvania State University*
Leanne Powner, *College of Wooster*
Tonya Putnam, *Columbia University*
Stephen Quackenbush, *University of Missouri*
John Quinn, *Truman State University*
Robert Rauchhaus, *University of California, Santa Barbara*
Chad Rector, *George Washington University*
Dan Reiter, *Emory University*
Stephen Saideman, *McGill University*
Idean Salehyan, *University of North Texas*
Todd Sechser, *University of Virginia*
Megan Shannon, *University of Mississippi*
Randolph Siverson, *University of California, Davis*
Oleg Smirnov, *Stony Brook University*
Mark Souva, *Florida State University*
Patricia Sullivan, *University of Georgia*
Hiroki Takeuchi, *Southern Methodist University*
Aleksandra Thurman, *University of Michigan*
Kelly Wurtz, *Trinity College*

David Lake class-tested the entire volume in his Introduction to World Politics courses at UCSD in Spring 2007 and 2008. For their helpful comments, suggestions, and corrections, he would like to thank the over 700 students in those classes as well as his teaching assistants, Molly Bauer, Mark Farrales, Danielle Jung, Jennifer Keister, James Long, Sam Seljan, and Benjamin Tang. For research assistance, we thank Eric Belz, Jeffrey Bengel, Charles Frentz, Oliver Kaplan, Alexander Noonan, and Priya Rajdev.

We also thank Helena de Bres of Wellesley College for her thoughtful ideas and hard work on the "Controversy" boxes, and David Singer of MIT for his work on the figures and boxes in the international political economy chapters. Nancy Frieden graciously hosted an authors' meeting. David Leblang of the University of Virginia developed simulations for the student Web site. Todd Sechser, also of the University of Virginia, created the PowerPoint set that accompanies the book, and Nancy Lapp of California State University, Sacramento, spent countless hours working on the test bank. Brian Potter of the College of New Jersey brought his experience as a teacher to the instructor's manual. We are grateful for their contributions to the project.

What Is World Politics and Why Do We Study It?

In the spring of 1921, Arabs and Jews living in Palestine came to the brink of war.[1] Angered by the influx of Jewish settlers, a group of Arabs set out to attack Jewish homes near their settlement at Tel Aviv. The Jews rushed out to confront them, and shots were exchanged. But the two parties did not go to war on that day. A rabbi named Ben Zion Uziel donned his rabbinical robes, walked out between the two sides, and implored them to go back to their homes. Uziel reminded both sides how the land over which they fought was once a barren desert plagued with disease and famine. By working together, he observed, Jews and Arabs had created a rich and fertile land whose natural resources were only starting to be enjoyed. The rabbi urged both sides to forswear war and instead focus on creating a prosperity that all could enjoy: "We have the entire land in front of us, let us work shoulder to shoulder to cultivate her, uncover her treasures, and live together in brotherhood." The appeal worked: both sides put down their arms and returned home.

We know now, of course, that the peace of that day would not last. Fighting between Arabs and Jews would begin anew only eight years later. In 1948, the state of Israel was created on that land, and that state has since seen frequent conflict with neighboring Arab states and with the stateless Palestinian people who once lived there. The Arab-Israeli conflict is one of the most intractable and dangerous rivalries in the world today. Still, as one scholar notes, "on that day in 1921, some men who otherwise would have died went home to enjoy life with their families."[2]

---

1. This story is told in Abraham Joshua Heschel, *Israel: An Echo of Eternity* (New York: Farrar, Strauss, and Giroux, 1969), 175–78. We are grateful to Arthur Stein for making us aware of this anecdote. See Arthur A. Stein, *Why Nations Cooperate* (Ithaca, NY: Cornell University Press, 1990), 210.
2. Ibid., 210.

Though little more than a footnote in history, this anecdote illustrates what we study when we study world politics and why we study it. The field of world politics—also called international relations—seeks to understand how the peoples and countries of the world get along. As the account suggests, international relations can span the continuum from open warfare to peaceful cooperation. Some countries fight wars against one another and, when they are not fighting, spend significant resources preparing to fight; other countries have managed to live in peace for long periods. Sometimes countries engage in lucrative economic dealings, selling each other goods and services and investing in one another's economies. These interactions can make some people and nations very rich, while others stay mired in poverty. Like the people in the anecdote, the countries of the world are also increasingly aware of the natural resources they share and depend on: the atmosphere, the water, the land. The common threat of environmental degradation creates a need for international cooperation; in some cases, governments have responded to this need, and in other cases, they have not. And, as the story of Rabbi Uziel suggests, small groups—even individuals—can sometimes make a difference, whether through the work of a mediator, the lobbying of human rights groups, or more ominously, the activities of terrorist organizations. Understanding this varied landscape of conflict and cooperation is the task of those who study world politics. Getting students started down this path is the task of this book.

Why study world politics? The nineteenth-century Scottish historian Thomas Carlyle once wrote of economics that it was not a happy science but rather a "dreary, desolate, and, indeed, quite abject and distressing one; what we might call . . . the dismal science." Those who study world politics often think that Carlyle's criticism applies equally well to the field of international relations. The history of world politics offers its fair share of distressing observations. International wars have claimed millions of lives; civil wars and genocides have claimed millions more, and in most cases outsiders who might have prevented these deaths have chosen not to get involved. Since 1945, international politics have taken place under the threat of nuclear war, which could destroy the planet, and fears about the potential use of these weapons have intensified since the terrorist attacks of September 11, 2001. International economic relations have in some cases been harmonious and generated great wealth for some countries. And yet, as one looks around the globe today, the inequality in living standards is stark. About half of the world's population—around 3 billion people—live on less than two dollars a day. Most countries have signed treaties promising to protect the basic human rights of their citizens, but some governments still kill, arrest, and torture their people—and outsiders usually do little to stop these violations. And despite increasing awareness of threats to the global environment, international efforts to do something about these threats often fail.

Still, the picture is not entirely bleak. One can point to a number of examples in which the world has changed for the better. For hundreds of years, the continent of Europe experienced horrific warfare, culminating in the first half of the twentieth century in two world wars that claimed tens of millions lives. Today, the countries of Europe are at peace, and a war between, say, Germany and France in the forseeable future is inconceivable. After World War II, many countries emerged economically shattered by war or destitute after decades of colonial rule, but some have experienced extraordinary prosperity in the decades since. For example, in the 1950s, South Korea had one of the world's poorest economies, with a per capita national income of less than $150 a year. Today, South Korea boasts the sixteenth largest economy in the world, with a per capita national income of over $26,000 a year.[3] At the beginning of the twentieth century, only a handful of countries worldwide had political systems that guaranteed the civil rights of their citizens and gave people a say in government through free and fair elections. By the beginning of the twenty-first century, more than half of the world's population lived in democratic countries. And despite the uneven track record of efforts to protect the global environment, cooperation in this area was virtually unknown a few decades ago. In recent years, the number of international environmental treaties and organizations has grown dramatically, as has awareness of the common challenges we face.

We study world politics because the bad things that happen in the world distress us and because the good things give us hope that, through understanding and effort, the world could be a better place.

Eleven Puzzles in Search of Explanations

This book is organized around what we consider to be the most compelling and pressing puzzles in the study of world politics. Puzzles are observations about the world that demand an explanation. In some cases, they arise because the world does not work the way that we might expect. Some things that happen seem like they should not, and other things that don't happen seem like they should. War, for example, is a puzzling phenomenon. Given the enormous human and material costs that wars impose on the countries that fight them, one might wonder why countries do not settle their conflicts in other, more reasonable ways. The difficulty of international cooperation to end genocides or to protect the environment presents another such puzzle: given the widespread agreement that genocide is horrific and that the environment needs protecting, why is it so hard for countries to do something about these issues? Other puzzles arise because of variation that needs to be explained. Some countries today are enormously wealthy, with living standards more opulent than ever experienced in world history; in many other countries, people scrape by on meager incomes and suffer from malnutrition, poor health, and inadequate schooling. What accounts for these vastly different outcomes? The study of world politics is the effort to make sense of these puzzles.

To that end, this book seeks to understand eleven puzzles:

1. Given the human and material costs of military conflict, why do countries sometimes wage war rather than resolving their disputes through negotiations? (Chapter 3)

---

3. Figures are 2008 estimates from U.S. Central Intelligence Agency, *The World Factbook*, www.cia.gov/library/publications/the-world-factbook/ (accessed 5/29/09).

2. What if there are actors within a country who see war as beneficial and who expect to pay few or none of its costs? Do countries fight wars to satisfy influential domestic interests? (Chapter 4)
3. Why is it so hard for the international community to prevent and punish acts of aggression among and within states? (Chapter 5)
4. Why are trade barriers so common despite the universal advice of economists? Why do trade policies vary so widely? (Chapter 6)
5. Why is international finance so controversial? Why are international financial institutions like the International Monetary Fund so strong? (Chapter 7)
6. Why do countries pursue different currency policies, from dollarizing or joining the euro, to letting their currency's value float freely? (Chapter 8)
7. Why are some countries rich and some countries poor? (Chapter 9)
8. How could relatively small transnational groups, from advocacy groups like Amnesty International to terrorist networks like Al Qaeda, bring about policy change within and among countries? (Chapter 10)
9. Given that nearly everyone wants a cleaner and healthier environment, why is it so hard to cooperate internationally to protect the environment? (Chapter 11)
10. Why do countries sometimes try to protect the human rights of people outside their borders? In light of widespread support for the principle of human rights, why has the movement to protect those rights not been more successful? (Chapter 12)
11. Why are some periods marked by extensive global conflict while others experience robust efforts at cooperation? Which of these patterns will hold in the future? (Chapter 13)

theory: A logically consistent set of statements that explains a phenomenon of interest.

After setting out one of these puzzles, each chapter shows how we can build theories to make sense of them. A **theory** is a logically consistent set of statements that explains a phenomenon of interest. When we confront the puzzle "Why did this happen?" theories provide an answer. They specify the factors that play a role in causing the events we are trying to understand, and they show how these pieces fit together to make sense of the puzzle. A theory of war explains why wars happen and identifies the conditions that make war between countries more or less likely. A theory of trade explains why countries sometimes choose to trade with each other and identifies what factors increase or decrease the amount of that trade. A theory of international environmental policy identifies the factors that foster or impede cooperation in this area.

In addition to this primary role of explanation, theories also help us to describe, predict, and prescribe. They help us to *describe* events by identifying which factors are important and which are not. Since it would be impossible to catalog all of the events that precede, say, the outbreak of a war, we need theories to filter the events that are worth including from those that are not. Theories help us to *predict* by offering a sense of how the world works, how a change in one factor will lead to changes in behavior and outcomes. And theories may help *prescribe* policy responses by identifying what has to be changed in order to foster better outcomes. Once a good understanding has been established of why wars happen, it might be possible to take steps to prevent them. Knowing what factors help countries emerge from poverty makes it possible to advocate policies that have a chance of helping. Just as an understanding of how the human body works is important for curing diseases, developing theories of how the world works is a first step in the quest to make it a better place.

Theories also provide manageable explanations for complex phenomena. Given how complicated the world is, simplifying it in this way may seem like a misguided pursuit. Whereas the movement of a falling object might be characterized by mathematical equations dictated by the laws of physics, the decisions of individuals and groups are influenced by factors too innumerable to list, yet alone predict. Any theory, therefore, is doomed to oversimplify things. But this is precisely the point of theorizing. We do not build theories because we believe the world is simple or mechanical. Rather, we build them because we know the world is extraordinarily complex, and the only way to understand important phenomena is to cut away some of the complexity and identify the most important factors. As a result, any general explanation will not be right in every single case.

Given this outlook, we generally aspire for probabilistic claims. A probabilistic claim is an argument about the factors that increase or decrease the likelihood that some outcome will occur. For example, while we cannot predict with certainty whether a given conflict will end in war or peace, we can identify conditions that increase or decrease the danger of war. Similarly, we use theories to identify factors that make trade protection, or international investment, or cooperation to protect human rights or the environment more or less likely. Given the world's complexity, developing a compelling probabilistic argument is no small feat.

The Framework: Interests, Interactions, and Institutions

No single theory adequately answers all of the puzzles posed in this book. Instead, we offer a framework—a way of thinking about world politics that will be useful in building theories that shed light on our puzzles. The framework rests on three core concepts: interests, interactions, and institutions. **Interests** are the goals that actors have, the outcomes they hope to obtain through political action. A state may have an interest in protecting its citizens or acquiring more territory; businesses generally have an interest in maximizing profits; an environmental activist has an interest in protecting the atmosphere, the oceans, or whales. **Interactions** are the ways in which two or more actors' choices combine to produce political outcomes. The outcomes that we observe—wars, or trade and financial exchanges, or cooperation to protect human rights or the environment—reflect the choices of many actors, each looking out for his or her own interests, but also taking into account the interests and likely actions of others. War is the product of an interaction because it requires at least two sides: one side must attack, and the other must decide to resist. Similarly, efforts at international cooperation require multiple states to coordinate their policy choices toward a common goal. An **institution** is a set of rules,

interests: What actors want to achieve through political action; their preferences over the outcomes that might result from their political choices.

interactions: The ways in which the choices of two or more actors combine to produce political outcomes.

institutions: A set of rules, known and shared by the community, that structure political interactions in particular ways.

known and shared by the relevant community, that structure political interactions. Institutions define the "rules of the game," often embodied in formal treaties and laws or in organizations like the United Nations. Institutions create procedures for making joint decisions, such as voting rules; they also lay out standards of acceptable behavior and often include provisions for monitoring compliance and punishing those actors that violate the rules.

Applying this framework to any particular puzzle is straightforward. We first think about who the relevant political actors are and what interests they have. We think about the choices, or strategies, available to each actor, how those choices interact to produce outcomes, and how the strategic interaction influences what the actors actually decide to do. And we think about what institutions, if any, might exist to govern their behavior.

The framework is intentionally flexible, pragmatic, and open to a variety of assumptions about which interests, interactions, and institutions matter. A theory emerges when we identify the specific interests, interactions, and institutions that work together to account for the events or pattern of events we hope to explain.

In building explanations, we do not precommit to any one set of actors or interests as being the most important regardless of issue area. Sometimes, it is most useful to think about states as actors pursuing goals such as power, security, or territorial aggrandizement. In other situations, we get more leverage thinking about politicians concerned about holding on to their office, or businesses interested in maximizing profits, or labor unions interested in protecting their members' jobs, or groups of like-minded individuals with strong ideological interests in, say, protecting human rights or extending the dominion of a particular religion. We cannot judge whether any particular assumption about actors and interests is right or wrong; rather, we judge whether that assumption is useful or not useful in explaining the puzzle. Indeed, assumptions are simplifying devices, which means that, strictly speaking, none captures the exact, entire truth. Since all decisions are made by individuals, it is not precisely accurate to say that a state or an interest group or an institution is an actor; and yet, sometimes, it is quite useful to assume precisely that. Similarly, when we ascribe interests to individuals—such as assuming that politicians care primarily about holding on to office—this is a sweeping generalization that cannot be right 100 percent of the time; and yet, very powerful insights can be drawn from this assumption.

We focus on two broad types of interactions that arise, to one degree or another, in all aspects of politics: bargaining and cooperation. **Bargaining** describes situations in which two or more actors try to divide something that both want. States may bargain over the allocation of a disputed territory; finance ministers may bargain over how high or low to set the exchange rate between their currencies; rich countries may bargain with poor countries over how much aid the former will give and what the recipients will do in return; governments may bargain over how much each will pay to alleviate some environmental harm. **Cooperation** occurs when actors have common interests and need to act in a coordinated way to achieve those interests. Governments that want to stop one country from invading another may try to act collectively to impose military or economic sanctions on the aggressor. Governments that share an interest in preventing climate change or degradation of the ozone layer need to cooperate in restraining their countries' emissions of the offending pollut-

bargaining: An interaction in which actors must choose outcomes that make one better off at the expense of another. Bargaining is redistributive; it involves allocating a fixed sum of value between different actors.

cooperation: An interaction in which two or more actors adopt policies that make at least one actor better off relative to the status quo without making the others worse off.

ants. Individuals who want to lobby for a particular trade policy or an environmental regulation have to pool their time, money, and effort in order to achieve their common aim. In short, bargaining and cooperation are everywhere in political life.

The institutional setting can vary considerably depending on the issues at stake. In some areas of world politics, there are well-established rules and mechanisms for enforcing them. International trade, for example, is governed by the World Trade Organization (WTO): it sets out rules that determine what kinds of trade policies member countries can and cannot have, and it provides a dispute resolution mechanism that allows countries to challenge one another's policies. Other areas of world politics have weaker institutions. As we will see in Chapter 5, the United Nations (UN) theoretically governs the use of military force by states, but it has, in practice, had a hard time enforcing these rules on its strongest members. As we will see in Chapter 11, there is an extensive body of international human rights law setting out standards for how governments should treat their citizens; unfortunately, noncompliance is common, and offenders are rarely punished. We will also at times focus on institutions at the domestic level—that is, the rules that govern who rules within countries and how they make decisions. Domestic political institutions determine which actors have access to and influence on the policy-making process. In some cases, differences in domestic political institutions can have profound effects on world politics. In Chapter 4, for example, we will encounter a phenomenon known as the "democratic peace": the observation that mature democratic states have rarely, if ever, engaged in a war against one another.

LEVELS OF ANALYSIS

The variety of actors and institutions that play a role in world politics means that we will see important interactions at three levels:

- At the *international level,* the representatives of states with different interests interact with one another, sometimes in the context of international institutions such as the UN or WTO.
- At the *domestic level,* subnational actors with different interests—politicians, bureaucrats, business and labor groups, voters—interact within domestic institutions to determine the country's foreign policy choices.
- At the *transnational level,* groups whose members span borders—such as multinational corporations, transnational advocacy networks, terrorist organizations—pursue interests by trying to influence both domestic and international politics.

These levels are interconnected. The interests that states pursue at the international level often emerge from their domestic politics. For example, whether or not a country's representatives push for liberalizing trade agreements with other countries depends on whether the interests within that country that support freer trade prevail over those that oppose it. Similarly, the relative influence of actors within domestic politics may depend on international conditions. Leaders may be able to use militarized conflict with other states in order to enhance their hold on power at home. International institutions that promote trade liberalization enhance the power of domestic interests that benefit from trade. Finally, transnational actors operate at all levels. Transnational networks like Amnesty International or Greenpeace try to change national policies by lobbying governments or mobilizing public opinion within key countries, and they try to change international outcomes by working with (or against) international institutions.

Because of these interconnections, we do not automatically privilege one level of analysis over others. Although international relations scholarship has experienced vigorous debates over which level of analysis is the "right" or "best" one,[4] we find that no single level is always superior to the others in making sense of our puzzles. In some cases, it is possible to build useful explanations from the bottom up, in a two-step process: (1) domestic interests, interactions, and institutions determine the interests that state representatives bring to the international level, and then (2) these interests combine in international interactions and institutions to determine the final outcome. The chapters on international political economy in Part Three generally rely on this two-step logic. In other cases, however, it is more useful to start elsewhere. In Part Two, we start the analysis of war on the international level: given that states have conflicting interests over things like territory or one another's policies or regime composition, why does the bargaining interaction sometimes lead to war? Only after laying out this basic logic do we turn to some of the domestic factors that push states toward more or less belligerent policies. In Part Four, transnational actors play a central role, and we show how they pursue their goals by altering domestic interests and by changing the prospects for international cooperation.

INTEGRATING INSIGHTS FROM REALISM, LIBERALISM, AND CONSTRUCTIVISM

In adopting a flexible framework based on interests, interactions, and institutions, we depart from the way the field of world politics is often organized. Many textbooks and courses on world politics emphasize the contrast between three schools of thought: realism, liberalism, and constructivism. In contrast to our framework, which holds few preconceptions about how the world works, these three "-isms" represent very different worldviews about the nature of international politics. Much ink has been spilled over the years by proponents arguing for the superiority of their preferred approach.

We can understand the differences among realism, liberalism, and constructivism by mapping them into our framework. Each school of thought is defined by a cluster of assumptions about what interests, interactions, and institutions are most important to understanding world politics.

Realism

Realist ideas can be found in the writings of Thucydides (ca. 460–400 BCE), Niccolò Machiavelli (1469–1527), Thomas Hobbes (1588–1679), and Jean-Jacques Rousseau (1712–1778). Realism was most forcefully introduced to Americans by Hans Morgenthau, a German expatriate whose 1948 book *Politics among Nations*

---

4. For a classic statement of this debate, see J. David Singer, "The Levels-of-Analysis Problem in International Relations," *World Politics* 14, no. 1 (October 1961): 77–92.

remains a classic statement of the realist approach. Realism was given its modern and scientific guise by the contemporary scholar Kenneth Waltz.[5]

Realism starts with two key assumptions: that states are the dominant actors—indeed, some would say the only relevant actors—on the international stage, and that the institutional setting of world politics is characterized by anarchy. **Anarchy**, a term we will revisit in Chapter 2, refers in this context to the absence of a central authority in the international system, the fact that there is no world government ruling over states the way that countries have governments that rule over their citizens.

Realists assume that anarchy profoundly shapes the interests and interactions that matter in world politics. Because there is no central government and no international police force, states must live in constant fear of one another. With no external restraint on the use of military force, every state must first and foremost look out for its own survival and security. Hence, all states have an interest in security, and this interest dominates other possible interests because no other goal can be realized unless the state is secure. In practice, the interest in security leads to an interest in acquiring power—primarily, military capabilities. By accumulating power and by ensuring that potential enemies do not become more powerful, states can ensure that they are not vulnerable to attack and conquest. The quest for power, unfortunately, inevitably brings states' interests into conflict with one another: when one state improves its military capabilities to enhance its own security, it typically undermines the security of its now comparatively weaker neighbors. For realists, then, international politics is, as Hobbes described the "state of nature," a war of "every man, against every man" in which life is "nasty, brutish, and short."

Because states are concerned with security and power, nearly all interactions involve bargaining and coercion. Each state tries to get a bigger share for itself; one state's gain is another state's loss; and the threat of war looms over everything. Even when the potential gains from cooperation are large, realists argue, states worry more about the division of the benefits than about the overall gain. Each must fear that the state gaining the most will be able to exploit its gains for some future advantage. As a result, states may forgo mutually beneficial exchanges if they expect to be left at a disadvantage. Cooperation, realists conclude, is difficult and rare.

Finally, realists assert that because of the anarchic nature of the international system, international institutions are weak and exert little independent effect on world politics. Institutions like the UN and the WTO merely reflect the interests and power of the dominant countries, which had the most say in their creation and design. Although realists may recognize that institutions can matter at the margin, they conclude that rules are unlikely to be followed and that states will always bow to interests and power in the end.

Liberalism

An equally venerable tradition, liberalism is rooted in the writings of philosophers John Locke (1632–1704) and Immanuel Kant (1724–1804), and economists

> **anarchy:** The absence of a central authority with the ability to make and enforce laws that bind all actors.

---

5. Hans Morgenthau, *Politics among Nations: The Struggle for Power and Peace* (New York: Alfred A. Knopf). First published in 1948, this book has been released in many editions since then. Kenneth N. Waltz, *Theory of International Politics* (Reading, MA: Addison-Wesley, 1979).

Adam Smith (1723–1790) and David Ricardo (1772–1823). Contemporary advocates include Bruce Russett and John R. Oneal, who make the modern case for the pacifying effects of democracy, international commerce, and international law, and Robert O. Keohane and Joseph S. Nye, whose work helped bring the study of international institutions to the fore.[6]

Liberal theorists accept many different types of actors as important in world politics: individuals, firms, nongovernmental organizations, and states. Unlike realism, liberalism does not require that any one interest dominate all others. Instead, liberal theory, like the framework presented in this book, is quite flexible in ascribing goals to actors. Moreover, since wealth can be used to purchase the means to accommodate many different desires, liberals assume that for many practical purposes actors can be treated as if they desire to maximize wealth.

Liberals are generally optimistic about the possibilities for cooperation in world politics. Whereas realists see most situations as involving conflicting interests, liberals see many areas in which actors have common interests that can serve as the basis for cooperation. Although liberals acknowledge that world politics is often wracked by conflict, they do not believe that conflict is inevitable; rather, conflict arises when actors fail to recognize or act on common interests.

Whether or not actors can cooperate to further their common interests depends a great deal on institutions, both domestic and international. At the domestic level, liberals believe that democracy is the best way to ensure that governments' foreign policies reflect the underlying harmony of interests among individuals. In this view, which we will revisit in Chapter 4, conflict and war are the fault of selfish politicians, voracious militaries, and greedy interest groups, whose influence can be tamed only by empowering the people through democratic institutions. At the international level, the scope for cooperation gives rise to a demand for institutions. Liberals posit that international institutions facilitate cooperation by resolving a host of dilemmas that arise in strategic interactions and by making it easier for states to make collective decisions. In Chapter 2, we will consider these dilemmas and the ways in which institutions might resolve them.

Constructivism

A relatively new approach, constructivism has roots in critical theory and sociology, and several of its most forceful proponents in world politics have been Peter J. Katzenstein, John G. Ruggie, and Alexander Wendt.[7] Constructivists assume that interests are not innate but are constructed through social interaction. Actors do not have fixed and predetermined interests; rather, they acquire interests from interacting with others within their social environment. Whether or not two states have conflicting or harmonious interests is something they discover as their re-

---

6. Bruce Russett and John R. Oneal, *Triangulating Peace: Democracy, Interdependence, and International Organizations* (New York: Norton, 2001). Robert O. Keohane and Joseph S. Nye, *Power and Interdependence: World Politics in Transition* (New York: Longman). First published in 1977, this volume is now available in a third edition published in 2000. Robert O. Keohane, *After Hegemony: Cooperation and Discord in the World Political Economy* (Princeton, NJ: Princeton University Press, 1984).

7. Peter J. Katzenstein, ed., *The Culture of National Security: Norms and Identity in World Politics* (New York: Columbia University Press, 1996); John G. Ruggie, *Constructing the World Polity: Essays on International Institutionalization* (New York: Routledge, 1998); Alexander Wendt, *Social Theory of International Politics* (New York: Cambridge University Press, 1999).

lationship unfolds. This means that the way states define their interests can be powerfully shaped by their social environment. For example, if a large number of countries decide that using a certain kind of weapon is barbaric, then states that wish to be seen as civilized may decide to forgo those weapons as well—even if using those weapons would enhance their security. Whereas the other schools of thought assume that actors are purposive, selecting among possible alternatives according to their anticipated effects, constructivists assume that social actors pursue what they believe is right and proper given their conceptions of who they are and how they wish others to view them. Institutions, in turn, embody the rules appropriate for behavior in different identities, and thus they exert a profound effect on action and observed outcomes.

For constructivists, however, neither interactions nor institutions are themselves fixed. Rather, both evolve continuously and, more important, can be transformed by actors through the introduction of new understandings of their interests or identities. The rough-and-tumble international system described by realists, for example, is not, according to constructivism, foreordained by the condition of anarchy. If actors come to understand their interests differently, their conception of appropriate behavior could change dramatically.

All three of these approaches offer insights into important problems of world politics. Nonetheless, each tends to emphasize particular aspects of our framework at the expense of others, and all make strong assumptions about which interests, interactions, and institutions matter the most. As a result, each sacrifices explanatory power and flexibility for the sake of intellectual purity. Not surprisingly, most international relations scholarship in recent years has moved away from arguments based on a single approach, instead borrowing insights from more than one. Indeed, as the field progresses, it has become harder to pigeonhole scholars and their work into any one category. For example, many contemporary scholars believe that coercive power plays a fundamental role in international politics (realism) but that power is often used in pursuit of goals that arise from the interplay of domestic interests (liberalism) and ideas (constructivism).[8] Hence, rather than trying to promote one school of thought over others, our goal is to answer important puzzles of international politics and, in the process, use the tools developed here to help us understand today's complex world.

The Plan of the Book

This book has five parts. The first part, Chapters 1 and 2, introduces the broad patterns of conflict and cooperation in international history and lays out the text's framework. Part Two, Chapters 3 through 5, deals with the central puzzles in the study of war: why wars happen, whether war serves the interests of actors within the state, and why the international community has such a hard time cooperating to prevent wars. Part Three, Chapters 6 through 9, discusses the main puzzles

---

8. See, for example, Jeffrey W. Legro and Andrew Moravcsik, "Is Anybody Still a Realist?" *International Security* 24, no. 2 (Autumn 1999): 5–55.

in international economic relations: why countries trade with one another, why financial investments flow across borders, why some countries have separate national currencies, and why some countries are rich while others are poor. Part Four, Chapters 10 through 12, considers the relatively new issues associated with "global civil society"—that is, issues in which nonstate entities such as terrorists, human rights activists, and environmental groups are important actors. Part Five presents the concluding chapter, which reviews the broad historical trends in world politics and considers what that experience, together with our theories, can tell us about the future.

By the end of the course, students should not only know a lot about international politics; they should also know how to *think* about international politics. When bad or puzzling things happen, they should be able to ask: "Whose interests did that outcome serve? Why were the people or countries involved not able to cooperate to achieve something better? How might new institutions be created, or existing institutions reformed, so that this does not happen again?"

Ultimately, we study world politics because doing so lets us grapple with important and interesting questions about ourselves and our world. This book cannot provide definitive answers to all of the questions. After all, while we are confident that we understand certain things, in other cases our understanding is still evolving and our theories are tentative—perhaps waiting to be overturned by the next generation. Instead, this book seeks to equip students with the tools they need to develop their own understanding. In the "information age," in which facts (and assertions masquerading as facts) are cheap and plentiful, the most valuable skill is the ability to think critically and carefully about what shapes our world.

Key Terms

theory, p. xxii
interests, p. xxiii
interactions, p. xxiii
institution, p. xxiii
bargaining, p. xxiv
cooperation, p. xxiv
anarchy, p. xxvii

World Politics

INTERESTS, INTERACTIONS, INSTITUTIONS

PART ONE

Foundations

The study of world politics does not take place in a laboratory with petri dishes or Bunsen burners. But like all fields that seek to understand the natural or social world, ours rests on two principal foundations: observation and theory. Observation involves a careful examination of past events, both distant and recent, to identify the puzzles that require explanation and the possible answers to those puzzles. A theoretical framework provides concepts and analytical tools to make sense of what we observe. Developing these two foundations is the task of this book's first part.

Chapter 1 traces the main developments in the evolution of world politics over the last 500 years. This history not only tells us what shaped our world, but also lays out the main patterns that students of international relations need to explain. The modern international system has experienced periods of intense warfare and competition as well as periods of relative peace and cooperation. Some regions and countries have grown wealthy and militarily powerful, while others have suffered from conquest and poverty. There have also been dramatic changes in the way countries are governed and in the interactions between politics and economics. This historical narrative provides the raw material for the study of world politics.

But history does not speak for itself; it needs all the help it can get from theory. Understanding the complex world requires that we identify a manageable set of

History and theory can help us understand events like the recent war in Afghanistan. These British soldiers took part in the conflict that began in 2001, but the British fought three colonial wars in Afghanistan in the past.

concepts, an analytical framework on which to build explanations. Chapter 2 develops such a framework, introducing the book's three core concepts: interests, interactions, and institutions. These concepts allow us to explore the puzzles of world politics by posing three main questions: Who are the relevant actors and what are their interests? How do their actions combine to produce cooperation or conflict? How do institutions, both international and domestic, structure the choices that actors make and help or hinder their efforts to cooperate? Developing these ideas and showing how they can be used to understand actual events is a crucial first step in the study of world politics.

CHAPTER 1

What Shaped Our World?

A HISTORICAL INTRODUCTION

During the nineteenth century, global trade grew at a rapid rate. While the increase in international trade was most pronounced in the advanced economies of Europe, many people in Asia also found themselves integrated into the global economy in new ways during this period. By the time this painting was done, around 1840, Canton, China (present-day Guangzhou), had become a significant international trading port

M ost western Europeans and North Americans born around 1800 spent their adult lives in an atmosphere of peace and economic growth. So too did their children, and their children's children, and their children's children's children. Between the end of the Napoleonic Wars in 1815 and the start of World War I in 1914, peace and prosperity by and large reigned in western Europe and North America. There were periodic wars among the European Great Powers, but they were relatively short; there were brutal conflicts with the indigenous peoples of the Americas, but they were on sparsely inhabited frontiers; there was a bloody civil war in the United States, but it was confined to one country. There were occasional financial panics and recessions, but between 1815 and 1914 the advanced economies of western Europe and North America grew more than eightfold, while output per person quadrupled.[1] This was the fastest growth in world history by a very long shot—it roughly equaled in a hundred years what had been achieved in the previous thousand.

Europeans and North Americans born around 1900 had a very different experience. While they were in their teens, the world plunged into a horrific, protracted war that wiped out the better part of a generation of young men. If those born around 1900 were fortunate enough to survive World War I, they and their children spent the next ten years whipsawed between postwar violence, economic uncertainty, fragile democracy, financial boom, and ethnic conflict. In 1929, the world spiraled even farther downward into economic depression, mass unemployment, dictatorship, trade wars, and eventually another global war.

1. Angus Maddison, *The World Economy: A Millennial Perspective* (Paris: Development Centre of the Organization for Economic Co-operation and Development, 2001).

If they, and their children and their children's children, were again lucky and survived World War II, their world was divided into two hostile camps, one led by the United States and the other led by the Soviet Union. These two contending alliances carried on a cold war that included the deployment of enough nuclear weapons to annihilate life on earth several times over.

International relations profoundly affected these many generations of Europeans and North Americans—as they did, in different ways, generations of people in Africa, Asia, and Latin America. During the nineteenth century, the inhabitants of many poor countries found themselves absorbed into a world economy for the first time; some prospered, others foundered. Latin Americans achieved independence from their colonial masters, while much of Africa and Asia was subjected to new colonial rule and domination by Europeans. The twentieth century brought industrialization and urbanization to much of the developing world and eventually saw the end of colonialism. For people north and south, east and west, global events beyond their control—Great Power war, international financial crises, colonial expansion, the division of

The start of World War I in 1914 marked the end of a century of relative peace and prosperity for much of Europe and North America. As international relations broke down and violent conflict erupted, Europeans and North Americans found their lives dramatically changed by world politics.

the world into warring camps—changed their lives profoundly, as they continue to change ours, and as they have changed lives for centuries.

Whether in the military realm or in that of international economics, the world's experience ranges from deadly conflict to fruitful cooperation. At times, nations have engaged in bitter armed battles over everything from territory to theology, and in equally bitter commercial conflicts over markets and money. At other times, the same nations have worked together in harmony on everything from geopolitics to trade, investment, and finance.

What will the future bring for those born around 2000? Will they experience general peace and prosperity, or war and deprivation? Will those born in the world's poor nations come closer to the living standards of the rich, or fall farther behind? Will governments cooperate or clash? These are the kinds of questions that the study of international politics hopes to illuminate. We do not aspire to predict the future; but we do propose to understand the past and present more fully, and to provide some guidelines to understand the choices available to people and governments, and how they decide among those choices.

Conflict and cooperation among nations have ebbed and flowed. So too have individual countries varied in their own relations with other nations—sometimes hostile, sometimes collaborative. Explaining the ebbs and flows over time, and the differences among countries, is the principal purpose of the scientific study of international relations. Our explanations focus on understanding how the interests of the world's countries, and of the people in them, lead the world's nations to interact with one another and to what effect. We also study the kinds of international institutions that arise from and mediate these interactions. This chapter reviews the modern history of international political and economic affairs in order to clarify the general patterns of interests, interactions, and institutions that have structured the world's political and economic orders.

The Emergence of International Relations: The Mercantilist Era

The world as a meaningful political and economic unit only emerged after 1500. Before then, most major societies existed in practical or complete isolation from all but those on their immediate borders. To be sure, there was some trade among societies: China to Constantinople, Central Africa to North Africa, Constantinople to Europe. But this trade was extraordinarily difficult and expensive, and therefore it involved only the most valuable and easily transported goods.

All that changed after 1492, as wave upon wave of explorers, conquerors, traders, and settlers went forth from Europe's Atlantic nations. First Spain and Portugal, then England, France, and the Netherlands sent soldiers and traders all over the New World, Africa, and Asia in search of possessions and profit. By 1700, the world was unquestionably controlled by western Europeans. They exercised direct rule over vast colonial possessions in the Western Hemisphere, India, Southeast Asia, and elsewhere; and their military might allowed them to assert their will on local rulers even where they did not establish colonial domain. Western Europe's economic influence was global, and it dictated the character and direction of economic activity on every continent.

The centuries of European expansion after 1492 meant that world politics was dominated by European politics. In fact, the Europeans used their military prowess to control much of the rest of the world, with formal empires or without them. The European economies were the world center of economic activity. Important as developments outside Europe may have been for the people living there, the analysis of world politics after 1492 of necessity has Europe at its core. This would only change in the twentieth century, with the rise of militarily and economically important non-European powers: the United States, Japan, the Soviet Union, and eventually China.

For several hundred years beginning in the 1500s, however, it was the rulers of western Europe who held sway over the rest of the world. These governments, almost all of them absolute monarchies, had two main interests. First, they wanted to ensure their own political and military power. These interests led them to desire control over ever greater territories and ever greater resources. Second, the European governments wanted access to markets and resources in other parts of the world. The European societies had thriving commercial classes, typically strongly allied with their respective monarchies, and each crown was hungry for revenue. There were rich natural treasures to be had abroad—precious metals, spices, tropical crops—and customers for the products of Europe's growing industries.

Western Europeans' economic and military interests were closely related and were reflected in the colonial order they established, known as mercantilism. **Mercantilism** was a system by which imperial governments used military power to enrich themselves and their supporters, then used those riches to enhance their military power. Mercantilism's principal mechanism was the establishment of monopolies that controlled trade and other economic activities, manipulating them so as to direct money into the coffers of the government and its business supporters.

mercantilism: An economic doctrine based on a belief that military power and economic influence were complements; applied especially to colonial empires in the sixteenth through eighteenth centuries. Mercantilist policies favored the mother country over its colonies and over its competitors.

The British imposed mercantilist policies on their colonies in North America. For example, the tobacco being loaded onto these ships in the Virginia Colony could be exported only to Britain, where the American producers received a lower price for their crops than they would on world markets.

Some mercantilist monopolies were held by a government itself, such as the Spanish crown's control over many of its colonies' gold and silver mines. Other mercantilist monopolies were granted by a government to private businesses, such as the Dutch East Indies Company and the Hudson's Bay Company. These private enterprises held exclusive rights to economic activities in vast areas of the colonial world.

Perhaps the most wide-ranging monopolistic features of mercantilism were its controls on trade. These controls typically served to manipulate the terms of trade, the prices paid for imports and received for exports. In the case of mercantilist policies, the goal was to turn the terms of trade against the colonies and in favor of the mother country—to reduce the prices that the mother country paid its colonists for what it bought, and to raise the prices the mother country charged its colonists for what it sold. One common way of achieving this effect was to require colonies only to buy and sell certain goods from and to the colonial power. In colonial Virginia, for example, farmers could only sell their tobacco to England, which artificially reduced demand for their tobacco and therefore its price; and Virginians could buy many manufactured goods only from England, which artificially reduced the supply of manufactures and therefore raised their price. Subjects received less for what they produced and paid more for what they consumed, but in return they obtained the protection of a powerful empire. Supporters of mercantilism argued that it benefited both the empire, which got richer and more powerful, and its subjects, who got protected. Not all colonial subjects agreed, as "What Do We Know?" on page 9 explains.

The mercantilist powers' international political and international economic interests were closely intertwined. For mercantilism's proponents, this was one of its great attractions. The English philosopher Thomas Hobbes wrote, "Wealth is power, and power is wealth." One of his fellow mercantilist thinkers drew out the connections: "Foreign trade produces riches, riches power, power preserves our trade and religion." And a French mercantilist was even more explicit: "Our colonies depend on our navy, our trade depends on our colonies, and our trade allows the state to maintain armies, increase the population, and provide for ever more glorious and useful functions."[2]

As the European powers took control of ever larger portions of the world, they also battled with one another over wealth and power. The struggle for supremacy in Europe was inextricably linked to the battle for possessions elsewhere, and the search for military advantage was closely tied to economic competition. International politics and markets were battlegrounds on which the major powers contended.

First the Spanish and Portuguese fought for predominance in the New World and elsewhere. After the Spaniards emerged victorious, they faced new contenders. The British challenged Spain continually from the 1580s onward, defeating the Spanish

---

2. All cited in Jacob Viner, "Power versus Plenty as Objectives of Foreign Policy in the Seventeenth and Eighteenth Centuries," *World Politics* 1, no. 1 (October 1948): 15–16.

Mercantilism and the Thirteen Colonies

British colonialism in North America followed the patterns of mercantilism, the system adopted by European colonial powers after about 1500. Mercantilist controls on trade restricted both where the colonists could sell the goods they produced, and where the colonists could buy the goods they consumed. Economic historian Robert Paul Thomas has estimated the cost to the colonies of these economic restrictions in 1770, a representative year in the decade leading up to the outbreak of the American Revolution (see table below).

The most costly restriction was the "enumeration" of certain goods, which meant they could only be exported to Britain. This measure artificially increased the supply of the enumerated goods to the British market, which caused their price to drop; and it kept American producers from selling in markets with higher prices. In fact, almost all of the enumerated goods sold by Americans to the British were then reexported to other European countries for much higher prices, with the British merchants making substantial profits as a result of these monopolistic policies. There were additional restrictions on what could be imported in the colonies, with the result that certain goods were only available if they were bought from Britain—at a higher price than available elsewhere. British mercantilist rules also forced the colonists to use British shipping and related services, and they limited colonial manufacturing.

The principal cost to the thirteen colonies was the lower price received for enumerated goods, especially the tobacco and rice that made up most of the colonies' exports. Thomas calculated that without enumeration the colonists would have been able to sell their tobacco at a price 49 percent higher than what they actually received, and their rice for more than double. If prices had been higher, we can also assume that the colonists would have

produced more of the goods, so the forgone production is factored in as well. The total cost of these export controls, almost all due to tobacco and rice, was $2.4 million—roughly 1.2 percent of the colonies' total gross domestic product (GDP),[a] at a time when annual income was probably under $100 per person. Thomas further estimated that the restrictions on imports raised the price of goods that the colonists bought from abroad by more than one-third, a total burden of $560,000. Thomas was unable to estimate accurately the cost of the other controls, but the import and export barriers were probably the principal problems. Thomas then took into account rewards ("bounties") the colonists earned for producing favored goods. The total net cost was about $2.7 million, approximately 1.5 percent of colonial GDP.

However, the thirteen colonies received benefits from being in the British Empire. Most important was the fact that the colonists were protected by the British army and navy. Thomas calculated these benefits in two ways. First, he estimated the cost to the British government of stationing its troops in the region, along with how much American shippers would have had to pay for private insurance if they had not had the protection of the world's greatest navy. Second, Thomas calculated how much the American government spent to provide these services itself after independence. The lower of the two estimates was $1,775,000 in 1770. Subtracting the benefits from the costs, Thomas figured that the colonies' net burden from imperial rule in 1770 was about $885,000—or 42 cents per person, less than 0.5 percent of a colonist's average annual income.

It hardly seems worth fighting a revolution over 42 cents a year. Even in today's money, the total burden of mercantilist controls would come to about $1,200 per person, and the net burden (costs minus benefits) to about $200. Some scholars think that Thomas's estimates of net costs are too low and could be doubled or even tripled; but still, the amounts are relatively small compared to the overall economy.[b]

The burden of mercantilism did not fall evenly on all colonists. The principal losers were the tobacco and rice planters of Virginia and South Carolina, as well as the merchants and craftsmen of New England. The former lost due to export controls, the latter due to restrictions on shipping and manufacturing. Thus, it is perhaps not surprising that the principal supporters of independence were in Virginia, South Carolina, and New England—precisely the regions where the costs of colonialism were highest.[c] ■

MERCANTILISM: COSTS AND BENEFITS

	1763–1772 (average/year)	1770
Burdens		
Burden on colonial foreign commerce	$ 2,255,000	$ 2,660,000
Burden per capita	$ 1.20	$ 1.24
Benefits		
Benefit of British protection	$ 1,775,000	$ 1,775,000
Benefit per capita	$ .94	$ .82
Balance	$ −.26	$ −.42

Source: Robert Paul Thomas, "A Quantitative Approach to the Study of the Effects of British Imperial Policy on Colonial Welfare," *Journal of Economic History* 25, no. 4 (December 1965).

a. Gross domestic product measures the total value of all goods and services produced in a country in a given year.
b. Roger L. Ransom, "British Policy and Colonial Growth: Some Implications of the Burden from the Navigation Acts," *Journal of Economic History*, 28, no. 3 (September 1968): 427–35.
c. Larry Sawers, "The Navigation Acts Revisited," *Economic History Review*, n.s., 45, no. 2 (May 1992): 262–84.

Peace of Westphalia:
The settlement that ended
the Thirty Years' War in 1648;
often said to have created the
modern state system because it
included a general recognition
of the principles of sovereignty
and nonintervention.

sovereignty: The expectation
that states have legal and
political supremacy—or ultimate
authority—within their territorial
boundaries.

hegemony: The predominance
of one nation-state over others.

Armada in 1588. Meanwhile, the Spanish possessions in the Netherlands revolted and formed the new Dutch Republic. Finally, in the Thirty Years' War (1618–1648), the French, Dutch, and other allies sealed the decline of Spain. This war ended with the **Peace of Westphalia,** which stabilized the borders of the belligerents and attempted to resolve some of the religious conflicts that had complicated their relations. Because the peace treaties called on governments not to interfere in the internal affairs of other countries, some scholars regard this as the beginning of the modern system of states, which are expected to respect each others' **sovereignty** within their borders.

Once the anti-Spanish alliance had defeated Spain, its members turned on each other. The English and the Dutch fought each other in a series of wars, and both the wars and rapid English commercial growth meant that by the 1660s the English had surpassed the Dutch as the world's leading trading and maritime power. This launched a 150-year conflict between England and its allies, on the one hand, and France and its allies, on the other. Anglo-French rivalry culminated with the Seven Years' War (1756–1763, also called the French and Indian War in North America), which effectively ended the French presence in the New World and established British predominance. The French challenge to Britain resurged during the French Revolution, which began in 1789 and led to the Napoleonic Wars (1804–1815). The British and their supporters finally defeated Napoleon at Waterloo in 1815, sealing British international **hegemony**.

For three centuries after 1492, world politics was dominated by the efforts of the principal European states to overpower one another and to control the non-European parts of the world. They pursued their economic and military interests by creating formal mercantilist colonial empires in some areas, by exercising less formal military and economic dominion elsewhere. Meanwhile, the principal European powers battled each other for their possessions and for global predominance. The rulers of western Europe fought on two fronts—to subdue the populations of their empires, and to expand at the expense of other European rulers.

By the end of the Napoleonic Wars in 1815, however, both central organizing principles of the mercantilist eras were being challenged. With the defeat of France by the anti-Napoleon coalition, conflict among the principal powers in Europe subsided and their security interests evolved. Meanwhile, the Industrial Revolution gathered force in Britain and on the Continent, and this started to alter the economic interests of the industrializing nations.

The Pax Britannica

The century from 1815 to 1914 was remarkably different from those that preceded it and the one that followed. The major powers were far more interested than they had been in trading and investing worldwide, including with each other. Instead of imposing strict restraints on the movement of goods and money around the world, most governments welcomed ever greater links among their economies. Their economic interactions became more cooperative as they pursued a common interest in global economic integration. This contributed to the accelerated economic growth that much of the world experienced during this period (see Figure 1.1). On the military front, global conflicts among the major

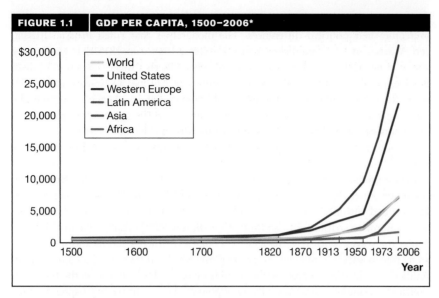

FIGURE 1.1 | **GDP PER CAPITA, 1500–2006***

*1990 International Geary-Khamis dollars, internationally comparable dollars of 1990.
Source: Angus Maddison, *The World Economy: Historical Statistics* (Paris: OECD, 2004); 2006 data provided at www.ggdc.net/Maddison/(accessed 2/28/2009).

powers gave way to generally peaceful ties among the countries of Europe (and, eventually, North America and Japan). To be sure, Europeans continued to use military and economic means to tighten and expand their control over people in their colonies and other poor countries. But interactions among the industrialized nations were generally pacific, and the world economy became very tightly integrated.

THE HUNDRED YEARS' PEACE

Between 1815 and 1914, relations among the European powers—and such rising non-European powers as the United States and Japan—were far calmer than they had been for three hundred years. While powerful nations certainly continued to care about their security interests, their relations became much less volatile and much less belligerent.

There were several sources of the greater cooperation among European powers. The first was a convergence in their interests. The French Revolution and the ensuing wars had, among other things, pitted democratic revolutionaries against absolutist and autocratic governments, and the autocrats had won. Few European nations were at all democratic, and those that were democratic were very partially so—in 1830, barely 2 percent of the British population was permitted to vote, and even then the disproportionate allocation of seats meant that those city-dwellers who could vote were unlikely to have much influence. All through the nineteenth century, however, movements for greater representation of the middle classes, farmers, and the working classes grew in strength. Sometimes, rulers acceded to these demands. But throughout Europe there was a common fear of revolution—by democratic forces originally, and eventually by the growing socialist and communist movements.

The common interest of the European rulers in suppressing revolution helped overcome their political differences. The monarchies that ruled Prussia, Russia, and Austria, in fact, established a formal Holy Alliance in 1815 that was largely aimed at facing the revolutionary threat. Eventually, this was extended to most of Europe, in what came to be called the Concert of Europe, a system under which the major powers consulted on important diplomatic affairs. At the same time, the growing integration of the markets of the European powers gave them some common economic interests as well, as we will discuss in the next section.

In addition to the convergence of interests among the principal powers, their interactions were also stabilized by the reality of British diplomatic, military, and economic predominance. In fact, the period is sometimes called the **Pax Britannica** (Latin for "British peace," by analogy with the Pax Romana that Rome was said to have created within its classical empire). British hegemony proved a stabilizing force among European nations. British military prowess was important—the British Navy "ruled the waves" with few challengers—but the country's significance rested also on its role in affecting interactions among European countries that had long been in conflict. Britain tried to prevent the supremacy of any one country on the European continent, acting to maintain a balance of power. (As we will see in Chapter 5, countries may form alliances in an effort to balance the power of a stronger country.) If one country or coalition seemed too strong, Britain would ally itself with an opposing country or coalition. This rough balance, which was the general goal of British foreign policy throughout the century, helped deter military conflict among the European powers.

Conflicts among the powers were muted, and there were few periods of open military strife. The age of massive intra-European war appeared to be over. To be sure, the power balance did not always serve to keep interactions peaceful, and European (and non-European) powers continued to compete with one another for military advantage and influence. The decline of one empire and the rise of another led to the century's biggest conflicts. The Ottoman Empire, which ruled much of the Middle East, North Africa, and southeastern Europe, weakened continually over the course of the nineteenth century. As the Ottoman state tottered, Russia attempted to expand its influence in the Middle East; and when other European countries sought to restrain Russia, the Crimean War (1853–1856) and Russian defeat were the result. Meanwhile, Prussia gradually unified a new German empire under its control. The French tried to discourage this process, but Prussia's victory in the Franco-Prussian War (1870–1871) settled the matter. The finalization of German unification indicated the arrival of a new power on the Continent. Despite these conflicts, the century from 1815 to 1914 was one of relative peace among the world's principal diplomatic and military powers.

FREE TRADE

Even as the absolutist European rulers—monarchs or others—could agree on a common opposition to democratic and other revolutionaries, so too could they agree on the desirability of ending the mercantilist economic controls of the earlier imperial period. To some extent, the reduction of barriers to trade among nations reflected the more peaceful nature of relations among the principal powers.

Pax Britannica: "British Peace," a century-long period beginning with Napoleon's defeat at Waterloo in 1815 and ending with the outbreak of World War I in 1914 during which Britain's economic and diplomatic influence contributed to economic openness and relative peace.

But much of the impetus for the reversal of mercantilism came from changes in the economic interests of the major powers themselves.

British desires for more open trade first displaced mercantilist interests. In the late eighteenth century, British inventors and industrialists introduced a flurry of technological innovations that revolutionized production. Employers brought workers together in large factories to use new machinery, new energy sources, and new forms of organization. Power looms and mechanical spinners transformed the textile industry. Improvements in the use of water power, and eventually the development of steam power, made the machinery more powerful still. By the 1820s, British industry was producing cotton and other textiles, iron, chemicals, and machinery at an unprecedented rate and at extremely low prices.

The economic interests created by Britain's Industrial Revolution saw mercantilist barriers to trade as irrelevant or harmful. Allowing foreigners to sell their products freely to Britain promised several positive effects. British manufacturers could lower their costs directly by importing cheaper raw materials, and indirectly because cheaper imported food would allow factory owners to pay lower wages without reducing workers' standard of living. And if foreigners earned more by selling to Britain, they would be able to buy more British goods. For these reasons, Britain's manufacturing classes and regions developed an antipathy to mercantilism and a desire for free trade. The City of London, which had become the world's financial center, added its influence to that of other free-trade interests. After all, Britain's international bankers had a powerful reason to open up the British market to foreigners: the foreigners were their customers. American or Argentine access to the thriving British market would make it easier for the Americans and Argentines to pay their debts to London. Of course, there were supporters of mercantilism and of barriers to trade more generally. Foremost among them were British farmers, who were protected by the Corn Laws. These were taxes, or tariffs, on imported grain. For twenty years, protectionist British farmers squared off against industrialists and other city-dwellers. Eventually, over the course of the 1840s, Parliament repealed most of the previous British mercantile controls on foreign trade.

After Britain, the world's most important economy, discarded mercantilism, many of the nation's customers and suppliers followed suit. In 1860, France joined Great Britain in a sweeping commercial treaty that freed trade between them and subsequently drew most of the rest of Europe in this direction. As the German states moved toward unification in 1871, they created a free-trade area among themselves and then opened trade with the rest of the world. Many New World governments also reduced trade barriers, as did the remaining colonial possessions of the free-trading European powers. Mercantilism was dead, and integration into world markets—trade liberalization—was the order of the day. Over the course of the 1800s, the trade of the advanced countries grew twice to three times as fast as their economies; by the end of the century, trade was seven or eight times as large a share of the world's economy as it had been at the beginning of the century.[3]

---

3. Angus Maddison, *Monitoring the World Economy, 1820–1992* (Paris: Development Centre of the Organization for Economic Co-operation and Development, 1995), 38. For an excellent survey of the period, see Peter T. Marsh, *Bargaining on Europe: Britain and the First Common Market, 1860–1892* (New Haven: Yale University Press, 1999).

The liberalization of world trade was encouraged by, and itself encouraged, major advances in transportation and communications. The railroad fundamentally changed the speed and cost of carrying cargo overland. The steamship revolutionized ocean-going shipping, reducing the Atlantic crossing from over a month in 1816 to less than a week in 1896. By the late 1800s, telegraphs, telephones, steamships, and railroads had replaced horses, carrier pigeons, couriers, and sails. The transportation revolution led to a twentyfold increase in the world's shipping capacity during the nineteenth century.[4]

THE GOLD STANDARD

gold standard: The monetary system that prevailed between about 1870 and 1914, in which countries tied their currencies to gold at a legally fixed price.

The monetary organizing principle of this global economic order was the **gold standard** (which we will examine in more detail in Chapter 8 on international monetary relations). When a country's government went "on gold," it promised to exchange its currency for gold at a preestablished rate. The country's currency became equivalent to gold, interchangeable at a fixed rate with the money of any other gold-standard country. Britain had had a gold-backed currency since 1717. As international trade and investment grew, more countries were drawn away from silver and other monetary metals and toward gold, the traditional international medium of exchange. Great Britain's status as the global market leader attracted other countries to use the same monetary system.

By the 1870s, most of the industrial world had adopted the gold standard. With all major currencies directly convertible into gold at fixed rates, the industrial world essentially shared one international currency. The predictability of the gold standard facilitated world trade, lending, investment, migration, and payments.

International trade, investment, and immigration grew dramatically. Citizens of rich countries invested huge portions of their savings abroad. Fifty million people left Europe for other continents, and another fifty million more left their homelands in Asia to live elsewhere. World markets for goods, labor, and capital were linked more tightly than they had ever been by free trade, the gold standard, and the new technologies of transportation and communications. In short, the world entered its first era of what we now call globalization.

COLONIAL IMPERIALISM

However pacific their diplomatic and economic relations may have been in Europe, the principal powers continued to use military force and economic controls on countries in the rest of the world. After a lull in the early part of the century, there was a burst of territorial expansion after 1870 that left most of Africa and Asia part of colonial empires.

The European powers, and eventually non-European powers such as the United States and Japan, were interested in the poor countries of Latin America, Africa, and Asia, for both security and economic reasons. The rich nations were interested in the resources and markets of the poor countries, in many cases wanting to secure

---

4. Peter Mathias and Sidney Pollard, *The Industrial Economics: The Development of Economic and Social Policies. The Cambridge Economic History of Europe,* Vol. 8 (Cambridge: Cambridge University Press, 1989), 56; Maddison, *The World Economy,* 95.

them for themselves (rather than sharing them with others). The major powers also saw the rest of the world as a sort of chessboard on which they could fight battles among themselves in their quest for military supremacy. The European (and American and Japanese) presence in the rest of the world expanded, contracted, and adjusted in accordance with the changing goals of the major powers and changes in the interactions among them.

The colonies had been central to the mercantilist system, but as mercantilism declined the economic interests in colonialism faded. For a hundred years after 1760, in fact, the European empires contracted dramatically. Many previous supporters of colonialism in the colonies began to favor independence, and many people in the metropolitan countries (such as the father of modern economics, Adam Smith, along with other free traders in Britain) came to see the colonies as unnecessarily burdensome. Eventually, Britain, France, Spain, and Portugal lost almost all their New World colonies, and by 1850 the only major colonial possessions remaining were British India, the Dutch East Indies (now Indonesia), and French Algeria.[5]

In the 1870s, however, colonial expansion started anew. The new powers that arose in and outside Europe—Germany, Italy, Japan, the United States—saw colonial possessions as a way of improving their military position. The established powers, especially Britain and France, did not want their newer rivals accumulating colonial power and wealth at their expense. At the same time, the growth of industry in the developed world increased the desire for overseas markets and resources. And there was an upsurge in nationalist sentiment, especially in such newly important nations as Germany, Italy, and Japan, which spurred governments to satisfy nationalistic demands for expansion.

The result was a scramble for new colonies. From a few scattered outposts in Africa, Europeans quickly spread out to occupy and rule the entire continent, leaving only Ethiopia and Liberia independent by 1890. Britain consolidated and extended its control of South Asia, while it, France, the Netherlands, Germany, Japan, and the United States took over almost all of the rest of Southeast and East Asia, leaving China, Persia (Iran), and Siam (Thailand) as the only major independent countries in the region (see Map 1.1). Within the space of a few decades, the industrialized nations had subjected most of the poor regions of the world to direct colonial control. The only major exceptions were Latin America and China, and even they had their sovereignty restricted by military and economic constraints imposed by the European nations, Japan, and the United States.

The Thirty Years' Crisis

A century of relative peace and prosperity in Europe ended with the most devastating military and economic conflicts in modern history. Generations of people in the advanced industrial world had their expectations of stability and security shattered

---

5. Britain's Canadian and Australian possessions had obtained effective autonomy by the 1850s, although they were still formally colonies. Within the British Empire, certain colonial areas were given extensive grants of self-government; for all intents and purposes, by the late nineteenth century, Canada, Australia, and New Zealand acted as if they were independent.

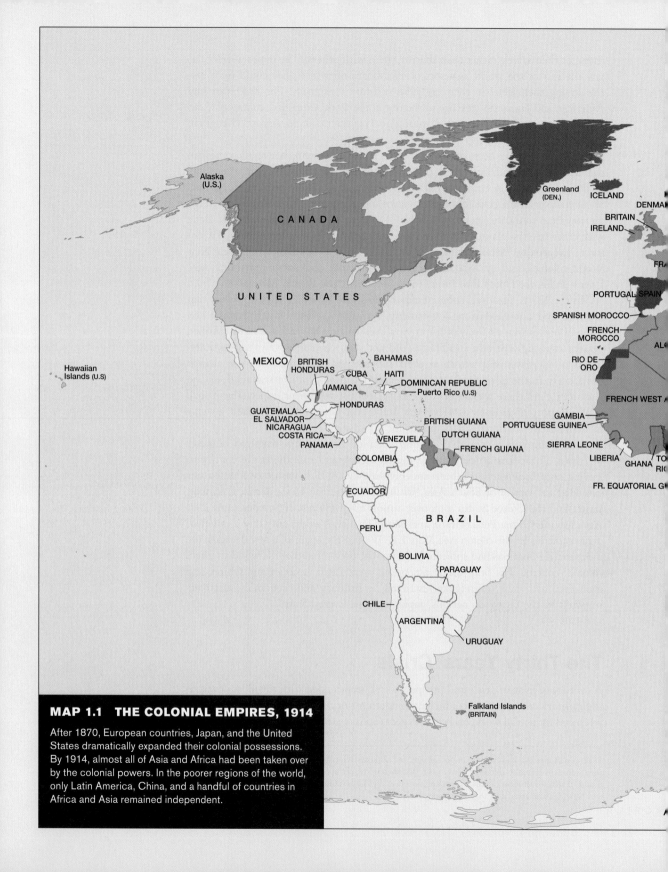

Alaska
(U.S.)

Greenland
(DEN.)

ICELAND

DENMA...

BRITAIN

IRELAND

CANADA

FR...

UNITED STATES

PORTUGAL SPAIN

SPANISH MOROCCO

FRENCH
MOROCCO

AL...

Hawaiian
Islands (U.S)

MEXICO

BRITISH
HONDURAS

BAHAMAS

CUBA

HAITI

DOMINICAN REPUBLIC

Puerto Rico (U.S)

RIO DE
ORO

JAMAICA

FRENCH WEST A...

GUATEMALA

HONDURAS

EL SALVADOR

NICARAGUA

COSTA RICA

PANAMA

VENEZUELA

BRITISH GUIANA

DUTCH GUIANA

FRENCH GUIANA

GAMBIA

PORTUGUESE GUINEA

SIERRA LEONE

LIBERIA

GHANA

TO...

RIO...

COLOMBIA

ECUADOR

BRAZIL

FR. EQUATORIAL G...

PERU

BOLIVIA

PARAGUAY

CHILE

ARGENTINA

URUGUAY

Falkland Islands
(BRITAIN)

MAP 1.1 THE COLONIAL EMPIRES, 1914

After 1870, European countries, Japan, and the United
States dramatically expanded their colonial possessions.
By 1914, almost all of Asia and Africa had been taken over
by the colonial powers. In the poorer regions of the world,
only Latin America, China, and a handful of countries in
Africa and Asia remained independent.

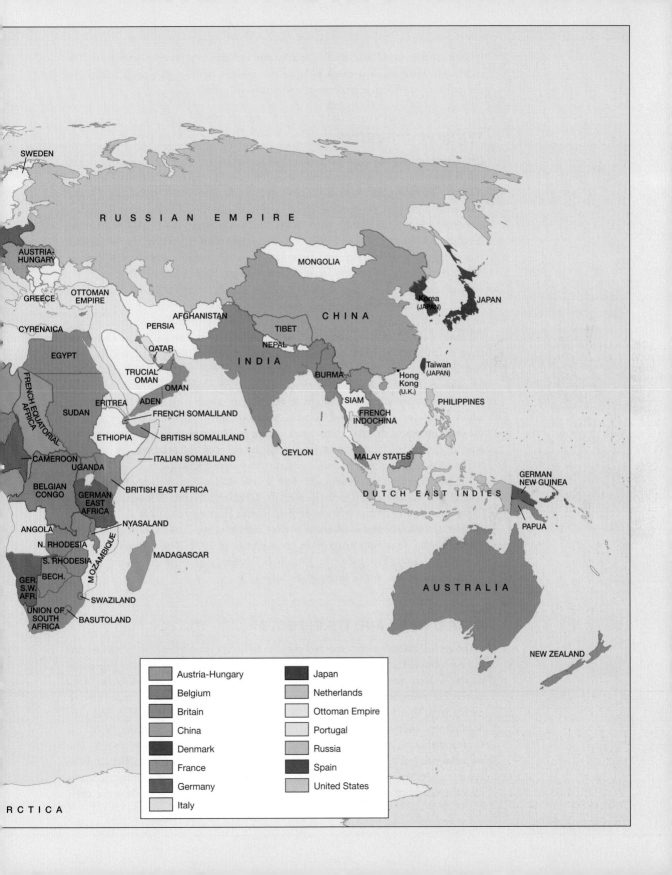

SWEDEN

RUSSIAN EMPIRE

AUSTRIA-
HUNGARY

GREECE

OTTOMAN
EMPIRE

MONGOLIA

Korea
(JAPAN)

JAPAN

CYRENAICA

AFGHANISTAN

PERSIA

TIBET

CHINA

QATAR

NEPAL

EGYPT

TRUCIAL
OMAN

INDIA

Taiwan
(JAPAN)

FRENCH EQUATORIAL AFRICA

OMAN

BURMA

Hong
Kong
(U.K.)

SUDAN

ERITREA

ADEN

FRENCH SOMALILAND

SIAM

PHILIPPINES

CAMEROON

ETHIOPIA

BRITISH SOMALILAND

FRENCH
INDOCHINA

UGANDA

ITALIAN SOMALILAND

CEYLON

BELGIAN
CONGO

GERMAN
EAST
AFRICA

BRITISH EAST AFRICA

MALAY STATES

GERMAN
NEW GUINEA

ANGOLA

NYASALAND

DUTCH EAST INDIES

N. RHODESIA

MOZAMBIQUE

PAPUA

S. RHODESIA

MADAGASCAR

GER.
S.W.
AFR.

BECH.

AUSTRALIA

UNION OF
SOUTH
AFRICA

SWAZILAND

BASUTOLAND

NEW ZEALAND

	Austria-Hungary		Japan
	Belgium		Netherlands
	Britain		Ottoman Empire
	China		Portugal
	Denmark		Russia
	France		Spain
	Germany		United States
	Italy		

RCTICA

by two terrible world wars and a catastrophic worldwide economic depression. The collapse of Europe's diplomatic balance led to three decades of global conflicts on the military, diplomatic, economic, and political fronts.

TENSION IN EUROPE

Contention among the principal powers had grown after 1900. One source of renewed conflict was the changing European power balance. On the one hand, the Ottoman, Austro-Hungarian, and Russian empires were weakening under the weight of socio-economic stagnation, political instability, and ethnic conflict. On the other hand, new economic and political actors were joining the world stage: the United States, after decades of insularity, was becoming more engaged with the rest of the world both politically and economically, and Japan had become a serious international force, as reflected in its decisive victory in the Russo-Japanese War of 1904–1905.

The most striking change in the European power balance was the rise of Germany. In 1870, the French and German populations and economies were of roughly similar size, and their economies were substantially smaller than Britain's, but by 1900 Germany's population and economy were the largest in Europe, larger even than those of Britain. This created frictions among European nations. The Germans, who had come late onto the world scene, felt that they had fallen behind in the race for colonies. Frustrated with their meager colonial possessions, Germany focused on Europe and appeared to have designs on neighboring lands with large German populations. These neighbors feared German expansionism and domination. For decades, the expectations of the major European nations had been of cooperative political and economic relations, largely under British hegemony; now, the prospect of a challenge to the previous arrangements made governments wary and suspicious.

Eventually, Europe divided into two hostile camps. On the one side were the central and southern European powers of Germany, Austria-Hungary, and the Ottoman Empire; on the other were Britain and France to the west and Russia to the east. Crises, whether in Morocco or the Caribbean, the Balkans or Africa, aggravated tensions until war erupted in the summer of 1914. The Central powers—Germany, Austria-Hungary, the Ottoman Empire, and Bulgaria—were arrayed against most of the rest of Europe (see Map 1.2).

WORLD WAR I AND ITS EFFECTS

Although all participants expected the war to be short and decisive, it turned out to be protracted and largely inconclusive—but extraordinarily bloody. Especially on the western front, in Belgium and northern France, huge armies settled into entrenched positions. Trench warfare was punctuated by attempts to break through enemy lines that typically led only to massive losses in dead, wounded, and captured troops on both sides. The first battle of the Marne, in September 1916, cost each side about a quarter million dead and wounded in the course of a week. The eventual entry of the United States in April 1917 on the side of the Allies, and the failure of German submarine warfare to cut Britain off from its supplies, guaranteed the defeat of the Central powers, but the victors had little to show for their

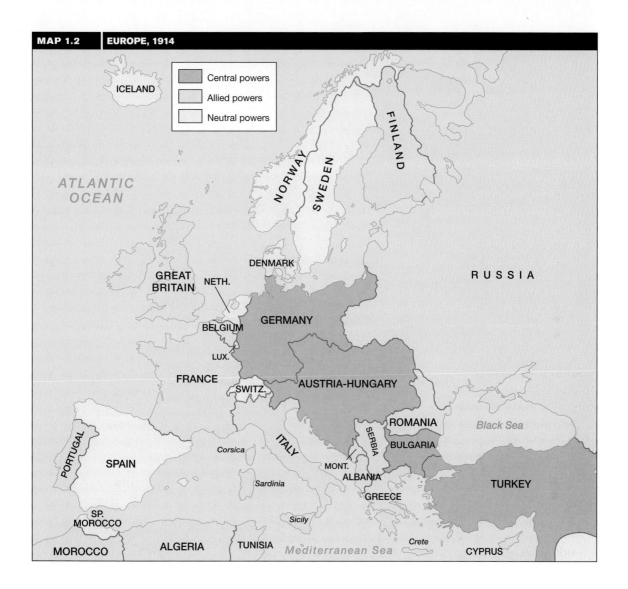

MAP 1.2   EUROPE, 1914

Central powers

Allied powers

Neutral powers

ICELAND

NORWAY

SWEDEN

FINLAND

ATLANTIC
OCEAN

DENMARK

RUSSIA

GREAT
BRITAIN

NETH.

BELGIUM

LUX.

GERMANY

FRANCE

SWITZ.

AUSTRIA-HUNGARY

PORTUGAL

SPAIN

Corsica

ITALY

Sardinia

ROMANIA

SERBIA

MONT.

ALBANIA

BULGARIA

Black Sea

GREECE

TURKEY

SP.
MOROCCO

Sicily

MOROCCO

ALGERIA

TUNISIA

Mediterranean Sea

Crete

CYPRUS

success. The war was far longer and far costlier than anyone had imagined it would be; it took of the lives of at least fifteen million people, including about seven million civilians.

Despite its immense cost, World War I did little to resolve the underlying political and military tensions that had unsettled Europe, and indeed exacerbated them. The war utterly disrupted European politics both among and within nations. It led to the collapse of the four great empires of central, eastern, and southern Europe. In the territory from Finland to Yugoslavia, the Austro-Hungarian and Russian empires shattered into pieces, and central and eastern Europe suddenly had a dozen new "successor states." The Ottoman Empire, which before the war had stretched from the Persian Gulf to Libya, and from Albania to Yemen, was reduced to the far

MAP 1.3   **EUROPE AFTER WORLD WAR I, 1920**

smaller country of Turkey. The German Empire lost what few colonies it had had, along with large portions of its European territory and population (see Map 1.3).

In addition to changing the political map of Europe, the war fundamentally altered domestic social and economic conditions. In most of the continent, economic recovery was slow and partial; many central and eastern European countries went through debilitating bouts of hyperinflation, with prices rising by thousands or millions of percentages. In the most dramatic case, that of Germany, prices rose to a level *one million million times*—that is, a trillion times—their immediate postwar level. The German mark, previously traded at 4.2 to the dollar, was eventually valued at 4,200,000,000,000—that is, 4.2 trillion—to the dollar. In the final months of the German hyperinflation, the central bank had to print so much currency that it used more than 30 dedicated paper mills, 29 plate manufacturers, and 132 printing plants.[6] This terrible experience bankrupted much of the central European middle classes and helped alienate them from the new democratic systems. Along with farmers, the disaffected middle classes grew to be an important base for extreme right-wing movements such as the fascists in Italy and the Nazis in Germany. At the same time, the war and its aftermath increased the power and organization of European labor movements and the socialist parties they supported. In Russia, a radical socialist movement took power, and soon there were communist parties everywhere, representing a revolutionary left-wing challenge to capitalism. The Communists favored government ownership of the means of production rather than capitalist private property, and a planned economy rather than a market system. Politics was polarized and nationalist sentiments inflamed, which contributed still further to tensions among European nations.

While it further weakened the bases of peace in Europe, the war demonstrated the international economic and military predominance of the United States. The entry of the United States into the war in 1917 effectively guaranteed the Allied victory, both with its millions of troops and with its billions of dollars in loans to the Allies. President Woodrow Wilson guided the negotiations that led to the **Treaty of Versailles,** which ended the war. Economically, while the Europeans were engulfed in war, the United States rushed into the vacuum they left in the rest of the world and seized a dramatically increased share of global trade and investment. In fact, the United States became the principal source of war loans to the Allies, so that between 1914 and 1919 America changed from being the world's biggest debtor to its biggest lender. The European powers were dependent on the United States for financial, commercial, and diplomatic leadership to rebuild from the most destructive war the world had ever known.

However, after this flurry of involvement in European politics and economics, the United States drew back. President Wilson could not convince the U.S. Senate to approve American entry into the **League of Nations.** Ironically, this was an international institution created, largely along lines defined by Wilson at Versailles, to bring the world's nations together to increase cooperation and guarantee the peace. In 1920, the Republican Party swept the presidency and both houses of Congress on a platform opposed to Wilson's internationalism and committed to an isolationist insulation of the United States from the uncertain vagaries of intra-European conflict.

Treaty of Versailles:
The peace treaty between the Allies and Germany that formally ended World War I on June 28, 1919.

League of Nations:
A permanent international security organization formed in the aftermath of World War I. The League was supplanted by the United Nations after World War II and was dissolved in 1946.

INTERWAR INSTABILITY

Europe was left to its own devices, without even the semblance of the pre-1914 balance. The French and British were weak in victory, Germany was bitter in defeat, Russia was isolated in its Communist experiment, and the Ottoman and Austro-Hungarian empires had dissolved into a series of small states beset by constant diplomatic and economic tensions. Economic conditions were unsettled, political systems were unstable, and diplomatic relations were tense when they were not downright hostile.

---

6. Gerald D. Feldman, *The Great Disorder: Politics, Economics, and Society in the German Inflation, 1914–1924* (New York: Oxford University Press, 1993), 782–85.

After World War I ended, the major economies of Europe and North America remained unsettled, and continuing tensions prevented cooperation on economic issues. Germany suffered hyperinflation that made its currency, the Deutschmark, virtually worthless. Here children play with bundles of useless Deutschmarks in the street.

The French and Germans, in particular, continued to clash diplomatically over issues left unsettled on the battlefield. These included control of the border regions of Alsace, Lorraine, and the Saar—the former two of which went to France, the latter to Germany. Another issue was Germany's commitment not to militarize the Rhineland, a region of Germany bordering on France. Germany took exception to this restriction on its sovereignty, while France regarded the movement of troops into a border region as a threat.

The former belligerents' interests also contended over the so-called war debts–reparations tangle. The Versailles treaty imposed payments of reparations, a fine levied on the losers for having started the war. This created great resentment in Germany, especially given the country's troubled economic conditions. The French argued, among other things, that they needed reparations to pay their debts to the United States. They would, they said, reduce demands on Germany if the United States would forgive some or all of these war debts—after all, the European Allies had paid a high price in lives and property. But the Americans were in no mood to give away billions of dollars to further their involvement with Europe's former belligerents. And so all throughout the 1920s and 1930s, the principals in World War I continued their battles in the diplomatic and economic realm.

The worst was yet to come: in 1929, the world spiraled downward toward further conflict. The global Great Depression that began in that year was more severe, lasted longer, and caused more hardship than any economic downturn in modern history. Industrial production dropped by half in the United States, and by 1932 one-quarter of the country's workers were unemployed. In Germany, unemployment topped one-third of the labor force. No country was untouched. The economic catastrophe deepened political polarization within nations, in many cases bringing extreme right-wing, highly nationalistic, often militaristic governments to power. By the late 1930s, the Nazis and their fascist allies controlled all of central, eastern, and southern Europe, as well as Japan. All these countries were hostile to the international economy and to the rich nations of western Europe and North America. In Latin America and in the colonial world, the collapse of the world economy drove nations in on their own devices, strengthening the hand of nationalist and anticolonial forces.

WORLD WAR II

Europe descended once again into war. World War II largely pitted the fascist governments that had turned against the global economy, on the one hand, against the democratic powers that remained committed to some form of international economic cooperation (along with the Soviet Union), on the other. The three major fascist powers—Germany, Italy, and Japan—formed an alliance, the Axis, aimed at restoring and increasing their military might and territory. By invasion, coercion, and persuasion, they built a network of followers, protectorates, and colonies—Japan in East Asia, Italy and Germany in Europe and North Africa.

An expansionist Nazi Germany annexed Austria in 1938 and occupied Czechoslovakia in 1939. In 1939, Germany attacked Poland and quickly overpowered it, leading Britain and France to declare war on Germany in support of their Polish ally. But in May 1940, Germany invaded France, which it defeated and occupied within six weeks. The Axis thus controlled virtually all of Europe and Asia except for Britain and Russia; the democratic allies were restricted to Britain, North America, Australia, and New Zealand. In June 1941, Germany invaded the Soviet Union, and soon German troops were on the outskirts of Moscow. In December, Japan—which had already occupied most of China and Indochina—attacked the American naval base at Pearl Harbor.

The United States had been supporting the British with supplies, but the Japanese attack on Pearl Harbor in 1941 overcame any lingering American reluctance to get involved in another world war. From then on, the war pitted the Axis against the three major Allies—the United States, Great Britain, and the Soviet Union. The bulk of the war in Europe was fought along the eastern front, between the Germans and the Soviets, where millions of troops faced each other over thousands of miles of territory. After an initial frenzied retreat, the Soviets battled back and turned the tide at Stalingrad in early 1943. Meanwhile, the British and Americans carried out operations in North Africa before invading Italy in 1943 and France in 1944, while American forces advanced against Japan in the Pacific. In May 1945, Germany surrendered unconditionally. In August, in an attempt to force a Japanese surrender, the United States dropped nuclear weapons on the Japanese cities of Hiroshima and Nagasaki; the Japanese surrendered several days later.

The human and economic costs of World War II were unimaginably large. About 110 million people served in the combined armed forces, of whom 25 million were killed. Approximately 30 million civilians were killed by the war directly, and this does not include the 7 million or more people, mostly Jews, whom the Germans and their allies murdered in a planned genocide. Four-fifths of the dead were from Allied nations, including some 20 million from the Soviet Union (13 million military, 7 million civilian). Most of Europe and Japan was left in ruins.

The Cold War

The impact of World War II on international politics was profound. Unlike in 1918, the results of the world war were conclusive, and they fundamentally altered international power relations. Germany, Japan, Italy, France, and Britain, which had defined Great Power politics before the war, were effectively finished as world powers; the only two nations with the ability to project significant military power were the United States and the Soviet Union. The question that remained was how this two-power world would be ordered. On the one hand, the two principal wartime allies had cooperated in defeating the Axis. On the other hand, they represented fundamentally different socioeconomic systems and had divergent interests in the organization of the postwar world.

THE SUPERPOWERS EMERGE

At war's end, the United States, the Soviet Union, Great Britain, and France were united in victory. The Allies defined the terms of the peace, carved up Germany into zones of occupation, and divided Europe into spheres of influence. Many people, including in the United States, felt that the four principal victors could, should, and would cooperate under the auspices of the new United Nations to manage international relations peacefully.

But within months, conflicts grew between the United States and the Soviet Union. Perhaps disagreements were inevitable between a capitalist democracy and a Communist one-party system. It may be that the two superpowers were driven toward discord by the very structure of their power relations, as they struggled for influence in Europe. Scholars continue to debate whether the source of the division was the inherently different economic or military interests of the two superpowers, or rather some failure in their attempts to interact productively.

By 1949, the two superpowers were consolidating control over their respective blocs. The United States drew together its new allies—including the defeated Axis nations—into a Western system. The Americans worked to solidify their coalition as a common military alliance, the **North Atlantic Treaty Organization (NATO)**, and as a collaborative economic order, the **Bretton Woods System**. The Soviet Union, for its part, now led a Communist alliance that stretched from central Europe to the Pacific, as China, North Korea, and North Vietnam had joined. The international order divided into Communist and capitalist parts, and the Cold War between them was the defining characteristic of international politics from the late 1940s until the late 1980s.

THE BLOCS CONSOLIDATE

The Cold War pitted the two superpowers against each other. Their military and economic interests were almost diametrically opposed. The United States favored market-based, capitalist economic activities, while the Soviet Union rejected markets and capitalism in favor of a centrally planned socialism. In the geopolitical sphere, the Soviets regarded a pro-American Western Europe as a threat to their western borders, and a pro-American Japan as a threat to their east; the Americans saw the Soviets and their Communist allies as a military menace to their European and Asian allies. In an atmosphere of trust and stability, it might have been possible for the two superpowers to work out an amicable understanding; but as it turned out, interactions between them quickly turned hostile and suspicious, and they devoted their efforts to fortifying themselves one against the other.

Each superpower went about building up its respective coalition. In the twenty years after World War II, the two major world alliances strengthened their internal

North Atlantic Treaty Organization (NATO):
A military alliance created in 1949 to bring together many Western European nations, the United States, and Canada, forming the foundation of the American-led military bloc during the Cold War. Today, NATO's role includes handling regional problems and developing a rapid reaction force.

Bretton Woods System:
The economic order negotiated among allied nations at Bretton Woods, New Hampshire, in 1944, which led to a series of cooperative arrangements involving a commitment to relatively low barriers to international trade and investment.

ties, added members, and fortified themselves against the rival bloc. The United States provided $14 billion in Marshall Plan and other aid to Western Europe and Japan in order to speed postwar reconstruction. It also led the Western world in creating a system of military alliances in the North Atlantic, Southeast Asia, Latin America, and elsewhere. The most important of these, the North Atlantic Treaty Organization (NATO), brought together North America and most of Western Europe in a collective military institution united against the Soviet Union and its allies (see Chapter 5 for more details on NATO and other military alliances).

The United States also guided its allies toward a newly integrated and strongly institutionalized Western economic order. The Bretton Woods System, so called because its founding documents were negotiated at the Bretton Woods resort in New Hampshire, included institutions intended to encourage the freer movement of goods and capital around the world. In trade relations, the General Agreement on Tariffs and Trade (GATT) oversaw a substantial reduction in trade barriers.[7] In monetary affairs, the International Monetary Fund (IMF) supervised a restored but reformed gold-dollar standard, in which the U.S. dollar was tied to gold and all currencies were tied to the dollar. The International Bank for Reconstruction and Development (IBRD or World Bank) worked to encourage a resumption of private investment, especially in the developing nations (these economic institutions are discussed in more detail in Part III). By the early 1960s, the Western world had rebuilt an integrated international economy—not a copy of the pre-1914 age of free trade and the gold standard, but something new. Particularly novel was that the commitment to economic integration was combined with social welfare programs such as unemployment insurance and the widespread public provision of health care, pensions, housing, and other social benefits. This expansive social safety net helped cushion workers from the harshest effects of global competition, and the Bretton Woods system thus represented a compromise between economic integration and national commitments to social reform and the welfare state.

The Soviet Union also consolidated its bloc. It created a military alliance with its European allies, the **Warsaw Pact.** It strengthened military ties with the Communist government that took power in China in 1949. In the economic realm, the Soviet bloc developed a socialist variant of economic integration in which different nations specialized in different products. This economic cooperation was overseen by an institution called the Council for Mutual Economic Assistance (CMEA or Comecon), which brought together the Communist nations and some of their supporters in the developing world. The Cold War, indeed, extended to competition over the support of many newly independent countries in Africa, Asia, and the Caribbean. Eventually, there was a rough division of the world between countries that tended to ally with the United States and those that tended to ally with the Soviet Union (see Map 1.4).

The defining feature of military relations between the two superpowers was the development of nuclear weapons. By 1954, both the United States and the Soviet Union had atomic and hydrogen bombs, possessing a destructive power far beyond anything previously possible. With the development of long-distance bombers and

Warsaw Pact: A military alliance formed in 1955 to bring together the Soviet Union and its Cold War allies in Eastern Europe and elsewhere; dissolved on March 31, 1991, as the Cold War ended.

---

7. The original institution was to be the International Trade Organization, but it encountered opposition in the United States. As a result, an "interim" institution, the GATT, took its place.

MAP 1.4　　THE COLD WAR AND ITS ALLIANCES, 1980

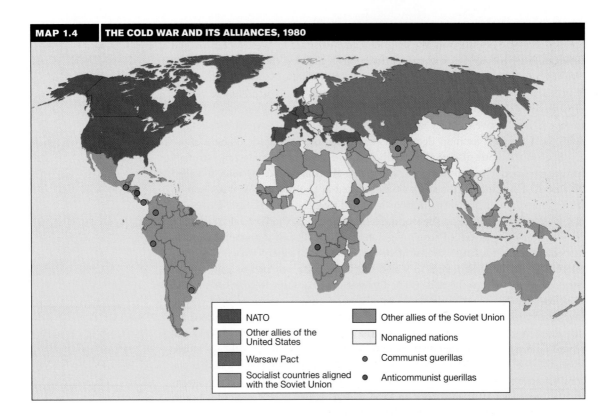

NATO

Other allies of the
United States

Warsaw Pact

Socialist countries aligned
with the Soviet Union

Other allies of the Soviet Union

Nonaligned nations

● Communist guerillas

● Anticommunist guerillas

missiles, eventually both superpowers had the ability to destroy each other (and their allies) many times over. This led to a real fear that war between the two superpowers might be unimaginably devastating and might threaten all of humanity.

However, the rough parity in nuclear weapons created something of a stand-off: each side's destructive capacity was sufficient to deter an attack on its homeland or its close allies. Since neither the United States nor the Soviet Union could really hope to conquer the other or its principal friends, their competition was limited to other regions of the globe.

Indeed, despite the absence of direct warfare between the superpowers, the Cold War was by no means a peaceful time for people in much of the world. On several occasions, crises between the two came to the brink of war, such as the 1949 Berlin airlift and the 1962 Cuban missile crisis. In the aftermath of the German surrender, Germany was divided into four zones, controlled respectively by the Americans, British, French, and Soviets. The country' s traditional capital, Berlin, which was located deep inside the Soviet zone, was also divided in four. Over time, the Western allies worked together in their zones, but there was constant friction between them and the Soviets. In June 1948, the Soviet Union blockaded land and rail routes into Berlin from the Western zones. This cut West Berlin (the American, British, and French portion) off from supplies of everything from food to coal. The Soviets clearly expected the Western allies to either withdraw or accede to several Soviet demands about the occupation. But the allies quickly organized a massive airlift that lasted nearly a year and involved almost 300,000 flights, providing millions of tons of supplies to the residents of West Berlin. In May 1949, the Soviets finally backed down and once again permitted transport between the Western occupation zones and West Berlin. But the level of tension between East and West had been raised substantially. Indeed, some scholars regard the Berlin blockade and airlift as the opening salvo in the Cold War.

Perhaps the most dramatic confrontation of the Cold War took place almost fifteen years later in Cuba. In 1959, a left-wing nationalist movement headed by Fidel Castro succeeded in ousting pro-American dictator Fulgencio Batista. Over the next several years, the new revolutionary government of Cuba moved quickly leftward and allied itself with the Soviet Union. An American-sponsored invasion in April 1961 failed, but the Cuban government was deeply fearful of American attempts to undermine it. Meanwhile, the Soviet government under Nikita Khrushchev was concerned that it was losing the nuclear arms race to the United States. In the summer of 1962, the Soviets secretly began installing nuclear missiles in Cuba; these were intended both to help protect the pro-Soviet Cuban government and, more important, to help redress the nuclear balance by putting Soviet missiles within easy striking distance of the United States. In October 1962, American spy planes spotted the missile installations, which the U.S. government regarded as a clear and present danger to American national security. American ships encircled the island, prepared to prevent Soviet naval vessels from reaching it, and plans for an American invasion were developed, even though many of the participants realized that this might lead to a nuclear war between the two sides. For about a week, the U.S. and Soviet governments bargained over the missiles in an atmosphere of extraordinary tension and widespread expectation that war would break out. Finally, the two sides agreed to a deal: the Soviets would dismantle their missiles in Cuba if the United States withdrew its nuclear missiles from Turkey. This represented a major concession by the Soviets, especially as the Turkish withdrawal was secret at the time; it appeared to most observers that Khrushchev had backed down. As Secretary of State Dean Rusk told President John F. Kennedy at the time, "We were eyeball to eyeball, and the other fellow just blinked."[8]

In addition to the threat of war between the two nations, each superpower routinely used military force in order to prevent other countries from falling into the sphere of its rival. The United States had its military and intelligence services undermine governments that were communist or seen as likely to come under communist influence: Iran in 1953, Guatemala in 1954, the Congo in 1961, Cuba in 1961, the Dominican Republic in 1962, Chile in 1971, and Nicaragua from 1979 to 1988. The Soviet Union similarly used military power to extend or preserve its own influence. Its forces invaded Hungary in 1956 and Czechoslovakia

---

8. One recent addition to the enormous literature on the crisis is Michael Dobbs, *One Minute to Midnight: Kennedy, Khrushchev, and Castro on the Brink of Nuclear War* (New York: Knopf, 2008). The tense showdown during the crisis is an example of brinksmanship, which we will discuss in Chapter 3.

in 1968 when these allies seemed likely to leave the Soviet orbit. The Soviet Union also invaded Afghanistan in 1979, leading to a decade-long war that sapped the country's military might.

In the colonial and postcolonial world, especially, the two superpowers constantly jockeyed for influence. Wars in Korea and Vietnam were the most obvious instances. In both cases, the Soviets supported one side of a civil conflict, while the Americans supported another side. The United States and some of its allies sent troops to both South Korea and South Vietnam; the Soviet Union and some of its allies sent supplies to both North Korea and North Vietnam. The same sort of "proxy war" was fought in many regions and over many decades. Much of the developing world became a Cold War battleground between pro-American and pro-Soviet forces.

DECOLONIZATION

The involvement of the two superpowers in the affairs of Africa, Asia, and Latin America was part of a broader emergence of these regions to a prominent place in world politics. This was a relatively new phenomenon in the modern era: between 1914 and the mid-1950s, the developing world was largely at the margins of world politics. Europe, North America, and Japan were preoccupied with two world wars, the Great Depression, postwar reconstruction, and the Cold War. Under these conditions, relations with the colonies and the independent developing nations were of less importance. The economic implications were particularly striking. For decades, Africa, Asia, and Latin America had supported themselves by exporting agricultural products and raw materials to the industrial world and importing manufactured products. But for much of the time between 1914 and 1955, the rich nations were unwilling or unable to continue normal trade relations—they were absorbed in war, devastated by economic crisis, or rebuilding after war.

The developing world thus was forced to rely less on its economic ties with the industrial nations and more on its own markets and products. While in the early stages it was external events—depression and war—that cut the developing world off, eventually governments encouraged the process. Many countries, and even some colonies, undertook substantial efforts at industrial development, providing at home what had previously been imported from Europe or North America. For example, by the early 1960s Brazil's industries supplied 99 percent of the country's consumer goods, 91 percent of its intermediate inputs (such as steel and chemicals), and 87 percent of its capital goods (such as machinery and equipment).[9] At that point the Brazilian economy, which was roughly the size of the Dutch economy, was close to self-sufficient in manufactured goods.

This economic turn inward was accompanied by an upsurge in nationalist sentiment. In Latin America, China, and Turkey, this brought to power governments that were unfavorable—even hostile—to foreign trade, foreign investment, and foreign finance. In many colonies, the rise in nationalism fed into dissatisfaction with continued colonial rule.

---

9. Werner Baer, *The Brazilian Economy: Growth and Development,* 3rd ed. (New York: Praeger, 1989), 70

After World War II ended, the colonial clamor for greater autonomy, and even independence, increased. The European empires had been weakened by the war, and their ability to sustain colonialism by force of arms had diminished. Meanwhile, many of the nationalist movements had grown in strength and resolve, and they demanded autonomy and even independence more insistently. **Decolonization** was on the agenda for the first time in years, as colonial subjects fought to leave the colonial empires. In some instances, such as British India, the colonial powers acceded to these demands, albeit reluctantly, recognizing that they had little alternative. But in other instances, such as British Kenya, French Algeria, and the Dutch East Indies (Indonesia), independence came only after violent conflict between the colonialists and the colonized.

Pressure on the colonial powers did not only come from the nationalist independence movements. In many instances, the United States encouraged its European allies to release their subjects. American anticolonialism had moral sources, but also more material origins. For example, American businesses welcomed a decolonization that would allow them fuller access to the markets of the developing world. And in the context of the Cold War, the United States was particularly concerned that colonialism would undermine American influence in the developing world. With so much of the world under European colonial control, it was hard for the United States to make a case for the evils of Soviet domination. The Soviet Union and China had good anticolonial credentials, and the Americans feared that colonialism would push Africans and Asians toward the Communists in the search for allies.

Developments within the colonies, within the imperial nations, and in international politics brought the end of colonialism more quickly than anyone had imagined possible. Within a few years of the end of World War II, almost all of colonial Asia and the Middle East was independent; North Africa gained its independence over the course of the 1950s, and by 1965 almost all of Africa was free. Colonialism was finished, and the world was made up of sovereign states.

decolonization: The process of shedding colonial possessions, especially the rapid end of the European empires in Africa, Asia, and the Caribbean between the 1940s and the 1960s.

THE RISE OF THE THIRD WORLD

Many of the newly independent nations of Africa, Asia, and the Caribbean resisted involvement in the battle between the American and Soviet blocs. They concentrated on problems in the relationship between the rich industrialized nations and the poor developing countries—the divide between North and South, rather than East and West. In the late 1950s and early 1960s, leaders of such countries as India, Egypt, Ghana, and the Philippines came together to form a nonaligned movement of nations that professed independence from either bloc. These members of the third world, so called to distinguish them from the capitalist first and communist second worlds, aimed to redress perceived inequities in their relationship with the advanced industrial world, especially in the nature of their economic ties.

Most third world attempts to reform the international economy were ineffectual, as they lacked the power to make their points any more than rhetorically. But in 1973, the success of the major oil-producing developing nations in manipulating world oil markets and dramatically increasing oil prices held out hope for more balance in North-South economic relations. The developing nations had raw materials that the industrialized world wanted, and if they could organize themselves as effectively as had the members of the Organization of Petroleum Exporting Countries (OPEC), they might be able to extract more resources from the rich nations. Some producers of raw materials followed OPEC in organizing cartels to try to raise prices (copper, bauxite, and bananas, for example), with mixed success. But the third world also agitated more generally for a New International Economic Order that would be more favorable to developing nations.

THE COLD WAR THAWS

Even as the developing world organized itself in ways that did not fit the East-West dimension, by the middle 1960s the two superpower alliances were themselves beginning to show signs of strain. France withdrew from NATO, and the United States got bogged down in a war in Vietnam that was unpopular both abroad and at home. The Soviet Union lost its most important ally when China broke with the rest of the Soviet bloc, while dissatisfaction in Eastern Europe and at home put pressure on the Soviet government to provide greater political and economic freedoms.

Although conflict persisted in relations between the United States and the Soviet Union, in the 1970s both sides warily attempted a relaxation of tensions. The two blocs built more political, economic, and cultural ties, and they negotiated a series of agreements to limit the arms race between them. This reduction in hostility, or détente, was set back by continued competition in the third world and Europe, but the threat of armed conflict seemed to recede.

After the Cold War

The relaxation of U.S.-Soviet tensions reduced the threat of superpower war. But the postwar patterns of international political and economic relations were soon disrupted by two decades of upheavals.

THE COLD WAR ENDS

In 1979, relations between the United States and the Soviet Union, which had been improving for over fifteen years, took a turn toward much greater hostility. In December of that year, Soviet troops entered Afghanistan to support a fragile pro-Soviet government. The United States and its allies responded vigorously to this first direct use of Soviet troops outside of the Warsaw Pact, imposing trade sanctions, financing Afghan insurgents, and boycotting the 1980 Olympic Games in Moscow. Soviet troops were soon bogged down in a guerrilla war that many observers compared to the American experience in Vietnam.

In 1981, Ronald Reagan took office as U.S. president, committed to a strongly anti-Soviet stance. The Reagan administration substantially increased military spending, especially spending connected to U.S.-Soviet rivalry. The United States

The fall of the Berlin Wall in 1989 provided a powerful symbol of the end of the Cold War. During the Cold War, the Berlin Wall divided West Berlin from communist East Berlin.

made plans to deploy a new generation of missiles in Western Europe, within a few minutes' striking distance of major Soviet cities. It also began work on a Strategic Defense Initiative, a "defensive shield" against potential missile attacks. These measures threatened to upset the rough balance between the United States and the Soviet Union; in reaction, the Soviets attempted to increase their own military spending.

The renewed tension put great strains both on international relations and the Soviet economic and political order. The Soviet economy was falling farther and farther behind that of the West, and the faltering Soviet system was finding it increasingly difficult to keep up militarily. Eventually, after Mikhail Gorbachev took power in the Soviet Union in 1985, he moved quickly to improve relations with the United States and to encourage greater political openness (glasnost) and economic reconstruction (perestroika) in the troubled Soviet system. In 1988, the Soviets relaxed their control over their Eastern European allies; in 1989, Soviet troops withdrew from Afghanistan, the Berlin Wall came down, and Communists began loosening their grip on governments all over central and eastern Europe. By 1991, the Soviet Union had dissolved into fifteen new independent non-Communist countries, and the Communist governments of the Soviet Union's European allies were out of power. The Cold War was over, and only one superpower was left standing.

WORLDWIDE ECONOMIC DEVELOPMENTS

It was not just in the world of East-West diplomacy that the 1970s and 1980s led to great change. After the OPEC oil shocks of 1973–1974, the industrialized capitalist world entered a decade of recession, high unemployment, and high inflation. In the early 1980s, austerity measures to cut government spending and restrain wages helped bring inflation under control, but many economies remained stagnant. The developing nations, too, ran into trouble as a global debt crisis erupted in 1982 and drove many heavily indebted poor nations into crisis. As mentioned, economic growth in the Soviet bloc slowed dramatically, and social unrest exploded into open protest.

Over the course of the 1980s, supporters and opponents of increasing the role of market forces in economic activity faced off in developed, developing, and Communist countries. In almost all instances, the crisis eventually led to a turn toward the market. The fact that international trade, finance, and investment were at very high levels probably increased the attractiveness of this evolution, as it held out the promise of access to lucrative global economic opportunities.

In the West, cross-border trade and investment increased very substantially. Regional trade agreements (RTAs) were strengthened. The European Union, first created as the European Coal and Steel Community (ECSC) by six Western European nations in 1951, grew to include almost all of Western Europe by 1995 (only Norway, Iceland, and Switzerland refrained from joining), removed all barriers to the movement of goods and capital among member states in 1991, and eventually replaced most of their national currencies, such as the French franc and the German mark, with a common currency, the euro, in 2002. The United States, Canada, and Mexico created a North American Free Trade Agreement (NAFTA) in 1994 that similarly removed many economic barriers among themselves. (See Figure 1.2 for an overview of RTAs established during the period 1959–2006.)

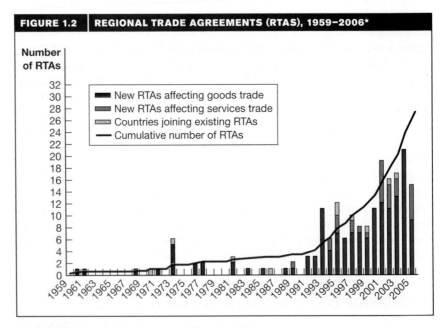

FIGURE 1.2 | REGIONAL TRADE AGREEMENTS (RTAS), 1959–2006*

* Includes RTAs currently in force, by year of entry into force.
Source: Roberto V. Fiorentino, Luis Verdeja, and Christelle Toqueboeuf, "The Changing Landscape of Regional Trade Agreements: 2006 Update," WTO Discussion Paper No. 12 (Geneva: World Trade Organization, 2007).

Most developing countries responded to the difficulties of the 1980s by jettisoning previous barriers to international economic involvement, welcoming foreign trade and investment. The watchword of the 1990s and early 2000s was *globalization,* with a level of international economic integration that had not been seen since 1914.

The most stunning changes took place in the Communist world. China and Vietnam embraced capitalist economic reform in the early 1980s but maintained their one-party systems. The Soviet Union under Gorbachev embarked on a program of economic reform, but the reforms were rapidly overtaken by events as the country fragmented into fifteen separate independent states. Some of them, and most of the Soviet Union's former allies in central and eastern Europe, quickly moved to integrate with the European Union. Russia remained somewhat aloof from Europe, and tensions with the United States continued.

Despite differences among regions and countries, by the turn of the millennium it was clear that the world economy was globalized and likely to remain so for the foreseeable future. Unlike in the interwar period or the Cold War era, every major country was committed to substantial involvement in world trade, investment, and finance. Although many aspects of globalization remained controversial, most people in most countries seemed to accept the general principle that national economies should, and would, be quite integrated with the rest of the world economy.

NEW DIPLOMATIC CHALLENGES

The end of the Cold War was not the end of military and diplomatic conflict in world politics. Even as the Soviet Union was disintegrating, a new crisis erupted in the Persian Gulf. In August 1990, Iraq, led by President Saddam Hussein, invaded its small neighbor Kuwait. The two countries had been embroiled in disputes over Iraqi debts to Kuwait, over oil policy, and over a contested border; but the invasion took almost everyone by surprise (for more on these events, see the discussion in Chapter 3). The international response to the Iraqi invasion was widely seen as an indication of how world politics might evolve in the new, post–Cold War environment.

Almost immediately, the United Nations Security Council and the Arab League condemned the invasion. The United Nations eventually established a deadline of January 15, 1991, for Iraq to withdraw from Kuwait, while the United States assembled a coalition of thirty-four countries willing to participate in military action to expel Iraqi troops from Kuwait. Two days after the deadline passed, the American-led coalition began a month of massive air attacks on Iraq, followed by a ground assault that defeated Iraqi forces within three days.

The overwhelming defeat of the Iraqi invasion seemed to presage an era in which the world community, acting through the UN, might act collectively to resolve diplomatic problems of general concern. This trend was visible in the expansion of UN involvement in a series of difficult military, diplomatic, and humanitarian issues over the course of the 1990s. In 1992, a UN mission went to Somalia to try to ensure that humanitarian supplies would reach the civilian population as the country descended into a state of lawlessness; the mission was a qualified success. In 1993, another UN mission went to Rwanda to try to mediate a resolution of that country's civil war. But a year later, the mission was powerless to halt a horrific genocide in which the Rwandan government orchestrated the murder of as many as a million Rwandan citizens, most of them from the minority Tutsi ethnic group. Meanwhile, UN peacekeeping forces were deployed in the former Yugoslavia to try to moderate continuing conflicts among the new governments, and disparate ethnic groups, in the region. These forces had some successes and some failures, including a very visible inability to keep Serbian forces from massacring some eight thousand Bosnian boys and men in Srebrenica, which the UN had declared a "safe area." Despite a mixed record, UN involvement in these and other conflicts held out the hope of further international collaboration to resolve difficult diplomatic and military problems.

At the same time, more traditional unilateral and alliance military actions continued. In 1995 and again in 1999, NATO launched air strikes in the former Yugoslavia to try to achieve diplomatic goals. In the first instance, the strikes were on Bosnian Serbian forces in the former Yugoslav province of Bosnia-Herzegovina; the strikes had the goal of ending ethnic fighting there. In the second instance, the attacks were on Yugoslav military forces, with the purpose of forcing the Yugoslav government to withdraw its troops from the contested, majority-Albanian, province of Kosovo. Both NATO undertakings were essentially successful: the Bosnian war ended with a peace agreement, and Yugoslav troops were withdrawn from Kosovo.

The tension between traditional and newer diplomatic approaches was high-lighted in 2002–2003, as the major powers debated how to deal with the Iraqi government of Saddam Hussein. As we will see in Chapters 2, 3, and 5, some policymakers wanted the UN to formulate a common response to Iraq's flouting of previous UN decisions. But the United States was dissatisfied with the speed and character of UN actions, and it and the United Kingdom organized an independent "coalition of the willing," which launched an invasion and occupation of Iraq in March 2003.

The record of the post–Cold War world is mixed. On the one hand, there has been a gradual growth of UN involvement in military and diplomatic conflicts. This may presage a new trend in world politics, especially in military affairs, toward greater use of the UN and other international institutions and less reliance on unilateral action. On the other hand, the Iraq War and other such conflicts resemble more traditional power politics, which is unlikely to disappear.

A development related to the greater involvement of international institutions in world politics has been the rise of such nonstate actors as transnational human rights and environmentalist groups. These groups, which will be discussed more thoroughly in Chapter 10, appear to have proliferated in recent years and, in the view of many analysts, have had an important impact on international politics. Such transnational groups are of many varieties—ranging from human and labor rights networks to terrorist organizations—and they are an increasingly prominent feature of the world political environment.

What Will Shape Our World in the Future?

Today, the two overriding realities of international politics are American supremacy and globalization. On the military and diplomatic front, there is no serious challenger to the United States, whose military spending is roughly equal to that of the rest of the world combined. Economically, the world is more tightly linked than it has been since 1914, and international trade and investment continue to grow rapidly. However, there remain important uncertainties about both the security and the economic dimensions of world politics. To understand where the world is likely to head, we need to identify the interests of the major actors in contemporary world politics, and to analyze how these interests interact as they play themselves out on the world stage.

AMERICAN PREDOMINANCE AND CHALLENGES TO IT

For the foreseeable future, the international political order will be unipolar, given the unchallenged diplomatic predominance of the United States. For the first time in modern history, there is no realistic prospect of armed hostilities among the world's major nations. The European Union, Russia, China, and Japan do not always like America's predominance, but conflicts among these powers have remained muted. Unchallenged American military superiority raises several questions about the future. The first set of questions has to do with American interests: To what purpose will the United States put its unaccustomed position? What are the security and economic goals it will attempt to further with its dominance?

Globalization and international economic institutions have provoked numerous controversies in world politics. Some people, like this Japanese farmer, believe that international institutions like the World Trade Organization (WTO) threaten their livelihoods.

The second set of questions has to do with the ways in which the United States, and other major countries, interact in the international arena: Will the general post-1945 American commitment to multilateral cooperation and to international institution-building be sustained? Or will the United States attempt to "go it alone" on military and economic ventures that may not meet with the approval of other countries? Will such other countries (or groups of countries) as the European Union, Russia, and China focus on collaborating with the United States in pursuit of common goals, or will they attempt to challenge its position in particular regions or issue areas?

In addition to relations among the principal powers, international politics has continued to be characterized by a wide variety of military, political, and ethnic conflicts. However, while during the Cold War these conflicts risked involving the two blocs and thus major war, today they appear not to represent a serious threat to peace among the principal powers. This does not mean that the conflicts are unimportant. Religious fundamentalists, hostile to many of the political, ideological, and economic values shared by industrial nations in both the East and the West, have launched armed campaigns to resist the penetration of Muslim societies by secular, capitalist values and institutions. In fact, the principal challenge to American international power in the twenty-first century has come not from Russia, China, or the European Union, but from a loose network of Islamic extremists who have used terror attacks around the globe to contest the role of the United States, and the West more generally, worldwide.

These two strands in international politics—America's predominance, and ethno-religious conflicts—came together with the American invasion of Iraq in 2003. This invasion marked a movement away from multilateralism on the part of American foreign policymakers; it also ended up involving the United States and its allies in a bitter and extended conflict with armed insurgents within and outside Iraq. Whatever the outcome of the Iraq conflict may be, it highlights issues that are likely to define international politics in the future: the interests of the United States, interactions between the United States and other major nations, and the future of anti-Western ethnic and religious extremism.

GLOBALIZATION

At the turn of the twenty-first century, whatever disagreements there may have been among the world's major nations, they all agreed on the general desirability of continued international economic integration—that is, globalization. Nonetheless, there are enduring issues in the international economy on the contemporary agenda.

There remain questions about the extent to which some countries see their interests tied to closer integration with the global economy. While almost all countries profess an interest in economic openness, continuing disputes may indicate that these interests are not so clear-cut. Up to now, for example, neither Russia nor China has been willing to open its borders fully to international trade, finance, and investment. Much of the developing world, after enacting a flurry of economic reforms, appears to be pulling back as the changes prove less effective, and more costly, than anticipated. There are Americans who worry that the European Union is turning in on itself, and Europeans who fear that the United States (and its close neighbors in the Americas) is also turning inward. Did enthusiasm for international economic engagement peak in the 1990s? Are countries (and regional groupings such as the EU and NAFTA) now more concerned with their own affairs than with global cooperation?

At the same time, globalization has brought challenges to the patterns of international interaction that have characterized the Western world since World War II. Conflicts over trade, investment, and finance have proliferated. Many developing countries, as well as China and Russia, feel that existing international institutions serve the rich nations rather than them. Will interactions among the world's major economies remain generally cooperative, or will they become more conflictual?

There is growing concern that international economic trends may pose a threat to social and environmental goals. Certainly, rapid growth in the developing world challenges the planet's ability to support more industry, more cities, more automobiles—more of the features of modern life to which billions of poor people aspire, but which may not be compatible with environmental sustainability. Is there enough interest among governments to deal with the problem? Is there an ability to work together to address the issues?

All of these apprehensions were heightened by the global economic crisis that began in 2008. Difficulties in the American financial system were quickly transmitted around the world, and within months the entire international economy was in recession. There were even fears that the recession might deepen into depression. The economic downturn raised the specter of economic conflicts among the world's major powers, as each nation focused its efforts on defending itself and its citizens from the fallout of the economic collapse. National governments and international economic institutions were confronted with problems of unprecedented breadth and scope. These events led many observers to wonder if the existing international economic order, and economic cooperation among the world's governments, would survive the most serious crisis since the 1930s.

LOOKING AHEAD

What will the lives of those born around 2000 be like? Will there be serious military threats, and will these threats come from such new powers as China, or from religious terrorists? Will the industrialized world collaborate in confronting such challenges, or will it splinter into contending blocs? For those born in the poor nations of Asia, Africa, and Latin America, will the next fifty years bring prosperity and a hope of catching up with the West, or will poverty persist and spread? Can the international economic order remain open and relations among the major economic centers remain collaborative, or will countries and regions turn toward self-sufficiency?

Our best hope for understanding the future of world politics is to develop analytical tools that accurately reflect the basic forces at play. This brief overview of the historical processes and events that created today's world shows how the interests of people and countries affect the way they interact with one another, as well as how their interactions influence and are influenced by the institutions of international politics. The chapters that follow suggest ways of thinking about the interests, interactions, and institutions that have shaped the world we live in, and that will continue to shape it for us, our children, and our children's children.

Key Terms

mercantilism, p. 7

Peace of Westphalia, p. 10

sovereignty, p. 10

hegemony, p. 10

Pax Britannica, p. 12

gold standard, p. 14

Treaty of Versailles, p. 21

League of Nations, p. 21

North Atlantic Treaty Organization
(NATO), p. 24

Bretton Woods System, p. 24

Warsaw Pact, p. 25

decolonization, p. 29

For Further Reading

Abernethy, David. *The Dynamics of Global Dominance: European Overseas Empires.* New Haven: Yale University Press, 2002. Explores the rise and decline of colonialism in the modern age.

Carr, E. H. *The Twenty Years' Crisis, 1919–1939.* New York: Harper and Row, 1964. Originally published in 1939, serves as a classic analysis of how and why the world collapsed into conflict over the decades after World War I.

Craig, Gordon, and Alexander George. *Force and Statecraft: Diplomatic Problems of Our Time,* 3rd ed. New York: Oxford University Press, 1995. Gives an overview of modern diplomatic history, with an analysis of basic concepts in diplomacy.

Findlay, Ronald, and Kevin O'Rourke. *Power and Plenty: Trade, War, and the World Economy in the Second Millennium.* Princeton: Princeton University Press, 2007. Surveys the interrelated development of international trade and international power politics since early medieval times.

Frieden, Jeffry A. *Global Capitalism: Its Fall and Rise in the Twentieth Century.* New York: Norton, 2006. Presents an overview of the development of the modern world economy from the 1890s to the present.

O'Rourke, Kevin, and Jeffrey Williamson. *Globalization and History: The Evolution of a Nineteenth-Century Atlantic Economy.* Cambridge, MA: MIT Press, 1999. Analyzes the development of the classical world economy of the nineteenth and early twentieth centuries.

 **FIND REVIEW AND STUDY MATERIALS ONLINE AT**
WWNORTON.COM/STUDYSPACE

CHAPTER 2

Understanding Interests, Interactions, and Institutions

After Saddam Hussein refused to give up power as the leader of Iraq in 2003, the U.S. military quickly defeated the Iraqi army. Hussein was eventually captured, turned over to the new Iraqi government, and executed. The demolition of this large statue of Hussein in Baghdad in April 2003 symbolized Hussein's fall from power. How can we understand Hussein's decision to risk war with a much more powerful country?

On March 19, 2003, the United States launched a preventive war against Iraq. Tensions between the two countries had remained high since August 1990, when Iraq invaded Kuwait—its small, oil-rich neighbor—and the United States led a multinational coalition to war to restore sovereignty to Kuwait. As a condition of the ceasefire that ended the 1991 war, Iraq agreed to eliminate its programs to develop nuclear, chemical, and biological weapons and permit United Nations inspectors to monitor its compliance. For most of the next decade, the United Nations and Iraq played a game of hide-and-seek as the weapons inspectors sought to enforce the ban on weapons of mass destruction (WMD) and the Iraqi government attempted to undermine the inspections regime and its attendant economic sanctions. In 2002, the administration of U.S. president George W. Bush argued that Iraq's WMD programs were rapidly reaching fruition. Concerned that Iraq might use its new weapons to assert itself in the region, the Bush administration decided to remove Iraq's dictator, Saddam Hussein, from power—by force if necessary. President Bush may also have been seeking to assert American power in the world, to demonstrate a new and more aggressive foreign policy, to secure supplies of oil from the Persian Gulf, and to transform the Middle East by building an effective democracy in an important but previously authoritarian country.

The United States turned to the Security Council of the United Nations (UNSC) to support its policy of regime change in Iraq, threatening that the organization would become irrelevant if it failed to enforce its own resolutions on Iraq's weapons programs. The United States faced determined opposition from France, Russia,

International institutions like the UN facilitate cooperation but are generally not able to enforce cooperation directly. Here, the UN Security Council meets in 2003 to discuss the showdown between the United States and Iraq.

and China, all of which can veto any substantive resolution within the UNSC.[1] Although these states shared concerns about the Iraqi regime and its suspected weapons programs, they were reluctant to endorse military action. As a result, the United States ultimately failed to obtain authorization from the UNSC for the war. Nonetheless, the United States claimed sufficient authority under past UN resolutions on Iraq and under the right of self-defense in the United Nations Charter. After Hussein rejected a U.S. ultimatum to step down, Washington led a "coalition of the willing" to a rapid military victory. The United States did not find the stockpiles of chemical and biological weapons it had claimed existed. The U.S.-led coalition also confronted a broad-based insurgency led by the previously powerful but now politically weakened Sunni religious minority

and Shiite militias determined to secure their new-found political strength. By early 2009, over 4,200 American troops had been killed in Iraq, along with over 300 coalition troops. As of early 2006, the last period for which systematic estimates are available, up to 600,000 Iraqis may have died directly or indirectly as a result of the war.[2]

This story is probably familiar to most readers of this book. Beneath the narrative, however, are important questions whose answers are not obvious: Why did the United States seek regime change in Iraq? Was the U.S. government motivated by concerns about American security, an economic interest in Middle East oil, the president's own political fortunes, or something else? Why did Saddam Hussein resist demands to cooperate fully with weapons inspectors

---

1. For more on the voting rules in the United Nations, see Chapter 5.

2. Estimates of Iraqi casualties vary widely. Gilbert Burnham, Riyadh Lafta, Shannon Doocy, and Les Roberts, "Mortality after the 2003 Invasion of Iraq: A Cross-Sectional Cluster Sample Survey," *Lancet* 368 (October 21, 2006): 1421–28, derive the estimate of 600,000.

and, later, to step down from power peacefully? The invasion drove him out of power, shattered his country, and led to his trial and, eventually, his execution on December 30, 2006. Certainly, Hussein would have been better off accepting the U.S. ultimatum and slinking into a comfortable retirement in exile. Why did the Bush administration attempt to pursue its policy through the UN, and why did it eventually abandon those efforts? Would the war in Iraq and its aftermath have unfolded differently if it had been carried out under the auspices of the UN? In more specific form, these are the same issues as the general questions raised in the previous chapter: Why do countries sometimes come into conflict, and why do those conflicts sometimes lead to wars? Why do states sometimes cooperate with one another, and why does cooperation sometimes fail?

We study international relations in order to gain insight into such questions. We seek to understand why states and their leaders make certain choices and why we observe certain outcomes. To help in our task, this chapter takes a closer look at three core concepts that enable us to think analytically about world politics: interests, interactions, and institutions. As we will see, this framework can be used to analyze and understand not only the Iraq War but also the puzzles described in the chapters that follow and, equally important, others that will arise in the future.

CORE OF THE ANALYSIS

▶ Interests are the fundamental building blocks of politics. Explanations of international political events begin by specifying the relevant actors and their interests.

▶ Cooperation is a type of interaction involving two or more actors working together to achieve a preferred outcome. Successful cooperation depends on the number and relative sizes of actors involved, the number of interactions among the actors, and the accuracy of the information they possess.

▶ Bargaining is a type of interaction involving the distribution of a fixed value. That is, if one actor gets "more," someone else necessarily gets "less." In bargaining, outcomes depend on what will happen in the event that no agreement is reached. Actors derive power from their ability to make the consequences of no agreement less attractive for the other side.

▶ Institutions are sets of rules. Actors comply with institutions because they facilitate cooperation and lower the cost of joint decision-making in the pursuit of valued goals.

▶ Institutions also bias policy outcomes. Rules restrain what actors can and cannot do, and thus they make some outcomes more or less likely. Actors struggle over institutions in efforts to bias policy toward outcomes they prefer.

Interests: What Do Actors Want from Politics?

Interests are what actors want to achieve through political action. For example, in international relations we often assume that states have an interest in security—that is, in preventing attacks on their territories and citizens. This interest prompts states to take steps to suppress potential enemies and to protect friends whose security is linked to their own. In the showdown with Iraq, such an interest might explain the U.S. government's desire to remove a regime that threatened American allies in the region and was suspected of developing WMD and to install a friendly regime in a part of the world that harbors great hostility toward the United States. As the primary motivations behind actors' choices, interests are the fundamental building blocks of any political analysis.[3]

More precisely, interests are the preferences of actors over the possible outcomes that might result from their political choices. Interests determine how actors rank the desirability of different outcomes, from most to least preferred. An actor motivated by an interest in money prefers outcomes in which it receives more money to those in which it receives less. A state interested in security prefers outcomes that strengthen it and weaken its adversaries over outcomes that have the opposite effect. For example, given the United States' general interest in security, it might prefer a democratic Iraq that is friendly toward American allies and encourages the democratization of other states in the Middle East (see Map 2.1). If this best outcome were to prove impossible, the United States' second-best result might be a pro-Western dictator in Iraq. This outcome would be preferable to an anti-American Islamist government, which, in turn, would be preferable to widespread instability and chaos in Iraq and the region more generally. Between each of these broad alternatives, of course, are many intermediate outcomes that can be similarly rank-ordered.

Interests can be many and varied depending on the specific policy or event under examination. In identifying the interests of an actor, analysts sometimes draw on prior theories of human nature or behavior; at other times they rely on the statements or actions of the actors themselves; and at other times still they simply assume that actors have a particular interest. At the most general level, analysts often group interests at the individual and collective levels into three categories: power or security, economic or material welfare, and ideological goals. In the first, all political actors are understood to require a degree of personal or collective security as a prerequisite to all other goals or, at an extreme, to desire power and the ability to dominate others either as part of human nature or as essential to survival in a competitive international environment. In the second category, political actors are presumed to desire a higher standard of living or quality of life, defined largely in terms of greater income, more consumable goods and services, or more leisure time (less work). This second set of interests is not incompatible with the first if we think of economic welfare as the long-term goal and security or power as a

---

3. For a more extensive treatment of the theoretical and methodological issues in studying interests, see Jeffry A. Frieden, "Actors and Preferences in International Relations," in *Strategic Choice and International Relations*, ed. David A. Lake and Robert Powell, 39–76 (Princeton, NJ: Princeton University Press, 1999).

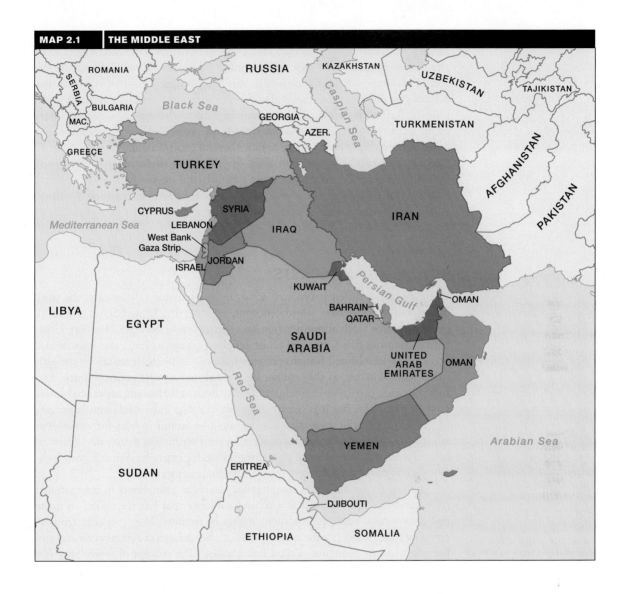

MAP 2.1   **THE MIDDLE EAST**

means to this end. Finally, political actors may also desire moral, religious, or other ideological goals, including democracy, human equality and dignity, the glory of a particular god, and so on. In this category, ideas often play a key role in shaping what actors want or believe to be good and desirable. Again, there is not necessarily a conflict between these interests and others, as power or wealth may be a means toward ideological ends.

Scholars have long debated whether one conception of interest is more universal, true, or useful than others. Indeed, the three sets of general interests roughly divide the three schools of realism, liberalism, and constructivism identified in this book's Introduction. In turn, various debates over what the interests of actors *should be* are often tied to debates over what policies should be pursued in specific contexts. For example, the Iraq War tapped into a longstanding debate in the United States over whether foreign policy should be narrowly defined to meet security threats or should also seek to undermine repressive regimes and promote the spread of democracy. Our approach in this book is agnostic—that is, we do not assume that one set of interests is always better in helping unravel puzzles of world politics. Rather, for some puzzles it may be sufficient to specify a general interest in security, increased international trade, or protecting the environment. For other puzzles, it may be necessary to move beyond general assumptions and specify interests over narrow sets of outcomes—say, between deploying 100,000 versus 200,000 troops, or between negotiating a multilateral international environmental treaty versus following a unilateral policy. Whichever level of detail or specificity is relevant depends on the purpose of the analysis, the questions being asked, and the puzzle under consideration.

ACTORS AND INTERESTS

There are many different types of actors in international relations. In the story of the Iraq War, we have already encountered *states* (the United States and Iraq), *governments* (the Bush administration and the regime of Saddam Hussein), *groups* within countries (the Sunni and Shiite religious groups in Iraq), and *international organizations* (the United Nations Security Council). Individuals are always the ultimate political actors, as they cannot be divided into smaller political units. And in some cases, particular individuals, such as Bush and Hussein, are crucial actors in their own right. But it is often convenient to group individuals into larger categories of people who share common interests (the Sunnis in Iraq, for instance) or who possess some mechanism for combining their conflicting desires into a joint or collective interest (the election of a government, for example). We call both individuals and these composite groups of individuals **actors**.

Of these composite actors, one that has particular prominence in international relations is the state. A **state** is a central authority that has the ability to make and enforce laws, rules, and decisions within its territory. Most countries are governed by states, though some may experience a breakdown of central authority and become what are sometimes called failed states.[4] The concept of sovereignty is a key part of the definition of the state. **Sovereignty** refers to the expectation that states have legal and political supremacy within their boundaries. To say that states are sovereign means that they have control over their own policies and political processes, such as the maintenance of domestic order and the provision of governance. In practice, outsiders sometimes do try to intervene in states' affairs—such as when the U.S. government demanded that Saddam Hussein step down from power in Iraq—so sovereignty is presumed, but not always respected.[5]

actors: The basic unit for the analysis of international politics; can be individuals or groups of people with common interests.

state: A central authority with the ability to make and enforce laws, rules, and decisions within a specified territory.

sovereignty: The expectation that states have legal and political supremacy—or ultimate authority—within their territorial boundaries.

---

4. On failed states, see Robert I. Rotberg, *When States Fail: Causes and Consequences* (Princeton, NJ: Princeton University Press, 2004).

5. On limitations on sovereignty, see Stephen D. Krasner, *Sovereignty: Organized Hypocrisy* (Princeton, NJ: Princeton University Press, 1999). For a theoretical treatment of variations in sovereignty, see David A. Lake, *Hierarchy in International Relations* (Ithaca, NY: Cornell University Press, 2009).

Referring to states as actors implies two different usages that are important to distinguish. When discussing states as actors, scholars sometimes assume that states are motivated by an interest in security—that is, safety from external and internal threats—and in accumulating power as a means to ensure security. These goals are said to be **national interests**, or interests that belong to the state itself. In this usage, the states-as-actors assumption sees international politics as driven by states' quest for security and power.

Alternatively, the states-as-actors concept serves as a convenient shorthand for sets of national leaders acting in the name of their countries. This usage reflects the fact that many actions in international politics are taken by individuals who represent the state: political leaders, diplomats, members of the armed forces, or others acting in an official capacity. Hence, we often lapse into language like "the United States threatened Iraq," when in fact it was certain representatives of the United States who threatened representatives of Iraq. In this usage, we make no prior assumption about where the interests pursued by those agents originate. Sometimes, the state's representatives might act on behalf of a particular domestic interest group—for example, when negotiating a trade agreement that is in the interest of exporting industries. Alternatively, state leaders might act to further their own personal or political agendas. In such cases, the interests that matter are those of the interest group or politician; but when those interests play out at the international level, they are pursued by people acting in the name of the state.

As this discussion suggests, there is no fixed or permanent set of actors in international relations. Like the concept of interest, an actor is an analytic concept that is imposed on explanations by observers seeking to understand why events happen in a certain way. Which sets of individuals get identified as the actors in any explanation is a pragmatic choice we make to help account for observed outcomes. There is no right or wrong way to specify the actors in any event or set of events. Like the concept of interests, we judge different conceptualizations only by whether they are useful in helping us understand world politics.

For example, we know that President Bush made the decision to invade Iraq, but how should we interpret his choice? We could think of him as the head of a state seeking to further the state's interest in security or access to a key natural resource; in this case, the state is the actor whose interests are driving choices. We could also understand Bush as a politician pursuing his personal interest in getting reelected to the presidency; in this case, the individual politician is the actor whose political interests are driving the choices. We might also focus on the interests of groups that could help support President Bush's reelection bid, such as oil companies or defense contractors that would benefit from war. Alternatively, we could think of Bush as an individual motivated by personal ideology about democracy. For any given policy choice, it may be difficult to know for sure which interests are being pursued; indeed, a single decision may further more than one interest. In these cases, we judge any assumption about actors by how useful it is in explaining the overall pattern of events we observe.

Table 2.1 presents a list of key categories of actors in world politics, the interests commonly ascribed to these actors by analysts, and specific examples. The list, of course, is not exhaustive. Any of the actors can be disaggregated into smaller sets

national interests: Interests attributed to the state itself, usually security and power.

TABLE 2.1	KEY CATEGORIES OF ACTORS AND INTERESTS IN WORLD POLITICS	
Actor	**Commonly ascribed interests**	**Examples**
States	Security, power, wealth, ideology	United States, Canada, China, Switzerland, India, Uruguay
Politicians	Reelection/retention of office, ideology, policy goals	President of the United States, Prime Minister of Great Britain, Speaker of the U.S. House of Representatives
Firms, industries, or business associations	Wealth, profit	General Motors, Sony, the pharmaceutical industry, National Association of Manufacturers, Business Roundtable
Bureaucracies	Budget maximization, influence, policy preferences; often summarized by the adage of "where you stand depends on where you sit"	Department of Defense, Department of Commerce, National Security Council, Ministry of Foreign Affairs
International organizations	As composites of states, they reflect the interests of member states according to their voting power. As organizations, they are assumed to be similar to domestic bureaucracies.	United Nations, International Monetary Fund, International Postal Union, Organization for Economic Cooperation and Development
Nongovernmental organizations (NGOs), often transnational or international in scope and membership	Normative, ideological, or policy goals; human rights, the environment, religion	Red Cross, Amnesty International, Greenpeace, the Catholic Church

of individuals for explanatory purposes. But we will encounter these actors again and again throughout this book. In subsequent chapters, we specify different sets of actors and their interests as needed to explain the puzzles being addressed.

Interactions: Why Can't an Actor Always Get What It Wants?

interactions: The ways in which the choices of two or more actors combine to produce political outcomes.

Actors make choices in order to further their interests. Yet political outcomes depend not just on the choices of one actor but on the choices of others as well. The United States might have preferred that Saddam Hussein step down peacefully, but the Iraqi dictator refused to yield, and it ultimately took a war to drive him from power. Interests are essential in analyzing any event in international relations because they represent how actors rank alternative outcomes. But to account for outcomes, we must examine the choices of all the relevant actors and how their choices interact to produce a particular result. As we use the term here, **interactions** refers to the ways in which the choices of two or more actors combine to produce political outcomes.

When outcomes are the product of an interaction, actors have to anticipate the likely choices of others and take those choices into account when making their own decisions. In March 2003, Saddam Hussein's interests in his personal well-being might have led to the following ordering of possible outcomes: (1) stay in power and continue present policies, (2) go into exile in some friendly state, (3) fight and lose a war with the United States. Hussein's only chance at getting his best possible outcome required that he resist U.S. demands to step down. But this risked bringing about his worst possible outcome: war. Whether resisting would lead to his best or worst outcome depended on what the United States would do in response. Would Bush carry out his threat to attack, or would he back down? Whether it made sense for Hussein to resist or step down depended crucially on the answer to this question. If he expected Bush to back down, then resisting U.S. demands would get him his best outcome; if Hussein expected Bush to carry out his threat, then resistance would lead to his worst outcome, and it would have been better to step down. Hence, in making his choice, Hussein had to consider not only what he himself wanted but also what he expected Bush to do. In this case, there is evidence suggesting that Hussein expected opposition on the part of other states, especially Russia and France, to prevent Bush from carrying out his threat—an erroneous expectation that led him to resist.[6] When combined with Bush's determination to invade, this choice ensured a war. Had Hussein been certain that Bush would act as he did, bringing about his eventual execution, he might have chosen differently even though his underlying interests would have been the same. We call such situations *strategic* interactions because each actor's strategy, or plan of action, depends on the anticipated strategy of others. Many of the most intriguing puzzles of international politics derive from such interactions.

We make two assumptions in studying interactions. First, we assume that actors are purposive, that they behave with the intention of producing a desired result. That is, actors are assumed to choose among available options with due regard for their consequences and with the aim of bringing about outcomes they prefer. Second, in cases of strategic interaction, we assume that actors adopt strategies to obtain desired outcomes given what they believe to be the interests and likely actions of others. That is, actors develop strategies that they believe are a best response to the anticipated strategies of others. In the example above, if Hussein believed that Bush would back down from his threat, the best response was to resist American demands; if he believed that Bush would carry out his threat, then the best response was to step down even though doing so would have meant accepting his second-best outcome. A best response strategy is the actor's plan to do as well as possible, in light of the interests and likely strategies of the other relevant actors. Together, these assumptions link interests to choices and, through the interaction of choices, to outcomes.

Formulating a strategy as a best response, of course, does not guarantee that the actor will obtain its most preferred or even a positively valued outcome. Sometimes,

---

6. Kevin Woods, Lacey James, and Williamson Murray, "Saddam's Delusions: The View from Inside," *Foreign Affairs* 75 (May/June 2006): 2–26.

the choices made by others leave actors facing a highly undesirable outcome, one that may leave them far worse off than the status quo. If one state chooses to initiate a war, for instance, the other state must respond by either capitulating to its demands or fighting back, and both options may leave the second state less well off than before the attack. Saddam Hussein was clearly better off before the U.S. attack in March 2003; but once the fighting began, the prewar status quo was no longer an option. A strategy is a plan to do as well as possible given one's expectations about the interests and actions of others. It is not a guarantee that one will obtain one's most preferred result.

Understanding the outcomes produced by the often complex interplay of the strategies of two or more actors can be difficult. A specialized form of theory has been invented, called game theory, to study strategic interactions. We offer a brief introduction to game theory in the appendix to this chapter, focusing on relatively simple games to communicate the core ideas behind strategic interaction.

COOPERATION AND BARGAINING

Interactions can take various forms, but most can be grouped into two broad categories: cooperation and bargaining. Political interactions usually involve both forms in varying degrees.

Interactions are cooperative when actors have a shared interest in achieving an outcome and must work together to do so. **Cooperation** occurs when two or more actors adopt policies that make at least one actor better off than it would otherwise be.[7] Opportunities for cooperation arise all the time in social and political life. A group of friends may want to throw a party, but none of them can spare the time or money to do so alone. If they all contribute a little, then they can all enjoy the benefits of throwing the party. The members of a community would all benefit if there were good roads to drive on and clean water to drink, but again, no individual may be able to provide these on his or her own. If they all agree to pay taxes to some central agency that will provide roads and water, then they can all be better off. A group of firms may share an interest in lobbying Congress for trade protection from foreign imports. By pooling their resources and acting together, they may be more effective at getting their way than they would be on their own. In the international system, states may have opportunities to cooperate to defend one another from attack, to further a shared interest in free trade or stable monetary relations, to protect the global environment, or to uphold human rights. We will look more closely at each of these types of situations in the following chapters. In the case of Iraq, a number of states in the international community loathed or feared Saddam Hussein's regime, and they may have seen his removal as preferable to the status quo. Some of these—especially the United States and Great Britain—chose to cooperate in a military effort to oust Hussein's regime. Both contributed significant military forces and other resources in the expectation that joint action would make them better off relative to either maintaining the status quo or acting alone.

cooperation: An interaction in which two or more actors adopt policies that make at least one actor better off relative to the status quo without making others worse off.

---

7. In many cases, successful cooperation makes all parties better off, but the strict definition requires only that some parties be better off while none be worse off.

Cooperation is defined from the perspectives of the two or more actors who are interacting. Even though their cooperation may make those actors better off, it may hurt other parties. The friends agreeing to throw a party together may disrupt their neighbors by making noise late into the night. Firms who cooperate to lobby Congress for trade protection may impose higher prices on consumers. The countries that cooperated to oust Saddam Hussein clearly made the dictator worse off. Indeed, cooperation is not always an unmitigated good; its benefits exist only for those who become better off by adjusting their policies to bring about an outcome they prefer.

Figure 2.1 presents a simple depiction of the problem of cooperation between two actors. Imagine that two actors can enact policies that have the potential to increase their overall income, or welfare. The income of the actors is depicted along two dimensions, with Actor A's income increasing along the horizontal axis and Actor B's income increasing along the vertical axis. All points within the graph represent possible outcomes produced by different combinations of policies chosen by the two actors. Assume that the most the two actors can make by cooperating is $1,000, a limit determined by the available technology and resources. This limit is depicted by the downward-sloping line in Figure 2.1, which shows all the different ways $1,000 can be divided between the two actors. The point at which the line touches the horizontal axis depicts a situation in which Actor A gets $1,000 and Actor B gets nothing; the point at which the line touches the vertical axis depicts a situation in which Actor B gets all the money; and every point in between represents different divisions of the maximum feasible income. This line is called the *Pareto frontier*, after the Italian economist Vilfredo Pareto (1848–1923), who developed these ideas.

At any moment in time, past policy combinations have produced an outcome referred to as the status quo (*q*). As *q* is depicted here, the actors are not doing as well as they could, meaning that they could potentially benefit by changing their policies to get closer to the maximum feasible income. Any policy combination

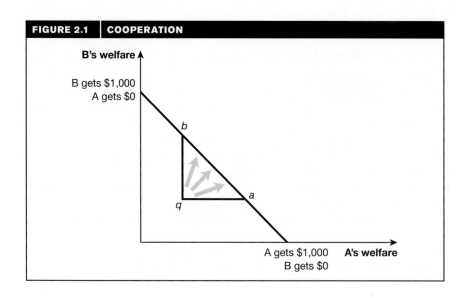

FIGURE 2.1 | **COOPERATION**

B's welfare

B gets $1,000
A gets $0

b

q

a

A gets $1,000   **A's welfare**
B gets $0

that leads to an outcome in the area *qba* would make both actors better off than they are under the status quo. Moving outward and/or upward from *q*, following the trajectory of the blue arrows, represents an improvement in the welfare of at least one actor. Policies along the line segment *qa* improve A's welfare at no loss to B, while policies along the line segment *qb* improve B's welfare at no loss to A. Any movement into the interior of the area of *qba* represents an improvement in the welfare of both actors, and any policy combination on the Pareto frontier between *b* and *a* makes the actors as well off as possible given the current status quo and available resources and technology. Cooperation consists of mutual policy adjustments that move actors toward or onto the Pareto frontier, increasing the welfare of some or all partners without diminishing the welfare of any one actor.

Whereas cooperative interactions involve the potential for mutual gain, **bargaining** describes an interaction in which actors must choose outcomes that make one better off at the expense of another. For example, two states may want the same piece of territory. Bargaining describes the process by which they come to divide the territory. They may negotiate, impose sanctions on one another, or fight. All these tactics are different forms of bargaining. Given the nature of the situation, the more territory one side gets, the less the other gets. Bargaining is represented in Figure 2.2. When actors bargain, they move along the Pareto frontier, as represented by the red arrow. On the frontier, any improvement in A's welfare comes strictly at the expense of B's welfare. For this reason, bargaining is sometimes called a *zero-sum game* because the gains for one side perfectly match the losses of the other. Bargaining is purely redistributive; that is, rather than creating additional value, as in the case of cooperation, it only allocates a fixed sum of value between different actors. We typically represent war as a bargaining interaction. In the case of the Iraq War, the United States and Iraq were not cooperating but bargaining over the latter's WMD programs and, ultimately, its regime. We will take a closer look at bargaining in war in Chapter 3.

bargaining: An interaction in which actors must choose outcomes that make one better off at the expense of another. Bargaining is redistributive: it involves allocating a fixed sum of value between different actors.

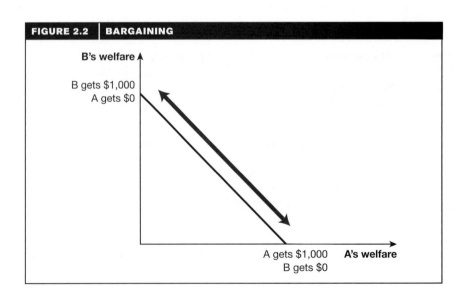

FIGURE 2.2 | BARGAINING

B's welfare

B gets $1,000
A gets $0

A gets $1,000
B gets $0

A's welfare

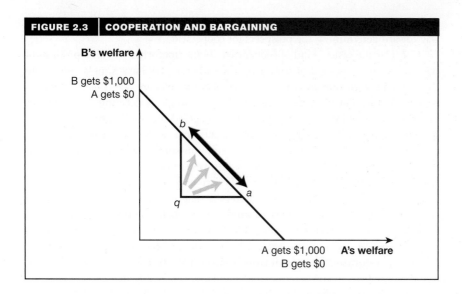

FIGURE 2.3 | COOPERATION AND BARGAINING

B's welfare

B gets $1,000
A gets $0

b

a

q

A gets $1,000   **A's welfare**
B gets $0

Most interactions in international relations combine elements of both coopera-tion and bargaining (see Figure 2.3). Although both may gain by moving to the frontier, A prefers bargains that leave it closer to *a* whereas B prefers bargains that leave it closer to *b*. Movement toward the frontier makes at least one actor better off, but where on the frontier they end up makes an important difference. For example, even as the United States, Britain, and other states had interests in coop-erating to defeat Iraq, they bargained over how much each would contribute to the effort. In many interactions, actors are cooperating and bargaining simultaneously, and the outcomes of both interactions are linked. Successful cooperation generates gains worth bargaining over. And if the actors cannot reach a bargain over the division of gains, they may end up failing to cooperate.[8]

Cooperation and bargaining can succeed or fail for many reasons. Just because actors might benefit from cooperation does not mean they will actually change their policies to realize the possible gains. And even though bargaining might seem doomed to fail—after all, why would one actor agree to reduce its welfare?—actors often do succeed in redistributing valuable goods between themselves. We now turn to some of the primary factors that influence the success or failure of cooperation and, later, bargaining.

WHEN CAN ACTORS COOPERATE?

If cooperation makes actors better off, why do they sometimes fail to cooperate? By far the most important factor lies in each actor's interests. Even when actors have a collective interest in cooperating, there are situations in which their individual interests lead them to "defect"—that is, to adopt an uncooperative strategy that

8. On bargaining and cooperating simultaneously, see James D. Fearon, "Bargaining, Enforcement, and International Cooperation," *International Organization* 52 (1998): 269–305.

undermines the collective goal. How strong the incentives are to defect goes a long way toward determining the prospects for cooperation.[9]

Consider the easiest kind of cooperative interaction, what we call a problem of **coordination**. This kind of situation arises when actors must simply coordinate their actions with one another, and once their actions are coordinated, there is no potential benefit from defecting. A classic example is deciding which side of the road cars should drive on. Drivers have a shared interest in avoiding crashes, so they are always better off if all drive on the right or the left, rather than some driving on each side of the road. It is largely immaterial which side of the road is selected; indeed, different countries have different rules: cars drive on the right side of the road in the United States and continental Europe, and on the left side in Great Britain and Japan. What matters is that all drivers in the region make the same choice. Moreover, no driver would intentionally deviate from that choice, since doing so would be very dangerous. In short, there is no incentive to defect from the coordinated arrangement. In the international economy, firms, industries, and even governments face coordination problems all the time, as suggested by the numerous agreements on international standards. There are many ways to encode information on a compact disc, for instance, but all firms producing CD-based products—home electronics equipment, computers, and the like—are better off coordinating on a single format so that products and CDs are interchangeable. Similarly, it is more important for international airline pilots to speak a single language so as to communicate effectively with one another and with air traffic controllers worldwide than which language they choose. In coordination situations, cooperation is self-sustaining because once coordination is achieved, no one can benefit by unilaterally defecting.

A more serious barrier to cooperation arises if the actors have an individual incentive to defect from cooperation, even though cooperation could make everyone better off. Cooperative interactions in which actors have a unilateral incentive to defect are called problems of **collaboration**. This kind of problem is often illustrated by a simple story called the Prisoner's Dilemma. Imagine that two criminals have robbed a bank and stashed the loot in a secret location. The two are caught by police, but the district attorney (DA) does not have enough evidence to convict them. She puts the prisoners in separate rooms and presents them with the following offer: "If you provide evidence against your accomplice, I will let you go and put him in jail for 10 years; however, I am making the same offer to your accomplice, and if he provides evidence against you, you will be the one behind bars. If you both squeal, then you'll both end up in prison." Collectively, the prisoners would do best by cooperating with each other and staying silent. In that case, the DA has to release them, and they get to split the loot. Unfortunately, each prisoner has an incentive to rat out his accomplice. Each prisoner reasons as follows: "If my partner stays quiet, I can likewise stay quiet and we will split the loot, or I can

coordination: A type of cooperative interaction in which actors benefit from all making the same choices and subsequently have no incentive to not comply.

collaboration: A type of cooperative interaction in which actors gain from working together but nonetheless have incentives to not comply with any agreement.

---

9. On the general forms of cooperation reviewed here, see Arthur A. Stein, "Coordination and Collaboration Regimes in an Anarchic World," *International Organization* 36 (1982): 299–324; Duncan Snidal, "Coordination versus Prisoner's Dilemma: Implications for International Cooperation and Regimes," *American Political Science Review* 79 (December 1985): 923–42; Lisa L. Martin, "Interests, Power, and Multilateralism," *International Organization* 46 (1992): 765–92.

provide evidence against him, in which case he goes to prison and I get to enjoy the loot myself." Assuming the prisoner cares only about money, then defection (that is, providing evidence to the DA) is the best response in the event that the accomplice stays quiet. Defection is also the best response if the accomplice defects, since the worst outcome is to go to prison while one's accomplice goes free and gets the loot. Since both prisoners will reason the same way, both will end up providing evidence against the other. Both will go to jail, and they will split the loot when they get out. This outcome, of course, is worse for both of them than the outcome they could have gotten by cooperating with each other; the dilemma is that each individual's incentive to defect undermines their collective interest in cooperation. This dilemma is explored further using game theory in the chapter appendix.

Although the dilemma of fictional prisoners may seem remote from the subject matter of this book, an analogous situation arises among states engaged in an arms race. Consider the nuclear arms race between the United States and the Soviet Union during the Cold War. Both countries built nuclear weapons at a furious pace, so that by the late 1980s the United States had about 14,000 strategic nuclear warheads, while the Soviet Union had around 12,000 (see Figure 2.4). Hence, the two states were in rough parity with one another, at the cost of billions of dollars. One might ask: why not agree to stop building when the United States had 1,400 warheads and the Soviet Union had 1,200? That would have kept the same ratio of forces, but at much lower cost. Both states might have been better off with such an agreement. The problem, however, is that each state had an incentive to cheat on such a deal in order to attain superiority over the other. If one stopped building, the other would be tempted to keep going. Therefore, each feared that its own restraint in building weapons would be exploited, leaving it vulnerable. Given these incentives and fears, the best strategy for each state was to go on amassing

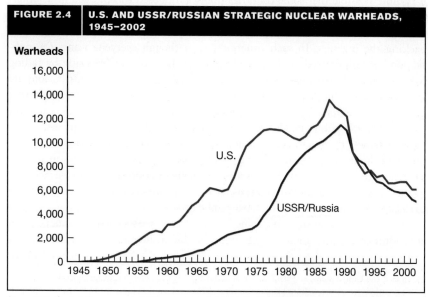

FIGURE 2.4 | U.S. AND USSR/RUSSIAN STRATEGIC NUCLEAR WARHEADS, 1945–2002

Source: Data for this figure are available at www.nrdc.org/nuclear/nubd/daFig2.asp (accessed 9/27/08).

weapons. This left both countries worse off than if they could have cooperated to limit their arms competition.[10]

A specific type of collaboration problem arises in providing **public goods**, which are socially desirable products such as national defense, clean air and water, and the eradication of communicable diseases. Public goods are defined by two qualities. First, if the good is provided to one person, others cannot be excluded from enjoying it as well (formally, the good is *nonexcludable*). If one person in a country is protected from foreign invasion, for instance, all other citizens are also protected. Second, if one person consumes or benefits from the public good, this does not diminish the quantity available to others (formally, the good is *nonrival in consumption*). Again using an example from national defense, one person's enjoyment of protection from foreign invasion does not diminish the quantity of security available to others. Many global environmental issues, such as ozone depletion and climate change, are also public goods (as we will discuss in more detail in Chapter 12). Public goods are contrasted with purely private goods, which are products that only one person can possess and consume. Your sandwich for lunch is a private good—that is, if it's available to you, it is not automatically available to all others; and if you eat it, it is not available to be eaten by others.

Efforts to produce public goods are bedeviled by **collective action problems**, which we will encounter many times in this book. Given that actors can enjoy public goods whether or not they contribute to the provision of those goods, each acts in anticipation that others will pay to produce the good while it gets to enjoy the good for free. That is, each aims to benefit from the contributions of others without bearing the costs itself. For example, individuals would prefer to benefit from national security without paying taxes or volunteering for military service. Alternatively, all states might want to end a genocide, but each would prefer that others assume the risks of the necessary military intervention. In the case of Iraq, it is quite possible that some countries publicly opposed the U.S.-led invasion *not* because they opposed ousting Hussein, but because they wanted to benefit from the regime change without paying the military, political, or diplomatic costs of backing the invasion. In such situations, even though everyone wants the public good to be provided, each individual has an incentive to **free ride** by failing to contribute while benefiting from the efforts of others. When contributions are voluntary, free riding leads public goods to be provided at a lower level than that desired by the actors.

This is why public goods are nearly always provided by governments, which have the power to tax citizens or otherwise mandate their contributions. Free riding is no longer so attractive if, say, the failure to contribute taxes can lead to steep fines or imprisonment. This is also why collaboration among governments on global issues can prove so difficult, as there is no international authority that can mandate their contributions to global public goods.

As this discussion suggests, some of the problems associated with cooperation are addressed by institutions, which might be able to alter actors' incentives so that

public goods: Individually and socially desirable goods that are nonexcludable and nonrival in consumption, such as national defense.

collective action problems: Obstacles to cooperation that occur when actors have incentives to collaborate but each acts in anticipation that others will pay the costs of cooperation.

free ride: To fail to contribute to a public good while benefiting from the contributions of others.

---

10. In fact, the United States and the Soviet Union did sign several arms control agreements, which may have prevented the arms race from being even worse. It was not until the collapse of the Soviet Union in 1991 that serious reductions in nuclear armaments took place.

their individual interests line up with the collective interest. The role of institutions in promoting cooperation is discussed later in this chapter. Even in the absence of institutions, though, we can identify several factors that facilitate cooperation.

Numbers and Relative Sizes of the Actors It is easier for a smaller number of actors to cooperate and, if necessary, to monitor each other's behavior than for a larger number of actors to do so. Two actors can communicate more readily and observe the other's actions better than a thousand actors can. Thus, the smaller the number of actors, the more likely they are to cooperate successfully. As we shall see in Chapter 6, firms can organize more easily to lobby their governments for trade protection than can consumers, who are typically more numerous. Environmental agreements are easier to monitor and enforce—thus, more likely to be agreed upon—among small groups of countries.

In the case of public goods, moreover, there may be groups in which a single member or a small coalition of members is willing to pay for the entire public good. This would happen if these members receive benefits from the public good sufficient to offset the entire costs of providing it. In such "privileged" groups, the single member or small coalition of members provides the public good despite free riding by others.[11] As we will see in Chapter 5, international efforts to enforce agreements in civil conflicts generally require that a very powerful state, such as the United States, be motivated to conduct a peacekeeping operation largely on its own. Similarly, success in limiting ozone emissions (see Chapter 12) stemmed in part from the disproportionately large role of the United States, Russia, and Japan in the industries responsible for the emissions. And as we will see in Chapter 6, some analysts attribute the economic openness of the international economy in the mid-nineteenth and mid-twentieth centuries to public goods like the international monetary regime provided unilaterally by Britain and the United States, which were the largest powers in those eras, respectively.

Iteration, Linkage, and Strategies of Reciprocal Punishment Cooperation is more likely to occur when actors have opportunities to cooperate over time and across issues. The incentive to defect or free ride in any given interaction can be overcome if actors expect to be involved in multiple, repeated interactions with the same partners.[12] In this situation—commonly known as **iteration**—actors can prevent one another from cheating by threatening to withhold cooperation in the future. Even when actors have incentives to defect in the current interaction, knowing that the other actor will refuse to cooperate with it in the future can offset those temptations. Thus, "good behavior" can be induced today by the fear of losing the benefits from cooperation tomorrow. The threat of reciprocal punishment can be a powerful tool for enforcing cooperation even when actors are tempted

iteration: Repeated interactions with the same partners.

---

11. On privileged groups, see Mancur Olson, *The Logic of Collective Action: Public Goods and the Theory of Groups* (Cambridge, MA: Harvard University Press, 1965). For an international application that later led to a theory that treated Great Britain in the nineteenth century and the United States in the twentieth century as privileged actors in the international economy, see Charles P. Kindleberger, *The World in Depression, 1929–1939* (Berkeley: University of California Press, 1973).

12. On iteration and international cooperation, see Robert Axelrod, *The Evolution of Cooperation* (New York: Basic Books, 1984).

The deep cooperation between the United States and Great Britain on a multitude of issues since 1945 has produced what many commentators call a "special relationship" between the two countries. For example, Britain, then led by Prime Minister Tony Blair, remained a stalwart ally and joined the United States in the Iraq War.

linkage: The linking of cooperation on one issue to interactions on a second issue.

to cheat.[13] You are more likely to leave a generous tip for the waiter at a local restaurant you are likely to frequent in the future—lest you get poor service on a another visit—than you are in a restaurant you will never visit again. Countries are less likely to cheat on a trade agreement with a country they trade with more often and expect to trade with again in the future.

Closely related to iteration is the concept of **linkage**, which ties cooperation on one policy dimension to cooperation on other dimensions. Whereas iteration allows victims to punish cheaters by withholding the gains from future cooperation, linkage allows victims to retaliate by withholding cooperation on other issues. Defection on military affairs, for instance, might be punished by withdrawing cooperation on economic matters. One of the reasons the United States and Great Britain are able to sustain their "special relationship" of deep cooperation, including on Iraq, is that they are bound together on so many different issues. The failure of cooperation on one dimension puts cooperation on other issues at risk and reinforces cooperation on all.

Information Finally, the availability of information affects the likelihood of cooperation. In some cases, it is easy to observe whether a partner has cooperated or defected, such as when cooperation entails a public act like participating in a military operation. In other cases, however, cooperative and uncooperative acts may be hard to observe or distinguish from one another. If cooperation involves reducing armaments, for example, the fact that states can build weapons in secret means that defection may not be observed.

When actors lack information about the actions taken by another party, cooperation may fail due to uncertainty and misperception.[14] A state might defect under the mistaken belief that it can get away with it. Alternatively, cooperation might unravel if cooperative acts are mistaken for defection. Suppose one party mistakenly believes that the other has defected and cuts off cooperation as punishment; the other party, which has been cooperating all along, then perceives the first actor's punishment as a new defection and then cuts off cooperation in retaliation. Simple misperceptions can lead to hostile punishments and the breakdown of cooperation even though all actors thought they were acting cooperatively.[15] In the years leading

---

13. For the expectation of future punishment to induce current cooperation, however, actors must value the future enough that future gains matter. Everyone discounts the future—that is, they value it somewhat less than the present. A dollar today is worth more to us than a dollar next year and much more than a dollar received in twenty years. The more actors discount the future, the less likely the threat of future punishment is to encourage them to cooperate today. Conversely, the more actors value the future, the more likely the threat of future punishment is to encourage cooperation now.

14. On the consequences of misperception, see Robert Jervis, *Perception and Misperception in International Relations* (Princeton, NJ: Princeton University Press, 1976).

15. George W. Downs, David M. Rocke, and Randolph M. Siverson, "Arms Race and Cooperation," in *Cooperation under Anarchy*, ed. Kenneth Oye, 118–46 (Princeton, NJ: Princeton University Press, 1986).

up to the Iraq War, Saddam Hussein really had dismantled his WMD programs as required by the United Nations, but he was reluctant to reveal this information because he wanted to use the possibility of such weapons to deter domestic insurgents and other regional powers, especially Iran.[16] Had Iraq's disarmament been more easily confirmed, the main rationale for the war would have been eliminated.

WHO WINS AND WHO LOSES IN BARGAINING?

Whereas cooperation has the potential to make actors collectively better off, bargaining creates winners and losers: each actor's gains come at the expense of someone else. When two or more actors covet the same good—for example, a sum of money or a piece of territory—it is impossible for all of them to get their best possible outcome at the same time. Why, then, are bargains ever reached? Why do actors consent to losses? What determines who wins and who loses?

Considering these questions introduces a core concept in international politics: power. In the standard definition, which we owe to the political scientist Robert Dahl, **power** is the ability of Actor A to get Actor B to do something that B would otherwise not do.[17] In the context of bargaining, power is most usefully seen as the ability to get the other side to make concessions and to avoid having to make concessions oneself. The more power an actor has, the more it can expect to get from others in the final outcome of bargaining.

> **power:** The ability of Actor A to get Actor B to do something that B would otherwise not do; the ability to get the other side to make concessions and to avoid having to make concessions oneself.

Power and, in turn, the outcome of any bargaining interaction are fundamentally influenced by what happens in the event that no bargain is reached. The outcome that occurs when no bargain is reached is often called the *reversion outcome.* In some cases, the reversion outcome is the same as the status quo. For example, if a car buyer and a prospective seller cannot agree on a price, then the seller is left with his car and the buyer keeps her money. What is lost is a chance to make a potentially profitable deal. When actors bargain over the terms of cooperation, a failure to agree can prevent the collective benefits from being enjoyed. For example, if states contemplating intervention in a civil war or negotiating an environmental treaty cannot agree on how to divide the costs, then the civil conflict will rage on or the environmental harm will continue. In other cases, the consequences of disagreement are more severe: the reversion outcome may be a war or some other kind of conflict, such as economic sanctions, that leaves one or even both actors worse off than before the dispute began.

The actor that is more satisfied with the reversion outcome generally has less incentive to make concessions in order to reach a successful bargain. Conversely, the actor that is less satisfied with the reversion outcome becomes desperate to reach an agreement and thus offers relatively bigger concessions in the hopes of inducing the more satisfied actor to agree. In short, bargaining power belongs to those actors most satisfied with, or most willing to endure, the reversion outcome. In the car buying example, if the seller needs money and is anxious to sell the car quickly, a more patient

---

16. This is the conclusion reached by the Iraq Survey Group, which examined Iraq's WMD program after the regime fell. See U.S. Central Intelligence Agency, "Comprehensive Report of the Special Advisor to the DCI on Iraq's WMD," September 30, 2004, www.cia.gov/library/reports/general-reports-1/iraq_wmd_2004/index.html (accessed 5/9/08).
17. Robert A. Dahl, "The Concept of Power," *Behavioral Scientist* 2 (July 1957).

buyer can extract a better deal. Internationally, in negotiations over global climate change, the United States has been less willing to go along with other countries in part because the expected costs of climate change to the United States are lower. Given its geography and economic resources, the United States is better equipped than many other states to weather the effects of a warming planet and rising sea levels. As a result, the United States has, so far, successfully shifted the burden of cutting greenhouse gas emissions onto others (see Chapter 12). In the case of Iraq, the United States has a great stake in rebuilding that country and ending the violence that has killed thousands of U.S. troops. Despite its enormous power in most respects, the United States has had a hard time convincing other countries, which are less directly hurt by the status quo, to share the costs of Iraq's reconstruction. Those most in need of agreement are likely to get worse bargains than those who can better tolerate the reversion outcome.

Because bargaining outcomes are largely determined by how each actor evaluates the reversion outcome, power derives from the ability to make the reversion outcome better for oneself and/or worse for the other side. Actors have three basic ways of exercising power—that is, shifting the reversion outcome in their favor.

coercion: The threat or imposition of costs on other actors in order to change their behavior. Means of international coercion include military force, economic sanctions, and embargos.

Coercion The most obvious strategy for exercising power is coercion. **Coercion** is the threat or imposition of costs on others to reduce the value of the reversion outcome (no agreement) and thus change their behavior. Thus, states can use their ability to impose costs on others to demand a more favorable bargain than they would otherwise receive. The demand of the United States that Saddam Hussein step down or be removed by force is an example of coercive bargaining that left the Iraqi dictator worse off than before the threat was made. The target, of course, can itself try to impose costs on the challenger. What matters is the net ability to impose costs on the other—that is, the difference between the coercion employed by one side and that employed by the other. If the costs each side can impose on the other are equal, neither party has power. The reversion outcome for both parties will be worse than the status quo and both will be more desperate to reach agreement, but neither will have any greater power over the other. It is the ability to impose greater costs on the other actor than that actor can impose on oneself that creates power through coercion.

Means of international coercion include military force and economic sanctions. The ability to impose costs on others, and to defend against others' efforts to impose costs on oneself, derives in large part from material capabilities: the physical resources that allow an actor to inflict harm and/or withstand the infliction of harm. In coercive interactions among states, these capabilities are often measured in terms of military resources—such as number of military personnel or level of military spending—as well as measures of economic strength, since economic resources can be readily converted into military power. The balance of such capabilities among states is a strong predictor (though not the only one) of who wins and who loses in warfare.[18] Similarly, the size of a country's economy has an impact on its ability to impose and/or withstand economic sanctions, which cut off a country's access to international trade.

Although material capabilities such as guns and money are important components of power, we will see in Chapter 3 that other factors can also be sources of

---

18. See, for example, Dan Reiter and Allan C. Stam, *Democracies at War* (Princeton, NJ: Princeton University Press, 2002).

power in coercive bargaining. Since the use of force is costly and risky, an actor's willingness to absorb costs and take risks can also generate an advantage. The economist Thomas Schelling famously described international crises as competitions in risk-taking likely to be "won" by the side that blinks second (see the game of Chicken described in this chapter's appendix).[19] This helps explain why weak states can at times defeat great powers. When France tried to reassert colonial control over Vietnam after World War II, the leader of the Vietnamese resistance, Ho Chi

In coercive bargaining, military capabilities are an important component of power. What matters is not the overall size and fighting prowess of one's own troops, but one's capabilities relative to an opponent's. During the Cold War, the Soviet Union held annual military parades to demonstrate its might relative to that of potential enemies.

Minh, warned the French that their superior military power would not matter: "You will kill 10 of our men, and we will kill 1 of yours, and in the end it will be you who tire of it."[20] The Vietnamese leader's optimism sprang from the belief that his people were more willing to bear the costs of war. His power stemmed not from military capabilities but from what we will refer to in Chapter 3 as resolve.

Outside Options Actors can also get a better deal when they have attractive **outside options**, or alternatives to reaching a bargain with a particular partner that are more attractive than the status quo. In this case, the reversion outcome is the next best alternative for the party with the outside option. The actor with an attractive alternative can walk away from the bargaining table more easily than an actor without such an option.

The actor with the better outside option can use its leverage, the threat to leave negotiations, to get a better deal. For example, even though the United States might have preferred to work through the United Nations to remove Saddam Hussein from power in Iraq in 2003, the U.S. government felt that it had an attractive outside option: acting unilaterally. The United States' military capabilities meant that even though it might benefit from international support, it did not feel that such support was necessary to prevail. Thus, while other countries on the UNSC tried to influence U.S. policy in the dispute, their bargaining power was greatly diminished by the fact that the United States felt that it could "go it alone."

Like coercion, however, it is the relative attractiveness of each actor's outside option that matters. Both actors may have alternatives, but the one with the more attractive outside option can more credibly threaten to walk away and, therefore, can get the better deal. In competitive economic markets with many buyers and sellers, for instance, there is little power exercised by any actor, as every buyer or seller has equally attractive outside options. In the case of the United Nations, again, the United States had an ability to act unilaterally that was not available to the UNSC, which had only the very unattractive alternative of fielding a military force of its own to stop the United States from invading Iraq. The UNSC could not, therefore, exercise any significant power over the United States.

outside options: The alternatives to bargaining with a specific actor.

19. Thomas C. Schelling, *The Strategy of Conflict* (Cambridge, MA: Harvard University Press, 1960).
20. This quotation is often cited, and the exact wording sometimes varies. The original source is Jean Sainteny, *Histoire d'une Paix Manquée: Indochine, 1945–47* (Paris: Amiot-Dumont, 1953), 231.

agenda-setting power:
A "first mover" advantage that helps an actor to secure a more favorable bargain.

Agenda Setting Similarly, actors might gain leverage in bargaining through **agenda-setting power**. Whereas an outside option is exercised in the event bargaining fails, agenda-setting involves actions taken prior to or during bargaining that make the reversion outcome more favorable for one party. A party that can act first to set the agenda transforms the choices available to others. For example, many computer users complain about Microsoft and believe its Windows operating system is less efficient than alternatives (Macintosh, Unix), yet the company used its initial advantage in the personal computer market to set the agenda for the entire personal computer industry and secure a position of continuing dominance for its product. Similarly, when the United States deregulated its airline industry to capitalize on its market position and benefit its domestic consumers, other countries were forced to deregulate their industries as well in order to remain competitive, often over the opposition of their national air carriers. In the Iraq War, the United States exercised its agenda-setting power both by bringing the inspections issue before the UNSC and by unilaterally initiating a war against Iraq, to which other countries were then forced to respond.

Even though bargaining creates winners and losers, bargains can be made as long as they give all parties more than (or at least as much as) they can expect to get in the reversion outcome. In other words, actors consent to painful concessions when the consequences of not agreeing are even more painful. As we will see in Chapter 3, the fact that there exist bargains that all sides prefer over, say, war does not guarantee that those bargains will always be reached. There are a host of problems that can prevent actors from finding or agreeing to mutually beneficial deals. For example, uncertainty about how each side evaluates its prospects in a war can make it hard to know which bargains are preferable to war. There may also be situations in which states cannot credibly promise to abide by an agreement that has already been made. Bargaining may also be complicated if the good being bargained over is hard to divide. (Since this is a broad topic, we leave fuller consideration of these issues for Chapter 3.)

In sum, both interests and interactions matter in politics. Political outcomes depend on the choices of two or more actors. Since political outcomes are contingent on the choices of two or more actors, any given actor does not always or even most of the time get its most preferred interest. Indeed, in bargaining, an actor may be worse off afterwards than if it had not entered the interaction at all. Interactions are often quite complex, but they are critical to understanding how interests get transformed into outcomes—often in paradoxical ways.

Institutions: Do Rules Matter in World Politics?

institutions: Sets of rules, known and shared by the community, that structure political interactions in specific ways.

Institutions play a major role in social and political life, domestically and internationally. We typically define **institutions** as sets of rules, known and shared by the relevant community, that structure political interactions in specific ways. Many institutions are embodied in laws or organizations. The United States Congress has rules that determine who gets elected to it and how it passes laws. Further rules determine how

Congress deals with other American political institutions, such as the presidency and the courts. The United Nations is an institution in which states make collective decisions about military actions or economic sanctions; the UN has rules that determine which states have a say over these matters and how their votes are counted. International economic institutions include the International Monetary Fund (IMF), the World Trade Organization (WTO), and the World Bank. Other institutions are more informal and exist only as shared understandings of principles and norms. These informal institutions, such as the widespread international norm against slavery, can also be important.

Institutions vary in their goals and rules, but they generally serve to facilitate cooperation among their members.[21] As discussed in the previous section, even when actors have common interests, there may be factors that make cooperation more difficult. Cooperation can flounder if the problems identified above—incentives to defect, large numbers of actors, nonrepeated interactions, and imperfect information—are not successfully resolved. Institutions can provide solutions to these problems. Indeed, it is precisely to facilitate cooperation that actors first create and subsequently comply with the rules embodied in institutions.

HOW DO INSTITUTIONS AFFECT COOPERATION?

In much of political and social life, the primary way that institutions promote cooperation is through enforcement, or the imposing of punishments on actors who fail to cooperate. Imagine, for example, that the prisoners in the Prisoner's Dilemma game were both members of an organized crime group, and it was understood that members who rat each other out will find themselves at the bottom of a river wearing cement shoes. In that case, the prisoners no longer have an individual incentive to defect on each other; the external enforcement by the organization changes the way they rank-order the possible outcomes, and cooperation between them now makes sense both individually as well as collectively. Similarly, governments provide public goods by compelling individuals to pay for them in the form of taxes; the threat of fines or jail time for failing to pay weakens the incentive to free ride on the contributions of others. Cooperation among private actors within a country may also be enforced by institutions. For example, a sales contract between a customer and a firm can be enforced by courts, whose rulings are backed by the police powers of the state. In short, when institutions have means of imposing punishments for defection, they can effectively enforce cooperation.

Institutions at the international level generally lack the capacity to impose punishments on states. The international system is characterized by **anarchy**, a term that in this context refers to the absence of formal government.[22] Whereas most countries are governed by states—a central authority with the ability to make and enforce laws within its boundaries—there is no such central authority at the

anarchy: The absence of a central authority with the ability to make and enforce laws that bind all actors.

---

21. See Robert O. Keohane, *After Hegemony: Cooperation and Discord in the World Political Economy* (Princeton, NJ: Princeton University Press, 1984).

22. The most forceful statement of the importance of anarchy in international relations is Kenneth N. Waltz, *Theory of International Politics* (Reading, MA: Addison-Wesley, 1979). For a critique, see Helen V. Milner, "The Assumption of Anarchy in International Relations: A Critique," *Review of International Studies* 17 (1991): 67–85.

global level. Some people think the UN is a world government, but as we will see in Chapter 5, this is not the case. Even poor, weak states have more enforcement power over their citizens than the UN has over actors in the international system. It cannot tax, raise its own military, or field its own police force.

The condition of anarchy means that international institutions do not generally enforce cooperation among their members. Instead, cooperation at the international level has to be self-enforcing: that is, the members have to police themselves and assume responsibility for punishing defectors. The fact that countries are largely dependent on self-help does not mean that international institutions are useless, but it does shape our understanding of the role they play. In general, international institutions, even informal ones, facilitate cooperation by making self-enforcement easier. They do so in at least four ways: by setting standards of behavior, verifying compliance, reducing the costs of joint decision-making, and resolving disputes. Different institutions may emphasize one or another of these tasks over the others, but all are important.

Setting Standards of Behavior Clear standards of behavior reduce ambiguity and enhance cooperation. For example, parents who tell a teenager, "Don't stay out too late, or else," invite continuing conflict. What does "too late" mean? Also, "or else" is ambiguous. If the parent grounds the teenager for a week, is this "unfair," as the aggrieved youth will likely claim, or "letting her off easy," as the parent will likely retort? The costs of this conflict could have been avoided by making clear that the teenager should "be home by midnight, or you'll be grounded for a week." The teenager might still choose to stay out later, but the criterion for evaluating lateness and the consequences are no longer in dispute.

International institutions set standards of behavior in similar ways. The North American Free Trade Agreement (NAFTA) among the United States, Mexico, and Canada contains twenty-two chapters and seven annexes of detailed rules governing trade and investment among the three countries, as well as exceptions to general rules for particular practices and industries. Arms control agreements between the United States and Soviet Union during the Cold War often ran to hundreds of pages detailing precise numbers for different types of weapons systems and limits on their capabilities. Following the 1991 Persian Gulf War, the United Nations Security Council passed Resolution 661 prohibiting Iraq from possessing or developing all chemical, biological, and nuclear weapons and any ballistic missile with a range greater than 150 kilometers and banning all facilities for the development, support, or manufacture of such weapons, their precursors, or their subcomponents. This resolution defined carefully what weapons Iraq was and was not allowed to possess.

Clear standards of behavior allow others to determine whether or not an actor is violating an agreement. The aggrieved parties can call violators to account; and if violations are not corrected, such parties can withdraw from cooperation entirely or impose sanctions. Clear standards are especially important for international agreements, which must be enforced by participants (as opposed to third parties, as in domestic affairs). Without an authoritative third-party enforcement mechanism, such as the courts or the police, there is a real potential for disputes to escalate on account of imperfect or inaccurate information. International institutions can help defuse potentially costly cycles of reciprocal punishments set off by misperceived violations by accurately identifying violations and violators.

Clear standards of behavior cannot eliminate all disputes. Rules can never address all possible circumstances, and there may well be ambiguous situations that those looking to evade the rules can exploit. Saddam Hussein skirted his obligations under UNSC Resolution 661 and played on divisions among the permanent members of the Security Council to avoid complying with restrictions, especially in reporting and inspections. But the resolution was nonetheless important in setting the standard against which his behavior was ultimately judged. Although disputes occur, clear standards help support cooperation by identifying violations and allowing enforcement procedures to function.

The IAEA was formed in 1957 to promote safe and peaceful nuclear technologies. Under the auspices of the United Nations, IAEA inspectors failed to find any evidence in 2002 of renewed nuclear progams in Iraq.

Verifying Compliance In addition to standards against which actors can judge compliance, institutions often provide ways to acquire information on compliance. President Ronald Reagan famously said about arms control agreements with the Soviet Union, "trust, but verify"—a rough translation of an old Russian proverb.

In many international institutions, self-reporting is common practice: countries are required to submit reports documenting their compliance. Such a procedure might appear weak, but it allows other parties to the agreement to inspect the self-reporting of others, assess those reports against their private knowledge of others' compliance, and publicize and criticize any inconsistencies. Discrepancies between self-reports and later verified accounts open the country to further disrepute and possible sanctions. In the fall of 2002, for example, the United States asked the UNSC to demand of Iraq a detailed accounting of its WMD programs, and then the United States highlighted inconsistencies within the hundreds of thousands of pages of documents, between the documents and past inspection reports, and between the documents and its own intelligence estimates.

At the other extreme, some international agreements permit on-site inspections. The International Atomic Energy Agency (IAEA), for instance, inspects declared nuclear material facilities in over seventy countries under the Treaty on the Non-Proliferation of Nuclear Weapons (NPT). This treaty, adopted in 1968, prohibits most countries from diverting fissionable material from civilian nuclear reactors for use in making nuclear weapons. The IAEA inspectors help to monitor compliance with this prohibition. UNSC Resolution 661 also provided for the IAEA to lead inspection teams in Iraq to search for possible nuclear weapons and development sites.

Finally, institutions protect the ability of countries to verify compliance independently. Rules specifying the status of embassies and the treatment of embassy personnel allow for diplomatic representation of one country on the territory of another, but they also permit embassy officials on-site access to collect information and track developments in the foreign state. Similarly, the Treaty on Open Skies, signed in 1992 and ratified by the United States and thirty-four other countries, formally permits states to use "national technical means," including satellites and high-flying spy planes, to observe developments on the ground below in foreign territories. Such national technical means were an important tool in verifying the arms control agreements between the United States and the Soviet Union during the Cold War. The treaty, which was negotiated just as the Cold War was ending, formally acknowledged and ratified what had been long-standing practice. National technical means remained important—even if misleading and incomplete—in monitoring Iraq's WMD programs in the 1990s.

Reducing the Costs of Joint Decision-Making Institutions make it easier for actors to make decisions collectively. Recall the example of the "rules of the road" from the discussion of coordination earlier in this chapter. In a society in which the side-of-the-road rule has not been established, each driver would have to negotiate with each oncoming car over who would drive on the left and who would drive on the right. Stops would be frequent, and crashes would be inevitable. The time lost in arriving at a destination as a result of negotiating these individual encounters, as well as the crashes, would be the costs of joint decision-making. Given the huge costs, societies establish institutions—rules of the road—to routinize decision-making, avoid conflicts, and reduce the costs of driving. The smooth flow of traffic, and faster commutes, are the benefits of the institution.

Domestic political institutions similarly operate to reduce the costs of joint decision-making. Imagine that a society needed to decide collectively on all matters of policy in the absence of any agreed-upon rules. Every time someone wanted to propose a new policy, he or she would have to get all citizens to figure out how they would decide. Should the policy be enacted by popular referendum? If so, who could vote? Would it pass by a simple majority (50 percent plus one vote), by a supermajority (greater than 50 percent, usually two-thirds), or by unanimous consent? Alternatively, would policy be decided by some subgroup of society? Would this subgroup be a representative body, only the most highly affected individuals, or a single individual? What powers would this subgroup have? Would it be able to not only establish the policy, but also tax others if necessary to implement the policy? The list of possible decision-making rules and the alternatives to be considered for each policy are virtually endless. In the absence of some agreed-upon rules on collective decision-making, the costs of any policy initiative would be enormous. These might be so large, in fact, that no policy would ever generate sufficient benefits to offset the costs of enacting that policy. Nothing would ever get done. As a result, societies create political institutions—rules of the political game—that define how joint political decisions will be made. These institutions are useful because they reduce the costs of joint decision-making.

International institutions serve to reduce the costs of joint decision-making among nations in the same way. The United Nations was created as a permanent forum in which countries could come together to deliberate and attempt to resolve disagreements. Since its founding, the UN and its associated agencies have undertaken sixty-one peace-keeping operations, fought the Korean War, authorized the 1991 Persian Gulf War, rewritten the law of the sea, managed refugee problems worldwide, fed people displaced by conflict or famine, helped eliminate smallpox worldwide, and undertaken a host of other activities. There is a relatively clear set of rules on which issues get referred to the General Assembly and which to the Security Council, as well as specific voting rules for each body. These rules reduce the costs of joint decision-making among member states just as they do in other social settings. A host of other international institutions help reduce the costs of joint decision-making on a broad range of other issues.

Resolving Disputes International institutions also facilitate cooperation by providing mechanisms for resolving disputes. When parties disagree about whether one or more of them have violated an agreement or how to interpret the terms of an agreement (and indeed, diplomats and lawyers can be very creative), it can be helpful to have prior agreement on how to handle such differences. Domestically, disputes are routinely referred to courts for authoritative resolution; in fact, courts are the default forum for dispute resolution unless the parties to an agreement have specifically agreed to other provisions, such as arbitration. Most international agreements, however, do not contain explicit dispute resolution procedures, and each party may seek to interpret the agreement according to its own interests and be limited only by its desire for a reputation as a "good partner."

Nonetheless, many international economic transactions regularly delegate dispute resolution to national courts—for instance, agreeing in advance that disputes will be decided according to the laws of the state of New York—or to one of many international arbitration boards. In a limited number of cases, states will create new dispute settlement procedures as part of an agreement, as in the World Trade Organization and regional economic blocs such as NAFTA. By creating mechanisms to resolve disputes, actors increase their expectations that others will uphold their commitments, prevent retaliation from escalating out of control, resolve ambiguities in their agreements, and allow mutually beneficial cooperation to occur. This does not, it should be noted, hinge on the dispute resolution body itself enforcing the rules by punishing violators. Rather, by interpreting rules when they are ambiguous or subject to conflicting interpretations, dispute settlement bodies help identify violator and victim, permit actors to employ self-help sanctions more efficiently, and potentially keep disputes from escalating.

In sum, institutions facilitate international cooperation in important ways. International institutions do not, however, directly enforce cooperation, except in extremely rare cases when they are empowered to punish defectors directly. Rather, despite a well-developed infrastructure of institutions, international politics remains largely a realm of self-help in which states alone must choose whether and how to penalize those who fail to cooperate. What international institutions do, however, is make compliance more likely by clarifying the terms of cooperation, providing information, and lowering the costs of joint decision-making—including the costs of deciding when to punish those states that choose not to follow the rules.

The European Union and the United States each have enough votes within the IMF to veto any major decision by the organization. Many critics charge that the IMF, as a result, is biased in its policies toward the interests of the developed countries. Here, various finance ministers and IMF officials meet to discuss the international financial crisis.

WHOM DO INSTITUTIONS BENEFIT?

Institutions may help states cooperate, and in that sense they can make all their members better off. But institutions rarely benefit everyone equally. Institutions are themselves a product of the cooperation and bargaining that brought them into being. They reflect past political bargains, with the winners getting to write the rules or, at least, having a disproportionate say over the rules. As a result, the rules are never neutral; instead, they embody the bargaining strength of the actors at the time the rules were written or amended. Thus, all institutions contain a policy bias.[23]

Institutions bias outcomes in many ways. In the United States, for instance, citizens' interests are aggregated, or summed, at the national level by different electoral institutions. These institutions themselves are a reflection of bargaining within the constitutional convention of 1787. The more populous states at the time sought a legislature in which representatives were allocated by population, which would give them a larger voice. The less populous states, knowing they would be routinely outvoted, wanted some form of guaranteed representation. The result was a compromise, with seats in the House of Representatives being determined by population and seats in the Senate being reserved two for each state. The larger states were forced to compromise by the unwillingness of the smaller states to agree to the Constitution without this provision.

These rules matter. Being elected by and responsive to different subsets of the national population, it is hardly surprising that the majority of the House of Representatives, the majority of the Senate, and the president—with the largest constituency—often differ in their interests. Indeed, the framers of the Constitution explicitly intended to create competing branches of government with different constituencies and policy preferences. Institutions that represent many smaller constituencies are likely to produce policies that favor particular groups in society through large, omnibus "logrolls" that contain something for everyone. Institutions that represent larger constituencies are more likely to enact policies that benefit society as a whole. For this reason, Congress is often thought to be more beholden to "special interests," while the president is expected to act more in the general interest. One manifestation of this difference is that members of the House of Representatives are typically more responsive to import-competing industries in their districts, and thus more protectionist in trade policy, whereas the president is more likely to support freer trade, which promotes the interests of consumers as a whole.

---

23. For a review of the effects of institutions, including policy bias, see Ronald Rogowski, "Institutions as Constraints on Strategic Choice," in *Strategic Choice and International Relations*, ed. David A. Lake and Robert Powell, 115–36 (Princeton, NJ: Princeton University Press, 1999).

International institutions differ widely in their rules and in their policy bias. Many institutions, including the General Assembly of the United Nations, have a one country–one vote rule, with China, population of over 1.3 billion, having the same official weight as Tuvalu, population about 11,000—giving each citizen of Tuvalu the same voice in the General Assembly as about 120,000 Chinese. The UNSC, by contrast, has voting rules that privilege five particular states—the United States, Great Britain, France, Russia, and China—by giving them a veto over any action the UNSC might take. This means that even if a majority of states on the UNSC, or around the world, want the UN to enact a particular policy, it can nevertheless be blocked by any one of these five states. Why these particular states? They were the five major victors of World War II, and hence they were in a position to write the rules when the UN was created in the aftermath of that war (see Chapter 5). The privileged position of these states helps explain why French and Russian opposition to the U.S.-led invasion of Iraq was so consequential—without their support, the UNSC could not authorize the use of force.

Other organizations have weighted voting rules, which give the largest contributors the most influence. In the International Monetary Fund, for example, the United States contributes about 17 percent of the fund's resources, and consequently it gets 17 percent of the votes on the organization's Board of Governors—by far the largest vote share of any individual country. The weights have been periodically renegotiated to reflect changes in the contributions and bargaining power of states, but the United States and the European Union still retain large enough shares of the votes to each block any important decision within the organization. Still other institutions operate by unanimous consent, permitting any member to veto an action. In its early decades, the Council of Ministers of the European Economic Community (later the European Community, now the European Union) used a unanimity rule. As the policy-making demands of deeper economic integration became more intense, the Council made a historic decision to adopt a qualified majority voting rule in the Single European Act signed in 1986. This was understood to be a major transfer of power away from member states, who could previously veto any initiative they found objectionable, to the Community as a whole. As in domestic institutions, rules matter in international institutions.

Because institutions matter and bias policy in consequential ways, states struggle over their rules. Institutions are both the shapers of politics (by facilitating cooperation) and the products of political action. Given the relative consistency in the basic institutions of government in the United States and many other countries, we often attribute a "taken for granted" or natural quality to political institutions. But it is important to understand that all institutions reflect particular policy biases and, as a result, are always the object of continuing political debate and battle.

WHY FOLLOW THE RULES?

Why do actors follow rules? If they have incentives to defect from rules and ignore institutions, why do they not always do so? If the rules are biased against them, why would they go along with them anyway? These have been key questions for many scholars of international relations. Some analysts argue that states ignore institutions whenever they do not serve their interests, so that the institutions we see merely reflect the current bargaining strength of states and do not affect policy.[24] Others argue that if institutions did not matter, states would not devote so much energy to writing the extensive rules we observe. In this view, as international lawyer Louis Henkin points out, "almost all nations observe almost all principles of international law and almost all of their obligations almost all of the time."[25] Rates of compliance in international politics are surprisingly high. Indeed, although this finding remains contested, other international lawyers argue that when states do violate international rules it is more often from a lack of capacity to live up to their obligations than from an attempt to seize an advantage over others.[26]

Actors comply with institutions for two reasons. First, since many problems in international relations combine both cooperation and bargaining, actors may agree to comply with rules for the cooperation they facilitate even though the outcome of those rules is biased against them. In these situations, the value of the cooperation created by the institution outweighs the costs of a relatively disadvantageous bargain. States observe the rules of the WTO not just because other countries might be authorized to punish them for violations, but because the system of free trade that the WTO supports and promotes is of great benefit to them (see "What Shaped Our World?" on p. 71). They fear that defiance of its mandates would place at risk the whole edifice of trade rules and the gains from trade. Similarly, countries abide by the NPT not just because the inspections of the IAEA may reveal cheating that could then be referred to the UNSC for possible sanctioning, but because the restraints on all countries make the world a safer place. In such cases, the prospect of continued, mutually beneficial cooperation restrains the short-run temptation for countries to ignore rules they do not like.

Second, actors comply with institutions because they are already in place and cheaper to use, even if they are biased, than are the costs of creating a brand new institution that might more fully reflect their interests. In the case of an existing institution, the costs of creating that set of rules have already been paid, but the costs of any new institution, however better suited to the matter now under discussion, would have to be paid anew. If the policy bias of an institution is not too large, actors may choose to work within the existing rules rather than create new ones from scratch. If the policy bias is too large, of course, actors will choose to disband the institution, ignore it, or reform it.[27] In many circumstances, however, they recognize that maintaining the institution is far from ideal but less costly than creating a new one.

The benefits of an established forum and set of rules for joint decision-making are substantial. Indeed, the United States continues to work through the UN even

24. For a skeptical view of international institutions, see John J. Mearsheimer, "The False Promise of International Institutions," *International Security* 19 (1994): 5–49.

25. Louis Henkin, *How Nations Behave: Law and Foreign Policy*, 2nd ed. (New York: Columbia University Press, 1979), 47.

26. See Abram Chayes and Antonia Handler Chayes, "On Compliance," *International Organization* 47, no. 2 (1993): 175–205. This view is criticized by George W. Downs, David M. Rocke, and Peter N. Barsoom, "Is the Good News about Compliance Good News about Cooperation?" *International Organization* 50, no. 3 (1996): 397–406.

27. Joseph Jupille and Duncan Snidal, "The Choice of International Institutions: Cooperation, Alternatives, and Strategies" (paper presented at the annual meeting of the American Political Science Association, Washington, DC, September 2005).

Costa Rican Underwear:
A Tale of WTO Compliance

On December 22, 1995, Costa Rica brought a suit against the United States through the World Trade Organization's (WTO) dispute settlement process. Six months earlier, the United States had imposed restrictions on the import of cotton and synthetic fiber underwear from Costa Rica and several other countries. The U.S. government claimed that these import restrictions were needed to prevent serious damage to its domestic underwear industry. Costa Rica claimed that these restrictions violated the rules of the WTO because the United States had acted unilaterally and without proof that its domestic industry was actually in danger. In bringing the case before the WTO, Costa Rica became the first small developing country to initiate a dispute settlement action against the United States, the world's largest trader and military power.[a] The following year, the panel that was appointed to adjudicate the case ruled in Costa Rica's favor. The United States appealed the decision, but on February 10, 1997, the WTO's appellate body confirmed the ruling. The United States subsequently allowed its import restrictions to expire, bringing its trade policy into compliance with the ruling.

Why would the United States comply in a case like this? After all, the WTO cannot punish a country for noncompliance. Instead, enforcement is left to the aggrieved states. But it is implausible that Costa Rica—with a far smaller economy and no military to speak of—could force the United States to comply. So why would the U.S. government override the demands of its domestic underwear producers and lift their protection from imports?

States have incentives to comply with institutional rules, even if inconvenient, if they value the benefits from the institution as a whole. The short-term incentive to disobey the rules can be outweighed by the long-term benefits provided by the institution. In this case, the WTO benefits the United States by helping to open other countries' markets to U.S. exports, and the United States is a frequent user of the dispute settlement mechanism. As of November 2007, the United States had been the complaining party in eighty-four cases brought before the WTO. It had prevailed in fifty-five of these cases and lost only four; the remaining cases were still in progress or had been dropped.[b] Even though Costa Rica could not punish the United States for noncompliance, the incentive for the United States to not comply in this one instance was tempered by the long-term advantages of having a system of rules that is generally respected. Protecting U.S. underwear manufacturers was not worth the risk that noncompliance would jeopardize those rules and the benefits they bring. ■■

a. For more on this case, see John Breckenridge, "Costa Rica's Challenge to US Restrictions on the Import of Underwear," www.wto.org/english/res_e/booksp_e/casestudies_e/case12_e.htm (accessed 2/9/07).

b. United States Trade Representative, "Snapshot of WTO Cases Involving the United States," November 29, 2007, www.ustr.gov/assets/Trade_Agreements/Monitoring_Enforcement/Dispute_Settlement/WTO/asset_upload_file24_5696.pdf (accessed 5/24/08).

though the other member states have failed to approve policies it supports. Despite failing to get UN approval for its invasion of Iraq, by 2006 the United States was once again working vigorously through the UNSC to condemn Iran's past violation of IAEA safeguards and to prevent its progress toward acquiring a nuclear weapon. In this case, the cooperation of all major powers is required for effective sanctions should Iran not halt its uranium enrichment program. The UN remains the most effective forum for negotiating a common position with other states. Even though the United States has not gotten its way in the past and may not ultimately sway others to its position on Iran's nuclear weapons program, the institution remains sufficiently valuable that the United States often prefers to work within rather than outside its rules or to create yet another organization.

Institutions are the rules of the political game. Valued and respected for the cooperation they facilitate, institutions are not, however, a panacea for problems of international cooperation. When the temptation to defect becomes too large, or the fear of being taken advantage of grows too severe, countries will violate the rules—just as individuals, firms, and other actors within countries choose at times to disobey the law. Yet, institutions do make international cooperation more likely, and countries that desire cooperation follow the rules more often than we might otherwise expect.

Conclusion: Thinking Analytically about World Politics

This chapter has outlined the basic concepts of interests, interactions, and institutions that serve throughout the book to unravel a variety of puzzles of international politics. The table at the end of chapter summarizes key points about each of these concepts.

To illustrate how this analytic framework can be used in concrete ways, we return to the example that opened this chapter. In the Iraq War of 2003, the interests of the United States and Iraq were diametrically opposed, thus throwing the two countries into an interaction of pure bargaining. The United States wanted, at a minimum, to eliminate Iraq's ability to deploy weapons of mass destruction and, at a maximum, to eliminate the regime of Saddam Hussein. The maximum demand of the United States was rooted in a belief that even though he might be successfully contained today, Hussein could not be trusted not to develop or use WMD in the future. These interests were reinforced by (1) the personal interests of the U.S. president and others in his administration to stand tough in international politics and promote democracy abroad, especially in the Middle East, (2) the desire for stable and cheap oil from Middle East suppliers, and (3) a general sense of insecurity on the part of many Americans after the terrorist attacks of 9/11. This confluence of interests combined to justify taking a hard-line stance against Iraq's purported weapons programs. The Iraqi ruler, in turn, wanted to remain in power and perhaps build Iraq into a regional power. Given these opposing interests, the United States and Iraq were bargaining over the extent of international controls on the latter's weapons programs and the nature of its government. With its coercive power and ability to set the agenda by increasing pressure on Iraq and, ultimately, initiating war, the United States was unwilling to accept anything less than Iraq's complete capitulation.

As we shall see more fully in Chapter 3, war is always a case of bargaining failure in which the parties are unable to reach an agreement on acceptable terms. In this case, the United States and Iraq were unable to devise a set of institutions, or to use existing ones, that would set agreed-upon standards for Iraq's weapons programs or effectively monitor and enforce the restrictions desired by the United States. In retrospect, it also became clear that the United States suffered from a serious lack of information—not only about Iraq's weapon's program and military capabilities, but also about the costs of rebuilding the country and ensuring internal political stability after the war. Despite facing almost certain defeat, in turn, Saddam Hussein gambled that he would be no worse off after the war than if he voluntarily left power and went into exile. In either case, he would lose office and likely be killed either in battle or in retribution for his crimes against the Iraqi people—as he eventually was in December 2006. He had little to lose by choosing to stand and fight. He also misjudged the United States' willingness to fight a war to remove him from power.

The great tragedy of the Iraq War of 2003 is that the previous inspection and disarmament efforts after the 1991 Gulf War conducted through the UN had effectively disarmed Iraq. The inspection regime—an international institution—had worked. But for a variety of reasons, Iraq could not allow the UN open access to all possible weapons sites. For Saddam Hussein to admit that he did not have stockpiles of WMD might have emboldened domestic insurgents and other regional powers, especially Iran. In turn, the United States, after a decade of failed Iraqi promises and thwarted inspections, did not believe it could trust Hussein to honor any agreement. As a result, there was no way Iraq could credibly demonstrate to the United States that it had, in fact, dismantled its weapons programs. The United States only discovered the truth for itself after it had begun what has turned into a long and costly war.

Reviewing Interests, Interactions, and Institutions

INTERESTS	INTERACTIONS	INSTITUTIONS
Interests are what actors want to achieve through political action.	Interactions are defined by the ways in which the choices of two or more actors combine to produce political outcomes.	Institutions are sets of rules, known and shared by the relevant community, that structure political interactions in particular ways.
Interests can be many and varied depending on the specific policy or event under examination.	Cooperation occurs when two or more actors adopt policies that make at least one actor better off without making any actors worse off.	Institutions facilitate cooperation by setting standards of behavior, verifying compliance, reducing the costs of joint decision-making, and resolving disputes.
We judge any particular specification of interests only by how well it explains the puzzle or set of events under consideration.	Cooperation is more likely to occur the smaller are the incentives to defect, the smaller is the group of actors, the more interactions are repeated or linked to other issues, and the greater is the information available to all parties.	All institutions bias outcomes, typically in ways favorable to those who write the rules. As a result, actors struggle over who gets to write and amend the rules.
	Bargaining arises when the choices of two or more actors will make at least one actor better off at the expense of at least one other actor.	Actors are more likely to comply with even biased rules the greater the value of the cooperation they facilitate, and the more costly it is to establish new institutions.
	Actors will gain more in bargaining the more attractive their reversion outcome, the lower their net costs of coercing others, the more attractive their outside options, and the greater their agenda-setting power.	

Key Terms

interests, p. 44

actors, p. 46

state, p. 46

sovereignty, p. 46

national interests, p. 47

interactions, p. 48

cooperation, p. 50

bargaining, p. 52

coordination, p. 54

collaboration, p. 54

public goods, p. 56

collective action problems, p. 56

free ride, p. 56

iteration, p. 57

linkage, p. 58

power, p. 59

coercion, p. 60

outside options, p. 61

agenda-setting power, p. 62

institutions, p. 62

anarchy, p. 63

For Further Reading

Bueno de Mesquita, Bruce, Alastair Smith, Randolph M. Siverson, and James D. Morrow. *The Logic of Political Survival.* Cambridge, MA: MIT Press, 2003. Integrates interests, interactions, and institutions to explain a wide range of behaviors in domestic and international politics.

Dixit, Avinash, and Barry J. Nalebuff. *Thinking Strategically: The Competitive Edge in Business, Politics, and Everyday Life.* New York: Norton, 1993. Presents concepts of strategic interaction applied in a variety of social settings.

Gordon, Michael R., and General Bernard E. Trainor. *Cobra II: The Inside Story of the Invasion and Occupation of Iraq.* New York: Pantheon, 2006. Along with Ricks (see below), offers a good contemporary history and analysis of the Iraq War.

Keohane, Robert O. *After Hegemony: Cooperation and Discord in the World Political Economy.* Princeton, NJ: Princeton University Press, 1984. Presents a classic statement on the role and importance of international institutions.

Lake, David A., and Robert Powell. *Strategic Choice and International Relations.* Princeton, NJ: Princeton University Press, 1999. Examines interests, interactions, and institutions in more detail within the context of international relations theory.

Milner, Helen V. *Interests, Institutions, and Information: Domestic Politics and International Relations.* Princeton, NJ: Princeton University Press, 1997. Explores the effects of interests, domestic institutions, and information asymmetries on international cooperation.

Ricks, Thomas E. *Fiasco: The American Military Adventure in Iraq.* New York: Penguin, 2006. Along with Gordon and Trainor (see above), offers a good contemporary history and analysis of the Iraq War.

Watson, Joel. *Strategy: An Introduction to Game Theory,* 2nd ed. New York: Norton, 2008. Explains fundamentals of game theory very well.

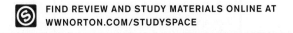

FIND REVIEW AND STUDY MATERIALS ONLINE AT WWNORTON.COM/STUDYSPACE

A Primer on Game Theory

Game theory is a tool for analyzing strategic interactions. Over the last fifty years, it has been developed and applied broadly in nearly all of the social sciences as well as in biology and other physical sciences—and it is even making inroads in the humanities. Among its earliest and most useful applications is to international politics. We provide here a brief overview of game theory to introduce strategic thinking and illustrate concepts discussed in the text.

Imagine two actors, Actor 1 (A1) and Actor 2 (A2), with only two choices, which we call cooperation (C) and defection (D). Since each actor has two choices, there are four possible outcomes to this "game": both might cooperate (CC), both defect (DD), A1 might cooperate while A2 defects (CD), and A1 might defect while A2 cooperates (DC). The mapping of choices into outcomes is best depicted using a 2 × 2 matrix, as shown in Figure 2A.1.[a1] As defined in the text, the actors' interests determine how they rank the four possible outcomes from best (4) to worst (1), with higher "payoffs" representing more preferred outcomes. A1's payoffs are given first in each cell, A2's second.

Both actors choose simultaneously without knowledge of the other's choices but with knowledge of their own preferences and those of the other actor.[a2] The outcome we observe is a function of the interaction—that is, the choices of both actors. Each actor can choose only C or D, but their payoffs differ across all four possible outcomes. A1 may desire or rank CC (mutual cooperation) over CD and decide to choose C, but in doing so it only partially controls which outcome arises. Having chosen C, A1's actual payoff depends crucially on whether A2 chooses C (creating CC) or D (creating CD). This highlights a key point: that *strategic interaction depends*

FIGURE 2A.1	A GAME MATRIX

a1. The same games can be represented in extensive form as a "game tree." Both are common in the larger literature.

a2. In some of the games discussed here, the outcome does not depend on the assumption that the actors move simultaneously.

on the choices of *all relevant actors,* and it is most important in explaining situations in which outcomes are contingent on the choices of all parties.

In such a setting, rational actors—that is, actors who seek their highest expected payoff—choose strategies, or plans of action, that are a best response to the anticipated actions of the other. In some cases, it makes sense for an actor to make the same choice (C or D) regardless of what the opponent does; in this case, the actor is said to have a *dominant strategy.* In other cases, each player's best choice depends on what the opponent does. For example, it might be a best response to cooperate when the other side cooperates and defect when the other side defects. Since each player is trying to play a best response, and since each expects the other to play a best response, the outcome of the game is given by two strategies each of which is a best response to the other. An outcome that arises from each side playing best response strategies is called an *equilibrium.* An equilibrium outcome is stable because the actors have no incentive to alter their choices; since in equilibrium both are playing their best responses, by definition they cannot do better by changing their choice. In all of the games below, the equilibrium (or *equilibria,* when there is more than one) is denoted by an asterisk (*) in the appropriate cell.

THE PRISONER'S DILEMMA

As we saw in the text (pp. 54–55), the Prisoner's Dilemma is a commonly cited game in international relations because it captures problems of collaboration, including arms races and public goods provision. Reread the full story on pages 54–55, and keep in mind that each prisoner can either *cooperate with his accomplice* and refuse to provide evidence to the district attorney, or *defect on his accomplice* by ratting him out. As a result, there are four possible outcomes for each player, ranked from worst to best as follows: (1) the prisoner cooperates while his partner defects (CD), meaning that he goes to jail while his partner goes free; (2) the prisoner and his partner both defect, end up in jail, and split the loot when released (DD); (3) the prisoner and his partner both cooperate, go free, and split the loot; (4) the prisoner defects while his partner cooperates (DC), meaning that he goes free and enjoys the loot while his partner does time in jail. In

FIGURE 2A.2	THE PRISONER'S DILEMMA

		A2				A2	
		C	D			C	D
A1	C	Both prisoners get out and split the loot.	A1 goes to jail; A2 goes free and keeps all the loot.	A1	C	3, 3	1, 4
	D	A1 goes free and keeps all the loot; A2 goes to jail.	Both go to jail and split the loot later.		D	4, 1	2, 2*

short, each prisoner has identical interests and ranks the four possible outcomes as DC > CC > DD > CD, as depicted in Figure 2A.2 (the "greater than" symbol should be read as meaning that the first outcome is "preferred to" the second).

What each prisoner should do is unclear at this point, but here is where the techniques of game theory help. As is evident once the matrix is examined carefully, each criminal has a dominant strategy of defecting regardless of his partner's actions. If his partner cooperates (that is, stays quiet), he is better off defecting (that is, talking to the district attorney) (DC > CC). If his partner defects, he is also better off defecting (DD > CD). The equilibrium that results from each prisoner playing his best response is DD, or mutual defection. The paradox, or dilemma, arises because both criminals would be better off remaining silent and getting released than both providing evidence and going to jail (CC > DD). But despite knowing this, each still has incentives to defect in order to get off easy (DC) or at least safeguard against his partner's defection (DD). The only actor who wins in this contrived situation is the district attorney, who sends both criminals to jail.

Although it is a considerable simplification, many analysts have used the Prisoner's Dilemma to capture the essential strategic dilemma at the core of the collective action problem. Each individual prefers to free ride while others contribute to the public good of, say, national defense, rather than contributing if everyone else does and receiving the good, to not contributing if no one else does, and finally to contributing if no one else contributes (DC > CC > DD > CD). As with the prisoners, each individual has a dominant strategy of not contributing (that is, defecting); thus, the public good of national defense is not provided voluntarily. The dilemma is solved only by the imposition of taxes by an authoritative state.

CHICKEN

The game of Chicken represents a second strategic dilemma. The animating story here is the game played by teenagers in the 1950s (and perhaps today by teenagers not yet familiar with game theory!). Two drivers speed down the middle of the road toward one another. The first to turn aside, the "chicken," earns the derision of his or her peers. The other driver wins. If both swerve simultaneously, neither is humiliated. If neither turns aside, both risk death in a serious wreck. If turning aside is understood as cooperation and continuing down the middle of the road as defection, the actors' interests are DC > CC > CD > DD, as shown in Figure 2A.3 (note that this is the same preference ordering as in The Prisoner's Dilemma, except for the reversal of the last two outcomes).

Lacking a dominant strategy, the key to one's strategy in Chicken is to do the opposite of what you think the other driver is likely to do. If you think your opponent will stand tough (D), you should turn aside (C). If you think your opponent will turn aside (C), you should stand tough (D). Two equilibria exist (DC and CD). The winner is the driver who by bluster, swagger, or past reputation convinces the other that she is more willing to risk a crash.

Chicken is often taken as a metaphor for coercive bargaining (see pp. 60–61 of text). Nuclear crises are usually thought of as Chicken games. Both sides want to avoid nuclear disaster (DD), but each has incentives to stand tough and get the

FIGURE 2A.3 | **CHICKEN**

		A2				A2	
		C	D			C	D
A1	C	Both drivers swerve; neither is humiliated or harmed.	A1 is "chicken"; A2 "wins."	**A1**	C	3, 3	2, 4*
	D	A1 "wins"; A2 is "chicken."	Both drivers are killed in a serious wreck.		D	4, 2*	1, 1

other to back down (DC). The state willing to take the greatest risk of nuclear war is therefore likely to force the other to capitulate. The danger, of course, is that if both sides are willing to run high risks of nuclear war to win, small mistakes in judgment or calculation can have horrific consequences.

THE STAG HUNT

A final game, which is often taken as a metaphor for problems of coordination in international relations (see p. 54 of text), is the Stag Hunt. This is one of a larger class of what are known as assurance games.[a3] The motivating parable was told by political philosopher Jean-Jacques Rousseau. Only by working together can two hunters kill a stag and feed their families well. One must flush the deer from the forest, and the other must be ready to fire his arrow as the animal emerges. In the midst of the hunt, a lone rabbit wanders by. Each hunter now faces a decision: he could capture the rabbit alone, but to do so he must abandon the stag, ensuring that it will get away. A rabbit is good sustenance, but not as fine as the hunter's expected share of the stag. In this game, both hunters are best off cooperating (CC) and sharing the stag. The next best outcome is to get a rabbit while the other tries for the stag (DC); however, if both go for the rabbit (DD), they then split the rabbit. The worst outcome for each hunter is to spend time and energy hunting the stag while the other hunts the rabbit (CD), leaving him and his family with nothing. Thus, each hunter's interests create the ranking CC > DC > DD > CD, as depicted in Figure 2A.4.

Despite the clear superiority of mutual cooperation, a coordination dilemma nonetheless arises. If each hunter expects that the other will cooperate and help

---

a3. Another common assurance game is Battle of the Sexes. In this game, a couple desires to spend the evening together, but one partner wants to attend a sporting event and the other a movie. The worst outcome for each is to spend the evening alone. Interested readers should model this game and describe its dynamics in terms similar to those for the Stag Hunt and the other games in this appendix.

FIGURE 2A.4 | THE STAG HUNT

		A2	
		C	D
A1	C	Both hunters split the stag.	A1 goes hungry; A2 eats the rabbit.
	D	A1 eats the rabbit; A2 goes hungry.	Both hunters split the rabbit.

		A2	
		C	D
A1	C	4, 4*	1, 3
	D	3, 1	2, 2*

bring down the stag, each is best off cooperating in the hunt. But if each expects that the other will be tempted to defect and grab the rabbit, thereby letting the stag get away, he will also defect and grab the rabbit. Lacking a dominant strategy, each can do no better than what he expects the other to do—creating two equilibria (CC and DD).

The Stag Hunt resembles the problem of setting international standards (see text p. 54). If a firm expects all others to use one format (C) for encoding compact discs, it should also use that format; if it expects others to use a different format (D), even if that format is inferior, it should use the second format as well. The worst outcome is for it to manufacture a product using the opposite format, leaving it with no compatible users. The Stag Hunt also captures situations in which the primary barrier to cooperation is not an individual incentive to defect, but a lack of trust. If we define trust in this context as an expectation that the partner will cooperate, then trust leads to mutual cooperation while a lack of trust leads to mutual defection. (By contrast, in the Prisoner's Dilemma, it never makes sense to trust an accomplice, and if one accomplice expects the other accomplice to cooperate, the best response is to defect.)

As this brief survey suggests, game theory helps clarify the core dilemmas in certain types of strategic situations. Many games are far more complex than the examples noted here, with more possible actions than "cooperate" or "defect," information asymmetries, random chance, and many more devices to capture elements of real-world strategic situations. The games presented here are more like metaphors than accurate representations of actual situations in international relations. But they illustrate how thinking systematically about strategic interaction helps us understand why actors cannot always get what they want—and, in fact, often get rather disappointing outcomes even though all actors might prefer other results. In both the Prisoner's Dilemma and the Stag Hunt, for instance, all actors prefer CC to DD, and this is known in advance. Nonetheless, in the Prisoner's Dilemma mutual defection is the equilibrium result, and in the Stag Hunt it is one of two expected outcomes. In all three games, outcomes are the result of the choices not of one actor, but of all.

PART TWO

War and Peace

In August 1914, as the armies of Europe fought the opening rounds of World War I, German prince Karl von Bülow paid a visit to the chancellor of Germany, Theobald von Bethmann-Hollweg, whose fateful decisions over the previous month had helped plunge the continent into war. "Well, tell me, at least, how it all happened," Bülow asked. Bethmann-Hollweg, with a look of pain and anguish, answered in an exhausted voice, "Oh—if I only knew!"[1]

Understanding the causes of war has been a pressing concern among scholars, policymakers, and regular citizens for as long as recorded history, and probably longer. At least since the Greek historian Thucydides wrote the *History of the Peloponnesian War* in the fifth century BCE, people have sought to explain why human groups—tribes, city-states, nations, and empires—sometimes fight one another in bloody contests. And as the machinery of warfare has advanced to the point where thousands, even millions, can now be killed in the blink of eye, the quest for understanding—and the hope that understanding will lead to prevention—has become more urgent.

Given the enormity of this topic, the three chapters that follow can only begin to grapple with the puzzle of war. The chapters in this section are organized around three of the most important questions for understanding

the origins and prevention of war: Why do countries sometimes fight wars rather than resolve their conflicts peacefully? In whose interests are wars fought? And what, if anything, can the international community do to prevent or stop the violence? To answer these questions, each chapter uses the framework of interests, interactions, and institutions, but each emphasizes a different component of the framework.

We begin with the central puzzle: given that war entails enormous human, material, and economic costs, why do states nonetheless use warfare as a strategy for resolving their conflicts? Surely the costs of war mean that states would be better off settling their conflict some other way, such as through negotiation? These questions force us to consider the bargaining *interaction* among actors with conflicting interests. Why are peaceful bargains sometimes reached, and why does bargaining sometimes fail? In Chapter 3, we show how features of the strategic situation can make it impossible for states to find deals that they prefer to war or to a strike a deal that will last.

Once we understand the dilemmas at the international level, we turn to domestic politics to explore the *interests* that might drive countries into conflict. Even if war is costly for the country as a whole, the costs and benefits of war do not fall equally on all citizens. In particular, there are times when political leaders seeking office, bureaucratic actors seeking budgets and influence, and economic interest groups seeking profits expect to benefit from war while paying few, if any, of the

---

1. This exchange is recorded in Bernhard von Bülow, *Memoirs of Prince von Bülow*, vol. 3, translated by Geoffrey Dunlop (Boston: Little, Brown, 1932), 166.

In the twentieth century alone, two world wars devastated the countries involved and killed tens of millions of people—including the 70,000 Japanese who were killed instantly in 1945, when the United States dropped an atom bomb on Hiroshima, shown here shortly after the blast.

costs. Chapter 4 examines the extent to which states' interests in war and peace derive from the interests of domestic actors, the interactions between those actors, and the political institutions that determine who governs within the country. This question also lets us consider whether democracy at home promotes peace abroad, a claim that has played an important role in recent events, like the Iraq War.

The final piece of the puzzle revolves around international efforts to prevent wars. In our private lives, we count on the police to protect us from acts of violence and to punish those who engage in violence. But what happens when violence takes place between states or within states, such as civil war or genocide? In the absence of an international police force, can outsiders cooperate to prevent, stop, or punish the violence? Chapter 5 examines two kinds of international *institutions* that try to foster such cooperation: alliances and collective security organizations. Alliances are institutions that make it easier for states with common interests to cooperate

militarily in defense of those interests. Collective security organizations, like the United Nations, seek cooperation within the international community in defense of peace and security. Neither institution provides a perfect solution to the problem of war, but under the right conditions, both can tilt the scales in favor of peace.

The analysis in this part helps us not only to understand war, but also to identify the factors that make war more or less likely. How can the bargaining interaction be shaped so as to improve the chances for peace? What kinds of domestic arrangements make countries less belligerent? When can states cooperate to prevent the outbreak of war? Ultimately, the persistence of warfare in human relations makes it hard to be optimistic that the scourge of war can ever be entirely eliminated. Nonetheless, by understanding the interests, interactions, and institutions that affect the likelihood of war, we have a chance of containing and reducing this danger. And we need not feel as helpless or bewildered as Bethmann-Hollweg was in August 1914.

CHAPTER 3

Why Are There Wars?

The deadliest international conflict since World War II is the war in the Democratic Republic of Congo (DRC), which has been called "Africa's World War." The war officially lasted from 1998 to 2003, but fighting continues to this day. Troops from eight different African nations—the DRC, Namibia, Zimbabwe, Angola, Chad, Uganda, Rwanda, and Burundi—were involved, as well as numerous rebel groups. The war and its aftermath have claimed over 5 million lives.

War is an extremely costly way for states to settle their disputes. Given the human and material costs of military conflict, why do states sometimes wage war rather than resolving their disputes through negotiations?

I n August 1914, the major countries of Europe embarked on a war the likes of which the world had never before seen. Convinced that the war would be over by Christmas, European leaders sent a generation of young men into a fight that would last four years and claim more than 15 million lives. The fighting was so intense that in one battle the British Army lost 20,000 soldiers in a single day, as wave after wave of attacking infantrymen were cut down by German machine guns. At the time, it was called the Great War. Those who could never imagine another such horrific event dubbed it the "war to end all wars." Today, we know this event as the First World War, or World War I, because twenty years later the countries of Europe were at it once again. World War II (1939–1945) claimed 30 to 50 million lives.

There is no puzzle in the study of international politics more pressing and important than the question of why states go to war. It is the most tragic and costly phenomenon that we observe in social and political life. The costs of war can be counted on a number of dimensions. The most obvious cost is the loss of human life. By one estimate, wars among states in the twentieth century led to 40 million deaths directly from combat plus tens of millions more deaths due to war-related hardships.[1] In addition, wars have left untold millions injured, displaced from their homes and countries, impoverished, and diseased. There are economic and material costs associated with war as well. By the middle of 2008, the United States had spent almost $6.3 trillion fighting ten wars in its history, and the bills for the wars in

---

1. Bethany Ann Lacina and Nils Petter Gleditsch, "Monitoring Trends in Global Combat: A New Dataset of Battle Deaths," *European Journal of Population* 21 (2005): 145–66.

What Is the Purpose of War?
▶ What Do States Fight Over?
▶ Bargaining and War
▶ Compellence and Deterrence: Varieties of Coercive Bargaining

Do Wars Happen by Mistake? War from Incomplete Information
▶ Incentives to Misrepresent and the Problem of Credibility
▶ Communicating Resolve: The Language of Coercion

Can an Adversary Be Trusted to Honor a Deal? War from Commitment Problems
▶ Bargaining over Goods That Are a Source of Future Bargaining Power
▶ Prevention: War in Response to Changing Power
▶ Preemption: War in Response to First-Strike Advantages

Is Compromise Always Possible? War from Indivisibility

How Can We Make War Less Likely?
▶ Raising the Costs of War
▶ Increasing Transparency
▶ Providing Outside Enforcement of Commitments
▶ Dividing Apparently Indivisible Goods

Conclusion: Why War?

Iraq and Afghanistan continued to mount.[2] Large sums of money are also spent every year to prepare for the possibility of war. In 2007, military expenditures by all countries amounted to about $1.3 trillion—a sum that represented about $202 per person.[3] Wars can also disrupt the international economy. The U.S. war in Iraq and tensions with Iran contributed to a run-up in the price of oil that caused gas prices to reach record highs in 2008. In short, as U.S. Civil War general William Sherman famously declared, "war is hell."

But if everyone recognizes that war is hell, why do wars happen? The very costs that make the puzzle of war so pressing also make the phenomenon so puzzling. Given the enormous costs associated with war, why would states sometimes choose this course?

At first glance, the answer might seem straightforward: states fight wars because they have conflicting interests over important issues. Often, two states desire the same piece of territory. Nazi Germany wanted to expand into Central Europe; World War II started when the Poles, who did not want to give up their territory, fought back. In 1980, Iraq coveted Iran's southern oil fields, and Iran refused to give them up, leading to the Iran-Iraq War. Alternatively, one state might object to the policies or ideology of another. World War I grew out of Austria-Hungary's demand that Serbia end nationalist agitation that threatened to tear the multiethnic empire apart. The war between the United States and Afghanistan in 2001 occurred because the United States wanted Afghanistan to hand over Osama bin Laden and dismantle terrorist training camps on its territory, something that the Afghans refused to do. Clearly, part of the explanation for any war requires that we identify the conflicting interests that motivated the combatants.

Although such explanations are correct, they are also incomplete. By identifying the object or issue over

which a war was fought, they neglect the key question of why war was the strategy that states resorted to in order to resolve their dispute. In each case, the conflicts were disastrously costly to at least one and, in some cases, all of the states involved. In addition to the millions of dead mentioned earlier, World War I led to the ouster of three of the leaders that brought their countries into to the war, and it hastened the breakup of the Austro-Hungarian, Russian, and Ottoman empires. World War II brought about the defeat and occupation of its main instigators, Germany and Japan. Nazi leader Adolf Hitler committed suicide, and his Italian ally, Benito Mussolini, was hung by his own people. Iran and Iraq fought to a stalemate for eight years, causing 1 to 2 million casualties and leaving Iraq on the brink of economic collapse. The Afghan government's refusal to hand over bin Laden led to its removal from power. Given these grave consequences, it makes sense to wonder whether all participants would have been better off if they could have come to some settlement that would have allowed them to avoid the costs of war. Explaining war thus requires us to explain why the participants failed to reach such an agreement.

To illustrate this puzzle even more concretely, consider the case of the Mexican-American War, which grew out of the United States' desire to expand its territory to the southwest. In 1845, relations between the two neighbors were quite tense, as the United States had just annexed Texas against Mexico's will, and a dispute grew up over whether the border between the countries was the Rio Grande River, as the United States claimed, or further north at the Nueces River, as Mexico claimed. In the midst of these tensions, U.S. president James K. Polk sent an emissary to offer the cash-strapped Mexican government money in exchange for a settlement of the outstanding disputes and to purchase additional territory. The offer: $25 million in exchange for California, New Mexico, and the disputed territory in Texas. The Mexican government, however, refused to entertain this offer or even to negotiate, and a war broke out in April 1846. The United States won every major battle that ensued, and U.S. forces seized Mexico City in September 1847. Not surprisingly, the

2. Stephen Daggett, "Costs of Major U.S. Wars," Congressional Research Service Report for Congress, July 24, 2008. Available at fpc.state.gov/documents/organization/108054.pdf (accessed 3/5/09). The Revolutionary War and American Civil War are not included in this total. The total reported is in 2008 dollars.
3. See www.sipri.org/contents/milap/milex/mex_trends.html (accessed 3/5/09).

settlement that ended the war, the Treaty of Guadalupe Hidalgo, was worse for Mexico than the original offer that it had rejected. The United States annexed what we know today as California, New Mexico, Arizona, and Utah and paid in return only $15 million, or $10 million less than it had been willing to pay before the war. Even on the U.S. side, however, victory came with a price: the deaths of 13,000 Americans and a financial outlay of $100 million. Given this outcome, it seems clear that *both* sides would have been better off if Mexico had accepted the initial American offer or if the United States had made a more generous offer at the outset.

And indeed, most disputes between states are settled without resort to war. Although wars tend to capture our attention, it is important to remember that war is an exceedingly rare phenomenon: most countries are at peace with each other most of the time. Figure 3.1 (p. 87) shows the number of states involved in interstate wars in each year from 1820 to 2008, expressed as a percentage of the total number of states in existence at the time. As the figure indicates, war is a recurrent feature of international politics in the sense that its frequency fluctuates up and down but never disappears completely. And yet war is the exception rather than the rule: in most years, the percentage of states involved in war is quite low. All of this peace cannot be explained by an absence of issues to fight over.

Hence, when seeking to explain war, we need to ask not only "What are they fighting over?" but also "Why are they fighting?"[4] In terms of the framework laid out in Chapter 2, answering the first question requires that we understand how states' interests can give rise to conflicts over things like territory, policies, and the composition or character of each other's government. The answer to the second question lies in the strategic interactions that determine whether or how these conflicts are resolved. As we saw, the international system lacks institutions—such as legislatures, courts, or international police forces—that can resolve conflicts between states through legal, judicial, or electoral mechanisms. As a result, interstate conflicts have to be settled through bargaining. Understanding why wars occur requires that we identify the factors that sometimes prevent states from settling their conflicts through peaceful bargains that would permit them to avoid the costs of war.

CORE OF THE ANALYSIS

▶ Even though states may have conflicting interests over goods like territory, policies, or the composition of one another's governments, the costs of war ensure that there generally exists a peaceful settlement that all sides prefer to war. War occurs when the bargaining interaction fails to reach such a deal.

▶ States may be unable to find negotiated settlements that they prefer to war when there is incomplete information about how each side evaluates the likely outcome and costs of waging war.

▶ Even if states can find a mutually acceptable bargain, peace can break down if they cannot commit to abide by the terms of the agreement, especially if their relative power is expected to change in the future.

▶ Bargaining may also fail if there are features of the disputed good that make it hard to divide, so that compromise agreements are impossible to reach.

▶ Given this logic, promoting peaceful conflict resolution requires efforts to increase the costs of conflict, to promote transparency and communication between disputants, to bring in third parties to enforce states' commitments to one another, and to find creative ways of sharing apparently indivisible goods.

---

4. The theory of war developed in this chapter relies extensively on James Fearon, "Rationalist Explanations for War," *International Organization* 49 (Summer 1995): 379–414.

What Is the Purpose of War?

A **war** is an event involving the organized use of military force by at least two parties that satisfies some minimum threshold of severity.[5] All of the components of this definition are important. The requirement that force be organized rules out spontaneous, disorganized violence, such as large-scale rioting. The requirement that force be used by at least two sides distinguishes war from mass killings perpetrated by a government against some group that does not fight back. The minimum threshold—scholars often require that a war have at least 1,000 battle deaths—excludes cases in which military force is used at low levels, such as brief skirmishes or minor clashes that fall short of our intuitive notion of war. If the main parties to the conflict are both states, then we refer to the event as an **interstate war**; if the main parties to the conflict are actors within a state—such as a government and a rebel group— then the event is a **civil war**.[6] In the main body of this chapter, the discussion will focus on understanding interstate wars. The Special Topic appendix at the end of the chapter extends this analysis to the case of civil wars.

WHAT DO STATES FIGHT OVER?

At the root of all wars lies a conflict over things that states value. The purpose of warfare is not to fight but rather to obtain, through fighting or the threat of fighting, something the state wants. Hence, we should think about the problem of war as a problem of bargaining over objects or issues that are of value to more than one state. Using the framework developed in the previous chapter, we focus on situations in which states' interests conflict, giving rise to a strategic interaction that involves bargaining over the distribution of whatever is in dispute. The analysis thus starts by assuming that there is some object of value—what we will sometimes refer to as a "good"—and that each state prefers more of the good to less.

What kinds of goods do states fight over? *Territory* has historically been the most common source of trouble. Indeed, a study of 155 wars over the last three centuries found that over half (83) involved conflicts over territory—more than any other single issue.[7] States come into conflict if more than one wants the same piece of territory. There are a number of reasons why a piece of territory may be valuable to more than one state. First, it might contribute to the wealth of the state, particularly if it contains valuable resources such as oil, natural gas, or minerals. Iran and Iraq fought a lengthy war from 1980 to 1988 in part because Iraq coveted Iran's southern oil fields. Territory can also be economically valuable simply by adding to the industrial or agricultural resources at the state's disposal. A second reason that territory can cause conflict between two states is if it has military or strategic value.

---

5. See, for example, J. David Singer and Melvin Small, *The Wages of War, 1816–1965: A Statistical Handbook* (New York: Wiley, 1972).

6. There are also cases that have elements of both kinds of wars. In the Vietnam War, South Vietnam, with the support of the United States, fought a civil war against a communist insurgency, while at the same time it was fighting an interstate war against communist North Vietnam, which was supporting the rebellion.

7. Kalevi J. Holsti, *Peace and War: Armed Conflicts and International Order, 1648–1989* (Cambridge: Cambridge University Press, 1991).

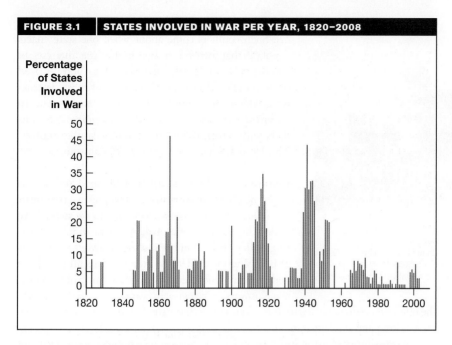

FIGURE 3.1 | STATES INVOLVED IN WAR PER YEAR, 1820–2008

Sources: For 1820–1992, the Correlates of War Interstate War data (version 3.0): see Meredith Reid Sarkees, "The Correlates of War Data on War: An Update to 1997," *Conflict Management and Peace Science* 18 (2000): 123–44. For 1993–2001, the Correlates of War Militarized Interstate Dispute data (version 3.1.): see Faten Ghosn, Glenn Palmer, and Stuart Bremer, "The MID3 Data Set, 1993–2001: Procedures, Coding Rules, and Description," *Conflict Management and Peace Science* 21 (2004); 133–54.

For example, the Golan Heights, on the border between Israel and Syria, have a commanding position over northern Israel from which it is possible to launch devastating attacks on the towns below. Israel seized the Golan Heights from Syria in the 1967 Six Day War, and this territory has been a source of conflict between the two states ever since. Finally, a piece of territory might be valuable for ethnic, cultural, or historical reasons. The long-standing conflict between Israel and its Arab neighbors stems from the latter's resistance to the creation of a Jewish state on a land where many Arabs lived. In this case, the dispute goes beyond simply the location of a border, as some Arab states have refused to recognize Israel's right to exist.[8] Similarly, the long-running conflict between India and Pakistan is driven by the fact that both have historical and ethnic claims to the region of Kashmir. When the two countries gained their independence from Britain in 1947, India forced Kashmir's Hindu leader to join with India, which is predominantly Hindu; however, because the people of Kashmir, like the people of Pakistan, are predominantly Muslim, Pakistan has claimed the territory on the basis of religious ties. In territorial disputes, states threaten or use military force to compel concessions and/or to seize and hold disputed land. "What Do We Know" on page 89 explores disputes over different types of territory in more detail, in light of the theory of war developed in this chapter.

---

8. Egypt recognized Israel in 1979, and Jordan did likewise in 1994.

States may come into conflict if they fear that the composition of another country's government will threaten their interests. For example, during the Vietnam War, the United States sought to prevent the establishment of a communist regime in South Vietnam. The Americans feared that a communist government would become an ally of their Cold War rival, the Soviet Union.

Wars can also arise out of conflicts over states' *policies*. Such conflicts come about when one state enacts a policy that benefits it but harms the interests of another. The conflict that led to the Iraq War centered on Iraq's alleged pursuit of weapons of mass destruction, which the United States saw as threatening to its broader interests in the region. Ongoing U.S. conflicts with North Korea and Iran have similar sources. The United States' war against Afghanistan in 2001 stemmed from the latter's support for the Al Qaeda terrorist organization. In 1999, the United States went to war against Serbia because of its repressive treatment of civilians in the Kosovo region. When states have policy disputes, war may be a mechanism for compelling policy change; in the case of Kosovo, two months of bombing by the United States and its allies led the Serb government to end its military campaign against the Kosovars. Alternatively, war may be used to replace the offending regime with a friendlier one that will pursue different policies, as in the cases of Iraq and Afghanistan.

The possibility of using military force to change regimes suggests a third kind of conflict between states: conflicts over *regime type*, or the composition of another country's government. During the Cold War, the United States saw communist regimes as natural allies of the Soviet Union, and hence it sought to prevent the establishment of such regimes. U.S. involvement in the Vietnam War was driven by the desire to protect the pro-American South Vietnamese government from internal and external enemies bent on overthrowing it. As we saw in Chapter 1, during this period both superpowers intervened regularly in other states to prop up friendly governments or to remove unfriendly ones.

As this last example suggests, conflicts over territory, policy, and/or regime may spring from deeper conflicts that give rise to concerns about relative power. The specific conflict that started World War II was a territorial dispute between Germany and Poland over a small strip of territory that lay between them. However, Britain and France were concerned that a victory over Poland would further strengthen and embolden Germany, making it a more formidable foe in their ongoing struggle for influence and territory in Europe. Hence, the German-Polish territorial dispute impinged on the interests of other states because of its potential impact on their relative power vis-à-vis Germany. The Cold War rivalry between the United States and the Soviet Union similarly imbued many local conflicts with global importance due to their perceived impact on the relative strength of the superpowers.

BARGAINING AND WAR

Conflicting interests over the distribution of a good are clearly necessary for wars to happen, but they are not sufficient to explain why wars actually do happen. To understand why some conflicts become wars and others do not, we have to think

Bargaining and Conflict over Territory

Disputes over territory have historically been the most common source of interstate violence. But not all pieces of territory are valuable for the same reason, and the different interests at stake in different territorial disputes affect the likelihood that these interactions will lead to war. Conflicts over territory may be rooted in three kinds of interests: economic, security, and ethno-religious. Two countries' economic interests can clash when a territory contains valuable resources such as oil, minerals, or rich soil for agriculture. National security interests can diverge when a piece of territory gives the state that controls it a military-strategic advantage, such as a hill with a commanding position over the area below or a mountain pass that is the only possible invasion route. Finally, countries may dispute a territory because there are ethnic or religious ties between the people who live in that territory and the inhabitants of the state that wants it; in these cases, states generally want the territory in order to bring these people—and any sites that might have ethnic or religious significance—within their borders.

The theory of war developed in this chapter suggests that these three kinds of disputes may present different challenges as states bargain over territory. Territory that has military-stategic value can present an obstacle to bargaining because possession of the territory imparts a strategic advantage and affects future bargaining power. States will be reluctant to make concessions if they cannot trust the other not to exploit that advantage to make further demands later on. (As we will see later, this is known as a commitment problem.) Territorial claims that involve core identities such as ethnicity or religion can make the territory hard to divide. Governments that base their claims on the idea of uniting with ethnic or religious kin may find it hard to split the disputed territory and thereby leave some behind.[a] By contrast, territory that is economically valuable does not face these types of challenges, unless the economic benefits are so large that possessing the territory dramatically alters the relative power between the states. Given this logic, it should be easier to reach peaceful bargains over economically valuable territories than over the other two kinds.

Is this true? In part to answer this question, political scientist Paul K. Huth collected information on 129 territorial disputes in the period 1950–1990.[b] In each of these cases, two states had conflicting claims to a piece of territory. For each dispute, Huth determined whether the territory in question had a strategically valuable location, whether it contained economically important resources, and whether it was home to people who shared ethnic or linguistic ties to the state that sought it. To determine how dangerous each kind of dispute was, Huth collected information on whether and when each dispute led to political or military conflict. (Political conflict includes hostile rhetoric, diplomatic or economic sanctions, and support for efforts to destabilize the adversary's government. Militarized conflict involves the threat or use of military force.) Huth also took into account a number of variables that influence the escalation of these disputes (for example, the military balance).

The data revealed a consistent pattern. On average, political and military conflict was most likely to occur when there were ethnic or linguistic ties between those in the disputed territory and the state claiming that territory; the risk of conflict was slightly lower for disputes involving strategic territory; and disputes involving economically valuable territory were, of the three, the least likely to lead to political or military conflict (see figure). Thus, the nature of the interests at stake has important consequences for the bargaining interaction and whether it will lead to peace or war. ∎

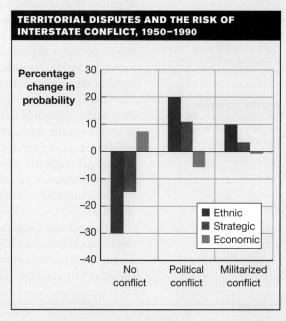

TERRITORIAL DISPUTES AND THE RISK OF INTERSTATE CONFLICT, 1950–1990

Percentage change in probability

Legend: ■ Ethnic ■ Strategic ■ Economic

(x-axis: No conflict, Political conflict, Militarized conflict)

Note: The bars indicate the percentage change in the likelihood of the possible outcomes associated with each kind of territorial dispute. A negative value, or bar, indicates a decrease in the likelihood of the given outcome, while a positive value, or bar, indicates an increased likelihood.
Source: Huth, p. 109.

a. Stacie E. Goddard, "Uncommon Ground: Indivisible Territory and the Politics of Legitimacy," *International Organization* 60 (2006): 35–68.
b. Paul K. Huth, *Standing Your Ground: Territorial Disputes and International Conflict* (Ann Arbor: University of Michigan Press, 1996).

about the strategic interactions that states engage in when they seek to settle their disputes. In a well-functioning domestic political system, the kinds of disputes that lead to wars are often settled through any number of institutional mechanisms. Property disputes can be adjudicated by courts backed by effective police powers. If one person engages in actions that harm another, the latter may have recourse to legal remedies. Policy disagreements and conflicting ideas over who should govern can be settled by elections. As noted in Chapter 2, however, the international system lacks reliable legal, judicial, and electoral institutions. As a result, states must generally try to settle their conflicts through bargaining.[9]

Bargaining describes a class of interactions in which actors try to resolve disputes over the allocation of a good. They may bargain over the distribution of a disputed territory to determine whether there is a division that is acceptable to both sides. Or they may bargain over each other's policies so that objectionable policies might be modified or eliminated. Although we often think of bargaining as entailing compromise or give-and-take, the process of bargaining does not always imply that differences will be split. Indeed, in many cases, states assume "all or nothing" bargaining positions. For example, when President Bush demanded in October 2001 that the Afghan government hand over Al Qaeda leaders and dismantle the terrorist training camps on their territory, he declared that "these demands are not open to negotiation or discussion."

A crisis occurs when at least one state seeks to influence the outcome of bargaining by threatening to use military force in the event that it does not get what it wants. At this point, we enter the domain of coercive bargaining, in which the consequences of not reaching an agreement can involve the use of force, including war. We sometimes refer to bargaining under the threat of war as **crisis bargaining** or **coercive diplomacy**. In all such interactions, at least one state sends the message "Satisfy my demands, or else"—where the "or else" involves imposing costs on the other side through military action. In some cases, this message takes the form of an explicit ultimatum, such as Bush's March 2003 ultimatum giving Iraqi leader Saddam Hussein 48 hours to leave the country or face an invasion. U.S. demands against Afghanistan were similarly backed by an explicit threat: "They will hand over the terrorists, or they will share their fate." In other cases, the threat is conveyed implicitly, through menacing actions such as mobilization of troops or military maneuvers. In either event, the purpose of such threats is clear: they seek to wrest concessions from the other side by making the alternative seem unacceptably costly.

The costs and likely outcome of a war define the range of acceptable outcomes from crisis bargaining. We can generally assume that the best possible outcome for a state in a crisis is to get the entire good without having to fight. Capitulation by the other side gives the state its most preferred settlement of the underlying issue

crisis bargaining:
A bargaining interaction in which at least one actor threatens to use force in the event that its demands are not met.

coercive diplomacy:
The use of threats to influence the outcome of a bargaining interaction.

---

9. Although some interstate disputes have been adjudicated through institutions like the International Court of Justice (ICJ), these institutions lack strong enforcement mechanisms to guarantee compliance with their rulings, and disputants often engage in bargaining after an ICJ ruling to determine whether and how its terms will be implemented. Hence, these rulings are a part of, rather than a substitute for, the bargaining process. See, for example, Cole Paulson, "Compliance with Final Judgments of the International Court of Justice since 1987," *American Journal of International Law* 98 (2004): 434–61.

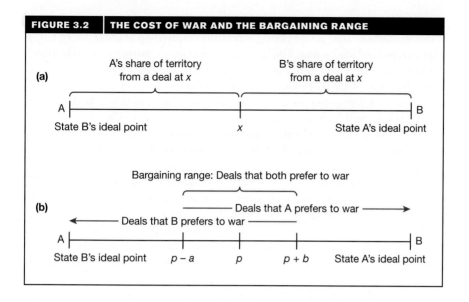

FIGURE 3.2 | THE COST OF WAR AND THE BARGAINING RANGE

(a)

A's share of territory from a deal at x

B's share of territory from a deal at x

A ———————————————— B

State B's ideal point x State A's ideal point

Bargaining range: Deals that both prefer to war

(b)

——— Deals that A prefers to war ——→

←——— Deals that B prefers to war ———

A ———————————————— B

State B's ideal point $p - a$ p $p + b$ State A's ideal point

and avoids the need to pay the costs associated with war. It is quite likely, though, that a state would also accept something less than full capitulation by the other side, given that the alternative of fighting is costly. For example, imagine a conflict over a piece of territory worth $100 million. Assume that a state believes that in the event of a war, it is certain to win the territory; however, the costs of war, if put in monetary terms, would amount to $20 million. In that case, the expected value of going to war for that state is $100 million − $20 million = $80 million. Hence, the state should be willing to accept any deal that gives it at least $80 million worth of the territory. Since a state has the option to wage war if it determines that it is in its interests to do so, a state will only accept a bargain that gives it at least as much as it can expect to get from war. And for any deal to prevent a war, it must satisfy all sides in this way: each state must decide that it prefers the deal to fighting a war. Hence, in our simple example, war can only be averted if the other state is willing to settle for the remaining $20 million worth of territory or less.

The discussion at the outset of this chapter implies a very simple proposition: *because war is costly, a settlement that all sides prefer to war generally exists.*[10] Figure 3.2 illustrates the simple idea behind this proposition. Assume that two states, call them State A and State B, both want a piece of territory that is represented by the line. Any point on the line, such as the point labeled x in (a), represents a possible division of the territory such that State A receives all of the territory to the left of the point and State B receives all territory to the right of the point. Since both states prefer more territory to less, A wants to get a deal that pushes x as far to the right as possible, and B wants to get a deal that pushes x as far to the left as possible. Put another way, A's most preferred outcome, or ideal point, is at the far right of the line, and B's ideal point is on the far left. Now, consider what happens if the

---

10. See Fearon, "Rationalist Explanations for War."

two states fight a war. Moving to (b), let p denote the actual or expected outcome of a violent conflict. That is, the point p represents the division of the territory that is expected to hold after a war. The higher p is (that is, the farther it is to the right), the better A is expected to fare in the event of war; the lower p is (the farther it is to the left), the better B is expected to fare.

Crucially, fighting entails costs. Let a and b denote the costs that State A and State B, respectively, will have to pay in the event of war. Costs have the effect of diminishing the value of the expected war outcome to each state. Hence, to determine the expected value of war for State A, we start at the outcome, p, and move away from A's ideal point by the amount a, arriving at the point $p - a$. Similarly, to determine the expected value of war for State B, we start at the outcome, p, and move away from B's ideal point by the amount b. Since B prefers outcomes that are farther to the left, or at the low end of the scale, this means we add the cost term b in order to diminish B's value for war. By rendering the costs in this way, we must interpret a and b as capturing the costs of war relative to the value of the good. For example, imagine that State A expects to win half the territory (that is, $p = 0.5$) at the cost of 5,000 lives. State A's war value, $p - a$, hinges on how much A values those lost lives relative to the value of the territory. If A thinks that losing those soliders is equivalent to losing 20 percent of the territory, then its value for war is $0.5 - 0.2 = 0.3$, or 30 percent of the value of the territory. The effective costs of war would go up if either the number of lives lost went up or the value attached to the territory went down.

As the figure shows, State A would prefer to war any division of the good that gave it more than its war value, $p - a$, while State B would prefer to war any division of the good that fell to the left of its war value, $p + b$. Notice that the set of deals that A prefers to war and the set of deals that B prefers to war overlap, creating a region called the **bargaining range**. Any division of the territory in this bargaining range gives both states more than they expect to get from fighting a war. Because war imposes costs on both sides, such a range of deals always exists. Hence, in theory, there are bargains that both sides would prefer to war.

This simple model is useful not because it is right, in the sense that it correctly describes the complexity of real-world bargaining interactions. Rather, the model is useful because it forces us to think about all of the ways in which it could go wrong. Understanding why wars happen in spite of this compelling logic is the main purpose of this chapter.

bargaining range: The set of deals that both parties in a bargaining interaction prefer to the reversion outcome. When the reversion outcome is war, the bargaining range is the set of deals that both sides prefer to war.

COMPELLENCE AND DETERRENCE: VARIETIES OF COERCIVE BARGAINING

The model is also useful for thinking about the conditions under which states might have an interest in initiating a crisis in the first place. The precrisis distribution, or status quo, can be represented as a point on the line. Where the status quo is located relative to the states' values for war determines which state, if any, might have an interest in changing the status quo through a threat of force. If a state is already getting from the status quo at least as much as it expects to get through war, then it generally cannot gain by threatening war to change the status quo.

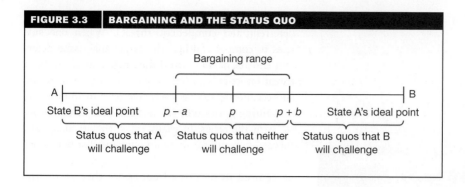

FIGURE 3.3 | BARGAINING AND THE STATUS QUO

Bargaining range

A ── B
State B's ideal point $p - a$ p $p + b$ State A's ideal point

Status quos that A will challenge | Status quos that neither will challenge | Status quos that B will challenge

However, if a state expects to get more through war than it has in the status quo, then it has an interest in making a challenge. This does not mean that there will be a war since, after all, a bargaining range still exists. But in this situation, the dissatisfied state can profit by threatening war in order to get a better deal. As Figure 3.3 shows, this logic divides the line into three segments. If the status quo is to the left of State A's value for war, $p - a$, then A would rather fight a war than live with things as they are; in this case, A has an interest in threatening war and trying to get a better outcome. Similarly, if the status quo is to the right of State B's value for war, $p + b$, then B prefers war to the status quo and thus has an interest in sparking a crisis. Finally, if the status quo is between the two states' war values—that is, in the bargaining range—then both prefer the current situation to war, and neither can expect to gain by waging war.

We often classify threats according to whether they are intended to preserve or change the existing relationship between states. An effort to change the status quo through the threat of force is called **compellence**. A compellent threat is intended to coerce the target state into making a concession or changing a current policy. Compellent threats take the form of "Give me Y, or else" (where Y is something that the threatener values) or "Stop doing X, or else" (where X is an objectionable policy). The U.S. demand that Afghanistan hand over Osama bin Laden and stop harboring the Al Qaeda terrorist network after the 9/11 attacks is an example of compellence.

Deterrence, by contrast, is used to preserve the status quo by threatening the other side with unacceptable costs if it seeks to alter the current relationship. A deterrent threat takes the form of "Don't do X, or else" (where X is some possible future action that the threatener finds objectionable). The most common deterrent threat is one that all states make implicitly all of the time: "Don't attack me, or I'll fight back." The effort to deter attack on one's own country is referred to as *general deterrence*, and it is an activity that states are constantly engaged in. Another form of deterrence occurs when a state seeks to protect a friend. In this case, the deterrent message takes the form of "Don't attack my ally X, or else." This kind of threat is generally referred to as *extended deterrence* because in this case the threatener attempts to extend protection to another state. Extended deterrence is crucial in the context of alliances, a subject that we will consider in Chapter 5.

compellence: An effort to change the status quo through the threat of force.

deterrence: An effort to preserve the status quo through the threat of force.

A deterrent threat is meant to send the message that a state can and will fight back if provoked. In 2006, Iran test-fired long-range missiles during a standoff with the United States and other countries over its nuclear program. The test was likely intended to convey that Iran was ready to impose unacceptable costs on its enemies if they took steps to interfere with Iran's nuclear program.

In general, crises may involve a combination of deterrent and compellent threats. When one side tries to compel another, the target may issue deterrent threats, or some third state may issue a deterrent threat on its behalf. Crises often involve such threats and counterthreats, as each side tries to improve its bargaining position by bringing to bear its capability to harm the other. In many cases, threats alone will succeed in bringing about an outcome that both sides find acceptable. Indeed, the most effective threats never need to be carried out, since they coerce the target into making the desired concessions or refraining from objectionable actions. It is when this contest of threats fails to generate an outcome that both sides prefer to fighting that we observe the descent into war.

Do Wars Happen by Mistake?
War from Incomplete Information

In July 1990, Iraq was engaged in coercive diplomacy with its small neighbor to the south, Kuwait. Two years earlier, Iraq had emerged from a disastrous, eight-year war with Iran, and Iraqi leader Saddam Hussein desperately needed to rebuild his shattered economy. Given that Iraq was sitting on oil deposits containing an estimated 112 billion barrels of oil, it was not hard to imagine where money for reconstruction would come from. But Hussein was not content simply to pump and sell Iraq's own oil, and he quickly turned his gun sights on Kuwait. Kuwait's 95 billion barrels of recoverable oil reserves made a tempting target, and, moreover, Hussein felt that his neighbor was standing in the way of his plans for economic recovery. For one thing, Kuwait was pumping more oil than it had previously agreed to. This extra supply meant that the price of oil was lower than it would otherwise be, depriving Iraq of needed revenue. Iraq also charged that Kuwait was stealing oil from oil fields that straddled the countries' shared border. Finally, Kuwait had loaned Iraq substantial sums of money during the war, and Saddam Hussein hoped to get this debt forgiven. When Kuwait refused these demands, Iraq flexed its military muscle. Beginning in mid-July, Iraq started moving its forces closer to the border with Kuwait, at one point moving an entire division per day. By the end of the month, 100,000 Iraqi troops, supported by thousands of tanks, were in position near the border.

With the help of spy satellites, American officials watched the buildup, and they passed on their intelligence to the Kuwaitis. Despite their concern, most officials in the U.S. government did not anticipate that Iraq would invade, nor did the Kuwaitis bow to Hussein's demands. To many observers, the Iraqi moves looked like an effort to intimidate, not a prelude to invasion. According to reporter Bob Woodward's account, "everything Saddam had to do to prepare for an invasion was exactly what he also had to do if his intention was simply to scare the Kuwaitis. There was no way to distinguish the two."[11] On July 31, with Kuwait still holding out, Hussein revealed that he had not simply been bluffing: Iraqi forces swept into Kuwait and fully occupied the country in a matter of hours.

In retrospect, it is clear that Iraq was able and willing to wage war against Kuwait if its demands were not met. At the time, however, key decision-makers in Kuwait and Washington were not sure of Hussein's intentions. Would he really risk the wrath of the world by gobbling up his small neighbor? Would he be willing to put his military and his country through another war so soon after the last one? The invasion of Kuwait happened in part because, unsure of the answers to these questions, the Kuwaitis decided that calling Hussein's bluff was preferable to giving in to his demands. When it became apparent that the threat was not in fact a bluff, war was already upon them.

When Saddam Hussein threatened to invade Kuwait in 1990, the Kuwaiti and U.S. governments were unsure if he was bluffing, as they had incomplete information about Hussein's intentions. The Kuwaitis refused to negotiate, hoping to call Hussein's bluff. It turned out that Hussein was not bluffing, and the Iraqi invasion of Kuwait started the Gulf War.

This episode illustrates one reason that bargaining can fail to resolve disputes short of war. When states have poor and incomplete information about one another's willingness and ability to wage war, two mistakes are possible, both of which can lead to war. First, a state confronted by demands may mistakenly yield too little or not at all—just as Kuwait failed to budge in the face of Hussein's threats. In these cases, bargaining can break down because at least one state feels that it can achieve more through fighting (in this case, Iraq) than the other is willing to offer in the negotiations (Kuwait). The second, related danger is that a state may demand too much (Iraq) under the mistaken belief that the other side will cave in (Kuwait, and its protector, the United States). In this event, the state may not realize its mistake until war is already upon it. In either case, even though there might be a settlement of the issue that both sides would prefer to war, uncertainty about one another's willingness to wage war can prevent such a settlement from being reached.

Where does this uncertainty come from? Recall that the main issue in crisis bargaining is how each state evaluates its prospects in a war. How likely is it that the state will be able to win the war? What will the human, financial, and political costs be? These assessments are important because each state's value for war determines what bargains it prefers to fighting. If one state is uncertain of how much its adversary values war, then it is also uncertain of how much it must concede in order to prevent a war. This uncertainty will arise whenever a state lacks information about any of the myriad factors that determine its adversary's evaluation of war.

A poker analogy is useful here. In poker, the fact that at least some cards are hidden from view means that each player knows more about the strength of her

---

11. Bob Woodward, *The Commanders* (New York: Pocket Star Books, 1991), 200.

own hand than do her opponents. The hidden cards are what might be called private information: important facts that are known only to the player who observes those cards. Because no player sees all of the cards, the game is played under a condition known as **incomplete information**. Every player lacks information about his or her opponents' hands and has private access to information about his or her own hand.

Incomplete information arises in crisis bargaining when states cannot readily observe or measure the key political and military factors that determine their adversaries' expected value for war. The hidden cards in this context can be many and varied, and we typically differentiate between two broad classes of unknowns: capabilities and resolve. *Capabilities* refers to the state's physical ability to prevail in war: the number of troops it can mobilize, the number and quality of its armaments, the economic resources it has to sustain the war effort. We might also include in this list the quality of the country's military leadership and military strategies. In addition, since third parties sometimes join wars on one or both sides, any uncertainty about what those third parties will do can lead to uncertainty about the capabilities each side will bring to bear in the event of war (see Chapter 5).

Resolve, a more abstract concept, refers to a state's willingness to bear the costs of fighting and how much the state values the object of the dispute relative to those costs. How many people is the country willing to lose in order to obtain, say, a given piece of territory? How much is it willing to pay in blood and money in order to win policy concessions or change another country's regime? Resolve has a direct impact on how much of the state's potential capabilities are actually mobilized in the event of war. We often make the distinction between *total wars*—in which states mobilize their entire military and economic resources—and *limited wars*—in which states fight with something less than their full potential, often because their aims are limited or of relatively low value. How a state evaluates the stakes of conflict determines where on this continuum its effort will be. World War II, for example, was seen as a war of national survival, and during those years (1942–1945) the United States spent more than one-third of its gross domestic product (GDP) on defense; by contrast, total U.S. defense spending in 2008 amounted to about 4 percent of GDP, and only a portion of that paid for the wars in Iraq and Afghanistan. Resolve is obviously a difficult quality to measure, as it hinges on a variety of political, ideological, and psychological factors. Indeed, it may be difficult for a leader to accurately assess his own country's resolve, much less the resolve of its adversary.

How could such uncertainty lead to war? When states have incomplete information about the capabilities and/or resolve of their opponents, bargaining over goods that they both desire may fail to achieve peaceful settlements. A central dynamic of bargaining under this kind of uncertainty is a phenomenon known as a **risk-return tradeoff**: essentially, there is a tradeoff between trying to get a good deal and trying to minimize the possibility that war will break out. On the one hand, a state can generally ensure peace by capitulating to its adversary's maximal demands. "Peace at any price" might not be a very attractive outcome, however. Kuwait, for example, could have given in to all of Iraq's demands and would likely have avoided war. On the other hand, a state can hold firm and yield nothing to its

incomplete information: A situation in which parties in a strategic interaction lack information about other parties' interests and/or capabilities.

resolve: The willingness of an actor to endure costs in order to acquire some good.

risk-return tradeoff: In crisis bargaining, the tradeoff between trying to get a better deal and trying to avoid a war.

adversary. This strategy promises a good deal if it works, but doing so runs a risk that the adversary will decide to fight rather than settle for nothing—as Iraq did when Kuwait refused to give in. Between these extremes, a state will generally find that it can reduce the risk of war only by making more generous offers, moving farther from its ideal outcome. Put another way, a state can improve the bargaining outcome for itself only by embracing a higher risk of war. Although war is costly and regrettable in retrospect, bargaining strategies that entail a risk of war can be perfectly rational given the uncertainty states face.

INCENTIVES TO MISREPRESENT AND THE PROBLEM OF CREDIBILITY

Given that incomplete information can lead to war, why can states not simply tell each other how capable and resolved they are and thereby avoid war? Actually, a large part of what goes on in a crisis consists precisely of such efforts at communication. Crises are generally characterized by diplomatic exchanges, threats and counterthreats, mobilization of forces, movement of troops and weaponry. These actions in part have a military purpose: one cannot wage war, after all, without first mobilizing the necessary forces and putting them in place. But these actions also have a political purpose: they are the language of coercive diplomacy, the vocabulary that states use to convince one another that they are willing to back their bargaining positions with the threat of force.

The problem that arises in this context is that as much as states may have an interest in communicating their hidden information, they may not always be able to do so effectively. A crucial question that arises in crisis bargaining is whether the messages a state sends have **credibility**. A credible threat is a threat that the target believes will be carried out. We say a threat lacks credibility if its target has reason to doubt that the threat will be carried out. The credibility of a threat refers not only to the belief that the threatener will start a war; the target also has to believe that the threatener is actually willing to put up a fight commensurate with its demands. In the case of the U.S. war against Afghanistan, the Taliban government probably had little doubt that President Bush would implement his threat to invade. However, the Taliban, and its Al Qaeda allies, were in all likelihood heavily influenced by their formative experiences confronting the Soviet Union after it invaded Afghanistan in 1979. At that time, a ragtag group of militants bled the superpower dry over the course of an eight-year war and eventually forced the Soviets to withdraw. The Taliban may have been encouraged to resist Bush's threat through their belief that once the fighting started, he would find that the payoff from war did not justify his extensive demands. In other words, the threat to start a war was credible, but the threat to remove them from power was, in their eyes, not.

Note that the credibility of the threat refers to the target's beliefs, not the actual intentions of the state issuing the threat. A state may fully intend to carry through on a threat, but it may have a hard time conveying that fact in a credible manner. Saddam Hussein genuinely intended to invade Kuwait if his demands were not met; observers in the United States and Kuwait, however, did not see

credibility: Believability. A credible threat is a threat that the recipient believes will be carried out. A credible commitment is a commitment or promise that the recipient believes will be honored.

the threat conveyed by his mobilization as credible. Similarly, a state may have no intention of carrying out its threat, but the target may mistakenly believe otherwise. In such cases, the bluff can succeed.

Why is credibility hard to achieve? There are two interrelated reasons. First, carrying through on threats is costly. A state may say that it will wage war if its demands are not met, but the costs of war might be such that it would not make sense to fulfill this threat if called on to do so. This concern about credibility was particularly pronounced during the Cold War between the United States and the Soviet Union. With both sides in possession of large arsenals of nuclear weapons, it was well understood that war could quickly escalate into total annihilation. Given this situation, officials in the United States worried a great deal about how they could deter the Soviet Union from attacking Western Europe. Would the United States really risk New York to save London or Paris? If the Soviets believed the answer to this question was no, then the U.S. commitment to defend Western Europe would lack credibility. It was precisely these kinds of concerns that led Great Britain and France to develop their own nuclear capabilities in order to deter the Soviets; after all, it was much more credible that France would risk Paris to save Paris.

Even without the prospect of nuclear annihilation, threats may lack credibility because their targets appreciate the costs of carrying them out. In the midst of the crisis between Iraq and Kuwait in 1990, the United States announced joint naval exercises with the United Arab Emirates. On the same day, the State Department spokesperson issued an extended deterrent threat by reaffirming the U.S. commitment to protect its friends in the Persian Gulf. Iraq's response was contemptuous. Hussein called the U.S. ambassador to his office the next day and told her that he was not scared by American threats. After all, he reportedly said, "Yours is a society which cannot accept 10,000 dead in one battle."[12] Thus, the U.S. deterrent threat had little credibility in Hussein's eyes because he believed that the United States would be unwilling to bear the costs of war.

The second reason that credibility is hard to achieve stems from the conflicting interests at the heart of the bargaining interaction. Even though states have a common interest in avoiding war, each also wants the best possible deal for itself, and this means that they have incentives to hide or mispresent their information.

In some cases, this incentive means that states will conceal information about their true strength. After Iraq invaded Kuwait, the United States massed a large force in Saudi Arabia and threatened war unless Iraq retreated. It was widely assumed that if war came, U.S. forces would attack Iraqi positions in Kuwait head-on. Such a strategy would have provided the most direct route to the objective, but there were clear costs involved: the Iraqi forces in Kuwait were dug in behind strong defenses, including trenches filled with oil that could be lit on fire as soon as U.S. troops tried to cross. Saddam Hussein's resistance to U.S. pressure stemmed in part from his belief that his defenses would make the liberation of Kuwait very costly. In fact, war planners in the United States decided early on that they would not attack directly into the strength of the Iraqi positions. Instead, they secretly shifted the bulk of

---

12. A transcript of this meeting was published in the *New York Times*, September 22, 1990.

the U.S. force into the desert west of the Kuwaiti border. The military plan called for a "left hook": U.S. tanks would enter Iraq on the western flank of Iraqi forces in Kuwait and then swoop around behind them, thereby outflanking the enemy's fortifications. A smaller force was positioned directly in front of the Iraqi forces in order to sustain the illusion that the main attack would come from that direction. This tactical decision meant that the United States expected to incur lower casualties than Iraq expected to be able to inflict.[13]

Theoretically, if the United States could have communicated these expectations to Iraq, its threat would have been more credible and perhaps Hussein would have decided to back down. But it is easy to see why the United States could not say to Hussein: "You think that war will be too costly for us, but you are mistaken. Rather than attack your forces head-on, we will go around them on the western flank." Had the United States sent such a message, Iraq could have taken measures to counter the tactic, such as by repositioning its forces to the west. Hence, any bargaining advantage the United States might have reaped by revealing its strength would have been nullified. In the strategic context of the crisis, it made sense for the United States to hide its strongest cards.

In other cases, states misrepresent in order to hide their weakest cards. Anyone who has played poker knows that it sometimes makes sense to bluff—that is, to act as if one has a strong hand in the hopes that others will fold. A similar incentive exists in international crises. In this context, a bluff is a threat to use force that the sender does not intend to carry out. In a crisis, a successful bluff could reap large rewards. In 1936, German military forces marched into a region on its border with France known as the Rhineland—a region that, by the 1919 treaty that ended World War I, Germany was required to keep demilitarized. Hitler sent his forces in anyway, daring the Western powers to stop him. Though alarmed by this move, both France and Great Britain chose not to risk a full-scale war over the issue, and the remilitarization of the Rhineland took place unopposed. Interestingly, there is good reason to believe that Hitler's move was a bluff. Although there is some controversy on this point—and the intentions of a dictator like Hitler are hard to know with great certainty—there is evidence that German troops were under orders to retreat if confronted.[14] If so, then one of the key moments in the lead-up to World War II was a well-executed bluff.

This observation raises a dilemma: how can states credibly convey their information in order to diminish the risk of war due to uncertainty? Given a strategic environment that sometimes rewards misrepresentation, how can a genuine threat be made believable?

COMMUNICATING RESOLVE:
THE LANGUAGE OF COERCION

To help us answer these questions, another example will be helpful. On June 25, 1950, without any warning, North Korea invaded South Korea. Korea had been

---

13. For a discussion of Persian Gulf War strategy, see Lawrence Freedman and Efraim Karsh, "How Kuwait Was Won: Strategy in the Gulf War," *International Security* 16 (Autumn 1991): 5–41.
14. James Thomas Emmerson, *The Rhineland Crisis, 7 March 1936* (Ames: Iowa State University Press, 1977), 98–100.

split in two after World War II, divided at the 38th parallel between the communist North and the noncommunist and pro-Western South. North Korea's attack was a bold attempt to reunify the country under communist rule, and the United States quickly joined the South in repelling the attack. After three months, the U.S. efforts were largely successful, and North Korean forces began to retreat to their side of the 38th parallel. At this point, the United States decided to press the attack, cross into North Korea, and topple the communist regime there. This possibility raised grave concerns in neighboring China, which had only the previous year been taken over by a communist government. On October 3, 1950, Chinese diplomats conveyed a message through the Indian ambassador that a move across the 38th parallel would trigger Chinese intervention.[15] Nonetheless, the threat went unheeded. The U.S. operation had been planned and authorized under the assumption that the Chinese would not intervene, and the October 3 warning did nothing to change any minds.[16] U.S. forces crossed into North Korea on October 7 and advanced rapidly. In response, 600,000 Chinese troops poured into the Korean peninsula, leading to three more years of fighting and a costly stalemate.

Why was the Chinese threat dismissed, in the words of Secretary of State Dean Acheson, as "a Chinese Communist bluff"? An October 4 memorandum describes Acheson's rationale:

> The Secretary pointed out that the Chinese Communists were themselves taking no risk in as much as their private talks to the Indian Ambassador could be disavowed. . . . [I]f they wanted to take part in the "poker game" they would have to put more on the table than they had up to the present.[17]

Acheson's reasoning for downplaying the Chinese threat is instructive. The Chinese government was making an extended deterrent threat: "Don't invade North Korea, or we will intervene to defend it." From the U.S. perspective, it was possible that China would actually make good on this threat, but it was also possible that China was simply trying to bluff the United States into staying out of North Korea. Regardless of which of these possibilities was true, the message conveyed through the Indian ambassador was cheap and easy to send. There was nothing in the message or the way it was sent that would give American decision-makers reasons to think that China was not simply bluffing. Unless the Chinese were willing to pay some costs—"to put more on the table"—there was little reason to take their threat seriously. In the same way, no one would believe a poker player who simply announced, "I have a strong hand." In poker, it is the willingness to put large amounts of money at risk that might convince the other players that one has a strong hand.

---

15. The United States did not recognize the People's Republic of China as a legitimate government, so they did not have direct diplomatic contacts.

16. See, for example, William Stueck, *Rethinking the Korean War* (Princeton, NJ: Princeton University Press, 2002), chap. 4.

17. U.S. Department of State, *Foreign Relations of the United States*, vol. 5 (Washington, DC: U.S. Government Printing Office, 1976), 868–69.

This example suggests a more general insight: for threats to be credible, they have to be costly in such a way that the sender would only make the threat if it really intended to carry the threat out. Consider the problem that the United States faced in October 1950 in these, admittedly oversimplified, terms:

> It is possible that the Chinese government is resolved to intervene if we attack North Korea, and it is possible that it is not so resolved. How can we know if we are facing a "resolute" China or an "irresolute" China? Or, to put it another way, what would we look for to distinguish these two "types" of adversary? The answer is: we would want to look for actions that a resolute China would be willing to take but an irresolute China would be unwilling (or, at least, less likely) to take. If we see such actions, then we are more likely to be facing a resolute China, and we have to take its threat seriously. If we do not see such actions, then there may be reason to doubt China's resolve.

The message that the Chinese actually sent did not have much credibility because an irresolute China could just as easily have made the same claim.

What kinds of actions would help an opponent to distinguish whether its adversary is resolved or not? In general, the literature has identified two primary mechanisms that states use to make their threats credible: brinksmanship and tying hands.

Brinksmanship: The "Slippery Slope"

Some of the earliest scholarship on the question of how to make threats credible took place in the 1950s, when policymakers and academics were preoccupied by the credibility of threats in the nuclear age. If everyone understood that nuclear war would bring total annihilation to each side, then under what conditions could threats between nuclear powers ever be credible? Since no state would ever

Leaders may use brinksmanship to make the threat of nuclear war credible. In the 1962 Cuban Missile Crisis, American president John F. Kennedy took steps toward nuclear war—for example, putting missile crews on alert—in order to pressure the Soviets to dismantle nuclear missile sites in Cuba.

intentionally "pull the trigger" and bring about Armageddon, the threat to do so was not credible. This observation raised the question of whether nuclear weapons had any utility at all in the emerging Cold War between the United States and the Soviet Union, and particularly whether these weapons could be wielded for bargaining leverage in crises between the superpowers.

The most important insight into this issue came from Thomas Schelling, an early theorist of the strategy of crisis bargaining. In Schelling's view, although it was understood that no state would intentionally bring about its own destruction by starting a total nuclear war, these weapons could nonetheless be wielded for diplomatic effect through a strategy known as **brinksmanship**. The basic idea was that states could signal their resolve in the crisis by approaching the "brink" of war through provocative actions. As Schelling describes this concept,

> The brink is not, in this view, the sharp edge of a cliff where one can stand firmly, look down, and decide whether or not to plunge. The brink is a curved slope that one can stand on with some risk of slipping, the slope gets steeper and the risk of slipping greater as one moves toward the chasm.[18]

The costs of war are such that if faced with a discrete choice of whether to jump or not, no sane decisionmaker would jump. But rational leaders might decide to step out onto the "slippery slope" and thereby increase the risk that war would start inadvertently. Schelling famously referred to such an act as a "threat that leaves something to chance."[19] The willingness to take such a chance separates resolute from irresolute adversaries. After all, the less the state values the good in dispute, and the more it fears a war over that issue, the less willing it would be to step onto the slope and embrace a risk of war.

In a brinksmanship crisis, each side bids up the risk of war—moving further and further down the slippery slope—until either one side decides to give in or they fall together into the precipice (as in the game of Chicken discussed in the appendix to Chapter 2). Exactly how a war might start "inadvertently" is not always clear; fortunately, in the case of nuclear war, we do not know the answer to that question. Absent a computer glitch, it still takes a human hand to pull the trigger. The general idea was that as tensions rose in an international crisis, the risk of accidents would increase. A limited skirmish between forces could inadvertently escalate if a nervous local commander thought his position was about to be overrun and decided to launch his tactical nuclear weapons in order not to lose them to the enemy. Or, in the midst of a tense crisis, a flock of geese might be mistaken on the radar for incoming bombers (as actually happened in the 1950s), leading to a decision to launch rather than risk being disarmed by a first strike (which, fortunately, did not happen in this incident). Alternatively, the tension of a nerve-wracking crisis might cause leaders to give in to passion and fury and lose their cool, rational heads. In any event, it was precisely the willingness to court this risk that would credibly separate the genuinely resolved opponents from the bluffers.

18. Thomas Schelling, *The Strategy of Conflict* (Cambridge, MA: Harvard University Press, 1960), 199.
19. Ibid., chap. 8.

brinksmanship: A strategy in which adversaries take actions that increase the risk of accidental war, with the hope that the other will "blink," or lose its nerve, first and make concessions.

Tying Hands

A second way in which states can send credible signals of their willingness to fight is by making threats in ways that would make backing down difficult. For example, after Iraq invaded Kuwait in August 1990, President Bush repeatedly and publicly stated that the conquest "will not stand." He made this commitment first on August 5, 1990, and reiterated it throughout the crisis, including during his State of the Union address on January 29, 1991. These words were also matched by deeds, particularly the deployment of over 500,000 U.S. troops to the region and an extensive diplomatic effort to build international consensus for an attack. Unlike the Chinese threat that Acheson felt could be disavowed, Bush was clearly on record as asserting that the policy of his administration was to reverse the Iraqi invasion. By taking such clear, public statements and actions, Bush put his reputation, and that of the country, on the line. It was not unreasonable to expect that in doing so he had made it quite costly to retreat from this position—to decide, in the face of Iraqi resistance, that the invasion would be allowed to stand after all. Doing so would have been embarrassing for him as a leader and for the country as a whole; it would have called into question the credibility of future U.S. threats, and Bush could expect his political opponents to use such a retreat against him at the next election.

The general insight here is that under some conditions, threats can generate what are known as **audience costs**—that is, negative repercussions that arise in the event that the leader does not follow through on the threat.[20] Two audiences might plausibly impose these costs. The first is the international audience: other states that might doubt future threats made by the president or by the country. Such international audience costs would be felt through an inability to convince future adversaries of one's resolve. For example, one of the reasons that U.S. decisionmakers were skeptical of the Chinese threat to intervene in the Korean War was that it came in the wake of a series of unfulfilled threats over a different issue: Taiwan. As early as March 1949, the Chinese Communist government began issuing threats to "liberate" Taiwan from the Nationalist Chinese forces that had fled there. These threats, repeated several times over the course of the next year and half, combined with China's failure to carry them out, led some analysts in the United States to discount the threats over Korea as similarly empty bluster.[21] A second audience that might punish a leader for backing down from a threat is in the leader's own country: voters and political opponents who might seek to punish a president who has tarnished the country's honor and reputation by making empty threats.

In either event, if threats expose state leaders to audience costs, they can have the effect of "tying their hands." This phrase comes from a famous scene in Homer's *Odyssey* in which the main character, Odysseus, asks to have his hands tied to the mast of his ship as they sail past the sirens. The call of the sirens is so beautiful that sailors who hear it are bewitched into steering their ship into the rocks. By tying his hands to the mast, Odysseus hoped to experience the sirens' call without

audience costs: Negative repercussions for failing to follow through on a threat or to honor a commitment.

---

20. James D. Fearon, "Domestic Political Audience Costs and the Escalation of International Disputes," *American Political Science Review* 88 (September 1994): 577–92.
21. Anne Sartori, *Deterrence by Diplomacy* (Princeton, NJ: Princeton University Press, 2005), 33–39.

succumbing to this enchantment. State leaders in a crisis tie their hands for similar reasons: because threats are costly to carry out, they know that they might choose not to follow through if faced with that decision. By exposing themselves to audience costs, they blunt the temptation to back down from their threats and thereby tie their own hands.

In the process of tying their hands, of course, state leaders also send a powerful message to their opponents: "I cannot back down; hence, my threat is completely credible." As with acts of brinksmanship, engaging in actions that generate audience costs separates the resolute from the irresolute. Those most likely to back down from a threat are less willing to take steps that will make backing down costly.

We started this section by noting that a condition of incomplete information is dangerous because states might miscalculate in bargaining, such as by mistakenly resisting threats that turn out to be genuine. Such mistakes played a role in the Iraqi invasion of Kuwait in 1990 and in the onset of war between the United States and China in 1950. Both brinksmanship and tying hands are strategies for communicating a willingness to fight: they are mechanisms that help states to figure out which threats are genuine and which are not. Interestingly, though, these cures for incomplete information entail risks that can be just as dangerous as the underlying problem they address. This is clearest in the case of brinksmanship strategies, through which states bid up the risk of accidental war in order to prove their resolve. The hope in doing so is that the adversary will blink and, thus, war will be averted. But there is no guarantee that the states will not lose control and fall into the precipice. Ironically, then, to avoid a war driven by uncertainty, states have to embrace some risk of accidental war. Hand-tying strategies can have similar risks. In this case, states take actions that make it costly to back down from their threats. Although these actions can convince the other side to give in, there is also a risk that both sides will tie their hands in a contest of threats and counterthreats. Both sides can then become locked into intransigent and incompatible bargaining positions from which it is too costly to retreat. Once each side has eliminated its ability to compromise, war may be inevitable—even if the initial uncertainty that led to the crisis has been removed.

In the case of the Persian Gulf War, it is quite possible that President Bush's hand-tying actions between August 1990 and January 1991 eventually convinced Saddam Hussein that the United States was willing to fight, in spite of his original belief to the contrary. He may have resisted nonetheless because his own pattern of defiance and counterthreats in those months had served to tie his own hands as well. Hussein may have feared domestic repercussions for a retreat in the face of American threats, or he may have been concerned that such a retreat would embolden Iraq's neighbor and long-standing enemy, Iran. By January 15, 1991, neither side was willing to compromise, and the U.S.-led war to liberate Kuwait began. We thus see that incomplete information can cause war both directly, through miscalculation, and indirectly, by forcing states to communicate their resolve in ways that can foreclose successful bargaining.

This discussion generates several predictions about the conditions that make war more or less likely. In general, the harder it is for states to learn about each other's capabilities and resolve, the more severe the problem of incomplete information will be. When states are relatively opaque, in the sense that it is hard for outsiders to observe their military capabilities or their political decision-making processes, there is likely to be greater scope for uncertainties of this kind to arise and bedevil the quest for negotiated settlements. The strategic situation might also influence the degree of uncertainty that states face. For example, as the number of states that might potentially get involved in a particular crisis increases, the number and importance of the "hidden cards" increases dramatically: in the event of a war, who will join and who will not? Finally, this discussion sensitizes us to the question of whether states can find ways to signal their intentions in a credible manner. Problems of incomplete information are more likely to be overcome when states can find costly ways to signal their intentions and thereby convince their adversaries to make concessions.

Can an Adversary Be Trusted to Honor a Deal? War from Commitment Problems

Incomplete information can cause bargaining failures by making it difficult for states to agree on a settlement that all sides prefer to war. The ability to identify such a settlement, however, does not always guarantee that war will be avoided. What happens if the states do not trust one another to abide by those settlements in the future? The sources of bargaining failure considered in this section all arise from a common underlying challenge: the difficulty that states can have making credible promises *not* to use force to revise the settlement at a later date. In this context, credibility has the same meaning as before, but we use it here to describe not a threat to use force, but rather a promise not to. A credible commitment to abide by a deal is a commitment that assures the other side that the state will not threaten force to revise the terms of the deal. A commitment problem arises when a state cannot make such a promise in a credible manner.

The Prisoner's Dilemma introduced in Chapter 2 is a quintessential example of such a problem. Although the prisoners in this game would like to commit to cooperate with each other, their incentives are such that such a commitment is not credible: when given the choice, they will prefer to defect. Commitment problems are particularly common in the absence of any enforcement mechanism, such as a court, that can hold people to their commitments. In the international system, external enforcement of commitments can be difficult to arrange (though not impossible, as we will see in the concluding section to this chapter). We now consider three ways in which an inability to make credible commitments to a bargain might undermine the search for a peaceful settlement of international disputes.[22]

---

22. The ideas are introduced in Fearon, "Rationalist Explanations for War," and are further elaborated by Robert Powell, "War as a Commitment Problem," *International Organization* 60 (2006): 169–203.

BARGAINING OVER GOODS THAT ARE A SOURCE OF FUTURE BARGAINING POWER

The clearest place to see the role of commitment problems is in the context of disputes over objects that can serve as a source of future bargaining power. The best examples of such goods are strategically important pieces of territory and weapons programs. States bargain over territory all the time, but in some cases the piece of territory in question is militarily significant, perhaps because it contains high ground from which one would be able to launch an effective attack. As mentioned earlier, the Golan Heights, on the border between Israel and Syria, is such a piece of territory. Because this territory gives its occupier a commanding position over northern Israel, any deal that might hand the Golan Heights back to Syria would make Israel more vulnerable to attack. (For further discussion of bargaining over territory, see "What Do We Know?" on p. 89.)

Bargaining over weapons programs has a similar quality. In recent years, the United States has sought to pressure several states—including Iraq (prior to 2003), Libya, Iran, and North Korea—into abandoning the development of weapons of mass destruction. These efforts have met with varying levels of success. Libya agreed to dismantle its weapons programs in December 2003. North Korea has twice agreed to end its nuclear program, in 1994 and 2007, but both deals fell apart, and North Korea had effectively entered the nuclear club. (See "Controversy" on p. 107.) Iran has so far resisted U.S. pressure. As with strategically important territory, a deal on this matter does not simply resolve a dispute—it also directly affects the military capabilities of the participants. A country that agrees to give up a weapons program makes itself weaker by doing so.

The obvious difficulty in bargaining over such objects is that a state will be reluctant to render itself more vulnerable to attack without credible promises that the other side will not exploit that vulnerability in the future. The state may be able to avoid war now by making concessions, but doing so entails a risk that its adversary, made stronger by the deal, will then press new claims. Unless there is some way for the other side to credibly commit not to use its newfound power, a threatened state may decide that it would rather fight today than face a future in which it is considerably weaker. Thus, even if there is some deal that is preferable to war now, if this deal will lead to a change in capabilities that can be exploited later on, the state that would be rendered weaker may decide to forgo that deal and gamble on a war.

This strategic dilemma has presented an important obstacle in U.S. efforts to convince countries like North Korea and Iran to give up their nuclear programs peacefully. It is important to remember that the United States had hostile relations with these countries prior to their seeking nuclear weapons. As we already saw, the United States fought a war against North Korea from 1950 to 1953. That war ended with a ceasefire, but not a peace treaty; and ever since, more than 30,000 U.S. troops have been stationed in South Korea. U.S. hostility toward the North is driven not only by the lingering issue of Korea's division but also by the odious nature of its regime, which is one of the most repressive systems in the world. Similarly, hostility between the United States and Iran dates back

Should We Negotiate with Rogue Regimes?

North Korea has one of the most oppressive regimes on the planet. It has been governed by a draconian dictatorship led first by Kim Il-Sung, who ruled for 46 years, and then by his son, Kim Jong-Il. The regime has murdered, tortured, and starved its people into submission. It has sealed them off from the outside world, denying virtually all contact with foreign visitors and media and keeping them separated from relatives in South Korea. In foreign affairs, North Korea has waged war on its southern neighbor, spewed threats at others in the region, and kidnapped Japanese citizens. North Korea has also been developing nuclear weapons, and the United States and other countries have worked for two decades to ensure that this regime does not acquire the world's most destructive weapons.

These efforts have had mixed results. In 1994, the United States and North Korea signed an Agreed Framework, under which North Korea pledged to freeze construction and operation of all nuclear reactors. In return, the United States promised oil, two pro-liferation-resistant nuclear reactors, and a normalization of trade and diplomatic relations. While this agreement initially appeared to work, neither party fully carried out its obligations. In 2002, the deal collapsed after the United States accused North Korea of circumventing the agreement by engaging in uranium enrichment. In 2006, North Korea tested a nuclear device, signaling its entry into the nuclear club. Renewed negotiations led to a deal in 2007,

which provided for North Korea to dismantle its nuclear reactors. Although this deal seemed promising at first, it too unraveled in the spring of 2009, when North Korea test launched a long-range missile. North Korea responded to international criticism by expelling inspectors, claiming to restart plutonium production, and then testing a second nuclear device. Even if this deal can be salvaged, it remains doubtful that North Korea will give up its existing weapons and plutonium stocks.

The strategy of bargaining with North Korea is fraught with problems. North Korea has repeatedly demonstrated its willingness to break agreements, and the regime's secretive nature fuels mistrust. At the same time, North Korea fears the consequences of disarmament. Given the longstanding hostility between the United States and North Korea, Kim Jong-Il worries that losing the nuclear option will leave him vulnerable to subsequent American pressure. To ease these concerns,

Washington would have to credibly commit to not seek regime change if North Korea lowers its defenses. Such a commitment would involve economic and energy assistance to help bolster the regime and promote development. North Korea has also sought security guarantees, including a formal promise that the United States will not attack it and a reduction of the U.S. military presence in South Korea and Japan.

Should the United States and its allies pursue such a bargain? Detractors of this strategy raise several objections. First, some argue that negotiating with a dictator like Kim Jong-Il is like "making deals with the devil," rewarding the regime for its odious behavior. The package of aid and security guarantees that might entice North Korea to disarm would, by propping up this regime, make outsiders complicit in the suffering of its people. Moreover, such a policy could encourage other tyrants to aspire to a similar deal. Critics also argue that North Korea's closed, aggressive regime presents a fundamental impediment to bargaining, since Pyongyang cannot be trusted to honor any agreement. In this view, regime change is a *precondition* for successful negotiations, not a bargaining chip to be given away.

Those who support negotiations acknowledge these concerns but argue that there is no feasible alternative to bargaining and that regime change, however desirable, is not a workable strategy. Prior to the 1994 Agreed Framework, some policy makers considered a preventive strike against North Korea. But even without nuclear weapons, North Korea has a strong military that is capable of retaliating against South Korea (a close ally of the United States) with devastating effect. Moreover, while refusing to bargain with North Korea may let the United States avoid a moral compromise, it does nothing to prevent the building of weapons. Indeed, Kim Jong-Il used the period of start-and-stop talks from 2003 to 2006 to build and test a weapon. The 2007 deal has at least temporarily brought plutonium production to a halt. Finally, imposing comprehensive economic sanctions not only would result in further catastrophe for North Korea's already desperate population, but, to be successful, would require international cooperation that is currently elusive. China, North Korea's largest trading partner, has no interest in seeing its neighbor collapse, especially given the risk of massive refugee flows. Hence, policy makers and other observers continue to debate the issue. ■

to the 1979 revolution that toppled Iran's pro-American leader and installed an Islamic fundamentalist government. To the extent that these states see their nuclear programs as a counterweight against American (and, in the case of Iran, Israeli) power, they would be reluctant to give up those programs if, by doing so, they would render themselves more vulnerable to U.S. demands on other issues. The success of any effort to end these programs peacefully requires the United States to find a way to commit credibly not to exploit the power shift brought about by disarmament.

PREVENTION: WAR IN RESPONSE TO CHANGING POWER

A second, and related, problem arises if the balance of military capabilities is anticipated to change because of factors external to the bargaining process. A common source of this kind of power shift is different rates of economic growth. As noted in Chapter 1, uneven economic development has led to the relative rise and decline of states over time. The growth of Germany's power in the late nineteenth and early twentieth centuries had a dramatic impact on that country's ability to challenge its neighbors. Similarly, as we will discuss in Chapter 13, China's impressive economic growth since 1980 has greatly increased its influence in international politics. If a state is growing much more rapidly than its adversary, then the military capabilities that it can bring to bear in future disputes will be greater than those it can bring to bear today. A second important source of large shifts in military capabilities is the development and acquisition of new technologies, such as nuclear weapons. The acquisition of nuclear weapons can cause an abrupt and profound shift in a state's capacity to impose costs on its adversaries.

Regardless of their exact source, anticipated changes in military capabilities can present an insurmountable dilemma in crisis bargaining. To see this, we revisit the bargaining model introduced earlier. Figure 3.4 illustrates what happens to the bargaining interaction when the power of one state, in this case State A, is expected to increase. In (a), the expected outcome of the war, which we label p_1, is initially close to State B's ideal point. Let's assume, however, that State A's power is expected to grow, so that, at some time in the future, the new war outcome, which we label p_2, will be closer to A's ideal point, as in (b). In the initial period, the states could agree to some distribution, labeled x, inside the bargaining range. But everyone can anticipate that in the future State A will no longer be satisfied with x and will demand a new deal in the new bargaining range. As this example is constructed, however, State B prefers the war outcome it could obtain under the initial power distribution, $p_1 + b$, over any outcome that falls in the future bargaining range (that is, $p_1 + b$ is closer to B's ideal point than any point in the future bargaining range). Hence, State B would rather fight a war now than face worse terms in the future. Notice that this logic is only compelling if it is believed that war will halt, or significantly delay, the anticipated change in power, as might happen if war could successfully disarm the other state or cripple its economic growth. If the shift in power from (a) to

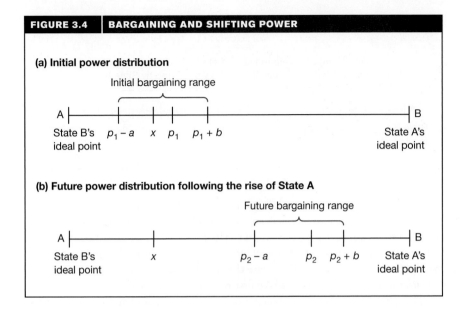

FIGURE 3.4 | BARGAINING AND SHIFTING POWER

(a) Initial power distribution

Initial bargaining range

A | B

State B's ideal point $p_1 - a$ x p_1 $p_1 + b$ State A's ideal point

(b) Future power distribution following the rise of State A

Future bargaining range

A | B

State B's ideal point x $p_2 - a$ p_2 $p_2 + b$ State A's ideal point

(b) will happen anyway, then there is nothing to be gained by fighting now only to have the outcome revised later in A's favor.

Thus, even if the states can locate a deal that they prefer to war today, such as x, the state that is getting stronger will face a strong temptation to use its future power to try to revise the deal at some later date. Unless there is some way for the growing state to make a credible commitment not to do that, then its adversary may decide that it is better to gamble on war today in order to stop or slow the anticipated shift. A war that is fought with the intention of preventing an adversary from becoming relatively stronger in the future is a **preventive war**.

The U.S. war against Iraq in 2003 had a preventive logic, even if much of the motivating intelligence turned out to be flawed. Saddam Hussein's regime was believed to have some minimal capability—and a demonstrated intention—to develop weapons of mass destruction. The preventive argument for attacking was that it would be easier to oust Hussein before he had fully developed these capabilities than to do so after he had succeeded in deploying them in his arsenal. Of course, the uncertainties surrounding Iraq's weapons program illustrate a major risk of engaging in preventive war, since the rationale for doing so is only as strong as the evidence that a disadvantageous shift in relative capabilities is coming.

PREEMPTION: WAR IN RESPONSE TO FIRST-STRIKE ADVANTAGES

A final commitment problem that can prevent states from reaching negotiated settlements of their disputes arises due to first-strike advantages. A **first-strike advantage** exists when there is a considerable benefit to being the first to launch an attack. This type of situation arises when military technologies enable a state to launch a

preventive war: A war fought with the intention of preventing an adversary from becoming stronger in the future. Preventive wars arise because states whose power is increasing cannot commit not to exploit that power in future bargaining interactions.

first-strike advantage: The situation that arises when military technology, military strategies, and/or geography give a significant advantage to whichever state attacks first in a war.

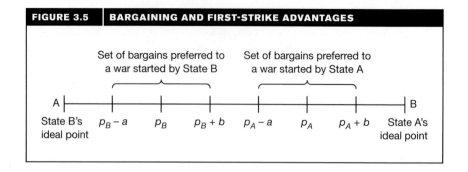

FIGURE 3.5 | BARGAINING AND FIRST-STRIKE ADVANTAGES

Set of bargains preferred to a war started by State B

Set of bargains preferred to a war started by State A

A ⊢———————————————————⊣ B

State B's ideal point $p_B - a$ p_B $p_B + b$ $p_A - a$ p_A $p_A + b$ State A's ideal point

blow that disarms the other state's military or renders it incapable of responding effectively. For example, if one state could launch its nuclear missiles and destroy all of its adversary's missiles on the ground before they could be launched, then that state would enjoy a first-strike advantage. A state that can land a disarming blow may be tempted to do so, and the state that is vulnerable to such a blow may feel a "use it or lose it" imperative to strike first rather than be disarmed.

This situation can create a potentially insurmountable commitment problem. Unless each state can credibly promise the other not to act first, there is a danger that bargaining will break down as each side rushes to get in the first blow. Each side may be confident that if it manages to strike first, it can do better in war than by accepting the deal that is currently on offer. Indeed, there may be no deal that both sides prefer to a war that they start. An example of this situation is depicted in Figure 3.5. Here, we assume that there are two different war outcomes depending on which state lands the first blow: the expected outcome of a war started by State A is p_A, and the expected outcome of a war started by State B is p_B. The first-strike advantage is captured by the assumption that each side expects to do better in a war that it starts than in a war started by the adversary (that is, p_A is closer to A's ideal point than p_B, and p_B is closer to B's ideal point than p_A).[23] As constructed, this advantage is quite large relative to the costs of war. As a result, while there exists a set of deals that both states prefer to a war started by State A and a set of deals that both prefer to a war started by State B, there is no deal that is preferable to both of these possible wars. A deal within the bargaining range around p_B would satisfy State B but gives State A less than it expects to get by attacking first ($p_A - a$). Similarly, a deal within the bargaining range around p_A would satisfy State A but gives State B less than it expects to get by striking first ($p_B + b$). Under these conditions, neither state will make concessions to the other at the bargaining table; instead, both will likely rush to the exits, each trying to beat the other to the punch. Negotiations in this context may be seen as nothing more than a ploy to delay the other side from mobilizing. A war that arises in this way is a **preemptive war**.[24]

preemptive war: A war fought with the anticipation that an attack by the other side is imminent.

---

23. It is likely that the costs of war also depend on who starts it, but for the purposes of this example, we do not vary the cost terms, *a* and *b*.

24. It should be emphasized that this example assumes a very large first-strike advantage relative to the costs of war, so it is possible that this kind of situation arises only rarely. For a historical overview of preemptive war, which finds that very few wars start this way, see Dan Reiter, "Exploding the Powder Keg Myth: Preemptive Wars Almost Never Happen," *International Security* 20, no. 2 (Autumn 1995): 5–34.

The 1967 Six Day War between Israel and four Arab states (Egypt, Syria, Jordan, and Iraq) is a classic case of a war that started this way. In May 1967, Egypt responded to border skirmishes between Israel and Syria by massing troops on the Israeli border and imposing a partial blockade. On June 5, fearing that war was likely, Israel launched a surprise, preemptive attack on the Egyptian air force, destroying 300 aircraft while they were still on the ground. With Egypt's main offensive threat crippled, the ensuing war lasted six days and left Israel in control of large swaths of formerly Arab-held territory.

Both preemption and prevention arise from the difficulty states can have in making credible commitments not to use their military power. The difference between the two concepts revolves around timing. Preemption is a response to an imminent threat when there is an already existing first-strike advantage. Prevention is a response to anticipated changes in the distribution of power that might result in an increased threat sometime in the future. For a discussion of how such considerations contributed to the outbreak of World War I, see "What Shaped Our World?" on page 112.

We have seen, then, that even if states can locate a deal that both prefer to war at the moment, concerns about their willingness to abide by the deal in the future can cause bargaining failure and war. Although these concerns can arise for different reasons, all of the paths to war discussed in this section have at their root a common commitment problem: the difficulty of committing not to use one's power to one's advantage in the future. In addition to shedding light on the general problem of war, this discussion generates a number of predictions about the conditions under which war is more or less likely to occur. First, war is more likely to occur when the good in dispute is a source of power to those who possess it. For example, it is harder to strike bargains over strategically important territory than over territory that is valuable for other reasons. Second, preventive incentives arise when there are relatively rapid and dramatic changes in the military balance between two countries. Hence, war is more likely when such changes are anticipated or under way. Finally, bargaining failures are more common when the military-strategic situation creates substantial advantages for striking first. These advantages generally arise from the nature of military technology, which sometimes imparts large advantages to the actor who goes on the offensive first—although, as we saw in the case of World War I, particular military strategies can also generate preemptive logics.

Is Compromise Always Possible?
War from Indivisibility

A final problem that can prevent states from reaching mutually beneficial settlements of their disputes arises from a feature of the issue that is contested: whether or not it is a good that can be divided. A good is divisible if there are ways to split it into smaller shares; an **indivisible good** cannot be divided without destroying its value. Imagine, for example, the difference between having 100 pennies and having one dollar bill. Although the amount of money available is the same in both

indivisible good: A good that cannot be divided without diminishing its value.

Prevention and Preemption in World War I

On June 28, 1914, Archduke Franz Ferdinand, heir to the throne of the Austro-Hungarian Empire, was assassinated during a visit to Sarajevo in neighboring Serbia. A month later, most of the states of Europe were embroiled in a war that would claim more lives than any previous war in human history. The chain of events that led to World War I is a complicated story about which many volumes have been written. Here, we consider the preventive and preemptive considerations that played a major role in the outbreak of this war.

Europe in 1914 was divided into two hostile camps: Germany and Austria-Hungary versus Great Britain, France, and Russia. In this combustible atmosphere, the assassination of the archduke by Serb terrorists created a dangerous spark. Austria-Hungary was a multiethnic empire with a substantial Serb minority, and agitation by Serb nationalists threatened to tear the empire apart. Austria-Hungary sought an end to Serbia's support for these militants and threatened war. This threat brought a deterrent response from the Russians, who felt threatened by Austrian designs in the region. Germany then promised to protect the Austrians, giving them a "blank check" to deal harshly with Serbia.

Although German leaders did not relish the idea of war with Russia, they also feared Russia's growing power. Russia had by far the largest population and land mass of any country in Europe. What kept it from being the dominant military power was its economic and industrial backwardness. But in the decades prior to the war, Russia had made great strides, building its heavy industries and constructing an impressive railroad network. Germany's leaders watched these developments with great concern. Shortly before the crisis broke, Chancellor Theobald von Bethmann Hollweg warned gloomily that "[t]he future belongs to Russia, which grows and grows and becomes an even greater nightmare for us."[a] German leaders came to believe that they had a short "window of opportunity" in which to confront this growing menace. The crisis of July 1914 provided the chance to wage preventive war while this window was still open.

In contemplating war with Russia, however, there was a significant obstacle: France. Since 1894, France and Russia had pledged to defend each other in the event of a war. Hence, the

Germans knew that a war would have to be fought on two fronts: against Russia to the east and France to the west. To deal with this possibility, German military planners came up with an audacious solution. The Schlieffen Plan, so named after the general who crafted it, sought to exploit the fact that Russia's vast size and still underdeveloped railway system meant that its military machine, though immense, was also very slow. After the Russians started mobilizing, it would take six weeks before their forces would be ready to join the fight. The Germans hoped to take advantage of this delay to invade and quickly defeat France. German troops could then be shifted to the east, in time to meet the Russian advance.

Success depended on timing and rapid execution. If the Russians started mobilizing, there was no time to waste: the trigger had to be pulled. Moreover, it was vital that the German advance go quickly and smoothly. This meant that strategic bridges and tunnels in Belgium had to be seized quickly and intact so that German forces could pass through them on the way to France. If a delay permitted the Belgians to fortify or destroy these bridges, then the German advance could bottleneck and precious time would be lost.

Hence, the strategic situation imparted a significant advantage to whoever struck first. If the Germans acted quickly, they could surprise the Belgians, defeat the French, and ultimately, they hoped, vanquish the Russians. If they waited, their troops would get bogged down in the west while the Russian "steamroller" crushed them from the east. Under these conditions, negotiations to settle the crisis were seen as an intolerable delay. Moreover, the preemptive incentives meant that military mobilizations were not a useful instrument of crisis diplomacy. When the Russians ordered their mobilization on July 30, they held out some hope that signaling their resolve would lead the Austrians to reduce their demands. Given the strategic situation, however, Russia's mobilization spurred the adversaries not to the bargaining table, but to the battlefield.

By August 3, 1914, most of Europe was at war. When the Russian army mobilized, the Germans enacted the Schlieffen Plan, bringing them into war with Belgium and France. Great Britain, which was allied to both of those states, joined the fray. Successful at first, the German offensive stalled and a stalemate arose. In a war they could not wait to start, the adversaries would have to endure four bloody years to reach the end. ◼

---

a. Quoted in Stephen Van Evera, "The Cult of the Offensive and the Origins of the First World War," *International Security* 9 (Summer 1984): 80.

cases, the pennies can de divided up between two people in many different ways, while the dollar bill cannot be split. When the good in question is indivisible, compromise solutions are impossible to reach, and the bargaining becomes "all or nothing." It is easy to see how indivisible goods could create an insurmountable obstacle in crisis bargaining. Consider a situation in which each state would prefer to fight a war rather than get none of the good. Even though there might be deals that both sides prefer to war—such as, say, a fifty-fifty split—an inability to divide the good into the necessary shares renders such a deal unattainable. In an "all or nothing" bargaining situation, one state must get nothing. And if both states prefer war to getting nothing, then war becomes inevitable.

Although the logic of indivisibility is quite clear, what is less clear is whether or how often indivisibility is actually a problem in international politics. What goods are truly indivisible? A key point is that indivisibility is not a physical property of a good, but rather of the way in which it is valued. This point is made most dramatically by the biblical story in which King Solomon, confronted by two women claiming to be the mother of the same baby, decides that the only fair solution in the face of these incompatible claims is to "cut the baby in half." This solution strikes us as odd not because it cannot be physically implemented, but because the process of doing so will kill the baby. (Fortunately, in King Solomon's case, the decision did not have to be carried out, since one woman insisted that she would rather let the other woman have her child than see it killed—whereupon Solomon decided that this woman must be the true mother.) Similarly, in a dispute over a valuable painting, one could slice the painting in two, but doing so would presumably destroy the object's value. Hence, when we say that a good cannot be divided, we generally do not mean this literally. Rather, we mean that that the good loses much, if not all, of its value when it is divided.[25] This can be the case with core values that cannot be compromised or with divisible goods that are closely linked to such core values.

A commonly cited example of an indivisible good in international relations is the city of Jerusalem.[26] It is a city that contains some of the holiest sites of Christianity, Islam, and Judaism and has historical, cultural, and religious significance unlike any other piece of territory in the world. As a result, the status of Jerusalem is a major stumbling block in efforts to bring about peace in the Middle East. For many Jews, Jerusalem is the focal point of the desire—sometimes symbolic, sometimes literal—to return to the promised land of Zion. Every year at Passover, Jews all over the world utter the words "Next year in Jerusalem," which underscores the role of that city in forging a connection between the land of Israel and the Jewish identity. The centrality of this city has been given political expression as well: a Basic Law passed by Israel in 1980 declares that "Jerusalem, complete and united, is the capital of Israel." For Muslims, East Jerusalem, or Al-Quds, is the third holiest city (after Mecca and Medina in Saudi Arabia) and the site of the Dome of the Rock, where the Prophet Mohammed is believed to have ascended to Paradise. Palestinians claim East Jerusalem, which Israel annexed after the 1967 Six Day War, as the capital of an eventual Palestinian state. This claim clearly clashes with the Israeli position

---

25. H. Peyton Young, "Dividing the Indivisible," *American Behavioral Scientist* 38, no. 6 (1995): 904–20.
26. See, for example, Cecilia Albin, "Negotiating Indivisible Goods: The Case of Jerusalem," *Jerusalem Journal of International Relations* 13, no. 1 (1991): 45–76.

MAP 3.1 **THE DIVISION OF JERUSALEM, 1949–1967**

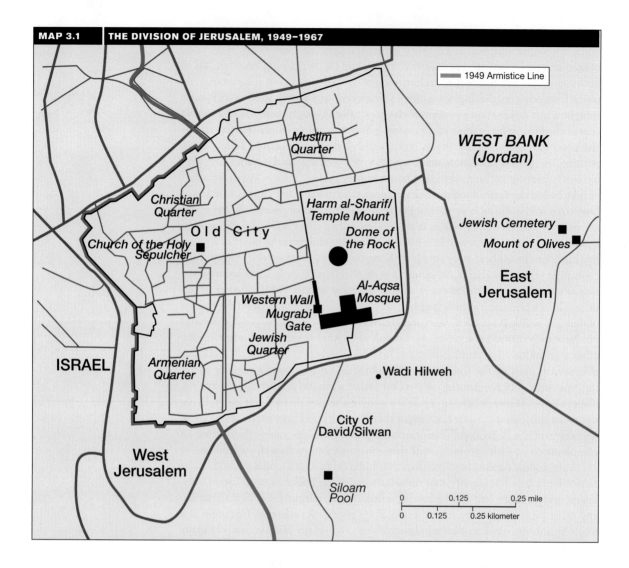

that the city is indivisible and the capital of the Jewish state. Moreover, some of the holiest sites for Jews—including the Western Wall and the Temple Mount—are located in the Old City in East Jerusalem (see Map 3.1). From 1949 to 1967, when East Jerusalem was controlled by Jordan, Jews could not worship at these sites. The question of whether or how to divide the city, and how to ensure that people of all faiths have access to their holy sites, is one that has so far defied resolution.

It is important, however, not to place undue emphasis on indivisibility as a source of bargaining failures. First, as we will see in the next section, there can be ways of dividing apparently indivisible goods that do not involve physical division. King Solomon's quandary is one that divorcing parents routinely face when each wants custody of their children. These disputes are settled not by dividing the children physically but by dividing the time they spend with each parent. Hence, an otherwise indivisible good is split by relying on the fact that time is easy to divide.

Alternatively, one actor may be able to compensate the other by making concessions on another issue or by paying money. Since money is generally divisible, it might be possible to change the bargaining from who gets an indivisible good to how much each party needs to be compensated in order to live without it.

A second reason to be skeptical of claims of indivisibility is that states may have strategic incentives to claim that they cannot compromise on a particular issue, even if they actually could. Recall that one of the strategies that states employ in crisis bargaining is to tie their hands through public pronouncements from which it would be costly to back down. It is quite possible that claims of indivisibility—such as the Israeli Basic Law mentioned above—have a strategic quality: they represent an effort to tie the government's hands so that it will find compromise difficult, if not impossible. In doing so, the hope is that the other side will realize that it has no choice but to capitulate entirely. In this sense, objects may take on the appearance of indivisibility in the course of the bargaining process, through the public positions that states take.[27]

The point of this discussion is not to suggest that indivisible goods do not exist in international politics. Rather, it is to suggest that we be appropriately skeptical when the participants in a dispute claim that the good in question is indivisible and hence no compromise is possible. Such a claim may reflect a bargaining position adopted for strategic reasons, rather than a true description of the fundamental nature of the good in question.

How Can We Make War Less Likely?

War arises from a variety of factors that can prevent states from reaching peaceful settlements of their disputes. Of course, the reason we study war is not just to understand why it happens; we also study war in the hope that understanding is the first step toward reducing or eliminating its occurrence. What, then, have we learned that might be useful in managing international disputes so that they are less likely to escalate into wars? The following discussion identifies four sets of mechanisms that can facilitate conflict management.

RAISING THE COSTS OF WAR

One of the main disincentives for engaging in war is the abhorrent human, economic, material, and psychological costs it imposes. Indeed, the costs of war generally ensure that states can do better by finding a negotiated settlement of their disputes. As war becomes less attractive, states will be more willing to make compromises in order to avoid it. Hence, raising the costs of war can expand the set of settlements that all sides prefer to fighting. Perhaps the best illustration of this effect is the apparently pacifying effect of nuclear weapons, a topic to which we

---

27. See Stacie E. Goddard, "Uncommon Ground: Indivisible Territory and the Politics of Legitimacy," *International Organization* 60 (2006): 35–68.

will return in Chapter 13. It is striking that despite five decades of intense hostility between the United States and the Soviet Union during the Cold War, the two superpowers never waged war directly against one another. Although there are many theories about the cause of this so-called long peace, it is certain that nuclear weapons and the threat of "mutually assured destruction" induced a dose of caution that helped the superpowers defuse numerous crises without resorting to war.[28] A more benign argument along these lines holds that trade and financial relations between states can promote peace by increasing the economic costs of going to war. The more two countries value one another as trading partners, the more incentive they will have to avoid conflicts that will disrupt those profitable exchanges. The argument and evidence in favor of this proposition are considered in Chapter 4.

INCREASING TRANSPARENCY

Although uncertainty is commonplace in world politics, mechanisms that increase the transparency of states can reduce some of the dangers of miscalculation. Transparency refers to the ability of outsiders to peer into a state and learn about the factors that influence its decision-making about war and peace. A state's military capabilities are probably the easiest factor to render transparent. The advent of satellite technology, for example, has made it possible for advanced states to learn a great deal about one another's weapons systems and force levels. States may also agree to send military officials to each other's country in order to observe one another's activities. International organizations may also enhance transparency by providing neutral observers of a state's military activities. The International Atomic Energy Agency, for example, conducts inspections of members' nuclear energy programs in order to determine whether nuclear fuel has been diverted to produce weapons. None of these mechanisms is foolproof, of course, as the U.S. experience with Iraq from the 1991 Gulf War to the 2003 invasion clearly showed. Weapons can be hidden from view, satellite images can be ambiguous, international observers can be obstructed or misled, and bureaucratic failures can lead to misinterpretation, whether deliberate or not.

Even so, generating information about capabilities is easy relative to the task of creating transparency about the many and complex factors that determine a state's resolve. Trying to observe how much an adversary values the object in dispute, what costs it is willing to pay to obtain the good, and what risks it is willing to run constitutes a much more daunting task than counting the other side's soldiers, tanks, and airplanes. Since resolve can emerge from the political factors within the state, it is likely that the best hopes for transparency on this dimension are likewise to be found within states. Some political systems are by nature very transparent, allowing outsiders ample opportunity to observe the internal debate about what values are at stake and whether they are worth fighting for. Other states are relatively opaque, with decisions made by a small number of individuals who operate with little or no public accountability. We will revisit this line of reasoning in Chapter 4, when we consider the possible effects of domestic political institutions on international conflict.

---

28. See, for example, John Lewis Gaddis, "The Long Peace: Elements of Stability in the Postwar International System," *International Security* 10 (Spring 1986): 99–142.

PROVIDING OUTSIDE ENFORCEMENT OF COMMITMENTS

A promise not to use one's power to one's advantage is a very difficult commitment to make in a credible fashion. A major part of the problem lies in the fact that states cannot generally rely on repeated interaction to hold one another to such a promise, as they can in the case of compliance with WTO rulings (see Chapter 2). Repeated interaction can make help make promises credible if the prospect of future dealings leads a state to forgo the temptation to break a promise today because it fears retaliation by the other state tomorrow. Under conditions of shifting power, however, the state that is becoming more powerful has less to fear from the other side's retaliation. Furthermore, if a state can use its increased power to destroy the other state, then there may be no "shadow of the future" to stay the growing state's hand. The same holds in situations involving first-strike advantages: the temptation to deliver a crippling blow is hard to blunt if the other side's retaliatory capability will be rendered ineffective in the process.

Because adversaries generally cannot solve this commitment problem on their own, any solutions are most likely to come from outside the bilateral relationship—that is, through the assistance or intervention of third parties. In this context, a third party constitutes any state or group of states, including international organizations, that are not directly involved in the bargaining game between the opponents. In some cases, such outsiders may be able to help build credibility for the opposing states' commitments not to exploit power or first-strike advantages. Third parties can play this role by monitoring and enforcing agreements, by providing security guarantees to one or both sides, and sometimes by interposing their forces directly between two potential combatants.

For example, after World War II, security guarantees extended by the United States played a large role in reassuring the Western European countries that they had little to fear from the postwar reconstruction of West Germany. Although the war had left Germany devastated and divided, France in particular feared that it was only a matter of time before Germany would recover and once again be in a position to threaten its neighbors. What made a final settlement between the two states possible was an extensive American commitment to station troops in West Germany and to guarantee the security of both states. With a sizable American troop presence monitoring Germany's reconstruction and remilitarization, France could undertake improved relations with its neighbor without fear of Germany's postwar recovery. The U.S. presence and the alliance system it built made credible Germany's commitment to live peacefully with its western neighbors. We will revisit this issue in Chapter 5, when we examine the role of international institutions in preventing the outbreak of war.

DIVIDING APPARENTLY INDIVISIBLE GOODS

As suggested earlier, there may be ways to allocate apparently indivisible goods that do not involve physical division. Rotating or alternating possession, used

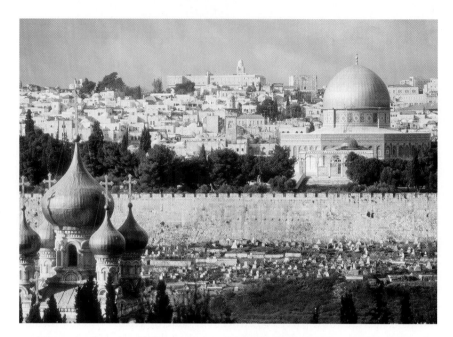

As we saw earlier in the chapter, the city of Jerusalem—which is home to important holy sites for Jews, Muslims, and Christians—is sometimes cited as an example of an indivisible good that causes conflict. However, there may be ways of dividing apparently indivisible goods, such as shared control or compensation. Some have proposed that conflict over Jerusalem could be resolved if Israelis and Palestinians shared control of key areas.

to resolve child custody disputes, is one such mechanism, though we rarely see it used in world politics. One possible mechanism for dividing apparently indivisible goods is joint or shared control. It has been proposed, for example, that Israelis and Palestinians jointly control certain portions of Jerusalem to ensure that all people have access to the sacred sites. A second mechanism for dealing with indivisible goods is through compensation on another issue. Although a rare painting cannot be physically divided, a dispute over it can be resolved by having one party compensate the other in exchange for the good. In this case, the object is made divisible by adding a new dimension to the deal: rather than arguing about who gets the painting, the issue becomes how much money one is willing to pay to the other to get it. Since money is generally divisible, adding this new dimension creates the possibility for compromise where none previously existed. Hence, disputants may be able to find a second issue dimension on which the loser in the main issue can be compensated. The strategy of making one dispute easier to solve by bringing in a second issue is known as linkage, as we saw in Chapter 2.

Conclusion: Why War?

This chapter posed the puzzle of why states fight wars in spite of the enormous costs associated with fighting. The answer involves two ingredients: a conflict in states' interests, and some factor or factors that prevent states from reaching a peaceful solution to that conflict. States' underlying interests in power, security, wealth, and/or national identities can give rise to disputes over territories, policies, and the composition of one another's governments. In the absence of authoritative institutions that resolve interstate disputes, states engage in a bargaining interaction over these issues, sometimes invoking the threat of military force to enhance their leverage. War occurs when features of this strategic interaction prevent states from reaching a settlement that both prefer to war, with all its uncertainties and costs.

Three kinds of problems can prevent states from settling their disputes in ways that allow them to avoid the costs of war: problems arising from incomplete information, those arising from the difficulty of committing to honor a deal, and those arising from goods that are hard to divide. Since these obstacles occur in different degrees and in different combinations from one crisis to the next, there is no single answer to the puzzle at the heart of this chapter. Instead, the discussion has sought to identify and explore a set of mechanisms that can bedevil the effort to resolve disputes peacefully. Having done so, we are in a better position to understand and interpret behavior and outcomes in international crises. The concepts introduced here highlight some of the key factors that determine whether a dispute can be settled without resort to war.

In particular, we need to pay attention to (1) what the adversaries in a dispute believe about one another's willingness and ability to wage war, and how uncertain those beliefs are; (2) how each side seeks to communicate its resolve, whether those efforts are credible, and to what extent they either entail a danger of accidental war or "lock in" incompatible bargaining positions; (3) whether the good in the dispute is a source of future bargaining power; (4) whether the distribution of power between the adversaries is expected to change as a result of different economic growth rates or technological progress; (5) whether the military technologies and strategies of the adversaries generate sizable first-strike advantages; and (6) whether the good in question is indivisible because of its close connection to core values, such as religious identity.

In spite of the many things that can go wrong and prevent a peaceful solution, it is important to remember a point we made early in this chapter: wars are rare. Even though information is often incomplete, credible commitments are hard to make, and core values are hard to compromise, most states most of the time are at peace with one another. The costs of war mean that not every disagreement is worth fighting over or even threatening to fight over. Hence, the very costs that make war hell also ensure that war is not the most common way that states settle their disputes.

At this point we must recognize, however, that the costs and benefits of war do not fall equally within states. Indeed, while we have assumed that the key actors in international bargaining are states, wars are in fact declared by leaders, planned by generals, fought by soldiers, and paid for by taxpayers. Because not everyone within a country has the same interests over matters of war and peace, we must turn our attention to the inner workings of state to think about who benefits from war, who pays the costs, and how domestic interests, interactions, and institutions affect the calculus of war.

Reviewing Interests, Interactions, and Institutions

INTERESTS	INTERACTIONS	INSTITUTIONS
States' interests in power, security, wealth, and other needs can lead to conflicts over territory, policies, and the composition/character of their governments.	States bargain over the allocation of disputed goods. War occurs when states cannot agree to a mutually beneficial bargain.	Because the international system lacks reliable legal, judicial, and electoral institutions, states try to resolve disputes through bargaining.
The costs associated with war ensure that states generally have a common interest in allocating the disputed good peacefully.	Bargaining can fail if states have incomplete information about one another's willingness and ability to wage war.	International institutions may help resolve information and commitment problems by providing monitors or organizing intervention by other states.
Hence, interest conflicts are necessary, but not sufficient, to explain why wars happen.	Bargaining can fail if states cannot commit to live by a deal in the face of changing power or first-strike incentives.	
	Bargaining can fail if the disputed goods cannot be divided without losing their value.	

Key Terms

war, p. 86

interstate war, p. 86

civil war, p. 86

crisis bargaining, p. 90

coercive diplomacy, p. 90

bargaining range, p. 92

compellence, p. 93

deterrence, p. 93

incomplete information, p. 96

resolve, p. 96

risk-return tradeoff, p. 96

credibility, p. 97

brinksmanship, p. 102

audience costs, p. 103

preventive war, p. 109

first-strike advantage, p. 109

preemptive war, p. 110

indivisible good, p. 111

For Further Reading

Blainey, Geoffrey. *The Causes of War*, 3rd ed. New York: Free Press, 1988. Presents a historical examination of war informed by bargaining theory.

Fearon, James. "Rationalist Explanations of War." *International Organization* 49 (1995): 379–414. Serves as the seminal statement of the theory of war developed in this chapter.

George, Alexander, and Richard Smoke. *Deterrence in American Foreign Policy*. New York: Columbia University Press, 1974. Offers a theoretical and historical overview of deterrence and its use in major U.S. foreign policy crises.

Goddard, Stacie E. "Uncommon Ground: Indivisible Territory and the Politics of Legitimacy." *International Organization* 60 (2006): 35–68. Argues that territories can become indivisible because of the way states try to legitimize their claims.

Powell, Robert. *In the Shadow of Power: States and Strategies in International Politics.* Princeton, NJ: Princeton University Press, 1999. Presents a formal analysis of shifting power and its effects on the potential for war.

Reiter, Dan. "Exploring the Bargaining Model of War." *Perspectives on Politics* 1 (2003): 27–43. Evaluates the argument that war is a product of, as well as a continuation of, interstate bargaining.

Schelling, Thomas. *Arms and Influence*. New Haven, CT: Yale University Press, 1966. Serves as an accessible introduction to the strategic problems that arise in coercive interactions, including problems of credibility and commitment.

Van Evera, Stephen. *Causes of War*. Ithaca, NY: Cornell University Press, 2001. Explores how power shifts and first-strike advantages contributed to major wars throughout history.

Walter, Barbara. *Committing to Peace: The Successful Settlement of Civil Wars.* Princeton, NJ: Princeton University Press, 2002. Shows how commitment problems present a significant obstacle to the resolution of civil wars.

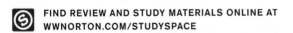 **FIND REVIEW AND STUDY MATERIALS ONLINE AT WWNORTON.COM/STUDYSPACE**

Understanding Civil Wars

When we think of wars, the examples that come to mind are usually wars between states, such as the two world wars or, more recently, the United States' wars against Afghanistan and Iraq. However, a great deal of armed conflict in the contemporary world takes place not between states but *within* them. Civil wars pit two or more groups within a country against one another. Typically, this means that one or more rebel groups fight against the central government or, in the absence of a government, against one another. Sometimes, these factions receive support from external actors, but the primary fighting takes place within the boundaries of a state.

For all the attention that we devote to interstate wars, civil wars are generally bloodier, harder to resolve, and, in recent years, much more common. At the end of 2007, there were, by one count, 30 civil wars under way and no interstate wars.[a1] A study published in 2003 reported that while there had been 25 interstate wars involving 25 different states since 1945, the same period witnessed 127 civil wars involving 73 states (some of which experienced multiple wars). In this period, interstate wars were responsible for the deaths of 3 million people; civil wars killed more than 16 million. And while the median duration of interstate wars was three months, the median duration of civil wars was six years.[a2]

The United States' experience in Afghanistan and Iraq illustrates this larger pattern. Both cases started out as interstate wars pitting the United States and its allies against the governments of these countries. In both cases, the interstate phase of the war was quick: both regimes were ousted in a matter of weeks. At that point, both countries descended into civil war as rebellious factions, including elements of the previous regimes, took up arms against one another and the U.S.-installed governments. The U.S. role thus shifted from trying to defeat the military of another state to trying to quell a domestic rebellion against a friendly regime. The civil phase of these conflicts has lasted for years and will likely continue even after the United States pulls out.

How do we understand civil wars? Are the concepts introduced to explain interstate war useful in this context, or is civil war an entirely different beast? The answer is that these two kinds of war are very similar in terms of the interests that underlie them, the interactions that lead to them, and the potential role of institutions in preventing or ending them.

ISSUES BEHIND CIVIL WARS

The main issues that underlie civil wars are very similar to those that underlie international wars: territory, policy, and regime. Territorial conflict in this context takes the form of secessionism or irrendentism. Both arise when a rebel group seeks

---

a1. Project Ploughshares, *Armed Conflict Report 2008*, www.ploughshares.ca (accessed 3/5/09).
a2. James D. Fearon and David Laitin, "Ethnicity, Insurgency, and Civil War," *American Political Science Review* 97 (2003): 75.

to carve out a piece of the state's territory for its own. A group is secessionist if it wants to create its own independent state out of the new territory. For example, Eritrean rebels fought within Ethiopia for years in order to carve out their own state; in 1993, they finally succeeded, and the new state of Eritrea was born. A rebel group is *irredentist* if it seeks to attach its territory to that of a neighboring state, usually because it shares ethnic ties with that state. For example, India faces a long-running rebellion in the Kashmir region fueled by Muslim militants who want Kashmir to join with Pakistan.

Civil wars can also arise when groups within the state contest policies pursued by the central government. Rebels may seek an end to discriminatory practices, promotion of their language and culture, or simply a greater share of government largesse. For example, the civil war in Iraq is fueled by concerns of the Sunni minority about how it will be treated by the Shia majority that was empowered by the U.S. invasion. The primary aim of this group is to ensure that it enjoys an equitable share of Iraq's oil revenues and that its religious and civil rights are protected.

Finally, civil wars may arise when rebel groups hope to seize control of the central government altogether. The civil war in Afghanistan is driven by the desire of those loyal to the former Taliban regime to reclaim power from the new government. Similarly, South Africa experienced a civil conflict in the 1980s pitting the white minority government over groups pushing for a democratic system that would pave the way for black majority rule.

Of course, most states contain dissatisfied actors who would like greater control over their territory, more influence over policy, a larger role in government, or a bigger share of the country's wealth. But many states are also strong enough internally to prevent such actors from organizing and arming themselves. The preconditions for a coercive bargaining interaction—i.e., the existence of at least two actors capable of threatening violence against the other—are more likely to be met in states that have fragile control over their people. Hence, we tend to see civil conflict in states that are poor, have weak police and military forces, and have a hard time projecting government authority throughout the country due to insufficient infrastructure or rugged terrain.[a3]

PROBLEMS OF CONFLICT RESOLUTION

As with interstate conflicts, civil conflicts can, in theory, be resolved through compromises that would allow the actors to avoid the horrendous costs associated with these wars. A territorial dispute could lead to a negotiated secession or a grant of autonomy that would give the rebel group many of the benefits of self-rule. Regime and policy disputes can be diffused through policy concessions or power-sharing arrangements that give rebels greater representation in the government. The puzzle of civil war is thus the same as the puzzle of international war: why do the actors—in this case, rebel groups and governments—sometimes fail to reach bargains that would permit them to avoid the costs of war?

---

a3. Ibid.

The three mechanisms discussed in the chapter—incomplete information, commitment problems, and indivisibility—are all relevant in answering this question. If we were to replace "State A and State B" with "government and rebel group," much of the logic we developed in the chapter text would continue to apply. The capabilities and resolve of each side may be hard to observe. Anticipated shifts in power can heighten incentives to fight preventively. And the conflict may take place over pieces of territory that are imbued with religious or ethnic significance and hence are hard to divide. There are, in addition, some issues in the context of civil conflicts that make them especially hard to resolve.

The first problem arises from potentially frequent changes in the relative power of the actors. We have seen that anticipated changes to the relative power of two states can generate incentives for preventive war. When power is changing, the rising actor cannot credibly commit not to exploit its power in the future to revise any deal made today; as a result, the actor that expects to grow weaker may prefer war now to a less desirable deal in the future. In the context of civil conflicts, changes in the relative power of rebels and the government can arise regularly due to shocks to the state's economy. When the economy falters, the government's tax revenue falls, depriving it of resources that could be used to combat a rebellion; at the same time, popular discontent associated with a poor economy makes it easier for rebels to attract new recruits. As a result, a downturn in the economy creates a window in which rebels are relatively strong and have incentives to press demands. And the government, facing a strong rebellion, has incentives to make concessions. A problem arises if the economic downturn is expected to be temporary, a result of short-term shocks such as a change in the price of oil or, in countries that depend heavily on agriculture, too little rainfall in a given year. If everyone anticipates that the economy will recover in the near future, then the rebels' newfound strength is known to be temporary. The rebels may expect that any concessions the government makes under these conditions will be withdrawn once conditions improve. As with a rising state, the government may not be able to commit credibly to abide by the deal in the future. Hence, the anticipated economic recovery creates incentives for rebels to fight now in the hopes of obtaining an irreversible victory while they are relatively strong. This logic suggests that economic downturns should be associated with a higher risk of civil wars. For example, one study of political violence in Africa found that a 5 percent drop in economic growth led, on average, to a 50 percent increase in the risk of civil conflict in the subsequent year.[a4]

A second commitment problem arises from the fact that settlements of civil disputes generally require rebel groups to lay down their arms. A rebel group mobilizes and arms in order to make demands on the government. The government, hoping to avoid war, may make concessions but also requires, as part of the deal, that the rebels demobilize and disarm. This is a sensible demand to ensure civil peace and order; after all, unless a new state is created through secession, rebel forces will have to be integrated into the existing state. The demand, however, gives rise to a severe commitment problem: once the rebels have disarmed, how can they be sure that the government will continue to abide by the deal? The government might simply exploit the rebels' disarmament to crack down and eliminate them as a threat altogether. Hence, any

---

a4. Edward Miguel, Shanker Satyanath, and Ernest Sergenti, "Economic Shocks and Civil Conflict: An Instrumental Variables Approach," *Journal of Political Economy* 122 (2004): 725–53.

deal that requires disarmament by the rebel group directly affects the future bargaining power of the actors. As we saw in the case of interstate conflict, this dynamic can create an insurmountable obstacle to reaching a negotiated settlement, either before or during the conflict. In part for this reason, civil wars rarely end with negotiated peace agreements. Indeed, the vast majority of civil wars end only when one side achieves an outright military victory.[a5] Reaching an agreement either before or during fighting requires some mechanism to ensure that the government will live by the deal once the rebels lay down their arms. The most likely mechanism for these purposes is the presence of a third party, such as peacekeepers from the United Nations, who can monitor and enforce the terms of the deal. As we will see in Chapter 5, UN peacekeeping missions do have a track record of success in this regard.

A final problem that is particularly acute in the case of civil conflicts arises when a government faces many potential rebel groups. Consider the case of Russia, which has been involved in a bloody civil war against the breakaway region of Chechnya since its predominantly Muslim inhabitants declared independence in 1993. Given the costs of this war, which has claimed tens of thousands of lives and sparked terrorist attacks by Islamic militants, Russia might have been better off letting the Chechens take their land and go. If Russia were facing a single possible separatist group, the dangers of such a concession might not be too large. But in a large, multiethnic country, concession to one group might encourage others to mobilize for similar reasons. And Russia is home to more than 100 different ethnic groups, many of whom seek separation or greater autonomy from the center. If potentially rebellious groups are uncertain about the government's resolve to resist their demands, then concession in one case might lead potential claimants to conclude that the government lacks the will to resist their demands. Although any one set of concessions might not be too painful, the collective costs of making concessions to multiple groups could be quite large. In this case, a state may choose to fight a rebel group rather than make concessions in order to convince all potential challengers that they will similarly face resistance. By fighting, the state sends a credible signal to potential challengers that it is tough and unlikely to make concessions; this signal may convince other groups to back down and/or dissuade potential challengers from mobilizing in the first place. Hence, even if concessions are preferable to war in any isolated conflict, the fact that other potential rebels are watching means that fighting may have informational value. This suggests that the more potential challengers a government faces, the less likely it is to make concessions to any one challenger, a prediction that has been confirmed in recent research.[a6]

In sum, the dynamics that drive civil wars are very similar to those that drive interstate wars. The kinds of interest conflicts that underlie civil disputes are the same, and the bargaining interactions are plagued with similar commitment and information problems, even though these problems arise for somewhat different reasons in this context. As a result, both kinds of conflict create a demand for institutions capable of bringing in third parties to monitor and enforce peace agreements.

---

a5. Barbara Walter, *Committing to Peace: The Successful Settlement of Civil Wars* (Princeton, NJ: Princeton University Press, 2002).

a6. Monica Toft, *The Geography of Ethnic Violence* (Princeton, NJ: Princeton University Press, 2005), especially Chapter 5 on Russia and Chechnya. Barbara F. Walter, "Building Reputation: Why Governments Fight Some Separatists but Not Others," *American Journal of Political Science* 50 (2006): 313–30.

CHAPTER 4

Domestic Politics and War

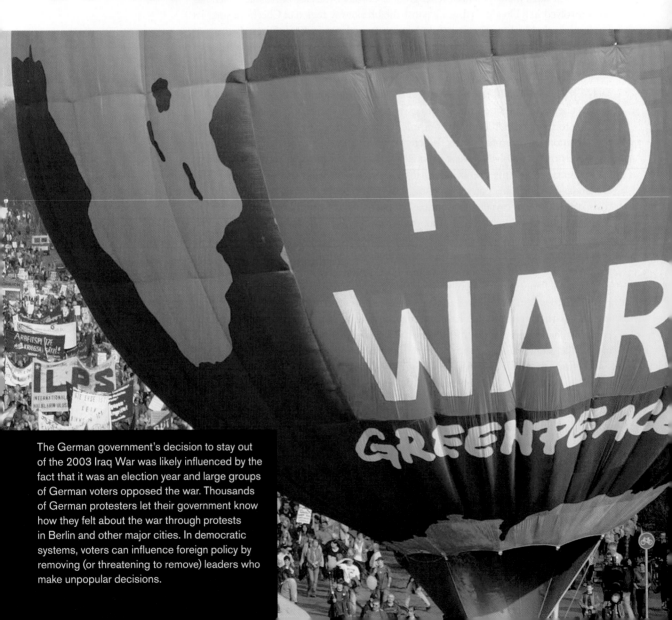

The German government's decision to stay out of the 2003 Iraq War was likely influenced by the fact that it was an election year and large groups of German voters opposed the war. Thousands of German protesters let their government know how they felt about the war through protests in Berlin and other major cities. In democratic systems, voters can influence foreign policy by removing (or threatening to remove) leaders who make unpopular decisions.

War is costly for states, but what if there are actors within the state—such as politicians, businesses, or the military—who see war as beneficial and who expect to pay few or none of its costs? Do states fight wars to satisfy influential domestic interests?

O n March 30, 1982, thousands of demonstrators marched in the streets of Buenos Aires, the capital of Argentina, denouncing the military government that had ruled the country with an iron fist since taking over in a coup in 1976. Riot police used tear gas, rubber bullets, and water cannons to break up the protests, and over 2,000 people were arrested. A week later, the streets of Buenos Aires filled with demonstrators once more, but this time the demonstrations voiced enthusiastic support for the military regime, as many of those who had earlier called for the government's ouster now joined in the outpouring of praise. What had changed in the course of a week? On April 2, Argentine naval forces invaded a small group of islands 300 miles off the Argentine coast that were the subject of a long-standing dispute between Argentina and Britain. Is there any connection between these events? Could the Argentine government have provoked a war with Britain in order to revive its popularity with its people?

In 1954, representatives of the United Fruit Company went to Washington, D.C., to voice their concerns about the leader of Guatemala, a man named Jacobo Arbenz. Arbenz had pushed a land reform program that led to the seizure of almost 400,000 acres that belonged to the company. Arbenz offered to compensate United Fruit to the tune of $1.2 million, the value of the land that the company claimed for tax purposes. The U.S. government insisted on behalf of United Fruit that the company be paid almost $16 million. In June of that year, rebels armed and trained by the U.S. Central Intelligence Agency invaded Guatemala. Fearing a full-scale American invasion, parts of the Guatemalan military revolted, Arbenz resigned from office and fled the country, and a pro-American leader was installed. The operation cost the CIA just under $3 million.[1] Did the United States overthrow a foreign leader to benefit a single company at the expense of American taxpayers?

In the century after the United States fought for and won its independence from Britain, the two countries clashed on numerous occasions: in the War of 1812, in several crises over the border with Canada (which was a British colony until 1867), and even during the American Civil War, when the British government contemplated intervening on the side of the Confederacy in order to foster the split of its rival. Since the early twentieth century, however, the United States and Britain have become close allies, to the point that we often refer to a "special relationship" between the two. Interestingly, the shift from conflict to peace in this relationship coincided with political reforms that made the two countries more democratic. In the United States, this period witnessed the end of slavery and the enactment of women's suffrage in 1920. Similarly, in Britain, major reforms in this period eliminated restrictions on the right to vote, ensured the secrecy of the ballot, and established universal suffrage. Could these changes in the countries' political systems have contributed to the lasting peace between them?

Our first look at the puzzle of war in Chapter 3 considered this problem from the perspective of states. We posited two states in conflict over some good, such as a piece of territory, and trying to arrive at a settlement that avoids the costs of war. This kind of analysis is very common in international relations scholarship, where it is often referred to as the *unitary state assumption:* the treatment of states as coherent actors with a set of interests that belong to the state. While this assumption can be a useful starting place for analysis, we must remember that states are legal and political constructs, not beings capable of taking actions. The choices and actions of states are made by people. Decisions about waging war are made by a state's political leaders. Military plans are drawn up by military officials and carried out by soldiers. Others within the country may also be able to influence foreign policy choices, even if they have no direct say over them. There may be interest groups, such as business or ethnic lobbies, that influence decision-making through their organizational and financial resources. In democratic systems, voters influence policy decisions because of their ability to remove leaders who make unpopular choices. Looking inside the state reveals new actors with varied interests, as well as variation across states in the political institutions that determine who affects decision-making.

How does our understanding of the causes of war change when we look inside the state and consider the interests, interactions, and institutions within it? In Chapter 3, we argued that to understand why wars happen, we need to understand why states at times cannot solve their conflicts peacefully, in a way that avoids the costs associated with fighting. This argument rested on the assumption that war is costly to those engaged in the interaction. These costs create a bargaining range, or a set of deals that both states prefer to fighting. The assumption that war is costly makes

Although France and Germany were once bitter enemies, they now cooperate closely, and war between them has become virtually unthinkable. Some scholars attribute this to the fact that both countries have had democratic governments since they last fought, in World War II. Here, German chancellor Angela Merkel and French president Nicolas Sarkozy wind up a press conference at the Franco-German Ministers Council in November 2008.

1. The cost information is from U.S. Central Intelligence Agency, "CIA's Role in the Overthrow of Arbenz," Job 79-01025A, Box 153, Folder 3, www.state.gov/r/pa/ho/frus/ike/guat/20181.htm (accessed 11/7/07).

sense when we think of the state as a unitary actor, but once we look inside the state, it is clear that the costs and benefits of war are not distributed equally within the country.

Different actors within the state may place more or less value on the issue in dispute. A disputed territory might represent a source of livelihood, profit, or national pride to some, a tract of worthless land to others. The persecution of a minority group in a foreign country might arouse outrage in some, perhaps due to ethnic attachment to the victims, while others greet it with indifference. Most Americans in 1954 had little or no stake in the land reform policies of the Guatemalan government; to the United Fruit Company, on the other hand, millions of dollars worth of land were at risk.

The costs of war are also distributed unevenly. Some people, such as those who might be drafted to serve in the military, can expect to pay very high and direct costs from war. Others may see the costs of war in economic terms, if the need to finance the conflict leads to higher taxes. In contrast, there are some groups within a country that may profit from war financially or professionally. Arms manufacturers benefit from increased purchases of their products. For military officers, combat experience leads to opportunities for medals and promotions. And for unpopular governments, such as the Argentine junta in 1982, war can build support domestically and solidify their hold on power.

These observations raise a number of questions. To what extent is war rooted, not in the information and commitment problems discussed in Chapter 3, but rather in the interests of domestic actors who see personal benefit and little or no cost to war? Do wars serve the national interest, or the parochial interests of office-hungry politicians, multinational companies, and/or a "military-industrial complex" composed of glory-seeking militaries and profit-seeking arms merchants? How do domestic institutions, such as democracy, influence a government's calculus and the likelihood of war between states?

To answer such questions, we must consider the different interests that domestic actors have in terms of war and peace. Simply identifying these interests is not enough, however, since not all actors within the state have equal say over foreign policy choices and hence not all interests are represented equally. Which domestic interests drive foreign policy choices depends on two things: the strategic interactions between actors, which determine which individuals and groups can exert effective influence and which cannot; and the institutions within the state, which determine how different actors have access to the decision-making process. Further, we have to recall that war is not the choice of a single state, but rather an outcome of the interaction between or among multiple states. Hence, as we consider domestic influences on foreign policy, we need to examine how these factors shape bargaining at the international level. This chapter will develop four major points.

CORE OF THE ANALYSIS

▶ There can be actors within the state who perceive high benefits from war and expect to pay little or none of its costs. In particular, there are conditions under which political leaders, business and ethnic lobbies, and the military will see conflict as furthering their narrow interests.

▶ Moreover, these actors have a variety of institutional and organizational advantages that make it possible for them to exert more influence than the general population.

▶ Except in rare circumstances, these hawkish interests are not sufficient to cause war on their own. Rather, their main effect is to increase the aggressiveness of the state's foreign policy and the scope of its ambitions, thereby creating more opportunities for conflict.

▶ Democratic political institutions—in particular, free and fair elections, party competition, and free media—can diminish the influence of hawkish interests and provide mechanisms for overcoming the strategic problems that can cause the bargaining interaction to end in war.

Whose Interests Count in Matters of War and Peace?

In the previous chapter, we observed that international disputes generally arise over territory, policies, and the characteristics of countries' domestic regimes. Why these conflicts of interest arise in the first place is a complicated question with no single answer. One view, referred to in the book's Introduction as realism, is that in world politics states' interests are largely, if not entirely, dictated by external factors. States want to preserve their sovereignty and territorial integrity. In order to do so, they need power—primarily, military power. Hence, they seek opportunities to expand their own power and/or to diminish the power of those that threaten them. In this view, states' interests are fixed, determined largely by their material resources and geographical position, and they are insensitive to domestic factors.

Although this argument is sometimes useful in understanding sources of conflict in the world, it is also overly simplistic. Conflicts between states often arise from the interests of domestic actors within them, interests that include more than the basic need for physical security. For example, some conflicts cannot be understood without reference to the ethnic identities and religious beliefs that prevail within states. In early modern Europe, wars often pitted Catholic countries against Protestant countries. A change in the official religion of a country could radically alter who its friends and enemies were. In the present day, ongoing rivalries between India and Pakistan or between Israel and its Arab neighbors are similarly fueled by religious differences. This observation suggests that the interests that states bring to international bargaining cannot be considered in isolation from the interests of actors within the states.

NATIONAL VERSUS PARTICULARISTIC INTERESTS

In considering the kinds of domestic interests that can influence foreign policy, it is useful to distinguish between general interests and narrow or particularistic interests. A general interest is something that most, if not all, actors within the country share. For example, virtually everyone has an interest in their country's physical security and economic well-being. If most people within the state share a common religious or ethnic identity, then the state's foreign policy interests likely reflect those identities. It makes sense to call such interests national interests, or interests that are so widely shared that they can be attributed to the state as whole. Narrow or particularistic interests are those held only by a relatively small number of actors within the country, such as a particular business, an ethnic minority group, or individuals within government.

To make this distinction concrete, consider the case of oil. The United States has long professed, and acted on, an interest in ensuring a steady supply of oil, particularly from the oil-rich countries in the Middle East. In 1943, President Franklin Roosevelt declared that the defense of Saudi Arabia was vital to the defense of the United States, and an American company, the Arabian-American Oil Company (Aramco), became the main player in developing and exploiting the oil fields there. The commitment to defend Saudi Arabia was reinforced on a number of occasions. In 1979, the Soviet Union invaded Afghanistan, putting Soviet forces on the doorstep of

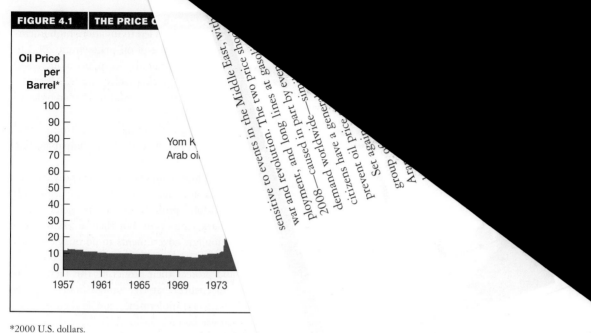

FIGURE 4.1   **THE PRICE C**

2000 U.S. dollars.
Source: International Monetary Fund, International Financial Sta

the Middle East and American allies in the Persian G
by articulating what became known as the Carter 1
outside force to gain control of the Persian Gulf region   ...n assault
on the vital interests of the United States of America,   ...n assault will be
repelled by any means necessary, including military force. And, of course, the need
to preserve stability and American influence in this region was cited to justify both
the 1991 Persian Gulf War and the more recent Iraq War.[2]

Why has the United States had such a consistent interest in oil and the Middle
East? One national interest–based argument hinges on the observation that oil is vital
to U.S. power because a modern military of tanks and airplanes consumes large quantities of fuel. It is no coincidence that Roosevelt's concern for Saudi Arabia arose during
World War II, at a time when American war planners were worried about running out
of gas. The Cold War that followed did nothing to alleviate concerns about maintaining access to this strategically valuable material that was crucial to the economic and
military might of the United States and its allies. In this view, the U.S. interest in oil
stems from a national interest in ensuring its military power and security.

An alternative argument, also based on general interests, revolves around the
U.S. economy's dependence on stable and plentiful oil supplies. The U.S. economy
runs on oil—to fuel cars, to transport goods around the country, to heat homes
and power businesses. Shocks to the price of oil can thus have substantial effects
on the economic welfare of U.S. citizens, influencing inflation, unemployment, and
disposable income. As Figure 4.1 shows, the price of oil over time has been highly

---

2. For a comprehensive history of the role of oil in international politics, see Daniel Yergin, *The Prize: The
Epic Quest for Oil, Money, and Power* (New York: Free Press, 1991).

major spikes occurring during times of
ks in the 1970s led to inflation, high unem-
ne stations; the rise of oil prices from 2002 to
ts in the Middle East, but also a product of increased
arly ate into consumers' pocketbooks. Hence, American
interest in ensuring stability in the Middle East in order to
shocks that would hurt the economy.

st these views is one that sees the pursuit of oil as benefiting a small
businesses: oil companies. After World War II, U.S. companies like
nco played a direct role in pumping and selling Middle Eastern oil, making
huge profits. Since the 1960s and 1970s, producer countries have generally nationalized their oil industries, meaning that oil companies have to negotiate deals with
these governments. U.S. firms like ExxonMobil profit from their participation in
the exploration, drilling, refining, and marketing of oil, but their access to these
activities depends on the willingness of foreign governments to do business with
them. It is possible, then, that U.S. foreign policy toward the Middle East is driven
by these companies' desire to expand and protect their profits. In this view, firms
use their influence over policymakers to ensure that the United States defends
friendly regimes (like that of Saudi Arabia) and undermines hostile regimes (like
that of Iraq under Saddam Hussein) that are bad for business. Because these policies can impose costs on American soldiers and taxpayers, this view sees U.S. foreign policy in the Middle East as benefiting a narrow set of interests within the
country at the expense of everyone else.

As our discussion suggests, the distinction between national and particularistic
interests is easy to make in the abstract but harder to observe in practice. Nonetheless,
the distinction is crucial for thinking about what causes war. Recall from Chapter 2
that an actor is a group of individuals with similar interests. To the extent that
groups or individuals within the state have different interests over the outcomes of
international bargaining, the analytical utility of assuming that the state is an actor
diminishes—and we have to start looking within the state for new actors. This quest
is important because the analysis of war in Chapter 3 assumed that war is a costly
outcome for the actors engaged in international bargaining. These costs ensure the
existence of deals that all sides prefer to war, and they underpin an understanding of
war that focuses on the information, commitment, and divisibility problems that can
prevent such deals from being reached. If, however, the benefits of war are enjoyed by
a different set of actors from those that pay the costs, then this view may need to be
revised. Does war arise, not because of obstacles to the bargaining interaction, but
because war furthers the interests of particular actors within the country?

INTERACTIONS, INSTITUTIONS, AND INFLUENCE

When we drop the unitary actor assumption and look within states, an enormous
number of individuals and groups, with a variety of interests, comes into focus.
How can we know which actors matter and which interests are likely to influence
foreign policy decisions? The answer lies in institutions and interactions. Domestic
institutions determine how decisions are made, and therefore, which actors' interests are taken into account. In some countries, decisions are made by a very small

number of individuals, perhaps even a single person, who do not have to consider the interests of anyone else. They can act on the basis of their personal interests or whims. More commonly, a ruler may only have to worry about maintaining the loyalty of the military by catering to that organization's interests. In other countries, institutionalized rules force decisionmakers to be sensitive to the interests of other actors. Democratic political institutions, for example, require leaders to win free and fair elections. This requirement forces leaders to think about how the voting public will respond to their policy choices. It also makes them dependent on organized groups that are willing to donate money and time to election campaigns. Although voters and organized interest groups are not literally in the room when decisions are made, democratic institutions force those who *are* in the room to take those actors' interests into account. Thus, institutions determine which actors and interests have a (figurative) seat at the table.

Some domestic actors may also have strategic advantages. In Chapter 2, we introduced a strategic dilemma known as the collective action problem. This problem arises when a group of individuals with common interests seeks to act collectively to further that interest. As we saw, such efforts can fall short if each individual prefers to free ride on the efforts of others. One implication of this insight is that relatively small groups can be more effective at cooperating to further common interests than large groups. Indeed, small groups of highly motivated and informed individuals are better able to organize and coordinate their activities and prevent others from free riding. By contrast, large, dispersed groups in which each individual has only a small stake in or knowledge about the policy decision are generally very hard to organize. For example, whereas United Fruit stood to lose millions of dollars of property in Guatemala, the intervention cost each U.S. taxpayer only a few pennies. Had taxpayers been opposed to having their money spent this way, they would have had a hard time cooperating, since no individual had any incentive to spend time and money on such an effort. To the extent that a group's political influence depends on the ability of its members to cooperate, this strategic problem favors the few over the many. This explains why a relatively narrow interest group can successfully demand a policy that benefits it at the expense of everyone else.

Appreciating the role of institutions and interactions, we can organize a discussion of domestic interests around three different kinds of actors. The first are the leaders who make foreign policy decisions. State leaders decide when to make threats, what demands to issue, and, ultimately, whether to wage war. These individuals matter the most because, by whatever rules of politics operate in their country, they have the authority to make these decisions. The second set of actors to consider are groups within the country that have sufficient organization and resources to influence the decisions made by the political leaders. Two such groups are of particular relevance: bureaucratic actors and interest groups. The state apparatus is made up of a variety of different organizations collectively known as the **bureaucracy**. These organizations—which include the military, the diplomatic corps, and the intelligence agencies—may wield considerable influence due to their institutional resources and knowledge. The military in particular, by virtue of its coercive power, organizational discipline, and expertise in war-fighting, can shape decisions about the use of force both through its role in implementation and through its influence over political leaders. **Interest groups** are groups of

bureaucracy: The collection of organizations—including the military, the diplomatic corps, and the intelligence agencies—that carry out most tasks of governance within the state.

interest groups: Groups of individuals with common interests that organize to influence public policy in a manner that benefits their members.

individuals with common interests that have organized in order to push for policies that benefit their members. Of particular importance in the present context are economic interest groups, such as companies or groups of companies, and ethnic lobbies composed of people with similar policy interests due to their common ethnic background. In later chapters, when we turn to issues like human rights (Chapter 11) and the environment (Chapter 12), interest groups that organize around other principles will come to the fore.

The third set of actors to consider is the general public. As already suggested, the influence of ordinary citizens varies considerably with domestic institutions. In democratic countries, free and fair elections provide individuals with a low-cost way to participate in deciding who governs. In other kinds of countries, it is harder for individual citizens to have much influence, since political leaders do not depend on their support. As long as the regime can count on the repressive power of the police and military, then general public interests can be ignored. Given this situation, the question of how the general public matters is largely a question of how democracy matters. (The "Controversy" box on page 135 asks if the costs of conflict should be imposed only on those with a direct role in foreign policy making.)

Do Politicians Spark Wars Abroad in Order to Hold On to Power at Home?

As noted early in this chapter, Argentina sparked a war with Great Britain in 1982 when it invaded a set of nearby islands: the Falkland Islands to the British, the Malvinas to Argentineans. This war was surprising in a number of respects. First, the islands in dispute were not particularly valuable pieces of territory. At the time of the war, the islands' population was under 2,000, and their primary source of income was sheep farming. Indeed, just prior to the war Britain had taken steps to weaken its hold over the islands. In 1981, Britain readied plans to withdraw the last of its naval vessels in the region and passed an act that stripped Islanders of full British citizenship. Second, the war was surprising given the enormous imbalance in military power between the two states. Though separated from the islands by a larger distance, Britain had a far superior naval force. After Argentina invaded and occupied the Falklands on April 2, 1982, it took only 74 days for British forces to retake the islands. There were 255 dead on the British side, 635 on the Argentine side. So why did Argentina pick a fight with such a formidable foe, and why did Britain react so strongly to defend its right to islands that seemed to be of diminishing importance?

A large part of the answer to this puzzle lies not in international considerations, but in the domestic political interests of the countries' governments. At the time, leaders in both countries had pressing domestic problems to which military conflict may have seemed the perfect solution. The Argentine government—a group of military officers known as a junta—had seized power in 1976, and its rule became increasingly repressive and unpopular over time. In the early 1980s, Argentina suffered a severe economic downturn, which led to civil unrest and splits within the ruling group. Facing a dire threat to its rule, the junta decided that an attack on

Should We Assassinate Leaders Rather Than Fight Their Armies?

On April 15, 1986, U.S. president Ronald Reagan ordered a bombing campaign on the domestic compound of Libya's head of state, Colonel Mu'ammar Quaddafi. Although Quaddafi escaped, 60 people died, including Quaddafi's 15-month-old daughter. The strike followed an interception of communications linking the Libyan government to the April 5 bombing of a West Berlin nightclub, which had left one American serviceman dead and 50 others injured. White House officials interpreted the Berlin attack as the latest in a string of belligerent actions taken by Quaddafi since his 1969 coup d'état, including his widespread financing of international terrorism, the invasion of Chad, and death threats toward the U.S. president. Although American hostility toward Quaddafi was widely known at the time of the April 15 attack (Reagan had described the colonel only days earlier as "the mad dog of the Middle East"), the White House vigorously denied that the operation was targeted at Quaddafi personally, rather than at the regime's military buildings.

As Washington's efforts at concealment suggest, the deliberate murder of a head of state for political reasons provokes outrage in modern international relations. However, two arguments hold that assassination is in fact preferable to conventional war. One argument cites the nature of the domestic interests and interactions that cause interstate conflict to occur. Even when citizens vote, foreign policy is largely determined by the interactions among self-interested politicians, military leaders, and—possibly—economic or ethnic interest groups, excluding the vast majority of the citizenry. Acccording to this view, a choice of assassination over troop combat appropriately reflects this fact by concentrating the costs of conflict on those who make foreign policy decisions. Critics of this argument reject its key claim that foreign policy is exclusively driven by the interests of hawkish officials and minority political groups. In healthy democracies, the populace does exert some impact on foreign policy decisions—through the mechanism of electoral accountability.

And in nondemocratic states, there may be cases in which the majority of the population desires aggression against foreign states (perhaps for nationalist reasons), even if they have not been formally consulted.

A second argument for the use of assassination over conventional war cites the common interests of warring states in achieving a bargaining outcome that minimizes the suffering and death of their populations. Whereas the murder of a single leader kills one, military battles may kill thousands on both sides. If political objectives are achievable just as readily by assassination, the argument goes, the additional harms caused by full-scale combat have no ethical justification. Again, this argument is controversial. For a policy of assassination to prevent suffering and save lives, assassination attempts would have to be effective at eliminating the initial cause of conflict, making a later war unnecessary. But this outcome is open to doubt. To begin with, assassination attempts are often unsuccessful at achieving even their immediate goal: the death of their target. Each known U.S. attempt since World War II to assassinate a senior foreign official outside a war has failed. Quaddafi survived intact and continued his international terrorist activities, including the 1988 bombing of Pan Am flight 103. Moreover, even when the target's death is secured, the removal of a single individual has generally not had the desired effect on state policy. Other officials have simply stepped into the breach, either continuing the status quo or worsening matters. Finally, some scholars argue, even if particular assassination attempts may save lives, the general policy of allowing assassinations would have a destabilizing effect on international politics as a whole. International cooperation, it is argued, rests on an assumption on the part of heads of state that their personal security is not at risk. The norm against assassination can therefore be understood as an institution that promotes everyone's interest in a stable and predictable international order. ■

Just a few days before invading the Falkland Islands, the Argentine government faced massive protests and calls for the overthrow of the ruling junta. Rioters confronted police, and thousands were arrested. The war with Britain provided the Argentine junta a (temporary) reprieve from these problems by shifting the public's attention away from domestic issues.

the Falkland Islands might help solve its problem. Knowing that most Argentineans resented British control of the islands, the junta leaders hoped that a bold move to seize the islands would stir up nationalist sentiment, distract people from their economic hardships, and give the military government a popular achievement that would bolster its prestige and legitimacy. Indeed, the invasion of the Malvinas had precisely this effect. Hence, the Argentine junta was seeking more than just territory when it seized the islands—it was also looking to solidify its hold on power.[3]

On the British side, Prime Minister Margaret Thatcher may also have been thinking in terms of political survival. Like Argentina, Britain in 1982 was in the midst of a severe recession. With unemployment soaring, Thatcher's popularity dropped precipitously. In February 1982, the month before the invasion, only 29 percent of Britons said that they approved of the job she was doing. Thatcher's firm response caused her poll numbers to soar. By May, with British operations to retake the Falklands under way, Thatcher's approval rating jumped to 44 percent. By the end of the war, her approval stood at 51 percent. The British prime minister rode this wave of popularity to electoral victory a year later. Hence, Thatcher's unexpectedly strong response to the Argentine invasion not only restored British control over the Falklands, but it also revived her political fortunes.[4]

WHAT DO LEADERS WANT?

The leaders of states are not solely, if at all, statesmen or stateswomen looking out for the best interests of the nation; they are also individuals with many varied interests of their own. Some may have very strong ideological beliefs that increase their willingness to pay costs or run risks in foreign policy. It is hard to understand World War II, for example, without reference to German leader Adolf Hitler's extreme ideology, which motivated him to seek out *lebensraum* ("living space") for the German people by attacking Poland and then the Soviet Union.[5]

Even in the absence of such extreme ideological interests, state leaders may have more prosaic personal motivations. As the story of the Falklands War reminds us, leaders

3. Jack Levy and Lily Vakily, "External Scapegoating in Authoritarian Regimes: Argentina in the Falklands/Malvinas Case," in *The Internationalization of Communal Strife,* ed. Manus Midlarski, 118–46 (London: Routledge, 1992).

4. Approval figures are from David Butler and Gareth Butler, eds., *British Political Fact 1900–1994,* 7th ed. (London: MacMillan, 1994), 256. There is some controversy over how much the Falklands War contributed to the Conservative victory in 1983. See Harold D. Clarke, William Mishler, and Paul Whiteley, "Recapturing the Falklands: Models of Conservative Popularity, 1979–83," *British Journal of Political Science 20,* no 1. (January 1990): 63–81.

5. There is a debate among historians about how much of Hitler's foreign policy is explained by his personal ideology. For a balanced view on this, which ultimately concludes that ideology played an important role, see Allan Bullock, "Hitler and the Origins of the Second World War," in *The Origins of the Second World War: A. J. P. Taylor and His Critics,* ed. Wm. Roger Louis, 117–45 (New York: Wiley 1972).

are also politicians, people who benefit from holding political office. Being in office confers all manner of benefits: the ego boost of having power, opportunities to enrich oneself and one's friends, the ability to shape policy in desired ways. As a result, politicians think a lot about how to obtain office and, once in power, how to secure their hold on it. This means that political leaders make choices with an eye toward how those choices will influence their chances of staying in power.

How could office-seeking motivations affect leaders' decisions about war and peace? At the most general level, the desire to stay in power means that leaders have to be responsive to the interests of those who control their political fate, whether they be voters, organized interest groups, the military, or some other groups. As a result, office-seeking by political leaders plays a key role in almost every aspect of this chapter, since it helps account for the influence of special interest groups that can provide resources that are useful for maintaining power; it contributes to an understanding of the role of the military, whose support is often necessary for a government to stay in power; and it is a necessary element in arguments about the effects of accountability in democratic political systems. In short, the desire to hold office explains how the interests of actors within the country can matter at the level of policy-making.

But office-seeking motivations do not turn political leaders into mere instruments of other actors. Strategic politicians can use their control of policy to shape their political constraints, rather than just respond to them. In the case of war and peace, the most common argument to this effect concerns the political use of force by leaders, not to further any national interest but, rather, to enhance their hold on power.

British prime minister Margaret Thatcher benefited politically from the Falklands War. Before the war, poor economic conditions in Britain had helped bring Thatcher's public approval rating down to just 29 percent. Once the war began, the British public rallied behind their leader, sending her approval rating up to 51 percent.

THE RALLY EFFECT AND THE DIVERSIONARY INCENTIVE

The idea that leaders can further their own political interest by fighting a war flows from the so-called rally-round-the-flag effect, or rally effect for short. The **rally effect** refers to people's tendency to become more supportive of their country's government when it experiences dramatic international events, such as wars. This effect is most apparent in countries in which public opinion polling regularly measures the level of support for a leader. Often, approval ratings jump up at the onset of a war or some other international crisis, as in the case of Thatcher's approval ratings at the outset of the Falklands War. The most dramatic rally event ever recorded followed the terrorist attacks of September 11, 2001, which caused President George W. Bush's approval rating to jump immediately from 51 to 86 percent, eventually reaching as high as 90 percent (see Figure 4.2). Even in countries without opinion polls and approval ratings, we see cases in which the start of war caused an upsurge of national unity and support for the government. As we saw at the outset of this chapter, in 1982 Argentina's military government reversed a tide of public discontent by invading the Falkland Islands.

rally effect: The tendency for people to become more supportive of their country's government in response to dramatic international events, such as crises or wars.

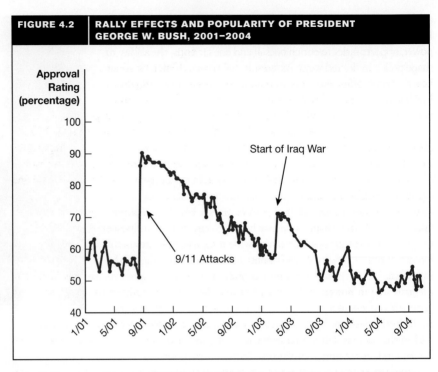

FIGURE 4.2 | RALLY EFFECTS AND POPULARITY OF PRESIDENT GEORGE W. BUSH, 2001–2004

Source: Gallup, www.gallup.com/poll/1723/Presidential-Job-Approval-Depth.aspx (accessed 10/15/08).

Why do people rally around the flag at times of international crisis? There are a number of explanations. Social psychologists have shown that members of a group often feel greater attachment and loyalty to the group when they experience conflict with outsiders.[6] Hence, international conflict can cause an upwelling of patriotism, and the leader derives increased support as the protector of the group's interests. At the same time, political opponents may decide to dampen their criticism of the government at a time of national crisis, and the government may use the emergency to crack down on dissent. This means that the government has a virtual monopoly on political discourse and can frame the public's evaluation of its policies without fear that opposing voices will split public opinion.[7] International conflict can also create a diversion from problems that might otherwise drag down a leader's popularity, such as economic troubles or scandals. Foreign policy crises tend to drive other issues out of the news headlines, redirecting people's attention away from the domestic issues that divide and disappoint them and toward the more unifying challenge of meeting a foreign threat. Finally, international conflict may give embattled leaders an opportunity to blame foreigners for the country's problems, a phenomenon known as scapegoating.

---

6. See, for example, Lewis A. Coser, *The Functions of Social Conflict* (New York: Free Press, 1956). The pioneering work of the rally effect in the United States is John E. Mueller, *War, Presidents, and Public Opinion* (New York: Wiley, 1973).

7. Richard A. Brody and Catherine R. Shapiro, "A Reconsideration of the Rally Phenomenon in Public Opinion," in *Political Behavior Annual*, ed. S. Long, 77–102 (Boulder, CO: Westview Press, 1989).

The existence of rally effects suggests that political leaders may at times face a **diversionary incentive:** a temptation to spark an international crisis in order to rally public support at home. This idea was popularized in the 1997 movie *Wag the Dog,* in which a scandal-plagued national leader hires a movie director to produce news footage of a fake war in order to boost his approval ratings. The logic, however, long precedes Hollywood. In William Shakespeare's *Henry IV,* Part II, a dying King Henry advises his son, Prince Hal, that to prevent plots against him he needs to "busy giddy minds / With foreign quarrels." This advice echoes in the words of a Russian minister who, during a 1904 dispute with Japan, reportedly told the tsar, "What this country needs is a short, victorious war to stem the tide of revolution."[8] Whether the tsar found this argument persuasive or not, Russia and Japan declared war on each other on February 10, 1904.

The danger posed by the rally effect should be clear from the discussion in Chapter 3. There, it was assumed that a state's first best outcome in a crisis is to get its way without having to fight. Fighting, after all, imposes costs that the state should prefer to avoid. A diversionary temptation could alter this calculus. If those who control the state's foreign policy think that using force abroad would greatly improve their chances of staying in power, then they may prefer war to a negotiated settlement, even one that gives them most of what they want.

These benefits may be particularly tempting to leaders who are insecure domestically, because of discontent with their policies or hard economic times. Such a leader may decide that she will surely lose office if she does nothing, so waging war and invoking the rally effect may be an appealing gamble. This phenomenon has been called gambling for resurrection: taking a risky action, such as starting a war, when the alternative is certain to be very bad. A sports analogy is useful here. Hockey teams trailing in the final minutes of a game sometimes pull their goalie in order to replace him with an additional attacker. Doing so increases the chances that they can even the score, but it also makes it easier for the other team to score against their undefended net. The gamble makes sense because a loss is a loss regardless of whether a team loses by one goal or many. Consequently, the downside risk of pulling the goalie is small compared to the upside potential of tying the game. Political leaders who are certain they will lose office because of poor economic conditions, such as the Argentine junta in 1982, might similarly see a large upside to starting a war and gambling that the outcome will turn out well.

DO LEADERS "WAG THE DOG"?

Do leaders "wag the dog," or gamble for resurrection? Given the intuitive nature of this argument, it may come as a surprise to learn that scholars have found little consistent support for the hypothesis that leaders systematically resort to force when they are in trouble domestically. Numerous studies have sought to determine whether the likelihood that a state will get involved in military conflict increases

diversionary incentive:
The incentive that state leaders have to start international crises in order to rally public support at home.

---

8. This quotation is attributed to Russian interior minster Vladimir Plehve. However, the authenticity of the quotation is unclear, and it has been suggested that it was attributed to Plehve only later by his political enemies.

when the leader is unpopular or the country is in a recession or facing high unemployment or inflation, or, in the case of democratic countries, shortly before an election, when a well-timed rally could be particularly useful. Although some studies have shown such effects, the results have been neither consistent nor particularly strong. As one scholar lamented while surveying this literature, "seldom has so much common sense in theory found so little support in practice."[9] Indeed, a growing body of evidence suggests that the relationship between international conflict and the leaders' political security may be the opposite of what diversionary theory suggests: international conflict is more likely to be initiated by leaders who are politically secure—that is, leaders whose hold on office is relatively strong.[10] For example, in democratic systems war initiation is more likely, not right before elections as diversionary theory would suggest, but right *after* them. A democratic leader is most secure just after an election, since the next election is at that point several years away.[11]

This is not to say that diversionary incentives never play a role in particular cases; in fact, historians cite many examples in which such logic contributed to the onset of war. What these results do suggest, however, is that leaders do not *systematically* use international conflict for diversionary purposes or to gamble for resurrection. In other words, even if diversionary incentives have contributed to war in some cases, they account for only a small portion of the conflict behavior we observe.

Why might this be the case? If sparking international conflict serves leaders' political interests, why do we not see stronger evidence of this effect? One possible answer is that most political leaders are not as cynical as we assumed and that they would not actually start a war simply to maintain their hold on power. Although we cannot rule out this possibility, other possible explanations do not force us to reject the assumption that leaders are office-seeking.

The first explanation is that the domestic political benefits of war relative to peace have to be large—perhaps unrealistically large—in order to eliminate the possibility of a peaceful bargain. Recall the simple bargaining framework we illustrated in the previous chapter, now depicted in Figure 4.3. As shown in (a), the size of the bargaining range is determined by the sum of the war costs to both sides, or $a + b$. Now, imagine that the leader of State A expects political benefits from waging war equal to some amount r, so that the total cost of war to A, after subtracting this benefit, is $a - r$. Even if the benefit r is greater than the costs a—so that State A sees no net cost to war—a bargaining range could still exist, as shown in (b). The size of this new bargaining range is given by the sum of the net costs, or $a + b - r$. Only if r exceeds the sum of the war costs to both states $(a + b)$ does the bargaining range vanish, making war inevitable. Hence, even if the leader of one state expected large political benefits from waging war, these benefits would be sufficient to cause war only if they outweighed the war costs to *both* sides.

9. Patrick James, "Conflict and Cohesion: A Review of the Literature and Recommendations for Future Research," *Cooperation and Conflict* 22, no. 1 (1987): 22.
10. See Giacomo Chiozza and Hein E. Goemans, "Peace through Insecurity: Tenure and International Conflict," *Journal of Conflict Resolution* 47 (August 2003): 443–67.
11. Kurt Taylor Gaubatz, "Election Cycles and War," *Journal of Conflict Resolution* 35, no. 2 (June 1991): 212–44.

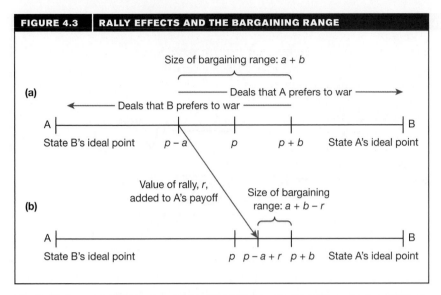

FIGURE 4.3 | RALLY EFFECTS AND THE BARGAINING RANGE

(a)

Size of bargaining range: $a + b$

Deals that A prefers to war →

← Deals that B prefers to war

A | | | | | B

State B's ideal point · $p - a$ · p · $p + b$ · State A's ideal point

(b)

Value of rally, r, added to A's payoff

Size of bargaining range: $a + b - r$

A | | | | B

State B's ideal point · p · $p - a + r$ · $p + b$ · State A's ideal point

Note: In this figure, p indicates the expected outcome in the event of a war, while a and b denote the costs of war to States A and B, respectively. For a fuller discussion of how to interpret these figures, see Chapter 3.

This observation reminds us that war is the product of an interaction between at least two actors, and not the choice of single actor. Of course, this condition becomes more likely if the leaders of both states expect political benefits from war, as was the case in the Falklands War.

THE POLITICAL COSTS OF WAR

A second reason why diversionary effects might be weak is that war can impose domestic political costs in addition to promising benefits. This is evident from the Falklands case as well. While Thatcher rode her postwar wave of support to a resounding electoral victory in Britain, the Argentine junta that lost the war met a very different fate. Following Argentina's defeat, protestors once again filled the streets, and members of the junta resigned or were stripped of their posts and several went to prison. The story of the Russo-Japanese War has a similar ending. Far from the short, victorious war the Russians hoped for, the war actually lasted almost two years, and the Russians suffered a humiliating defeat at the hands of the Japanese. Rather than stemming the tide of revolution, successive defeats on the battlefield increased unhappiness with the tsar's regime and helped usher in the Revolution of 1905, when the tsar was forced to make political concessions to his opponents. Full-scale revolution would hit Russia in 1917, in the midst of yet more battlefield defeats in World War I. Indeed, the initial surge of patriotism that generally accompanies the onset of war can quickly give way to discontent and rebellion if the war goes badly.

One way to see the relationship between the costs of war and its domestic political repercussions is to consider how public support for war changes as the costs mount. Figure 4.4 shows the relationship between public support and battle deaths

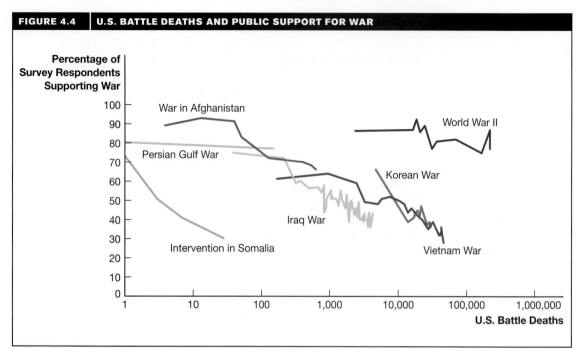

FIGURE 4.4 U.S. BATTLE DEATHS AND PUBLIC SUPPORT FOR WAR

Percentage of Survey Respondents Supporting War

War in Afghanistan
World War II
Persian Gulf War
Korean War
Iraq War
Intervention in Somalia
Vietnam War

U.S. Battle Deaths

Sources: WWII, Korea, Vietnam, Gulf War, and Somalia from Eric V. Larson, *Casualties and Consensus* (Santa Monica, CA: RAND, 1996). Other poll numbers from Gallup, www.gallup.com/poll/1633/Iraq.aspx (accessed 3/12/09). Casualty figures for Iraq and Afghanistan from www.icasualties.org (accessed 3/12/09).

for major U.S. military operations since and including World War II. As the graph shows, most operations started with very high levels of public support, but support generally fell off as the number of U.S. battle deaths mounted. The only wars that remained popular throughout were World War II—a war of national survival that followed the Japanese attack on the U.S. homeland—and two wars with relatively low numbers of U.S. casualties: the Persian Gulf War and the war in Afghanistan. Moreover, in cases in which support for the war collapsed, the presidents' approval ratings also suffered. During the Korean War, President Truman saw his approval rating fall to as low as 22 percent, and he declined to run for reelection in 1952. The unpopularity of the Vietnam War similarly doomed the presidency of Lyndon Johnson, who dropped his bid for reelection in March 1968. The Iraq War dragged down President Bush's approval ratings, causing his Republican party to lose control of Congress in 2006 and contributing to the election of Democrat Barack Obama in 2008. More generally, research has shown that leaders who fight losing or costly wars are more likely to be removed from office than those who win wars, as the "What Do We Know?" box on page 145 explains.

The evidence suggests that in terms of their political interests, leaders should see war not as a pure opportunity but as a gamble—and one that has a downside risk. Hence, in thinking about how reelection incentives influence the calculus of war and peace, we need to set the costs of losing a war against the potential benefits of the rally effect. These costs may explain why we do not see strong or systematic evidence that politically insecure politicians engage in diversionary conflict.

In light of this observation, it is worth recalling that the scandal-plagued leader in the movie *Wag the Dog* does not start an actual war; instead, he hires a movie producer to stage a fake war for public consumption. The attraction of doing this is clear: when you script the war yourself, you can make sure the right side wins. In the real world, war is a risky gamble—not just for the state, but also for the political interests of its leaders.

Do Countries Fight Wars to Satisfy the Military or Special Interest Groups?

From 1898 to 1902, Great Britain engaged in a costly and divisive war with the Boer states in South Africa. The Boer War, which lasted three years and claimed about 50,000 lives, was a climactic episode of a larger process in which the European states carved up and colonized the continent of Africa, as described in Chapter 1. To the British economist J. A. Hobson, this scramble for colonies and the bloody war that it gave rise to presented a puzzle. Why had Britain expended so many young lives and so much money to acquire and defend an empire in Africa, as well as in Asia and the Americas?

The answer that Hobson arrived at was unsettling. He calculated that although imperialism did not benefit the British nation as a whole, it was extremely profitable for a few small groups within the country. The primary beneficiaries, he argued, were rich people with the ability to invest overseas. With colonial possessions came many opportunities for profitable investments. Rich people could invest in railroads, mines, and other properties and receive very high rates of return. They could loan money to colonial governments at favorable interest rates. In pushing for colonial possessions, Hobson argued, financial interests found allies in powerful places: military leaders seeking glory and larger budgets, and arms manufacturers seeking profits. In his view, these groups used their power and influence to force British governments to pursue a policy that benefited them at the expense of the greater good.[12] Hobson's theory of imperialism is not without critics, but the general thesis—that wars are fought to benefit military and business interests—is a familiar one. It echoes famously in the words of U.S. president Dwight Eisenhower, who warned of the influence of a **military-industrial complex:** an alliance of military leaders and arms manufacturers who presumably have a vested interest in an aggressive foreign policy.

In this section, we consider the influence of the military and interest groups with respect to questions of war and peace. As we will see, there are times when these actors might be expected to have hawkish interests, because they anticipate benefits from war and/or pay few of the costs. These two sets of actors also have strategic advantages that they can exploit in their interaction with political leaders and others within the country. That said, we will see that the primary effect of hawkish actors is not to cause wars per se—that is, by eliminating the bargaining

military-industrial complex: An alliance between military leaders and the industries that benefit from international conflict, such as arms manufacturers.

---

12. J. A. Hobson, *Imperialism: A Study* (London: James Nisbet and Co., 1902).

range—but rather to expand the scope of the state's ambitions, to increase the conditions under which the state would consider fighting a war. Hence, hawkish domestic interests do not lead directly to the breakdown of bargaining, but they do create more opportunities for such failures to occur.

BUREAUCRATIC POLITICS AND THE MILITARY

Although the ultimate decision to wage war may lie in the hands of a few individuals, the actual machinery of government that deals with matters of war and peace is much larger and more complex. The leader of a modern state sits atop a large bureaucratic apparatus: a collection of organizations that manage many of the details of governance. Wars are planned and implemented by the state's military—usually a massive organization with thousands and, in some cases, millions of individuals. Negotiations with other countries are conducted by a host of diplomats around the world, typically overseen by a ministry of foreign affairs (known, in the United States, as the State Department). Information about other countries' military capabilities and intentions are collected and analyzed by intelligence organizations, like the United States' CIA, Britain's MI6 (Military Intelligence, Section 6), or Russia's SVR (Foreign Intelligence Service). Given all the tasks that governments have to perform and all the individuals that are needed to carry out those tasks, such organizations are a necessary part of any modern state.

This observation opens up the possibility that decisions about war and peace are shaped not only by state leaders, but also by the interests of the bureaucratic organizations involved in the decision-making process.[13] While such organizations care about what is best for the country, they may also care about the resources and influence that they wield themselves. They generally seek bigger budgets, more input into policy-making, and opportunities for personal promotion. As a result, they may press for policies that elevate their own status or fit their own worldview. For example, prior to the 2003 Iraq War there were serious disagreements within the U.S. government between the Defense Department and the State Department. Civilian leaders at the Pentagon generally expected war to be easy, while those at State were more cautious and emphasized the need for international diplomacy. There were also disagreements over which agency should take the lead role in rebuilding Iraq politically and economically in the aftermath of the conflict. These debates reflect a common aphorism about bureaucratic politics that "where you stand depends on where you sit"—that is, the leaders of bureaucratic agencies often take policy stands that reflect their own organizations' needs. In the end, the Defense Department won these scuffles.[14]

As this example suggests, the military is usually the most influential bureaucratic actor in matters of war and peace. To this point, our discussion has treated

---

13. The classic investigation of bureaucratic politics, now revised and updated, is Graham Allison and Philip Zelikow, *Essence of Decision: Explaining the Cuban Missile Crisis,* 2nd ed. (New York: Longman, 1999).

14. See, for example, Bob Woodward, *Plan of Attack* (New York: Simon and Schuster, 2004).

War and the Fate of Political Leaders

It is very rare in the modern world for state leaders to fight alongside their militaries and face the direct costs of war—that is, threat to life and limb. Instead, leaders feel the costs of war politically, through its effect on their survival in office. What happens to leaders who take their countries into war? Does winning or losing abroad affect whether they win or lose at home?

One systematic study of almost 200 leaders who took their countries to war in the last two centuries shows that losing a war can be very costly indeed.[a] In this study, war outcomes were classified into three categories: victories, small losses, and big losses, with small and big losses distinguished by how costly the war was in terms of dead soldiers. For each war, the study examined the fate of the wartime leader within one year of the war's termination. Table A summarizes the main results. There is a large difference between the political fate of leaders who win wars and those who lose, especially if the loss is very

costly. About 85 percent of leaders who lost costly wars also lost office within a year of the war's end. By contrast, more than two-thirds of war victors were still in office a year after the war ended. Moreover, the type of political system makes a difference in this regard. As Table B shows, democratic leaders who took their countries to war were significantly more likely to lose office within a year of the war's end than were their nondemocratic counterparts—regardless of whether they won or lost.

Losing office, however, is not the only or the worst thing that can happen to a leader. Indeed, some leaders are imprisoned, exiled, or even killed upon being removed from office. Table B shows the percentage of such leaders who faced additional punishment. The results are striking: although democratic leaders are more likely to be removed from office, nondemocratic leaders face a much greater risk of additional punishment such as going to prison, being sent into exile, or being executed. ■

TABLE A	WAR AND THE FATE OF LEADERS	
	Fate of Leader	
War Outcome	Stayed in Power	Lost Power
Victory	68%	32%
Small loss	47%	43%
Big loss	16%	84%

TABLE B	DEMOCRACY AND THE FATE OF WARTIME LEADERS			
	Democratic Leaders		Nondemocratic Leaders	
War Outcome	Lost Power	Punished If Lost Power	Lost Power	Punished If Lost Power
Victory	31%	11%	19%	38%
Loss	88%	43%	48%	88%

a. Hein Goemans, *War and Punishment* (Princeton, NJ: Princeton University Press, 2001); Table A and Table B are derived from the data on p. 58 of this text.

the military as an instrument of the state—a tool that states use to increase their leverage in international bargaining. What happens when we think about the military as an actor in its own right?

There is a compelling—although, as we will see, incomplete—argument to be made that the more influence the military has over foreign policy decision-making, the more belligerent the state will be. This argument rests on the assumption that members of the military have ideological, organizational, and professional interests in policies that make war more likely. Ideologically, leaders in the armed forces may be predisposed to seeing military solutions to foreign policy problems, overestimating the efficacy of force relative to other alternatives. As an organization, the military can demand larger budgets and more enlisted personnel under arms when the state is frequently engaged in international conflict than when it is at peace. And professionally, military officers find that combat experience is crucial to being promoted to the highest ranks. All these considerations suggest that the military sees benefits to war that other actors may not.

The most dramatic example of how military influence can lead to aggressive foreign policy is the case of Japan in the 1930s. Japan in this period pursued a relentless campaign of expansion against its neighbors, ultimately bringing the country into war with China, France, Britain, the Netherlands, and the United States. This belligerent turn in foreign policy coincided with a creeping takeover by the military, which undermined the nascent democratic system that had been developing in the country. In 1931, elements of the Japanese military provoked a war with China and seized a region known as Manchuria, which military leaders prized for its coal and iron. A year later, the prime minister of Japan was assassinated by a group of naval officers, an event that ushered in the end of civilian control of Japanese politics. The Japanese military became the main instigator of that country's expansionist policies. This case is an extreme example, but there is broader evidence to suggest that countries in which civilian leadership has weak control of the military are more likely to initiate militarized conflicts.[15]

Having said this, it is important not to automatically equate the military with militarism. One study examined the advice that military leaders gave U.S. decisionmakers in about 20 key crises during the Cold War, comparing how aggressive the officers were relative to the president's civilian advisors. The study showed that the advice from military officers was generally very similar to the advice from civilians; indeed, the military was less aggressive than civilians just as often as it was more aggressive. The author concluded that the "stereotype of a belligerent chorus of generals and admirals intimidating a pacific civilian establishment is not supported by the evidence."[16] Similarly, a study of elite opinion in the United States shows that military leaders are inclined to advocate the use of force in a narrower set of cases than are civilian leaders without any military experience.[17] Indeed, by all accounts, U.S. military officers were much more reluctant to go to war against Iraq in 2003 than was the civilian leadership at the Pentagon and White House. Many top commanders thought that war with Iraq would be costly and that conducting it successfully would require larger commitments of manpower and money than the civilian leadership was willing to make.[18] Such observations suggest that in some contexts at least, the military's interests push in a conservative direction: more appreciative of the limits of what can be achieved through force and more sensitive to the human costs of war, which are, after all, borne by its personnel.

---

15. Todd S. Sechser, "Are Soldiers Less War-Prone Than Statesmen?" *Journal of Conflict Resolution* 48, no. 5 (2004): 746–74.
16. Richard K. Betts, *Soldiers, Statesmen, and Cold War Crises* (New York: Columbia University Press, 1991), 4.
17. See Peter D. Feaver and Christopher Gelpi, *Choosing Your Battles: American Civil-Military Relations and the Use of Force* (Princeton, NJ: Princeton University Press, 2004).
18. See, for example, Michael R. Gordon and General Bernard E. Trainor, *Cobra II: The Inside Story of the Invasion and Occupation of Iraq* (New York: Pantheon, 2006).

INTEREST GROUPS: ECONOMIC AND ETHNIC LOBBIES

The possibility that special interest groups can influence foreign policy in a manner that furthers their particular interests is familiar to most people. In the wake of the 2003 U.S. invasion of Iraq, Vice President Richard Cheney's former company, Halliburton, was awarded contracts worth billions of dollars to rebuild Iraq's infrastructure and supply American troops. By the end of 2006, the company's stock was worth four times its value when the war started. Considering also that President Bush himself was once an oil industry executive, observations such as these have led to speculation that the Iraq War was fought at the behest of oil companies interested in Iraq's oil and military contractors interested in taxpayer dollars. Such charges are not new. U.S. interventions in Latin American countries have often been ascribed to the influence of American businesses whose properties in those countries were at risk. The previously mentioned case of Guatemala, where United Fruit feared a major loss at the hands of an unfriendly government, was by no means unique. The United States also intervened in Cuba (1961), the Dominican Republic (1965), and Chile (1973)—all places where American investors had substantial assets.

Although economic actors such as companies and industries figure most prominently in such stories, not all interest groups organize around economic motives. Interest groups that organize around ethnic ties are another influence on foreign policy, particularly in the United States. There is, for example, a very sizable and influential pro-Israel lobby in the United States: a collection of individuals and groups who want the U.S. government to support and defend the state of Israel—a stance that often brings the

Business groups may try to influence foreign policy to protect their interests. When the Guatemalan government seized extensive property belonging to the United Fruit Company in 1954, arguing that it belonged to the workers of Guatemala, United Fruit asked the U.S. government to intervene. Here, a banner with slogans from Guatemala's General Confederation of Workers hangs in front of a United Fruit hiring hall.

United States into conflict with Israel's adversaries in the Arab world. The main lobbying arm of this group is the American-Israel Public Affairs Committee (AIPAC), which is considered one of the most effective lobbying groups in Washington.[19] Other influential lobbying groups represent Cuban Americans opposed to the communist regime in Cuba. Most of these people fled Cuba after Fidel Castro took over in 1959 and seized the property of many wealthy Cubans. Cuban American groups have lobbied the U.S. government to take strong actions to contain and undermine the Castro regime, including supporting a failed invasion by exiles in 1961 and imposing a strict economic embargo on the country. In 2008, after almost half a century in power, Castro stepped down due to poor health and handed control to his brother, Raúl. Nonetheless, political pressure to maintain the island's isolation continues.

Why do interest groups care about the state's foreign policy? In cases like the pro-Israel and anti-Castro lobbies, group members are motivated by ethnic attachment or ideological interests to support or oppose a particular country or regime. In the case of economic actors, preferences over foreign policy arise whenever an actor's income depends on events in other countries or on the relationship between countries. A multinational company, like United Fruit Company, may have production facilities in numerous countries. If those countries experience political instability that threatens to disrupt the company's business, or if they have unfriendly regimes that might confiscate the company's property, then it might lobby for some form of intervention to protect its interests. Similarly, an investor who owns stocks in a foreign company or a bank that has loaned money to a foreign government might lobby its own government to use military force to ensure the return on its investment or the repayment of its loan. Such lobbying could lead to intervention against unstable or unfriendly regimes. In the extreme case that Hobson considered, economic actors with international investments might even lobby their governments to extend direct imperial control over other countries. Although establishing and maintaining such control was costly, imperialism made it safer to invest overseas, since there was less danger that investments would be wiped out by instability or hostile governments. A smaller set of economic actors, primarily those that make and sell military armaments, also has a direct interest in their country's foreign policy, since a belligerent foreign policy keeps them in business.

However, the interests of economic actors need not always lead to a preference for belligerent policies. Indeed, economic actors who depend on peaceful relations with other countries in order to do business could press their governments to pursue friendly relations or even formal alliances with profitable partners. For example, American banks and companies that had important trade, financial, and investment interests in Western Europe played a significant role in lobbying for a strong U.S. commitment to defend Western Europe at the outset of the Cold War. Similarly, banks that depended heavily on loans to Asia lobbied for strong alliance commitments to Japan and South Korea.[20] More recently, U.S. corporations interested in selling goods to China have been a potent

---

19. For a recent study arguing that the pro-Israel lobby wields a great deal of influence on U.S. foreign policy, see John J. Mearsheimer and Stephen M. Walt, *The Israel Lobby and U.S. Foreign Policy* (New York: Farrar, Straus and Giroux, 2007). This book generated a great deal of controversy. For a thoughtful response, see Walter Russell Mead, "Jerusalem Syndrome: Decoding the Israel Lobby,'" *Foreign Affairs* (November/December 2007).

20. Benjamin Fordham, *Building the Cold War Consensus* (Ann Arbor: University of Michigan Press, 1998).

political force lobbying for more cooperative relations with that country. In fact, an extensive literature suggests that trade between countries decreases the likelihood of war between them, in part because businesses that profit from the trade lobby against policies that could lead to conflict.[21] In sum, depending on where and how they do business, economic actors can have an interest in peaceful relations with some countries and/or hostile relations with others.

HOW CAN SMALL GROUPS HAVE A BIG INFLUENCE ON POLICY?

We have seen that militaries seeking budgets and prestige, businesses seeking profits, and ethnic groups looking out for their kin may all, at times, see particular benefits to war. What is remarkable about each of these actors is how small they are relative those who pay the costs of war. The generals and admirals who run military organizations are greatly outnumbered by the enlisted personnel who bear the brunt of the fighting, as well as by the rest of the population. Multinational companies and ethnic lobbies tend to make up a small fraction of society. Given how extensively they are outnumbered, when and how can these narrow interests prevail? The answer lies in the nature of the interactions between these different actors and the institutions that regulate their relations.

The military's influence on foreign policy decision-making derives from the fact that it controls a vast portion of the state's coercive resources. While militaries are generally created in order to defend a state from foreign threats, their capabilities inevitably make them key players domestically as well. In many states, the military plays a direct role in ensuring the continuation of the government. This role can either be very explicit (as with military dictatorships, in which military officers take direct control of executive power) or more subtle but no less potent. In many countries, the military is able and willing to intervene in politics to ensure that the government is to its liking; as a result, a nominally civilian government may have to cater to the military's interests in order to avoid being ousted in a coup d'état. A number of countries in Latin America, Africa, the Middle East, and Asia have experienced frequent alternations between direct military rule and civilian governments that lived under the constant threat of a coup. Moreover, authoritarian regimes that actively suppress popular dissent may rely heavily on the military to put down challenges to their rule. In such systems, the regime's dependence on the armed forces for its continued survival gives military leaders a prominent role in decision-making.

Even when the government does not depend so heavily on the military to stay in power, the military can have strong influence over foreign policy decision-making. All political leaders rely on the information and expertise of bureaucratic actors within the state. No political leader is an expert in every policy area; even if she were, there would not be enough time for her to focus on every task the government has to do. Instead, the job of making policy proposals and analyzing the implications of different decisions

21. For a review of this argument and supporting evidence, see Bruce Russett and James Oneal, *Triangulating Peace: Democracy, Interdependence, and International Organizations* (New York: Norton, 2001), chap. 4.

rests with the specialists who staff the bureaucratic agencies. When making decisions about war, a leader has to rely on experts within the military and other agencies (such as those dealing with intelligence and diplomacy) to provide key pieces of information: what the country's capabilities are, what the capabilities of potential adversaries are, what plans there are to wage war with a given country and deal with any contingencies that might arise. The political leader's dependence on the military for this kind of information gives the military leadership the ability to shape decisions to their liking. A military bent on war could, for example, give the leader skewed advice about how easily the war could be won and how low the costs would be. Conversely, military officials opposed to war could give conservative estimates of the likelihood of success and magnify the potential costs. In this way, the military would shape the outcome by manipulating the information that the leader uses to calculate the expected value of war and its alternatives.

Organized interest groups also rely on their superior resources and access to information in order to exert influence over policy. Consider an intervention like the one in Guatemala mentioned at the outset of this chapter. In that case, intervention cost U.S. taxpayers about $3 million, and it protected property for which United Fruit Company demanded $16 million. Given that the taxpayers who footed the bill vastly outnumbered the stockholders of the company that benefited, it is useful to think about why the latter would get their way at the expense of the former. How could economic interest groups "hijack" a state's foreign policy for their own, narrow interests?

Much of the answer lies in how the costs and benefits of international conflict are distributed in such situations. Precisely because taxpayers are more numerous, the costs of intervention to any individual are quite low. As a result, no individual citizen has much incentive to become informed about the situation, to call his member of Congress to weigh in on the policy, to go to Washington to bang on the doors of the State Department, and so on. Indeed, in the case of Guatemala and United Fruit Company, most U.S. citizens were likely unaware of what the CIA was up to (in arming and training Guatemalan rebels) and how much taxpayer money was being spent. By contrast, the company that stands to benefit from intervention has a very large stake in the outcome. Company representatives have every incentive to become informed, to lobby representatives, and to exploit contacts within the government. Hence, in the interaction between the many who pay the costs and the few who stand to benefit, the latter have a significant advantage.

Organized interest groups can prevail because they can provide political leaders with things they need and want in exchange for favored policies. Sometimes, what interest groups provide is money, which leaders can use to line their pockets or, if that is prohibited, to finance political campaigns. Concerns about the military-industrial complex center around the flow of money: industries give money to elected officials, who then allocate taxpayer money to the military, which then spends the money in ways that benefit the industries, such as by purchasing their arms or intervening to protect their foreign assets.[22]

In democracies, interest groups also wield clout by promising the support of motivated voters. For example, the Cuban American lobby does not give large sums

---

22. This is an example of a larger phenomenon known in the American politics literature as an "iron triangle": the mutual dependence that arises among members of Congress, interest groups, and government agencies.

of money relative to big economic interest groups like companies, labor unions, and professional organizations. When representatives of this lobby go to Washington, they primarily remind politicians that 1 million Cuban Americans care enough about U.S. policy toward Cuba that they vote on the basis of that issue. Moreover, these voters are concentrated in Florida—a crucial state in U.S. presidential elections, where a margin of only 500 votes swung the 2000 election to George W. Bush. By contrast, most other voters pay little attention to this issue and do not base their votes on it. Hence, when representatives of the Cuban American or pro-Israel lobby say "this is an issue our voters care about," politicians tend to listen.

Although our discussion suggests that it is possible in theory for relatively small interest groups to influence government policy in their preferred direction, to what extent does this influence actually take place? Giving a definitive answer is difficult because any connection between interest groups and foreign policy decision-making is often hard to observe directly. One should not commit the fallacy of assuming that because a policy decision benefits a particular group, the policy must have been enacted in order to benefit that group. For example, just because Halliburton benefited from the invasion of Iraq, we cannot automatically infer that the company actively lobbied for the invasion or that the Bush administration chose to invade in order to benefit the company.

The evidentiary challenge here is significant. For most foreign policy decisions that one might suspect were made to serve a narrow interest, there are alternative arguments based on national interests. Hobson's theory of nineteenth-century imperialism has been disputed by other scholars who argue that imperialism was a product of military-strategic competition among the principal powers.[23] U.S. interventions in Latin America during the Cold War were part of a larger pattern in which the United States sought to undermine communist regimes or prevent the spread of communism—sometimes in countries in which U.S. investors had no significant assets. Thus, scholars debate whether the United States overthrew Arbenz in order to protect United Fruit's interests or to prevent Guatemala from becoming a Soviet ally.[24] The Bush administration argued for war with Iraq as a response to that country's alleged nuclear, chemical, and biological weapons programs and its possible ties to international terrorism; when those allegations were shown to be unfounded, the revised justification turned on the need to promote democracy in the Middle East—a region whose stability serves a variety of possible interests. In short, it can be very difficult to accurately determine whether national interest justifications reflect genuine motivations or serve as a smokescreen to conceal a more cynical agenda.

HOW DO DOMESTIC INTERESTS AFFECT INTERNATIONAL BARGAINING?

We have seen that it may be possible for hawkish actors to push a state's foreign policy in a direction that suits their interests. How does the influence of such actors

---

23. See, for example, Benjamin J. Cohen, *The Question of Imperialism* (London: MacMillan, 1974).
24. For an argument against the interest group interpretation of these cases, see Stephen D. Krasner, *Defending the National Interest* (Princeton, NJ: Princeton University Press, 1978), esp. chap. 8.

affect the likelihood of war? The general answer is that domestic interests affect the likelihood of international conflict primarily by determining the extent of the state's ambitions. By influencing the costs and benefits of conflict, such interests can widen or narrow the scope of goods over which the state's leaders might be willing to wage war; they affect when and how often the state's foreign policy interests will come into conflict with those of other states; they determine the size of the demands that the state will make and the risks that it is willing to run. In short, variation in the nature of domestic interests that influence policy-making will increase or decrease the opportunities for conflict. Except in rare circumstances, however, these interests will not be sufficient to cause war in any given interaction. Thus, the influence of hawkish interests gives states more things to consider worth fighting over, but they are generally not sufficient to explain why bargaining over those goods fails in some cases but not in others.

To illustrate this point, we return in Figure 4.5 to the bargaining model introduced Chapter 3 and ask what would happen if the interests of State A changed in response to the influence of hawkish actors. For example, imagine that the object in dispute is a piece of territory with oil in it. In the interaction depicted in (a), the government in State A is led by a party whose core supporters are pacifists and environmentalists. As a result, the government considers the costs of war over this territory to be rather high; we let a_D denote the cost of war in the eyes of a dovish government. Recall that this term measures the costs of war relative to value of the good in dispute, so it is large when the human and economic costs of war loom large and/or when the benefit associated with possessing the territory is low.

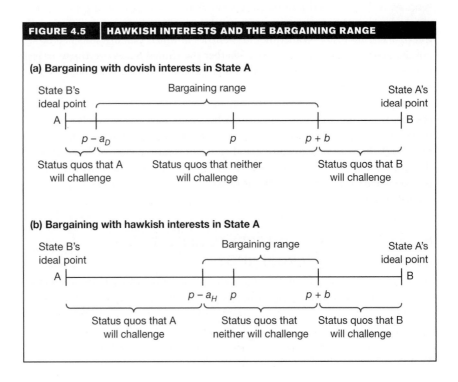

FIGURE 4.5 | HAWKISH INTERESTS AND THE BARGAINING RANGE

(a) Bargaining with dovish interests in State A

State B's ideal point — Bargaining range — State A's ideal point

$p - a_D$ p $p + b$

Status quos that A will challenge   Status quos that neither will challenge   Status quos that B will challenge

(b) Bargaining with hawkish interests in State A

State B's ideal point — Bargaining range — State A's ideal point

$p - a_H$ p $p + b$

Status quos that A will challenge   Status quos that neither will challenge   Status quos that B will challenge

Because the dovish interests that control the state see war as very unattractive, they are highly unlikely to start a crisis over this territory. Only if the status quo distribution of the territory is located at the far left of the line—very far from State A's ideal point—would the government in A see any potential benefit from sparking a crisis.

What happens to the international interaction if the dovish leader in State A is replaced by a leader of a party that draws support from oil companies who would profit from State A's control of the territory? Because of the influence of these actors, the new leader places more weight on the value of the land and less on the costs of war. In terms of our model, the costs of war relative to the value of the good are smaller. Let a_H denote the costs of war in the eyes of this hawkish government. Since the costs of war have gone down, A's value for war shifts to the right, as shown in (b). Notice two things about this panel. First, status quo distributions that would have been tolerated by the dovish leader are unacceptable to the hawk. As a result, State A becomes more likely to initiate a crisis, and it will make larger demands on its adversary. Second, even after this shift, a bargaining range still exists. As before, the costs of war ensure the existence of a set of mutually acceptable bargains.

This means that absent the information, commitment, or divisibility problems discussed in Chapter 3, there is no reason why the shift from (a) to (b) should, on its own, lead to a war. However, the shift does create a danger of war that did not exist before. The new government in State A is more willing to threaten force to change the status quo. The change in governance increases the state's demands and creates a risk of conflict where none previously existed. Whether or not this potential conflict will lead to an actual war depends on features of the bargaining interaction, such as how information is distributed and whether the states can credibly commit to live by any deal they reach.

The one exception to this claim would arise if there are actors who derive benefits from war that cannot be part of a negotiated settlement, as in the case of diversionary conflict. For example, assume that the leader of State A represents arms manufacturers. If there is a war, they get paid to build weapons and to replace those that are destroyed. Since they get these profits only if there is a war, then it is peace, rather than war, that these actors find costly. Would the influence of such interests change the above logic? As we saw when considering the diversionary incentive, the answer is yes—but only if the net benefits from war are high enough to offset *both* states' costs of war.

Hence, except in rare circumstances, the influence of groups within the state that place high value on the goods that can be acquired through force and/or see little cost to war does not itself ensure that war will happen. When such interests hold sway, they will make the state's foreign policy more belligerent, in the sense that it will make larger demands and come into conflict with more states, but such interests alone are not sufficient to cause war in the absence of the strategic dilemmas discussed in Chapter 3. Thus, when we think about how oil interests influence U.S. policy in the Middle East, it is reasonable to say that oil interests explain why there are issues in the region that American leaders are willing to fight over. It is harder to argue that these interests alone explain why crises over these issues sometimes become wars.

Why Don't Democracies Fight One Another?

At the outset of the chapter, we noted the dramatic turn in relations between the United States and Great Britain at the turn of the twentieth century—a change that coincided with political reforms that made both countries more democratic. The pattern is not unique to this case. For example, France and Germany were bitter rivals during the nineteenth and early twentieth centuries. France resisted the creation of a unified German state in 1870, and the two countries fought three major wars since then: the Franco-Prussian War, World War I, and World War II. Today, however, France and Germany are close friends and allies; it is almost unthinkable that there could be another war between them. As in the U.S.-British case, a turning point in relations between France and Germany came when Allied powers occupied what was then West Germany following World War II, eradicated the vestiges of Nazi rule, and established a democratic constitution.

Far from being isolated examples, these cases are part of a larger phenomenon that scholars and policymakers refer to as the **democratic peace**. The term refers to a well-established observation that there are few, if any, clear cases of war between mature democratic states. Our choice of words reflects some caveats about this observation. We say "few, if any, clear cases of war" because the strength of the claim depends in part on how one defines democracy and what events one considers wars. Since there are some ambiguous cases, there is not a universal consensus on whether wars between democratic states are nonexistent or simply rare.[25] We say "mature democracy" because some studies have suggested that countries in the process of becoming democracies do not fit this overall pattern.[26] Even taking these qualifications into account, this is still a remarkable observation: over the 200 or so years in which democracies have existed in their modern form, they seem not to have engaged in war with one another—or, at least, they have done so less frequently than we might expect given the overall frequency of war.

Another noteworthy aspect of this observation is that democracies are not, overall, less war-prone than other kinds of states. That is, while they rarely, if ever, fight wars against other democratic states, their overall rate of war participation is roughly the same as that of nondemocratic states.[27] This means that although democracies seldom find themselves at war with one another, they are more frequently at war with nondemocratic states. Hence, there is something special about the relationship between democracies that does not carry over to their relationships with other kinds of states.

---

25. For a discussion of the democratic peace finding, definitional issues, and some cases that raise questions, see Bruce Russett, *Grasping the Democratic Peace* (Princeton, NJ: Princeton University Press, 1993): chap. 1.
26. Edward D. Mansfield and Jack Snyder, *Electing to Fight: Why Emerging Democracies Go to War* (Cambridge, MA: MIT Press, 2005).
27. Although there has been some controversy over the issue, this statement reflects the general consensus in the literature. See, for example, Nils Peter Gleditsch and Havard Hegre, "Peace and Democracy: Three Levels of Analysis," *Journal of Conflict Resolution* 41 (1997): 283–310.

This observation is so striking and important that it has entered into policy discussions in the United States and elsewhere. In his 1994 State of the Union address, President Clinton cited the democratic peace in arguing for a foreign policy of promoting democracy abroad: "Ultimately, the best strategy to ensure our security and to build a durable peace is to support the advance of democracy elsewhere. Democracies don't attack each other."[28] Similarly, President George W. Bush argued that democracy promotion should be a central aspect of American policy in the Middle East because "democracies don't go to war with each other."[29] This interest in democratic peace has been particularly salient in recent decades, which have seen a remarkable growth in the number of democracies worldwide, as Figure 4.6 shows (p. 166).

Is this absence of wars among democracies a coincidence, or is there something about democratic institutions that facilitates peaceful relations among states that have them? In what ways might shared democracy influence the calculus of war and peace that we have developed here?

WHAT IS DEMOCRACY?

To answer these questions, we turn to the third leg of our framework: institutions. Domestic institutions determine the rules of political decision-making within the state. They govern the relationship between the leadership and the people, and they help determine the extent to which citizens' interests matter when it comes to war and peace. Although there are many different kinds of political systems, the distinction that has attracted the most attention is that between democratic and nondemocratic, or autocratic, systems. A **democracy** is a political system in which candidates compete for political office through frequent, fair elections in which a sizable portion of the adult population can vote. This definition encompasses two major aspects of democracy: contestation, or the ability of different individuals and groups to compete for political office; and participation, or the ability of a large portion of the country to be involved in the selection process through voting. The mechanism of choosing leaders through election also rules out alternative paths to power, such as hereditary succession. Countries that fall short of this definition have tight restrictions on who can compete for political office, or they greatly restrict the number of people who have any effective say over the selection process.

democracy: A political system in which candidates compete for political office through frequent, fair elections in which a sizable portion of the adult population can vote.

Another term that often accompanies democracy is *liberal,* which we use here in its classic sense to refer to a philosophy that emphasizes the value of individual liberty. Most modern democracies are also liberal democracies because, in addition to allowing competition and voting, they have numerous protections of individuals' civil and political rights, such as rights to free speech, religion, political association, and a free press. Hence, liberal democracies not only choose their leaders by democratic means, but they also impose restrictions on what those elected governments can do by giving citizens rights that cannot be transgressed. We should note

---

28. William Clinton, "1994 State of the Union Address."
29. Office of the Press Secretary, "President and Prime Minister Blair Discussed Iraq, Middle East," White House Press Conference, November 12, 2004, www.whitehouse.gov/news/releases/2004/11/20041112-5.html (accessed 11/19/07).

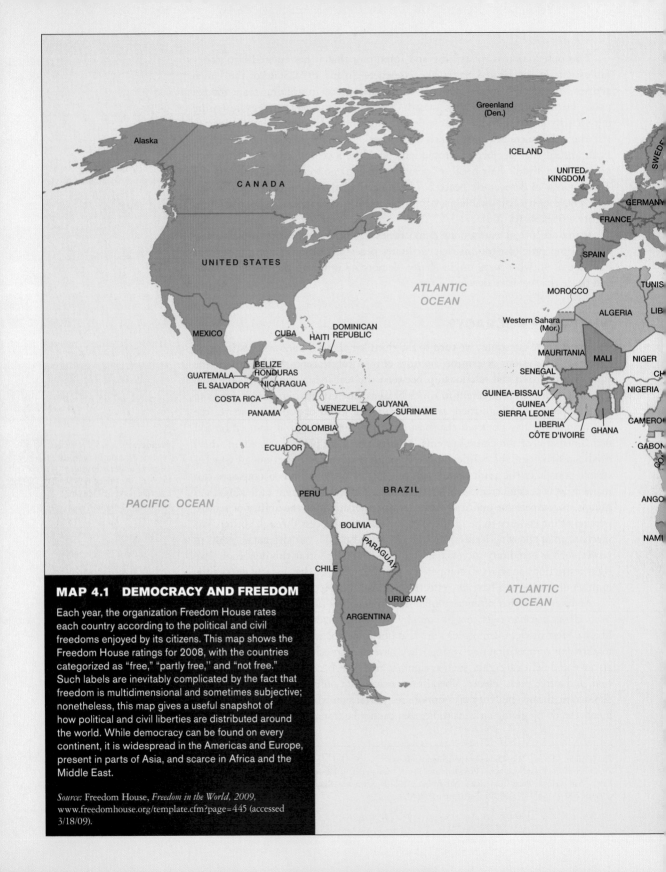

Greenland
(Den.)

ICELAND

Alaska

CANADA

UNITED
KINGDOM

SWED-

GERMANY

FRANCE

SPAIN

UNITED STATES

ATLANTIC
OCEAN

MOROCCO

TUNIS

ALGERIA

LIB

Western Sahara
(Mor.)

MEXICO

CUBA

HAITI

DOMINICAN
REPUBLIC

MAURITANIA

MALI

NIGER

BELIZE
HONDURAS

SENEGAL

CH

GUATEMALA
EL SALVADOR

NICARAGUA

GUINEA-BISSAU

NIGERIA

COSTA RICA

GUINEA
SIERRA LEONE

PANAMA

VENEZUELA

GUYANA
SURINAME

LIBERIA
CÔTE D'IVOIRE

GHANA

CAMERO

COLOMBIA

GABON

ECUADOR

CO

PERU

BRAZIL

ANGO

PACIFIC OCEAN

BOLIVIA

NAMI

PARAGUAY

CHILE

ATLANTIC
OCEAN

URUGUAY

ARGENTINA

MAP 4.1 DEMOCRACY AND FREEDOM

Each year, the organization Freedom House rates
each country according to the political and civil
freedoms enjoyed by its citizens. This map shows the
Freedom House ratings for 2008, with the countries
categorized as "free," "partly free," and "not free."
Such labels are inevitably complicated by the fact that
freedom is multidimensional and sometimes subjective;
nonetheless, this map gives a useful snapshot of
how political and civil liberties are distributed around
the world. While democracy can be found on every
continent, it is widespread in the Americas and Europe,
present in parts of Asia, and scarce in Africa and the
Middle East.

Source: Freedom House, *Freedom in the World, 2009,*
www.freedomhouse.org/template.cfm?page=445 (accessed
3/18/09).

ARCTIC OCEAN

RUSSIAN FEDERATION

KAZAKHSTAN

MONGOLIA

UZBEKISTAN
TURKMENISTAN
KYRGYZSTAN
TAJIKISTAN

N. KOREA
S. KOREA
JAPAN

TURKEY
SYRIA
RAEL
IRAQ
GYPT
KUWAIT
SAUDI
ARABIA
IRAN
AFGHANISTAN
Kashmir

CHINA

PACIFIC OCEAN

PAKISTAN

NEPAL

BANGLADESH

INDIA

MYANMAR
(BURMA)

VIETNAM

TAIWAN

OMAN

YEMEN

THAILAND

CAMBODIA

PHILIPPINES

SUDAN

SRI
LANKA

TRAL
ICAN
ETHIOPIA

SOMALIA

UGANDA
KENYA

MALAYSIA

TANZANIA

GO

INDONESIA

PAPUA
NEW
GUINEA

INDIAN OCEAN

BIA
MALAWI

MADAGASCAR

EAST
TIMOR

BABWE
WANA

AUSTRALIA

TH
CA
MOZAMBIQUE

NEW
ZEALAND

Free
Partly Free
Not Free

that not all democratic countries are liberal, as some have restrictions on religious or press freedoms, or they give rights to ethnic or religious groups at the expense of individual rights. Map 4.1 shows how countries were judged, in 2008, in terms of the political and civil freedoms they offered their citizens.

With these definitions in place, we turn to the central question: how could democracies be different when it comes to war and peace? Not surprisingly, the democratic peace observation has generated a great deal of scholarly interest in this question, and there is no single, settled answer. But the framework of this book suggests two broad ways in which domestic institutions can affect the likelihood of war: either by influencing the interests of states and their leaders, or by influencing the bargaining interaction between and among countries.

REPRESENTATION, ACCOUNTABILITY, AND INTERESTS IN WAR AND PEACE

A common argument for the distinctiveness of democracy is rooted in the idea that domestic institutions shape leaders' interests in war and peace. This argument starts with the observation that the costs of war are paid by society at large but generally not by the leader who makes the decision to wage war. It is the people who lose lives or loved ones on the battlefield, who suffer the economic hardship of wars, and who may have to pay higher taxes to support a war effort. The leader, by contrast, rarely has such direct exposure to the costs of war. This disjuncture between the ruler and the ruled was humorously illustrated in the 2001 movie *Shrek,* when the evil Prince Farquaad tells his knights that he is going to send them on a mission to rescue from a fire-breathing dragon a princess whom he wants to marry. Exhorting his men to combat, the prince declares, "Some of you may die, but it's a sacrifice I am willing to make."

Over 200 years before this scene was digitally animated, the German philosopher Immanuel Kant noted a similar dilemma. Kant wrote in the late eighteenth century, when most countries were ruled by monarchs. For such rulers, he noted, "the easiest thing in the world to do is to declare war." Kant reasoned:

> war does not affect [the ruler's] table, his hunt, his places of pleasure, his court festivals, and so on. Thus, he can decide to go to war for the most meaningless of reasons, as if it were a kind of pleasure party, and he can blithely leave its justification (which decency requires) to his diplomatic corps, who are always prepared for such exercises.[30]

In other words, a basic problem in such political systems was that the interests of the ruler and the ruled were not aligned: the former enjoyed the benefit of war, while the latter paid its costs. In Kant's view, the solution to this problem was to establish a representative government, one in which the ruler would be accountable

---

30. Immanuel Kant, "To Perpetual Peace: A Philosophical Sketch," in *Perpetual Peace and Other Essays on Politics, History, and Morals* (Indianapolis, IN: Hackett, 1983), 113.

to the people: if "the consent of the citizenry is required in order to determine whether or not there will be war, it is natural that they consider all its calamities before committing themselves to so risky a game."[31] In this view, political institutions that foster representation would serve to align the interests of the ruler and the ruled, making those with the power to decide on war sensitive to the costs their decisions impose on others.

There are two ways in which representative institutions, such as elections, could put a brake on the decision to go to war. The first mechanism, which Kant envisaged, was that the people, through their elected representatives, would share in the decision to go to war. That is, the issue of war would be openly debated, the costs and benefits weighed, and the country would only commit to war once the people, through their representatives, gave their consent. In this way, the decision to wage war would be made cautiously, with widespread input from those who would bear the costs, rather than at the whim of an individual leader. Generalizing this point in light of our earlier discussion, electoral institutions make it easier for individual voters to make their collective voice heard and thereby weaken the influence of small groups who see concentrated benefits, but few costs, from waging war.

A second mechanism that comes with representation and elections is **accountability**: the ability to punish or reward leaders for their decisions. Even if political leaders do not directly bear the costs of war, they can be punished politically if they lead the country into a failed or costly venture. Elections, in this view, provide a rather simple mechanism for people to impose these punishments, and leaders who are subject to frequent and fair elections have to take such risks into account. By contrast, removing a leader in a nondemocratic system generally requires risky actions, such as participating in a revolution or a coup, making it harder for average citizens to oust such leaders. As a result, nondemocratic leaders are often politically, as well as personally, insulated from their policy failures and thus from the costs of war.

In this view, then, democracies are different because their leaders face systematically higher costs from war than do nondemocratic leaders. Holding equal the probability of victory in war, a democratic leader values war less than the nondemocratic leader because the political implications of losing are worse. Holding equal the human and material costs of war, a democratic leader values war less because that leader is more likely to be held accountable for those costs.

Although this logic is compelling, we must point out that losing office is not the worst or only consequence of losing a war. When democratic leaders lose an election, they can generally retire in good comfort, collect their pension, perhaps go on the lecture circuit, and even continue to participate in politics if they want. Nondemocratic leaders, by contrast, often find that life after losing office is not so pleasant. Because their removal often occurs through violent means, such as a coup or revolution, nondemocratic leaders often suffer additional punishment above and beyond simply losing office. For the Russian tsar in 1917, the disastrous showing in World War I not only contributed to his removal from office, but he and his family were executed at the hands of the revolutionaries. The German emperor similarly

accountability: The ability to punish or reward leaders for the decisions they make, as when frequent fair elections enable voters to hold elected officials responsible for their actions by granting or withholding access to political office.

31. Ibid.

In nondemocratic states, like North Korea, a small group of leaders typically makes foreign policy behind closed doors, often limiting what can be reported to the media and the public. This lack of transparency can make it harder for foreign states to gauge the state's capabilities and resolve.

faced popular uprisings in the wake of his country's defeat in that war, prompting him to abdicate his throne and flee into exile. And the leader of the military junta that led Argentina into the Falklands War was later tried for mishandling the war and spent five years in prison. Indeed, death, exile, and imprisonment are common punishments meted out to autocratic leaders who run afoul of their people. This suggests that the relationship between the political institutions and the costs of losing a war may not be as straightforward as the Kantian logic suggests. (For more on this point, see "What Do We Know?" on p. 145.)

How would this argument about accountability explain the democratic peace? If in fact war is costlier for democratic leaders, this could influence the likelihood of war in several ways. As we saw, an increase in the costs of war diminishes a state's willingness to contest the status quo, reducing the opportunities for conflict. If there are fewer things that a state is willing to fight for, the scope for it to come into violent conflict with other states decreases. Moreover, the logic of political accountability suggests that democratic leaders should be more selective about starting wars—that is, they should be willing to wage war when their chances of victory are sufficiently high. Leaders in nondemocratic political systems may be more willing to gamble on wars in which they have a low chance of winning. This logic would lower the probability of war between two democratic states because in such interactions it is unlikely that both leaders would simultaneously judge their chances in war to be high enough.[32]

But how could this argument explain the fact that, overall, democratic states are just as war-prone as other states, meaning that they are particularly likely to fight wars against nondemocracies? A possible answer lies in the observation that constraints on the use of force can make democratic states appear to be tempting targets to their nondemocratic foes. Recall how Saddam Hussein dismissed U.S. deterrent threats prior to the Persian Gulf War: "Yours is a society which cannot accept 10,000 dead in one battle." Although he does not say so explicitly, this statement seems to reflect a sense that American leaders would find war politically too costly to fight. This belief made Hussein more likely to resist U.S. efforts to coerce him out of Kuwait. Similarly, Japanese leaders who decided to bomb Pearl Harbor in 1941 did so in part under the mistaken impression that the American public would respond by opposing a war and would therefore constrain President Franklin Roosevelt's ability to respond. In this view, the constraints that make democracies peaceful in their relations with one another can have the opposite effect when democracies square off against less constrained adversaries, who may seek to exploit democracies by making larger demands and discounting their threats, thereby increasing the risk of war.

---

32. See Bruce Bueno de Mesquita, James D. Morrow, Randolph M. Siverson, and Alastair Smith, "An Institutional Explanation for the Democratic Peace," *American Political Science Review* 93 (December 1999): 791–807.

DEMOCRACY AND THE BARGAINING INTERACTION

Another view of democracy focuses on how institutions influence bargaining interactions between states and, particularly, their ability to solve the information and commitment problems that can cause war. Recall from Chapter 3 that states may fail to find mutually beneficial bargains if they have incomplete information about the military and political factors that determine their value for war. Resolving this informational problem is not trivial because the strategic context of a crisis generates incentives for states to conceal or misrepresent their information in the hopes of getting a better deal. Could domestic institutions help solve this problem and thereby lessen the danger of war?

There are several reasons to think that democratic institutions and processes do make it easier to overcome informational problems. First, democratic political systems are much more transparent than nondemocratic systems because democratic processes are more open and observable. For example, major policy decisions are frequently subject to public and/or legislative debate. A relatively unfettered press can disseminate information about what decisionmakers are thinking, the level of popular support for war, and even details about the state's military capabilities. Opposition parties can freely voice approval or dissent from the government's actions, thereby revealing the strength (or weakness) of the government's political support within the country. Such practices exist primarily to ensure that the public can scrutinize what its leaders are doing—an essential element of democratic accountability. An inevitable by-product of such openness is that foreign states can also glean relevant information about a democratic state's capabilities and resolve. This is not to suggest that democratic states hide nothing—either from their own people or from outside eyes. Rather, the point is that democratic states are *relatively* more transparent than most nondemocratic systems, in which decision-making occurs without broad participation, there are restrictions on what can be reported in the media, opposition groups are actively suppressed, and disagreements within the governing group are rarely aired in public. Thus, it is reasonable to expect that all other things being equal, there is less uncertainty about the capabilities and resolve of democratic states.[33]

Another argument about the informational effects of democracy addresses the ability of states to send credible signals in crises. Recall from Chapter 3 that when states have private information, communicating their resolve in a credible manner often requires that they take costly actions—actions that a resolute state would be willing to take but an irresolute one would not. One way in which they can do so is by making statements or taking actions from which it would be difficult to back down. As we saw, such threats are costly if leaders expect to lose

In contrast, policy making in democratic states, like Germany, often involves public and legislative debate, resulting in a more open and observable process. This greater transparency makes it easier for other states to accurately assess the democratic state's capabilities and resolve.

---

33. Kenneth A. Schultz, *Democracy and Coercive Diplomacy* (Cambridge: Cambridge University Press, 2001).

domestic political support for failing to follow through on them. A recent study of U.S. public opinion demonstrates this effect. One group of survey respondents was presented with a hypothetical scenario in which a president threatened to defend another country from invasion and then failed to do so. Another group was presented with a similar scenario in which the president failed to defend another country but had never threatened to do so. When asked to assess the president's actions, respondents in the first group gave the president a lower approval rating than those in the second—a result that is consistent with the idea that it is politically costly to back down from a threat.[34]

If backing down creates public disapproval, then there is reason to think that democracy magnifies the political importance of this effect. Mechanisms of accountability mean that public disapproval is more likely to result in some kind of punishment for the democratic leader, in the form of either diminished support for his agenda or a greater chance of losing office at the next election. Nondemocratic leaders, by contrast, are more politically insulated from whatever disapproval their actions might engender. If so, then public threats of democratic leaders are more informative because they are costlier to make. This suggests that institutions of accountability make it easier for democratic leaders to credibly communicate their resolve and thereby overcome problems associated with incomplete information.[35]

A related argument holds that transparency can reduce the risk of preemptive wars between democracies. As we saw Chapter 3, preemptive wars occur when each side fears that the other can deliver a potent first strike. While first-strike advantages are partly a product of military technology, they can also arise when states have the ability to prepare for attack in secret, so as to gain strategic surprise. However, if each state knows that the other faces large costs from attacking, and neither can mobilize its forces in secret, then each may be sufficiently reassured that there is no need to act preemptively. If so, the commitment to refrain from attacking is made credible by the knowledge that neither state can effectively renege on that promise.[36]

DOMESTIC INSTITUTIONS OR STRATEGIC INTERESTS?

The preceding arguments all suggest a causal connection between democratic institutions and the peace that has prevailed among states that possess them. It is possible, however, that democracy is not responsible for the democratic peace. For example, perhaps some other factor both causes states to become democratic and causes them not to fight. In this case, the relationship between democracy and

---

34. Michael Tomz, "Domestic Audience Costs in International Relations: An Experimental Approach," *International Organization* 61, no. 4 (Fall 2007): 821–40.
35. There is some controversy over whether democracies are really special in this respect or whether some kinds of autocrats may also be able to tie their hands by invoking audience costs. See Jessica Weeks, "Autocratic Audience Costs: Regime Type and Signaling Resolve," *International Organization* 62 (Winter 2008): 35–64.
36. Russet, *Grasping the Democratic Peace,* 38–40. See also Bruce Bueno de Mesquita and David Lalman, *War and Reason: Domestic and International Imperatives* (New Haven, CT: Yale University Press, 1992), chap. 4.

peace could be a product of the fact that both democracy and peace share a common cause. What could this common cause be? It is sometimes argued that economic development accounts for the democratic peace. Democracy does tend to go hand in hand with economic development: it generally emerges and endures only in countries that are relatively wealthy. In poorer countries, by contrast, democratic institutions are more likely to break down. There is less evidence to suggest, however, that wealth alone promotes peace between countries. Hence, it is unlikely that what appears to be a democratic peace is actually a peace among rich countries.

A more plausible alternative argument is that historically the main democratic states have had relatively similar interests. From the late nineteenth century on, the main democratic countries were united against common threats, first against Germany and then against the Soviet Union. During the Cold War, most democracies had similar strategic interests due to a common perceived threat from the Soviet Union and the communist bloc (see Chapter 5). Such common interests reduced the opportunities for conflict between democratic states and provided a strong incentive to resolve peacefully any conflicts that did arise. In addition to fighting with each other less often, democratic states in these periods also tended to form alliances with each other—an indication that they perceived common strategic interests.[37]

Could such common interests, and not shared democracy, account for the democratic peace? The verdict is mixed. On the one hand, evidence suggests that the democratic peace is a relatively recent phenomenon whose onset dates to the late nineteenth or early twentieth century. Although there are no clear cases of war between democratic states in the nineteenth century, there were also very few democracies at that time. Given that war itself is a very rare phenomenon, it may not be surprising that there were no wars between democracies in this period. Moreover, democratic states in the nineteenth century did experience a relatively high number of militarized disputes short of war, as the main democratic countries—Great Britain, France, and the United States—clashed frequently over colonial holdings. This suggests that the democratic peace effect emerged with the rise of the common enemies at the turn of the twentieth century. On the other hand, one has to ask if it was purely coincidence that the democratic states found themselves united first against Germany and then against the Soviet Union. Did these common threat perceptions arise by chance, or did something about these countries' political systems lead them to see each other as natural allies rather than as threats? One could argue that the constraints operating on these states, as well as their relative transparency, made them less threatening to one another, particularly when compared to the closed and relatively unconstrained autocratic rivals.[38]

In short, the democratic peace raises tantalizing questions for both scholars and policymakers, and we are likely to be debating this issue for some time.

---

37. Joanne Gowa, *Ballots and Bullets: The Elusive Democratic Peace* (Princeton, NJ: Princeton University Press, 1999).
38. David Lake, "Powerful Pacifists: Democratic States and War," *American Political Science Review* 86 (March 1992): 24–37.

The Kargil War and the Limits of Democratic Peace

In April and May 1999, Pakistani military forces infiltrated across the Line of Control (LoC) that separates the Pakistani- and Indian-controlled areas of the disputed Kashmir region. When the incursion was discovered, India mobilized 200,000 troops to repel the attack. Over the next several weeks, the two countries fought a war in the high mountains near the town of Kargil, a war that ended when Pakistan agreed to withdraw behind the LoC. At least 1,000 soldiers died in the combat.

In one respect, the Kargil War was not a particularly surprising event: India and Pakistan had already fought three wars since their independence in 1948, and there had been frequent clashes along the LoC for years. In another respect, however, the Kargil War was quite unusual: at the time of this event, both countries had democratically elected governments. The Kargil War thus represents an exception to the general pattern of peace between democratic states.[a] Why did two democracies go to war in this case?

There are several possible answers. One line of argument focuses on the role of religious differences in fueling the conflict. When the Indian subcontinent became independent in 1947, it was partitioned into two new states largely on the basis of religion: the secular but Hindu-dominated India, and the Islamic Republic of Pakistan. The partition not only created two states with different prevailing religions, but it also generated tremendous bloodshed and a legacy of conflict. Not surprisingly, there is a great deal of enmity between not just the governments but also the people in these states.

Given this history, it is easy to see why democratic institutions might not prevent conflict in this relationship. If democracy influences foreign policy by making leaders accountable to the preferences of voters, then democracy acts as a brake on war only if those voters are themselves against war. In the Kargil case, the war was popular with people on both sides. In India, success in the war revived the political fortunes of a government that was on the verge of electoral defeat; in Pakistan, people were disappointed only that their country did not prevail.

Another important factor is the influence of the military in Pakistan. The military is very powerful in Pakistani politics and has on several occasions ousted civilian leaders that it did not like. The historical experience suggests that Pakistani leaders have more to fear from the military than from voters. Indeed, shortly after the Kargil War, the democratically elected prime minister, Nawaz Sharif, was deposed and replaced by the army's chief of staff, General Pervez Musharraf.

Although there are many unknowns about Pakistan's decision-making in the lead-up to the war, there is good reason to believe that Musharraf and the military manipulated Sharif into starting a war he did not fully understand.[b] For some time, Muslim Kashmiris had been engaged in a low-level insurgency against Indian military forces and government figures in Kashmir. Pakistan supported these insurgents with training, money, and arms. When India accused Pakistan of crossing the LoC in May 1999, Sharif claimed that the invaders were local Kashmiris operating on their own initiative, without support of the Pakistani military. This was a cover story that Pakistan had used in previous wars as well. In this case, however, the evidence suggests that Sharif actually believed the cover story. Sharif and others claim that when he was briefed on the plan, no mention was made of the fact that Pakistani forces would cross the LoC in large numbers. Some of the former prime minister's denials may be an attempt to deflect blame for a policy that eventually failed, but nonetheless it seems clear that he did not understand the full scope of the operation and that military secrecy led to inadequate civilian control. There also seems to have been little civilian oversight of the diplomatic ramifications of the operation. Pakistan's Foreign Office was not alerted or consulted on how India and the rest of the world might react.

In sum, the Kargil War suggests an important amendment to theories of democratic peace. For democracy to prevent international conflict, elected leaders must have knowledge of and control over the state's military actions. If decisions about when and how to start a war rest with the military, then the accountability of civilian leaders is largely irrelevant. ■

a. For a discussion of how this case is judged as a war between democracies, see Scott Sagan, "Introduction: Inside Nuclear South Asia," in Sagan (ed.), *Inside Nuclear South Asia* (Stanford, CA: Stanford University Press, 2009).

b. This discussion is based on Owen Bennett Jones, *Pakistan: Eye of the Storm* (New Haven, CT: Yale University Press, 2003), 87–109.

Conclusion: What If All the World Were Democratic?

When diplomats and state leaders come to the bargaining table with one another, they inevitably bring a great deal of baggage from their home countries. The interests that state representatives advance in international negotiations are themselves a function of interests, interactions, and institutions within the state. Political leaders may care about what is best for their country, but they also care about staying in office. As a result, they must think about how their foreign policy choices will impact the interests of important domestic constituents such as the military, organized interest groups, and, in some cases, the general public. When these actors have a stake in the outcome of international bargaining, and when they have the strategic and/or institutional resources to punish or reward the leader, then their interests will be represented at the bargaining table. In particular, when groups with hawkish interests have superior organization and resources, they can push the state toward greater international ambition, with a greater attendant risk of war. As we have seen, there are times when military organizations and economic or ethnic interest groups have both the interests and the ability to push foreign policy in such a direction.

In contrast, when interactions and institutions empower those who bear the costs of war, they can exert a pacifying effect at the international level. Economic actors who benefit from international commerce and investment may lobby for peaceful relations with profitable partners. Representative institutions give voice to the people who bear the costs of war, thereby weakening the influence of concentrated interests who might promote conflict for their own reasons. Free, fair, and frequent elections provide a relatively low-cost mechanism for people to punish leaders who engage in failed or costly wars. The relative openness and transparency of democratic political processes can reduce informational and commitment problems that can cause bargaining to fail. Although these features may make democracies tempting targets for autocratic foes, they also help account for the relative rarity of war among democratic states.

Does this mean that a world full of democratic states would be a world without war? Certainly, the evidence to date is encouraging, although not definitive. There are at least two reasons to be cautious. First, although the number of democracies in the world has generally increased over time, the spread of democracy has experienced reversals. As Figure 4.6 shows, there have been several periods in which democracy has broken down, particularly in the 1930s and 1970s. During these periods, economic and international upheaval caused some democratic systems to fail. It is worth remembering that Adolf Hitler came to power in Germany through relatively democratic institutions—which he then subverted before embarking on his campaign of foreign expansion. Hence, democratic systems have given birth to forces that undermined democracy and engaged in aggressive foreign policies. Even if there are no cases of war between two democratic states, there have been wars between democracies and states that were once democratic.

FIGURE 4.6 | THE SPREAD OF DEMOCRACY, 1810–2007

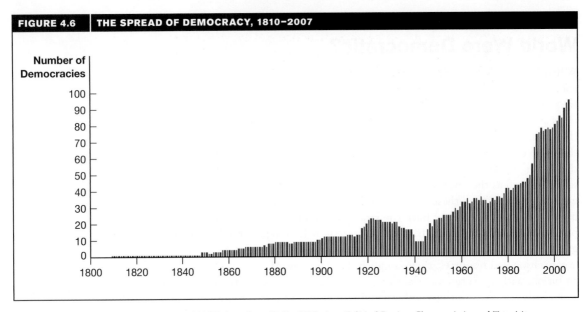

Number of Democracies

Source: Monty G. Marshall, Keith Jaggers, and Ted Robert Gurr, "Polity IV Project: Political Regime Characteristics and Transitions, 1800–2007," www.systemicpeace.org/polity/polity4.htm (acccessed 3/24/09).

A second reason for caution centers on the interests that will come to be represented by the spread of democracy. Most of the original democratic states were also liberal, in the sense that they enshrined policies and ideologies that emphasized the value of individuals rather than groups. Not all democratic countries are liberal, however, as some are built on ethnic or religious group identities that can foster conflict with other nations.[39] For example, the rivalry between India and Pakistan is fueled by religious differences and historical hatreds. In spite of the fact that both countries have been democratic in some periods, there is not much evidence that shared democracy has exercised a restraining effect on this rivalry. Indeed, India and Pakistan fought a war in 1999 when both were nominally democratic, an exception to the democratic peace that is discussed further in "What Shaped Our World?" on page 164.

Recall that democratic institutions make leaders more sensitive to the interests of the citizenry. Kant, and those who follow in his tradition, assumed that citizens are generally cautious, since it is they who bear the costs of war. But what if the public is motivated by nationalist, ethnocentric, or even genocidal ideas? In that case, accountability is likely to induce belligerence rather than caution, and leaders may fear domestic political retribution for being overly "soft" toward the nation's ethnic or religious enemies. The costs of war might,

---

39. See Fareed Zakaria, "The Rise of Illiberal Democracy," *Foreign Affairs* 76 (November/December 1997): 22–43.

as a result, be offset by the political costs of compromise. For example, imagine what would happen if Saudi Arabia became democratic. Would this increase or decrease the likelihood of conflict with democratic Israel? Would shared political institutions negate hostility fueled by conflicting religious views and historical hatreds? A strong argument could be made that democracy in a country like Saudi Arabia would enfranchise people who are, in general, even more hostile to Israel than are those in the current ruling family. Indeed, Saudi Arabia's relatively moderate stance toward Israel in recent years has been made possible precisely because the monarchy does *not* have to satisfy popular pressures. Hence, the international effects of democracy's spread may very well depend not only on the institutions that take root but also on the interests of those they empower.

Reviewing Interests, Interactions, and Institutions

INTERESTS	INTERACTIONS	INSTITUTIONS
States' foreign policy interests can derive from national interests that are shared by virtually everyone in the country or by particular interests of individuals or small groups.	Small groups often have an advantage over large groups in their ability to organize collectively and influence policy. As a result, small, organized interests can push governments to enact policies that benefit them at the expense of everyone else.	Democratic institutions make elected leaders accountable to people who pay the costs of war. This can weaken the influence of hawkish actors and make leaders more cautious about waging war.
Office-seeking politicians at times have an interest in sparking international crises to increase their hold on power. But losing a war can harm a leader's political and personal interests.	The military and economic or ethnic interest groups often enjoy superior organization, information, and resources relative to the general public.	Democratic institutions increase the transparency of the political process, which can help resolve information and commitment problems that sometimes lead to war.
The military's organizational interest in larger budgets and greater control can lead it to advocate more aggressive foreign policies.	The influence of hawkish actors generally does not, on its own, cause wars. Instead, these interests increase the state's demands on other states, creating more opportunities for conflict.	
Actors engaged in international trade and investment can have economic interests in undermining hostile governments and supporting countries with whom they do business.		

Key Terms

bureaucracy, p. 133

interest groups, p. 133

rally effect, p. 137

diversionary incentive, p. 139

military-industrial complex, p. 143

democratic peace, p. 154

democracy, p. 155

accountability, p. 159

For Further Reading

Allison, Graham, and Philip Zelikow. *Essence of Decision: Explaining the Cuban Missile Crisis,* 2nd ed. New York: Longman, 1999. Presents a classic study of the effects of bureaucratic politics on foreign policy-making in one of the most dramatic crises of the Cold War.

Doyle, Michael. "Liberalism and World Politics." *American Political Science Review* 80 (December 1986): 1151–69. Offers an influential discussion of how liberal political systems might affect foreign policy choices; this analysis brought the study of the democratic peace to the forefront of political science.

Feaver, Peter D., and Christopher Gelpi. *Choosing Your Battles: American Civil-Military Relations and the Use of Force.* Princeton, NJ: Princeton University Press, 2004. Presents a systematic study of how civilians and military officers differ in their views about the use of force.

Fordham, Benjamin. *Building the Cold War Consensus.* Ann Arbor: University of Michigan Press, 1998. Examines how different economic interests came together to underpin the United States' international commitments during the Cold War.

Gowa, Joanne. *Ballots and Bullets: The Elusive Democratic Peace.* Princeton, NJ: Princeton University Press, 1999. Offers a skeptical take on the democratic peace, arguing that strategic interests—and not democratic institutions—account for this observation.

Reiter, Dani, and Allan Stam. *Democracies at War.* Princeton, NJ: Princeton University Press, 2002. Carefully examines an unanticipated finding that grew out of the study of democracy and war: democracies tend to win the wars they fight.

Russett, Bruce, and James Oneal. *Triangulating Peace: Democracy, Interdependence, and International Organizations.* New York: Norton, 2001. Gives a comprehensive review and analysis of the effects of democracy, trade, and international institutions on violent conflict between states. Find review and study materials online at wwnorton.com/web/fls.

Snyder, Jack. *Myths of Empire: Domestic Politics and International Ambition.* Ithaca, NY: Cornell University Press, 1991. Explores how domestic interest groups and military organizations can push great powers to adopt expansionist foreign policies—often with disastrous consequences for the state as a whole.

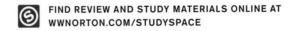

FIND REVIEW AND STUDY MATERIALS ONLINE AT WWNORTON.COM/STUDYSPACE

CHAPTER 5

International Institutions and War

Collective security organizations like the United Nations can influence interactions between adversaries in ways that promote peaceful outcomes. However, these institutions face significant challenges in achieving their goals, and they have a mixed record when it comes to preventing war and other violent conflicts. Here, the UN General Assembly convenes in 2006.

In a well-governed country, the police prevent and punish acts of violence between individuals. Where are the police in international politics? Why is it so hard for the international community to prevent and punish acts of aggression?

When North Korea invaded South Korea in June 1950, the United Nations responded by authorizing member states to use military force to resist this act of aggression. Although North Korea had some influential supporters, including the Soviet Union and China, a coalition of 20 nations led by the United States successfully expelled the North Koreans from South Korea by October 1950. At that point, the United Nations expanded the forces' mandate and pushed into North Korea. This act provoked China to intervene in order to save its ally, and the Korean War dragged on for another three years.

Around the same time, Chinese forces also invaded Tibet, which neighbors China on the west. China long claimed sovereignty over this vast, mountainous region, but Tibet had declared independence from China in 1911. Although China never recognized this declaration, Tibet was in practice an independent state for the next several decades as China, distracted by civil war and the Japanese invasion in the 1930s, was unable to resist. Not long after the Communists gained control of mainland China in 1949, they sought to reassert the country's historic claim over Tibet. Units of the People's Liberation Army swept into the region in October 1950, quickly defeating the Tibetan army and forcing Tibet's leaders to accept Chinese rule. Tibet's political and religious leader, the Dalai Lama, appealed to the United Nations to meet the Chinese attack on Tibet with the same kind of response that it had mustered against North Korea. But, in this case, the United Nations took no action, and the Chinese conquest of Tibet was allowed to stand.

In our everyday lives, we generally count on the police to protect us from acts of aggression by other people. If someone breaks into your house, you can call the police. Assuming you live in a place with an effective police force, the police may come in time to stop the person from harming you or your property. Even if the police cannot always stop a crime in progress, they can investigate and try to bring the perpetrator to justice. This has a deterrent effect on would-be criminals, who can be dissuaded from committing aggression by the expectation that they might be caught and punished. Although total security is rarely possible, people who live in societies with well-functioning police and judicial systems rarely experience acts of violence, and they rarely have to commit acts of violence to defend themselves. Unfortunately, the same cannot be said of actors in the international system.

Where are the police in world politics? The short answer is that the international system has no police force analogous to what exists in most countries. Each state possesses its own police and its own military, but there is no authoritative institution above states with an independent force that can police relations among them. As the examples above suggest, this condition of anarchy means that there is variation in the ways the international community responds to acts of aggression. And this variation has real consequences for people living in the states where such aggression occurs. Thanks to the international efforts that kept it independent, South Korea is today a thriving and prosperous country, with a living standard that far exceeds that of the impoverished North. Tibet, on the other hand, remains a part of China in spite of the fact that many Tibetans want their independence and an active movement for independence continues to this day. Indeed, in the spring of 2008, protestors calling for a free Tibet shadowed the Olympic torch as it made its way around the globe to the summer games in Beijing, China.

Understanding this variation in international responses requires that we explore the institutions that govern whether and how outside actors respond to acts of violence in the international system. The most obvious of these outside actors are bodies like the United Nations or its predecessor, the League of Nations (1919–1946). Formally known as collective security organizations, these institutions are the closest approximation to a world government that we have. Collective security organizations try to govern relations among their members, providing them with tools for peaceful conflict resolution and a mechanism for organizing collective responses to acts of aggression. To answer the question "Where are the police

When China invaded Tibet in 1950, the United Nations did not intervene, and the Chinese rule of Tibet remains a source of conflict today. These Chinese soldiers are marching in front of the Potala Palace, the traditional residence of the Tibetan leader, the Dalai Lama. The current Dalai Lama fled Tibet in 1959 and lives in exile in India.

in international politics?" collective security organizations are a natural first place to look.

For much longer than such organizations have existed, however, states have used an alternative institution to arrange for help from others: alliances. If collective security organizations are like governments, alliances more closely resemble neighborhood associations: relatively small groups of actors who work together to meet common threats or address common needs. Alliances are institutions that help states cooperate militarily, such as by coming to one another's defense in the event of war. In the absence of an effective world police, alliances represent attempts by small numbers of like-minded states to look out for one another.

This chapter completes our inquiry into the puzzle of war by looking at the role of international institutions. In Chapter 3, we laid out a general theory of war by considering the bargaining interaction between states. In Chapter 4, we looked inside the state to see how domestic interests and institutions affect international bargaining and war. Here, we examine how international institutions affect interactions between states as they try to cooperate to prevent or stop international and civil conflict.

Both alliances and collective security organizations influence whether or not outsiders will intervene in the event that war breaks out. As a result, they play a role in the bargaining that precedes a war, the bargaining that seeks to end an ongoing war, and the bargaining that takes place in the aftermath of fighting. But, despite these common features, these two kinds of institutions also differ greatly in how they operate. They form in response to different kinds of interests that third parties have in international disputes. And while both kinds of

institutions try to facilitate cooperation among states, they address different aspects of the strategic interactions that surround third-party involvement in international disputes. Hence, the factors that predict their success or failure are quite different. This chapter will develop four major points.

CORE OF THE ANALYSIS

▶ Alliances form when states have common interests that lead them to cooperate militarily. They are institutions created between or among states to facilitate cooperation for the purpose of influencing the outcomes of disputes with outsiders.

▶ Alliances are successful when allies have a strong interest in coming to one another's aid in the event of war, and when they are able to signal this interest to the opponent in a credible manner.

▶ Collective security organizations form around a common interest, which all states are presumed to share, in promoting peace. As broad-based institutions, their primary role is to facilitate collective action within the international community so that states can respond effectively to prevent or stop the outbreak of violence whenever and wherever it may occur.

▶ Collective security organizations are successful when leading states perceive a common and compelling interest in stopping an act of aggression; they fail when leading states have conflicting interests in the outcome of a particular dispute or when they have too little interest in the matter to justify the costs of intervention.

Alliances: Why Promise to Fight Someone Else's War?

World War II in Europe started as a territorial dispute between Germany and Poland but quickly grew into something much larger. After Germany invaded Poland on September 1, 1939, Britain and France responded two days later by declaring war on Germany. On September 17, the Soviet Union joined the fray, invading Poland from the east, and Poland was quickly swallowed up by its larger neighbors. Several months later, in June 1940, Italy joined the war on the German side and launched an invasion of southern France as German forces attacked France in the north. In each case, states that joined the war were carrying out the terms of alliance treaties that they had signed earlier. France and Poland had long-standing promises, codified in treaties from 1921 and 1925, to help each other in the event of war with Germany. Britain made a similar commitment to Poland in March 1939. Italy and the Soviet Union, for their parts, had each signed treaties pledging support for German military activities. Italy and Germany forged the so-called Pact of Steel in May 1939. Germany and the Soviet Union unveiled the Molotov-Ribbentrop Pact (so named for the two countries' foreign ministers) only days before the invasion of Poland. In that treaty, the two countries pledged not to attack one another, they agreed to divide Poland between them, and Germany promised the Soviets control over Finland, Estonia, Latvia, and Lithuania.

alliances: Institutions that help their members cooperate militarily in the event of a war.

Alliances are institutions that help their members cooperate militarily in the event of a war. Like all institutions, alliances specify standards of behavior, or expectations about how states are to behave under certain conditions. They may include provisions for monitoring and verifying each member's compliance and procedures for joint decision-making. Alliances also codify bargains between their members that settle distributional issues, such as how much each member will contribute to the common cause.

These provisions can vary considerably depending on the needs of the allies. Some alliances are offensive, while others are defensive. An offensive alliance is an agreement by which states pledge to join one another in attacking a third state. The Molotov-Ribbentrop Pact is a classic example of such an agreement. It not only specified the nature of Soviet-German military cooperation, but it also spelled out how the spoils of conquest would be divided. More commonly, alliances are defensive: states pledge to come to one another's defense in the event that either is attacked. The British and French pledges to Poland had this character. Defensive alliances may be open-ended, in the sense that allies pledge to defend each other against any and all attackers, or they may be targeted only at specific countries. Alliances may also differ in what the member states are required to do in the event of attack. A typical defensive alliance requires states to come to one another's aid militarily—that is, to treat an attack on the ally as an attack on oneself. Other alliance agreements specify merely that the states will consult one another in the event of war.

The United States currently has defensive alliances with a number of countries: South Korea, Japan, and—through the North Atlantic Treaty Organization (NATO)—Canada and many states in western and central Europe. If any of these states should come under attack, they could invoke the U.S. alliance commitment and ask Americans to come to their aid. In turn, the United States can appeal to others if it is attacked. NATO invoked its mutual defense provision for the first time in the alliance's history after the terrorist attack on the United States in September 2001. European NATO members assisted in flying Airborne Warning and Control Systems (better known as AWACS) over U.S. skies from October 2001 to May 2002.

In addition to spelling out their offensive or defensive character, alliances may codify bargains over how much and what each state will contribute to the common defense. Some alliances are symmetric, meaning that the members have similar responsibilities and contribute in roughly equal amounts. Other alliances are highly asymmetric, typically because one of the members is much more powerful than the others. For example, while the United States has pledged to defend South Korea, there is little expectation that South Korea would be in a position to return the favor if the U.S. homeland were attacked. In exchange for protection, South Korea provides bases for American troops in East Asia, has contributed to U.S. military efforts in the region, and generally supports U.S. foreign policy diplomatically and economically.

The United States maintains numerous military bases in South Korea, including this one in Seoul, as part of a defensive alliance between the two countries. Countries form alliances when they have common interests that motivate them to cooperate.

ALLIANCES AND ALIGNMENTS

Given that alliances can drag a country into other countries' wars, why do states sign them? Alliances form when states have common interests that motivate them to cooperate. Often, this common interest arises because states have a stake in the outcome of other countries' disputes. In the lead-up to World War II, the leaders of Britain and France did not agree to defend Poland simply out the goodness of their hearts; they did so because they believed that protecting Poland from Germany was crucial to their own interests. These countries feared that a German conquest of Poland would make Germany militarily stronger and economically more self-sufficient, making it a greater threat to their own security. Similarly, the United States formed the NATO alliance after World War II in order to protect Western European countries from the Soviet Union. The United States feared that countries like Britain, France, and West Germany were vulnerable to the massive Soviet army, and if those countries fell under its sway, the Soviet Union could use its mastery of Europe to threaten the United States.

We can understand the role of alliances by recalling the bargaining framework from Chapter 3. There, we imagined two states, A and B, interacting in a dispute over some good. Possible allocations of the good, and the two states' ideal points, are depicted on a line, as shown in (a) in Figure 5.1. Now, imagine that some third state, C, also has a stake in the dispute. Say that C has common interests with B, meaning that C's ideal point, like B's, is on the far left end of the line, as shown in (b). This means that the better the deal that B gets, the happier C is. In such a circumstance, we say that B and C's interests are aligned.

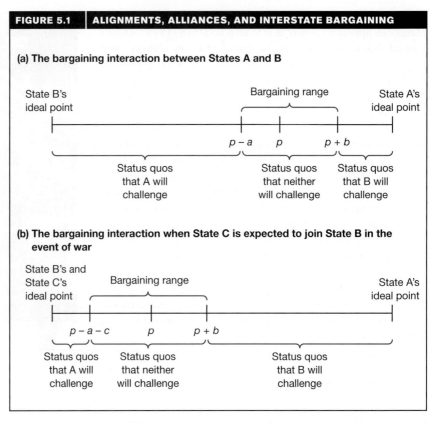

FIGURE 5.1   ALIGNMENTS, ALLIANCES, AND INTERSTATE BARGAINING

(a) The bargaining interaction between States A and B

State B's ideal point

Bargaining range

State A's ideal point

$p-a$ p $p+b$

Status quos that A will challenge

Status quos that neither will challenge

Status quos that B will challenge

(b) The bargaining interaction when State C is expected to join State B in the event of war

State B's and State C's ideal point

Bargaining range

State A's ideal point

$p-a-c$ p $p+b$

Status quos that A will challenge

Status quos that neither will challenge

Status quos that B will challenge

Note: In the figure, p indicates the expected outcome in the event of a war, while a and b denote the costs of war to States A and B, respectively. For a fuller discussion of how to interpret these figures, see Chapter 3.

How these common interests arise is a complicated question without a single answer. A long tradition in the study of international relations holds that alliances form to create or preserve a **balance of power**—that is, a situation in which the military capabilities of two states or groups of states are roughly equal.[1] When a balance of power exists, no state or bloc has a clear military advantage over the other. A power imbalance, in contrast, is considered threatening to the weaker side's interests. According to this view, alliances form when two or more states need to combine their capabilities in order to match the capabilities of another state and thereby counter the threat to their security. Common interests thus arise from a common threat posed by the power of a stronger state or bloc. In the late nineteenth century, both France and Russia feared the growing power and ambition of imperial Germany. Not only did each state want help in defending itself against a

balance of power: A situation in which the military capabilities of two states or groups of states are roughly equal.

1. See, for example, Edward Gulick, *Europe's Classical Balance of Power* (New York: Norton, 1955). For a more recent and influential statement of the theory, see Kenneth Waltz, *Theory of International Politics* (New York: McGraw Hill, 1979). For a historical analysis of balancing and its alternatives, see Paul Schroeder, "Alliances, 1815–1945: Weapons of Power and Tools of Management," in *Historical Dimensions of National Security Problems*, ed. Klaus Knorr (Lawrence: University Press of Kansas, 1976).

possible German attack, but each also feared that if Germany managed to conquer the other, then it would face an even more formidable foe in the future. As a result, each felt that its own survival depended in part on the survival of the other. The 1894 alliance between these states was formed on basis of this common interest.

Although this dynamic can explain some aspects of alliance formation, the balance of power theory does not fully account for all alliance decisions that we observe. First, not all alliances form with the intent of balancing a stronger state. When the Soviet Union allied with Nazi Germany against Poland, it joined the stronger state, exacerbating rather than alleviating the imbalance of power in Central Europe. We refer to such behavior as bandwagoning.[2] **Bandwagoning** occurs when states team up with the more powerful side in a dispute in order to share the spoils of conquest. Bandwagoning alliances are often offensive, as the shared interests that underlie them arise not from a common fear, but from a desire to cooperate for a common gain.

bandwagoning: A strategy in which states join forces with the stronger side in a conflict.

A second limitation of the balance of power theory is that states can often choose many potential partners in order to balance the capabilities of a stronger state. The arithmetic of balancing capabilities does not explain why some partners are more desirable than others. For example, when Saudi Arabia sought allies against Egypt in 1957, why did it choose to ally with fellow Arab monarchies Jordan and Iraq, rather than with Israel, a state with much more impressive military capabilities and which also had reason to fear Egypt? The answer lies not in the balance of power, but rather in the ideological and religious incompatibility between Saudi Arabia and the Jewish state, which made an alliance between the two unthinkable.[3]

A final problem for the balance of power theory is that not all strong powers provoke similar balancing responses. For example, the United States today has unparalleled military power, accounting for roughly half of all world military spending. And yet, despite some tensions associated with the Iraq War, there has not been a marked tendency toward creating balancing alliances in response. Indeed, the U.S.-led NATO alliance, rather than falling apart after the collapse of the Soviet bloc, has expanded both its membership and the scope of its missions (see "What Shaped Our World?" on p. 187). A likely explanation is that while many states complain about American arrogance and bullying, very few see the United States as an actual threat to their interests. Whatever differences the United States has had with France, for example, there is virtually no danger of war between them. Commercial, cultural, and ideological ties between the countries are strong, and there are no disputed goods in their relationship that are valuable enough to risk war over. In short, whether or not two states share a common interest vis-à-vis a third state depends on much more than whether or not the latter has an advantage in military capabilities. Other factors such as geographic proximity, ideological and cultural similarity, and the existence (or not) of high-value disputes play a large role in determining which states are considered threatening, and hence worth allying against, and which are not.[4]

---

2. Randall Schweller, "Bandwagoning for Profit: Bringing the Revisionist State Back In," *International Security* 19 (1994): 72–107.
3. Stephen M. Walt, *The Origins of Alliances* (Ithaca, NY: Cornell University Press, 1987), 204–6.
4. Ibid.

ALLIANCES AND THE LIKELIHOOD OF WAR

The possibility of intervention by an ally influences the outcome of international bargaining by changing the likely outcome and costs of war for each side. Returning to the example in Figure 5.1, imagine that if State A and State B were to fight a war, the expected outcome would be p and the costs of war to each side would be a and b, as shown in (a). In this interaction, A is assumed to be more powerful, so p is close to its ideal point. This means that A can extract a favorable bargain from B and is likely to challenge B to try to realize that bargain (in other words, there is a large range of status quo outcomes in which A will make a demand of B). If State C were expected to intervene in this war, however, the outcome and costs could be quite different. With C's military power added to B's, the likely outcome would shift in the latter's favor, as shown in (b). In addition, it is likely that A's costs of war will be higher, shown here by the inclusion of additional costs, c. These changes shift the bargaining range in a way that benefits B and C. War becomes less attractive to A, and it can no longer extract a lopsided deal. Indeed, as p shifts to the left, A's incentive to challenge B declines (there are fewer status quo outcomes in which A will make a demand). In this way, A is deterred from challenging B. Hence, C's willingness to intervene influences the bargaining interaction between A and B by shifting each side's evaluation of war.

In addition, the possibility of intervention can affect whether or not the opposing sides reach a bargain. In the example just given, the shift in the bargaining range was based on the assumption that both A and B believe that C would intervene in the event of war. In other words, it assumed that the two sides form their expectations on the basis of the same information about C's intentions. What would happen if this were not the case? For example, what if B expected C to join a war, but A did not?

When the parties to a dispute have different information about what third parties will do, this uncertainty can heighten the probability of a bargaining failure leading to war, for reasons discussed in Chapter 3. As we have seen, Iraq in August 1990 did not know whether the United States would defend Kuwait, and its doubts about U.S. threats to that effect helped bring about the Persian Gulf War. Similarly, we saw in the case of the Korean War that the United States was uncertain about whether China would come to the aid of North Korea if U.S. troops crossed the 38th parallel. In the lead-up to World War I, Germany was unsure until the last moment whether Britain would join its allies, France and Russia, in the event of war.

This observation suggests that alliances influence the bargaining interaction between states by influencing the states' beliefs about what third parties will do. While common interests are necessary for alliances to form, the main reason that states sign alliances is to signal those common interests to others. After all, if it were completely obvious to everyone which states would come to the defense of others, then there would be little need to negotiate and sign treaties to this effect.

Because of their role as signals, alliances face the same challenge of credibility discussed in Chapter 3 with respect to threats. Indeed, an alliance entails an implied threat: "If you attack my ally, I will fight you." Just because a state has an interest in the outcome of its ally's bargaining interactions does not ensure that the

In May 1939, Germany and Italy entered into an alliance known as the Pact of Steel. Here, German leader Adolf Hitler and the Italian Foreign Minister publicly celebrate the alliance between the two fascist powers in a ceremony in Berlin. States often publicize their alliances in order to influence bargaining with potential adversaries.

state will actually fight alongside its ally in the event of war. As a result, an alliance commitment may be questionable for the same reasons that threats are questionable: they are costly to carry out, and there can be incentives to bluff. Alliances are not, after all, binding contracts. There is no external mechanism to compel states to fulfill their treaty obligations. Rather, the promise to come to another's defense in the event of war is precisely that: a promise, which may or may not be fulfilled. In fact, there are many instances in which allies have not lived up to their commitments. Indeed, in June 1941, less than two years after signing the Molotov-Ribbentrop Pact, Germany broke its side of the agreement by invading the Soviet Union and grabbing all of Poland for itself.

This observation suggests that when we talk about alliances, we should be clear to treat them as institutions and not as actors in their own right. It sometimes serves as a useful shorthand to talk about alliances as cohesive actors; for example, we might say that "NATO intervened in Afghanistan." This simplification should not obscure the fact that alliances are institutions formed by states in response to common interests. These institutions may shape states' interests in a way that helps them to act as a cohesive group, but at all times decision-making power rests with the states, not the alliance per se.[5]

5. This characteristic distinguishes alliances from empires and more hierarchical relationships between states in which the capabilities of two or more actors are combined but decision-making power rests in a dominant state. On security hierarchies, see David A. Lake, *Entangling Relations: American Foreign Policy in Its Century* (Princeton, NJ: Princeton University Press, 1999).

HOW ALLIANCES ESTABLISH CREDIBILITY

Whether or not an alliance can successfully further the interests of allied states depends on their willingness to fight on one another's behalf and on their ability to signal this willingness in a credible manner. As a result, alliances must accomplish two key tasks in order to enhance their chances of success. First, they must make it more likely that allies will fight on each other's behalf than they would in the absence of an alliance. This can be accomplished by decreasing the costs of fighting, increasing the benefits of fighting, and/or increasing the costs of not fighting—that is, of abandoning the ally. Second, alliances must do these things in a way that leads adversaries to believe that the allies will indeed fight together. Hence, the goal is both to heighten the allies' interests in aiding one another and to influence the interaction with the rival state by shaping its expectations.

Alliances typically exhibit a number of features designed to further these goals. They increase the benefits and decrease the costs of war by improving the member countries' ability to fight effectively together. Allies may engage in joint military planning and joint military exercises, and they may station troops on one another's soil. By doing so, they make the expected value of fighting together higher than it would be in the absence of an alliance. This coordination is publicly revealed (even if actual warfighting strategies are not), which serves to put potential adversaries on notice. Some alliances also contain provisions for joint decision-making that further enhance their collective war-fighting abilities. NATO appoints a Supreme Allied Commander, Europe, for instance, who is responsible for all troops under the organization's authority.

Alliances can also increase the costs of abandonment—that is, of failing to fight on an ally's behalf. Prior to the nineteenth century, it was common to cement alliances through a marriage between royal families—under the theory that a king would have special motivation to defend an ally if his daughter was married to that ally's monarch. More commonly, the fact that alliance treaties are generally made public—often accompanied by public signing ceremonies and, in some countries, open ratification processes—can bring states' reputations into play.[6] States may fear that the failure to come to an ally's defense, after making such a public commitment, would hurt their credibility in future conflicts. Such hand-tying strategies seek to bolster the credibility of alliances just as they do the credibility of other threats.

Despite the challenges of establishing credibility, states have historically honored their alliance commitments in war about 75 percent of the time. Although it is hard to know with certainty how often states would have fought alongside their allies even in the absence of a formal alliance commitment, this is an impressive success rate given the lack of any formal enforcement mechanism for treaties and the often substantial costs states must bear once the fighting starts. Moreover, those states most likely to violate agreements are those that have, in some sense, outgrown their commitments because of changes either in interstate power or in their domestic regimes. This suggests that institutional mechanisms that heighten states' interests in coming to an ally's aid when called on to do so are often effective.[7]

---

6. This is generally true of defensive alliances. Offensive alliances, in contrast, may be kept secret if the intended target would otherwise take countermeasures to blunt the effectiveness of the alliance.

7. Brett Ashley Leeds, "Alliance Reliability in Times of War: Explaining State Decisions to Violate Treaties," *International Organization* 57 (Fall 2003): 801–27.

WHY AREN'T ALLIANCE COMMITMENTS IRONCLAD?

If states have common interests that lead them to form alliances and create institutional mechanisms for enhancing the credibility of their commitments to one another, why is there often uncertainty about whether or not members will actually fulfill their obligations? Why do allies and other states that are the targets of alliances sometimes have different expectations about whether allies will actually come to one another's aid? The answer to these questions is not obvious, demonstrating the need to think about the choices facing all sides of a strategic interaction.

Ironclad alliance guarantees that effectively deter challenges to the weaker party also enhance the risk that the weaker party will demand more of the target or become intransigent in negotiations. To see this, consider again (b) in Figure 5.1. Alliances have two effects. As mentioned above, an alliance deters a challenger, in this case State A, by reducing the probability that it will win a combined war against States B and C. This is why States B and C are interested in forging the alliance in the first place. At the same time, the alliance strengthens B in its bargaining with A. Indeed, as shown in the diagram, as p moves to the left, the range of status quo outcomes in which B has an incentive to challenge A expands. As a result, B is likely to demand a better bargain from A and, following the risk-return tradeoff explained in Chapter 3, run a risk of war to obtain its demands. In other words, while the alliance between B and C weakens A and deters it from challenging B, the same alliance strengthens B and gives it an incentive to demand more of A.

This situation presents a dilemma. State C may want to assist State B in defending itself against a stronger State A, but it may not want to see B make larger demands or run a risk of war to fulfill those demands. In such cases, State C must worry about becoming "entrapped" in a war by a reckless ally.[8] In response, states attempt to avoid entrapment by limiting their commitments or leaving those commitments purposely ambiguous. In other words, in an effort to control opportunism by their allies, states rarely forge ironclad agreements that they must fulfill. Rather, states attempt to reserve a measure of discretion for themselves on when, how, and to what extent they will meet their alliance obligations.

An important example of this challenge can be found in the United States' relations with China and Taiwan. Since 1949, the United States has sought to defend Taiwan from mainland China, which regards the island as a renegade province. China has repeatedly warned that if Taiwan officially declares independence, that act would be a cause for war. The dilemma for the United States has been this: how to deter China from attacking without, at the same time, making Taiwan feel that it could declare and win its independence with the help of the United States. On the one hand, China might attack if it believes the United States would abandon Taiwan. On the other hand, an ironclad promise to defend Taiwan might encourage pro-independence politicians there to take the fateful step that would risk a war. In order to navigate this dilemma, the United States has at times pursued a policy of "strategic ambiguity": making its intentions less than fully clear

---

8. On entrapment and other forms of opportunism by allies, see Glenn H. Snyder, "The Security Dilemma in Alliance Politics," *World Politics* 36 (1984): 461–95.

in the hopes that China would be deterred from attacking, while Taiwan would act with restraint.

This dilemma shows that there can be a tradeoff between the *credibility* of alliances (which requires ironclad promises) and efforts to *control* alliance partners (which can require ambiguity and flexibility). There is seldom any way to avoid this tradeoff. The more credible the guarantee to an ally, the greater the incentive for that ally to behave opportunistically. As we shall see, Germany learned this lesson too late in giving a "blank check" to Austria-Hungary in 1914. But the greater the discretion the state retains in an effort to limit the risk of entrapment, the less credible is the alliance and the less successful it will be in deterring challengers.

THE SUCCESS AND FAILURE OF ALLIANCES IN EUROPE, 1879–1990

As we have seen, alliances are institutions that states create in order to facilitate cooperation in support of common interests. They form when states' interests are aligned to an extent that they may be willing to fight on each other's behalf. They work by making it more likely that the states will in fact fight together in the event of war and by signaling this willingness to the adversary. As a result, the success or failure of an alliance depends on (1) the strength of the common interests that brought the allies together, (2) the ability of the alliance to alter the members' preferences so that in the event of war, fighting is preferable to abandonment, (3) the effectiveness of the alliance in convincing the adversary of this fact, and (4) the ability of the partners to limit the risk of entrapment.

We can see how this explanatory logic has played out historically by analyzing some of the major events of the last century through the lens of alliance politics. As noted in Chapter 1, the first and second halves of the twentieth century were markedly different in terms of warfare between the world's major powers. In both periods, international politics was shaped by conflicts among the large, industrialized countries in Europe. In both periods, states that felt threatened formed alliances in the hopes of protecting themselves from rivals. Yet, the outcomes in these two periods were quite different. The first half of the century witnessed two world wars of unprecedented destructiveness; the second half was remarkable for the absence of war between the two superpowers, in spite of the intense hostility between them. What explains this variation? A complete answer is, of course, quite complicated. Nevertheless, the logic of alliances laid out in the previous sections gives us considerable insight.

Pre–World War I: Two Armed Camps

The story of European alliance formation preceding World War I is driven primarily by the rapid growth of Germany following that country's unification in 1871. Indeed, Germany experienced dramatic industrial development and population growth over the decades following unification. These were accompanied by a corresponding increase in the country's international ambitions.

As Germany became more assertive internationally, it collected both friends and enemies. In 1879, Germany signed an alliance with neighboring Austria-Hungary, uniting the two central powers. In 1882, Italy, angered by France's seizure of

Tunisia and looking for a powerful friend, joined the Austro-German pact to form the Triple Alliance. It would not take long, however, before Germany's newfound power and ambition would lead to the formation of a countercoalition against it. In the late 1880s, relations between Russia and Germany worsened, and Germany increasingly threw its support to Austria in the latter's disputes with Russia. In response, Russia went looking for allies. The most likely place to look was France, which was still smarting from its defeat at the hands of Germany in their war of 1871. The common fear of Germany led to the formation of the Franco-Russian alliance in 1894. Britain, too, became fearful of Germany, particularly when the latter began a massive ship-building effort designed to erode Britain's naval superiority. In 1904, Britain and France formed a pact known as the Dual Entente.[9] The final piece fell into place in 1907, when Britain and Russia signed an agreement settling some outstanding issues in their relationship and pledging military cooperation—thereby creating the Triple Entente.

Hence, by the first decade of the twentieth century, Europe was essentially divided into two armed camps: the Triple Alliance of Germany, Austria-Hungary, and Italy facing off against the Triple Entente of Britain, France, and Russia. Although the apparent symmetry between the two alliances would appear to have created a stable balance, the system was in fact fraught with danger. The alliance network created the possibility that any small conflict could drag all of the European powers into war. Of course, since European decisionmakers understood that a small spark could lead to general conflagration, this system did engender some caution and mutual deterrence by raising the expected costs of war to each side. And indeed, several crises in the first decade of the twentieth century were all resolved peacefully, in spite of much saber-rattling.

Nonetheless, the system had several features that made it unstable. First, as we saw in Chapter 3, the strategic situation created a number of preventive and preemptive incentives. Germany feared the rise of Russian power, causing some strategists to argue that war with Russia would be better now than later. In addition, Germany's need to plan for a two-front war against France to the west and Russia to the east gave rise to the Schlieffen Plan, with its precise timetables and preemptive logic. Second, the delicate balance made each of the major powers highly dependent on its allies for security; the prospect of losing an ally was seen as particularly dangerous. Hence, the threat to Austria-Hungary from Serbia—a threat that could have caused the empire to break up from within—was also felt keenly in Germany. This explains why Germany gave its ally a blank check in the July crisis, promising to back Austria-Hungary in whatever the latter chose to do. This commitment, however, emboldened Austria-Hungary in its conflict with Serbia, leading Austria-Hungary to issue a harsh ultimatum to Serbia.[10] The set of interconnected alliances, Austro-Hungarian intransigence, and a small spark

---

9. The word *entente* is French for "understanding." An entente is generally seen as a weak form of alliance in which the states agree to cooperate and consult, but they do not pledge automatic military assistance to one another.

10. Some historians argue that Germany issued the blank check precisely to incite Austrian-Hungarian intransigence and, thus, provoke war. Among others, see Fritz Fischer, *Germany's Aims in the First World War* (New York: Norton, 1967).

turned an otherwise local crisis between Austria and Russia over Serbia into a war that consumed most of Europe. Finally, the sheer number of states involved magnified the possibility of miscalculations. Whether or not an ally would actually fight in the event of war was a crucial question in determining how hard a state could push or how much it should give. Uncertainty about who would join a prospective war created considerable scope for errors.

Probably the most important source of uncertainty in this event was how Great Britain would react in the event of war. Because it had the most powerful navy in the world—larger, in fact, than the next three largest navies combined—whether or not Britain would join a continental war was a crucially important question, and one over which there was a good deal of uncertainty until the very last minute. Although the Entente committed Britain to cooperate with France and Russia in the event of war, the public and many policymakers in government were not keen to shed British blood over what appeared to be a distant matter. As a result, German decisionmakers believed for some time that Britain would stand aside while Germany took on France and Russia. Moreover, suggestions by British leaders that Britain would join its allies in war were discounted by German leaders as bluffs. It is unclear whether German leaders would have backed off from war had they been certain that Britain would intervene; it is clear, however, that Germany was stimulated by British wavering to take an intransigent, belligerent position in the crisis. When Britain belatedly made clear that it would join in the fight, the military actions and diplomatic commitments already made by Germany and Austria were hard to reverse. Once war started, the network of the alliances brought all of Europe into war.[11]

The Interwar Period, 1919–1939

Germany was defeated in World War I, but the underlying problem of its growing power and ambition remained. Still recovering from the devastating war, the European powers "passed the buck" among themselves, hoping others would bear the costs of containing Germany, and failed to form a set of alliances to balance Germany until another war was already imminent.[12]

Until 1939, the alliance system that formed to contain Germany rested on a few thin reeds that easily snapped under Hitler's pressure. By the Treaty of Locarno (1925), Britain pledged to defend Belgium and France in the event that either was attacked by Germany and to ensure that Germany respected the demilitarization of the Rhineland region, which bordered on those countries. France also signed alliances with several of Germany's neighbors to the east: Poland, Czechoslovakia, Yugoslavia, and Romania. The first of these treaties was tested, and failed, in 1936 when Hitler remilitarized the Rhineland and Britain refused to support France in taking any action to stop it. Public opinion in Britain would not tolerate a risk of war since, after all, Germany was simply moving troops into its own backyard.

---

11. In a final example of how the alliance system failed, Italy refused to join its allies, Germany and Austria, when war broke out. After sitting on the sidelines for several months, Italy decided that the Entente powers were more likely to win. Hence, Italy decided to side with the Entente and, in May 1915, attacked its former ally, Austria-Hungary, with whom it had a long-standing territorial dispute.
12. Thomas Christensen and Jack Snyder, "Chair Gangs and Passed Bucks: Predicting Alliance Patterns in Multipolarity," *International Organization* 4 (1996): 137–68.

The French guarantees to the eastern European countries were also suspect due to the geographic separation between them. The German invasion in World War I, which almost led to the fall of Paris, caused France to adopt a defensive posture in the interwar period, with most of the French forces positioned along a fortified line on the frontier. This meant that France was in a weak position to defend its distant allies from the German threat. The weakness became all too clear in September 1938, when France and Britain acquiesced to German demands for a section of Czechoslovakia called the Sudetenland. Six months later, in March 1939, Germany invaded and conquered the rest of Czechoslovakia, and France did not lift a finger to save its ally. Not until Germany attacked Poland in September 1939 did France and Britain, which pledged to defend Poland on August 25, find the resolve to fulfill their commitments.

Hence, rather than being deterred by the states that sought to contain him, Hitler exploited weak alliances that were not backed up by sufficient resolve or capabilities, highlighting the lack of common interests and credible commitments among the allies. Bandwagoning alliances with Italy, the Soviet Union, and eventually Japan only strengthened his hand. The resulting imbalance between a bloc of revisionist powers and a fragmented group of buck-passing allies, combined with a leader ideologically bent on conquest, cast the world into war once more.

In August 1939, Britain formed a defensive alliance with Poland. One month later, Germany invaded Poland, Britain stepped in to defend its ally, and World War II began.

The Cold War: The "Long Peace" in Europe, 1945–1990

Whereas the first half of the twentieth century witnessed two world wars that grew out of European conflicts, the second half of that century was a period of relative peace in Europe. Indeed, the more than five decades that followed the end of World War II are sometimes referred to as the period of the Long Peace, since there were no wars among the major European powers in this period. Of course, the period of relative peace was not due to an absence of conflicts, since most of this time coincided with the Cold War between the United States and the Soviet Union, a rivalry that once again led to the division of Europe into two opposing blocs. Although the Long Peace has a number of causes, some credit must go to the nature of the alliance system that formed in this period.[13]

Within ten years after the end of World War II, most countries in Europe belonged to either the **North Atlantic Treaty Organization (NATO)** or the **Warsaw Pact** (see Map 5.1). NATO covered most of the states of Western Europe and bound them in a collective defense treaty with the United States. Its core

North Atlantic Treaty Organization (NATO): An alliance formed in 1949 among the United States, Canada, and most of the states of Western Europe in response to the threat posed by the Soviet Union. The alliance requires the members to consider an attack on any one of them as an attack on all.

Warsaw Pact: A military alliance formed in 1955 to bring together the Soviet Union and its Cold War allies in Eastern Europe and elsewhere. It dissolved on March 31, 1991, as the Cold War ended.

---

13. John Lewis Gaddis, "The Long Peace: Elements of Stability in the Postwar International System," *International Security* 10 (Spring 1986): 99–142.

MAP 5.1 | **NATO EXPANSION, 1949–2009**

NATO Membership
- Founding members (1949)*
- Cold War era enlargement
- Unification of Germany (1990)
- Enlargement 1st round (1999)
- Enlargement 2nd round (2004)
- Enlargement 3rd round (2009)
- Former Warsaw Pact countries

*NATO members also include the United States, Canada, and Iceland.

NATO after the Cold War

When the Cold War ended in the late 1980s, many analysts thought that NATO's days were numbered. With the Soviet Union unable to maintain its control over Eastern Europe, the communist regimes in that region fell, the Red Army retreated behind its borders, and the Warsaw Pact dissolved. Germany reunited, with the communist East absorbed into the pro-Western, democratic West. In December 1991, the Soviet Union disintegrated. Given these earth-shattering changes to the international system, it seemed plausible that the NATO alliance would crumble as well. The common interests and fears that originally brought the alliance into being had vanished.[a]

NATO's obituaries turned out to be premature. The United States did reduce some of its troop presence in Europe, but over 100,000 U.S. military personnel remain stationed there today. Rather than withering away, NATO actually expanded. In 1999, three former Soviet satellites—Poland, Hungary, and the Czech Republic—joined. In 2004, seven more Eastern European states—Bulgaria, Estonia, Latvia, Lithuania, Romania, Slovakia, and Slovenia—became members. In 2009, Albania and Croatia became the alliance's newest members, and further expansion has been proposed.

NATO has expanded its mission as well. Although designed to protect its members from external attack, NATO has become a vehicle for military cooperation not directly related to this core function. From 1993 to 1995, NATO conducted air strikes in support of UN operations in Bosnia (see text). In 1999, NATO went to war against Yugoslavia—not because Yugoslavia had attacked a NATO member, but because that country was mistreating some of its own citizens: the ethnic Albanians living in a province of Yugoslavia called Kosovo. Hence, as the "Controversy" box on p. 206 describes, the first war in NATO's history was a humanitarian intervention in a purely internal matter in a state that was not a member of the alliance and that did not directly threaten any member of the alliance. NATO's mission and reach extended even further after the September 11, 2001, terrorist attacks on the United States. The next day, the alliance invoked Article 5 of the North Atlantic Treaty, declaring that the entire alliance had been attacked. NATO countries have since played a role

in helping to stabilize Afghanistan after the U.S. war against the Taliban regime in 2001–2002. In 2008, about half of the international troop presence in Afghanistan came from NATO countries other than the United States.

These operations suggest that while NATO is no longer held together by a common fear of the Soviet Union, its members are still bound by common interests. Those interests include a basic concern for security, but with an expanded conception of where the main threats lie: particularly, terrorism and the ability of terrorists to take root in chaotic, war-torn regions. Moreover, the Bosnia and Kosovo operations showed that the alliance could act on other shared interests, such as a common commitment to democracy and human rights. In taking on these "out of area operations"—that is, operations not confined to territory of the member states—NATO has been transformed from a purely defensive alliance into something more akin to a collective security organization.

Whether shared interests and values will continue to hold together the NATO alliance remains to be seen. The 2003 Iraq War exposed cracks within the alliance.[b] The U.S. and British governments argued that Iraq's suspected weapons of mass destruction, together with possible (but unproven) ties to terrorist organizations, created a dire threat that had to be extinguished. They were supported by other NATO allies, including Italy, Spain, Denmark, and the newest members from Eastern Europe. Other NATO countries, however, most prominently France and Germany, opposed the use of military force, arguing that it would cause instability in the region and inflame Muslim extremism. France also had economic ties with Saddam Hussein's regime. The United States was also unable to win the support of Turkey, a NATO ally but also a country with a predominantly Muslim population. Turkey's refusal to allow U.S. troops to use its territory to launch an attack prevented the opening of a second, northern front against Iraq and may have contributed to U.S. difficulties in securing the country after the fall of the regime. Hence, the Iraq War showed that the shared interests and values that have so far held the NATO alliance together do not rule out conflicting viewpoints that can divide the members and prevent cooperation. ■

a. For an example of this argument, see John J. Mearsheimer, "Back to the Future: Instability in Europe after the Cold War," *International Security* 15 (Summer 1990): 5–56.

b. See, for example, Phillip H. Gordon and Jeremy Shapiro, *Allies at War: America, Europe, and the Crisis over Iraq* (New York: McGraw-Hill, 2004).

provision was in Article 5 of the North Atlantic Treaty, which specified that each member would consider an attack against one or more members to be an attack against them all. The Warsaw Pact covered the states of Eastern Europe and the Soviet Union. Germany, which was split after the war into two countries, was also split between the blocs: with West Germany in NATO and East Germany in the Warsaw Pact. Each bloc formed in response to a perceived threat from the other. NATO was established in 1949 in response to the Soviet military presence in Eastern Europe—a presence that the Soviets used to install puppet governments in those countries. The Warsaw Pact formed in 1955 after West Germany was admitted into NATO, raising the fear in Moscow that its nemesis in the two world wars would again be rearmed and active on the European stage.

Although the experience of World War I would seem to suggest that two alliance blocs, roughly evenly divided, can be a cause of war, the Cold War alliance system had a number of features that made it different, and more stable, than what came before. First, the world in 1914 was much more complicated, with several major powers in competition and highly dependent on their allies for security. During the Cold War, by contrast, the system was dominated by the two superpowers. This meant that there was less scope for miscalculation, as the outcome of any conflict was dependent on the choices of fewer key actors. It also meant that neither superpower would be as threatened by the loss of an ally as the states of Europe were before 1914. Germany at that time considered the possible loss of Austria-Hungary to be extremely threatening, worth risking war over. The United States and Soviet Union, by contrast, had less to fear from the possible defection of allies.[14] And indeed, France's departure from NATO's joint military command in 1966, Yugoslavia's defection from the Soviet orbit in 1948, and Romania's increasingly independent foreign policy starting in the 1960s did not upset the relatively stable equilibrium between the two sides.

A second major feature of the Cold War alliances was their highly institutionalized nature. Both were more than just pieces of paper promising mutual aid in the event of war. Rather, they included a dense set of military, political, and economic relationships. The United States in particular needed to demonstrate that it would uphold its commitment to defend its allies an ocean away, as any uncertainty about the U.S. commitment was seen as inviting Soviet aggression against Western Europe. As a result, the NATO alliance provided for close integration of the American and European militaries, a joint command led by an American officer, and the basing of over a quarter of a million U.S. troops on European soil, primarily in West Germany. This forward deployment of U.S. forces served both military and political purposes. It ensured that the United States had capabilities in place to slow a Soviet offensive until much larger reinforcements could come across the sea. It also served to signal the American commitment to the region. In the event of a Soviet attack, U.S. troops would have been quickly involved in the fighting, ensuring that the United States could not remain indifferent.

This political aspect of the American presence in Europe was most clearly evident in the Berlin Brigade, a garrison of about 7,000 troops in West Berlin. Like the rest of Germany, the capital city of Berlin had been divided into western

---

14. Kenneth Waltz, *Theory of International Politics* (Reading, MA: Addison-Wesley, 1979), 169–70.

and eastern portions after the war. The city sat in the midst of communist East Germany, however, so West Berlin was a small island of Western and American influence surrounded by a "red" sea. Given its geographic isolation, the American garrison would have been quickly overrun in the event of a war. Nonetheless, its presence was seen as a crucial signal of the U.S. commitment to defend Western Europe. The theorist Thomas Schelling described its role vividly:

> The garrison in Berlin is as fine a collection of soldiers as has ever been assembled, but excruciatingly small. What can 7,000 American troops do . . . ? Bluntly, they can die. They can die heroically, dramatically, and in a manner that guarantees that the action cannot stop there. They represent the pride, the honor, and the reputation of the United States government and its armed forces; and they can apparently hold the entire Red Army at bay.[15]

Hence, the military presence was a kind of hand-tying strategy (see Chapter 3): an effort to ensure that if the American commitment to NATO were triggered by a Soviet attack, the United States would have little choice but to fulfill that commitment. The strength of this pledge, clearly signaled to the Soviet Union, had a deterrent effect that contributed to the relative stability of Europe during the Cold War. The "What Shaped Our World" box on page 187 explores NATO's role since the Cold War.

Collective Security: Why Can't the United Nations Keep the Peace?

As World War I was coming to a close, world leaders began to think about what the postwar world should look like. U.S. president Woodrow Wilson argued that the only way to prevent another such war was to change the nature of world politics. Wilson was convinced that the prewar pattern, in which major powers jockeyed for advantage against one another in shifting alliances, had to go. Alliances could not prevent wars; they could only cause wars to spread into larger, more destructive events. In their place, there should be a permanent institution that would enable countries to police the international system in the name of peace and security for all. From this vision, in 1919, the **League of Nations** was born; although it limped along until 1946, it effectively died in 1939 with the onset of World War II.

As World War II was coming to a close, world leaders once again turned their thoughts to the question of how to prevent another such war. Like his predecessor, U.S. president Franklin Roosevelt championed the idea of a permanent governing body that would enable the major powers to police the international system. The **United Nations (UN)** was created in 1945 as a successor to the League of Nations. The United Nations still functions to this day, but its track record in responding

League of Nations:
A collective security organization founded in 1919 after World War I. The League ended in 1946 and was replaced by the United Nations.

United Nations (UN):
A collective security organization founded in 1945 after World War II. With over 190 members, the UN includes all recognized states.

---

15. Thomas Schelling, *Arms and Influence* (New Haven, CT: Yale University Press, 1966), 47.

Collective security organizations like the United Nations work to prevent war and violence. These soldiers were sent to East Timor as part of a UN mission to ensure a peaceful transition to independence in 2002. Indonesia invaded East Timor in 1975 and occupied the country until 1999, subjecting the people to violence and brutality.

collective security organizations: Broad-based institutions that promote peace and security among their members. Examples include the League of Nations and the United Nations.

genocide: Intentional and systematic killing aimed at eliminating an identifiable group of people, such as an ethnic or religious group.

to acts of aggression is, at best, mixed. Why is this? Why have efforts to build an effective international organization capable of policing international politics failed to create a lasting peace?

The League of Nations and the United Nations are both examples of collective security organizations. Like alliances, **collective security organizations** are institutions that facilitate cooperation among their members. These two kinds of institutions, however, form in response to different kinds of interests. Alliances form when two or more states have a common interest in the outcome of bargaining with an adversary or a set of adversaries. They are based on alignments in interests that prompt states to cooperate against a common foe. Collective security organizations, by contrast, form under the presumption that all states have a common interest in preventing war and aggression, regardless of who the perpetrator and victim are. Unlike alliances, their primary purpose is not to alter bargaining outcomes in favor of one state or another, but rather to ensure that changes to the status quo, if they occur, happen peacefully. They forbid the use of military force by one member state against another, and they generally provide mechanisms, such as mediators or arbitrators, to help member states resolve their disputes peacefully. An attack by one member against another is considered to be a threat to the whole community. As a result, the entire membership is responsible for coming to the aid of the victims of aggression. This collective response is intended to deter would-be aggressors in the first place and, in the event that deterrence fails, ensure that those who wrong the community by engaging in war will not benefit from the transgression.

Although collective security organizations were born out of the desire to prevent interstate wars, they have also sought to prevent violence within states. Indeed, the United Nations has been quite active in dealing with civil wars and maintaining peace in their aftermath. In recent years, there also has been pressure to expand its scope to deal with gross violations of human rights, such as cases of **genocide,** the systematic slaughter of an identifiable group of people. In fact, genocidal conflicts have led to the sharpest criticism of the United Nations in recent years: for inaction in such places as Rwanda, Bosnia, and, more recently, Darfur (more on these cases below).

Unlike alliances, whose membership is restricted to a small number of states with common interests, the membership of collective security organizations is generally universal, or nearly universal. The United Nations, for example, includes all internationally recognized states. Universal membership reflects the presumption of a community with universally shared interests in international peace and security. There are also numerous regional security organizations—such as the Organization of American States, the African Union, and the Organization for Cooperation and Security in Europe—that include all or most of the states in each relevant region.

HOW DOES COLLECTIVE SECURITY WORK?

In theory, collective security works as follows. The mechanism is triggered when one state attacks or threatens to attack another or, in the event of a civil conflict, when there is an outbreak of large-scale violence within a country. If it is determined that these events constitute an act of aggression—or, in the language of the

United Nations, a "threat to international peace and security"—then all members of the organization are called on to act against the state or government that has committed the offending action. Depending on the circumstances, the prescribed action can range from economic sanctions to full-scale military intervention. This threat of intervention is primarily intended to deter actors from making aggressive demands against or attacking one another. A state that knows its actions will be opposed by the full weight of the international community should be reluctant to engage in aggression. In addition, collective security organizations provide other services intended to prevent violence from breaking out. For example, they may offer mediators to help states identify mutually beneficial bargains, and they can provide peacekeeping troops—troops from neutral third parties—to help monitor and enforce peace agreements.

These different strategies can influence the bargaining interaction between adversaries in at least three ways, all of them intended to foster peaceful outcomes. First, as with alliances, the prospect of outside involvement makes war less attractive by changing the likely outcome of the interaction between states or, in the case of civil wars, between groups. At the extreme, the combined weight of the entire international community means that the defeat of the challenger is virtually certain. The status quo is stable if both sides know that they will surely lose if they attempt to change the status quo by force. Under such conditions, neither side can shift the bargain in its favor by threatening war.

One way that UN forces promote peace is by interposing themselves between hostile factions, making it harder for fighting to resume. Here, UN peacekeepers patrol southern Lebanon. The UN Interim Force in Lebanon was established in 1978 to enforce peace between Israel and Lebanon following fighting over territory in southern Lebanon along the Israeli border.

Second, outsiders can help resolve the commitment problems identified in Chapter 3 by promising to enforce what would otherwise be an unbelievable commitment by one state not to exploit its power against another. A shift in relative power between two states might be rendered less dangerous if the weakened state can count on others to defend it, thus diminishing any preventive incentive it might have. Likewise, a state may feel secure handing over a piece of strategic territory if it knows that others will come to its aid in the event that its adversary exploits this territory to attack or press further claims. In other words, the state that is made more powerful by the deal can more credibly commit not to exploit its newfound power if it knows that any attempt to do so will be countered by the international community. For example, as noted in Chapter 3, Israel and Syria have a conflict over the strategically valuable Golan Heights, which Israel seized from Syria in 1967. Since control of this territory imparts a military advantage to its owner, Israel has been reluctant to return the land to Syria without guarantees that it (Israel) will remain safe from attack. In 1974, however, the two states agreed to withdraw their forces from the Golan Heights, and the UN inserted over 1,000 peacekeeping troops into observation posts in the hills between the two sides' positions.[16] These troops, who remain in position to this day, help to ensure that both sides live up to their commitment not to deploy military forces into the Heights. By making it costlier for either side to break this promise, the UN eased a source of tension in this volatile region.

Third, collective security organizations may play a positive role in promoting peace not through a threat of direct intervention for or against any particular side, but by serving as neutral observers and peacekeepers. Peacekeepers diminish first-strike advantages by interposing themselves between two adversarial factions, as in the Golan Heights. Such operations are particularly useful in cases in which previously warring parties have each pledged to disarm and demobilize, but each fears that if it disarms and the other does not, it will be at a dangerous disadvantage. As we saw in the appendix to Chapter 3, the commitment problem associated with disarmament is a major obstacle to preventing and ending civil wars. The United Nations often deploys peacekeeping missions into precisely such situations in order to make sure that both sides uphold their promise to disarm and that neither side attempts to exploit the other in the process. For example, following the end of the civil war in Liberia, which claimed almost 150,000 lives from 1989 to 2003, the UN inserted 15,000 peacekeepers to facilitate disarmament and demobilization.

THE DILEMMAS OF COLLECTIVE SECURITY

Regardless of the specific ways in which the organization chooses to intervene, it faces two major challenges: a collective action problem, and a joint decision-making problem. The collective action problem arises from the fact that collective security organizations, unlike their members, do not have the power to

---

16. For more information on the UN peacekeeping mission in the Golan Heights, see www.un.org/Depts/dpko/missions/undof/index.html.

tax or to raise and field military forces. As a result, the organizations are wholly dependent on their members to provide troops, funds, and military equipment for any operation. The member states that contribute then face the costs and risks associated with sending troops into combat or foregoing trade due to economic sanctions. Crucially, the international peace and stability that these actions are intended to provide is a public good. Recall from Chapter 2 that a public good can be enjoyed whether or not one actually contributed to its creation. If the community succeeds in preventing or reversing an act of aggression, all members of the community enjoy the benefit—whether or not they took costly action. After all, even if all states have an interest in seeing aggression halted, their first preference will often be to have the aggression halted by someone other than themselves. Hence, collective security organizations necessarily face a free-rider problem: the temptation that member states face to let the burden of providing the public good fall on others. Because of this problem, even if everyone shares an interest in cooperating to stop or prevent a war, their collective effort may fall well short of what is required to do so. Indeed, UN peacekeeping missions are often underfunded and undermanned relative to their mandates; the temptation to free ride, to pass the costs to other states, leads to low levels of cooperation.

The challenges of joint decision-making are also very severe. Members of the organization need to be able to determine which acts constitute a threat to the community, which states are aggressors, and what actions to take in response. This determination is not always straightforward since collective security organizations permit states to use force in self-defense. Of course, states generally justify their military actions as being in self-defense, so determining which acts are acts of aggression and which are self-defense is necessary for the organization to function. Otherwise, the entire system can collapse under mutual recriminations. A finding that a particular act constitutes a threat to international peace and security not only delegitimizes that act as a violation of community interests, but it also grants legitimacy to those who use force to reverse it. As we will see, this grant of legitimacy can be an asset to states that operate under the organization's seal of approval.[17]

Determining whether a given act merits an international response is complicated by the mix of interests that member states have. Although they may share a general interest in halting aggression and promoting the peaceful settlement of disputes, they may also have specific interests that diverge in any particular conflict. Recall that collective security organizations, due to their universal membership, often include states with varying, even opposing, interests. Whereas NATO during the Cold War included only states that perceived a common threat from the Soviet Union, the UN during this period included not only the United States and its NATO allies but also the Soviet Union and its allies, as well as states that were neutral in the superpower rivalry. This mix of interests means that in many situations the members of a collective security organization may not all be neutral outsiders to a particular military action. Some may have reasons to favor one side or the other in a dispute, meaning that some will be motivated to see aggression

17. On the UN's legitimacy role, see Ian Hurd, *After Anarchy: Legitimacy and Power in the United Nations Security Council* (Princeton, NJ: Princeton University Press, 2007), and Alexander Thompson, *Channeling Power: The UN Security Council and American Statecraft in Iraq* (Ithaca, NY: Cornell University Press, 2009).

where others will not. Collective security works best when all states are satisfied with the current status quo, a condition that is rarely met.

INSTITUTIONAL RESPONSES TO THE CHALLENGES OF COLLECTIVE SECURITY

The design of collective security organizations reflects the challenges posed by the dilemmas of collective action and joint decision-making. Recall that institutions facilitate cooperation in situations that arise repeatedly. Rather than treating each new crisis in an ad hoc manner, requiring renegotiation of standards and rules each time, institutions embody a lasting set of standards and decision-making rules.

In the two most ambitious collective security organizations attempted in the last century—the League of Nations and the United Nations—the problems of collective action and joint decision-making were addressed by vesting the main decision-making power in the hands of relatively small councils dominated by the strongest states in the system. These councils were given the authority to determine whether a particular action was a threat to international peace and security and to prescribe the organization's response. The League Council began with four permanent members—Great Britain, France, Italy, and Japan—and four nonpermanent members who were elected every three years.[18] Germany later joined as a fifth permanent member, and the council was expanded to 15. When the United Nations replaced the League in 1946, its **Security Council** had a similar structure—five permanent members and six (later 10) nonpermanent members—although the identity of the **permanent five (P5)** changed: the United States, Great Britain, France, the Soviet Union (now Russia), and China. In both cases, the privileged few shared a common trait: with the exception of Germany, which was admitted to the League only belatedly, they were the victors of the global wars that gave birth to these organizations.

The voting rules of both councils amplified the influence of these permanent members. In the case of the League Council, all decisions had to be unanimously approved by all 15 members. As a result, any member of the council could block the organization from acting by withholding its support. In other words, every member of the council had **veto power,** and permanent members had permanent veto power. This voting rule was modified slightly in the UN Security Council. Enacting a substantive resolution in the Security Council requires majority support among all Council members *and* the support of every one of the P5. This change was intended to make decisive action easier—by eliminating the requirement that all 15 members agree—but it also magnified the asymmetrical role of the P5, each of which can block a resolution it does not like.

These arrangements have several virtues. First, vesting decision-making power with a relatively small group of states means that it is not necessary to obtain consensus within the entire membership (which, in the case of the UN, now numbers 192). This both reduces the costs of coming to an agreement and, in theory at least,

18. Originally, the United States was intended to be the fifth permanent member, but the United States never joined the League because of congressional opposition.

makes it possible for the organization to respond to crises quickly. Second, these rules ensure that when the organization acts, it does so with the consent of the strongest powers in the international system. This arrangement can alleviate the collective action problem by ensuring that any operation that is approved will enjoy cooperation and contributions from those members with the greatest resources and capabilities. Moreover, the veto ensures that at a minimum, the organization's actions will not be forcibly opposed by any of these powerful members.

As with all institutions, however, the effects of these rules are not neutral; rather, they bias policy outcomes in a direction that favors the states that were in a position to dictate the rules at the outset. The organization cannot act on its core mission without unanimity among the most powerful states in the system, any one of which can block action by exercising its veto. Such unanimity can be difficult to achieve. When the major powers disagree among themselves, the permanent member veto introduces a bias toward inaction. The veto also ensures that the organization cannot act in ways that harm the interests of any of the permanent members. As a result, the organization wields its policing powers unevenly: it may respond to the crimes of those who are weak, or who have no friends among the permanent members, while the crimes of the strong, or those with friends in high places, may go unpunished. In the case of Tibet, mentioned at the outset of this chapter, any effective action by the UN against China could have been blocked by its ally, the Soviet Union.[19] More recently, China has resisted efforts by the UN to impose tough economic sanctions on the government of Sudan for its genocide in Darfur. Because China is the main customer for Sudan's oil (it purchases about 70 percent of Sudan's oil exports), China has an interest in protecting the Sudanese government from the full weight of international disapproval.

In sum, collective security organizations help states cooperate to further their collective interests in international peace by providing rules and standards to address the challenges of collective action and joint decision-making that inevitably bedevil this enterprise. Nonetheless, these institutions operate under constraints that limit their ability to act effectively. Collective security organizations are most likely to succeed when two conditions are met. First, the powerful member states that are central to their decision-making processes must all agree on the desirability of collective action. At a minimum, none of these states can be sufficiently opposed that it will block such action. Second, at least some members must value the collective good highly enough that they are willing to pay the costs in lives and money to ensure that the good is provided. The latter condition is most likely to hold either when the

Because of its institutional rules, the UN is unlikely to undertake missions that harm the interests of any of its most powerful members. For example, UN efforts to impose economic sanctions on the government of Sudan, in response to the genocide in the Darfur region, have been blocked by China. As a big buyer of Sudanese oil, China has an interest in sparing Sudan from punishment.

19. Communist China was not, at that time, on the Security Council. Until 1971, China's seat on the Council was held by Taiwan.

anticipated costs of intervention are low or when states have some private interest in contributing above and beyond the public interest in stopping aggression. In other words, collective security institutions are useful at promoting cooperation when their key members have strong common interests in protecting the peace; unfortunately, the existence of such common interests is not guaranteed.

THE EXPERIENCE OF COLLECTIVE SECURITY: THE UNITED NATIONS

To see how these predictions have been borne out historically, we consider the experience of the most ambitious collective security organization ever created: the United Nations. This organization arose from the ashes of World War II and embodied the aspiration, articulated in its founding charter, to "save succeeding generations from the scourge of war"—a goal that had become all the more pressing with the advent of nuclear weapons, which had the capacity to kill millions in the blink of an eye. Although the world has not since seen a repetition of global warfare, or the nightmare of nuclear war, the role of the UN in preventing these outcomes is not clear. Indeed, the UN has had uneven and sporadic success in fulfilling its creators' aspirations. In this section, we briefly review the experience of the UN. As we will see, the challenges facing collective security organizations discussed above play a large role in accounting for this organization's limited success historically.

What Does the United Nations Do?

When countries join the UN, they sign on to the organization's charter.[20] Members pledge not to use force in disputes with one another and to seek assistance from the organization in resolving their conflicts peacefully. Chapter VII of the UN Charter authorizes the Security Council to identify acts of aggression and threats to peace and to determine what measures should be taken in response. The charter first provides for economic and diplomatic sanctions to be applied against aggressor states, but it also authorizes the Security Council to "take such action by air, sea, or land forces as may be necessary to maintain or restore international peace and security."

In practice, the Security Council can authorize two different kinds of military operations: peacekeeping and peace-enforcement. A **peacekeeping operation** typically follows the conclusion of an interstate or civil war. The combatants have agreed to end the fighting, but it is considered valuable to have an impartial force in place to make sure that the war does not resume. In such instances, the UN may assemble a multinational peacekeeping force with the mandate to verify that the terms of the peace agreement are kept: that the ceasefire holds; that any temporary ceasefire lines are respected; that troops are withdrawn or demobilized, if there are provisions to that effect; and so on. In the aftermath of civil conflict, peacekeeping forces have also helped to ensure the fairness of elections. Their deployment typically requires that the parties to the conflict agree to invite them in, a requirement known as *host nation agreement*. Hence, except in rare cases, peacekeepers are not imposed on warring parties; rather, they deploy only with those parties' consent. Although peacekeepers

peacekeeping operation: An operation in which troops and observers are deployed to monitor a ceasefire or peace agreement.

---

20. The entire UN Charter can be viewed at www.un.org/aboutun/charter/.

may be physically interposed between the adversaries or may patrol in areas where fighting could recur, they are typically lightly armed. Their purpose is not to fight a war, but to make sure that a war does not restart. For this reason, their main resource is not military power, but rather their perceived impartiality—that is, they are neutral brokers, favoring neither side in the dispute. As a result, peacekeepers are often drawn from distant countries with only weak interests in the conflict, and rarely from the P5. To illustrate, Table 5.1 provides a list of the top ten contributors to peacekeeping missions in February 2009, none of which is a permanent member; the ranking of the permanent members is also shown.

A **peace-enforcement operation,** by contrast, is used to make peace among warring parties that have not yet agreed to end their fighting. The Security Council can authorize such an operation under Chapter VII of the charter, after finding that a particular situation is a threat to international peace and security. The invasion of one state by another is a classic example of the kind of act that was intended to trigger intervention under Chapter VII. In recent years, the Security Council has also authorized action under Chapter VII for purely civil conflicts when the state in question could not or did not request intervention. Because peace-enforcement operations are generally targeted against one or more sides that are viewed as aggressors, they are not impartial, and the expectation is that troops involved in such operations will engage in combat. Hence, unlike peacekeeping, peace-enforcement operations tend to be more heavily armed, and a P5 member may be

peace-enforcement operation: A military operation in which force is used to make and/or enforce peace among warring parties that have not agreed to end their fighting.

TABLE 5.1	TOP CONTRIBUTORS TO UN PEACEKEEPING OPERATIONS, FEBRUARY 2009	
Rank	**Country**	**Number of personnel**
1	Pakistan	10,687
2	Bangladesh	9,425
3	India	8,633
4	Nigeria	5,993
5	Nepal	3,888
6	Rwanda	3,597
7	Ghana	3,250
8	Jordan	3,122
9	Uruguay	2,539
10	Italy	2,515
CONTRIBUTIONS FROM THE P5		
Rank	**Country**	**Number of personnel**
13	France	2,174
14	China	2,168
42	Great Britain	292
45	Russia	248
66	United States	97

Source: United Nations, Department of Peacekeeping Operations, www.un.org/Depts/dpko/dpko/contributors/2009/feb09_2.pdf (accessed 3/17/09).

centrally involved. The UN efforts in the Korean War and the Persian Gulf War both fall within this category.

Cold War Paralysis

The UN was born with high hopes but soon found its most ambitious aspirations dashed by conflict among the powerful states in the system. The Cold War between the United States and the Soviet Union, which lasted from approximately 1946 to 1989, meant that the Security Council was largely incapable of dealing with issues that cut across this key divide. On many matters that came before the Council, one side or the other had an interest in blocking effective action. For example, when the United States put forward proposals in 1947 to help Greece in its civil war against communist rebels, the Soviet Union exercised its veto. The United States, for its part, wielded its veto quite frequently to stop resolutions that it saw as harmful to Israel, such as those censuring Israel for its treatment of Palestinians in the occupied territories. France, Great Britain, and China also exercised their vetoes, though on significantly fewer occasions. All in all, during the period 1946–1989, there were 192 vetoes cast on substantive issues before the Council. This compares to 646 resolutions passed in the same period. The UN was most active in cases that did not cut across the Cold War divide, in which case one or both superpowers had little direct interest.

The one major exception to this generalization, the UN-sponsored intervention in the Korean War, is the exception that proves the rule. Two days after North Korea invaded South Korea, the Security Council passed Resolution 83 authorizing member states to assist South Korea in repelling the attack. While the United States provided the bulk of the forces for this operation, it was joined by 19 other states. Given that North Korea was an ally of the Soviet Union, the latter should have been expected to veto the Security Council resolution. This act would not have prevented American intervention, but it would have denied the operation UN blessing and perhaps some multilateral support. The veto failed to materialize because the Soviet Union was boycotting meetings of the Security Council at the time due to a dispute over China's representation on the body. When the UN was created, mainland China was ruled by the pro-American Nationalist government. In 1949, however, Communist forces defeated the Nationalists in a civil war, and the latter fled to the island of Taiwan. A year later, when the Korean War broke out, China's seat on the Security Council was held by a representative of the Nationalist government on Taiwan. The Soviet Union argued that China's seat should be filled by a representative of the Communist government on the mainland, and it refused to attend meetings of the Security Council until that demand was met. Hence, when Resolution 83 came to a vote on June 27, 1950, the Soviet representative was not present to cast a veto. Needless to say, the Soviet Union ended its boycott of the Security Council not long afterwards.[21]

The Cold War divide thus crippled the UN for the first five decades of its existence. Although the organization did have a constructive role at times—brokering ceasefires on several occasions and deploying 18 peacekeeping missions—the organization sat on the sidelines of many of the most dangerous conflicts of this period.

---

21. China's seat on the Security Council remained in the hands of Taiwan until 1971, when warming relations between the United States and the People's Republic of China paved the way for the seat to be transferred to the mainland's control.

The Gulf War and the "New World Order"

The end of the Cold War created new possibilities for the UN. In 1989, the central source of the East-West rivalry, Soviet domination of Eastern Europe, receded. And in December 1991, the Soviet Union itself dissolved and was replaced by 15 new independent states, the largest of which, Russia, inherited the Soviet Union's seat in the UN, along with most of its military capabilities. The dramatic realignment of interests and reduction in conflict among the P5 meant that the UN could take on a more active role. And indeed, 1990 marks a major turning point in the activity of the organization. As Table 5.2 shows, the post–Cold War period saw a marked drop in the number of vetoes cast and a corresponding increase in the number of peacekeeping missions and resolutions passed by the Security Council. Map 5.2 shows where UN peacekeeping missions were deployed in 2008.

Optimism about the UN's role in the post–Cold War period hit a high point very early on, in the wake of Iraq's invasion of Kuwait in August 1990. As we have seen, U.S. president George H. W. Bush committed almost immediately to ensuring that the conquest of Kuwait would not stand. Bush also made a concerted effort to line up UN support at every step of the way. Between Iraq's invasion of Kuwait and the U.S.-led military operation to reverse it, the Security Council passed 12 resolutions on the crisis. The most important of these, Resolution 678, authorized member states to use "all necessary means" to bring about the unconditional withdrawal of Iraqi forces from Kuwait if Iraq did not comply voluntarily by January 15, 1991. The Security Council's approval of this resolution owed a great deal to the reduction of conflict in the international system with the end of the Cold War. The Soviet Union had long been an ally of Iraq, and in an earlier period it might have been expected to veto a resolution like 678. In the post–Cold War environment, however, when the Soviet Union desired better relations with the West, it was relatively easy to overcome that country's reluctance to approve the use of force against its former ally.

The blessing of the UN meant that the United States had substantial international assistance in the ensuing war. The coalition that fought Iraq included troops from 35 nations. As shown in Figure 5.2, the United States supplied the vast majority of the troops for the operation, but the multinational cast and UN blessing had political, if not much military, significance. The participation of a number of Arab and Muslim states was seen as important in blunting Iraq's argument that the United States was waging a war against Islam. The limited mandate of the operation—to liberate Kuwait and not to occupy Iraq—was intended to reassure states in the region that the United States

TABLE 5.2	THE UNITED NATIONS DURING AND AFTER THE COLD WAR	
	Cold War, 1946–1989	Post–Cold War, 1990–2008
Security Council resolutions approved	646	1,213
Vetoed resolutions	192	22
Peacekeeping missions	18	45

Sources: United Nations Security Council, un.org/Docs/sc/unsc_resolutions.html. Great Britain, Foreign and Commonwealth Office, www.fco.gov.uk/resources/en/pdf/4175218/vetoes-2008-2. United Nations, Department of Peacekeeping Operations, un.org/Depts/dpko/dpko/ (accessed 3/17/09).

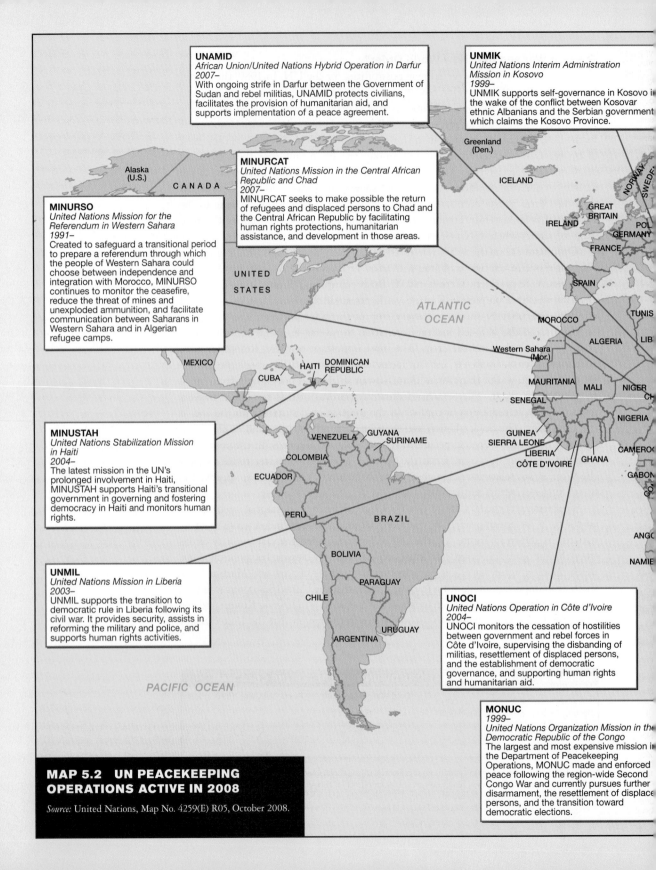

UNAMID
African Union/United Nations Hybrid Operation in Darfur
2007–
With ongoing strife in Darfur between the Government of Sudan and rebel militias, UNAMID protects civilians, facilitates the provision of humanitarian aid, and supports implementation of a peace agreement.

UNMIK
United Nations Interim Administration Mission in Kosovo
1999–
UNMIK supports self-governance in Kosovo in the wake of the conflict between Kosovar ethnic Albanians and the Serbian government which claims the Kosovo Province.

MINURCAT
United Nations Mission in the Central African Republic and Chad
2007–
MINURCAT seeks to make possible the return of refugees and displaced persons to Chad and the Central African Republic by facilitating human rights protections, humanitarian assistance, and development in those areas.

MINURSO
United Nations Mission for the Referendum in Western Sahara
1991–
Created to safeguard a transitional period to prepare a referendum through which the people of Western Sahara could choose between independence and integration with Morocco, MINURSO continues to monitor the ceasefire, reduce the threat of mines and unexploded ammunition, and facilitate communication between Saharans in Western Sahara and in Algerian refugee camps.

MINUSTAH
United Nations Stabilization Mission in Haiti
2004–
The latest mission in the UN's prolonged involvement in Haiti, MINUSTAH supports Haiti's transitional government in governing and fostering democracy in Haiti and monitors human rights.

UNMIL
United Nations Mission in Liberia
2003–
UNMIL supports the transition to democratic rule in Liberia following its civil war. It provides security, assists in reforming the military and police, and supports human rights activities.

UNOCI
United Nations Operation in Côte d'Ivoire
2004–
UNOCI monitors the cessation of hostilities between government and rebel forces in Côte d'Ivoire, supervising the disbanding of militias, resettlement of displaced persons, and the establishment of democratic governance, and supporting human rights and humanitarian aid.

MONUC
1999–
United Nations Organization Mission in the Democratic Republic of the Congo
The largest and most expensive mission in the Department of Peacekeeping Operations, MONUC made and enforced peace following the region-wide Second Congo War and currently pursues further disarmament, the resettlement of displaced persons, and the transition toward democratic elections.

MAP 5.2   UN PEACEKEEPING OPERATIONS ACTIVE IN 2008

Source: United Nations, Map No. 4259(E) R05, October 2008.

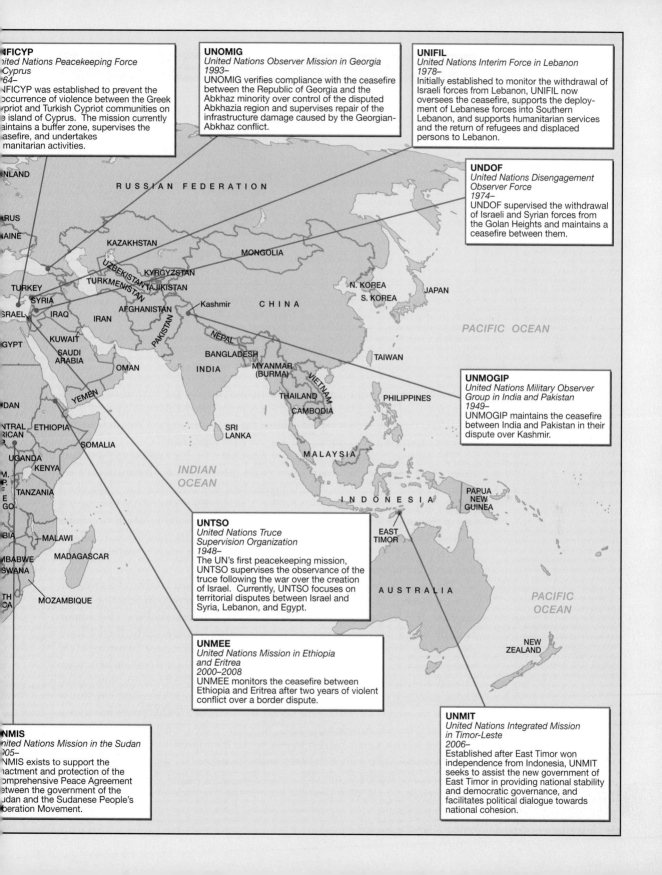

NFICYP
United Nations Peacekeeping Force Cyprus
964–
NFICYP was established to prevent the occurrence of violence between the Greek ypriot and Turkish Cypriot communities on e island of Cyprus. The mission currently aintains a buffer zone, supervises the asefire, and undertakes manitarian activities.

UNOMIG
United Nations Observer Mission in Georgia
1993–
UNOMIG verifies compliance with the ceasefire between the Republic of Georgia and the Abkhaz minority over control of the disputed Abkhazia region and supervises repair of the infrastructure damage caused by the Georgian-Abkhaz conflict.

UNIFIL
United Nations Interim Force in Lebanon
1978–
Initially established to monitor the withdrawal of Israeli forces from Lebanon, UNIFIL now oversees the ceasefire, supports the deployment of Lebanese forces into Southern Lebanon, and supports humanitarian services and the return of refugees and displaced persons to Lebanon.

UNDOF
United Nations Disengagement Observer Force
1974–
UNDOF supervised the withdrawal of Israeli and Syrian forces from the Golan Heights and maintains a ceasefire between them.

UNMOGIP
United Nations Military Observer Group in India and Pakistan
1949–
UNMOGIP maintains the ceasefire between India and Pakistan in their dispute over Kashmir.

UNTSO
United Nations Truce Supervision Organization
1948–
The UN's first peacekeeping mission, UNTSO supervises the observance of the truce following the war over the creation of Israel. Currently, UNTSO focuses on territorial disputes between Israel and Syria, Lebanon, and Egypt.

UNMEE
United Nations Mission in Ethiopia and Eritrea
2000–2008
UNMEE monitors the ceasefire between Ethiopia and Eritrea after two years of violent conflict over a border dispute.

UNMIT
United Nations Integrated Mission in Timor-Leste
2006–
Established after East Timor won independence from Indonesia, UNMIT seeks to assist the new government of East Timor in providing national stability and democratic governance, and facilitates political dialogue towards national cohesion.

NMIS
nited Nations Mission in the Sudan
005–
NMIS exists to support the nactment and protection of the omprehensive Peace Agreement etween the government of the udan and the Sudanese People's beration Movement.

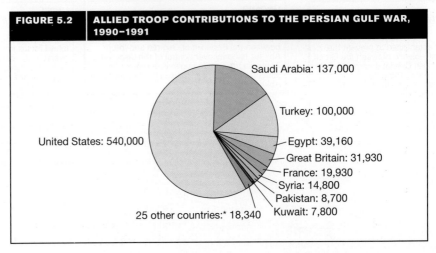

FIGURE 5.2 | **ALLIED TROOP CONTRIBUTIONS TO THE PERSIAN GULF WAR, 1990-1991**

Saudi Arabia: 137,000

Turkey: 100,000

Egypt: 39,160

Great Britain: 31,930

France: 19,930

Syria: 14,800

Pakistan: 8,700

Kuwait: 7,800

United States: 540,000

25 other countries:* 18,340

*Bangladesh, Morocco, Qatar, United Arab Emirates, Canada, Italy, Australia, Netherlands, Oman, Spain, Bahrain, Germany, Belgium, Senegal, Niger, Argentina, Philippines, Greece, Poland, South Korea, Czechoslovakia, Denmark, Norway, New Zealand, Hungary.
Source U.S. General Accounting Office, *Persian Gulf: Allied Burden Sharing Efforts,* GAO/NSIAD-92-71, Appendix II, 16-7, www.gao.gov/products/NSIAD-92-71 (accessed 10/20/08).

did not have expansionist objectives. International support also reduced the financial costs of the war. Contributions from other countries covered about 90 percent of the $61 billion the United States spent fighting the war—making the Persian Gulf War the least expensive war in America's history on a per capita basis.

The successful operation of the UN machinery in this case led to great optimism about the role this organization could play in the new international environment. Bush, in his State of the Union address just before the war, spoke of the opportunity to create "a new world order, a world where the rule of law, not the law of the jungle, governs the conduct of nations"—a world in which "a credible United Nations can use its peacekeeping role to fulfill the promise and vision of the UN's founders." Indeed, the UN had seemed to meet the first challenge of this new era quite successfully.

The optimism would turn out to be overblown. The Iraqi invasion of Kuwait was in many respects an easy case for effective international action. By invading a weak neighbor, Iraq had committed a flagrant violation of international law. More important, the attack was seen as directly threatening the interests of the United States and its allies. After gobbling up Kuwait, Iraq was in possession of 20 percent of the world's known oil reserves. Furthermore, the attack put Iraq in a position to threaten Saudi Arabia, home to another 25 percent of the world's oil. All told, the Persian Gulf region contained two-thirds of this valuable natural resource. The possibility that so much of the world's oil could come under the control of a hostile power was seen as threatening to vital American interests. As a result, the United States was strongly motivated to take forceful action to reverse the Iraqi invasion. In all likelihood, it would have done so even if it had been unable to secure UN approval.

Hence, the success of the UN in this case owed a great deal to the fact that the United States, the most powerful actor in the international system, perceived a direct threat to its own interests. The international community was, in this instance, what we called in Chapter 2 a privileged group, since a single member was strongly motivated enough to provide the public good. The next several years would provide ample evidence that when such incentives are lacking, the community's collective interests in stopping aggression and/or ending gross violations of human rights are generally not enough to compel effective international intervention.

The "Triumph of the Lack of Will": Bosnia, Somalia, Rwanda, and Darfur

The hard tests of the new world order came only a few years after the victory in the Persian Gulf. The 1990s witnessed a number of bloody and heart-wrenching crises that transfixed the international community but also exposed the limits of that community's willingness to do much about them.[22]

One visible example of the limited will of the international community played out in the former Yugoslav republic of Bosnia-Herzegovina. The civil conflict in Bosnia was the bloodiest of several violent acts in the breakup of Yugoslavia. Originally composed of five republics—Serbia, Slovenia, Croatia, Bosnia-Herzegovina, and Macedonia—the Yugoslav federation began to dissolve in 1991 as Slovenia, Croatia, and Bosnia sought independence and Serbia, the largest republic, tried to hold the multiethnic state together by force. The conflict in Bosnia was the most complicated and bloody because this republic was home to three ethnic groups with different aspirations: Serbs (comprising 31 percent of the prewar population), Croats (25 percent), and Bosnian Muslims (44 percent). See Map 5.3. Many Serbs did not want to live in an independent Bosnia; rather, they wanted to carve out portions of that republic and join with Serbia. The more radical Croats had similar thoughts of joining Croatia. When Bosnia declared its independence from Yugoslavia in March 1992, militant Serbs and Croats rebelled, triggering a three-way war. Although most of the fighting was among Bosnians of different ethnic groups, there was also an international component to the war, since Serbia supported the Bosnian Serbs and Croatia (which had gained its independence in 1991) supported the Bosnian Croats.

The three-year war was incredibly brutal, with 300,000 killed, mostly civilians, and at least 2 million refugees displaced from their homes. In addition, the combatants engaged in widespread atrocities against civilians: shelling cities, herding men and boys into detention camps where they were malnourished and mistreated, raping women and girls in order to terrorize the population. While crimes were committed by all sides, the greatest offenders were the Serbs, who engaged in a systematic campaign of what became known as "ethnic cleansing": clearing coveted territory of all non-Serbs by either killing them or scaring them into flight.

The international response to these events was feeble and at times counterproductive. Although there was unanimous condemnation of the violence, no one was willing to exert on behalf of Bosnia the kind of effort that had been had marshaled to save Kuwait only one year earlier. Absent compelling interests, such as securing an important natural resource (that is, oil), the UN, at the behest of the United States and European powers, responded in a half-hearted way. A peacekeeping

---

22. We take our heading for this section from the title phrase of an insightful analysis of this period; see James Gow, *Triumph of the Lack of Will: International Diplomacy and the Yugoslav War* (New York: Columbia University Press, 1997).

MAP 5.3   ETHNIC DIVISIONS IN THE FORMER YUGOSLAVIA

AUSTRIA

HUNGARY

SLOVENIA
★ Ljubljana

ROMANIA

Zagreb
★

CROATIA

VOJVODINA
(autonomous
province)

Belgrade
★

BOSNIA AND
HERZEGOVINA

SERBIA

Sarajevo
★

MONTENEGRO
Podgorica
★

Pristina
★

KOSOVO

BULGARIA

Legend
- Albanian
- Bulgarian
- Croat
- Hungarian
- Macedonian
- Montenegrin
- Muslim
- Serb
- Slovak
- Slovene
- No majority present

*Adriatic
Sea*

MACEDONIA

ALBANIA

GREECE

ITALY

force, composed mostly of European troops, was deployed to the area—despite the fact that there was no peace to keep. Imposed into the war zone under Chapter VII, the UN Protection Force (UNPROFOR) nonetheless had many of the qualities of a traditional peacekeeping force: it was lightly armed, dispersed throughout the country, required to be neutral, and ordered to fire only in self-defense. Its main mission was to distribute food and medicine to civilians and to help keep them out of harm's way. Hence, UNPROFOR sought to treat the symptoms of the war, but it had neither a mandate nor the requisite capabilities to end the war. In fact, the peacekeepers often had to bribe combatants in order to move about the country without being molested, and on several occasions Serb forces took peacekeepers hostage and chained them to artillery pieces in order to deter air strikes against their positions. The UN also declared several Bosnian cities to be "safe havens" where civilians could find safety from the war under its protection. The hollowness of this promise became evident in the worst atrocity of the war. In July 1995, Serb forces overran the safe haven of Srebrenica and proceeded to massacre 7,000 Muslim men and boys. The 600 Dutch peacekeepers charged with defending the city could do little to resist. When Serb forces threatened to kill some Dutch hostages, the

Dutch government and the UN commanders on the ground decided to negotiate their troops' surrender.[23]

The massacre at Srebrenica did finally spark tougher international intervention. In August–September 1995, the United States and NATO conducted sustained air strikes against Serb forces. These attacks helped bring about a peace conference in Dayton, Ohio, that led to the Bosnian war's end in December 1995. With a peace to keep, U.S. and NATO forces were deployed as peacekeepers, with the blessing of the UN and alongside international police forces organized by the UN. In a pattern repeated elsewhere (see below), the UN mechanism had more success in maintaining a peace already achieved than in ending aggression and gross violations of human rights.

The United Nations' halfhearted response to war and atrocities in the former Yugoslavia had little effect. As part of an "ethnic cleansing" campaign, Serbian fighters forced Muslim men and boys into detention camps. Eventually, NATO stepped into the ongoing crisis, in 1995, ending the conflict.

A similar lack of will by the international community was manifest in Rwanda in 1994 and in the ongoing conflict in the Darfur region of Sudan. In Rwanda, conflict between the county's principal ethnic groups, the Hutu and the Tutsi, erupted in genocide in April 1994. In the course of three months, an estimated 800,000 people were killed—many hacked to death by machetes—including 75 percent of the Tutsi population. The international response to this tragedy was very weak. A small UN peacekeeping force already on the ground was overwhelmed. After 10 of its peacekeepers were killed on the first day of the conflict, Belgium withdrew its forces, and other nations followed suit. As the death toll rose, the international community stood by and watched. The killing stopped only after a Tutsi rebel force succeeded in defeating the Hutu forces responsible for much of the slaughter.

The case of Darfur is equally tragic. Since 2003, a bloody conflict has raged in western Sudan, where government-supported militias have carried out systematic killings of the people there. In another widely acknowledged genocide, it is estimated that 200,000 to 400,000 people have died, and another 2.5 million have been displaced from their homes. In spite of widespread outrage, the response of the UN has been weak. Member states have been unwilling to support or contribute troops to a robust military operation to end the violence.

This discussion is not meant to imply that the UN mechanism never works. Rather, it suggests that absent compelling national interests, member states are reluctant to pay heavy costs or embrace high risks to further the community's interest in stopping aggression or ending humanitarian crises. In all of these cases, the member states cared about the suffering, but they did not care enough to undertake the kind of military operation that would have been needed to end the conflicts that were the cause of the suffering. The "Controversy" box on page 206 discusses the conflict in Kosovo that came to international attention in 1999 and the challenges that international organizations face when it comes to such interventions.

---

23. Samantha Power, *"A Problem from Hell": America and the Age of Genocide* (New York: Perennial, 2002), 399–400.

Should the International Community Intervene Militarily in Civil Conflicts?

In the early morning of January 15, 1999, Serbian forces entered the village of Račak, in the country's southern province of Kosovo. In the ensuing massacre, 45 ethnic Albanian civilians were shot at close range, and their decapitated corpses left to decompose in the fields. This atrocity culminated nine years of punitive measures by Slobodan Milosevic's Serbian government against Kosovo's Albanian majority—including acts of murder, rape, and deportation—and led to pressure for international action to halt a brewing genocide. On March 24, the NATO alliance launched an air campaign against Serbia that ultimately resulted in the expulsion of Serbian troops from Kosovo, the establishment of an interim administration under the United Nations, and the return of hundreds of thousands of Albanian refugees.

Despite this success, the moral legitimacy of NATO's war remains contested. The controversy can be partly explained by the complex and sometimes conflicting interests that are at stake in any humanitarian intervention.

The main argument in favor of war rested on the urgent moral imperative to protect the interests of Milosevic's victims. It was argued that where a state has failed in its obligation to protect its citizens from massacre, ethnic cleansing, and other "crimes against humanity," other states have the responsibility to intervene—by force, if necessary. A second argument appealed to the interests of NATO's member

states. Political instability in the Balkans threatened the security of surrounding nations, including NATO members Greece and Turkey, thereby justifying military action under the alliance's charter.

Opponents of the intervention pointed to other interests that the NATO campaign jeopardized. Humanitarian intervention threatens the interests that states have in exercising sovereign control over internal matters. Serbia argued that Albanians were engaged in a violent terrorist campaign that sought to dismember the country. Although the atrocities committed against civilians were unacceptable, states have a legitimate interest in maintaining order domestically and preserving their territorial integrity. Humanitarian intervention erodes that right. And while the NATO operation served a moral purpose, there is no guarantee that foreign states will not abuse the principle of intervention to pursue less noble interests. Critics also argue that the Kosovo case could threaten international

stability. Although Kosovo's independence was not the goal of the operation, it will likely be the eventual outcome. Kosovo declared its independence in February 2008, and while the legality of this act is contested, most NATO members have recognized the new state. As much as one can sympathize with the desire of the Kosovars to be free of Serbia, the precedent could be destabilizing, as there are many groups around the world that would similarly like a state of their own.

A second source of controversy over the NATO campaign was the strategic merits of military force as a means of promoting humanitarian interests. Even if intervention is justified, war is a blunt and costly instrument for achieving policy change. Outside governments worried about casualties to their own forces may not intervene in an effective manner. To minimize the risks, the NATO campaign was conducted entirely from the air, using high-altitude bombing. Although this strategy did prevent NATO casualties, its immediate effect on the ground was a brisk escalation of Milosevic's campaign of extermination. Even if an intervention succeeds in easing a crisis, an enduring solution requires a long-term commitment by outside actors that may not be credible. When the foreigners go home, conflict may recur.

Finally, humanitarian intervention raises the institutional question of who should decide when the international community can get involved. The United Nations is the natural venue for such a determination. Even so, for the Security Council to authorize intervention in purely domestic conflicts requires an expansive interpretation of what constitutes a "threat to international peace and security." Moreover, two members of the Security Council, China and Russia, have been loathe to endorse humanitarian intervention, in part because their own human rights records are spotty. For this reason, the UN Security Council never authorized the Kosovo operation. Supporters argued that NATO, as an alliance of democracies, was well qualified to act in support of human rights. But, as a matter of international law, the alliance does not have the authority to undertake such an operation. Although, to some, this means that the intervention in Kosovo was illegitimate, others would suggest that it points to a fundamental problem with the United Nations mechanism. ∎

The Quiet Successes

In other cases, however, the costs of intervention are seen as relatively low, and the UN's track record has been more impressive. These cases generally fall under the category of traditional peacekeeping: monitoring and assisting in the implementation of peace agreements. Because the existence of a peace agreement indicates that the opposing parties are ready to stop fighting and resolve their differences, the risks associated with getting involved are not that high. Keeping peace after a war is generally easier than making peace during a war.

For this reason, UN efforts have been most successful in the area of post-conflict reconstruction.[24] In the case of El Salvador, for example, a UN peacekeeping operation played an important role in that country's recovery from a 12-year civil war that had claimed 75,000 lives. The UN Observer Mission in El Salvador (ONUSAL) comprised about 700 military observers and civilian police from 17 countries, but it had an expansive mandate to help rebuild the country. ONUSAL not only helped to monitor the demobilization of the warring factions after a 1992 peace agreement, but it also assisted in implementing political reforms designed to address the root causes of the conflict, such as reforming the judiciary, forming and training a new civilian police force, and redistributing land to former combatants. ONUSAL also monitored an election in 1994 to ensure that it was free and fair and that all sides would respect the result. The mission's mandate ended in April 1995, leaving in its wake a country that is generally considered free and democratic. Similar stories of success in post-conflict reconstruction can be found in Mozambique, Liberia, Sierra Leone, East Timor, Cambodia, and even Bosnia, where a NATO-led peacekeeping force with a UN blessing went in after the 1995 peace deal and was deemed to have fulfilled its mission and departed in December 2004.[25]

It is quite likely that people following the news have heard much more about the UN's failings in Bosnia, Rwanda, and Darfur than about the quieter victories in places like El Salvador and Bosnia after 1995. Bloodshed naturally draws more attention than do peace and reconciliation, so the failures of the UN get more publicity than do its successes. For more evidence on the success of peacekeeping operations, see "What Do We Know?" on page 208.

From 9/11 to Iraq: Consensus Lost

During the 1990s, civil conflicts such as the ones in Bosnia and Rwanda were much more prominent on the UN agenda than were cases of international aggression like the Persian Gulf War. As we have seen, the main impediment to effective action in these cases was a lack of will—the absence of compelling national interests that could have justified committing resources and taking risks. The September 11, 2001, terrorist attacks against the United States changed this focus, exposing a threat that many UN member states, including all of the P5, had reason to fear. (For more on the nature and origins of the terrorist threat, see Chapter 10.) The

---

24. See Michael W. Doyle and Nicholas Sambanis, *Making War and Building Peace: United Nations Peace Operations* (Princeton, NJ: Princeton University Press, 2006).

25. The United Nations force was replaced by a European Union force (EUFOR Althea, named after the Greek goddess of healing).

Does Peacekeeping Keep the Peace?

Since its creation in 1946, the United Nations has undertaken 63 peacekeeping missions in the wake of interstate and civil conflicts. About 2,600 peacekeepers have died in the course of these operations, whose total cost has been estimated at around $54 billion. At the time of this writing, over ninety-one thousand uniformed personnel from 120 countries were deployed in 16 ongoing operations around the globe.[a] Given this expenditure of time, blood, and treasure, it is reasonable to ask: do peacekeeping operations actually work?

A series of studies by Virginia Page Fortna represent a systematic attempt to answer this question.[b] Fortna collected information on ceasefires in interstate and civil wars since 1946. There is a good deal of variation in how long ceasefires last. Some break down almost immediately, others last for years, and still others form the basis for a permanent peace between the adversaries. To determine whether peacekeepers can affect how long a ceasefire will last, Fortna recorded, for each case, whether or not a peacekeeping force was sent in to monitor and/or enforce

the agreement. She also collected information about the severity, duration, and outcome of the war, the issue it was fought over, and features of the combatants—all factors that might affect the durability of a ceasefire.

When these factors are taken into account, the presence of a peacekeeping operation has a substantial effect on the likelihood that a ceasefire will endure. Looking at the 48 ceasefires in interstate wars that ended between 1946 and 1998, Fortna found that the presence of peacekeepers reduced by 85 percent the probability that a ceasefire would break down in any given year.[c] In the case of civil wars, Fortna's analysis focuses on the period 1989–1999, which witnessed an explosion in the number of peacekeepers sent into civil conflicts (see figure below). An analysis of 94 ceasefires in 60 civil wars during this period shows that the presence of peacekeepers reduced the risk of renewed fighting in any given year by around 60 percent.[d] Considering the enormous human and economic costs associated with warfare, peacekeeping operations appear to be well worth their price. ■

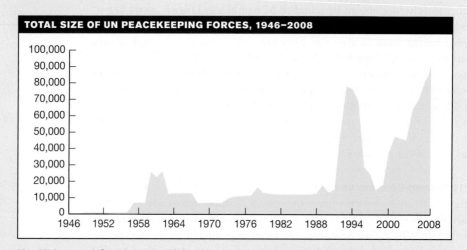

TOTAL SIZE OF UN PEACEKEEPING FORCES, 1946–2008

Note: Highest month for each year, rounded to the nearest hundred. Figures include troops, military observers, and police.
Source: Global Policy Forum, "Size of UN Peacekeeping Forces, 1947–2009," www.globalpolicy.org/security/peacekpg/data/pcekprs.htm (accessed 3/18/09).

---

a. Data are from www.un.org/Depts/dpko/dpko/bnote.htm (accessed 3/18/09).
b. See Virginia Page Fortna, *Peace Time: Ceasefire Agreements and the Durability of Peace* (Princeton, NJ: Princeton University Press, 2004); Fortna, "Interstate Peacekeeping: Causal Mechanisms and

Empirical Effects," *World Politics* 56 (July 2004): 481–519; Fortna, *Does Peacekeeping Work? Shaping Belligerents' Choices after Civil War* (Princeton, NJ: Princeton University Press, 2008).
c. Fortna, "Interstate Peacekeeping," 500.
d. Fortna, *Does Peacekeeping Work?* 105.

unanimous condemnation of the terrorist attacks and international support for the United States' war in Afghanistan suggested that once again the UN mechanism could work effectively in the new international environment.

This optimism would prove short-lived, however. Slightly over a year after the 9/11 attacks, the U.S. effort to mount a war against Iraq divided the Security Council and left the organization alienated from its most powerful member. Although all members were on record demanding that Iraq fully account for its past weapons programs, they parted ways on the desirability of using military force to enforce this demand. For a variety of reasons—some high-minded, some less so—a majority of the Security Council members, including France, Russia, and China, refused to back a proposed resolution in January 2003 authorizing the use of force against Iraq. France has a large Muslim population and was worried about the effects of a war on Islamic militancy. France and Russia also had long-standing economic ties to Saddam Hussein's regime and may have been concerned about jeopardizing those relations; indeed, both countries had advocated loosening the economic sanctions on Iraq in part for those reasons. Moreover, many members of the Council were reluctant to endorse the U.S. doctrine of preventive war (defined in Chapter 3) or its argument that Iraq posed an imminent threat. Although the U.S.-sponsored resolution never came to an official vote, it looked likely that 11 of the 15 Security Council members, including three of the P5, would have voted against it. Anticipating this defeat, the United States withdrew the draft resolution. Claiming authorization under prior UN resolutions and Article 51 of the UN Charter permitting self-defense, the United States went ahead with the invasion without explicit UN support.

As this overview suggests, the United Nations faces two essential requirements if it is to work as intended. First, none of the veto-wielding members can see a potential operation as threatening to its interests. If this requirement is not met—as it was not through much of the Cold War and in the case of Iraq—then action can be blocked thanks to the voting rule. Second, member states, and particularly the powerful member states, must care enough to devote the necessary resources and take the necessary risks. If those risks are low, as in the case of post-conflict peace-keeping, this requirement may not be hard to satisfy. In the more costly cases of reversing aggression or stopping genocides, a strong interest, such as existed in the Gulf War case, is necessary to ensure that sufficient resources are brought to bear. Thus, effective action can be thwarted in two ways: by self-interest, as in the case of Tibet, or by apathy, as in the case of Rwanda.

A cynical conclusion that one might draw from this observation is that the UN mechanism is most likely to be effective precisely when it is needed least— that is, when the powerful states agree enough and care enough to take action. In a case like the Gulf War, one could argue, the UN served simply to give a stamp of approval to actions that the United States would have taken anyway. Moreover, it is also clear from the experience of the Iraq War that the failure to get UN approval will not always stop a great power from taking actions that it wants to take.

In light of this conclusion, one might question whether the UN matters at all when it comes to war and peace. The answer is that although the UN matters less than one might hope, the organization does indeed make a difference. First, as already noted, it has played a constructive role in organizing peacekeeping missions to help countries reconstruct in the wake of conflict. In these cases, the UN's perceived impartiality bestows a legitimacy on peacekeepers' efforts that is needed for them to play the role of an honest broker. Second, the American experience in its two wars against Iraq, in 1991 and 2003, shows that the UN's blessing can be a valuable resource. In the Gulf War, UN support helped build both domestic and international support for the war effort, which contributed to the United States' ability to prevail at low cost to itself. In the case of the Iraq War, the absence of UN support had important implications for the United States' ability to stabilize the country after toppling Hussein's regime. One study of post-conflict reconstruction showed that in order to have a nation-building effort in Iraq that was the same size per capita as the one that was deployed in Bosnia in 1995, the United States would have needed 480,000 combat troops and 12,600 international police.[26] The absence of UN backing, however, meant that some countries that often contribute peacekeeping or police forces to these kinds of missions, such as Pakistan and India, refused to do so in this case. As a result, the U.S.-led coalition had, in March 2004, 154,000 total combat troops, 85 percent of whom were American. And those troops had to serve double duty as an international police force, because there was no separate deployment of police. Hence, there are costs of going to war without the backing of the UN—even if these costs are not always sufficient to prevent a great power from doing so.

Finally, although cooperation is uneven, the UN facilitates joint decision-making. Its rules of procedure in the Security Council and established mechanisms for fielding peacekeeping and peace-enforcement operations keep countries from having to "reinvent the wheel" each time a crisis arises. Vetoes may interfere with decision-making; but without clearly established rules, decisions would be harder to reach even in those instances where cooperation has been successful. Indeed, if the UN did not exist, states would need to create some organization very similar to the one we already have.

Conclusion: Are Poor Police Better Than None?

At the outset of this chapter, we asked whether and when international institutions can prevent or stop wars between and within states. The track record of both alliances and collective security organizations has been uneven, at best, in this regard. Both are imperfect substitutes for an effective police force of the kind that we take for granted in a well-governed country.

---

26. James Dobbins, John G. McGinn, Keith Crane, Seth G. Jones, Rollie Lal, Andrew Rathmell, Rachel M. Swanger, and Anga Timilsina, *America's Role in Nation-Building: From Germany to Iraq* (Santa Monica, CA: RAND, 2003).

Alliances form in response to common interests—generally, the perception of a common threat. For this reason, allies are often better able to work together in concert than are the more fractious members of, say, the UN. However, the existence of alliances does not ensure that allies will fight together, nor does it ensure that other states will be deterred from making threats. Not all alliances are created equally, as the capabilities and resolve underlying the commitment to defend an ally can vary quite considerably. When these are in doubt, as in the case of the French alliance to Czechoslovakia in the interwar period, the alliance can fail in both deterring threats and defending against them. When states are strongly resolved and take the necessary steps to lock in and demonstrate that commitment, as in the case of NATO, then the alliance institutions can be a source of peace through credible deterrence.

For collective security organizations, like the UN, the primary challenge involves providing a public good in an environment in which there can be competing private interests and the costs of providing the good may be more than anyone is willing to pay. Moreover, the joint decision-making rules set down by the organizations' founding members gave those states important privileges to block actions that they do not like. Hence, these organizations have been most effective only when there has been relatively strong agreement among the powerful states, and they have been crippled when those states are in conflict. They have had their greatest successes when at least one powerful state had a sufficient interest that it was willing to pay costs and take risks to provide the public good for everyone. They have also had more quiet successes when those costs and risks were relatively low, such as in cases of post-conflict reconstruction.

Former UN secretary general Dag Hammarskjold reportedly said, "The UN was not created to take humanity to heaven but to save it from hell." This statement reflects a pragmatic understanding of the limits of governance in the international system. States have conflicts of interests that they are willing to fight over, as do people within states. In the absence of an impartial police force, the ability of third parties to enforce peace depends on whether those parties are willing and able to step in. Do outsiders have an interest in intervening? Do the available institutions promote intervention by lowering the costs of getting involved or by increasing the costs of staying out? Does the intervention influence the interaction between combatants in a way that resolves the information and commitment problems that can lead to violence? All of these questions have to be answered in the affirmative for outside intervention to have a chance at preventing or reversing acts of violence. In cases like the wars in Korea and the Persian Gulf, these conditions were met, and South Korea and Kuwait owe their continued existence to this fact. Similarly, in places like El Salvador and Liberia, effective outside assistance has helped these countries rebuild after decades of civil conflict. But in many other cases these conditions are not met, and the results can be disastrous, as in Bosnia, Rwanda, and Darfur.

And yet, as we survey this uneven record, Hammarskjold's statement reminds us that even an imperfect police force may be better than none. Although the international system has no central authority analogous to that of a well-governed domestic system, the institutions that have developed in its place have a beneficial—albeit imperfect and uneven—impact on world politics. Alliances and collective security organizations are poor substitutes for an effective and neutral police, but it is likely that the world would be an even more violent place in their absence.

Reviewing Interests, Interactions, and Institutions

INTERESTS	INTERACTIONS	INSTITUTIONS
States' interests become aligned when they face a common threat and/or have shared goals.	Alliances influence bargaining by changing the expected outcome and costs of a war. A state with an ally can generally get a better deal than it could get alone.	Alliances facilitate military cooperation in support of members' shared interests by specifying what each state is expected to do in the event of war.
Aligned states have an interest in the outcomes of one another's disputes and, consequently, an incentive to cooperate militarily.	Alliances affect the likelihood of war by providing information about the behavior of third parties. An alliance is more likely to deter war if the allies' commitment to fight for one another is credible.	Alliances make it more likely that states will cooperate by improving their war-fighting ability and/or making it costly to renege. Alliances include public provisions in order to signal this commitment to potential adversaries.
States may also have a collective interest in promoting peace and protecting human rights.	Collective security organizations seek to deter acts of aggression by threatening an overwhelming response by the international community.	Collective security organizations facilitate cooperation in support of a (presumed) collective interest in civil and international peace.
	Collective security organizations can resolve commitment problems that lead to interstate and civil wars by making it costly to break agreements.	Collective security organizations face severe challenges of collective action and joint decision-making. They have responded to these challenges by vesting authority in a relatively small number of powerful states.
	States in a collective security organization may face a collective action problem stemming from the incentive to free ride on the efforts of others.	The design of the UN Security Council means that the UN cannot take strong action when one or more of the permanent members is opposed or when none of them cares enough to pay the costs of intervention.

Key Terms

For Further Reading

Doyle, Michael W., and Nicholas Sambanis. *Making War and Building Peace: United Nations Peace Operations.* Princeton, NJ: Princeton University Press, 2006. Examines the track record of UN peacekeeping and peace-enforcement operations in civil wars; finds that while the UN is not well equipped to end wars, it has been helpful in peacekeeping and post-conflict reconstruction.

Lake, David. *Entangling Relations: American Foreign Policy in Its Century.* Princeton, NJ: Princeton University Press, 1999. Considers the different ways that states can institutionalize their relationship with other countries, from empire to informal alignments.

Leeds, Brett Ashley. "Alliance Reliability in Times of War: Explaining State Decisions to Violate Treaties." *International Organization* 57 (2003): 801–27. Offers empirical evidence about the conditions under which states do or do not come to the aid of their allies in the event of war.

Morrow, James D. "Alliances: Why Write Them Down?" *Annual Review of Political Science* 3 (2000): 63–83. Reviews the literature on alliances with a view toward understanding why they have to be institutionalized.

Power, Samantha. *"A Problem from Hell": America and the Age of Genocide.* New York: Perennial, 2002. Graphically details the failings of the United States and the UN in the face of genocide, including the cases of Bosnia and Rwanda.

Snyder, Glenn H. *Alliance Politics.* Ithaca, NY: Cornell University Press, 1997. Offers a comprehensive presentation of theory and historical evidence on the origins and maintenance of alliances.

Voeten, Erik. "The Political Origins of the UN Security Council's Ability to Legitimize the Use of Force." *International Organization* 59 (Summer 2005): 527–57. Seeks to explain why people care whether or not the UN authorizes a military operation.

Walt, Stephen M. *The Origins of Alliances.* Ithaca, NY: Cornell University Press, 1987. Tests balance of power theory and offers a reformulation that hinges on perceptions of threat, not just power.

Waltz, Kenneth N. *Theory of International Politics.* New York: McGraw Hill, 1979, esp. chaps. 6 and 8. Presents a modern formulation of balance of power theory and argues that it explains the relative stability of the pre-1945 and Cold War international systems.

FIND REVIEW AND STUDY MATERIALS ONLINE AT WWNORTON.COM/STUDYSPACE

International Political Economy

During Bill Clinton's successful race for the American presidency in 1992, a sign on the wall of Clinton headquarters read "It's the economy, stupid." The idea was that the presidential election would be determined by voters' views of the state of the economy, and what the candidates would do about it. Indeed, one scholar has developed a formula that he claims correctly predicts the outcome of almost every U.S. presidential election since 1916 with the use of a few simple economic measures—primarily, the rate of economic growth and the inflation rate.[1] Whether or not the relationship is quite that simple, there is little doubt that economic conditions have a powerful impact on politics, and that politics has a powerful impact on the economy. This is as true internationally as it is within countries.

Up to now, we have focused largely on how states interact with one another in diplomatic and military matters. But interactions among states, and between states and other international actors, take place on many other dimensions. One of the most prominent, especially in today's world, is economic affairs. Some countries cooperate and create trade blocs like the European Union or NAFTA, but there are also many bitter disputes among nations over their trade policies. Developing nations run into international debt and currency crises that force them to turn to the International Monetary Fund

(IMF)—at the risk of provoking "IMF riots" from disgruntled citizens. Governments rise and fall on their ability to fulfill the promise of delivering prosperity to their people—and this often depends on their ability to navigate the international economy effectively, dealing successfully with world markets and with foreign governments.

To analyze the politics of international economic relations, we once more look to interests, interactions, and institutions. We pay particular attention to how these factors work at both the domestic and the international levels. Domestic politics matters to all of international politics, to be sure—we have seen in Chapter 4 how domestic politics can affect military relations among nations. However, domestic politics are particularly important in the international political economy. This is because, in almost any area of economic policymaking, there are likely to be profound conflicts of interest *among* domestic actors. The role of groups with contending interests is in fact central to the national politics of economic policy, and to the politics of foreign economic policy as well.

The next four chapters look at the politics of international economic relations—known in international relations as the subfield of *international political economy*. We use a common approach to analyze issues in the international political economy. Because economic policies typically implicate contending groups within a society, we begin each of the next four chapters at the domestic level, looking at the interests affected by particular policies. We ask how these contending interests interact at the domestic level, and how national

---

[1] Ray Fair, *Predicting Presidential Elections and Other Things* (Palo Alto: Stanford University Press, 2002).

As a deep financial crisis first struck the United States in 2008 and then spread around the world, economic policy was at the center of political debates both within and among countries. These British protesters demonstrated against policies designed to help ailing financial firms at the expense of taxpayers. At the same time, disagreements emerged between governments over the appropriate response to the crisis.

political institutions affect the clash and collaboration of such interests. This allows us to understand how national goals in the global economy are determined—whether a country desires more foreign trade or less, whether it welcomes or restricts foreign investors, or whether it wants to keep a separate national currency.

On the basis of this analysis of the domestic politics of foreign economic policy, we turn to interactions at the international level. This involves relations among national governments, of course. But it also includes such powerful private actors as international banks and multinational corporations, which can mobilize more financial resources than many countries. In addition, there are a large number of important international economic organizations, such as the IMF, which some observers believe are more powerful than many governments. At times, the interaction among states, private corporations, and international

organizations leads to cooperative outcomes; at other times, serious conflict erupts over economic issues.

The chapters that follow analyze the sources of conflict and cooperation, domestically and internationally, in economic affairs. Chapter 6 deals with trade among nations, traditionally the foundation of international economic relations. Chapter 7 considers the movement of capital across borders, especially lending and investments made by private investors to developing countries—one of the most contentious topics in the international political economy. In Chapter 8, we consider the policies that countries pursue toward their currencies, both on their own and with other nations—including the emergence of such new currencies as the euro. Chapter 9 looks at the broad issue of economic development, examining the reasons why some countries have been so much more successful than others at industrializing.

CHAPTER 6

International Trade

While free trade benefits economies as a whole, trade policies often create winners and losers. Freer trade under NAFTA has helped the American, Mexican, and Canadian economies in general, but certain groups in each country have suffered as a result. In 2008, these Mexican farmers protested against allowing cheaper corn to be imported freely from the United States, arguing that it would force them out of business.

All economic analysis concludes that trade is economically beneficial. Why, then, does every country restrict trade in some way? Why, too, have policies toward trade varied so much from country to country and over time?

Sugar costs at least twice as much in the United States as on world markets. The U.S. government uses trade barriers to keep the price of sugar high to help American sugar producers, keeping less expensive foreign sugar off of supermarket shelves. This affects the budget of every American, essentially at least doubling the price of a common food product. Here are the facts: The government's protection of America's 15,000 or so sugar cane and beet growers and processors brings the farmers over a billion dollars a year in additional earnings beyond what they would earn without such protection. But the program costs 300 million American consumers and taxpayers more than $2.3 billion a year. Clearly, the government's efforts on behalf of the sugar industry harm American consumers.

The sugar industry is hardly alone in being protected from imports, to the benefit of producers and the detriment of consumers. Footwear, dairy products, motorcycles, clothing, cotton, automobiles, and steel are among the many other goods whose import has been restricted by the U.S. government. One group of scholars has estimated that if all barriers to international trade were removed, the U.S. economy would gain between $500 billion and $1.5 trillion dollars a year, equivalent to between $5,000 and $15,000 a year for every American household.[1] And the United States is hardly alone in erecting obstacles to international commerce: to varying degrees, every country has such trade barriers.

1. Scott Bradford, Paul Grieco, and Gary Hufbauer, "The Payoff to America from Global Integration," in *The United States and the World Economy: Foreign Economic Policy for the Next Decade*, ed. C. Fred Bergstein (Washington, DC: Institute for International Economics, 2005). Figures have been updated from their original 2003 dollar terms. It should be noted that these numbers have been questioned by other scholars, who think they are either too high or too low.

What's So Good about Trade?
▶ Why Do Countries Trade What They Do?
▶ Trade Restrictions Are the Rule, Not the Exception

Why Do Governments Restrict Trade? The Domestic Political Economy of Protection
▶ Winners and Losers in International Trade
▶ Economic Interests and Trade Policy
▶ Domestic Institutions and Trade Policy
▶ Costs, Benefits, and Compensation in National Trade Policies

How Do Countries Get What They Want? The International Political Economy of Trade
▶ Strategic Interaction in International Trade Relations
▶ International Institutions in International Trade

Explaining Trends and Patterns in International Trade
▶ Why, within a Country, Are Some Industries Protected and Some Not?
▶ Why Have National Trade Policies Varied over Time?
▶ Why Do Some Countries Have Higher Trade Barriers Than Others?
▶ Why Has the World Trading Order Been More or Less Open at Different Times?

Conclusion: Trade and Politics

People have traded across borders for as long as borders have existed. In the modern world, international trade has been one of the two most important economic relationships among countries (the other is international investment, which we will examine in Chapter 7). Much of the focus on the globalization of the contemporary world economy reflects dramatic reductions in trade barriers and dramatic increases in international trade itself. Yet, governments have always attempted to control trade across their borders. In fact, trade policy—the restriction of imports and the promotion of exports—has long been one of the most important economic policies, foreign or domestic, that governments undertake. Today's very high levels of international trade, and the continued attempts of governments to control trade, serve as the basis for this chapter's discussion.

We first ask why international trade takes the form it does. Most poor countries export almost exclusively farm products and raw materials, and import manufactured goods. Most rich countries, in contrast, import much of

One pattern that we can identify in international trade is that rich countries have typically exported manufactured goods, especially sophisticated products like airplanes. This French factory builds Airbus jets, many of which will be sold to foreign buyers.

their food and raw materials, and export mainly manufactured goods. Those poor countries that do export industrial products typically sell such simple goods as clothing, footwear, and furniture, while rich countries' manufactured exports primarily include sophisticated goods such as commercial aircraft and elaborate machinery. How can we explain these patterns of international trade?

Our exploration of this question raises the further question of why international trade is so commonly restricted. Although many of us take for granted that protecting national products is good, why should a government purposely raise the prices that domestic consumers pay? This point was captured by the economist John Maynard Keynes, who wrote that protectionism "rests on the principle of making things relatively scarce. To those who are concerned with making these things, this is no doubt advantageous. But it causes an amount of distress more than equivalent elsewhere. The community as a whole cannot hope to gain by making artificially scarce what the country wants."[2] Given that every country has far more consumers than producers of traded goods, we might wonder why trade barriers are so common.

Another question results from the fact that barriers to international trade vary a great deal. Some countries restrict trade very little, while others come close to prohibiting it. In addition, trade barriers have changed dramatically over time: both globally and in individual countries, trade has gone from generally unhindered to tightly regulated over relatively short periods. Today, international trade is quite free (that is, unrestricted). Finally, government trade policies themselves often differ among industries, with some goods being strongly protected and others not at all.

Because trade policy stands at the intersection of international and domestic politics, it involves powerful interests, important interactions, and influential institutions at both the domestic and international levels. Foreign trade has powerful effects on domestic producers, consumers, and others. Those who sell or buy from abroad have a great deal at stake in international

2. Cited in Robert Skidelsky, *John Maynard Keynes*, vol. 1, *Hopes Betrayed 1883–1920* (New York: Penguin, 1983), 227.

trade; so too do those who face competition from foreigners that can threaten their jobs or businesses. Indeed, the conflicts of interest between those in a country who want access to world markets and those who want protection from foreign competition help determine a nation's trade policy. Discussions of international trade often overlook the fact that while it takes place among countries, it really involves individuals and firms with well-defined interests. We say that "Mexico" exports a million tons of steel to "the United States," but in fact companies in Mexico sell the steel to companies in the United States. Companies in one country profit from the sale, and companies in the other profit from the purchase. This point is important in analyzing political conflict over trade, inasmuch as it pits the foreign and domestic actors who benefit from the sale against those who are harmed by it—such as American steel producers, who would prefer that customers buy from them rather than from their Mexican competitors.

Domestically, trade interests interact in a battle over national policy, with supporters and opponents of freer trade squaring off according to their own economic interests. Interactions among contending domestic interests are mediated through the national political institutions of trade policy-making: parties, legislatures, executives, and bureaucracies.

While important domestic interests, interactions, and institutions determine a country's goals in world trade, this is only half the story. In addition, a given nation's trade policies affect other nations' trade, such that all national policies are made in interaction with those of other governments. Sometimes, governments cooperate closely to maintain and expand their trade relations; at other times, bargaining among governments over trade policy is conflictual and even hostile. Indeed, international trade interactions have often spilled into broader interstate relations—sometimes in a positive way, sometimes negatively.

A network of global and regional institutions has evolved to facilitate bargaining over trade policies. These institutions include treaties among countries, as well as regional and global trade agreements. The most prominent trade institutions have been the two international organizations that have governed world trade for sixty years: first, the General Agreement on Trade and Tariffs (GATT); and, since 1995, the World Trade Organization (WTO). At the regional level, trade-based institutions include the European Union (EU), which addresses many other issues as well as those relating to trade, the North American Free Trade Agreement (NAFTA), and the Southern Common Market (Mercosur). This chapter develops several points about the interests, interactions, and institutions that structure the political economy of international trade. All these factors help determine how open a country will be to trade and which domestic industries it will likely protect. When we consider global networks, these factors affect how open or closed international trade as a whole will be.

CORE OF THE ANALYSIS

▶ Economists are virtually unanimous in concluding that international trade brings important benefits to national economies and that barriers to trade hurt economic growth and well-being. Reducing trade barriers—trade liberalization—is good for a nation's economy.

▶ While trade is almost certainly beneficial for a country as a whole, it can harm the interests of groups and individuals in the society. Trade, as well as trade liberalization, can create both winners and losers.

▶ The nature of a country's economy determines which groups have an interest in expanding or restricting the country's trade with the rest of the world. National political institutions affect the extent to which interest groups that stand to lose from world trade will prevail over those that stand to gain.

▶ The politics of international trade also involves strategic interaction among national governments. Governments can face difficult problems of bargaining and cooperation, which sometimes lead to trade conflicts among nations.

▶ The institutions of the international trading system can facilitate cooperation among governments as they confront the demands of both their own constituents and their foreign counterparts.

What's So Good about Trade?

Actors engage in foreign trade for the same reason that they trade with each other within countries: to realize the benefits of specialization. Only a household that produces everything it wants to consume, at a lower cost than available elsewhere, would have no reason to trade. But such a household is unlikely to exist. For example, a farm family could make its own tractor but is better off expending its energy in farming and using the proceeds to buy or rent a tractor. Modern societies are based on specialization—some people farm or manufacture, others transport or build—and on trade among people with different specialties. The division of labor permits diverse segments of society to focus on different economic activities, in ways that benefit society as a whole. After all, if all households or all villages had to be self-sufficient, they would produce only a fraction of what they could if they specialized.

The Scottish thinker Adam Smith's ideas about division of labor help explain the benefits of trade. Smith (1723–1790) showed that the division and specialization of labor among workers improves productivity. Similarly, if individual countries specialize in the goods they are best at producing, and trade these goods, they gain economically.

Adam Smith, in his 1776 founding text of classical economics, *The Wealth of Nations*, made specialization—that is, the division of labor—the centerpiece of his argument. Smith and his fellow economic liberals argued, against the then-dominant mercantilists, that self-sufficiency was foolish because a greater division of labor made societies wealthier. In a famous example, Smith pointed out that an individual pin maker working alone could make at best 20 pins a day. However, in the manufactories of Smith's time, pin making was divided into about 18 steps, with each worker specializing in one or two steps. In this way, a pin factory with 10 workers produced 48,000 pins a day—making each individual some 240 times as productive as he would be if working alone.[3] Specialization increased productivity, and productivity fueled economic growth.[4]

The classical economists emphasized that specialization required access to large markets—after all, a village could hardly use 48,000 pins a day. They argued that restricting market size slowed economic growth. A village cut off from the rest of the world and forced into self-sufficiency would have to produce everything it needs; but if that village were part of a larger national or global market, it could specialize in what it does best. Producers need ample markets to specialize; the division of labor depends on the size of the market.

The division of labor allows gains from international trade. In farming, temperate countries such as the United States and Argentina specialize in temperate crops such as wheat, while tropical countries such as Brazil and the Philippines specialize in tropical crops like sugar cane. The nations around the Persian Gulf, with their rich oil deposits, base their economies on oil, while countries with plentiful iron ore gain economic advantages by mining it. Similarly, countries with many

---

3. Adam Smith, *An Inquiry into the Nature and Causes of the Wealth of Nations* (New York: Modern Library, 1937), 4–5. Originally published 1776.
4. Productivity in this context refers to the amount produced by one unit of labor with the other factors of production—especially land and capital—at its disposal. In farming, for example, the same amount of labor is more productive on good soil than on poor, more productive with machinery and fertilizer and irrigation than without.

unskilled laborers, such as Bangladesh and Egypt, produce goods that require lots of unskilled labor: clothing, footwear, furniture. Countries with many skilled technicians, such as the European nations, produce goods that require sophisticated technical skills: complex machinery, aircraft. Such specialization among countries leads to economic gains based on trade.

Comparative advantage is the core concept of the economics of trade (see the Special Topic appendix to this chapter). It applies the principle of specialization to countries: like people, they should do what they do best. Thus, comparative advantage implies that a nation gains most by specializing in producing and exporting what it produces most efficiently. By doing so, it can earn as much as possible in order to pay for imports of the best products of other countries. It is not necessary for a country to have an **absolute advantage** (that is, the ability to do something better than others) in producing something for it to be profitable to produce and export it; all that is necessary is a comparative advantage.

The principle of comparative advantage has clear implications for free trade. Since a country gains from following its comparative advantage, and since barriers to trade impede its ability to do so, trade protection is harmful to the economy as a whole. Government policies that keep out imports force the country to produce goods that are not to its comparative advantage to produce. Indeed, trade protection raises the price of imports and reduces the efficiency of domestic production.

Many people find the economic argument for free trade counterintuitive. Policymakers often argue, like the mercantilists did 300 years ago, that exports are good because they create jobs, that imports are bad because they take away jobs, and that governments should stimulate the national economy by restricting imports and encouraging exports. Economic logic insists the opposite: that imports are the gains from trade, while exports are its costs. A country imports goods that it cannot make very well itself, which allows the nation to focus its productive energies on making (and exporting) the goods that it produces best.

Free trade induces a country to follow its comparative advantage, and economic logic implies that it is the ideal policy. This is true even if free trade is pursued unilaterally. Protection only serves to raise costs to consumers. If other countries impose trade barriers that raise prices to their own consumers, that is no reason for us to harm our own consumers in response.

There is a clear parallel between the comparative advantage argument and the choices available to a household. A farm family, for example, "exports" (sells its crops) in order to "import" (buy the goods and services it wants). Because the farm family wants to maximize the imports it buys, it needs to earn more; the best way to do so is to produce more of what it produces best. The principle of comparative advantage illustrates how farmers, workers, and firms gain by specializing and trading, just as countries do.

WHY DO COUNTRIES TRADE WHAT THEY DO?

The principle of comparative advantage suggests that countries will produce and export what they do best. But how can we know what a country does best, other

comparative advantage: The ability of a country or firm to produce a particular good or service more efficiently than other goods or services, such that its resources are most efficiently employed in this activity. The comparison is to the efficiency of other economic activities the actor might undertake, not to the efficiency of other countries or firms.

absolute advantage: The ability of a country or firm to produce more of a particular good or service than other countries or firms using the same amount of effort and resources.

than by observing what it exports? And if the only way to predict a country's exports is to observe them, the theory is not of much value—especially given that trade flows are affected by many noneconomic factors, such as trade barriers. In the 1920s, Swedish economists Eli Heckscher and Bertil Ohlin addressed this puzzle and extended the classical approach.

The Heckscher-Ohlin approach tries to explain national comparative advantage, and therefore national trading patterns. The two economists recognized that comparative advantage is not simply a result of effort: for example, the productivity of farmers depends primarily on characteristics of their land, not on how hard they work. In countries where land is in short supply and expensive, farming is costly; where it is plentiful and cheap, farming is low in cost.

Heckscher-Ohlin trade theory characterizes the basic economic characteristics of a country in terms of its factor endowments, the material and human resources it possesses. Typically, these endowments are summarized in terms of basic factors of production, resources essential for economic activity. Such factors of production include the following:

- land, an essential input into agricultural production
- labor, typically understood to refer to undifferentiated and unskilled labor
- capital for investment, which refers both to the machinery and equipment with which goods are produced and to the financial assets necessary to employ this machinery and equipment
- human capital, which refers to skilled labor, so called because the labor has been enhanced by investment in training and education

Countries differ greatly in their factor endowments. Some are rich in land, others have abundant unskilled labor, others have abundant skilled labor (human capital), still others are wealthy in investment capital. These endowments, according to Heckscher-Ohlin trade theory, determine national comparative advantage and, in turn, what countries produce and export. A country with a large population and poor farmland is likely to have a comparative disadvantage in farming; a country with few people but vast supplies of farmland is likely to have a comparative advantage in agriculture. Different products, too, require different mixes of endowments: typically, farm goods require a lot of land, simple manufactured goods require a lot of unskilled labor, complex machinery requires a lot of investment capital.

Heckscher-Ohlin trade theory argues that a country will export goods that make intensive use of the resources the country has in abundance; likewise, a country will import goods that make intensive use of the resources in which the country is scarce. Countries with lots of land, where land is cheap, specialize in producing farm goods: for example, the United States in the nineteenth century was relatively sparsely populated, but it had huge endowments of very fertile land and exported massive quantities of cotton, tobacco, and wheat. In contrast, countries with very little arable land import many farm goods—such as Great Britain in the nineteenth century, which relied heavily on imports for its food. Countries rich in investment capital focus on making products whose production requires a great deal of capital: for example, most North American and Western European nations' industries today specialize in sophisticated manufactured

Heckscher-Ohlin trade theory: The theory that a country will export goods that make intensive use of the factors of production in which it is well endowed. Thus, a labor-rich country will export goods that make intensive use of labor.

According to the Heckscher-Ohlin trade theory, developing countries that are rich in unskilled labor should export labor-intensive manufactured goods. Indonesia's primary exports are textiles and clothing—the textile industry definitely benefits from Indonesia's vast supply of cheap labor.

goods such as complex machinery, construction equipment, and commercial aircraft. Regions with abundant labor produce labor-intensive goods: China and other rapidly developing labor-rich nations concentrate on making products that require a great deal of labor, such as clothing, toys, furniture, and other relatively simple manufactures.

This pattern of specialization leads to analogous trade patterns. Poor countries with little capital import the capital-intensive products they need: today, for example, poor agricultural nations tend to import their farm machinery from capital-rich industrialized nations, just as the United States did in the early nineteenth century. China and India export their labor-intensive manufactures to North America and Western Europe and import capital-intensive industrial goods—including the complex machinery needed to operate their domestic factories.[5] Within North America, the capital-rich United States exports capital-intensive machinery (and capital) to Mexico, while labor-rich Mexico sends labor-intensive manufactured products (and labor) to the United States.

The Heckscher-Ohlin theory does relatively well at explaining the broad outlines of international trade. The industrial countries are rich in capital and skilled labor (human capital), and they export manufactured goods that make intensive use these endowments. Most developing countries are rich in land, raw materials, or unskilled labor (or some combination of the three), and they export agricultural products, minerals, or labor-intensive manufactures. In addition to explaining aspects of world trade patterns, Heckscher-Ohlin trade

---

5. This argument applies to movements of capital and people as well as to trade. Countries rich in capital should export capital, and countries rich in labor should export labor (land, of course, cannot be traded across borders without changing the borders!).

theory has important implications for the domestic politics of trade policy, as we discuss below.[6]

Other economic links among countries also encourage trade. Countries that share a currency, such as those in the European Union that use the euro, trade with each other much more than those that do not. Countries that invest heavily in one another's economies also tend to trade heavily with one another.

Noneconomic factors also affect trade. For example, diplomatic and military relations between nations influence their trade patterns. Countries whose governments are hostile to one another are likely to trade little, whereas those on friendly terms are likely to trade more. There are two reasons for this. First, trade between hostile nations is riskier than trade between friendly nations: businesses avoid engaging in trade that may very well be disrupted by the outbreak of hostilities. Second, governments often pursue close economic ties with their allies in order to cement the alliance and help friendly nations. After all, if trade is good for a national economy, a government might shy away from encouraging trade with an unfriendly nation in order to keep from strengthening a potential enemy. During the Cold War, as we mentioned in Chapter 5 when discussing NATO, the United States and its allies purposely limited their economic ties with the Soviet Union, just as they encouraged ties among themselves.

Indeed, trade relations tend to track alliances. Some analysts believe that trade encourages friendly relations as much as friendly relations encourage trade. For example, Cordell Hull, American secretary of state before and during World War II, wrote: "It is a fact that war did not break out between the United States and any country with which we had been able to negotiate a trade agreement. It is also a fact that, with very few exceptions, the countries with which we signed trade agreements joined together in resisting the Axis. The political line-up followed the economic line-up."[7] After World War II, the two superpowers used their trade relations to reinforce their alliances: the United States and the Soviet Union each encouraged its allies to build a common trading order that excluded members of the other alliance. After the Cold War ended, many policymakers in Europe wanted to encourage trade with the former communist countries of Eastern and Central Europe as a way to encourage cooperative diplomatic relations with them. Regardless of the pattern of cause and effect, international diplomatic realities and international trade are closely related.

But the most important noneconomic source of international trade patterns is national trade policies, undertaken to address the interests of domestic

---

6. There are other potential economic sources of patterns of international trade. A great deal of modern international trade is related to the activities of multinational corporations, such as sales from overseas affiliates of American corporations to their headquarters. This sort of "intra-firm" trade may not be due primarily to the forces Heckscher-Ohlin trade theory suggests, but rather to production and distribution networks within firms. In addition, a great deal of international trade is in goods whose attraction to consumers has to do as much with brand name, reputation, or other related considerations as it does with price. North America, for example, both imports automobiles from Europe and exports automobiles to it. This sort of "intra-industry" trade is not the result of fundamentally different factor endowments (and prices) between Europe and North America—both regions are rich in capital and skilled labor, and poor in unskilled labor—but rather of European consumer interest in American car brands and American consumer interest in European car brands.

7. Quote in Richard Gardner, *Sterling-Dollar Diplomacy in Current Perspective: The Origins and Prospects of Our International Economic Order,* expanded ed. (New York: Columbia University Press, 1980), 9.

constituencies. For trade is the stuff of domestic politics, as governments attempt to address the interests of corporations and consumers, farmers and bankers, all of whom have something at stake in their countries' policies toward foreign trade. We now consider how domestic political and economic factors affect trade policy and trade itself. In this context, we examine the interests, institutions, and interactions that lead to national trade policies.

TRADE RESTRICTIONS ARE THE RULE, NOT THE EXCEPTION

Despite the powerful economic arguments for free trade, every country currently has at least some restrictions on trade with the rest of the world. Some countries have very high barriers to trade; others have much lower ones. Yet, government policies to control and contain trade are the norm, today as in the past. **Protectionism,** the use of specific measures to shield domestic producers from imports, has long been one of the most common government policies worldwide.

Virtually all governments restrict at least some imports. For hundreds of years, governments have imposed a wide variety of **trade barriers,** impediments to the import of foreign goods. Historically, the most common barrier is a **tariff,** a tax on imports levied at the border and paid by the importer. A tariff raises the price of the import directly, so that a consumer of the imported good has to pay more for it. Another common form of trade barrier is a **quantitative restriction, or quota,** which limits the quantity of a foreign good that can be sold domestically. Because the reduced quantity typically causes an increase in its domestic price, a quantitative restriction has an effect like that of a tariff: it makes the imported good more expensive to domestic consumers. There are many other **nontariff barriers to trade,** such as regulations targeted at foreign goods or requirements that governments purchase from national producers. In all instances, the effect of these policies is to shelter domestic producers from foreign competition. Before we analyze the effects of these policies, it is important to emphasize how common they have been and continue to be.

The degree of openness of the world trading order has varied greatly over time and among countries (for an illustration of this varying openness in terms of countries' exports as a percentage of gross domestic product, see Table 6.1). As we saw in Chapter 1, for more than 300 years after 1492 the major European nations followed the trade policies of mercantilism, a system by which great powers used their military might to control trade with and extract wealth from their colonial possessions. The colonial powers' mercantilist regulations kept foreign goods out of their markets and reserved their colonies' markets for themselves.

However, around the middle of the nineteenth century, Great Britain and other leading industrial countries moved in the direction of trade liberalization: they pursued policies that involved fewer restrictions on trade. Great Britain adopted free trade, permitting foreigners to sell anything to Britain without tax or restriction. More generally, from the 1860s until 1914 international trade among the principal industrialized nations was quite free.

protectionism: The imposition of barriers to restrict imports. Commonly used protectionist devices include tariffs, quantitative restrictions (quotas), and other nontariff barriers.

trade barrier: Any government limitation on the international exchange of goods. Examples include tariffs, quantitative restrictions (quotas), import licenses, requirements that governments only buy domestically produced goods, and health and safety standards that discriminate against foreign goods.

tariff: A tax imposed on imports; this raises the domestic price of the imported good and may be applied for the purpose of protecting domestic producers from foreign competition.

quantitative restrictions (quotas): Quantitative limits placed on the import of particular goods.

nontariff barriers to trade: Obstacles to imports other than tariffs (trade taxes). Examples include restrictions on the number of products that can be imported (quantitative restrictions, or quotas); regulations that favor domestic over imported products; and other measures that discriminate against foreign goods or services.

TABLE 6.1	MERCHANDISE EXPORTS AS A PERCENTAGE OF GDP, 1820–1992*						
	1820	**1870**	**1913**	**1929**	**1950**	**1973**	**1992**
France	1.3%	4.9%	8.2%	8.6%	7.7%	15.4%	22.9%
Germany	n.a.	9.5	15.6	12.8	6.2	23.8	32.6
Great Britain	3.1	12.0	17.7	13.3	11.4	14.0	21.4
Canada	n.a.	12.0	12.2	15.8	13.0	19.9	27.2
United States	2.0	2.5	3.7	3.6	3.0	5.0	8.2
Brazil	n.a.	11.8	9.5	7.1	4.0	2.6	4.7
Mexico	n.a.	3.7	10.8	14.8	3.5	2.2	6.4
China	n.a.	0.7	1.4	1.7	1.9	1.1	2.3
India	n.a.	2.5	4.7	3.7	2.6	2.0	1.7
Japan	n.a.	0.2	2.4	3.5	2.3	7.9	12.4
Korea	0.0	0.0	1.0	4.5	1.0	8.2	17.8
World	1.0	5.0	8.7	9.0	7.0	11.2	13.5

*Exports and GDP at 1990 prices
Source: Angus Maddison, *Monitoring the World Economy* (Paris: OECD, 1995), Table 13.

There were tariffs and other barriers, to be sure, and some countries were very protectionist—especially such industrializing nations as the United States. Nonetheless, most of the world's major economies were open, and world trade grew at a very rapid rate.

With the outbreak of World War I in 1914, however, international trade relations entered 30 years of crisis and closure. Efforts to rebuild the trading system after the war were not very successful, especially once the Great Depression hit in 1929. The major powers divided up the world into more or less hostile trading blocs: the British, French, Italian, Japanese and other empires, along with the less formal German and American spheres of influence.

After 1945, the Western world under American leadership moved gradually to reduce trade barriers among the developed nations. The communist countries and most developing countries protected themselves from world markets, but the industrialized world significantly liberalized its trade. Although the reduction of trade barriers has remained controversial, by the 1980s the rich countries had become very open to world trade, as part of the broader march toward economic globalization. Eventually, most developing and formerly communist countries joined the liberalizing and globalizing trend. Since the early 1990s, international trade has once more—as before 1914—been quite open. Thus, in terms of global trade relations over time, we see a pattern in which mercantilist closure gave way to freer trade, then to interwar closure, then to liberalization after 1945, and further liberalization leading to globalization after 1980.

Many nations have, at some point, gone from very closed to very open to trade, or in the opposite direction. Great Britain jettisoned mercantilism in the 1840s. The United States was one of the the most protectionist nations in the world through most of the nineteenth and early twentieth centuries, started moving toward freer

FIGURE 6.1	IMPORTANCE OF TRADE TO THE U.S. ECONOMY, 1960–2005

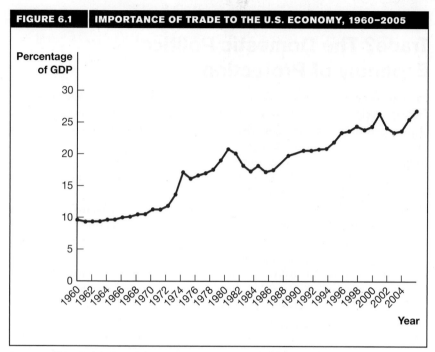

Source: World Bank, World Development Indicators, http://econ.worldbank.org (accessed 3/17/09).

trade in the 1930s, and by the 1950s and 1960s was leading the charge for trade liberalization. As Figure 6.1 shows, trade became an increasingly large part of the U.S. economy after the 1960s. Developing nations such as Brazil and India were among the world's most closed economies until the 1980s, after which they reduced their trade barriers dramatically. Trade among European countries was quite free from the 1860s until 1914; in the 1920s and 1930s, the region's nations erected highly strict barriers to trade among themselves; today, trade among the 27 members of the European Union is completely unrestricted.

Even within a single country, there can be significant differences among policies toward trade in different goods—some protected, and some not. Almost all developed nations protect agricultural producers much more heavily than manufacturers. Developing nations, meanwhile, tend to protect manufactured products more than farm products. The United States, as well as many other industrial nations, generally protects the steel industry more than most other industries. And despite the industrial countries' rhetoric in favor of freer trade, they have imposed restrictions on many goods that might be imported from developing nations. Why are some producers—farmers, or certain kinds of farmers; industries, or certain kinds of industries—more favored by trade policy than others? Why do different countries' trade policies vary so much? Why has the world's general openness to trade changed so dramatically over time? And, perhaps most central, why have governments almost always, and almost everywhere, ignored economic analysis and advice and imposed restrictions on foreign trade?

Why Do Governments Restrict Trade? The Domestic Political Economy of Protection

For over 200 years, economic analysis has been unambiguous about the benefits of trade for national income, output, and efficiency. This is reflected in the opinions of professional economists, more than 90 percent of whom believe that barriers to trade reduce national well-being (according to a recent American survey).[8] Yet, economists' confidence in the benefits of trade is not shared by most people. Public opinion is much less favorable to trade: 60 percent of respondents in another survey of American views were favorable to trade protection, as opposed to less than 5 percent of economists.[9] Indeed, many people seem wary of openness to international trade, despite the overwhelming support of economists. Such wariness is evident in the fact that almost all countries, almost all of the time, have substantial barriers to trade that protect their own producers.

Trade barriers usually reflect domestic concerns, despite the fact that they implicate foreign relations. William McKinley, a leading protectionist member of the U.S. Congress before he became president, once said of a tariff he was shepherding through the House of Representatives, "This is a domestic bill; it is not a foreign bill."[10] This statement remains a common view of protection for domestic interests.

Trade policy typically reaches the public consciousness, and the media, when some national producers complain that there is too much or too little trade in the goods they produce. Often, producers are concerned because imported goods cut into their profits or cost them their jobs. Other producers may complain that foreign barriers to their goods keep them out of markets abroad and similarly cut into profits and cost jobs at home. To understand the domestic politics of trade, we need to know the interests in question, the institutions through which these interests are expressed, and how contending interests interact with one another.

There are both benefits and costs to trade barriers. Virtually all tools of trade protection—tariffs, quotas, and other restrictions—make imports more expensive, which allows domestic producers to sell more of their products, to raise their prices, or both. When tariffs are imposed on foreign steel imported into the United States, American steelmakers can expand sales at higher prices. This may allow them to increase profits, raise wages, and hire more workers. Quotas, which restrict the quantity of foreign goods sold in the national market, ultimately have a similar impact in that the reduction in imports reduces supply, thus raising price. So trade barriers assist national producers. What could be wrong with that?

The most direct cost of protection is to consumers of the protected good. Tariffs and quotas raise the domestic price of imported goods and may lead to price increases for similar domestically produced goods: for example, a barrier to steel imports makes imported steel more expensive and allows domestic steelmakers to raise prices, too.

---

8. Cletus C. Coughlin, "The Controversy over Free Trade: The Gap between Economists and the General Public," *Federal Reserve Bank of St. Louis Review* 84, no. 1 (January/February 2002): 1.
9. Ibid.
10. Cited in David Lake, *Power, Protection, and Free Trade: International Sources of U.S. Commercial Strategy, 1887–1939* (Ithaca, NY: Cornell University Press, 1988), 111.

The former Soviet Union imposed strict controls on trade, effectively requiring many goods to be produced domestically even if the country was not well-equipped to do so. This photo from 1986 shows a worker in a shoe factory in Armenia. Today, the former Soviet Republics are more likely to import shoes and clothing, as they can be produced more efficiently in other countries.

Producers gain and consumers lose from protection; this is its *redistributive effect*—income is redistributed from domestic consumers to the protected domestic industry. But there is another cost as well: in this case, to efficiency or aggregate social welfare—the ability of society to use its resources most effectively. For a trade barrier introduces economic distortions. It leads domestic producers to make more goods that they are not particularly good at making (otherwise, they would not need protection). It also leads consumers to consume less of those goods that protection has made artificially expensive. Trade protection leads to an allocation of domestic resources—labor, capital, land, skills—that is not to the country's comparative advantage. Protection of European wheat leads European farmers to use their land for wheat farming when it might make more sense, from the standpoint of the region's overall economy, to use that land for dairy or vegetable farming, or to build houses. (For more on the economic effects of trade restrictions, see the Special Topic appendix at the end of this chapter.)

WINNERS AND LOSERS IN INTERNATIONAL TRADE

The domestic politics of trade is infused with battles between winners and losers from protection, and with debates over the importance of any inefficiencies it may promote.

Domestic industries protected by trade barriers receive clear and concentrated benefits. Protection creates returns above the normal rate of profit by artificially restricting competition and supply. However, at least three groups stand to lose from trade protection. First are consumers of the imported good. This group includes consuming industries, which—unlike average consumers—may be powerful and well organized. When the U.S. government imposed tariffs on imported steel in 2002, the American users of this steel—especially in the automobile industry—mobilized strongly against it (as did foreign governments), and the policy was eventually reversed. A second group that tends to oppose protection is exporters. They worry that their country's protective barriers might provoke retaliation in foreign markets. American farmers, for example, have opposed American barriers to Chinese goods—largely to avoid Chinese retaliation against the many billions of dollars of American farm goods that China imports. Third, citizens in general may be willing and able to punish politicians for the costs that protection imposes on them, especially if the connection is clear and the issue is prominent. In the 1980s, many people in Soviet-bloc (communist) countries blamed the stagnation of their economies on their governments' pervasive trade controls, and this may have created popular sympathy for the subsequent opening of these nations to international trade. Also, there is evidence that consumers in developing countries favor freer trade because they understand that it will lead to reduced prices for themselves.[11]

Because of the diverse array of industries that compete with imports, use imports, and sell exports, as well as the range of producers and consumers, trade is politically controversial. Who do we expect to have an interest in supporting and opposing trade protection within national political systems?

ECONOMIC INTERESTS AND TRADE POLICY

The socioeconomic characteristics of a country, and of particular groups within it, help explain who might be in favor of and against trade. There are two leading theories of trade-policy interests. The first grows out of the Heckscher-Ohlin approach. If a country exports goods that make intensive use of a factor of production that the country has in abundance, then trade is particularly good for those who own that factor of production. For example, if a capital-rich country opens to trade, it will export capital-intensive goods, which will increase the demand for capital and therefore its return (profits); a land-rich country will export land-intensive goods (farm products), which will make landowners (such as farmers) better off. By the same logic, artificially restricting trade will *hurt* owners of abundant factors by artificially restricting the market for the goods they make: reducing trade in a land-rich, food-exporting country will hurt landowning food producers.

The Stolper-Samuelson Approach This explanation of supporters and opponents of protection is the **Stolper-Samuelson theorem,** which is simply stated as: protection benefits the scarce factor of production. Consider Bangladesh, a poor country with lots of unskilled labor and very little capital. Bangladesh exports mainly clothing and leather goods, which make intensive use of its abundant unskilled labor; it imports such capital-intensive products as machinery, equipment, and chemicals. Trade barriers artificially restrict the supply of the imported capital-intensive goods, so that some of them at least will have to be produced in Bangladesh. In order to produce these capital-intensive goods, some Bangladeshi capital will have to be diverted from labor-intensive production and into capital-intensive production (from garment factories to chemical plants, for example). This raises the domestic demand

Stolper-Samuelson theorem: The theory that protection benefits the scarce factor of production. This view flows from the Heckscher-Ohlin approach: if a country imports goods that make intensive use of its scarce factor, then limiting imports will help that factor. So in a labor-scarce country, labor benefits from protection and loses from trade liberalization.

---

11. For example, Andy Baker, "Who Wants to Globalize? Consumer Tastes and Labor Markets in a Theory of Trade Policy Beliefs," *American Journal of Political Science* 49, no. 4 (October 2005): 924–38.

for capital and reduces the local demand for labor. And this, in turn, raises the return on Bangladeshi capital (profits) and reduces Bangladeshi wages. Thus, protection in capital-scarce countries helps owners of capital and hurts workers.

The application of the Stolper-Samuelson theorem to a labor-scarce country, such as the United States, is analogous. The United States has abundant capital but scarce unskilled labor, so it imports labor-intensive goods such as clothing and furniture. Protection restricts the American supply of these products and raises their price. This, in turn, increases American production of these labor-intensive products, raises the American demand for unskilled labor, and helps American unskilled workers (who own the scarce factor—labor). By the same token, protection in land-scarce countries (such as those of Western Europe, as well as Japan) helps farmers and hurts workers and owners of capital.

So who would we expect to support and oppose trade barriers? We would expect owners of the scarce factors of production in a country to be protectionist, and owners of the abundant factors to favor free trade. In rich societies, which typically have abundant capital and skilled labor but are scarce in unskilled labor, capitalists and skilled workers should be free traders while unskilled workers should be protectionists. In countries with abundant land, farmers should support trade; in countries where land is scarce, farmers should support protection. In poor societies, which typically have abundant unskilled labor and scarce capital, workers should support trade while capitalists should be protectionists. An important feature of the model is that attitudes toward trade vary with the country's factor endowments of land, labor, capital, and human capital (skills). Thus, the model expects farmers to be protectionists in land-poor Japan but free traders in land-rich Argentina.

These expectations appear to be borne out by a great deal of evidence. Labor movements in the United States and other rich countries do seem to be protectionist, while people with a lot of capital appear more favorable to free trade. Japan and Europe have relatively little land, and their farmers are strongly protectionist; Australia and Canada are rich in land, and their farmers usually favor free trade. Notice that the Stolper-Samuelson predictions are about very broad groups—owners of production factors (roughly the same as social classes) such as labor, investors, and farmers.

But observers of economic policy-making in the United States and elsewhere note that many demands for protection come from specific *industries*—the steel industry, sugar growers, shoe manufacturers. Often, everyone in an industrial sector—skilled and unskilled workers, managers, and owners of a group of firms—works together to ask for trade barriers or support for their exports. For example, we tend to think of the American steel industry as relatively protectionist because we group together everyone associated with the industry. This flies in the face of the Stolper-Samuelson focus on labor as a class or investors (capital) as a class. Indeed, one study of lobbying behavior by corporate and labor groups over a trade bill in the early 1970s found that labor and investors (capital) were almost always on the same side of the trade policy issue. Twenty-one industries appeared before the relevant congressional committee. Labor unions and corporate management both were in favor of protection in 14 industries, while they were both in favor of free trade in five industries. In only two industries were unions and management on opposite sides of the trade-policy debate.[12] Many detailed studies of trade policy, and of attitudes toward trade, confirm the idea that the industry in which people work has a powerful impact on their trade-policy opinions.[13]

Ricardo-Viner (specific-factors) model: A model of trade relations that emphasizes the sector in which factors of production are employed, rather than the nature of the factor itself. This differentiates it from the Heckscher-Ohlin approach, for which the nature of the factor—labor, land, capital—is the principal consideration.

The Ricardo-Viner or Specific-Factors Approach A second way of explaining trade-policy preferences, the **Ricardo-Viner** or **specific-factors model,** focuses on why whole industries often act together. This perspective has one key feature that differentiates it from Stolper-Samuelson: some factors of production tied to their industry are *specific* to their industry. For example, capital in the steel industry largely takes the form of steel factories and machinery; it cannot simply be turned into capital in the food-processing industry. Thus, steel manufacturers care not about the profits of capital *in general* and in the country as a whole, but rather about the profits available only in steel. The same may be true of workers or farmers, whose job skills or land can be inherently "specific to" (some might say "trapped in") a particular industry or crop. This gives the owners, workers, or farmers a strong incentive to safeguard their current use—for example, by obtaining government protection from foreign competition. In this model, the interests of an individual flow from the sector of the economy in which he or she is employed. A worker or manager in a industry that faces stiff import competition will be protectionist; a worker or manager in an exporting industry will want free trade. Unlike in the Stolper-Samuelson approach, people's interests are tightly bound up with the interests of others in their sector of the economy.

There is evidence that both sources of demand for trade protection matter. Broad classes—farmers, workers—sometimes mobilize for or against protection. But at the same time, much lobbying for protection is industry based, consistent with the view that the benefits of protection accrue to industries, not to broad classes or factors. The accuracy of each view may vary among industries and countries, and over time. One study has found, for example, that in the late nineteenth century American labor was quite interchangeable, which contributed to the working class having a clear, distinctive interest in trade policy; in contrast, today's American working class is much more differentiated, so that industry-based sectoral interests predominate.[14]

It can also be the case that groups support trade policies because they believe those policies complement or permit other policies they favor. Recall the words of economist John Maynard Keynes: "The community as a whole cannot hope to gain by making artificially scarce what the country wants."[15] This is a powerful argument; but later, in the midst of the Great Depression of the 1930s, Keynes came to believe that there could be equally powerful political arguments against free trade. In 1933, in fact, Keynes spoke in favor of "the policy of an increased national self-sufficiency . . . not as an ideal in itself, but as directed to the creation of an

12. Stephen Magee, "Three Simple Tests of the Stolper-Samuelson Theorem," in *Issues in International Economics,* ed. Peter Oppenheimer, 138–53 (London: Oriel Press, 1980).
13. See especially Anna Maria Mayda and Dani Rodrik, "Why Are Some People (and Countries) More Protectionist Than Others?" *European Economic Review* 49 (2005): 1393–1430.
14. Michael Hiscox, "Commerce, Coalitions, and Factor Mobility: Evidence from Congressional Votes on Trade Legislation," *American Political Science Review* 96, no. 3 (September 2002).
15. Cited in Skidelsky, *John Maynard Keynes,* vol. 1, 227.

environment in which other ideals can be safely and conveniently pursued." Keynes had come to believe that trade barriers might usefully give national governments breathing space as they attempted to combat mass unemployment and economic collapse. Governments confronted with serious foreign competition would be tightly constrained in what they could do to confront the economic emergency. But, Keynes felt, protectionism might permit governments to implement policy measures to alleviate the social and economic distress of the Great Depression.[16]

Understanding the economic interests that contend over trade is only a start to understanding national trade politics and policies. At best, this can tell us who wants more or less protection, and what the interests of different groups in trade policy might be. But what determines who wins and who loses in the battles among supporters and opponents of trade liberalization?

DOMESTIC INSTITUTIONS AND TRADE POLICY

Since there are always supporters and opponents of protection in any country, how are trade-policy decisions made? Why are some countries more open to trade than others? Why do governments protect some industries and not others? There are many steps between raw economic interests and the actual results in economic policy. Most of them have to do with the institutions of national politics, including the organization and representation of interests, and the ways in which policy decisions are made.

National political institutions can be of stunning variety and complexity, but a general rule of thumb can help orient our understanding of their implications for trade policy. Let's start with the observation that trade protection tends to help relatively narrow and concentrated groups—the steel industry, skilled workers—but harms the economy and consumers as a whole. Then, those political institutional forms that are particularly responsive to the interests of more concentrated groups—a particular class, a particular industry—will be more favorable to protection, while those that respond especially to broad national pressures will be less favorable. So an important question about domestic institutions has to do with whether they favor particularistic interests, in which case they would incline toward protectionism, or whether they favor broad economic and consumer interests, in which case they would incline toward less protectionist policies.

The Organization of Interests As we've discussed in previous chapters, the logic of collective action implies that smaller groups will be better able to organize than larger groups. We saw in Chapter 4 how smaller, highly motivated groups were better able to influence foreign policy in matters of war and peace. The same principle applies in matters of trade policy. This tends to favor supporters of protection over supporters of trade liberalization; in fact, one simple expectation is that concentrated producers will win over diffuse consumers in many circumstances. This helps explain, for example, how a very small number of sugar farmers are able to obtain a policy that benefits them at the expense of the vast mass of American sugar consumers (see "What Do We Know?" on p. 234).

---

16. John Maynard Keynes, "National Self-Sufficiency," *The Yale Review* 22, no. 4 (June 1933): 755–69.

The Political Economy of American Sugar Protection

U.S. government policy provides substantial benefits to sugar growers. It gives them subsidies guaranteeing a domestic price that is usually two or three times as high as world prices. The government maintains this artificially high domestic price with barriers to the import of cheaper sugar from abroad.

The beneficiaries of American sugar policy have been identified as follows:

- About 1,700 sugar cane farmers, mostly in Hawaii, Florida, and Louisiana, make an extra $369 million a year. About 60 percent of this goes to 17 large growers.
- About 14,000 sugar beet farmers (and a few processors), mostly in Minnesota and the Dakotas, make an extra $888 million a year. The bulk of this goes to about 10 percent of the growers.
- A few foreign producers, largely from countries that are close allies of the United States (Mexico, the Philippines, and the Dominican Republic), are permitted to sell small amounts of sugar in the United States at the artificially high price. Foreigners gain about $434 million a year.

These benefits to producers are profits arising directly from the sugar policies of the U.S. government. The added profits come at the expense of American taxpayers and consumers, who pay over $2.3 billion a year more for sugar that is twice or three times as expensive as on world markets (see figure). If you are paying close attention, you will notice that the extra profits earned above equal less than $2.3 billion—in fact, $640 million a year less.[a] The $640 million a year is what economists call *dead weight cost*, or inefficiency. This is the cost to the economy of (1) producing more sugar cane and sugar beets than is economically efficient given our country's climate and land, and (2) changing our use of sugar in inefficient ways (such as using corn syrup instead of sugar to sweeten soft drinks).

These policies are economically beneficial to producers, but they amount to only about two cents a day per American. The fact that they are much more important to producers than to consumers helps explain why they are politically attractive to politicians. This is reflected in the fact that the sugar growers make substantial campaign contributions to members of Congress.

THE COST OF SUGAR, 2004

One study found that during a single electoral season, in the run-up to an important series of votes, the sugar lobby gave about $1.7 million to members of Congress and the Senate, including about $9,000 for each member of the agriculture committees that controlled the sugar legislation. While average consumers had little reason to be involved, corporations that use sweeteners (such as soft drink producers) did counterlobby, but they were not as well organized and gave less than one-third as much as the sugar producers. The study looked at the impact of contributions on voting on the sugar bill, and it estimated that every $1,000 given to a senator or member of Congress by sugar producers increased the probability that the politician would vote for the sugar policy by between 4 and 7 percent.[b]

It seems that a small but well-organized group of sugar growers has been able to use lobbying and campaign contributions to obtain billions of dollars in support from American taxpayers and consumers. Few Americans are aware that they are paying so much more for their sugar because of the current trade barriers, and it is not clear whether they would object to paying a bit more in order to keep thousands of sugar growers in operation. But they are rarely presented with a clear, informed choice about the repercussions of this trade policy. ■

---

a. Data are from John Beghin, Barbara El Osta, Jay Cherlow, and Samarendu Mohanty, "The Costs of the U.S. Sugar Program Revisited," *Contemporary Economic Policy* 21 (2003): 1006–116; and from Center for Responsive Politics, "The Politics of Sugar: Sugar's Iron Triangle," www.opensecrets.org/pubs/cashingin_sugar/sugar02.html (accessed 6/1/07). Benefits calculations are for 1998, converted into 2006 dollars.

b. Jonathan C. Brooks, A. Colin Cameron, and Colin A. Carter, "Political Action Committee Contributions and U.S. Congressional Voting on Sugar Legislation," *American Journal of Agricultural Economics* 80 (1998): 441–54. Contributions reports are from the 1989–1990 cycle, converted into 2006 dollars, with probabilities recalculated accordingly.

Economic interests organize themselves very differently in different societies. In some Western European countries, for example, most workers are members of a centralized labor federation that devises policies for virtually the entire labor movement. Even where workers in different industries might disagree, the existence of a class-wide labor federation helps create a common working-class political position. In the United States, by contrast, labor unions tend to be organized by industry; even if there were common trade-policy interests among American workers, it might be difficult for them to express those interests in a common way.

The implication is that an organization reflecting the concerns of broad groups—such as all workers—is more likely to ignore the demands of specific groups or industries. In contrast, interests that are organized into narrower groups are more likely to pursue the particular goals of such special interests.

The Representation of Interests through Political Institutions Just as narrowly based social groups are more likely to favor protection than broader ones, so political institutions that are more closely tied to narrow interests are more likely to favor trade protection than institutions that reflect broader interests. Generally, inasmuch as democracies reflect broad interests while dictatorships are restrictive, we would expect democracies to be less protectionist than dictatorships. Indeed, scholars have found that democratic developing countries are much more likely to liberalize their trade than dictatorships are.[17]

Apart from such broad institutional features as democracy, societies differ in the ways their partisan, electoral, and legislative institutions represent the interests of their citizens, and these differences are likely to affect the way trade policy is made. For example, many European countries have strong class-based parties: the working class votes for the socialist parties, and other parties associate themselves more or less explicitly with farmers or business. Although the American labor movement has close ties to the Democrats and working-class voters tend to vote Democratic, these connections are weak by European standards. This affects the expression of interests and their bias toward special or general interests, toward protection or freer trade.

National electoral systems vary greatly, and indeed they may well cause differences among national party structures. Most industrial countries are parliamentary and have a legislature elected on a proportional basis in which voters choose the party they prefer rather than the individual local candidate. American voters elect the president on a national basis but elect individual local candidates (for the House of Representatives and the Senate) whose ties to the national party may be weak. And there are systems in between, such as the Westminster system (in Great Britain) and hybrid presidential-parliamentary systems (in much of Latin America).

How might these institutions affect trade policy? Politicians with local political constituencies tend to be more responsive to local interest groups, while nationally elected politicians have less reason to cater to particular local concerns. Consider two otherwise identical countries: one with strong national parties and a powerful

---

17. Helen V. Milner with Keiko Kubota, "Why the Move to Free Trade? Democracy and Trade Policy in the Developing Countries," *International Organization* 59, no. 1 (Winter 2005): 107–43.

national executive, and the other with weak parties and a weak executive. Politicians in the former are more likely to focus on national effects of policy and favor free trade, while politicians in the latter are more likely to emphasize local concerns and thus favor trade protection to local special interests.

The same holds within a country, where one branch of government may be more sensitive to local pressures than another. The American president, elected nationally, has a strong incentive to consider the impact of trade policies on the country as a whole, while members of Congress have little reason to think about anything other than the effects of the policy on their district. For example, most members of Congress or senators from Michigan feel bound to support protection for the automobile industry, while the president needs to consider the electoral implications of higher car prices nationally.

For an example of how the breadth of a politican's constituency can affect trade policy, let's look at the American experience. In 1934, Congress granted the president authority to negotiate certain trade agreements with other countries. Before this, only Congress had made trade policy. After 1934, the president was much more deeply involved. The contemporary version of this is a congressional grant of fast-track negotiating authority, under which the president negotiates a trade agreement with another country and then presents it to Congress for an up-or-down vote, so that members of Congress cannot change the agreement but must vote either yes or no. This institutional arrangement empowers the president at the expense of Congress, and many observers believe that it has allowed the president to impart a pro-trade bias instead of the protectionist bias favored by Congress. It follows that the institutional change that began in 1934, giving more influence to the president, helped direct the United States toward more liberal trade policies.[18]

Partisan features of government can also affect trade policy, especially inasmuch as parties are associated with well-defined social groups with preferences for particular trade policies. For example, in the Stolper-Samuelson framework, labor has well-defined interests in trade: if labor is scarce, it will be protectionist; if it is abundant, it will support free trade. In most of the world, labor typically supports left-wing parties. Given this observation, governments of the Left in labor-rich countries (mainly, poor nations) should be more open to trade than governments of the Left in labor-scarce countries (mainly, rich nations). Similarly, inasmuch as business typically is associated with right-wing parties, governments of the Right in capital-rich countries (usually, rich nations) should be more open, while in capital-poor countries (poor nations) they should be more protectionist. Thus, leftist governments should support free trade in poor countries and protection in rich countries; rightist governments should support free trade in rich countries and protection in poor countries. One study of a large number of countries indeed found strong support for this joint impact of partisan politics and Stolper-Samuelson interests. For example, Bangladesh and Senegal are similarly labor-rich and capital-poor; but in the 1980s,

---

18. See especially Susanne Lohmann and Sharyn O'Halloran, "Divided Government and U.S. Trade Policy: Theory and Evidence," *International Organization* 48, no. 4 (Autumn 1994): 595–632; and Michael Bailey, Judith Goldstein, and Barry Weingast, "The Institutional Roots of American Trade Policy," *World Politics* 49 (April 1997): 309–38. But for a skeptical view, see Michael J. Hiscox, "The Magic Bullet? The RTAA, Institutional Reform, and Trade Liberalization," *International Organization* 53 (Autumn 1999): 669–98.

Bangladesh's right-wing (presumably, anti-labor) government had tariffs twice as high as Senegal's left-wing (presumably, pro-labor) government.[19]

COSTS, BENEFITS, AND COMPENSATION IN NATIONAL TRADE POLICIES

Even if trade liberalization makes a country's economy as a whole better off, it can seriously harm groups within the country. Concentrated groups of potential losers with a lot at stake could conceivably block policy changes that would improve conditions for the nation overall. This means that the country would be better off if it "bought off" the negatively affected interests. Such a policy would represent a movement toward the Pareto frontier in the model presented in Chapter 2. Movement toward the Pareto frontier, called a Pareto improvement, makes everyone better off (or at least unharmed) and nobody worse off. Essentially, while trade liberalization might hurt some people in the first instance, the overall gains to the national economy are large enough that the losers can be fully compensated for their losses and the benefits will still be left over for the rest of society. Indeed, it is not uncommon for a government to arrange compensation for people who lose from trade liberalization, in order to diminish opposition to a removal of trade barriers that the government wants to pursue. The United States, for example, provides Trade Adjustment Assistance to workers harmed by the country's foreign trade; the assistance ranges from tax credits, to money for retraining, to outright grants.

More generally, the very structure of the post-1945 political economy of most Western societies has to some extent been based on the logic of compensation. As the industrialized world substantially reduced trade barriers after World War II, its governments implemented sweeping social policies that provided a safety net to workers, farmers, and others who might be negatively affected by the reopening of world trade. This strategy reflects a kind of compromise between supporters of economic integration, on the one hand, and defenders of the welfare state, on the other.[20] The Bretton Woods System permitted, even encouraged, this compromise, and it was quite successful at achieving its goal of an integrated world economy and extensive social welfare policies in the industrialized nations.

The issue of compensation has attracted recent attention because many observers believe that trade has led to reduced wages for unskilled workers in the industrial countries. Trade puts unskilled American workers in direct competition with unskilled workers in poor countries with much lower wages, which may depress the wages of the former. This is in fact a clear implication of the Heckscher-Ohlin approach: trade will tend to make wages, profits, and other earnings more similar across countries. The process is called factor price equalization, for the prices of factors of production (the wages of labor, the profits of capital, the returns to land) tend to become more equal. Trade leads countries

---

19. Pushan Dutt and Devashish Mitra, "Endogenous Trade Policy through Majority Voting: An Empirical Investigation," *Journal of International Economics* 58 (2002): 107–33.
20. John Ruggie called this compromise "embedded liberalism." See John Gerard Ruggie, "International Regimes, Transactions, and Change: Embedded Liberalism in the Postwar Economic Order," *International Organization* 36, no. 2 (1982): 379–415.

to export goods that use factors of production in which they are well endowed: labor-rich countries export labor-intensive goods. This increases the demand for labor and raises wages. At the same time, labor-poor countries import labor-intensive goods rather than producing them at home, and this reduces the demand for labor—thus lowering wages. The implication is that wages in poor countries will rise toward the levels of those in rich countries, while wages in rich countries will fall toward the levels of poor countries.

The wages of unskilled workers in the United States have in fact been stagnant or declining since the early 1970s, and trade with developing countries may have contributed to this process. The issue is controversial; some analysts think that the decline in unskilled wages in the United States is largely due to technological changes that have made facility with computers and other skills more valuable in the workplace. Nonetheless, there is little doubt that globalization has created winners and losers in rich countries, and that working people are more likely to be on the losing side. This observation has led some analysts to suggest that rich countries may face social and political conflict over economic openness unless they develop more extensive social safety nets to reduce the negative impact of the world economy on some groups in society. (We will return to this issue in Chapter 13.)

Clearly, the interests, interactions, and institutions that characterize different national political economies have a powerful impact on national trade policies. Nonetheless, a focus on the *domestic* sources of trade policies misses an important part of the story, because each country's trade relations are part of a broader international environment. While trends in French or Indian trade depend on French and Indian domestic politics, they also depend on the global economic and political situation. One could hardly understand the French turn toward protectionism in the 1930s without the context of the Great Depression, the country's reduction in protection after 1950 without situating it within the Cold War, or its current trade policies without knowing France's place in the single market of the European Union. Similarly, it would be difficult to explain India's protectionism upon independence in 1947, or its turn toward freer trade in the 1990s, without knowing that in both instances it was following policies shared by most other developing countries. The *international* environment—especially the global strategic and institutional setting—has a powerful impact on national trade policies and patterns.

How Do Countries Get What They Want? The International Political Economy of Trade

What a national government wants from trade is only a starting point, for every country's commercial relations depend on the international environment. Certainly, a country can pursue a unilateral trade policy; it can open its borders or close them, regardless of what other countries do. But what a country achieves depends powerfully on the actions of others. How can governments get what their constituents want out of the world economy? How do factors abroad, including the policies of other countries, affect the ability of a national government to deliver goods to its constituents? What is the international political economy of trade?

International economic conditions, for example, have a powerful impact on both the policies a country might like to pursue and their likely effects. The collapse of the world economy in the 1930s drove many countries inward—foreign markets were small and shrinking, and the benefits of openness shrank with them. In contrast, the rapid expansion of world trade since 1950 has given many countries strong incentives to link their economies to dynamic world markets. In addition to global market conditions, the policies of other governments can have an enormous impact: for example, the opening of China and India to world trade has profoundly affected other developed and developing nations. How, then, can we understand the national politics of trade within the broader international context? How does the strategic and institutional environment affect whether countries get what they want from world trade?

STRATEGIC INTERACTION IN INTERNATIONAL TRADE RELATIONS

When governments make national trade policies, they take into account what other governments are likely to do in response. A government that raises tariffs dramatically, for example, might find other countries retaliating with even higher barriers to its exports—so that the benefits to domestic producers sheltered from imports might be canceled out by costs to exporters frozen out of foreign markets. In 1930, for example, the U.S. Congress attempted to provide relief to farmers by raising the duty on eggs from eight to ten cents a dozen. This reduced the already-small number of Canadian eggs bought in the United States by 40 percent, from 160,000 to under 100,000. The British imperial trade area (which included Canada) countered by increasing the duty on eggs to the same ten cents a dozen (from the previously low three cents). This move drove America's very considerable egg exports to Canada down by 98 percent, from 11 million to under 200,000. The British-Canadian response meant that American protectionism had backfired.[21]

By the same token, attempts to create regional trading areas such as the European Union or NAFTA, or to affect the international commercial order such as the United States did after World War II, rely on the joint behavior of different nation-states. One government cannot achieve many of its trade policy goals without considering the actions of other governments. (For a discussion of the evolution of the European Union, see "What Shaped Our World?" on p. 240.)

Two or more governments involved in trade policy negotiations are engaged in strategic interaction and must take into account the behavior of other governments in trying to do their best. For example, suppose that American farmers decide they would be better off if they had access to Europe's market for farm goods and are willing to reduce American agricultural trade barriers in return. American trade negotiators offer the Europeans a joint reduction of farm trade protection, and the

---

21. Cordell Hull, *The Memoirs of Cordell Hull* (New York: Macmillan, 1948), 355–56.

The Creation of a Single European Market

Today, the 27 countries (and counting) of the European Union constitute a single market for goods, services, capital, and even people. In some respects, the EU is more economically integrated than the 50 U.S. states. How did the single European market emerge? Its evolution teaches us a great deal about the politics of trade policy and the challenges of economic integration.

The origins of the European single market can be traced back to the end of World War II and the famous Marshall Plan, in which the U.S. government channeled more than $14 billion (equivalent to over $500 billion in today's dollars) in food, raw materials, and capital to the war-torn economies of Western Europe beginning in 1947. The Europeans had to cooperate among themselves to distribute U.S. aid, and this spirit of cooperation continued into the next decade. In 1951, six countries—France, West Germany, Italy, Belgium, the Netherlands, and Luxembourg—created the European Coal and Steel Community (ECSC). The ECSC established a common market for coal and steel and placed these industries under the control of a supranational governing body. With the creation of the ECSC, France and West Germany finally resolved battles that had raged—often violently—for a century over the natural resources along their shared borders. Great Britain remained staunchly opposed to the ECSC for many years, fearing that the supranational ESCS would impede its autonomy to pursue national economic goals.

The original six countries moved toward greater integration upon the signing of the Treaty of Rome in 1957, which created the European Economic Community (EEC), or European Common Market. The EEC was a regional trade agreement of a particular type: a customs union. This meant that the members agreed to allow free trade among themselves for all goods and to impose a common external tariff on imported goods. The EEC also created several supranational governing bodies to help manage the affairs of the Common Market. The members of the EEC prospered as a result of the free exchange of goods, and British opposition to integration eventually waned. In fact, Great Britain joined the EEC in 1973, along with Ireland and Denmark.

Trade integration deepened as a result of the EEC. International trade among the original six countries more than doubled during the period 1960–1972. However, the customs union was not a single market in the same way that national

states, such as the United States, constitute a single market. Trade in services remained outside its scope, as did many informal barriers to trade in goods, such as product standards and regulatory differences. The next institutional steps—the 1986 Single European Act and the 1991 Maastricht Treaty—were designed to create a single European market for goods and services, along with capital and people. These treaties also paved the way for a common currency.

Today, the European Union (EU) is close to reaching the ideal of a truly open market, free of barriers to trade and investment. Citizens of an EU country can move freely to any other member country to live, work, study, or retire. There are no formal trade barriers among members, and nontariff barriers (such as licensing requirements and environmental safeguards) have been substantially harmonized throughout the EU. Crossnational investment occurs without impediment, especially among the 17 EU members that have adopted a common currency, the euro.

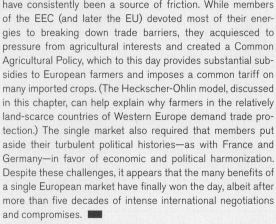

The evolution of European integration demonstrates both the attractions and the challenges of regional economic agreements. A six-country regional trade agreement in 1957 has now become a 27-country single market. Countries that join the union enjoy the benefits of increased trade and capital flows. The path to European integration, however, was not smooth. For example, agricultural interests have consistently been a source of friction. While members of the EEC (and later the EU) devoted most of their energies to breaking down trade barriers, they acquiesced to pressure from agricultural interests and created a Common Agricultural Policy, which to this day provides substantial subsidies to European farmers and imposes a common tariff on many imported crops. (The Heckscher-Ohlin model, discussed in this chapter, can help explain why farmers in the relatively land-scarce countries of Western Europe demand trade protection.) The single market also required that members put aside their turbulent political histories—as with France and Germany—in favor of economic and political harmonization. Despite these challenges, it appears that the many benefits of a single European market have finally won the day, albeit after more than five decades of intense international negotiations and compromises. ■

Europeans agree. But the Americans are wary: the Europeans might find hidden ways to maintain their barriers, such as by imposing regulations that apply only to American crops. In fact, some American farmers argue that European bans on the import of genetically modified food, or of meat from animals whose feed contains hormones, are in fact disguised trade barriers. In other words, the Europeans might find ways to "cheat" on the agreement and gain greater access to the American market without providing anything substantial in return. The Europeans, for their part, have analogous concerns: the United States, they fear, will promise them open markets but find devious ways to keep European goods out. Given this threat, both the United States and the European Union decide not to take the chance, farm trade is not liberalized, and both sides are left worse off than they would have been with an agreement. This scenario is an example of how international trade bargaining problems can resemble a Prisoner's Dilemma (see the appendix to Chapter 2): both sides would be better off cooperating to reduce trade barriers, but concern that the other side will cheat leads both sides to act noncooperatively, to their common detriment.

This sort of cooperation problem is common in trade relations among countries. To be sure, the logic of comparative advantage discussed above implies that countries would maximize their overall economic welfare by unilaterally liberalizing trade. However, governments respond to pressures other than that of the economy as a whole. For this reason, a government's first choice of trade policy is almost never to remove its trade barriers unilaterally; typically, it wants to get concessions from other countries in return for its own.

Yet, as we saw in Chapter 2, it can be difficult for political actors to arrive at a mutually beneficial accord when there is no way to guarantee compliance with the agreement. Just as in the security relations among countries discussed in Chapters 3–5, in the international trade realm governments that want to collaborate may be hampered by the fear that they will be taken advantage of in an interaction that can have very high stakes. No government can take lightly the possibility that its farmers, companies, or workers might lose money or jobs because the government mismanaged an international trade negotiation. Countries face inherent difficulties in making credible commitments to accommodate the desires of their trading partners; as in military matters, this can lead to a breakdown of trust and, eventually, an inability to cooperate.

Strategic problems can also arise when countries try to work out a common approach to a problem, such as what legal rules to use to govern trade. One of the most common difficulties arises when one country accuses another of unfairly subsidizing its exports. Disputes in world trade often involve accusations that one country's exporters are *dumping* their goods—that is, selling them below the true cost of production in order to drive out competitors. Dumping is widely accepted to be an unfair trading practice, but it is extremely hard to define, let alone measure. Similarly, government subsidies to exporters encounter widespread disapproval. But such subsidies can take many indirect forms (such as regulation of shipping costs, complicated accounting or tax rules, management of the currency), and there is often no easy way to determine whether in fact an actual subsidy is being used. In these cases, even where countries would like to work out their conflicts amicably, there may be serious disagreements about the standards to be used to govern fair trading relations.

For example, one of the longest-standing disputes in world trade has been between the United States and Canada, two countries with generally very friendly relations.

The U.S. government has charged that Canadian forestry policies constitute an unfair subsidy to the country's important exports of softwood lumber, a charge the Canadians reject. Both countries undoubtedly want to maintain their cooperative trade relations, but this cooperation has been threatened by conflicting interpretations of trade rules. In these cases of coordination problems, the parties typically want to find a common position or standard but have trouble deciding which one is best.

Overcoming Problems of Strategic Interaction The international politics of trade is full of examples of problems of cooperation and coordination; it is also full of attempts to make it easier for governments to overcome these problems. In Chapter 2, we saw that several factors can facilitate cooperation and coordination: small numbers, information, repeated interaction, and linkage politics. These all affect international trade relations.

Small numbers make it easier for governments to monitor each others' behavior; there is likely to be less free riding among small groups of countries than in the world at large. An extreme version of this observation is the theory of *hegemonic stability*, which argues that the existence of a single very powerful nation facilitates the solution of problems of collective action and free riding; the hegemonic power is large and strong enough to be both willing and able to solve these problems for the world as a whole. In economic affairs, the approach argues that when there was such a hegemonic power over the past two centuries (Great Britain after 1860, and the United States after 1945), trade liberalization was facilitated by the leadership of an overwhelmingly influential world economic power. Less extreme versions of the approach suggest, more modestly, that smaller numbers of countries—privileged groups (see Chapter 2)—will find it easier to monitor and enforce trade agreements than very large groups of nations or the world as a whole. Due to the greater ease of monitoring and enforcement, small numbers of countries are more likely to succeed at liberalizing trade.[22] This might help explain why so many trade agreements take the form of regional accords among a few neighboring nations, such as the European Union, NAFTA, and Mercosur.

Small numbers might also help explain why the United States and Canada have been able to negotiate successfully in even so acrimonious a dispute as that over softwood lumber, which involved billions of dollars and one of Canada's more important industries. In 1986 and again in 1996, despite long-standing conflict over whether Canada was in fact subsidizing its lumber industry, the two countries reached compromise agreements. In the first instance, the United States agreed to reduce its tariff on Canadian imports; in the second instance, Canada agreed to limit its exports to the United States.

Information can also be an important consideration in trade negotiations. Many failures of cooperation are due to fears of hidden actions—that one government might use its superior knowledge of its own domestic conditions to take advantage of other governments. In the case of dumping and subsidies, decisions are often made by national bureaucratic agencies about which foreigners may know little. For example, in 2001 the United States and Canada were unable to negotiate a renewal of the 1996

---

22. For a reasoned summary, see David A. Lake, "Leadership, Hegemony, and the International Economy: Naked Emperor or Tattered Monarch with Potential?" *International Studies Quarterly* 37, no. 4 (December 1993): 459–89.

Many trade agreements are based on cooperation among countries in the same region. Mercosur began as a trade agreement between Argentina, Brazil, Paraguay, and Uruguay in 1991 and has grown to include several other Latin American countries. Here, former Argentine president Nestor Kirchner meets with Chilean president Michelle Bachelet at the thirtieth Mercosur summit, in 2006.

Softwood Lumber Agreement. Immediately after the agreement expired, the United States International Trade Commission and the Department of Commerce found that Canadian lumber was being subsidized, so the United States unilaterally imposed a 27 percent tariff on Canadian imports, triggering a new round of acrimonious conflict. If the Canadians had known about this finding, perhaps they might have reached agreement with the Americans. This example suggests that transparency may lead to trade cooperation. It also suggests that establishing some manner by which partners can provide information to one another may facilitate cooperative relations.

Repeated interaction between governments on a continuing basis provides a reason to avoid cheating, or even the appearance of cheating. The possibility that the collapse of a current deal might sour future deals can impose a powerful discipline on government behavior and can encourage greater efforts to cooperate. This is especially the case in a trading relationship, which is likely to go on indefinitely. By the same token, governments with a long history of dealing with one another are likely to have more information about each other—and, in good circumstances, more reason to trust one another.

Governments may also facilitate trade agreements by *linking* concessions granted in one arena to concessions received in another. A government that would otherwise be uninterested in negotiating lower barriers in, say, steel might be willing to exchange concessions in steel if its partner gives it concessions in some other industry. Governments can, in other words, trade among trade policies—"giving" in an area they care less about, in return for "getting" in an area they care more about. These exchanges can benefit governments and their citizens. Countries might link agreements in trade (steel for apparel, for example), or they might link agreements in trade with agreements on something else, such as foreign aid or military cooperation.

All these considerations help explain why countries are more likely to have friendly, collaborative trade relations in some circumstances than in others. This is true of pairs or groups of countries: bilateral or regional trade agreements are more likely with smaller numbers, where information about the partners is readily available, when the partners have a long history of interaction, and where trade relations are linked to other economic or noneconomic relations. It may also be true for the world as a whole: when these conditions are met, at least for the leading countries in the international trading system, trade cooperation is more likely. But when there is great uncertainty about the true intentions of some of the major powers (such as Germany and Japan in the 1920s and 1930s), coupled with a real concern for the short term and the absence of a dense network of other relationships among the major powers, international trade cooperation is difficult or impossible.

Because it can be inherently difficult for governments to ensure cooperative trade relations among themselves, they have created international institutions that help overcome the variety of collective action and other strategic problems that have beset international trade relations. International institutions may indeed be the most powerful factor in affecting whether trade relations among countries are collaborative or conflictual. They run the gamut from global organizations, such as the World Trade Organization (WTO), to regional agreements, such as the North American Free Trade Agreement (NAFTA), to bilateral treaties between countries. Most such institutional arrangements have the goal of facilitating trade cooperation among their member states.

INTERNATIONAL INSTITUTIONS IN INTERNATIONAL TRADE

International organizations represent the principal systematic attempts to order contemporary international trade policy. As we saw in Chapter 2, institutions can play an important part in providing a setting within which cooperation is facilitated. They can help mitigate all of the problems that stand in the way of interstate cooperation on trade. Institutions can set standards of behavior that governments are expected to follow. They can gather information to assist member states in monitoring and enforcing compliance with their agreements. International institutions can reduce the costs to governments of making joint decisions—a real problem in the very complex trade realm—and can help governments resolve disputes. For all these reasons, over the years countries have developed institutional arrangements to facilitate their trade negotiations. One is the concept of **reciprocity,** by which a concession granted by one government is met by another, a sort of linkage politics that helps bind agreements. A more general provision of this nature has developed over the course of more than a hundred years to serve a similar purpose: **most favored nation (MFN) status.** Countries that confer MFN status on one another agree to extend to each other the same concessions that they provide to all other nations—for example, a tariff reduction given to one country is automatically given to all countries with MFN status. This system, called normal trade relations in the United States, serves to link negotiations between two countries to all their multilateral trade relations.

The most important international institution in commercial relations has a global reach: the **World Trade Organization (WTO),** which succeeded the **General Agreement on Tariffs and Trade (GATT)** in 1995. From their beginnings, both the GATT and WTO were intended to reduce barriers to trade among member nations. The institutions have been enormously successful in their stated purpose, with world trade growing faster than world output for virtually all of the postwar period.

Within the WTO, countries negotiate in rounds under a loose rule of reciprocity that balances the dollar value of concessions, which are then automatically extended

reciprocity: In international trade relations, a mutual agreement to lower tariffs and other barriers to trade. Reciprocity involves an implicit or explicit arrangement for one government to exchange trade policy concessions with another.

most favored nation (MFN) status: A status established by most modern trade agreements guaranteeing that the signatories will extend to each other any favorable trading terms offered in agreements with third parties.

World Trade Organization (WTO): An institution created in 1995 to succeed the GATT and to govern international trade relations. The WTO encourages and polices the multilateral reduction of barriers to trade, and it oversees the resolution of trade disputes.

General Agreement on Tariffs and Trade (GATT): An international institution created in 1948 in which member countries committed to reduce barriers to trade and to provide similar trading conditions to all other members. In 1995, the GATT was replaced by the World Trade Organization (WTO).

to all other member states under the MFN rule. There are also rules about when and how countries can use safeguards to temporarily protect domestic industries.

Although all members of the WTO have a formally equal vote, in practice negotiations are dominated by the largest trading states—in particular, the United States, the European Union (which negotiates as a single actor in the WTO), and Japan. Developing countries have found it difficult to get their concerns onto the international trade agenda. Their principal demand has been for the liberalization of agricultural trade, as many developing countries would benefit from greater access to rich-country markets for food. This, however, has been blocked by politically powerful farmers in the developed countries.

The WTO, like the GATT before it, acts in several ways to encourage cooperation among its members. It makes available a great deal of information about trade and trade policies, including monitoring national compliance with international agreements. The WTO monitors a country's compliance in two primary ways. First, members must report actions taken under the safeguards clause, as well as on any regional trade agreements they may enter into (such as the North American Free Trade Agreement). Second, countries that believe that foreign exporters or importers are not complying with the rules can file a complaint with the WTO. Complaints are referred to the Dispute Settlement Body, composed of all member states, which then appoints a panel of experts in consultation with all parties to the dispute. The panel investigates the alleged rule violation and issues a report that becomes a ruling within 60 days. Each side can appeal (but not block) the ruling to the WTO's standing seven-member Appellate Body. If not overturned, the ruling becomes binding. A country held to be in violation of WTO rules must bring its policy into conformity with the rules; if it does not, it is subject to sanctions authorized by the organization itself.

As the world's largest trader, the United States is the most frequent defendant at the WTO. It is surprising to some observers that the United States usually abides by WTO rules and rulings, even when the complainant is a small country like Costa Rica that the United States could easily ignore (see "What Shaped Our World?" in Chapter 2, p. 71). The reason is probably that the United States believes that it is more likely to be a complainant than a target and would like rulings in its favor to be obeyed, which is less likely to occur if the United States itself does not respect WTO rulings.

In addition to the global trade organizations, there are many similar institutions at the regional level. The three most prominent are the European Union, which started in 1958 as a customs union of six countries but now encompasses 27 nations in a single market; the North American Free Trade Agreement (NAFTA), made up of the United States, Canada, and Mexico; and Mercosur, or the Southern Common Market, originally composed of Argentina, Brazil, Paraguay, and Uruguay. There are many other such regional trade arrangements, of varying size and involving varying degrees of commitment to openness among their members (see Map 6.1).

Although the GATT and its successor, the WTO, have reduced barriers to international trade, these institutions have often provoked opposition from actors whose interests may be harmed by trade liberalization. These French farmers worried that they would be harmed by GATT policies that benefited the United States.

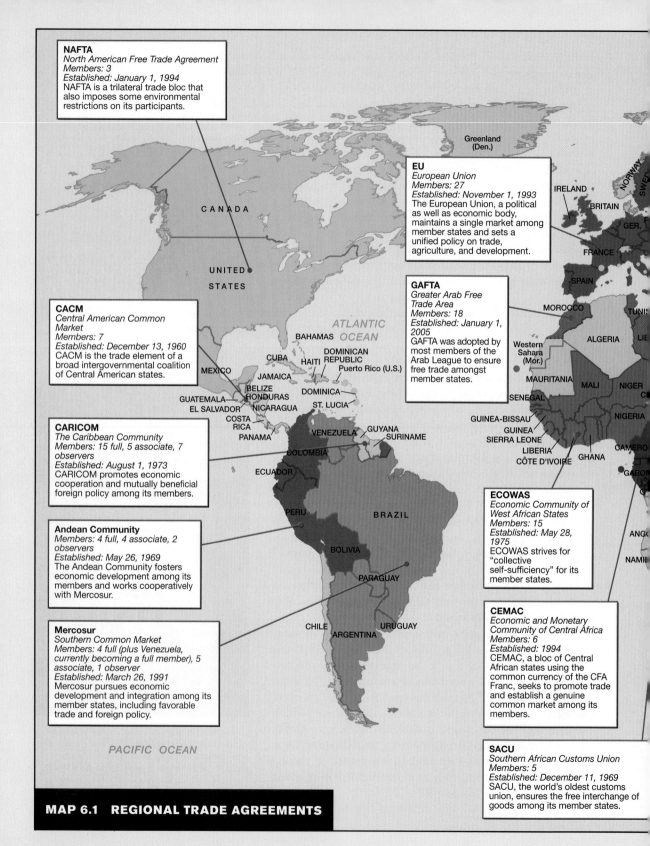

NAFTA
North American Free Trade Agreement
Members: 3
Established: January 1, 1994
NAFTA is a trilateral trade bloc that also imposes some environmental restrictions on its participants.

EU
European Union
Members: 27
Established: November 1, 1993
The European Union, a political as well as economic body, maintains a single market among member states and sets a unified policy on trade, agriculture, and development.

CACM
Central American Common Market
Members: 7
Established: December 13, 1960
CACM is the trade element of a broad intergovernmental coalition of Central American states.

GAFTA
Greater Arab Free Trade Area
Members: 18
Established: January 1, 2005
GAFTA was adopted by most members of the Arab League to ensure free trade amongst member states.

CARICOM
The Caribbean Community
Members: 15 full, 5 associate, 7 observers
Established: August 1, 1973
CARICOM promotes economic cooperation and mutually beneficial foreign policy among its members.

Andean Community
Members: 4 full, 4 associate, 2 observers
Established: May 26, 1969
The Andean Community fosters economic development among its members and works cooperatively with Mercosur.

ECOWAS
Economic Community of West African States
Members: 15
Established: May 28, 1975
ECOWAS strives for "collective self-sufficiency" for its member states.

Mercosur
Southern Common Market
Members: 4 full (plus Venezuela, currently becoming a full member), 5 associate, 1 observer
Established: March 26, 1991
Mercosur pursues economic development and integration among its member states, including favorable trade and foreign policy.

CEMAC
Economic and Monetary Community of Central Africa
Members: 6
Established: 1994
CEMAC, a bloc of Central African states using the common currency of the CFA Franc, seeks to promote trade and establish a genuine common market among its members.

SACU
Southern African Customs Union
Members: 5
Established: December 11, 1969
SACU, the world's oldest customs union, ensures the free interchange of goods among its member states.

MAP 6.1 REGIONAL TRADE AGREEMENTS

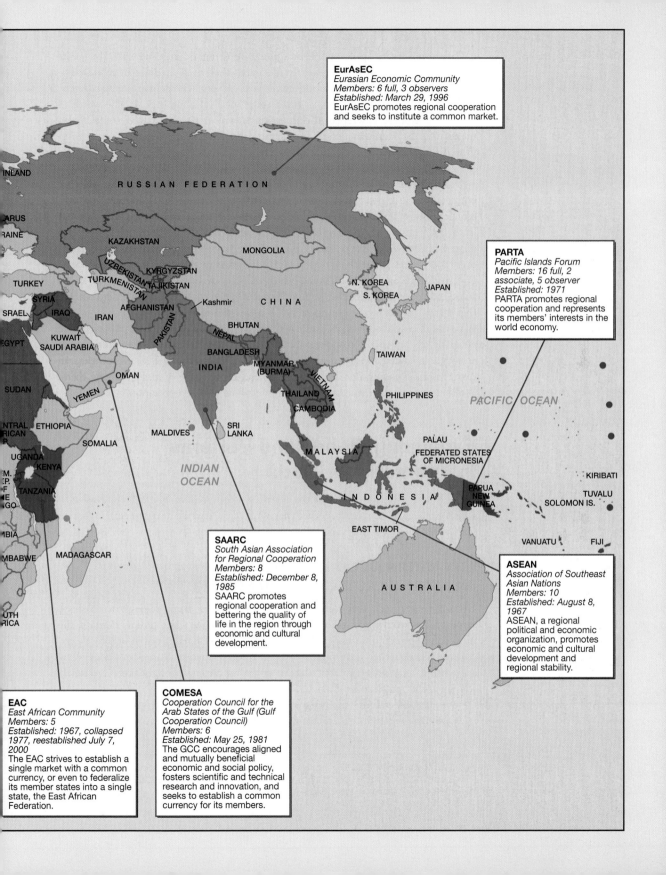

EurAsEC
Eurasian Economic Community
Members: 6 full, 3 observers
Established: March 29, 1996
EurAsEC promotes regional cooperation and seeks to institute a common market.

PARTA
Pacific Islands Forum
Members: 16 full, 2 associate, 5 observer
Established: 1971
PARTA promotes regional cooperation and represents its members' interests in the world economy.

SAARC
South Asian Association for Regional Cooperation
Members: 8
Established: December 8, 1985
SAARC promotes regional cooperation and bettering the quality of life in the region through economic and cultural development.

ASEAN
Association of Southeast Asian Nations
Members: 10
Established: August 8, 1967
ASEAN, a regional political and economic organization, promotes economic and cultural development and regional stability.

EAC
East African Community
Members: 5
Established: 1967, collapsed 1977, reestablished July 7, 2000
The EAC strives to establish a single market with a common currency, or even to federalize its member states into a single state, the East African Federation.

COMESA
Cooperation Council for the Arab States of the Gulf (Gulf Cooperation Council)
Members: 6
Established: May 25, 1981
The GCC encourages aligned and mutually beneficial economic and social policy, fosters scientific and technical research and innovation, and seeks to establish a common currency for its members.

Some observers applaud these regional agreements, arguing that they, like the WTO, constitute institutional structures that help mediate or avoid divisive trade policy conflicts among countries. Others see them more negatively, believing that they may serve to limit trade with nonmembers. In the words of economist Robert Lawrence, the question is whether the regional trade agreements will be "building blocs" or "stumbling blocks" on the road to an integrated world economy.[23] While questions remain, most observers today regard such regional institutions as complementary to the WTO.

To state that the WTO (or the EU or NAFTA) facilitates cooperation among governments on trade policy is not to pass judgement on whether its actions are ethically, economically, or otherwise good or bad. Governments may cooperate for purposes that leave some consumers, workers, or businesses worse off. Anti-globalization critics complain that the WTO is too pro-business, that it privileges international corporations over other interests. They charge that WTO rules and procedures are biased, especially in their disregard for environmental, health and safety, labor, and social policies. WTO rules, indeed, tend to focus on trade itself and exclude consideration of other concerns that many analysts regard as important. Whether this is justifiable depends largely on value judgments about the relative importance of trade, and economic relations more generally, as compared to concerns about human and social rights. (We will return to this issue in Chapter 13; see also the "Controversy" box on page 249.) Nonetheless, in many instances cooperation among governments is preferable to conflict among them, and the international institutions of trade contribute to this cooperation.

Explaining Trends and Patterns in International Trade

We can now return to some of the features of international trade relations with which we began, bringing together these analytical strands to try to explain them. Let's recall the major ways in which trade policies vary.

WHY, WITHIN A COUNTRY, ARE SOME INDUSTRIES PROTECTED, AND SOME NOT?

Governments often favor some industries over others, some regions over others, some groups over others—and this is certainly true of trade policy. Perhaps the most striking such difference is that virtually all developed countries protect agriculture, whereas they have relatively open trade in manufactured products. Why are America's farmers (in particular, its sugar producers) strongly protected while so many other producers are not?

We can look at the interests in play, to determine which groups or industries are most likely to benefit from protection. Land is scarce in most developed

---

23. Robert Z. Lawrence. "Emerging Regional Arrangements: Building Blocs or Stumbling Blocks?" In *Finance and the International Economy 5: The AMEX Bank Review Prize Essays,* ed. Richard O'Brien, 25–35 (New York: Oxford University Press, 1991).

Does the WTO Hurt the Global Poor?

In the late 1980s, Lee Kyung-Hae led a rewarding life as a thriving farmer in South Korea. He had succeeded in transforming a difficult area of land in the mountains south of Seoul into a prosperous cattle farm and a model of modern agriculture for the farmers in his poverty-stricken region. However, this success story ended abruptly when, under pressure from the WTO, South Korea opened its markets to imports of cheaper cows from Australia. Beef prices collapsed and, unable to make the repayments on his loans, Lee was forced to sell his farm. This experience, and the similar experience of many other farmers and fishermen in his country, caused Lee to become a prominent anti-globalization activist. After a series of hunger strikes over a period of years, on September 10, 2003, at a demonstration outside the WTO meeting in Cancún, Lee climbed a police barricade and stabbed himself in the heart, surrounded by 150 of his countrymen and the television cameras of the world.[a] Some observers consider Lee a hero for calling the WTO to account for its treatment of the global poor. His signature phrase, "The WTO Kills Farmers," continues to be displayed on placards by protestors worldwide. Others consider Lee's death a pointless tragedy. Well meaning as his action was, it displayed a fundamental misunderstanding of the impact of trade liberalization on the world's disadvantaged. Who is right?

When thinking about the effects of the WTO on the global poor, it helps to distinguish two questions. The first is whether trade liberalization has indeed hurt the world's poor. There is no doubt that certain people—such as Lee and the poor South Korean farmers he represented—have suffered great hardship as a result of some WTO-related policies. But assessing the overall effects of the WTO regime on the poor is difficult. Partly, this is because trade liberalization has varying impacts on a range of interests (income, food security, health, education, and life expectancy); some impacts are negative, others positive. Partly, it is because the interests of different actors, both within and across countries, are affected differently by trade liberalization. Lee's livelihood was sustainable only as a result of his government's agricultural protectionism—a policy that hurts not only South Korean consumers (including the poor) by raising the prices of agricultural goods, but also poor farmers in other countries, such as China, who are denied a market for their produce. Finally, the question is hard to answer because we are not sure what the global poor would have experienced under an institution, or set of rules, other than the WTO. Without the WTO, perhaps, their situation would have been even worse than it is today.

Whatever we decide on this first question, it leaves the following one unaddressed. Has the bargain represented by the WTO been fair to the global poor? Our interest here is not the nature of the benefits and burdens produced, but the way in which those benefits and burdens have been distributed. Some aspects of the WTO system may seem unfair in this sense. While rich countries have pressured poor or middle-income countries such as South Korea to open their markets to the developed world, they themselves have maintained extensive protectionism in precisely the markets that matter most to the developing world. And global inequality has, by some measures, increased over the past several decades, suggesting to some analysts that the gains of free trade have been unevenly distributed. These facts appear to violate, respectively, reciprocity and nondiscrimination, two core norms of fairness. However, proving this claim runs up against difficulties similar to those discussed above. While agricultural subsidies in richer countries have burdened the poor in food-producing countries, such subsidies may have helped people in less developed countries that import food, such as those of North Africa and the Middle East. And it is difficult to decisively attribute changes in the relative economic fortunes of different countries to the WTO system in the absence of knowledge of what the world would have looked like without it. Some scholars argue that any increase in inequality in recent decades is the result of technological change, the collapse of communism, or the AIDS crisis and civil war in Africa—rather than WTO policies.

Some scholars wonder, finally, whether it matters if the WTO is unfair, provided that the aggregate gains from free trade are large enough. One way in which it may matter is if the perception that the WTO is unfair undermines the public support necessary to sustain it—as instanced in the demonstrations in which Lee Kyung-Hae met his death. ∎

---

a. "Field of Tears," *The Guardian*, September 16, 2003.

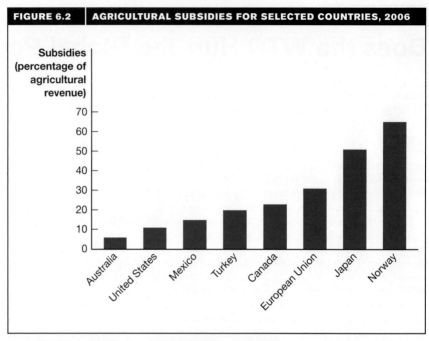

FIGURE 6.2   AGRICULTURAL SUBSIDIES FOR SELECTED COUNTRIES, 2006

Source: OECD Database of Producer and Consumer Support Estimates, www.oecd.org/document/
59/0,3343,fr_2649_33727_39551355_1_1_1_1,00.html (accessed 3/17/09).

countries, certainly relative to capital and skilled labor; this explains why their farmers are protectionist. We can then explore how well organized the interests are; the more cohesive and powerful interests are likely to get more government support. Farmers are well organized, while consumers of food are rarely organized at all. Perhaps the country's political institutions privilege some regions, classes, or industries over others. Many nations' electoral institutions favor farm regions over cities, as does the U.S. Senate, which allots a sparsely populated farm state the same number of senators (two) as a densely populated, mostly urban state. Farmers and their parties are often pivotal in parliamentary systems, as they occupy the crucial center of the political spectrum. All these considerations help explain why some sectors receive more trade protection than others and, in particular, why farmers in rich countries are so commonly favored. In the case of American sugar producers, they have very high stakes in protection—the country's sugar farms might shut down without it—and their numbers are small enough to be extremely well organized and well represented in Congress. Figure 6.2 shows selected examples reflecting the protection of farmers in various countries.

WHY HAVE NATIONAL TRADE POLICIES VARIED OVER TIME?

There have been many striking instances of countries shifting from openness to closure, or from protectionism to trade liberalization. The United States in the 1920s was one of the most protectionist industrial nations on earth; starting in the late 1940s, however, it led the Western world toward substantial trade liberalization. How can we explain such shifts?

Interests may change: for example, a nation's ability to compete in world markets might improve, creating less opposition to trade. Institutions may change, too: perhaps democratization gives more pro-trade groups, such as consumers, access to political influence. Some such national changes may be driven by changes at the international level that affect the nation in question, such as a dramatic change in the price of its principal export product. The distributional interests at play—whether factoral or sectoral—may alter in a manner that affects national policy, such as when one factor becomes more abundant or one sector develops powerful export interests. And national political institutions can affect policy by strengthening the hand of groups that want to push policy in a certain direction.

For example, several explanations have been offered for the American shift from very high levels of trade protection to support for liberalization. The destruction of foreign economies by World War II reduced support for protection: the United States faced very little serious industrial competition, which made it relatively easy for the country to opt for trade liberalization. As the Cold War began, the geopolitical concerns associated with a desire to bind together a pro-American Western alliance reinforced support for an open Western trading system. At the same time, the rise of powerful American manufacturing industries interested in exporting and in investing overseas created a base of support for increasing economic integration. This, too, was encouraged by institutional changes in the making of American trade policy in the 1930s, which gave the generally more trade-friendly president greater influence than the usually relatively protectionist Congress. All these factors and more may have affected American policy. Scholars continue to present arguments and evidence for and against these hypotheses. They may not, in fact, be mutually exclusive. National policy changes may be better explained in some cases by the global context, in others by the domestic interests engaged, in still others by domestic institutions.

WHY DO SOME COUNTRIES HAVE HIGHER TRADE BARRIERS THAN OTHERS?

Even within a common international trading system, national policies can differ. In the late 1930s, as the United States and some Western European nations began moving away from trade protection and toward liberalization, most other industrial countries—especially Germany, Italy, and Japan—erected extremely high barriers to trade. In the 1980s, China became a global exporting powerhouse, while many other developing nations remained very closed to trade.

Again, interests matter: these differences among nations may be driven by different factor endowments or sectoral features. In line with the Stolper-Samuelson approach, for example, the interests of landowners in two countries might be diametrically opposed: in favor of trade in a land-rich country, opposed to it in a land-poor country. If identical pro-farmer parties were in power in the two nations, one would reduce trade barriers while the other would raise them. A country whose economy is dominated by exporters will tend to be less protectionist than one that has very few exporters.

The source of the difference, however, might be in national institutions, such as a party system or legislative structures that favor the protectionist class (scarce factor) or protectionist sectors and regions. A democracy might give labor or consumers more influence than a dictatorship would. Anything that affects the domestic interests, institutions, or interactions of a country may well affect its trade policies.

WHY HAS THE WORLD TRADING ORDER BEEN MORE OR LESS OPEN AT DIFFERENT TIMES?

Global trends are usually best explained by international factors, and trade is no exception. Three causes of the ebb and flow of open trade relations are most prominent: international economic conditions, the role of one or a few very large countries, and the creation of international institutions. Forbidding world economic conditions in the 1930s were a major source of the protectionist turn of many countries' trade policies, just as global economic growth in the 1990s encouraged trade liberalization among developing and formerly communist countries. The ability of one or a few large countries to organize a leadership role in international trade relations—Britain and France in the late nineteenth century, the United States and its principal allies after World War II—also appears to have been important in affecting global trade. Further, the presence of such institutions as the WTO encourages and facilitates collaborative trade ties among governments.

Conclusion: Trade and Politics

International trade is the centerpiece of international economic relations, and government policies toward trade have long been among the most hotly contested. They are controversial *within a country,* as supporters and opponents of freer trade clash. Trade policies can also be controversial *among countries,* as governments contend over their respective policies. This contention often breeds further discord; as the American statesman Cordell Hull said of the 1930s, "The political line-up followed the economic line-up."[24]

National policies toward foreign trade have been important to the development of the world economy and to international politics more generally. How open a nation is to trade affects its pattern of economic and social development as well as its relations with other nations. In turn, a country's trade policies are determined by the nature of its prevailing economic interests and political institutions, and by its interactions with other nations.

---

24. Quoted in Gardner, *Sterling-Dollar Diplomacy,* 9.

Reviewing Interests, Interactions, and Institutions

INTERESTS	INTERACTIONS	INSTITUTIONS
Trade is in the interest of the society as a whole; it increases aggregate social welfare by making the economy more efficient.	National trade policies reflect interactions among domestic interests, such as the formation of coalitions among those in favor of protectionism or trade liberalization.	Domestically, national trade policies are strongly affected by their mediation through domestic political institutions.
There are, however, both winners and losers from trade: just because the country as a whole benefits does not mean everyone in it benefits.	Internationally, governments have many incentives to cooperate in trade policy; but they also face many obstacles to cooperation—such as the fear that other governments will cheat on trade agreements.	Differences among countries in their electoral institutions, legislatures, and bureaucracies affect national trade policies. Even within countries, different institutions can have different trade-policy orientations.
Winners include owners of abundant factors, exporters, and consumers.	Features of the bargaining environment—small numbers, good information—can make it easier for governments to develop cooperative trade relations.	Governments have created many international trade institutions, which facilitate cooperation by setting standards of behavior, providing information, and a giving a framework for settling disputes.
Losers include owners of scarce factors, and those who compete with imports.	Cooperation has often proved difficult, as trade negotiations have broken down and trade conflicts have erupted among countries.	The principal trade institution at the global level is the World Trade Organization (WTO). There are also regional institutions (NAFTA, the EU) and bilateral agreements between countries.
National trade policies also reflect such noneconomic concerns as geopolitical interests—the desire to support one's friends and isolate one's enemies.		

Key Terms

For Further Reading

Busch, Marc I. *Trade Warriors: States, Firms, and Strategic-Trade Policy in High Technology Competition*. New York: Cambridge University Press, 1999. Analyzes why governments intervene in trade to support industries and firms regarded as strategically important to their economies.

Chase, Kerry. *Trading Blocs: States, Firms, and Regions in the World Economy*. Ann Arbor: University of Michigan Press, 2005. Describes and analyzes why countries decide to form regional trade agreements such as NAFTA and the EU.

Davis, Christina. *Food Fights over Free Trade: How International Institutions Promote Agricultural Trade Liberalization*. Princeton: Princeton University Press, 2005. Analyzes the interests and institutions that have structured the complex politics of trade in farm products.

Destler, I. M. *American Trade Politics*. 4th ed. Washington, D.C.: Peterson Institute for International Economics, 2005. Surveys and analyzes the political economy of trade policy in the United States.

Hiscox, Michael. *International Trade and Political Conflict: Commerce, Coalitions, and Mobility*. Princeton: Princeton University Press, 2002. Evaluates the relative importance of factoral (class) and sectoral (industry) demands for protection and of variation among these considerations over time.

Irwin, Douglas. *Against the Tide: An Intellectual History of Free Trade*. Princeton: Princeton University Press, 1997. Presents the theory, economics, and politics of debates over trade in the modern era.

Milner, Helen. *Resisting Protectionism: Global Industries and the Politics of International Trade*. Princeton: Princeton University Press, 1988. Explores the impact of multinational corporations on trade policy, arguing that internationally active businesses can change the domestic alignment of forces in support of trade liberalization.

Rogowski, Ronald. *Commerce and Coalitions: How Trade Affects Domestic Political Alignments*. Princeton: Princeton University Press, 1989. Develops an analysis, based on the Stolper-Samuelson theorem, of how trade affects politics within nations.

FIND REVIEW AND STUDY MATERIALS ONLINE AT WWNORTON.COM/STUDYSPACE

Comparative Advantage and the Political Economy of Trade

Economists generally agree that international trade is good for the aggregate welfare of societies. Where does this consensus come from? In this section, we introduce the concept of comparative advantage, which for centuries has been the backbone of economic thinking on international trade. We also illustrate the redistributive and welfare effects of opening the domestic economy to international trade and the countervailing effects of imposing a tariff.

COMPARATIVE ADVANTAGE

At the heart of economic analyses of international trade is the concept of *comparative advantage*. In short, the idea of comparative advantage implies that all countries benefit from trade if each country specializes in the production of certain goods. Which goods should countries produce? Economist David Ricardo provided the straightforward answer in the early 1800s: countries should focus their production only on goods that they can produce most efficiently relative to other goods. If a country is good at mining copper, or growing coffee beans, or producing steel, then it should focus its productive capacities on producing these goods and rely on international trade to obtain all the other goods that it needs.

What if a country is not very good at producing anything? To answer this question, it is important to distinguish between *absolute advantage* and comparative advantage. A country has an absolute advantage if it can produce a good more efficiently than any other country. Comparative advantage, on the other hand, is determined within a country: of all the possible goods in the world, a country can produce some goods more efficiently than others. This means that *all* countries have a comparative advantage in something. A country might not be the most efficient in the world at producing coffee, but it still has a comparative advantage in coffee if it can produce coffee more efficiently than steel, airplanes, or any other good.

Consider the following example used by Ricardo himself to explain the concept of comparative advantage. Assume that there are two countries in the world, Portugal and England, and that these two countries can produce only cloth and wine. Further assume that the only input in the production process is labor, such that one unit of each good (a bolt of cloth or a barrel of wine) has a cost in manhours. For example, in England it takes 15 man-hours to produce a bolt of cloth and 30 man-hours to produce a barrel of wine. In Portugal, it takes 10 man-hours to produce a bolt of cloth and 15 man-hours to produce a barrel of wine. Note that it takes fewer man-hours to produce both cloth and wine in Portugal than in England; indeed, in this example, Portugal has an absolute advantage in the production of both goods, cloth and wine (see Table A).

To understand the impact of each country's choice of which goods to produce, it is helpful to examine the *opportunity cost of production.* This is the value that a country forgoes in order to make one product rather than another. The resources (in this

TABLE A		
Country	Cloth	Wine
	Cost in man-hours per bolt	Cost in man-hours per barrel
England	15	30
Portugal	10	15

TABLE B		
Country	Opportunity Cost of Producing...	
	One bolt of cloth	One barrel of wine
England	1/2 barrel of wine	2 bolts of cloth
Portugal	2/3 barrel of wine	1 1/2 bolts of cloth

example, labor) that each nation uses to make cloth are unavailable to make wine, so that it must forgo a certain amount of wine in order to make cloth. How many bolts of cloth must a country give up to produce a barrel of wine, and vice versa?

England must give up two bolts of cloth to produce an additional barrel of wine (30 divided by 15); alternatively, it can give up one-half a barrel of wine to produce a bolt of cloth (15 divided by 30). In contrast, Portugal must give up 1 1/2 bolts of cloth to produce an additional barrel of wine; alternatively, it can give up 2/3 of a barrel of wine to produce an additional bolt of cloth. Table B presents these results.

Note that the opportunity cost of producing cloth is lower in England than in Portugal, whereas the opportunity cost of producing wine is lower in Portugal than in England. From these figures, we can conclude that England has a comparative advantage in the production of cloth, and Portugal has a comparative advantage in the production of wine.

What happens if these two countries engage in international trade? If England focuses all of its man-hours on producing cloth, and Portugal does the same for wine, then the total world production of cloth and wine will be considerably higher than if the two countries did not specialize or engage in trade. Ricardo's simple model tells us that international trade based on comparative advantage increases aggregate welfare, measured by the total amount of goods produced in this two-country world. The increase in aggregate welfare occurs even though England does not have an absolute advantage in the production of either good.

DISTRIBUTIONAL AND WELFARE EFFECTS OF TRADE

Economists largely agree that international trade is welfare-improving for societies, whereas tariffs and other forms of trade protection are inefficient and costly for societies. A few simple graphs can illustrate the logic behind these claims. Consider first a country in a state of autarky, in which there is no international trade. The domestic price of any good is therefore determined by the intersection of the two lines of domestic supply and domestic demand. All else being equal, producers will supply more of a good as its price increases, and consumers will demand more of a

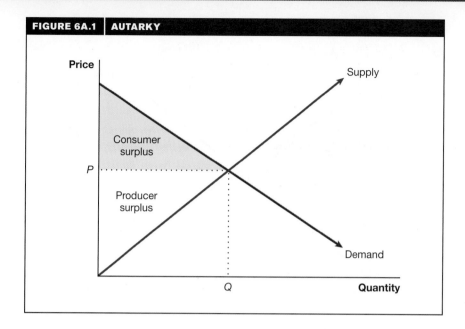

FIGURE 6A.1 | AUTARKY

Price

Supply

Consumer surplus

P

Producer surplus

Demand

Q

Quantity

good as its price falls. Therefore, the supply line is upward-sloping and the demand line is downward-sloping. The intersection indicates the good's domestic price (P) and quantity demanded (Q), as shown in Figure 6A.1.

The effects of the production of the good in autarky are measured by the concepts of *consumer surplus* and *producer surplus*. Consider first the fate of consumers. Based on the downward-sloping demand line, some people in the country would be happy to pay more than P for the good. The shaded region represents the aggregate welfare benefit for consumers; it is called a surplus because it represents the gains to consumers who would be willing to pay more than P for the good. Similarly, there are some producers in the country who would happily supply the good at a lower price than P. The region beneath P and bounded by the two lines represents the producer surplus. This region captures the gains to producers who benefit from a higher price than they would otherwise tolerate for selling the good.

Now, consider how the price and quantity of the good change as the country begins to trade freely with other countries. Note that the world price of the good will be lower than the domestic price in autarky. The world price is determined by the intersection of global, not domestic, supply and demand. For simplicity, we assume that the country in this example is small relative to the world economy. In other words, it is a "price-taker": its own domestic supply and demand of the good will not appreciably affect global supply or demand. Figure 6.A2 indicates that the new domestic price declines to the (lower) world price (P$_w$) after the country moves from autarky to international trade openness. At this lower price, domestic consumer demand increases to Q$_d$ because more people can enjoy the good at the new lower price. Domestic supply of the good decreases to Q$_s$ because fewer producers are willing to produce the good at the lower price. The larger consumer demand is satisfied by imports from the rest of the world (equal to the distance between Q$_s$ and Q$_d$). Note that under free trade, the consumer surplus increases considerably because consumers are better off with the lower price.

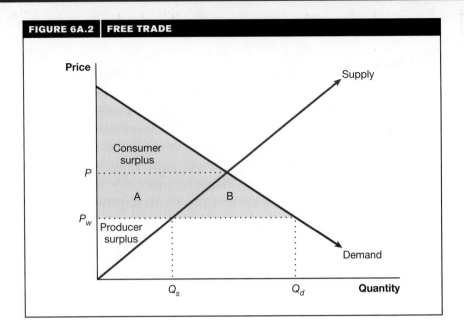

FIGURE 6A.2 | FREE TRADE

Price

Supply

Consumer
surplus

P ....

A   B

P_w ....
Producer
surplus

Demand

Q_s Q_d **Quantity**

The regions labeled A and B represent the additions to consumer surplus that result from free trade. The producer surplus declines as a result of the lower world price. However, note that the combination of consumer and producer surplus—an overall measure of aggregate welfare—is larger under free trade than in autarky. There are two important implications: opening to trade redistributes income from producers to consumers, and opening to trade makes society as a whole better off.

As a final exercise, consider the implications to redistribution and to aggregate welfare of a tariff on the good. The tariff—which is a tax by the government on the imported good—increases the domestic price of the good to P_t, as shown in Figure 6.A3. The quantity demanded by consumers falls to Q_d^t because of the higher price, whereas the quantity supplied by domestic suppliers increases to Q_s^t. As expected, the consumer surplus declines, because many consumers who wish to purchase the good cannot afford the higher price. The producer surplus increases by the amount represented by region A, as more producers benefit from a higher price than what they would normally receive. What of the remaining regions? The amount represented by C accrues to the government as a result of the tariff revenue. But the two dark triangular regions on either side of C do not benefit anyone! Known as the *deadweight loss*, of the tariff, they represent the efficiency losses to society of trade protection.

Where does the deadweight loss come from? The best way to understand this loss is to reflect on the concept of comparative advantage. The tariff causes an artificially higher price, which leads domestic producers to shift their production away from whatever they were previously producing and toward the higher-priced good. Suppose the country in question is England, which has a comparative advantage in the production of cloth. If England imposes a tariff on imported wine, then more English producers will shift their production away from cloth and toward wine to

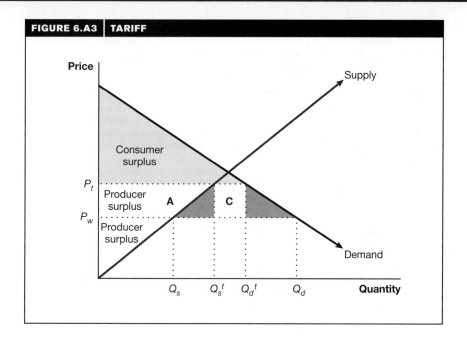

FIGURE 6.A3 | TARIFF

take advantage of the higher price, even though they are relatively inefficient in producing wine. In other words, a tariff interferes with the efficient allocation of production and works against the concept of comparative advantage. By the same token, the artificially high price of the protected good leads consumers to reallocate their consumption away from it and toward a good they would not otherwise purchase, which is another loss to society. The losses to efficiency are represented by the dark triangles in Figure 6A.3. When we combine these efficiency losses with the decline in domestic consumption caused by the higher price, we can see why economists are generally in agreement that tariffs cause society as a whole to be worse off compared to free trade.

This simple set of graphs captures the essence of the political economy of trade policy. First, international trade improves aggregate welfare. However, certain producers who previously produced exclusively for the domestic market can be harmed when the country moves toward free trade. Trade tariffs lead to a decline in aggregate welfare and cause deadweight losses to society. They also result in an increase in the producer surplus and a reduction in the consumer surplus. If producer groups can successfully lobby the government for protection, they can reap great benefits. These benefits come at the expense of consumers, in the form of a reduced consumer surplus (due to higher prices), and at the expense of the country as a whole, in the form of an efficiency loss.

CHAPTER 7

International Financial Relations

In the 1970s and early 1980s, Latin American governments borrowed hundreds of billions of dollars from foreign banks, using the money for roads, buildings, and other projects as they tried to catch up with the developed world. In 1982, Mexico ended the borrowing boom when it defaulted on its debt, causing foreign investors to panic. It took years for the debtor countries to recover from the financial crisis and for progress to resume in places like Mexico City (pictured here).

Every year, approximately $5 trillion is invested abroad. Why is so much money invested in foreign countries? And why do relations between foreign investors and the countries in which they invest often become hostile and politically controversial?

In the 1960s, the governments of Latin America discovered a valuable resource: foreign loans. International investors had not lent money to developing countries since 1929, having been burned during the Great Depression of the 1930s when most countries stopped paying their debts. But by 1965 memories had faded, and international banks were again willing to lend to governments in the developing world.

Latin American governments pursued foreign loans with great enthusiasm. They needed the money to build factories and roads, power plants and steel mills, schools and houses. For fifteen years, governments in Latin America, as well as a few other developing regions, borrowed frantically to try to catch up with the industrialized world. Loans poured in, public and private projects lined up for money, and economies expanded. The region's total debt grew in ten years, from 1973 to 1982, from $40 billion to $330 billion. In the peak year of 1981, at the height of the borrowing boom, over $50 billion flooded into Latin America (equivalent to over $110 billion in 2008 dollars), quantities never before seen in borrowing by developing nations.

The borrowing boom came to a crashing halt late in the summer of 1982. In August, the Mexican government announced that it could not pay the interest and principal on its $100 billion debt to foreign banks. International banks panicked. If Mexico, a major oil producer, couldn't or wouldn't pay its debts, perhaps other nations couldn't or wouldn't either. Investors stopped lending within weeks, and heavily indebted developing nations around the world were thrown into crisis. Within four months, about 40 countries had fallen behind on their debt payments.

How and Why Do People Invest Overseas?

▶ Why Invest Abroad? Why Borrow Abroad?
▶ What's the Problem with Foreign Investment?
▶ Concessional Finance

Why Is International Finance Controversial?

▶ Who Wants to Borrow? Who Wants to Lend?
▶ Debtor-Creditor Interactions
▶ Institutions of International Finance
▶ Recent Borrowing and Debt Crises
▶ A New Crisis Hits the United States, and the World

Foreign Direct Investment: What Role Do Multinational Corporations Play?

▶ Why Do Corporations Go Multinational?
▶ Why Do Countries Let Foreign Multinationals In?
▶ Host-Country Interactions with MNCs
▶ Why Aren't There International Institutions Related to FDI?

International Migration: What Happens When People—Rather Than Capital—Move across Borders?

Conclusion: The Politics of International Investment

The debt crisis that began in 1982 led to an economic collapse that was, for many countries, the most catastrophic in modern history. Latin America spiraled downward into recession and depression, unemployment, and hyperinflation (price increases of more than 50 percent a month). After decades of rapid growth, income per person in Latin America declined by 10 percent over the 1980s, real wages fell by at least 30 percent, and investment fell even further, while inflation in many nations went above 1,000 percent.[1] The 1980s became known in the region as "the lost decade." In Mexico, wages dropped, inflation soared, some of the country's biggest companies went bankrupt, and the government was forced to cut back many popular social programs. In 1983, as demonstrations and strikes roiled the country, Mexico's principal opposition party won control of some of the country's major cities for the first time.

Throughout the developing world, protests erupted over the debt crisis and the unemployment, inflation, and government cutbacks it had brought. Millions of citizens took to the streets in protest, often blaming their dire situation on foreign banks and the International Monetary Fund (IMF). The economic and political crisis eventually drove most of Latin America's military dictatorships from power. But this advance was overshadowed, in the view of many observers, by the fact that the debtor nations had fallen even farther behind economically as they struggled to shoulder their debt. What had originally seemed a golden opportunity—readily available foreign loans—now seemed a terrible burden.

This experience is no anomaly. International finance is arguably both the most widely sought and the most generally mistrusted feature of the modern world economy. Every country wants access to the enormous amounts of money that global investors can mobilize. But no country wants to be beholden to international bankers, the IMF, and other representatives of foreign creditors.

Today, capital flows around the world in unimaginably large quantities. Nearly half of all the world's investment goes across borders—every year, about $5 *trillion* in foreign loans or investments. Total international investments in 2008 were about $100 trillion, and *every day* many trillions of dollars in foreign currencies are traded. Even the United States has financed large trade and budget deficits with money from abroad, borrowing about $6 trillion between 2000 and 2008—increasing its debt to foreigners in those years by more than $50,000 for every American household.[2]

International finance has long been the leading edge of global economic integration. Massive investment flows drove the integrated world economy of the nineteenth and early twentieth centuries; then, they dried up during the years between World Wars I and II, when the world's nations turned inward. Since 1960, international finance has revived and is once again the most globalized component of the world economy, dwarfing international trade and migration.

Some analysts regard the emergence of a worldwide market for capital as one of globalization's main attractions. Companies, investors, and borrowers around the world now can tap into an enormous pool of capital.

International lending can help developing countries build up their infrastructure and take other steps to improve their economy. However, opponents of current lending practices argue that the promise of much-needed money lures developing countries into the "chains of debt" that they may not be able to repay without imposing significant suffering on their people.

1. Eliana Cardoso and Ann Helwege, *Latin America's Economy: Diversity, Trends, and Conflicts* (Cambridge, MA: MIT Press, 1995).
2. Except where otherwise noted, all data are from M. Ayhan Kose, Eswar Prasad, Kenneth Rogoff, and Shang-Jin Wei, "Financial Globalization: A Reappraisal" (IMF Working Paper 06/189, 2006).

Homebuyers in Arkansas can have their mortgages underwritten by investors in Germany; startups in India can be financed by Canadian pension funds; shopkeepers in South Africa can borrow money that comes from small savers in Japan.

Supporters of global economic integration see finance as a force that can knit together the world's nations in ways that are economically and politically desirable. They welcome the availability of huge amounts of capital to borrowers around the world, allowing poor countries to finance investments they otherwise could not afford. And international finance serves, in the view of some observers, to encourage responsible policies by otherwise unreliable governments.

Yet, international finance is also extremely controversial, and critics of global economic integration have long targeted international bankers. Vladimir Lenin, the Russian revolutionary and founder of the Soviet Union, blamed finance capitalism for colonial imperialism and for World War I. In the 1930s, parties of the Right and Left alike angrily criticized foreign bankers for their alleged mistreatment of Germany and other debtor nations. Today, many policymakers in the developing world see such international finance as a source of economic and political problems, and as a potential threat to their nations' sovereignty. In September 1997, in the midst of another massive financial crisis (this one in Asia), Malaysian prime minister Mahathir bin Mohamad charged that his nation's achievements were under attack by "the great fund managers who have now come to be the people to decide who should prosper and who shouldn't." The fault was clear: "the currency traders have become rich, very very rich through making other people poor."[3] Mahathir was not alone in blaming international financiers for the tribulations of the developing world: protests over the involvement of foreign financiers and the IMF in debt crises have become common.

Governments, firms, and individuals sometimes pursue international finance avidly and sometimes attack it mercilessly. This discrepancy raises questions about why international investment is so controversial. It also raises questions about the effects, and the implications, of today's globe-straddling financial markets. This chapter makes several key points about the interests, interactions, and institutions associated with international investment.

CORE OF THE ANALYSIS

▶ Within borrowing nations, there are many actors who value access to foreign funds. However, there are others who resent the constraints and burdens that foreign investments sometimes impose on debtors. Similar conflicting interests exist within lending nations.

▶ At the international level, both lenders and borrowers, like investors and recipients of investment, have a common interest in sustaining capital flows, which benefit both sides. Nonetheless, they may enter into conflict—especially over how the benefits from the loans or investments will be divided.

▶ Lenders and borrowers, and investors and recipients, bargain over the investments that tie them together. There is frequent disagreement over debt payments to foreign creditors and profit payments to foreign corporations.

▶ An array of important and influential international institutions structure interactions in the international financial realm. The most prominent is the International Monetary Fund, which has often played a major role in managing the problems of heavily indebted countries. Like international finance generally, the role of the IMF is very controversial: some analysts think it contributes to the cooperative resolution of financial problems, while others think that it takes unfair advantage of struggling debtor nations.

---

3. *Foreign Policy Bulletin* 8, no. 6 (November–December 1997): 24–26.

How and Why Do People Invest Overseas?

portfolio investment:
Investment in a foreign country via the purchase of stocks (equities), bonds, or other financial instruments. Portfolio investors do not exercise managerial control of the foreign operation.

There are many ways in which those with capital can invest in foreign lands. The principal varieties of foreign investments can be grouped into two broad categories: portfolio investment and direct investment. **Portfolio investments** give the investor a claim on some income, but no role in managing the investment. Loans are portfolio investments. So are shares of a company's stock (equities), for each share of stock represents a minuscule portion of ownership in the corporation.[4] If, for example, an investor buys the bonds of an Indian corporation or the Indian government, or if a bank lends money to an Indian corporation or the Indian government, the Indian debtor commits itself to make interest and principal payments but has no obligation to involve the creditor in figuring out how or when to use the borrowed money. Even if the Indian corporation or Indian government has a bad year, it is obligated to pay off its creditors at the preestablished interest rate.[5] Portfolio investors take little or no part in running their investment; their interest is simply in the rate of return.

sovereign lending:
Loans from private financial institutions in one country to sovereign governments in other countries.

Most of the portfolio investment that goes to developing countries is **sovereign lending,** that is, loans from private financial institutions to sovereign governments. Loans by European or American financial institutions to the governments of Indonesia or Brazil—or to government-owned or -controlled companies or agencies in those countries—are sovereign loans. Even loans made to private firms in foreign countries are sometimes considered to be sovereign loans. This is because the government of the debtor often has an explicit or implicit commitment to ensure the creditworthiness of its nation's borrowers: for example, loans to an Indonesian or Brazilian private bank or corporation may implicate the Indonesian or Brazilian government, because these governments can facilitate or impede repayment of those loans.

foreign direct investment (FDI): Investment in a foreign country via the acquisition of a local facility or the establishment of a new facility. Direct investors maintain managerial control of the foreign operation.

Foreign direct investment (FDI) is made by a company that owns facilities in another country, facilities over which the company maintains control. For example, when Toyota opens a truck factory in Thailand or when Disney opens a theme park in France, these are instances of FDI. In fact, FDI differs from foreign portfolio investment most importantly because the investor maintains managerial control—and also bears the full long-term risk of the investment. If a Toyota truck factory in Thailand is not profitable, Toyota loses money. Direct investors have full authority to run their investments, but they take most of the associated risks as well.

WHY INVEST ABROAD? WHY BORROW ABROAD?

Banks, corporations, and individuals make investments overseas with a clear goal: to make money. Those with capital want to move their money from where profits are lower to where profits are higher. Thus, many international investors want to

---

4. Equities (stocks) can be ambiguous; if an investor owns enough of the company's shares, he or she might in fact take control of the company, which would make the investment direct. But almost all international equity investment is of the portfolio variety, meaning that it does not involve actual managerial control of the firm.
5. This distinction is blurred in instances in which foreigners buy large quantities of corporate equities—so that at some point they could in fact exercise control over the corporation. Traditional portfolio investors, as discussed here, are not interested in control; they buy equities solely as financial instruments.

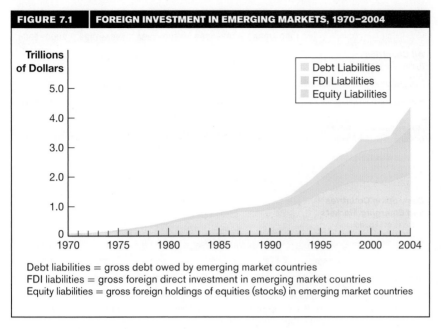

| FIGURE 7.1 | FOREIGN INVESTMENT IN EMERGING MARKETS, 1970–2004 |

Trillions of Dollars

- Debt Liabilities
- FDI Liabilities
- Equity Liabilities

Debt liabilities = gross debt owed by emerging market countries
FDI liabilities = gross foreign direct investment in emerging market countries
Equity liabilities = gross foreign holdings of equities (stocks) in emerging market countries

Note: These are stocks of investments outstanding, not flows of new investments. Emerging market countries are Argentina, Brazil, Chile, China, Colombia, Egypt, India, Indonesia, Israel, the Republic of Korea, Malaysia, Mexico, Pakistan, Peru, the Philippines, Singapore, South Africa, Thailand, Turkey, and Venezuela. *Source:* M. Ayhan Kose, Eswar Prasad, Kenneth Rogoff, and Shang-Jin Wei, "Financial Globalization: A Reappraisal" (IMF Working Paper 06/189, 2006).

take money from capital-rich developed countries to capital-poor developing ones. Banks, corporations, and individuals in rich countries invest more than $300 billion every year in developing nations, about half of it in direct investment from multinational corporations, the other half in loans and related investments.[6] (Figure 7.1 illustrates the rapid growth of foreign investment in emerging markets over recent decades.) The Heckscher-Ohlin theory presented in Chapter 6 explains why. A country's average profit rate depends on how plentiful capital is. Where land or labor are scarce, they are expensive; where they are plentiful, they are cheap. The same is true of capital, recognizing that the interest rate is the "price" of capital—more expensive capital means a higher rate of return. In a poor country, capital is scarce and therefore expensive: borrowers pay higher interest rates for something in short supply. In a rich country, capital is abundant, so interest rates and profit rates are much lower. For example, in 2008 the prevailing rate of interest on short-term loans in most developed countries was about 4 percent, while in Latin America it was typically 10 percent and often higher.

The greater scarcity of capital, as well as higher interest rates, in developing than developed countries encourages capital to flow from richer to poorer countries. For example, Mexico is poor in capital, while the United States is rich in capital. Thus,

---

6. This is an annual average as of the mid-1990s. Except where otherwise noted, all data are from Kose, Prasad, Rogoff, and Wei, "Financial Globalization: A Reappraisal."

TABLE 7.1	INTERNATIONAL INVESTMENT FLOWS, 1980–2004				
	1980–1984	1985–1989	1990–1994	1995–1999	2000–2004
All Countries (billions of U.S. dollars)	397	803	1,209	2,453	3,564
Foreign direct investment	12.9%	15.8%	15.6%	21.7%	19.6%
Foreign portfolio investment	87.1%	84.2%	84.4%	78.3%	80.4%
Advanced Economies (billions of U.S. dollars)	325	739	1,008	2,112	3,260
Foreign direct investment	12.3%	14.9%	13.9%	18.6%	16.9%
Foreign portfolio investment	87.7%	85.1%	86.2%	81.4%	83.1%
Developing Countries and Emerging Markets (billions of U.S. dollars)	72	64	201	341	304
Foreign direct investment	15.3%	21.2%	26.4%	40.8%	46%
Foreign portfolio investment	84.7%	78.8%	73.6%	59.1%	54%

Note: These are flows of new investments, not stocks of existing investments.
Source: M. Ayhan Kose, Eswar Prasad, Kenneth Rogoff, and Shang-Jin Wei, "Financial Globalization: A Re-Appraisal" (IMF Working Paper 06/189, 2006).

profits and interest rates are higher in Mexico, which helps explain why American investors have over time accumulated investments worth over $300 billion in Mexico.

If the only consideration in international investment were differential rates of return, as in our simple Heckscher-Ohlin discussion, then all foreign investment would flow from capital-rich countries to capital-poor countries. But it decidedly does not. In fact, most international investment is *among* rich countries, and only about 10 percent of all international investment in the past couple of decades has gone to the developing world. (See Table 7.1 for a breakdown of portfolio and direct investment flows since 1980.) This is due to the lower risk of crossborder investment in rich countries. International banks, corporations, and other investors care not just about the promised interest or profit rate on foreign investments, but also about the likelihood that they will actually get the money.

Although all investment is risky, international investment involves a very specific risk: that a foreign government over which the investor has no influence may do things that reduce the value of the investment. This is especially true about loans to a foreign government, which involve a government's promise to pay debt service (interest and principal). Unlike in domestic lending, this promise cannot be enforced by the threat of foreclosure or bankruptcy. For international corporate investment, the concern is that the local government will undertake policies that devalue the investment—up to and including taking over the investment itself.

Investment among rich countries is much less risky than investment in poor countries. After all, the industrialized nations are more economically and politically stable, and they have a longer and more reliable history of treating foreign investors well. For investors to be willing to take a chance on the greater risk in the developing world, they need either higher interest rates and profits, or some reason to think that they can effectively manage the investment risks. This need can lead to negotiations between lenders or investors, on the one hand, and developing countries, on the other hand, to try to ensure a more reliable investment environment. This effort, in turn, draws international investment into international politics.

WHAT'S THE PROBLEM WITH FOREIGN INVESTMENT?

International investment is controversial because not only can it provide great benefits to both investors and the countries they invest in, but it can also impose real costs on both sides of the relationship. This is yet another example of the fact, discussed in Chapter 2, that many issues in international politics contain elements of both cooperation and bargaining. Both sides stand to gain by an amicable resolution of their differences, so they have an interest in cooperating; but each side wants to get as much as possible out of the relationship, which leads to bargaining.

In international investment, there are many common interests among borrowers and lenders, among investors and the countries they invest in. Both sides of the arrangement gain from successful international investments and loans. The receiving country gets capital it would not otherwise have. Companies that borrow from abroad can expand their businesses. Governments that borrow from abroad can finance projects that spur development, such as roads and power plants. An inflow of foreign funds can increase the availability of credit to small business owners and homeowners. Meanwhile, the foreign investor who has sent the money overseas gets higher profits than are available at home. Borrowing and lending nations alike gain from the ability of capital to flow across borders.

But there may also be major conflicts of interest between the two sides of the relationship. Each party wants to get as much as possible from the other, and to give as little as possible. Lenders want their debts repaid in full, and corporations want to bring home high profits from their foreign investments. Poor nations, however, would rather pay less of what they owe and would rather that foreign corporations have less to take away. This situation creates both a commonality of interests in maintaining a flow of capital, and a conflict of interests in distributing the benefits of the flow.

Within countries, domestic politics may also contribute to conflict between capital-sending and capital-receiving nations. In most countries, there is little disagreement when money is flowing in. Foreign capital allows the country to consume more than it produces and allows the government to spend more than it takes in through taxes; the foreign capital increases domestic consumption, investment, and economic activity, and this outcome tends to be popular. However, eventually lenders must be repaid and profits taken out; this outcome is less universally popular. Making debt service payments can require raising taxes, reducing government services, restraining wages and consumption, importing less while exporting more, and generally imposing austerity on the national economy. The debt crisis that began in 1982 all over the developing world was associated with slow growth, unemployment, cuts in social spending, and general economic hardship. And there is no guarantee that the people and groups who are asked to bear the greatest burden of austerity will be those who benefit most from the capital inflow. Even if foreign borrowing and foreign investment are unambiguously good for a nation, the benefits and costs do not accrue equally to all people in the country. This fact has made international finance a contentious issue within developing countries.

Within lending and investing nations, too, overseas loans and investments can be controversial. While those making the foreign investments stand to gain, there are also firms and workers that resent money going abroad that could be lent or invested at home. And when debt crises erupt, it is common for creditor-country governments to expend time, energy, and money to try to resolve the crisis. This is partly because a crisis abroad can have grave repercussions at home: in the midst of the debt crisis of the 1980s, for instance, many Americans were shocked to learn that American banks had lent more money to Latin American governments than the value of the capital base of the entire American banking system. This meant that the Latin American debt crisis could conceivably have bankrupted many of America's largest banks and caused a more general financial and economic crisis in the United States itself. But even if it is in the general interest of creditor nations as a whole to "bail out" their troubled banks and their borrowers, it may not be in the interests of everyone in these nations. So international investment gives rise to plenty of potential sources of conflict, and these conflicts of interest give rise to complex interactions among the sources and targets of global capital movements.

CONCESSIONAL FINANCE

There is another, smaller and somewhat less controversial, part of international finance: money lent to developing countries by government agencies and intergovernmental organizations. Rich countries give to poor countries, or lend to them at below-market interest rates, something on the order of $100 billion a year. Such *concessional finance* differs from that discussed above because it is typically lent at interest rates well below those available in the marketplace—World Bank loans to the poorest nations, in fact, bear no interest. Many of the countries that borrow these concessional funds would not be able to borrow from private creditors, who are wary of particularly poor and unstable nations. Most countries in sub-Saharan Africa and South Asia have little access to private loans; to the extent that they can borrow, it is from North American, European, and Japanese governments, or from such institutions as the World Bank and the Asian Development Bank.

Concessional loans from foreign governments are more a form of aid than of finance. They reflect, as does aid generally, both economic and political motivations of the donors and lenders. The international development banks and related agencies—the **World Bank,** Inter-American Development Bank, Asian Development Bank, and so on—are somewhat less directly political, as they are controlled by a number of rich countries. Their lending programs emphasize basic development projects, such as economic infrastructure (power plants, dams, highways) and social infrastructure (schools, housing).

There has been less political controversy about this concessional finance, as loans from individual governments are negotiated directly and, like loans from the World Bank and its related institutions, are relatively cheap. Nonetheless, countries with severe economic problems often complain about the cost of these loans, and for extremely poor nations concessional debt can be a heavy burden—despite the loans' lower interest rates. This situation has led to calls for debt forgiveness, a measure

World Bank: An important international institution that provides loans at below-market interest rates to developing countries, typically to enable them to carry out development projects.

that would alleviate some problems in very poor nations but that would come at the expense of rich nations' taxpayers. These issues, ethically important as they may be, do not have much impact on private international finance. The amounts at stake are relatively small, and private investors are typically not involved. In any case, much government-to-government concessional debt has been canceled, and the World Bank and IMF are in the process of writing off the debt of the most heavily indebted poor countries.[7] Moreover, the major economic and political issues related to international investment have to do with other, non-concessional, finance.

Why Is International Finance Controversial?

We start our analysis with what has historically been the most important—and most politically conflictual—component of international investment: private lending to foreign governments. Shakespeare may have been right about the pitfalls of borrowing and lending when he wrote:

> Neither a borrower nor a lender be;
> For loan oft loses both itself and friend,
> And borrowing dulls the edge of husbandry.
> —Polonius, in Shakespeare's *Hamlet*

Indeed, the parties might end up enemies, and the borrowers could have little incentive to use the money wisely. However, there is nothing economically suspect about borrowing or lending in principle. In the case of a private corporation, it makes sense to borrow if the borrowed funds are used in ways that increase the firm's earnings by more than the money costs. If General Motors borrows at an interest rate of 10 percent but uses the money to make investments that only pay out 5 percent, it will suffer a loss; but if the investments pay out 15 percent, both the borrower and the lender can benefit. The logic is similar for a government.

WHO WANTS TO BORROW? WHO WANTS TO LEND?

Borrowing is usually quite popular within borrowing countries—at least while the money is flowing in. As more capital comes into the nation, it is cheaper and easier for people in the recipient country to borrow. Companies, consumers, and the government can benefit from this easier credit.

From the standpoint of the economy as a whole, it generally makes sense for a country to borrow if the borrowed funds are used productively, in ways that increase the country's output by more than it will take to repay the debt. Loans might be used to raise national output directly, such as to make productive use of a government-owned natural resource (oil or copper, for example). The money could also be used to

---

7. For further information on the reduction of debts owed by the heavily indebted poor countries (HIPC), see Daniel Cohen, "The HIPC Initiative: True and False Promises," *International Finance* 4, no. 3 (2001): 363–80.

increase national output indirectly, such as by building new roads that allow the opening or improvement of agricultural lands, or by building a hydroelectric power plant that makes national industry more efficient. As national output rises, the government gets more tax revenue and can service its debts more easily. If borrowed funds are used to increase the productivity of the national economy, they can pay for themselves.

Because developing countries are by definition short of capital, most of their governments are eager to borrow abroad. The prospect of using borrowed money to speed growth and increase national output gives developing economies today a powerful interest in attracting loans from international investors, and it makes borrowing relatively uncontroversial within debtor countries—so long as times are good.

But sovereign debts can quickly become a burden to debtor nations, which makes them much less popular. Governments attempting to service their debts often impose unpopular measures. They cut spending and raise taxes in order to earn the money they need to pay off loans. They raise interest rates to restrain wages, profits, and consumption, which in turn reduces imports and increases exports, so that the country can earn more foreign currency to pay its creditors. These austerity measures typically weaken the domestic economy in order to allow the government to continue paying debt service to foreign creditors. Such measures can cause **recessions** and even **depressions,** incurring the wrath of labor, business, and other groups. For example, in the wake of a 1997 debt crisis, the Thai government pushed interest rates to 25 percent, cut government spending by 20 percent, and raised taxes. The economy collapsed, shrinking by 12 percent in two years as unemployment more than doubled.[8] In Thailand, as in many such cases, people regarded debt-driven austerity as doubly unfair: they were being asked to sacrifice to repay borrowed money that did not help them, and their sacrifice was going to enrich huge international financial institutions.

One potential source of debt difficulties is international conditions, which can change in ways that make it harder for governments to pay their debts. Between 1980 and 1982, for example, American interest rates rose by 10 percent as the Federal Reserve attempted to reduce American inflation. Most of the debts owed by developing countries to international banks were at floating interest rates, adjusted every six months in line with American interest rates; as American rates went up, so did the cost of outstanding loans. This was, in fact, one of the causes of the debt crisis of the 1980s. Similarly, an international recession that reduces demand for debtors' exports can make it hard to service loans: when the Great Depression of the 1930s drove prices and demand for debtors' products down, almost every debtor nation **defaulted.** When circumstances, especially conditions beyond their control, make it harder for debtor governments to keep up their payments, some people in debtor nations prefer that their government simply default in order to force a reduction in the debt burden. There are, then, contending interests *within* debtor countries over whether to service foreign debt. Those who expect to benefit from maintaining access to international loans will disagree with those who have more to lose from the economic sacrifices required to maintain good relations with foreign creditors.

Within lending countries, when foreign debts are performing well there is usually little conflict over them. Some local companies and individuals may resent

recession: A sharp slowdown in the rate of economic growth and economic activity.

depression: A severe downturn in the business cycle, typically associated with a major decline in economic activity, production, and investment; a severe contraction of credit; and sustained high unemployment.

default: To fail to make payments on a debt.

8. Joseph Kahn, "I.M.F. Concedes Its Conditions for Thailand Were Too Austere," *New York Times,* February 11, 1998.

When the Indonesian government sought the IMF's help during the 1997–1998 Asian financial crisis, it was forced to cut spending on popular programs, and poor Indonesians suffered. These protesters in Jakarta hold a sign asking, "The country's debt—why should the people pay?"

the fact that money that could be lent to them is being sent abroad, but this is counterbalanced by the profits being brought home. Overall, creditor countries and their governments tend to support their lenders.

Domestic conflict within creditor nations over foreign debts arises most commonly when the loans run into trouble. In these conditions, creditors and their governments often step in with billions of dollars of new loans and aid to alleviate a debtor country's financial crisis. They do so in the belief that if such a crisis were allowed to broaden and deepen, it could spread to other nations and eventually hurt the creditor nation itself. But many people in North America, Europe, and Japan resent their governments' spending of billions of dollars to "bail out" debtors and creditors whose plight may be the self-inflicted result of greed, venality, and bad judgment.

For example, in 1994, in the aftermath of another Mexican crisis, the U.S. government provided many billions of dollars to the beleaguered Mexican government to try to keep the crisis from spreading and affecting American domestic finances as well. In reaction, conservative Republican political activist Patrick Buchanan charged: "What's going down is not just a bailout of Mexico, but a bailout of Wall Street. [President] Clinton and Congress are rushing to recoup for Wall Street bankers and brokers their enormous losses from the plunderings of [Mexican] ex-President Carlos Salinas and friends."[9] From the Left, the liberal *Progressive* magazine observed: "It's amazing how our government can find money for . . . bailing out some banks or shoring up some brutal regimes, but not for solving the pressing social needs of our own country, like health care, housing, and jobs at a living wage."[10]

Many people in creditor nations regard the hundreds of billions of dollars spent in financial rescue packages since the early 1980s as money doled out to

---

9. From www.buchanan.org/pa-95-0420.html (accessed 1/3/08).
10. "Bailout for Whom?" *The Progressive* 62, no. 2 (February 1998): 9–10.

undeserving banks and investors who benefited from their ability to put pressure on policymakers. In the aftermath of the Mexican and East Asian financial rescues, the U.S. Congress enacted a number of measures that limited the authority of the executive branch to use taxpayer money for such bailouts. Supporters of the bills presented them as a clear case of Wall Street versus Main Street: bailing out banks while many small farms and businesses were allowed to go under.[11]

Attitudes toward the IMF and other international financial institutions are often related to broader attitudes toward global economic integration. Both supporters and opponents of globalization tend to think of the IMF and its allies as important pillars of the contemporary international economy. Those wary of globalization distrust global finance and the IMF; those who favor globalization support them. (See "What Do We Know?" on p. 273.)

Whatever domestic disagreements there may be, in general the interests of debtor and creditor countries are clear. Both sides of the relationship stand to benefit from continued lending: borrowers get access to foreign money, and lenders get profits. But each side would prefer to gain more from the relationship. Thus, there are incentives to cooperate to keep the lending going, and incentives to bargain for the best possible deal. This sets the stage for complex interactions between debtors and creditors.

DEBTOR-CREDITOR INTERACTIONS

In the modern era, there have been many cycles of lending and debt crises. All through the nineteenth and early twentieth centuries, rapidly growing countries borrowed heavily from the major European financial centers—primarily London, but also Paris, Amsterdam, and Berlin. Foreign borrowing was in fact important to the economic development of the principal developing regions of the day: the United States, Canada, Australia, Argentina, Brazil, and others. In most instances, debts appear to have contributed to economic development, but there were plenty of crises and political disputes. The United States, the world's largest borrower throughout the nineteenth century, was not immune: many of its state governments defaulted in the 1840s, and the state of Mississippi, whose banks borrowed heavily from London financiers in the 1830s and defaulted in 1841, has ever since continued to refuse to make payments on its London debt.

Concern about getting embroiled in debt disputes helps explain why today's private international financial flows to the developing world are restricted to the more advanced and successful less developed countries (LDCs). Countries facing severe developmental difficulties, or about which there is little reliable information, are simply unattractive to private creditors. The world's biggest developing-country debtors today are Brazil, Mexico, and Argentina, which as of 2008 together owed about $600 billion to foreign private creditors.[12] Even in the case of well-known debtor countries, however, debtor-creditor interactions are inherently complicated by the strategic nature of the relationship.

---

11. J. Lawrence Broz, "Congressional Politics of International Financial Rescues," *American Journal of Political Science* 49, no. 3 (July 2005): 496–512.
12. World Bank, Quarterly External Debt Database, www.worldbank.org/data/working/QEDS/sdds_main.html (accessed 11/1/08).

What Motivates the IMF?

Whatever one may think about the ethical issues raised in the "Controversy" feature for this chapter (see p. 277), we may ask what motivates the International Monetary Fund to become involved in a debt problem and provide loans to a country in difficulties. Specifically, to what extent do IMF actions reflect political motivations rather than economic ones?

Two scholarly studies help us to evaluate the IMF's actions. The political scientist Strom Thacker looked at determinants of IMF lending to countries in crisis and found that macroeconomic conditions strongly affected the Fund's actions.[a] However, Thacker also found that IMF behavior seemed to reflect the geopolitical concerns of its largest member, the United States. Debtor governments were rewarded if their foreign policies were moving closer to those of the United States—as measured by the similarity of their voting behavior in the United Nations General Assembly. For example, in Thacker's analysis, a government that

had been neutral in the UN but moved toward close alignment with the United States would be three times as likely to receive IMF funding as one that remained neutral.

These findings were confirmed by political scientists Lawrence Broz and Michael Hawes in another study.[b] Like Thacker, Broz and Hawes found that political alignment with the United States made it more likely that governments would get IMF assistance.

But they also found that the Fund seemed to reflect American *economic* interests as well. Controlling for many other factors, they discovered that the more money debtor countries owed to American international banks, the more likely they were to get money from the IMF and the more money they were able to get. Every additional $3 billion that a country owed to American banks increased the likelihood of receiving IMF money by 5 percent and increased the amount received by about $0.5 billion.

Both studies showed that the IMF appears to take into account the strategic and economic interests of its largest and most powerful member state, the United States. But what determines American policy toward the IMF?

Broz and Hawes also examined the determinants of American policy in the IMF. They were particularly interested to know who in the United States was more likely to support the Fund's operations. So they analyzed a series of congressional votes on American contributions to the IMF, which were quite strongly contested in the United States. The researchers hypothesized that two groups would be particularly favorable to the IMF: (1) international banks based in the United States, whose activities the IMF tends to support (critics would say "bail out"); and (2) interest groups in the United States who would expect to benefit from the financial globalization that the IMF helps to supervise.

Broz and Hawes indeed found support for their hypotheses about the interest groups expected to support the IMF. Members of Congress who received substantial campaign contributions from large American international banks were much more likely to vote for more American money for the Fund. In addition, members of Congress from districts with more highly skilled workers—which were expected to benefit particularly from globalization—were also more likely to support the Fund. Members of Congress from districts with larger numbers of college-educated workers—who, analysts agree, are particularly likely to do well in international economic competition—were much more likely to support American funding for the IMF.

These studies help provide a picture of the sources of IMF policy. Although the Fund does indeed respond to underlying economic problems in debtor nations, it is also motivated to act by the foreign-policy and economic-interest concerns of the major powers, especially the United States. This finding is not surprising, as American support is crucial to the Fund's existence and functioning. Nonetheless, it implies that a full understanding of the role of the IMF in the international financial order must take into account both economic and political considerations. ■

a. Strom Thacker, "The High Politics of IMF Lending," *World Politics* 52, no. 1 (October 1999): 38–75.

b. J. Lawrence Broz and Michael Brewster Hawes, "Congressional Politics of Financing the International Monetary Fund," *International Organization* 60, no. 1 (Spring 2006): 367–99.

Sovereign lending itself involves a problem of commitment of the sort we discussed in the context of war and peace in Chapter 3. This commitment problem could, in fact, make lending impossible. Domestic debts can be enforced in national courts, but who can enforce debts—or other investor rights—across borders? Once a loan is made, the borrower has incentives to renege on its commitment to repay. In turn, creditors have reason to expect that the debtor will default, and they will not extend loans in the first place if they do not expect to be repaid. This makes the possibility of default a problem for the *borrower*. Unless the borrower finds some way to reassure creditors that the commitment will be honored, lenders will do something else with their money and the borrower will not get loans. Hence, just as puzzling as why debtors repay their loans is why any lender makes loans in the first place. The fact that international lending does in fact occur indicates that debtors and creditors have found ways to address the commitment problems inherent in lending across borders in the absence of a third-party enforcement mechanism.

Nonetheless, debtors and creditors often enter into conflict. The principal bargaining weapon available to the debtor government is the threat of default, or suspension of payment on the debt.[13] In August 1998, the Russian government responded to national economic difficulties with a default that affected as much as $80 billion in foreign debt; in December 2001, the Argentine government defaulted on $93 billion in foreign debt.[14]

Creditors also have financial weapons available: they can cut off debtor governments from future lending, and they may be able to retaliate in related areas, such as freezing debtor governments' bank accounts or taking other government-owned properties. Creditors can also try to get their home governments to use broader foreign policy considerations to induce compliance, such as threatening a cutoff of aid or even military action. The ability of each side to get concessions from the other depends on how powerful and how credible these threats are. In some instances, the issue is resolved amicably with a negotiated settlement; in other instances, the parties remain far apart. Debt-related conflicts have even been blamed for invasions, wars, and colonialism.

Just as with lending itself, conflict between creditors and debtors over existing debt is analogous to the conflicts between countries we described in Chapter 3, in which countries may end up going to war. There is usually a bargaining solution to their interaction short of debtor default, or creditor retaliation, that makes both sides better off than financial warfare. Both sides would prefer to restructure the debt so that payments can continue to be made; this is what negotiators, arbitrators, and bankruptcy courts do in the case of domestic debt problems. However, as in the case of security relations, international debtor-creditor interactions are characterized by incomplete information. The debtor may claim not to be able to make payments, but the creditor does not know if the claim is true; the creditor may threaten to retaliate, but the debtor does not know if the threat will be carried out. In these circumstances, cooperative relations between debtors and creditors can collapse into bitter conflict.

---

13. Legally, a default is invoked by the creditor when the debtor misses payments, but the term is used more generally to describe a suspension of debt service.

14. The amounts involved are unclear, especially for Russia. See International Monetary Fund, *World Economic Outlook* (Washington, DC: IMF, 1998), chap. 2.

Of course, cooperation between debtors and creditors is not necessarily a good thing for everyone involved. This is especially the case when the debtor country faces increasing macroeconomic difficulties, due either to international trends or to a deterioration of domestic conditions. Whether an amicable resolution of debtor-creditor interactions is a good thing or a bad thing, it is important to try to understand the conflict and how it develops. One prominent aspect of international debt interactions is that it has come to involve important international institutions that can play an important part in debtor-creditor relations.

INSTITUTIONS OF INTERNATIONAL FINANCE

During the twentieth century, there were frequent attempts to regulate debtor-creditor relations by creating institutions to mediate their interactions and, perhaps, facilitate mutually acceptable outcomes. In the interwar period, the League of Nations' Economic and Financial Committee attempted to work with debtors and creditors to manage the financial difficulties of troubled nations in central and eastern Europe, with mixed results. The **Bank for International Settlements (BIS)** was established in 1930 explicitly to help oversee relations between one of the world's most problematic debtor nations, Germany, and its international creditors; this, too, met with mixed results. Nonetheless, by the 1940s there was a common view that some form of international financial institution might be beneficial to the resolution of sovereign debt problems.

Bank for International Settlements (BIS): One of the oldest international financial organizations, created in 1930. Its members include the world's principal central banks, and under its auspices they attempt to cooperate in the financial realm.

The International Monetary Fund (IMF) Today, many aspects of international financial affairs are overseen by one of the world's most powerful international organizations, the **International Monetary Fund (IMF)**. The establishment of the IMF was agreed on at Bretton Woods (see Chapter 1) in order to manage the international monetary system. After the Bretton Woods monetary regime collapsed in the early 1970s (as we will see in Chapter 8), the IMF gradually took on a more directly financial role. Today, its principal concern is financial crises in developing nations, although it has also played a role during crisis periods in developed countries such as Great Britain and Italy.

International Monetary Fund (IMF): A major international economic institution that was established in 1944 to manage international monetary relations and that has gradually reoriented itself to focus on the international financial system, especially debt and currency crises.

Typically, a country facing debt difficulties turns to the IMF to negotiate a program of economic policies intended to address the sources of the difficulties. In return for implementing a program that meets the IMF's standards, the debtor government receives relatively inexpensive loans from the IMF. Probably more important, the debtor country is "certified" as being in compliance with IMF norms, which makes it more attractive to creditors. This certification is meant to encourage private lenders to renegotiate with the debtor government, and perhaps to extend it new loans to help it overcome temporary difficulties. For example, during the debt crisis of the 1980s, the IMF signed dozens of agreements with troubled debtors, typically requiring policies of economic austerity and adjustment in return for assistance with working out their debt problems. The IMF's agreement with Indonesia in the midst of the 1997–1998 Asian financial crisis obliged the Indonesian government to cut subsidies to—and therefore raise the prices of—sugar, wheat flour, corn, and soybeans, as well as fuel and electricity.

All of this imposed hardships on Indonesia's poor and working people. The IMF also required the government to shut down 16 banks controlled by relatives or cronies of the country's dictatorial president, Suharto. This move may have been less objectionable to ordinary people, but it was, of course, unpopular with the Indonesian government.[15]

The IMF, like other international institutions, can facilitate international agreements in a variety of ways. It provides a set of financial and macroeconomic standards that can be used to assess the behavior of debtor nations. The IMF can also help verify a debtor government's compliance with commitments to pursue economic policies that creditors want to see. And the IMF can act on behalf of the collectivity of creditor nations, who might otherwise have difficulties working out common decisions about how to deal with financial crises.

In one sense, though, the IMF is unusual. While many international institutions act primarily to facilitate bargaining among nation-states, the IMF negotiates agreements directly with an individual country's government. And, perhaps even more unusual, the IMF's involvement is typically closely tied to relations between the debtor government and private international creditors. While the IMF does not *represent* foreign creditors, there is normally an understanding that an agreement with the IMF will facilitate agreement with private lenders; and sometimes the IMF, member governments, and private creditors make this connection explicit. In this sense, the IMF plays a major part, directly or indirectly, in negotiations between sovereign governments and private financiers.

Supporters of the IMF believe that it plays an important role in managing the international financial system, allowing for an orderly resolution of debtor-creditor problems. They focus on the informational difficulties endemic in sovereign debt, as well as the need for reliable monitoring of compliance with agreements. Supporters emphasize how the IMF can help debtors and creditors arrive at cooperative arrangements. They believe that the IMF's power comes from its central role in resolving financial problems in ways that are beneficial to both debtors and creditors.

However, opponents see the IMF as a tool of international financiers. They regard the IMF as a biased agency whose actions reinforce the subordinate position of debtor nations and do little to assist them in achieving economic growth and development. (See "Controversy," p. 277.) Similar conflicts arise over the involvement of the home governments of creditors, primarily from North America, Europe, and Japan. Debtor nations often resent political pressure from these powerful governments, which they regard as unduly concerned with insisting that "their" bankers get repaid. Creditors can be politically influential at home, and defaults can threaten to bankrupt major financial institutions in industrial nations, which would in turn destabilize their own financial markets. This situation leads creditor governments and the IMF, in the eyes of many opponents, to serve as debt collectors for international banks.

---

15. Stephan Haggard, *The Political Economy of the Asian Financial Crisis* (Washington, DC: Institute for International Economics, 2000).

Is the IMF Unfair?

In February 1989, facing a protracted fiscal crisis, Venezuela's president, Carlos Andrés Pérez, negotiated a loan with the IMF. In a reversal of pre-election promises he had made only weeks earlier, Pérez implemented a package of market-based reforms under the IMF's recommendation, including import liberalization and tariff elimination measures, privatization of state companies, restrictions on state spending, relaxation of price controls, and deregulation of exchange and interest rates. On February 27, the people of Caracas took to the streets in violent protests that came to be known as El Caracazo ("the Caracas smash"). Considered by some observers to mark the birth of the antiglobalization movement, El Caracazo also played a key role in the demise of Pérez's government and the rise of Hugo Chávez to the Venezuelan presidency. In April 2007, Chávez, by now one of the world's most vocal critics of the IMF, announced that he would pull Venezuela out of the IMF.

The IMF provides a vital source of economic assistance to nations that would otherwise risk protracted fiscal crises and be cut off from the foreign capital that is vital to their development. Why, then, does such a useful institution cause such controversy? The answer stems in part from the IMF's nature as a bargaining forum. Although the IMF facilitates mutually beneficial international cooperation, critics claim that it distributes the benefits and burdens of that cooperation unevenly across member nations. Whereas IMF policies often appear to directly promote the interests of (certain influential investors within) creditor countries, benefits to debtor countries are not always as immediately apparent.

Two of the chief criticisms leveled by Chávez at the institution reflect these distributive concerns. The first charge is that the IMF violates national sovereignty (or, in Chávez's interpretation, that it is an "agent of U.S. imperialism"). This charge derives from the "conditionalities" routinely attached to IMF loans. For decades, the IMF has required that countries requesting balance-of-payments assistance commit to what are known as structural adjustment programs, designed to solve debtor nations' fiscal crises. Such programs have included not only economic reforms of the kind Venezuela enacted, but also specific political reforms. Pérez, for instance, was asked to institute direct elections of state governors in place of presidential appointments. Although acceptance of such conditions is supposedly voluntary, the high price of refusal—ineligibility for IMF assistance—creates an impression of coercion. Moreover, when developed countries sign on to the IMF, they do not suffer a similar risk of diminished sovereignty. As they are more often lenders rather than borrowers, developed countries impose rather than submit to the IMF's conditionalities.

Chávez's second main criticism derives not from the use of conditionalities per se, but from the particular nature of the conditions the IMF routinely imposes. Those conditions are said to exhibit scant concern for the most needy debtor nations. Indeed, the immediate result of IMF economic austerity measures is often hardship for such nations' poorest citizens, who face higher taxes, wage cuts, unemployment, and reduced social services—all at a time of rising prices. Again, the world's affluent countries, as lenders rather than borrowers in these situations, do not face comparable hardship through IMF membership.

Defenders of the IMF respond to both of these criticisms by stressing the mutual gains from cooperation. The IMF's policy recommendations are essential for restoring fiscal balance and access to foreign credit, they say, and the benefits of achieving these goals over the long term outweigh the temporary diminishment of a nation's sovereignty and the short-term suffering of its poorest citizens. Once these longer-term effects are taken into account, defenders argue, it becomes clear that debtor nations derive substantial benefit from membership in the IMF, so that talk of an unfair bargain is inappropriate.

The plausibility of this response depends on how well the IMF in fact delivers on its promise. It must be shown that standard IMF measures actually do rectify debtor nations' trade deficits, that this in turn contributes to economic growth, and that the growth in question benefits the poor. The evidence is currently mixed: while IMF programs may improve a nation's balance of payments, their record on economic growth and poverty reduction is unclear. ■

RECENT BORROWING AND DEBT CRISES

Lending to developing nations has been an important part of the international economy since the mid-1960s. At the same time, there have been many debt crises since international financial markets reopened to developing countries. The first such crisis started in 1982, with the Mexican default. Like most financial crises, this one had a self-reinforcing nature. As in a bank panic, as lenders worried that developing-country governments might not repay them, they stopped lending. This left developing-country governments without a financial cushion, and in desperation they stopped making payments to their creditors—thereby scaring international bankers even further. The more the developing countries ran out of money, the less bankers lent; and the less bankers lent, the more the developing countries ran out of money. In the space of weeks, some of the most rapidly growing economies in the world were suddenly cut off from the bank lending they had relied on for 15 years.

One after another, the major debtor governments struggled to generate the foreign currency and government revenue needed to pay their creditors, until eventually their economies collapsed. By 1983, as many as 34 developing and socialist countries were formally renegotiating their debts, and a dozen more were in serious trouble. Latin America was spending nearly half of its export earnings to pay interest and principal on its foreign debt, leaving little to buy the imports it needed. Most debtor economies remained depressed for years, and the crises were not fully resolved until 1990. A combination of austerity programs and economic reforms in debtor nations, and concessions from lenders to reduce the debt burden, gradually allowed the problems to be worked out.

Eventually, lending resumed, but debt crises continued to occur. In 1994, Mexican finances once again collapsed. In 1997–1998, combined debt and currency crises hit a series of East Asian countries from Indonesia and Thailand to the Philippines and Korea. This was a particularly startling shock, as these nations had long been regarded as models of developmental success. Their apparently endless potential had drawn in considerable amounts of foreign money: Thailand's foreign debt tripled from $30 to $90 billion in three years to 1996, while Indonesia's doubled from $25 to $50 billion. During the early 1990s, about $50 billion a year flowed into East Asia from global financial markets, with tens of billions more in direct investment from multinational corporations.

Once the crisis hit in the summer of 1997, however, money ran out of the East Asian debtor countries as fast as it had run in. The $50 billion annual inflow of the early 1990s turned into an outflow of over $230 billion between 1997 and 1999. After years of extraordinary growth—10 percent a year was common—the economies of Indonesia, Thailand, and Malaysia contracted by 15, 12, and 8 percent, respectively, in a matter of months. It would be years before they would recover their pre-crisis levels. (For more on the Asian crisis, see "What Shaped Our World?" on p. 279. For a graphic illustration of the economic ups and downs of the 1990s in Thailand, see Figure 7.2.)

The East Asian crisis was followed by crises in Russia and Brazil in 1998–1999, Argentina in 2000–2001, and others since then. In all of these cases, intervention by the IMF alone was not sufficient—the debt problems were so large that creditor

The Asian Financial Crisis, 1997–1998

In 1997, an international financial crisis ripped through the countries of East Asia. The roots of the crisis lay in the revival of capital flows in the 1990s. Recall that the debt crisis of the early 1980s led to a "lost decade" for Latin America and much of the developing world as international investment came to a halt. All of this began to change in the 1990s as an economic slowdown in the developed world prompted investors to seek out new investment opportunities overseas.

Investors steered a substantial share of their funds toward four countries with strong records of economic growth: Thailand, Indonesia, South Korea, and Malaysia. These countries had all eased, or *liberalized*, their restrictions on capital inflows and made it easier for domestic banks to borrow from foreign investors. A private business in Thailand, for example, could borrow money from its local bank, which in turn could borrow money from a foreign commercial bank. Some businesses could raise capital directly from foreign investors by listing their shares of stock on the domestic stock exchange. In either case, foreign investors benefited from higher returns, while domestic business owners reaped the benefits of greater access to capital. The arrangement seemed to be stunningly successful: the four Asian economies expanded at a rate of 8 to 9 percent per year through most of the 1990s, compared to less than 4 percent annually for developed countries.[a]

Despite the impressive statistics, investors became more cautious by 1997. They had two main worries. First, the value of their investments was dependent on the value of the domestic currency—whether it be the Thai *baht*, the Indonesian *rupiah*, the Malaysian *ringgit*, or the South Korean *won*. If these currencies were to fall in value, the value of their investments would decline as well (see Chapter 8 for a discussion of the effects of currency depreciation). For example, if a U.S. investor exchanged dollars for Thai *baht* to purchase stock on the Thai stock exchange, the investor would incur a loss if the *baht* had declined in value relative to the dollar at the time the stock

was sold. Foreign commercial banks were similarly sensitive to changes in the value of the domestic currency.

Second, foreign investors became concerned about the debtor government's involvement in the domestic economy in each of the four countries. Some Asian governments promised to bail out domestic banks if they found themselves in financial trouble. And, in some cases, the government actually owned the banks! If banks can count on a government rescue, they have little reason to be cautious in their lending behavior. Many banks therefore engaged in high-risk lending with the hope of reaping great profits.

Investors' concerns turned to panic in the spring of 1997 when one of Thailand's largest banks was declared insolvent (its liabilities were greater than its assets). Foreign banks suddenly refused to lend to any Thai banks, fearing that financial troubles were spread throughout the country. Investors also sold their stocks, liquidated their assets, and rushed to turn their Thai currency into dollars or some other, more stable, currency. The crisis quickly spread to the other Asian countries in a process known as *contagion*, by which investors fear that the domestic troubles in one country might be endemic to an entire region. Thailand, Indonesia, Malaysia, and South Korea were the hardest hit, but the crisis extended to the Philippines, Hong Kong, Taiwan, and even Japan. The value of the Asian currencies plummeted as investors collectively pulled out, and stock markets collapsed under the weight of the massive capital outflows.

The crisis led to a number of policy changes in the East Asian countries as well as the developed world. Governments shut down insolvent banks, imposed tighter regulations on lending, and relaxed restrictions on the entry of foreign banks. They also privatized many government-owned banks. In developed countries, banks became more cautious about lending to financial institutions in developing countries and instituted new rules to protect themselves against currency fluctuations and other investment risks. The crisis also led to a reevaluation of the IMF's advocacy of financial liberalization and triggered a vigorous—and still ongoing—discussion among economists and policymakers about the pros and cons of international financial integration. ■

---

a. Data from the World Bank's World Development Indicators online database, go.worldbank.org/U0FSM7AQ40 (accessed 11/2/08).

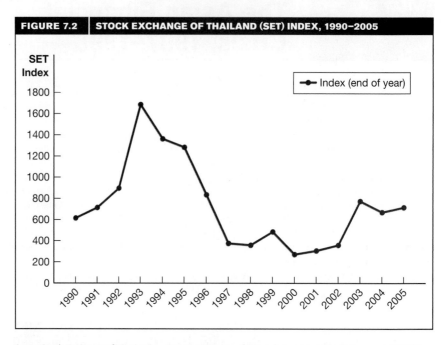

FIGURE 7.2 | STOCK EXCHANGE OF THAILAND (SET) INDEX, 1990–2005

SET Index

— Index (end of year)

Source: Stock Exchange of Thailand, www.set.or.th/en/market/market_statistics.html (accessed 12/2/08).

governments also stepped in, to the tune of over $50 billion for Mexico, almost $120 billion for the three principal Asian crisis nations (Indonesia, Korea, and Thailand), and another $70 billion for Russia and Brazil. Critics charged that taxpayers were being forced to bail out foolish investors and dissolute governments, but financial leaders insisted on the need for a quick response to avoid financial contagion.

The international politics of developing-country debt is a striking example of how actors with different interests interact strategically in a highly institutionalized context. The parties have not only clear conflicting interests, but also clear interests in common. Even though creditors want to be repaid and debtors want to pay as little as possible, both sides have an interest in continuing their relationship: the creditors to earn profits, the debtors to maintain access to foreign finance. This mix of cooperative and conflictual motives leads to complicated strategic interactions. And the role of the IMF highlights the role of international institutions—seen by some as effective at helping resolve conflicts, by others as tools of the powerful.

A NEW CRISIS HITS THE UNITED STATES, AND THE WORLD

In 2008, the world was stunned by the eruption of yet another financial crisis. This one originated in the United States, the world's largest economy and most developed financial system.

Many features of the initial crisis were familiar from previous episodes. The United States had embarked on a major foreign borrowing spree. In 2001, substantial tax cuts drove the American federal government into a large deficit.

Much of the deficit was financed by borrowing from abroad. Government borrowing spurred the economy, reinforced by a monetary policy of very low interest rates. These low interest rates in turn encouraged American households to borrow heavily. Much of the borrowing went for housing, as many Americans refinanced their homes or bought new homes. Foreigners eager to buy American investments they regarded as safe and profitable provided large portions of the lending directly or indirectly.

From 2001 to 2007, the United States experienced a traditional borrowing boom. Every year, the country borrowed between half a trillion and a trillion dollars from the rest of the world. A significant portion of the debt went to finance the government budget deficit; much of the rest went into the flourishing housing market. As financial markets grew at a dizzying pace, banks developed ever more complex ways of investing, borrowing, and lending. Some observers warned that not enough of the new debt was going into productive investments that would increase the efficiency of the U.S. economy, such as new factories or new technologies. Other observers were concerned that American regulators were inadequately supervising the free-wheeling, increasingly complex financial system. However, the U.S. government resisted stricter financial oversight, especially given its general commitment to deregulation. Meanwhile, most Americans were happy to enjoy a dramatic expansion in consumption, reduced taxes, increased government spending, and a striking increase in housing prices—all made possible by foreign borrowing.

America's debt-fed expansion eventually became an unsustainable bubble, especially in the housing market. In some parts of the country, housing prices doubled in the space of four or five years. Much of the lending was predicated on the unrealistic expectation that housing prices would continue to rise at this pace. For example, financial institutions extended mortgages to borrowers who would otherwise not have qualified, because they expected that the homes being bought would rise in value. Both borrowers and lenders were thus gambling that housing prices would continue to go up.

Eventually, housing prices stopped soaring and began to fall. Overextended mortgage-holders could not pay their debts; overextended lenders faced massive losses. During 2007 and 2008 financial difficulties spread, as hundreds of billions of dollars worth of mortgages and related financial assets went bad. Fear spread from bank to bank, culminating in September 2008, when Lehman Brothers, one of the world's leading investment banks, collapsed. This was the largest bankruptcy in American history; and it caused near panic in financial markets.

Within a few months, the crisis had been transmitted around the world, and virtually every economy was in decline. The U.S. government stepped in with trillions of dollars to bail out affected financial institutions, and try to get financial markets working again, taking over some of the country's largest financial corporations in order to avoid their collapse. And the U.S. government enacted a massive deficit-funded spending package to attempt to stimulate an economy facing its steepest recession since the 1930s.

Within the United States, political battles broke out over the response to the financial crisis. Many Americans were furious that the government was spending taxpayer dollars to bail out imprudent banks and corporations. As in other debt crises, many felt that the interests of working-class and middle-class Americans were being sacrificed to address problems created by wealthy financiers.

Internationally, too, the crisis caused tension among contending interests. Governments everywhere scrambled to protect their economies, even at the expense of other countries. For example, the U.S. Congress insisted that government spending to stimulate the failing economy be used preferentially to buy American goods; trading partners insisted that this was protectionist and violated the rules of the WTO. Developing countries complained that the heavy borrowing by industrialized-country governments to deal with the crisis was making it impossible for poor nations to get the funds they needed to confront their dire problems. The European Union was torn by conflicts among member states with widely different views as to the appropriate response to the crisis. Neither existing levels of international cooperation nor existing international institutions seemed adequate to address a global financial crisis of this magnitude.

As the crisis exacerbated disputes among major governments, many observers wondered whether the world would descend into the kind of trade, currency, and debt conflicts that characterized the interwar years. More generally, people everywhere wondered whether the deep recession that began in 2007–2008 might spiral downward into a global depression similar to that of the early 1930s. Whatever the outcome of the crisis, it demonstrated the potential for political controversy inherent in international financial affairs.

Foreign Direct Investment: What Role Do Multinational Corporations Play?

Foreign direct investment (FDI) is another important form of international capital movement. It differs from foreign lending because it is carried out explicitly by corporations that maintain control over the facilities they establish overseas; the corporations involved have come to be known as **multinational corporations (MNCs)**. FDI occurs when Volkswagen sets up an auto factory in Brazil, or Telefónica de España buys the Czech telephone company, or ExxonMobil drills for oil in Angola. In all these instances, what is involved is far more than a simple transfer of capital. Volkswagen could export cars to Brazil but chooses to build them there instead; individual foreign investors could buy shares in the Czech telephone company, but instead a global telecommunications corporation adds the Czech system to its network; the Angolan government could borrow money to drill for oil but instead gives a concession to an American company.

multinational corporation (MNC): An enterprise that operates in a number of countries, with production or service facilities outside its country of origin.

WHY DO CORPORATIONS GO MULTINATIONAL?

It is not easy for a corporation to set up facilities in a foreign country. Volkswagen could simply build cars in Europe and export them to Brazil, rather than building them in Brazil; and one might imagine that a local company could run the Czech telephone system better than a Spanish company could. There must be a reason for firms to invest abroad rather than exporting, and for a foreign firm to have some advantage over a domestic one, despite the inherent difficulties of doing business abroad. What makes it attractive for the corporation to establish or purchase subsidiaries across borders, and what gives the host country an interest in permitting this foreign investment?

Nike is one of Vietnam's largest private employers. Abundant cheap labor in countries like Vietnam makes it profitable for companies like Nike to invest in factories there.

Corporations may want to establish overseas affiliates to gain access to the local market or to take advantage of local resources—in both instances, presumably because doing so through trade is less attractive or impossible. Some FDI is driven by resource location: American and European oil companies, with ample experience in exploring for oil, may be more effective at getting Angola's oil out of the ground than local entrepreneurs could be. The case of Volkswagen in Brazil illustrates that there are often advantages to producing in the local market: cheaper transport costs, or the ability to avoid trade barriers, or better access to market information. In the decades right after World War II, most FDI was by American manufacturers and was motivated by trade protection in Europe and developing countries. Ford, GE, and other big U.S. corporations faced tariffs and other restrictions imposed on their exports to Europe and the developing world. To get around these barriers, they established local affiliates.

More recently, as trade barriers have come down, other motivations have surfaced. MNCs today often place different components of their production network in different countries: the labor-intensive work is done in countries with cheap labor, such as Vietnam, while the work that requires more skilled labor and technicians is done in countries with ample skilled labor, such as Ireland. Other types of FDI, such as that by Telefónica de España, are in service sectors in which companies may have substantial experience or a famous brand name—banking or entertainment, for example. What ties all FDI together is that the corporations involved believe that overseas direct investment is profitable.[16]

Within the home countries of multinational corporations (that is, the countries in which they are headquartered), there is generally support for their foreign activities. After all, American corporations are constituents of American politicians, and it is part of the job of the government to support their constituents, corporate or otherwise. So the U.S. government, like all governments, typically acts to promote and protect the interests of American corporations abroad.

However, FDI can be controversial in the countries from which it originates. Groups and people in North America and Western Europe often fault MNCs for not investing at home. Labor unions in North America and Western Europe often

---

16. For more on the economics of FDI, see Richard Caves, *Multinational Enterprises and Economic Analysis,* 3rd ed. (Cambridge: Cambridge University Press, 2007).

criticize MNCs, especially for "outsourcing" jobs to countries with lower wages. The American labor federation, the AFL-CIO, has complained: "Today, multinational corporations can move capital thousands of miles with the click of a mouse and send jobs halfway around the world in the time it takes numbers to travel along fiber-optic cable. These companies—many of them American—search the globe for the lowest possible labor costs and weakest environmental safeguards."[17] Labor unions and others have demanded stricter controls on "sweatshop labor" in the developing countries, reflecting both working-class solidarity and a more prosaic desire to reduce competitive pressure.

Some human rights activists and environmentalists also eye MNCs with apprehension. Just as corporations can seek lower wages, they can look for pollution-friendly regimes, dictatorships that allow violations of human rights, and other ethically lax governments. In the words of a European campaign to "clean up" the world garment industry, "incentives for foreign investors include not only low wages, but also the suspension of certain workplace and environmental regulations. If a government does attempt to strictly enforce these regulations, you can bet that many investors will quickly pack their bags for another country that is even less strict and is more accommodating."[18] And there is a cultural component to some complaints about MNCs, arguing that MNCs reduce diversity and encourage the homogenization of world culture. Nonetheless, in general home-country governments see their interests as closely tied to those of their corporations.

WHY DO COUNTRIES LET FOREIGN MULTINATIONALS IN?

Most countries that host FDI have an interest in allowing multinational corporations to operate within their borders—otherwise, of course, they would keep the corporations out. Certainly, in the nineteenth century it was common for such rapidly growing nations as the United States, Canada, Argentina, Russia, and Australia to rely on foreign companies to build up such important industries as railroads.

Today, governments generally welcome foreign corporations. This is because MNCs bring in managerial, technological, and marketing skills that might not otherwise be available, as well as investment capital. Some poor nations lack the trained personnel and capital necessary to access and develop their own natural resources; without foreigners, they might not be able to profit from their resources. However, if they allow foreign companies to pump oil or to mine copper, the government can then tax some of the profits. Other poor nations with weak or small private sectors may welcome foreign corporations to provide jobs for their citizens and to gain access to world markets for their products.

Most nations are eager to attract the technological or other expertise that MNCs can mobilize. This may especially be the case in high-technology industries, where such multinationals as IBM or Siemens can be the sole source of crucial modern technologies. When Intel opened production facilities in Costa Rica in 1997, it

---

17. From www.aflcio.org/globaleconomy/meaning.htm (accessed 8/21/04).
18. From www.cleanclothes.org/intro.htm#7 (accessed 8/21/04).

transformed that country's economy. The firm soon accounted for one-third of total exports, with Intel's sales alone surpassing the country's traditional banana and coffee exports. Overall, Intel has invested about a billion dollars in a country of 3.5 million people, and it employs about 5,000 people directly or indirectly; it has a network of almost 500 local supplier companies; and its presence has spurred the creation of a high-technology cluster with over 50 other companies. There have been years when Intel's activities alone have accounted for more than half of the growth of the Costa Rican economy.[19]

Yet, host countries—the countries in which MNCs invest—do not always have such positive views of FDI. There is always scope for disagreement over the division of the benefits. Conflict can arise over how much in taxes an oil company should pay to the local government, or over the wages an automobile factory should pay to local workers. Local competitors may complain about foreign firms' presence in the domestic market. Some people may be concerned that foreign managers will be insensitive to national social, cultural, and political norms. Interactions between MNCs and national governments have been particularly fraught in the case of developing countries, many of which have gross domestic products (GDPs) smaller than the sales of the multinational corporations they host.

Even where there is agreement when the investment is made, views may change over time. One common pattern is that when countries are very poor, they are eager to attract FDI to bring natural resources and other national products to market. Over time, however, as the local economy becomes more sophisticated, local investors become better able to undertake the activities dominated by the MNCs. As the LDC develops, its government may want its own citizens to get more of the benefits of the investment. National businesses may come to resent the foreign competition, and local managers and technicians may feel they no longer need the MNC. Even the case of Intel in Costa Rica is hardly clear-cut. Just as Intel's expansion spurred the country's economy, its difficulties have held it back: in 2000, when the firm's growth slowed, Intel's problems depressed Costa Rican growth to half of what it would have been otherwise. And in order to attract Intel, the Costa Rican government had exempted it from all taxes for eight years and from half of its taxes for another four, and had freed it from many regulations that apply to other domestic and foreign firms. Costa Rica has certainly gained from having Intel invest there; but the presence of this huge firm—whose total worldwide sales are larger than the GDP of Costa Rica—also has imposed real constraints on the small Central American nation. In this context, there is plenty of scope for conflict between MNCs and host governments.

HOST-COUNTRY INTERACTIONS WITH MNCS

Like debtors and creditors, foreign corporations and host-country governments have some common interests and some conflicting interests. This mix defines the scope of interactions between national governments and multinational corporations. As with foreign debt, each side has reasons to work to ensure that the investment can take

---

19. World Bank, Multilateral Investment Guarantee Agency, *The Impact of Intel in Costa Rica* (Washington, DC: World Bank, 2006).

place. But, again as with foreign debt, each side has strong incentives to bargain for a greater share of the benefits from FDI. This bargaining can involve negotiations over tax rates, or the company's training of local citizens for more skilled jobs, or the MNC giving some of its business to local suppliers. The host country's weapons include its ability to regulate and tax companies within its borders, up to and including nationalizing them—essentially, forcing them to sell out to local investors or to the government itself. The MNC's weapons include withholding its capital, its technology, or its expertise, and ultimately pulling out of the local economy.

Interactions between host countries and MNCs have gone through many phases. Among the most conflictual have been relations over foreign direct investments in the raw materials sector. Before World War I, most FDI was in mining, agriculture, or utilities. These investments, which may have been popular at the outset, eventually became controversial. The case of the United Fruit Company in Central America (see Chapter 4) is a good example: many people in developing nations came to see plantation and raw-materials investments as exploitative. Indeed, after the 1920s more and more LDCs tended to buy out, take over, or limit foreign investment in these sectors, favoring their own investors instead. One study of forcible takings of MNCs in developing countries between 1960 and 1976, for example, found that while FDI in extractive industries (agriculture and raw materials) and utilities was just one-fifth of the total, these sectors accounted for more than half of the takings.[20]

Political considerations about the role of FDI have added to purely economic concerns. Especially over the course of the 1960s, LDC governments began to believe that large foreign corporations could have a powerful and unwelcome impact on local politics. The activities of the U.S.-based International Telephone and Telegraph Company (ITT) in Chile demonstrated the threat. ITT first tried to keep Socialist Party candidate Salvador Allende from being elected president in 1970 for fear that his government would nationalize its investments. When this attempt was unsuccessful, ITT participated in a series of plots to try to overthrow President Allende. The story ended with a coup that destroyed one of Latin America's sturdiest democracies and brought the murderous dictatorship of Augusto Pinochet to power. The notion that American companies could be complicit in such matters, long derided by Westerners as feverish imaginings, was soon proven to be accurate by a congressional investigation, and this finding fueled sentiment against MNCs.[21]

For both economic and political reasons, many countries began restricting MNCs in the 1960s. This was even true of some developed nations: Canada monitored and controlled new investments, while both France and Japan limited foreign companies. But the most sweeping efforts were in the developing world, where foreign corporations were excluded from many industries and foreign ownership was strictly limited, often to a minority share. Many developing countries nationalized foreign corporations, transferring ownership to local private companies or to the government. Others allowed FDI only if the foreign company did not compete with local firms, shared ownership with local investors, or agreed to reinvest most of its profits in the host country. The turn away from MNCs in the 1960s and 1970s went hand

20. Stephen J. Kobrin, "Foreign Enterprise and Forced Divestment in LDCs," *International Organization* 34, no. 1 (Winter 1980): 65–88.
21. Paul Sigmund, *Multinationals in Latin America* (Madison: University of Wisconsin Press, 1980).

in hand with the turn toward foreign borrowing: by borrowing, developing countries could get foreign capital without allowing foreign ownership of the projects.

But the debt crisis of the 1980s, along with the increased acceptance of global economic integration in the 1990s, eroded resistance to multinational corporations. Developing countries were desperate for foreign capital, especially after loans dried up. And it appeared that attracting foreign corporations was important to ensuring a nation's integration into global markets. Previous restrictions on foreign direct investment were loosened or removed, and many LDCs actively sought to encourage foreign corporations to locate production facilities within their borders. The amounts involved were enormous: while MNCs invested about $2 billion a year in the developing world in the early 1970s, they have averaged over $150 billion a year since 2000. Even accounting for inflation, this is nearly a thirty-fold increase. As most developing countries have opened their economies to world markets, FDI has become less politically sensitive and more broadly desired.

This does not mean that MNCs are not controversial. Indeed, many people in the developing world continue to regard foreign corporations as economically, politically, or culturally undesirable. Restrictions persist on their activities in developing nations. In industrialized countries, too, there are continuing concerns about the exporting of jobs, and in some quarters about the possibility that foreign investors might compromise national sovereignty. Nevertheless, in the past 20 years the prevailing attitude toward FDI has been quite positive.

WHY AREN'T THERE INTERNATIONAL INSTITUTIONS RELATED TO FDI?

There are no effective international institutions associated with foreign direct investment. This is in striking contrast to international lending, where there are both regional and global multilateral institutions: the IMF, the World Bank, the Inter-American Development Bank, and so on. One possible reason is that there are fewer (if any) widely accepted truly global concerns associated with FDI than with international finance. In the latter area, it has been generally agreed for over a century that there is a risk of financial crises in one country affecting other countries. This risk creates incentives for countries to find ways, including institutionalized ways, to cooperate to avoid such financial contagion, and international institutions facilitate cooperation in pursuit of these types of common goals. Such incentives are not so strong in the case of FDI.

Nor is there a particularly strong demand for cooperation among countries in bargaining with MNCs. Individual countries that wish to limit or regulate MNCs can do so on their own, and it is not clear that IMF-style international institutions would help with this effort. The role of international institutions in providing information or establishing standards seems less relevant in the case of FDI, where each investment has different characteristics and where host governments are often well equipped to supervise foreign companies.

There have been occasional suggestions that some international agreement or organization might help to create a common set of standards for FDI. Codes of conduct have been proposed, and there has been an increase in private voluntary compliance with such codes of conduct, but this falls far short of an organized intergovernmental institution. Initiatives to institutionalize and regularize relations between multinational corporations and host nations have made little progress. There are thousands of **bilateral investment treaties** signed between two countries, providing protection for each other's investors, but nothing even remotely similar to an IMF has emerged.

Despite the absence of any multilateral institution, since the 1980s interactions between foreign corporations and national states have been less conflictual than they were before then. Certainly, FDI today leads to much less debate than conflict between debtors and creditors. Foreign direct investment is widely accepted as an important component of an integrated world economy and as a generally positive factor in economic development.

bilateral investment treaty (BIT): An agreement between two countries about the conditions for private investment across borders. Most BITs include provisions to protect an investment from government discrimination or expropriation without compensation, as well as establishing mechanisms to resolve disputes.

International Migration: What Happens When People—Rather Than Capital—Move across Borders?

Like capital, labor is a factor of production that moves across borders. In fact, international movements of labor and capital can be thought of as responding to similar economic factors and having similar economic effects. Capital can leave one country in order to hire workers in another—this is what happens when a corporation sets up production abroad. Alternatively, labor can leave one country in order to work for capital in another—this is what happens when workers migrate to a new country to be employed by a corporation there. Whether GM moves a factory to Mexico to hire Mexican workers, or Mexican workers move to Detroit to work for GM, the effect is similar. It therefore makes sense to think about the politics of immigration as part of the broader integration of the world economy, and as simply another example of the movement of factors of production from country to country.

In fact, international migration has long been a feature of a globalized world economy. In the nineteenth and early twentieth centuries, international labor migration occurred at much higher levels than today. Over the decades before World War I, some 100 million people left their homelands in Europe and Asia for other parts of the world. The cities of such rapidly growing countries as Canada, Australia, Argentina, and the United States were full of foreign-born workers. For the most part, before 1914 Europeans could move and work wherever they pleased, without complicated legal proceedings or documents (Asian immigration was much more heavily restricted). While international labor movements in recent years have been very large, they are proportionately much smaller than those of the nineteenth and early twentieth centuries. However, labor migration has been significant—and also politically controversial.

Today, about one American resident in eight was born in a foreign country, approximately half of them in Latin America. The immigrant share of the population of other developed countries is generally similar to that of the United

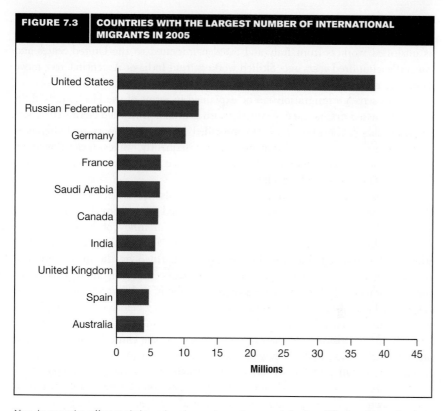

FIGURE 7.3 — COUNTRIES WITH THE LARGEST NUMBER OF INTERNATIONAL MIGRANTS IN 2005

Note: As countries collect statistics on immigrants in varying ways, it is often difficult to harmonize them across countries; differences in counting deeply affect rank orders.
Source: United Nations, *Trends in Total Migrant Stock: The 2005 Revision*, http://esa.un.org/migration/index. asp?panel=1.

States (12 percent). It is a bit lower in some countries (8 percent in Great Britain, 10 percent in France) and substantially higher in some others (20 percent or more in Canada, New Zealand, and Australia).[22] Figure 7.3 shows the countries with the largest number of immigrants. In almost every developed country, immigration is a politically contentious issue, with some residents favoring more open borders to immigrants and others wishing to limit immigration.[23] What explains these controversies over immigration?

There are many ways in which the movement of labor from one country to another is similar to the movement of capital, and it can be similarly analyzed. Labor, like capital, responds to differential rates of return: higher wages in rich countries attract workers from poor countries. This is true of both unskilled labor and skilled labor, which is typically called human capital because its "owners"

22. Organization for Economic Cooperation and Development, *A Profile of Immigrant Populations in the 21st Century: Data from OECD Countries* (Paris: OECD, 2008).
23. A useful resource on this highly controversial topic is the Migration Policy Institute, www.migration policy.org.

have invested in advanced skills. Unskilled workers from El Salvador or Morocco migrate to the United States or Germany in search of higher-paying jobs, just as unskilled workers from Italy and Sweden migrated to the United States and Australia a hundred years ago. Skilled workers from India or Argentina, too, move to Europe or North America in search of higher incomes.

In this sense, immigration can be explained in terms of the Heckscher-Ohlin theory discussed in Chapter 6. Countries with abundant unskilled labor will export unskilled labor; countries scarce in unskilled labor will import it. Differences across countries in labor endowments (and, consequently, wages) mean that there are economic incentives for a labor-rich country such as Mexico or China to export both labor-intensive goods and labor.

The economic impact of labor migration can also be understood in terms of the Heckscher-Ohlin theory. An inflow of unskilled labor from abroad will tend to reduce the wages of local unskilled workers, while an inflow of skilled labor will tend to reduce the wages of local skilled workers. Thus, for example, unskilled workers in developed countries are likely to be harmed by the immigration of unskilled workers from countries with lower wages. Concerns about this labor-market competition are one source of unease about immigration in developed countries. This is not a new phenomenon. In the century before 1914, immigration probably also exerted downward pressure on wages in migrant-receiving countries: two scholars have estimated that in such countries as the United States, Australia, and Argentina, unskilled wages were between one-eighth and one-third lower with immigration than they would have been without it.[24] While this outcome may have been bad for unskilled workers, it was probably good for the countries' economies as a whole, supplying them with much-needed labor.

Immigration benefits people in receiving countries in several ways. Employers gain from the lower wages they can pay. This is especially true for those who hire a lot of unskilled labor; in parts of the United States, sectors such as agriculture, restaurants, and construction have come to rely on cheaper immigrant labor. The economy as a whole profits from having a larger labor force and from the lower cost of production that lower wages can provide. As usual, the benefits for some are counterbalanced by costs to others: if immigration lowers the wages that employers have to pay, it also lowers the wages paid to native workers who compete with immigrants.

The domestic distributional effects of immigration, coupled with national political institutions, help explain changes in policies over time. In the nineteenth century, there was substantial anti-immigrant sentiment among workers in such countries as the United States, Canada, and Australia. But a century and more ago, employers were far more politically powerful than labor—after all, unions were barely organized. So while there were some restrictions on immigration, especially from Asia, most countries remained open. As the political influence of labor grew, restrictions on immigration expanded and until the 1960s were very stringent. During the 1960s, labor shortages began to develop in industrialized nations, and pressure to permit more immigration grew. The result was a loosening of

---

24. Kevin O'Rourke and Jeffrey Williamson, *Globalization and History: The Evolution of a Nineteenth-Century Atlantic Economy* (Cambridge, MA: MIT Press, 1999), tables 8.1 and 8.3.

restrictions; this may also have been due to the rising influence of skilled workers in rich countries, who are less concerned about competition from unskilled immigrants. Today, there are many countervailing economic interests at play: workers who would compete with immigrants and workers who would not, employers who depend on immigrant labor and those who do not.

The political economy of immigration involves other economic and noneconomic considerations. One economic consideration is the potential cost of social programs that immigrants may use disproportionately, inasmuch as they tend to be poorer than natives. However, immigrants typically pay taxes, so that the overall (net) effect may be hard to distinguish.[25] In some contemporary American debates, opponents of immigration express particular concern about the fiscal effects of large-scale immigration.

Supporters and opponents of immigration often raise noneconomic issues as well. Unlike capital, labor is a factor of production that inherently involves people. Capital can move across borders without having much, or any, noneconomic impact on sending or receiving nations. But immigration changes the nature of both the countries from which immigrants come and the countries to which they go. Some people feel that immigrants pose a cultural threat to host societies and that immigrant communities will change the social and political nature of the local society. Others welcome the diversity; for many citizens, new immigrants may well be family members or former neighbors. Some people regard immigrants as a threat to national security and national identity. Others see immigration as a way of spreading Western values and of rewarding allies in poor countries.

Certainly, immigration is one of the more prominent and visible features of contemporary globalization. It raises many of the same economic issues as do factor movements involving capital. But it also provokes responses on a very human level—about culture, rights, and identity. It promises to continue to be a controversial topic.

Conclusion: The Politics of International Investment

International finance is the most globalized portion of the international economy. People and governments worldwide try mightily to attract foreign corporations and to qualify for loans from foreign lenders. There are substantial advantages to having access to the world's enormous pool of capital. This gives governments powerful reasons to try to collaborate with foreign investors to smooth the path of capital as it moves from country to country.

---

25. Like many other aspects of immigration, the fiscal costs and benefits of immigrants are hotly debated, even among scholars. For two contending views, both from conservative think tanks, see Robert E. Rector, Christine Kim, and Shanea Watkins, *The Fiscal Cost of Low-Skill Households to the U.S. Taxpayer*, Heritage Foundation Special Report no. 12, April 4, 2007; and Daniel Griswold, "The Fiscal Impact of Immigration Reform: The Real Story," *Free Trade Bulletin* 30 (May 21, 2007).

However, international finance is not an unmitigated blessing. Foreign loans can be a boon to a developing nation, but they can become an oppressive burden that forces the population to make huge sacrifices in order for their government to keep up interest payments. Foreign investment by multinational corporations can bring a country valuable technology and expertise, but it can also impose severe constraints on the room for maneuver of the host nation. Governments have many interests in common with international financiers, but they also have many conflicting interests.

International finance is inherently political because powerful private actors, governments, and international institutions all come together to bargain over the terms of international financial relations. Such negotiations—over foreign loans, debt bailouts, IMF packages, the role of multinational corporations, and other financial issues—can be contentious. The policies associated with them are also often very controversial within nations, which adds to the problems' politicization.

Certainly, international financial flows can be a powerful force for development and economic progress. Many countries, past and present, have used foreign capital to finance rapid economic growth and development. And many individuals, groups, and companies have benefited from their access to international finance. However, when things go wrong in the international financial system, they can go spectacularly wrong in ways that can profoundly impact international politics—and the lives of billions of people.

Reviewing Interests, Interactions, and Institutions

INTERESTS	INTERACTIONS	INSTITUTIONS
Investors and receiving countries have a common interest in moving capital from where it is abundant to where it is scarce. Capital movements provide cheaper capital for borrowers and higher profits for investors.	There are strong incentives for host nations and international investors to cooperate to secure the property rights of foreigners.	The International Monetary Fund (IMF) often oversees sovereign debt renegotiations. It encourages debtor governments to change their domestic policies to enable them to sustain debt payments.
Conflicts of interest between investors and host countries arise over the division of profits from direct investments.	Governments and lenders often end up bargaining over international debt and over the terms of repayment. Debtors can threaten default and other reductions of payments, while creditors can threaten to cut off debtors from future lending.	Some analysts see the IMF's role as benevolent: it helps set standards and gather information to permit debtors and creditors to reach agreement and to allow international lending to take place.
There are potential conflicts of interest between creditors and debtors over the terms and timing of servicing of debt, and over the division of sacrifices to be made when times are difficult.	Governments and multinational corporations sometimes enter into conflict over foreign direct investments.	Other people see the IMF as an international financial policeman, collecting debts from poor countries for rich bankers.
Multinational corporations bring expertise and tax revenues to their host countries. But the corporations and their hosts may disagree over how to divide the benefits of these investments.		There are few or no international institutions in the FDI realm. There are, however, bilateral and multilateral treaties among countries to attempt to safeguard crossborder investments.

Key Terms

portfolio investment, p. 264
sovereign lending, p. 264
foreign direct investment (FDI), p. 264
World Bank, p. 268
recession, p. 270
depression, p. 270

default, p. 270
Bank for International Settlements
    (BIS), p. 275
International Monetary Fund (IMF), p. 275
multinational corporation (MNC), p. 282
bilateral investment treaty (BIT), p. 288

For Further Reading

Caves, Richard. *Multinational Enterprise and Economic Analysis*, 3rd ed. Cambridge: Cambridge University Press, 2007. Presents a classic summary of the economics of foreign direct investment.

Haggard, Stephan. *The Political Economy of the Asian Financial Crisis.* Washington DC: Institute for International Economics, 2000. Analyzes the widespread crisis that affected East Asian countries in 1997–1998.

Helleiner, Eric. *States and the Reemergence of Global Finance.* Ithaca: Cornell University Press, 1994. Shows how government policy was crucial to the development of the modern international financial system.

Jensen, Nathan. *Nation-States and the Multinational Corporation: A Political Economy of Foreign Direct Investment.* Princeton: Princeton University Press, 2006. Analyzes the politics and economics of national responses to foreign corporations.

Roubini, Nouriel, and Brad Setser. *Bailouts or Bail-ins? Responding to Financial Crises in Emerging Economies.* Washington DC: Peterson Institute for International Economics, 2004. Analyzes and evaluates the problems presented by countries facing severe debt crises, and potential responses from creditors, their governments, and the international financial institutions.

Obstfeld, Maurice, and Alan Taylor. *Global Capital Markets: Integration, Crisis, and Growth.* Cambridge: Cambridge University Press, 2004. Provides a detailed description and analysis of the history and contemporary nature of international financial markets.

Singer, David. *Regulating Capital: Setting Standards for the International Financial System.* Ithaca: Cornell University Press, 2007. Analyzes the economics and politics of international financial regulation in a world of global financial markets.

Tomz, Michael. *Reputation and International Cooperation: Sovereign Debt across Three Centuries.* Princeton: Princeton University Press, 2007. Explores the politics and economics of private lending to governments historically and in the present.

Vreeland, James. *The International Monetary Fund: Politics of Conditional Lending.* New York: Routledge, 2007. Presents an analytical survey of one of the world's most controversial international organizations.

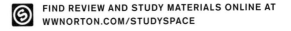

FIND REVIEW AND STUDY MATERIALS ONLINE AT WWNORTON.COM/STUDYSPACE

CHAPTER 8

International Monetary Relations

International monetary relations are often controversial. Although most of the countries in the European Union succeeded in working together to adopt the euro in place of their national currencies in 2001, the decision was hotly debated among the people and policymakers in each country. Today, the European Central Bank in Frankfurt, Germany, implements monetary policies for the entire euro zone.

In the absence of global government, how are international currencies supplied and international monetary relations regulated?

On December 18, 2001, rioters swept through the cities of Argentina. They were furious about three straight years of economic stagnation and government economic policies that seemed to make matters worse. Most recently, the government had frozen bank deposits, so that Argentines could take only small amounts of cash out of their bank accounts—and nothing out of the very popular accounts that many people had in U.S. dollars. In response to the rioting, President Fernando de la Rúa declared a state of siege, but the following day the disorder spread, as hundreds of thousands of middle-class Argentines joined the protests in the streets. That evening, the economy minister stepped down. A day later, violent clashes with the police led to more than two dozen deaths around the country, and huge crowds surrounded the presidential palace in Buenos Aires. At the end of the day, de la Rúa resigned and was evacuated by helicopter from the presidential palace to avoid the hostile crowds.

The president of the Senate, a member of the opposition Peronist Party that controlled both houses of Congress, assumed the interim presidency. Two days later, the Peronists installed provincial governor Adolfo Rodríguez Saá as president until national elections could be held. Rodríguez Saá declared the largest default in history—on $93 billion in sovereign debt. But he, too, faced protests and resigned a week after taking office. This time the president of the Chamber of Deputies, also a Peronist, stepped in as interim president. After further turmoil, the legislature appointed to the presidency Eduardo Duhalde, the Peronist candidate who had lost the 1999 presidential election to the now-disgraced de la Rúa. Meanwhile, the country had entered full-fledged economic collapse. Argentine gross domestic product (GDP), which had declined by 8 percent over the three previous years of recession, dropped by 11 percent in 2002, and unemployment soared above 20 percent.

The ultimate reason for these extraordinary events—nationwide riots, five presidents in less than two weeks, the biggest default in history, economic disintegration—was the Argentine government's policies toward its currency. Ten years earlier, the government had made the Argentine peso equal to one U.S. dollar and fixed it at this exchange rate. The currency policy led to rapid growth and many other economic achievements in Argentina. But by 2001 the commitment was dragging the economy downward. It was widely blamed for general economic stagnation and for the specific banking policies that provoked popular outrage. Argentina's fortunes rose dramatically, and fell even more dramatically, with its currency policies.

Many people who find currencies confusing or boring may be surprised that exchange rates could be responsible for such striking developments. But the Argentine events are not alone in illustrating the importance of currencies and currency policies to economics and politics—and to people's everyday lives. A couple of weeks after Argentine society exploded into violence over the exchange rate, and halfway around the world, came another, unrelated but equally remarkable, currency development. Twelve European countries abandoned their national monies, some of which had existed for centuries. In place of the Deutsche mark, franc, lira, and other currencies, they adopted the euro, a common European currency. The creation of the euro dominated European politics and economics for most of the 1990s, and its consolidation, management, and expansion have been central to the continent's political economy since then. Argentina and Europe are not alone: in many countries, currency policy is one of the most hotly contested economic and political issues.

National governments have pursued very different policies toward their national currencies. Today, most governments choose among three monetary paths. One option is to give up the national currency in favor of another money—as has occurred in a number of Caribbean and Latin American countries, which have adopted the U.S. dollar, and in most European countries, which have adopted the euro. Other governments have tied the national currency's value to that of

Currency policies and exchange rates can have dramatic consequences for ordinary citizens. The Argentine government's decision in 1991 to set the exchange rate for the Argentine peso such that it was equal to the U.S. dollar led to larger economic problems. By 2001, millions of Argentines faced significant hardships as a result of this currency policy, and mass protests erupted.

another country, such as the dollar or the euro (as we will discuss in more detail below). Finally, many governments continue to maintain a separate national currency whose value is allowed to change in response to markets and other forces. Given the importance of exchange rate policies for international economic and political relations, how and why do governments choose any one of these three monetary paths?

In addition to individual national choices, there are important global monetary issues. Indeed, international monetary affairs—the interrelationships among national monies—are central to the international economy and thus to world politics. Stable relations among national currencies allow actors in one country to make payments to actors in other countries, and therefore make it easier for goods, people, and capital to move across borders. Just as it is hard to imagine national economies without national money, it is hard to see how the modern world economy could function without some arrangement for the use of money among countries. Yet, while national governments supply national monies, there is no international government to organize international monetary affairs. How, then, is this crucial service provided? How is such a quintessentially governmental function as the provision of currencies carried out at the global level in the absence of global government?

The international monetary order has varied enormously over the years. As we saw in Chapter 1, from the 1870s until 1914 most of the world's major economies were on a classical gold standard that tied their currencies together. After World War II, a revised version of this approach, the Bretton Woods monetary system, reigned until 1973. Since then, international and regional currency arrangements have been in flux. They have always, however, been politically sensitive, and they have been the focus of a great deal of international attention among major national governments. This chapter makes the following points about the interests, interactions, and institutions associated with international monetary policy.

CORE OF THE ANALYSIS

▶ There are many contending interests over monetary affairs within countries, which leads to domestic conflict over the appropriate currency policy to pursue.

▶ Although every country can set currency policy as it wants, the fact that exchange rates value currencies relative to one another means that outcomes are the product of interactions among countries' policies. As a result, countries may have reasons to cooperate with one another to create arrangements that are mutually beneficial.

▶ Virtually everyone has an interest in the existence of a functioning international monetary system. But different arrangements benefit some actors more than others, which leads to disagreement about how such a system should be organized and about how the burdens and benefits should be distributed among countries.

▶ International monetary institutions, such as the gold standard, the Bretton Woods monetary system, or Europe's Economic and Monetary Union, can create rules that facilitate cooperation in international monetary policy.

What Are Exchange Rates, and Why Do They Matter?

A national monetary system allows for the convenient exchange of goods, services and capital. It is a classic public good (see Chapter 2): it benefits everyone, but because people cannot be excluded from its benefits and charged for them, there is little incentive for private firms to provide it. This is why national governments typically determine the currency, print bills, mint coins, and control the money supply. Almost everyone in a country can agree on the desirability of a recognizable, trustworthy national money, and of stable prices. But in addition to a currency's domestic use, it exists in relation to other national currencies. For example, the U.S. dollar can be used not only to buy goods and services in the United States, but also to buy euros, Canadian dollars, and Mexican pesos, among other currencies. The price of a national currency relative to other national currencies is its **exchange rate**, and like other prices, the exchange rate can go up or down. When the dollar goes up in value against some other currency—such that, for example, a dollar can buy more pesos—it is said to strengthen or **appreciate.** When the dollar's value goes down against that of some other currency—such that, for example, a dollar can buy fewer pesos—it is said to weaken or **depreciate,** or to be **devalued.**

When a country's currency appreciates, it is more expensive for foreigners to buy the country's goods and services; when the currency depreciates, it is cheaper to do so. The most direct experience that many people have with currency movements is as tourists or, if they live near a national border, with prices around the border. American travelers to Europe find, for example, that when the dollar is strong (that is, appreciates), local prices in Europe seem relatively low. The hotels they stay in, the restaurants they go to, and the souvenirs they purchase are relatively inexpensive. However, when the dollar weakens (that is, depreciates), local prices get much higher. For example, in early 2006 an American staying in an Italian hotel charging 100 euros a night would have been paying about $120 a night, because the euro was worth 1.2 dollars; in early 2008, with the euro worth 1.5 dollars, the same hotel room at the same euro price would have cost the American $150 a night. The dollar had depreciated by 25 percent against the euro, so goods and services in euro countries (such as Italy) cost 25 percent more. (See Figure 8.1 for an indication of how the value of the dollar has fluctuated over the past 30 years.)

The same is true of goods bought and sold across borders. If a currency goes up or down, the prices that foreigners pay for goods priced in that currency rise or fall as well. So a pair of Italian shoes that cost 100 euros in Italy in early 2006 could have been exported to the United States and sold for $120 dollars (plus shipping costs), while in early 2008, after the dollar had depreciated by 25 percent, the same 100-euro pair of shoes would have sold for $150 dollars. When the U.S. dollar is weak (depreciates) against other currencies, foreign goods are expensive to Americans; however, when the U.S. dollar is strong (appreciates) against other currencies, foreign goods are inexpensive to Americans.

Although the attractiveness of a given country to foreign tourists is not particularly important to most nations, the attractiveness of that country's goods, services, and investment opportunities is crucial. Thus, the exchange rate is a very important part of a country's international economic relations.

exchange rate: The price at which one currency is exchanged for another.

appreciate: In terms of a currency, to increase in value in terms of other currencies.

depreciate: In terms of a currency, to decrease in value in terms of other currencies.

devalue: To reduce the value of one currency in terms of other currencies.

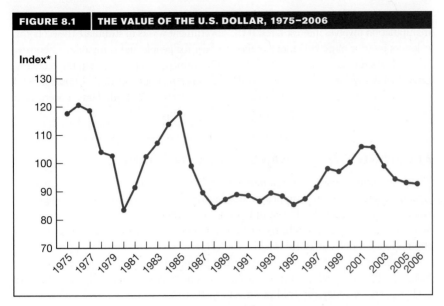

FIGURE 8.1 | THE VALUE OF THE U.S. DOLLAR, 1975–2006

*The base year (2000) is given the value of 100 in this index, which means that the values for other years tell us whether the dollar was stronger or weaker than it was in the year 2000. Higher numbers indicate a stronger currency.

Source: World Bank, World Development Indicators, go.worldbank.org/U0FSM7AQ40 (accessed 11/2/08).

HOW ARE CURRENCY VALUES DETERMINED?

Like other prices, an exchange rate goes up or down in response to changes in supply and demand. There are many factors that can affect supply and demand for a national money. Perhaps the most relevant is relative interest rates. As we saw in Chapter 7, foreigners considering investing in a country weigh relative interest rates; if interest rates are higher in the United States, investments in the United States are more attractive (everything else being equal).[1] But in order to invest in the United States, investors need dollars. Higher interest rates make it more profitable for people to put (or keep) their money in the country, so higher interest rates increase the demand for the currency and lead to its appreciation. Of course, the relationship works in the opposite direction as well: if people want fewer dollars, its exchange rate will go down. Lower interest rates can lead to a depreciation of the currency, just as higher interest rates can lead to an appreciation.

The relationship between interest rates and the value of the national currency is particularly important because governments routinely raise and lower interest rates as part of their **monetary policy.** Indeed, monetary policy is a powerful tool of national governments; in most developed countries, it is implemented by the central bank (for example, the Federal Reserve in the United States). National monetary policy refers to government attempts to affect macroeconomic conditions—unemployment, inflation,

> **monetary policy:**
> An important tool of national governments to influence broad macroeconomic conditions such as unemployment, inflation, and economic growth. Typically, governments alter their monetary policies by changing national interest rates or exchange rates.

---

1. We ignore trade-related sources of currency movements, for convenience. It should be clear that anything that makes a country's goods and services more attractive to foreigners will increase demand for the country's currency and lead to an appreciation (and vice versa).

overall economic growth—by manipulating monetary conditions. The most common manipulation involves interest rates. If the government wants to stimulate the economy, it lowers interest rates; this move makes it easier for people and companies to borrow, and it allows the economy to expand. If the government wants to restrain the economy, typically because prices are rising and there is concern about inflation, it raises interest rates; this move makes it harder to borrow and restrains demand. Thus, government policy can have a powerful impact on a currency's value.

ALLOWING THE EXCHANGE RATE TO CHANGE

There are other choices facing a national government with respect to its currency. Among these, the most important is whether and how to let the exchange rate change relative to others. The simplest choice is whether to "fix" the exchange rate or let it "float." A **fixed exchange rate** is one whose government promises to keep the national money at some established value in terms of another currency or of a precious metal such as gold. During the period of the classical **gold standard,** from the 1870s to 1914, a country's government "went on gold" by promising to exchange its currency for gold at an established rate (in the United States, it was one troy ounce of gold for $20.67). This move made the country's currency equivalent to gold and interchangeable at a fixed rate with the money of any other gold-standard country. Much of the world, as a result, essentially shared one currency. Gold-backed money invested by Germans in Japan, or by Belgians in Canada, would be paid back in equivalent amounts of gold-backed money. Contracted prices would not fluctuate, for exchange rates did not change.

At the other extreme is a **floating exchange rate,** under which a currency's value is allowed to change more or less freely, driven by markets or other factors. This is the regime currently in place for most major currencies, including the U.S. dollar, the Japanese yen, and the euro. If a government chooses this exchange rate regime, the price of the currency moves around in line with changes in supply and demand. Map 8.1 indicates which countries worldwide follow fixed versus floating exchange rate regimes.

There are intermediate steps between a fully fixed currency and a freely floating one. A government can allow its currency to vary, but only within limits; or it can fix the exchange rate for short periods, changing the currency's value as desired. This approach avoids some of the costs of each system but also forgoes some of the benefits. At the global level, the **Bretton Woods monetary system** that followed the classical gold standard and prevailed from 1945 to 1973 was something of a compromise. It was based on a fixed rate and a gold standard for the United States and on a "fixed but adjustable rate" for other currencies that were on a dollar standard. This system of fixed but adjustable rates (an **adjustable peg**) required that governments keep currency values fixed for relatively long periods but permitted them to alter ("adjust") them if and when governments found it desirable to do so. In practice, the Bretton Woods system meant that the U.S. dollar's value could not change (it was fixed at $35 per ounce of gold). Other governments also fixed their currency against the dollar, but the national government of a country other than the United States could devalue (depreciate) or revalue (appreciate) its currency's value if it felt a change was necessary. Typically, such changes were infrequent, occurring once every five to seven years.

The Bretton Woods system was seen as a middle ground between gold-standard rigidity and complete unpredictability. As under the gold standard, exchange rates were stable enough to encourage international trade and investment. As under a more flexible system, the exchange rates could be varied as necessary, albeit rarely.

As these examples indicate, a national government's decisions about the exchange rate often depend on international monetary conditions. While national policies are important, from the standpoint of international economics and politics more generally it is the *global* nature of international monetary relations that is most relevant. We will return to these international issues below. First, however, we evaluate the potential for *domestic* conflicts of interest over exchange rate policy.

Who Cares about Exchange Rates, and Why?

GOVERNMENTS

A government deciding what to do with its currency must consider important trade-offs and domestic interests that are often in conflict. One dimension of conflict involves whether the currency should be fixed, floating, or in between. Each choice helps some domestic actors and hurts others.

Fixed exchange rates, such as the gold standard or a peg to the dollar, provide currency stability and predictability, which greatly facilitate international trade, investment, finance, migration, and travel. Under the gold standard, businessmen, investors, and immigrants did not have to worry about changes in exchange rates or about major impediments to moving money around the world. The stimulus to trade was substantial; being on gold in this period is estimated to have raised trade between two countries by between 30 and 70 percent.[2] Generally speaking, a fixed currency provides stability that facilitates international economic exchange; it also provides a monetary anchor that keeps prices stable. It is thus very much in the interest of those engaged in crossborder trade, investment, finance, and travel, as well as those who want to keep inflation low.

However, there are costs to fixing the exchange rate, so that some people and governments are strongly opposed to it. By definition, a government on a fixed exchange rate is committed to maintaining its currency's value, even if economic conditions could be improved with a change. A fixed rate reduces or eliminates a government's ability to have its own independent monetary policy, which can be costly. For example, if an economy is in recession, a common economic policy response is to lower interest rates and thereby promote borrowing to expand consumption and investment. This move stimulates the economy, as mentioned

---

2. See, for example, A. Estevadeordal, B. Frantz, and A. M. Taylor, "The Rise and Fall of World Trade, 1870–1939," *Quarterly Journal of Economics* 118 (May 2003): 359–407; J. Ernesto Lopez-Cordova and Christopher M. Meissner, "Exchange-Rate Regimes and International Trade: Evidence from the Classical Gold Standard Era," *American Economic Review* 93, no. 1 (2003): 344–53.

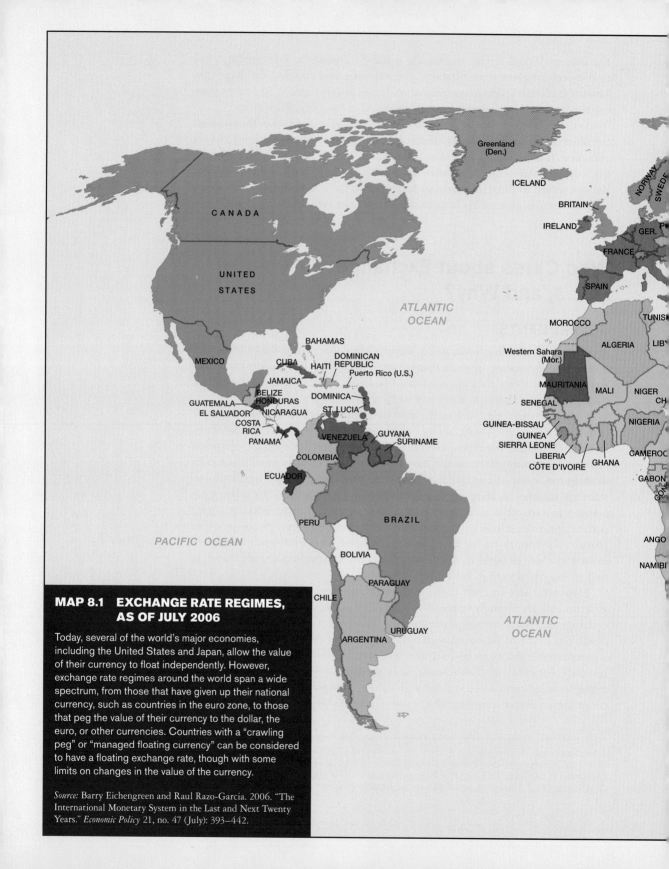

Greenland
(Den.)

ICELAND

BRITAIN

IRELAND

GER.

FRANCE

SPAIN

NORWAY

SWEDE

P

MOROCCO

TUNIS

Western Sahara
(Mor.)

ALGERIA

LIB

MAURITANIA

MALI

NIGER

CH

SENEGAL

GUINEA-BISSAU

NIGERIA

GUINEA

SIERRA LEONE

LIBERIA

CÔTE D'IVOIRE

GHANA

CAMEROO

GABON

CO

ANGO

NAMIBI

CANADA

UNITED
STATES

ATLANTIC
OCEAN

BAHAMAS

DOMINICAN
REPUBLIC

MEXICO

CUBA

HAITI

Puerto Rico (U.S.)

JAMAICA

BELIZE

DOMINICA

GUATEMALA

HONDURAS

EL SALVADOR

NICARAGUA

ST. LUCIA

COSTA
RICA

PANAMA

VENEZUELA

GUYANA

SURINAME

COLOMBIA

ECUADOR

PERU

BRAZIL

PACIFIC OCEAN

BOLIVIA

PARAGUAY

CHILE

ATLANTIC
OCEAN

URUGUAY

ARGENTINA

MAP 8.1 EXCHANGE RATE REGIMES, AS OF JULY 2006

Today, several of the world's major economies, including the United States and Japan, allow the value of their currency to float independently. However, exchange rate regimes around the world span a wide spectrum, from those that have given up their national currency, such as countries in the euro zone, to those that peg the value of their currency to the dollar, the euro, or other currencies. Countries with a "crawling peg" or "managed floating currency" can be considered to have a floating exchange rate, though with some limits on changes in the value of the currency.

Source: Barry Eichengreen and Raul Razo-Garcia. 2006. "The International Monetary System in the Last and Next Twenty Years." *Economic Policy* 21, no. 47 (July): 393–442.

FINLAND

BELARUS

UKRAINE

RUSSIAN FEDERATION

KAZAKHSTAN

MONGOLIA

UZBEKISTAN KYRGYZSTAN

TURKMENISTAN TAJIKISTAN

N. KOREA

S. KOREA

JAPAN

TURKEY

SYRIA

ISRAEL

IRAQ

IRAN

AFGHANISTAN

Kashmir

CHINA

PACIFIC OCEAN

EGYPT

KUWAIT

SAUDI ARABIA

PAKISTAN

NEPAL

BHUTAN

BANGLADESH

TAIWAN

SUDAN

OMAN

YEMEN

INDIA

MYANMAR
(BURMA)

VIETNAM

THAILAND

CAMBODIA

PHILIPPINES

CENTRAL
AFRICAN
REP.

ETHIOPIA

SOMALIA

MALDIVES

SRI
LANKA

INDIAN
OCEAN

MALAYSIA

PALAU

FEDERATED STATES
OF MICRONESIA

KIRIBATI

UGANDA

KENYA

DEM.
REP.
OF
THE
CONGO

TANZANIA

SEYCHELLES

INDONESIA

PAPUA
NEW
GUINEA

SOLOMON IS.

TUVALU

ZAMBIA

MALAWI

EAST TIMOR

VANUATU

FIJI

ZIMBABWE

BOTSWANA

MADAGASCAR

MOZAMBIQUE

SOUTH
AFRICA

AUSTRALIA

NEW
ZEALAND

FIXED RATE REGIMES

No national currency

- *Uses dollar*
- *Uses euro*
- *Uses CFA franc*

Fixed peg arrangements

- *Pegged to dollar*
- *Pegged to euro*
- *Pegged to "other"*

FLOATING RATE REGIMES

- Crawling peg
- Managed floating currency
- Independently floating currency

Travelers to foreign countries find that their money goes farther when their country's currency is strong relative to the local currency. The same is true when goods are traded across borders; buyers find that foreign goods are less expensive when their own currency is relatively stronger.

above, and may help alleviate the recession. But if national interest rates go down, people will sell the currency, and it will depreciate—which is not possible with a fixed exchange rate. By the same token, in difficult economic times there can be strong pressures for the government to allow the currency to depreciate so as to make the country's goods more attractive to foreign consumers; this, too, is not possible if the exchange rate is fixed. More generally, producers of goods that compete on import or export markets might want the government to be able to change the currency's value so that it becomes easier for them to sell their products. But this is impossible with a fixed exchange rate.

Both of these fixed-currency constraints were at work in the run-up to the 2001 Argentine crisis. In 2001, the Argentine peso had been tightly fixed to the U.S. dollar for 10 years, but the Argentine economy was in great distress. There were powerful pressures for the government to address broader economic conditions—in particular, to lower interest rates and to depreciate the currency so that Argentine goods would become more competitive on international markets. To carry out this strategy, the Argentine government needed to loosen the peso's link to the dollar. But at the same time, many Argentines did not want to see the peso's value change; among them were millions of homeowners whose mortgages were in dollars and who would have had to pay substantially more in pesos if the currency were devalued. With powerful interests on both sides, the Argentine government was paralyzed.

As this example demonstrates, the great advantage of a floating exchange rate is that it gives a government more freedom to pursue its own monetary policies, as it is not hampered by the need to keep the exchange rate fixed. But this advantage is countered by the fact that floating exchange rates can move around a great deal, which can impose costs on those engaged in international trade and investment, and which more generally can impede international economic exchange. Volatility in currency values almost certainly makes international trade and investment, travel, and finance more difficult.[3]

CONSUMERS AND BUSINESSES

Consumers and businesses have different views on how the national currency should be managed, depending on their position in the economy. Those whose economic activities are entirely domestic are likely to favor a floating exchange rate, because they are indifferent to currency fluctuations but want the government to be able to affect the national economy as necessary. Those with international economic concerns have an interest in a fixed currency, because too much volatility in exchange rates can be harmful to their activities.

---

3. These constraints are known as the Mundell-Fleming conditions, after the two economists who pioneered the approach; see, for example, Jeffry Frieden, "Invested Interests: The Politics of National Economic Policies in a World of Global Finance," *International Organization* 45, no. 4 (Autumn 1991): 407–31.

Just as people, firms, and groups may have conflicting interests over whether a currency should be fixed or floating, interests may also differ over a currency's desirable value (that is, whether it should be stronger or weaker). Government policy can have a powerful impact on whether a currency's value rises or falls in the short and medium run, which in turn can affect important domestic interests.

A strong (appreciated) exchange rate allows consumers and others to buy more of the world's products, thereby increasing national purchasing power. But there is a tradeoff: a strong exchange rate makes domestic goods more expensive to foreigners, which harms national producers who compete with foreigners on local or world markets. This is why manufacturers and farmers typically complain about a strong currency: it leads to a surge of cheaper imports, and it dampens exports. For example, the U.S. dollar appreciated by more than 50 percent between 1981 and 1985. This was associated with a big increase in Americans' purchasing power and ability to buy goods from the rest of the world—all of which contributed to a sense of prosperity among American consumers. However, the strong dollar led to a flood of cheaper imports into the United States and made American exports more expensive to foreigners. This caused serious problems in American manufacturing industries and led to the loss of 1.5 million manufacturing jobs. The strong dollar was particularly damaging to firms that either sold many of their products abroad or competed with imports; it led the president of one such firm, Caterpillar Tractors, to call the strong dollar "the single most important trade issue facing the U.S." Under this pressure, in 1985 the Senate passed a unanimous resolution calling on the administration to depreciate the dollar.[4] Eventually, the dollar did decline, and complaints subsided.

A weak, or depreciated, currency gives a big boost to national producers. This is why countries that are trying to encourage exports—such as many developing countries—typically keep their currencies weak. It is also why manufacturers and farmers, who compete with foreign producers both at home and abroad, have an interest in a relatively weak exchange rate. But there is a tradeoff here, too: a weak currency reduces national purchasing power, making consumers worse off. As the dollar declines, Americans can buy less of the world's products—and tourists cannot afford foreign vacations so easily. As a currency declines and prices of foreign goods rise, this can also contribute to overall price rises and inflation.

Both strong and weak currencies have advantages and disadvantages, and there is no particular reason that one or the other is better for a country. A strong currency helps consumers (and tourists) but hurts producers who compete with foreigners; a weak currency helps producers but hurts consumers. These conflicts of interest make currency policy controversial within countries and can make governments sensitive to the domestic political and economic effects of their currency arrangements. Such conflicts are evident when the possibility arises that a government might devalue its currency. Because the devaluation makes foreign goods more expensive and domestic goods relatively cheaper, it is in the interests of national producers. But the devaluation also reduces consumers' ability to buy goods and

4. Jeffry Frieden, "Economic Integration and the Politics of Monetary Policy in the United States," in *Internationalization and Domestic Politics*, ed. Robert Keohane and Helen Milner, 127–30 (Cambridge: Cambridge University Press, 1996).

services. In this context, it is perhaps not surprising that governments in democratic systems typically avoid currency devaluations or depreciations in the run-up to elections, for fear that the negative impact on consumers will cost them votes.[5]

A government's interest in exchange rate policy depends on the structure of its economy, its interest groups, and its political system. In a country with many firms and individuals engaged in economic activities across borders, the government is likely to face powerful pressure to stabilize or fix the currency's value. This is why the smaller economies of Europe that were extremely open to trade with other European countries (the Netherlands, Belgium, Luxembourg, Austria, Ireland) were among the strongest supporters of the creation of the euro. However, some larger European economies that traded and invested less across European borders (like France and Italy) were less enthusiastic. This is also why, in the Western Hemisphere, small countries that are tightly tied in to U.S. trade, investment, and tourism (such as Caribbean island nations, El Salvador, and Panama) have been the most likely to adopt the U.S. dollar or to fix their currencies to it. Larger, more self-sufficient economies (like Mexico and Brazil) have typically allowed their currencies to vary.

National currency policy implicates contending interests and complex institutions within countries. It is doubly complicated because one government's exchange rate policy inevitably affects other countries' policies. This observation takes us to the international level, where national governments with interests in conflict, and in common, interact over the structure of the international monetary system.

Can There Be World Money without World Government?

A monetary system is crucial to any modern economy; this is also true of the international economy, which requires some arrangement to permit trade, investment, and other payments across borders. A *national* monetary order provides predictability in the value of money and thus in the prices of goods. An *international* monetary order does the same for prices across borders—which means that it has to provide predictability in currency values. If traders, investors, tourists, and others had no idea what exchange rates would be tomorrow or next week, they would be very reluctant to engage in exchange across borders. For the international economy to work well, there must be some predictability to currency values, so that people can reasonably expect that the dollar or peso they are earning today will be worth something tomorrow.

However, there is no world government to provide a world money. In the absence of global government and a global money, many arrangements have emerged to provide this global public good. Under the classical gold standard of the nineteenth and early twentieth centuries, gold was the common denominator for international transactions. Under the Bretton Woods monetary system that prevailed from 1945

---

5. S. Brock Blomberg, Jeffry Frieden, and Ernesto Stein, "Sustaining Fixed Rates: The Political Economy of Currency Pegs in Latin America," *Journal of Applied Economics* 8, no. 2 (November 2005): 203–25.

to 1973, the dollar was the centerpiece of the monetary order. Some form of functioning global monetary system is in the interest of almost everyone.

But there can be disagreements over the nature of the international monetary system and every country's place in it. As we will see later in this chapter, the classical gold standard was popular with some people but unpopular with others. Similarly, Americans were quite satisfied with a Bretton Woods monetary system that put the dollar at its center, but Europeans were less enthusiastic. Just as there are conflicting interests within countries over national policy, there are tradeoffs and conflicts of interests among countries over international monetary arrangements.

INTERNATIONAL MONETARY REGIMES

National government decisions to float or to fix their currencies interact to create an **international monetary regime**—that is, an arrangement, which may be formal or informal, that is widely accepted to govern relations among currencies and that is shared by most countries in the world economy. There may also be regional monetary regimes that prevail in particular geographical regions, such as Europe with the euro.

The existence of a generally accepted international monetary regime has clear benefits for the international community in general, as it facilitates international economic exchange. It may come, however, at the cost of national sacrifices, which we will discuss below. First, we define the characteristics of international monetary regimes.

International monetary regimes have two principal features. The first makes clear whether currency values are expected to be fixed or floating, or a mix of both. As discussed above, the classical gold standard and the Bretton Woods monetary system were international fixed-rate regimes (although the Bretton Woods monetary system allowed for occasional adjustments). The contemporary regime is based on floating rates; there is no general agreement that national currency values should be fixed.

The second feature of an international monetary regime is agreement about whether there will be a mutually accepted benchmark against which values are measured, some common base or standard to which currencies can be compared. Three such standards have been used over time: a commodity standard, a commodity-backed paper standard, and a national paper currency standard.

A *commodity standard* uses a good with value of its own as the basic, monetary unit. Typically, this involves a precious metal such as gold or silver. Under the classical gold standard that prevailed from the 1870s until 1914, for example, all major national currencies had a fixed value in terms of gold, and they could be exchanged freely on the basis of their gold equivalent. This was a fixed-rate regime based on gold as the commodity standard.

A *commodity-backed paper standard* is similar to the Bretton Woods monetary system that prevailed from 1945 to 1973. Under such a regime, national governments issue paper currency with a fixed value in terms of gold (or some other commodity). This is one step removed from a pure gold standard, as it requires that governments be able to commit credibly to stand ready to redeem the currency for gold. Nonetheless, under such a standard, national currency values are comparable

international monetary regime: A formal or informal arrangement among governments to govern relations among their currencies, and which is shared by most countries in the world economy.

because they are all expressed in terms of a common commodity: gold. Under the Bretton Woods monetary system, the U.S. dollar was fixed to gold, while all other currencies were fixed to the dollar.

Under a *national paper currency standard*, national currencies are only backed by the commitments of their issuing governments to support them. In this context, people want to know that the government will act to ensure that the national currency continues be valuable. This may not mean committing to a fixed rate; it does mean committing to the currency not losing so much value as to become undesirable. Foreigners who hold dollars or euros, or who accept promises to pay in dollars or euros, do so with the expectation that even if exchange rates do change, dollars and euros will continue to be valuable national monies. Typically, only a few major currencies are used for international exchange—usually, the currencies of the world's most important trading and financial powers. This is the system that has prevailed since 1973. Today, most international exchange is measured and conducted in the dollar and the euro.

When and Why Do Governments Agree on the Monetary Order?

International agreement on a common monetary regime or system can be in everyone's interest, in that it facilitates international exchange. After all, almost everyone wants to have a stable and predictable monetary arrangement that allows firms and people to compare prices and transact business from one nation to another—whether in gold, a gold-backed national currency, or a paper national currency. Governments and people tend to share a desire for a general commitment to a common regime. However, governments and people often differ on the standard they would prefer. During the days of the classical gold standard, for example, there were many people and governments—including some powerful political movements—that preferred a silver standard to a gold standard. Supporters of silver typically believed that if money were the more plentiful silver, prices would be higher than with scarce gold and this would help raise the prices of goods they produced. During the decades of the Bretton Woods monetary system, there were frequent complaints by non-Americans over the role of the United States in the international monetary order. International monetary relations are infused with this tension between sources of conflict and reasons for cooperation.

INTERNATIONAL MONETARY COOPERATION AND CONFLICT

It can be difficult for governments to agree on global monetary relations. At the international political level, the difficulties stem from inherent characteristics of international monetary affairs. Agreement on a monetary regime has many features of a public good: everyone benefits if there is a smoothly functioning way to carry out international economic transactions. But, as with most public goods, the provision of this monetary order is not automatic or easy. A functioning monetary order can require conscious efforts by national governments to alter their policies, or to contribute funds to stabilize currencies, or otherwise to help sustain the system. However, it can be difficult to organize collaboration among governments to provide such a public good because there are powerful incentives to free ride on the efforts of others. Governments of smaller countries might reason that their contributions are too trivial to matter, and thus not participate; if enough governments follow this path, cooperation will break down. For example, a global fixed-rate system such as the gold standard can facilitate international trade and investment, but the government of a small country might decide that it can benefit from the global system without fixing its own currency and tying its hands. If enough countries take this route, the system will collapse.

A successful international monetary regime depends on interactions among the governments of the world's major economies. Their behavior sets the standards for the regime as a whole, and they need to address problems as they arise. However, governments also face major temptations to "cheat" on their international monetary commitments. In a fixed-rate regime, for example, one government might decide to devalue in order to make its producers' goods more competitive on world markets. Other countries might respond by also devaluing to allow their producers to match. The result is akin to the undesirable outcome of a Prisoner's Dilemma game (see the Special Topic appendix to Chapter 2). If every nation engages in competitive devaluations, the result is that all currencies end up being devalued, so that nobody gains any advantage. Meanwhile, the currency turmoil can throw international monetary relations into disorder and uncertainty, thereby interfering with normal economic activities.

Interactions among national governments, facing incentives both to cooperate and to enter into conflict, have determined the character of international monetary relations, including the emergence of global and regional monetary regimes. In the following section, we take a closer look at the evolution of international monetary arrangements over the past couple of centuries.

A SHORT HISTORY OF INTERNATIONAL MONETARY SYSTEMS

The modern international economy has experienced all three kinds of international monetary regimes described above.

The Gold Standard

Under the classical gold standard, most of the world's major economies had gold or gold-backed currencies tied together at exchange rates that did not change for decades. The portion of the world that was on gold—which eventually came to include every major economy except China and Persia—effectively had a common money: gold.

The stability of the classical gold standard relied on close ties among the three leading financial powers of the day—Britain, France, and Germany—along with support from smaller European nations. For example, when the 1890 collapse of

The gold standard was at the center of many political debates in the late 1800s and early twentieth century. American presidential candidate William Jennings Bryan called for a monetary system based on silver in his campaigns of 1896, 1900, and 1908. This poster shows the slogan NO CROSS OF GOLD to the right of Bryan's name.

Barings, a major British bank, threatened to destabilize the London markets, the central banks of France and Russia lent large sums to the Bank of England. The mere knowledge that enough money was available to address the problem helped calm investors. In 1898, the British and French helped stabilize German financial markets; a few years later, the Austrians helped calm the Berlin market. And at least seven more times between 1900 and 1914, the French stepped in to assist the British in order to stabilize the gold standard.[6]

The gold standard provided currency stability and predictability, which greatly facilitated international trade, investment, finance, migration, and travel. Most of the world's governments, and many countries' citizens, agreed that this common monetary standard was generally beneficial. Such confluence of interests among the major financial centers allowed them to interact cooperatively to sustain the gold standard for many decades.

However, there were costs to being on gold, so that some people and governments were less enthusiastic. As we saw in our discussion of a fixed-rate system, a government on the gold standard gave up its ability to run its own independent monetary policy, which implied a serious loss of economic policy influence. In the United States, the gold standard was very controversial; in fact, the 1896 presidential campaign was largely fought around it. William McKinley and the Republicans ran in favor of maintaining the American commitment to gold, but many Americans were hostile to the gold standard. The anti-gold forces, led by the Populists, wanted the government to take the dollar off gold and put it on silver at a different rate. This move would have accomplished two things: it would have devalued the dollar, making American exports more competitive, and it would have raised American prices. Farmers in particular liked the idea of a devaluation, as many of them produced for export markets. They, and others, also liked the idea of raising prices, as many of them were heavily indebted, and a rise in prices could have reduced their debt burden (the debts would have remained the same, while prices for farm products would have risen). As a result, the Democratic Party and the Populists united around William Jennings Bryan, who famously said to gold supporters, "You shall not crucify mankind upon a cross of gold!" Bryan lost in 1896 and again in 1900 and 1908, although the anti-gold movement he represented remained strong. (For more on this episode, see "What Shaped Our World?" on p. 313.) Nonetheless, there was enough domestic political support for the international cooperation necessary to sustain the gold standard that it was solid and extensive for almost fifty years, from the 1870s until 1914.

In the 1920s and 1930s, attempts to restore the classical gold standard were largely unsuccessful. Most countries did go on gold again after World War I ended, but the sort of international monetary cooperation that had allowed the classical gold standard

---

6. For a classic account of the gold standard era and its interwar collapse, see Barry Eichengreen, *Golden Fetters: The Gold Standard and the Great Depression, 1919–1939* (New York: Oxford University Press, 1992).

The *Wizard of Oz* and the Politics of Exchange Rates

The Wizard of Oz is one of the most famous children's stories of all time. First published as a book in 1900, it was turned into a film starring Judy Garland in 1939. The story chronicles the adventures of Dorothy, a young girl from Kansas whose house is suddenly swept up in a tornado and transported to a magical place populated by munchkins, witches, and other strange creatures. The Good Witch of the North counsels Dorothy to follow the yellow brick road to the Emerald City and seek the help of the Wizard of Oz to return home to Kansas. The Good Witch also gives her a pair of magic slippers. Dorothy skips along the yellow brick road and meets a brainless scarecrow, a tin man without a heart, and a cowardly lion. Together, this motley team battles the Wicked Witch of the West to gain access to the venerable Wizard. At the end of the story, they realize that the Wizard is a fraud; but fortunately the Good Witch reappears and informs Dorothy that she can return home simply by clicking together her magic slippers.

What does *The Wizard of Oz* have to do with exchange rate politics? Many observers believe that the story, which was written during the height of the U.S. experience under the gold standard, reflects the highly politicized debates over monetary policy in the late 1800s. A little background on the gold standard will help to elucidate the symbolism in the story.

Starting in the 1870s, the U.S. government officially agreed to exchange dollars for gold at a fixed rate of one ounce of gold for $20.67. One problem with this policy was that the domestic money supply was fixed based on the availability of gold. If businesses produced more goods and services but the stock of gold remained steady, then prices would fall. (In other words, if gold's value increases as it becomes more scarce relative to the economy, then the gold price of any good declines. An ounce of gold buys more and more goods.) This was indeed the case throughout much of the 1880s and 1890s. Falling prices harmed nearly everyone, but they were especially harmful to farmers who had borrowed money from banks to finance their operations. With the price of grain declining steadily, farmers had difficulty earning enough money to repay their

debts. Industrial workers also faced tough times as unemployment levels increased. Because the United States was on the gold standard, it was not able to lower interest rates or allow the currency to depreciate, both of which would have boosted prices and stimulated the economy.

The dire economic conditions of the 1890s helped to fuel the Populist movement, led by Democratic presidential candidate William Jennings Bryan. He wanted to replace the gold standard with an alternative system that would help increase the money supply—in particular, a system that included silver, a much more plentiful commodity. Bryan ultimately lost the election to William McKinley, a Republican who supported the gold standard.

With this background in mind, it is easy to see the symbolism in *The Wizard of Oz*, which was written just a few years after the 1896 election. Dorothy, representing the naïve American public, believes that her problems will be solved if she simply follows a winding road paved with gold bricks. She meets a scarecrow (a farmer), a tin man (an industrial worker), and a lion whose roar masks his cowardice (Bryan). When Dorothy finally meets the Wizard (McKinley), she realizes that he is a fraud. In response, she simply clicks her slippers together to transport herself back home. In the original book, the slippers were silver. (They were changed to ruby for the 1939 movie to take advantage of Technicolor technology.)

The symbolism in *The Wizard of Oz* (note that *oz* is an abbreviation for *ounce*) reflects the political and cultural importance of different monetary systems. In the late 1800s, the economic consequences of the gold standard helped to fuel the Populist movement, which played a prominent part in American presidential politics through the early 1900s. Gold continued to play a role in U.S. monetary policy through the early 1970s, but today the dollar is a *floating* currency. Could politicians revive the idea of a fixed exchange rate for the dollar? That remains to be seen—but in the meantime, politicians (and students) can use Dorothy's colorful experience as a reminder of the perils and promises of monetary policy-making. ■

to succeed had become difficult to organize. Countries such as France and Germany were on very poor terms diplomatically, which created an atmosphere of distrust that impeded efforts to negotiate monetary collaboration. As interests diverged, interactions among the major financial players became more hostile.

This failure to cooperate in the 1920s was exacerbated by the Great Depression that began in 1929. Faced with massive crises, governments were unwilling to forgo an economic policy that might allow them to alleviate the suffering of their citizens. After 1929, virtually all of the governments that had gone on gold in the 1920s went back off it as they tried to resuscitate their failing national economies. The result was a floating-rate system based on paper national currencies. This led to a great deal of currency volatility and instability, including many competitive devaluations, and probably contributed to the overall collapse of the international economy in the 1930s. In any case, monetary disorder was overwhelmed by the economic and military conflicts of the 1930s and 1940s.

The Bretton Woods System

As World War II drew to a close, the United States and Great Britain led the victorious Allies in designing an international monetary order—called the Bretton Woods monetary system because the agreements were negotiated at the Bretton Woods resort in New Hampshire—that represented a fundamental reform of the gold standard.[7] The Bretton Woods monetary system was organized around the U.S. dollar, and the dollar was tied to gold at the fixed rate of $35 per ounce. While other currencies were tied to the dollar, and thus indirectly to gold, they were permitted to be adjusted as necessary. This was seen as a middle ground between gold-standard rigidity and interwar insecurity. Like under the gold standard, exchange rates were stable enough to encourage international trade and investment. Unlike under the gold standard, governments other than the United States could change their currencies' values as needed, although frequent changes were frowned upon. The Bretton Woods monetary compromise kept currency values stable and currency markets open, contributing to the growth of international trade and investment while allowing national governments to pursue national policies in line with national conditions.

Like the gold standard, the Bretton Woods system relied on collaboration among its leading members. It was sustained in large part because the Western allies after World War II saw it as an important component of their economic and military alliance structure, just as the West's willingness to undertake international trade liberalization was related to its geopolitical alliance. There was thus a confluence of both economic and noneconomic interests among Western nations that facilitated cooperation. This cooperation was reminiscent of that which prevailed during the classical gold standard: under Bretton Woods, as under the gold standard, for example, it was common for the world's major national central banks to lend money to each other in times of crisis.

Under the Bretton Woods monetary system, cooperation on exchange rates was institutionalized under the auspices of the International Monetary Fund (IMF).

---

7. The term *Bretton Woods system* is sometimes used to describe the post–World War II international economic order more generally; we use the term *Bretton Woods monetary system* more narrowly to describe the currency order.

During this period, the IMF was charged with over-seeing currency relations and with providing support to countries in need of short-term assistance in keeping their exchange rates stable. The IMF made information available to members and provided standards of behavior that countries were expected to follow with respect to their currencies. The backing of the major Western financial powers, along with the institutional support of the IMF, were central to the stability of the Bretton Woods monetary system.

Eventually, however, international monetary cooperation foundered on fundamental disagreements among countries. By the early 1970s, the U.S. government was unwilling to make the sacrifices necessary to keep the dollar fixed to gold. President Richard Nixon felt that the Bretton Woods commitments constrained American economic policy more than was acceptable. The U.S. government felt itself too constrained by the rigid link between the dollar and gold, eventually breaking that link in order to give itself more monetary independence.

Representatives of 44 countries met at the Bretton Woods conference in 1944 and negotiated a new monetary system organized around the U.S. dollar. After the turbulence of the interwar years and World War II, the Bretton Woods system succeeded in bringing stability to currency values.

Today's International Monetary System

Since 1973, international monetary relations have been based on floating exchange rates among a small number of major currencies, typically those of the principal industrial and financial nations (especially the United States, Japan, Germany, and Great Britain). While today's international monetary system does not depend on explicit commitments to fixed exchange rates, its orderly functioning still requires the major national governments to work together, especially in times of crisis. When the major governments believe that exchange rates are fluctuating too wildly, they can coordinate their monetary policies to try to reduce these wide swings. At times, currency problems in developing countries have led the major financial powers to intervene to attempt to stabilize exchange rates and keep a crisis from spreading.

Different alignments of national interests, and different patterns of strategic interaction among states, help account for different international monetary outcomes. It is striking that both the gold standard and the Bretton Woods monetary system each relied in major ways on the leadership of one country—Great Britain and the United States, respectively. Nonetheless, the participation of other major financial and monetary powers was needed to keep the systems going, so that a sense of common interests was also crucial. As the collapse of both systems indicates, such participation can be difficult to sustain. It can be impeded by fundamental disagreements over how to share the costs of stabilizing the system, or by a lack of trust among governments that the commitments of others will be honored.

Today's world of floating exchange rates presents a related set of problems. While the major powers do interact, generally cooperatively, to try to avoid major monetary disturbances, exchange rates still fluctuate quite widely. Since 1980, for example, the U.S. dollar has risen and fallen by very large amounts against other major currencies. While few people in the United States seem overly worried about this volatility, in smaller countries that trade more with the rest of the world, these currency fluctuations can be widely unpopular.

The current system is not monolithic, as was the gold standard, or organized, as was Bretton Woods, but it does have some clear defining features. Countries can allow their currencies to float freely, and large countries typically do; but smaller countries appear less enthusiastic about this currency volatility, and they often link their currency to that of a larger nation or bloc. The absence of an established global monetary system has in fact led some countries to try to develop regional monetary systems that can at least stabilize exchange rates among groups of countries.

REGIONAL MONETARY ARRANGEMENTS: THE EURO

In the absence of a global agreement on stabilizing currencies, some countries have tried to work out regional arrangements. Where countries can resolve problems of cooperation, a more orderly system can be maintained regionally even as it disintegrates globally. This was the strategy pursued by most of the members of the European Union (EU) after the collapse of the Bretton Woods monetary system. Most EU countries trade and invest a great deal with one another, an arrangement that leads them to want to limit exchange rate fluctuations. Starting in 1973, they committed themselves to stabilize exchange rates among EU member countries and eventually to work toward a common currency.

But the road to the euro was not an easy one, for both domestic and interstate political reasons. Within countries, some interests were often less than enthusiastic about a common monetary policy. In practice, fixing EU exchange rates meant pegging them to the German currency (the Deutsche mark), for Germany was the largest economy in the EU and had a long-standing commitment to keeping its currency, as well as its prices, stable. In countries with higher inflation than Germany, pegging the currency to the Deutsche mark meant that governments would have to bring inflation down. This typically involved raising interest rates and implementing austerity measures, such as restraining wages and cutting government spending. In France and Italy, especially, labor unions and public employees felt that their interests would be sacrificed to the currency peg. It was not until 1985 that supporters of a fixed rate won out in these two countries. In Great Britain and Sweden, there were even fewer supporters of a fixed rate, and for most of the period these two nations kept their distance from the growing currency union. (See "What Do We Know?" on p. 318.)

At the regional level, interactions among the governments of the EU were complex and often conflictual. Because other EU currencies were fixed to the Deutsche mark, Germany's monetary policy had to be followed by other countries. This arrangement was satisfactory as long as they all agreed on the course of German policy. However, in 1991, in the aftermath of the reunification of the eastern and western parts of Germany, the German central bank was very concerned about inflation. To restrain prices, it raised interest rates very high. This measure, taken for entirely domestic reasons, forced the rest of the currency bloc to raise interest rates and thus drove most of Europe into recession. The eventual result was a currency crisis—and the decision by many EU members to break the Deutsche mark link.

Movement toward currency union continued, nonetheless, because there was a domestic consensus in most EU countries on the desirability of stabilizing currencies—even at the cost of giving up a national policy and even, in many cases, a powerful national symbol, the currency. The next move was to plan for a common currency, the euro, to be managed by a common European Central Bank (ECB). This measure appealed to countries other than Germany, because it meant that European monetary policy would be made by a European, rather than a German, central bank and would presumably take European conditions as a whole into account. Germany went along for several reasons. First, the ECB was to be based in Frankfurt, Germany, and its constitution was drafted so as to ensure that it would be very similar to the German central bank. This helped allay German fears that the new institution would stray too far from the low-inflation principles Germans preferred. Second, Germany itself wanted a reduction in currency volatility in Europe, and it was clear that other EU members would not accept a continuation of the Deutsche mark–based system. Third, the creation of the euro and the ECB was connected to a broad array of cooperative ventures among EU member governments on a wide range of issues. Just as economic cooperation between the United States and Western Europe was facilitated by their military alliance, monetary union among Western European countries was facilitated by the fact that they had come to cooperate on so many other dimensions, from trade policy and antitrust to foreign policy.

The combination of gradually emerging domestic consensus within most EU member countries and increasingly cooperative interaction among EU governments led to the adoption of the euro and its successful introduction as Europe's circulating money in 2002. As of 2009, most of the members of the EU share the euro, which is used by more than 300 million people in 17 countries. Britain and Sweden remain outside the monetary union, while Denmark has not adopted the euro but has fixed its own currency against the euro very tightly. Another dozen or so more recent and prospective members of the EU are considering joining the euro zone.

The creation of this regional currency union reflected the interests of many countries to stabilize their exchange rates in a time of turbulence. There are several other such regional currency arrangements. For example, fourteen central and west African countries share a common currency, which is pegged to the euro; and eight Caribbean island nations and territories share a common Eastern Caribbean dollar, pegged to the U.S. dollar.

Many other countries deal with concern over currency volatility by pursuing unilateral measures, such as adopting another currency (for example, Panama, Ecuador, and El Salvador use the U.S. dollar as their currency) or linking their currency to that of another country. All these strategies are aimed at achieving the desired balance between currency stability and policy independence—either on one's own, or in collaboration with other national governments. While they may succeed in reducing threats to individual countries or groups of countries, they do not address problems at the global monetary level, which some analysts regard as a matter for concern. Nor do they address the continuing problem of spreading currency crises, to which we turn in the next section of this chapter.

Who Wanted the Euro?

Currency arrangements have been central to the politics of the European Union (EU) since the 1970s. They have always been controversial, both within and among nations. Interest and controversy reached their high point in the 1990s, as most of the EU member states debated Economic and Monetary Union (EMU), the creation of a single European currency and a common European Central Bank. Within countries, there were strong supporters and opponents of currency unification everywhere. Three principal factors affected political positions on EMU: desires to reduce currency volatility, interests in maintaining national monetary independence, and concerns about EMU-induced austerity measures.

A series of studies has looked at public opinion on EMU in the 1990s, and their findings are quite consistent.[a] Some analyzed surv1eys to see what might affect individuals' attitudes toward EMU. Generally speaking, citizens with higher skills, and those whose economic activities were more involved in European trade, were more favorable to EMU. These people could expect to benefit from greater European integration and from stabilizing currencies to encourage more intra-European trade. Poorer and less well educated citizens were less enthusiastic; they were more likely to regard greater intra-European trade as a threat. By the same token, citizens who relied more on government social policies were less enthusiastic about EMU, which was seen as implying more constraints on government social spending.

There were also differences across countries. Of course, countries more integrated into European trade were more favorable to EMU. Where a country had been afflicted by high inflation, EMU was more generally welcomed as a way of helping to bring inflation down.

But EMU also implicated feelings about national pride and identity; after all, a national currency is often a powerful symbol of the nation itself. One study made use of an interesting comparison to evaluate this.[b] In 2000 and 2003, Denmark and Sweden, respectively, held national referendums on joining the euro zone. Denmark was already locked into a very fixed peg against the euro, so that for it the choice was largely symbolic, replacing the Danish krone with the euro.[c] In Sweden, the choice was much more meaningful: Sweden had remained outside of EMU, so that joining the euro zone would have meant both giving up the national currency (the krona) *and* joining the euro zone for the first time. Researchers surveyed voters to evaluate the role of national identity and personal self-interest in their attitudes toward the euro. (The referendums failed in both cases, by the way.)

In Sweden, there were important economic components to attitudes toward joining the euro zone. As elsewhere, individuals whose jobs or skills made them more oriented toward European trade and investment favored the euro. However, nationalistic sentiment mattered as well: at least some of the opposition to the euro was motivated not by economic concerns but by fears of a curtailment of national sovereignty. This makes sense, as there were real economic and symbolic components to the decision faced by Sweden.

In Denmark, individuals seem to have voted almost entirely in line with their views on Danish identity and autonomy. Those concerned to maintain the country's sovereignty were opposed to giving up the currency in favor of the euro. This, too, makes sense. There were no effective economic implications to adopting the euro (after all, Denmark was already a de facto member of the euro zone), so voters' economic characteristics played no apparent role in their decision. Given these findings, one can say that the Danes' views on the euro largely tracked their broader sense of national pride or identity.

As a dozen or more countries face the prospect of joining the euro zone over the next decade, these domestic political considerations will continue to significantly affect the character of the world's largest and most important currency union. (The map shows the EMU's members as of 2009.) ■

---

a. Matthew Gabel, "Divided Opinion, Common Currency: The Political Economy of Public Support for EMU," in *The Political Economy of European Monetary Unification,* ed. Barry Eichengreen and Jeffry Frieden (Boulder: Westview Press, 2000); Karl Kaltenthaler and Christopher Anderson, "Europeans and Their Money: Explaining Public Support for the Common European Currency," *European Journal of Political Research* 40 (2001): 139–70; Susan Banducci, Jeffrey Karp, and Peter Loedel, "The Euro, Economic Interests, and Multi-Level Governance: Examining Support for the Common Currency," *European Journal of Political Research* 40 (2003): 685–703.

b. Joseph Jupille and David Leblang, "Voting for Change: Calculation, Community, and Euro Referendums," *International Organization* 61 (Fall 2007): 763–82.

c. Legally, Denmark was a member of the Exchange Rate Mechanism II, and it committed to holding its currency within a 2.25 percent band around the euro. In practice, the two currencies were tightly fixed.

ICELAND

Countries using the euro*

ATLANTIC
OCEAN

NORWAY

SWEDEN

FINLAND

DENMARK

ESTONIA

RUSSIA

IRELAND

LATVIA

LITHUANIA

GREAT
BRITAIN

NETHERLANDS

BELARUS

BELGIUM

GERMANY

POLAND

LUX.

CZECH
REPUBLIC

UKRAINE

FRANCE

SWITZ.

AUSTRIA

SLOVAKIA

HUNGARY

MOLD.

SLOVENIA

CROATIA

ROMANIA

PORTUGAL

BOS.-
HERZ.

SERBIA

SPAIN

ITALY

BULGARIA

MONT.

MAC.

ALBANIA

GREECE

TURKEY

*Several other countries use the euro either formally or informally, but are not part of the European Union.

What Happens When Currencies Collapse?

Even those who pay little attention to international monetary affairs notice the occasional spectacular currency crises, such as those that affected Europe in 1992–1993, East Asia in 1997–1998, or Argentina in 2001. Indeed, currency crises have been a frequent feature of the modern international political economy. They are one of the more dramatic effects of national currency policy. Currency crises have been closely related to the financial and debt crises discussed in Chapter 7 and have been associated with all-encompassing economic and political upheavals.

Currency crises usually result when government exchange rate commitments are not fully credible. In this sense, they are analytically comparable to crises in military affairs that result when the threats and promises of governments are not fully credible (see Chapter 3). In the case of currency affairs, when private economic actors do not believe the promises of a government with respect to its exchange rate, they can react in ways that cause a major crisis.

EFFECTS ON GOVERNMENT

Up to now, we have assumed that when a government fixes its exchange rate, it stays fixed until the government decides, on its own, to alter the arrangement. But we also know that it can be economically and politically difficult for a government to sustain a fixed currency, because a government with a fixed exchange rate may not be able to undertake monetary policies desirable to address national economic conditions. This was the problem in Argentina in 2001, when the tight dollar-peso link made it virtually impossible for the Argentine government to reverse a three-year recession. In these circumstances, expectations that the government will not be able to sustain its commitment to a fixed rate can create concern among economic actors about the future course of the currency. And this concern can feed on itself until it becomes a panic.

A typical currency crisis follows a fairly predictable trajectory. In order to reap the benefits of a fixed currency, the government commits itself to a particular fixed exchange rate—a peg to gold, the dollar, or the euro at a specific rate. This move presumably has all the advantages we have identified, but it also imposes costs. Over time, for some reason, the government faces economic and political difficulties in maintaining a fixed exchange rate. Perhaps the local economy is doing poorly, or exporters are clamoring for a devaluation that will make their goods more attractive abroad, or the country's main exports are losing markets to competitors.

As the government faces increasing pressures to devalue the currency, people begin to doubt the credibility of the government's commitment to keep the exchange rate stable. This unease gives investors strong reasons to sell the nation's currency. After all, nobody wants to hold on to an asset, or a currency, that is going to lose value. So investors at home and abroad start converting the local currency into more reliable foreign currency. The government usually continues to assure the public that the exchange rate will be maintained, in an effort to keep people from selling the currency. But as doubts about the government's credibility grow, more and more people may go to the banks to exchange their local currency for more reliable dollars or euros.

The government itself is torn. On the one hand, there are powerful domestic interests in favor of keeping the currency's exchange rate where it is. Companies and others that have borrowed in a foreign currency, for example, are anxious to make sure the national currency is not devalued. For those with foreign currency debts, a devaluation would increase the cost of their debt by requiring more of the national currency to buy the foreign currency they must use to repay the debt. Also, a devaluation would reduce national purchasing power—an unpopular move with consumers, who would have to pay more for many goods as a result. On the other hand, there are good reasons to allow the currency's value to drop: it might alleviate the economic distress and help national farmers and manufacturers compete with foreigners. At the same time, sustaining the fixed rate can be very difficult. The government would have to take some action to convince people to hold on to the national currency rather than buying dollars or some other foreign currency. Most commonly, a government trying to convince investors and others to hold on to the national money has to raise interest rates in order to make the local currency more attractive—and raising interest rates is likely to exacerbate the country's economic difficulties.

Eventually, the government runs out of time, money, or patience, and the currency is devalued. When the currency drops in value, this may have a positive effect by helping national producers compete with foreigners. But it also usually has some very powerful negative effects. Anyone in the country with substantial foreign currency debts—including the government—faces serious trouble. As the local currency drops, the burden of foreign currency debt rises. In early 2002, the Argentine peso dropped from 1 to the dollar to 3 to the dollar in two months, so that a 1 million dollar debt went from being a 1 million peso debt to a 3 million peso debt. In these circumstances, large numbers of debtors go bankrupt, which in turn leads many banks to fail as their customers cannot pay their debts. A recession almost always ensues, which can even turn into a deep financial and debt crisis. Indeed, most currency crises eventually turn into broader banking crises. This scenario has been repeated dozens, perhaps hundreds, of times, from the nineteenth century through the present in developed and developing countries.

INTERNATIONAL REPERCUSSIONS

The international aspect of currency crises can be particularly troubling. Currency crises can be transmitted from one country to another, as uncertainties about one country feed uncertainties about others. Investors looking at countries that are economically or politically similar may believe that the collapse of one country's currency portends the collapse of others like it. Throughout the nineteenth century, currency crises (often originating in the United States, then a heavily indebted developing country) had repercussions all over the industrialized world. When, in 1931, Austria was hit by a currency and banking crisis, the resulting fears soon affected neighboring Hungary, leading to a follow-on crisis there. Then the crisis hit Germany, then the rest of Central Europe, then Great Britain; eventually, most of Europe was brought down by a "contagious" currency crisis that almost certainly deepened the Great Depression.

In the past 30 years, there have been many rounds of currency crises. The first was associated with the less developed countries' sovereign debt defaults of the early and middle 1980s. In this case, the currency crises followed, rather than led, the larger financial crisis. As country after country found itself unable to sustain its currency's value in the face of massive debt problems, currencies collapsed as well. Since the early 1990s, it has become more common for currency crises to be the source of broader financial and economic difficulties.

Case Study: Europe

One of the first major modern currency crises affected European countries that were moving toward currency union. In this process, most EU countries had pegged their currencies to that of Germany, the Deutsche mark. In 1991, the German central bank raised interest rates quickly and steeply to keep prices from rising after the eastern and western parts of the country had been unified. This forced other European countries whose currencies were tied to the Deutsche mark to raise their interest rates as well, a move that shoved them into a recession made in Germany. German policy confronted European governments with a stark choice between continued membership in the Deutsche mark bloc, on the one hand, and avoiding a recession, on the other. The rest of Europe was already mired in slow growth and double-digit unemployment, and there was little enthusiasm for more austerity measures that would slow inflation but also reduce wages and public spending.

In the summer of 1992, investors and currency traders began anticipating that Great Britain and Italy would not maintain their currencies' pegs to the Deutsche mark. Investors sold off their holdings of these currencies, which intensified speculation that the pound and the lira would be devalued. The British and Italian governments pushed interest rates up to try to convince investors to hold on to their pounds and lira, but eventually the cost seemed extreme and both devalued their currencies. Foreign exchange traders starting selling off other currencies in the months that followed. Governments tried to hold on to the link to the Deutsche mark (at one point, the Swedish central bank pushed interest rates to 500 percent), but the cost was too high. Eventually, six other European nations followed Britain and Italy in devaluing their currencies. The damage to monetary unification was repaired quickly and effectively enough to move forward with plans for the euro. But it was clear that even the world's richest nations were not immune from currency crises that could force governments to devalue and change policies. The perception began to grow that there might be a common interest in trying to limit the negative effects of currency crises, as they could be transmitted from nation to nation.

Case Study: Mexico

Within a year, this point was brought home to Mexico. With NAFTA in effect, the Mexican government wanted to hold the peso steady against the U.S. dollar. And in the run-up to a hotly contested presidential election campaign, the government wanted to keep the peso strong and Mexican incomes high. But in January 1994 a rebellion broke out in southern Mexico, and in March one of the ruling party's leading presidential candidates was assassinated. This worried investors, who came to believe that the government's position was shaky. As the election year of 1994 wore on, the government struggled to maintain its commitment to the peso, both to uphold its reputation and because the strong peso increased the purchasing power of Mexican consumers.

But currency traders did not believe that the government could hold to its promises. Investors became more and more skittish, and the narrowness of the victory won by the ruling Partido Revolucionario Institucional (PRI), or Institutional Revolutionary Party, in the August 1994 presidential election was not reassuring. The PRI's secretary general was assassinated in September, which further scared investors, who worried that the new government would be too unstable to commit credibly to the currency peg. As the new government took office in December, currency traders sensed they could take a "one-way bet" against the peso: if it was devalued, they won; if it wasn't, they didn't lose. As the speculators sold off the currency, the government tried desperately to keep the currency stable; but a few days before Christmas 1994, it floated the peso—which promptly sank. Yet another government had been forced to devalue its currency.

When currencies collapse, the crisis often spreads to other parts of the economy, with significant political repercussions. The events surrounding the collapse of the Mexican peso in 1994 forced a series of government leaders from office as the economic situation worsened. Economic minister Jaime Serra Puche resigned a few days after the government devalued the peso.

Following the common pattern of currency crises leading to financial crises, Mexico was next hit by a crippling banking crisis as a result of the currency collapse. When the peso was strong, many banks and companies borrowed heavily in dollars. The devaluation of the peso triggered mass bankruptcies as the real cost of dollar debts soared. The peso dropped in the space of a month from about 30 cents to about 15 cents, so the real burden on a Mexican company of a $1 million foreign debt doubled from about 3.3 million to 6.6 million pesos. Many indebted firms collapsed, followed by their domestic bankers, and within weeks the country was in the throes of a financial panic. The country's output dropped by 6 percent, and inflation soared above 50 percent. The fallout of the Mexican crisis affected all of Latin America, which plunged into recession.

Case Study: East Asia

The next round of currency and financial crises was even more dramatic. In 1997, the East Asian economies were booming, as about $50 billion a year flowed into East Asia from global financial markets, with tens of billions more in direct investment from multinational corporations. The region seemed well on the way to rapid economic development. But there were a few warning signs of slowing growth, and a bubble in housing and financial markets. By 1996 and early 1997, exports were lagging, inflation was rising, and banks were taking on more and more debt. Soon, investors began to anticipate devaluations and started selling off East Asian currencies.

In a now-familiar spiral, the movement away from the region's currencies became a flood, then a stampede, then a panic. The sell-off spread from Thailand and the Philippines to Indonesia and Malaysia, then to Taiwan and Korea. The size and efficiency of international financial markets seemed to facilitate the attacks by making it remarkably easy for investors to speculate against government attempts to defend their currencies. Joseph Stiglitz, then chief economist at the World Bank, gave an example of the process:

> Assume a speculator goes to a Thai bank, borrows 24 billion baht, which, at the original exchange rate, can be converted into $1 billion. A week later the exchange rate falls; instead of there being 24 baht to the dollar, there are now 40 baht to the dollar. He takes $600 million, converting it back to baht, getting 24 billion baht to repay the loan. The remaining $400 million is his profit—a tidy return for one week's work, and the investment of little of his own money. . . . As perceptions that a devaluation is imminent grow, the chance to make money becomes irresistible and speculators from around the world pile in to take advantage of the situation.[8]

As more and more investors did what Stiglitz suggests, within weeks of the initial attack the currencies of Korea, the Philippines, and Malaysia had dropped by 40 percent, that of Thailand by 50 percent, that of Indonesia by 80 percent. The political fallout was also intense: the government of Thailand fell, and after more than 30 years in power the Suharto dictatorship in Indonesia collapsed.

The dramatic economic and political effects of the crises in Europe, Mexico, Argentina, and East Asia, and of others in Turkey, Russia, Brazil, and elsewhere, caught the world's attention. So, too, did the fact that currency and banking crises could spread quickly from country to country, as they did in East Asia in 1997–1998. This realization led many of the world's economic leaders to see these currency crises as threats to the international monetary order and the world economy more generally. One nation's currency collapse could be transmitted to others, to an entire region, or to the whole world. Currency and financial instability had, after all, lengthened and deepened the Great Depression of the 1930s, and the world might not be better prepared to handle a truly major crisis in the twenty-first century than it had been in 1929. The currency crises of the 1990s led many to believe that in a globalized financial system, such attacks had the potential to destabilize the entire world economy. The "Controversy" box on page 325 explores the debate over what, if anything, should be done to prevent them.

CONTAINING CURRENCY CRISES

Concern that currency crises can have broad international effects make attempts to counter them something of an international public good. Thus, major governments have a common interest in containing such crises—although, as with all public goods, there is often conflict over how to distribute the cost of providing

---

8. Joseph Stiglitz, *Globalization and Its Discontents* (New York: Norton, 2002), 94–95.

CONTROVERSY

Should Currency Traders Be Permitted to "Attack" Weak Currencies?

In summer and early fall of 1997, Malaysia faced the gravest economic crisis in its history. Trouble had started when the currency of Thailand came under speculative pressures in early summer. On July 2, after months of desperate measures to maintain the value of the baht, Thai authorities devalued the currency. Within a few days, the Philippines, Malaysia, Singapore, and Indonesia faced attacks on their currencies; eventually Vietnam, Hong Kong, Taiwan, and South Korea joined the list of victims. By September 1997, all of East and Southeast Asia was engulfed in a financial crisis that threatened to reverse decades of economic progress. In a scorching speech at the annual meeting of the World Bank and the International Monetary Fund, the prime minister of Malaysia, Mahathir bin Mohamad, blamed international currency traders. "Society must be protected from unscrupulous profiteers," he raged.[a] International financier George Soros, whom Mahathir had previously singled out as a key culprit, lashed back the following day. Soros called the suggestion of a trading ban "so inappropriate that it does not deserve serious consideration," and he labeled Mahathir "a menace to his own country."[b]

Most people—including Mahathir in calmer moments—agree that international currency markets are, on balance, highly beneficial. By supplying liquidity, currency trade greases the wheels of international trade and investment, and the market signals sent by speculators provide a helpful check on unsustainable inflationary policies within domestic economies. The controversy is chiefly over the way in which the benefits and burdens of this generally useful institution are distributed across distinct interests, both within and across countries. Those who join Mahathir in condemning the current system make two main complaints. The first is that currency speculation can result in economic disaster in developing countries, especially for the poor. Devaluation allegedly spurred by speculation increases the prices of foreign goods, bankrupts debtors, and can cause a societywide recession. The second complaint is that in their

current form, international currency markets allow speculators to ride roughshod over the policy autonomy of developing nations. Not only do speculators have the power to decimate national budgets and disrupt economic planning, but they also appear to use that power to favor particular economic measures. Critics charge that it is only when economies violate the IMF's core tenets of liberalization, deregulation, balanced budgets, and privatization that currency speculators, sensing imminent trouble, step in.

Defenders of the current currency market system reject both of these criticisms. To begin with, they claim that currency speculation is hardly the chief cause of currency crises. In most cases, they argue, speculation simply hastens or exacerbates a crisis that would have happened anyway due to underlying domestic problems. Soros claimed, for instance, that Malaysia's crisis stemmed from an excessive expansion of credit, and that Mahathir was using Soros "as a scapegoat to cover up his own failure" to deal with that issue.[c] Second, defenders argue, the suggestion that international financiers intentionally mold the domestic policy of foreign nations and willfully impoverish the poor is overblown. Traders in international currency are no different from traders in other goods: their motivation is simply to realize profits through market exchange. Defenders characteristically finish by reemphasizing the idea that international currency markets are not solely of benefit to international financiers, but promote the interests of most everyone—including, ultimately, the poor.

How should we evaluate this debate? Soros's defenders may be right that individual traders, pursuing their own interests within an established system, are not necessarily doing anything wrong. However, Mahathir is arguably equally right to question the aggregate consequences of those individual actions—the product of their interactions. If the rapid flow of large amounts of money in and out of a country does not alone cause a crisis, it may nonetheless aggravate one, especially in the case of emerging economies such as Malaysia's. This pairing of individually rational actions with collectively undesirable effects suggests to some observers the need for institutional reform. ■

---

a. "Premier of Malaysia Spars with Currency Dealer," *New York Times*, September 22, 1997.
b. Ibid.

c. Ibid.

---

such containment. This challenge has given rise to complex interactions in which governments, private investors, and international institutions both cooperate and contend over attempts to limit the damage caused by currency crises.

Indeed, over the past 20 years, governments of the major financial centers and the leading international financial institutions have often cooperated to try to slow the spread of currency crises. The IMF, other international institutions, and creditor governments have often mobilized tens of billions of dollars to try to support governments facing a currency crisis. The reasons for major governments to cooperate in the face of currency crises are closely related to the reasons for cooperation to address sovereign debt crises, as discussed in Chapter 7. Cooperation among national governments can help avoid, or mitigate the international impact of, currency crises; indeed, developed-country governments and the IMF have spent hundreds of billions of dollars since 1980 in attempts to control these crises.

However, such cooperation has not always been easy to organize and sustain. As with all public goods, there are incentives for each government to free ride and hope that other governments will pay the price of stabilizing the monetary order. Even more, many people believe that it is not a good idea to spend billions to support a failed or failing currency: such an effort may prop up undeserving governments and banks. This highlights the fact that currency crises can be controversial in domestic politics: governments are often blamed for allowing the crisis to take place, for not dealing with it effectively, or for inappropriately setting the currency in the first place.

Supporters have regarded these currency crisis interventions as striking examples of international cooperation to sustain the global monetary order, and with it the global economy more generally, with a quick response to avoid the proliferation of contagious crises. But critics have charged that taxpayers were being forced to bail out foolish investors and overextended governments, encouraging a continuation of irresponsible government and private behavior. The clash has largely pitted contending interests against one another (see Chapter 7 for similar debates over financial bailouts), and it is sure to continue. The mix of common interests and contentious issues ensures that currency crises, and controversies over them, will continue to plague many currencies and globalized financial markets.

Conclusion: Currencies, Conflict, and Cooperation

Argentines are not alone in learning from experience that currency policy can make a significant difference to economic and political life. Over the past 20 years, billions of people in dozens of countries have experienced both the positive and negative effects of national currency policies. The exchange rate is controversial within countries because its impact differs among groups, firms, regions, and individuals with contending interests. There are many who benefit if the currency is fixed, and others who are harmed. For every firm that gains as a currency depreciates, there is another that loses. This clash of interests, mediated through national political institutions, determines national attitudes toward the exchange rate.

International monetary relations, too, have a profound impact on international economic and political affairs. There is a reason that the classical gold standard and the Bretton Woods monetary system gave their names to entire economic eras: the ordering principles of these currency regimes were central to their respective international economies. Without functioning international monetary arrangements, global economic activity would be immensely difficult.

Governments have powerful reasons to collaborate in devising international monetary arrangements, but they also have significant interests that conflict. Inasmuch as an international monetary regime is a public good, governments have strong incentives to free ride and let others provide it; they also have strong reasons to try to make sure it is provided; and they have reasons to want the regime to be organized in ways favorable to themselves. Such a mix of incentives for cooperation and incentives to bargain hard characterizes the politics of international monetary relations today, as it has for centuries. This can be seen through the currency policy issues that are likely to preoccupy national governments, and the world community, over the coming years.

The first contentious issue has to do with the overall structure and functioning of the international monetary system, and cooperation among the world's major financial and monetary powers. Many scholars believe that more organized collaboration among major governments is desirable to avoid future problems and crises. Certainly, there is a desire among many governments to collaborate in devising a new monetary order. Yet, there are also powerful interests in conflict, as governments disagree about the desirable characteristics of such an order.

In the absence of global agreement on international monetary relations, many countries in specific geographical regions continue to devise regional currency arrangements. The euro zone is expanding to incorporate new members of the European Union in eastern, central, and southern Europe, and many countries in Africa and the Middle East have already linked their currencies to the euro or have plans to do so. There have been similar proposals for informal or formal currency unions in Latin America, North America, and parts of Asia. As many governments find these regional proposals an appealing way to reduce currency instability, some observers have suggested that we may be heading toward a world of currency blocs: an expanded euro zone eventually encompassing all of Europe, much of the Middle East and Africa, and parts of Asia; a dollar zone in the Western Hemisphere; and an East Asian currency area. The future of such arrangements depends both on the interests governments have in developing them and on their interactions to pursue their monetary goals. Whether national governments come together on the global level to forge a new international monetary regime, or devise regional arrangements such as the euro, international monetary relations will profoundly shape the world economy.

Reviewing Interests, Interactions, and Institutions

INTERESTS	INTERACTIONS	INSTITUTIONS
There are conflicts of interest within countries over whether the exchange rate should be fixed, floating, or something in between. Generally, internationally oriented economic actors favor a fixed currency, while domestically oriented actors favor a floating currency to allow for an independent monetary policy.	At the international level, there is often cooperation to sustain a workable international monetary order. This cooperation includes collaboration among governments to assist each other in difficult times.	The International Monetary Fund (IMF) was established to oversee the Bretton Woods system. As the system fell, the IMF turned more toward sovereign debt management.
There are also conflicts of interest within countries over the desirable level of the exchange rate. Consumers like a strong currency: producers of goods that compete with foreigners prefer a weak currency.	There is also disagreement over how to manage the division of adjustment among countries. Each country would prefer others to bear most of the costs of supporting international monetary arrangements.	In recent years, the IMF has been involved in attempts to limit the international effects of currency crises in developing countries.
Internationally, countries share a common interest in a generally accepted international monetary regime in order to facilitate international trade, investment, and payments. However, there are powerful incentives to free ride and strong desires to craft such a regime to serve each nation's particular interests.	Some national governments, frustrated by disagreements at the global level, have decided to work out smaller-scale regional monetary arrangements, up to and including such currency unions as that of the euro.	Contemporary global monetary relations are not strongly institutionalized. However, there are significant regional currency institutions—such as the European Central Bank, which manages the euro.
	Governments have collaborated, but also clashed over, attempts to cooperate to reduce the harm done by currency crises.	

Key Terms

exchange rate, p. 300
appreciate, p. 300
depreciate, p. 300
devalue, p. 300
monetary policy, p. 301
fixed exchange rate, p. 302

gold standard, p. 302
floating exchange rate, p. 302
Bretton Woods monetary system, p. 302
adjustable peg, p. 302
international monetary regime, p. 309

For Further Reading

Eichengreen, Barry. *Globalizing Capital: A History of the International Monetary System*, 2nd ed. Princeton: Princeton University Press, 2008. Presents a general historical survey of the economics and politics of the international monetary order.

Eichengreen, Barry. *Golden Fetters: The Gold Standard and the Great Depression, 1919–1939.* New York: Oxford University Press, 1992. Serves as a classic analysis of how the gold standard collapsed in the interwar period.

Eichengreen, Barry, and Marc Flandreau, eds. *The Gold Standard in Theory and History.* New York: Routledge, 1997. Collects important articles on the economics and politics of the classical gold standard.

Eichengreen, Barry, and Jeffry Frieden, eds. *The Political Economy of European Monetary Unification*, 2nd ed. Boulder: Westview Press, 2001. Presents a collection of articles analyzing how and why European countries created the euro.

James, Harold. *International Monetary Cooperation Since Bretton Woods.* Oxford: IMF and Oxford University Press, 1996. Surveys the evolution of the international monetary system from the end of World War Two through the rise of the system of floating exchange rates, up to the mid 1990s.

Kenen, Peter, and Ellen Meade. *Regional Monetary Integration.* Cambridge: Cambridge University Press, 2008. Summarizes and analyzes international experience with the creation of regional monetary unions.

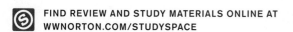 **FIND REVIEW AND STUDY MATERIALS ONLINE AT WWNORTON.COM/STUDYSPACE**

CHAPTER 9

Development:
Causes of the Wealth
and Poverty of Nations

Despite the overall growth of the world economy in recent decades, billions of people around the world live in poverty. For example, citizens of Zambia are significantly worse off today than they were when Zambia achieved independence in 1964. The average Zambian lives on the equivalent of about $600 per year.

Why are some countries rich and others poor? How do international politics and economics affect development?

I n 1964, the African nation of Zambia and the East Asian country of South Korea were at roughly equivalent levels of development. Indeed, when Zambia achieved its independence in 1964, its prospects appeared far more promising than those of South Korea. Zambia was rich in copper, and its newly elected president, Kenneth Kaunda, was popular at home and respected abroad for his intelligence and seriousness of purpose. South Korea, in contrast, had no resources to speak of, was ruled by a despised and ridiculed military dictatorship, and depended heavily on American aid that was being cut back.

Four decades later, the two countries could not be more different. The economy of Zambia has failed miserably. By the mid-1990s, the average Zambian had barely half the income he did at independence. Kaunda had been voted out of office in disgrace, political unrest was rife, and food riots were widespread. The government's failures were compounded by the AIDS epidemic that was sweeping throughout Africa. In 2008, Zambia has one of the lowest standards of living in the world. Life expectancy is barely 40 years, one-third of the adult population is illiterate, half of the population does not have access to adequate water or sanitation, and there is not even one telephone per 100 people.[1] Today, Zambia is a developmental disaster.

Meanwhile, South Korea has become a modern industrial nation. In 1996, the Organization for Economic Cooperation and Development (OECD) recognized Korea's progress and made the country a member of this club of rich countries. South Korea had "graduated" from the developing to the developed world. As of 2008, it has a standard

If Everyone Wants Development, Why Is It So Hard to Achieve?
▶ Geographic Location
▶ Domestic Factors
▶ Domestic Institutions

Are Rich Countries Responsible for the Problems of the Developing World?
▶ Did Colonialism Hamper Development?
▶ Is the International Economy Biased against LDCs?
▶ Are International Institutions Biased against LDCs?

Development Policies and Development Politics
▶ Import Substituting Industrialization
▶ Export-Oriented Industrialization
▶ The Turn toward Globalization
▶ Attempts to Remedy the Bias of International Institutions
▶ Is Foreign Aid an Answer?
▶ Globalization and Its Discontents

Conclusion: Toward Global Developments
▶ Addressing International Factors
▶ Addressing Domestic Factors

---

1. Data from the United Nations Human Development Reports, available at http://hdr.undp.org/en/ (accessed 11/26/08).

of living comparable to that of Spain or New Zealand. Life expectancy is 78 years, adult literacy is practically universal, virtually everyone has access to modern sanitation and water, and there are 1.3 telephones per person. Although the two nations had similar starting points over 40 years ago, today South Korea is an industrialized, developed nation, while Zambia is desperately poor.

This comparison illustrates two realities of contemporary economic development. First, billions of people live in conditions of poverty. For example, average incomes in Africa today are comparable to what they were in western Europe 200 years ago; African life expectancy and literacy rates are similar to those of western Europe 100 years ago. In sub-Saharan Africa, nearly one-third of all children under age five are malnourished, fewer than one-third of children of secondary school age attend school; and barely half the population has access to clean water.

Second, developmental experiences have varied widely, and there have been some striking successes in the last 50 years. In 1960, countries such as South Korea and Taiwan were dismally poor—poorer than most of Africa. Today, these two nations are advanced industrial countries with per capita incomes comparable to those in parts of western Europe. And the world's two most populous countries, China and India—home to over one-third of the world's people—have been growing very rapidly for over 25 years. China's living standards are today over five times higher than they were in 1980; India's are three times higher. The differences among developing nations are in fact enormous: for example, the gap between Latin America and sub-Saharan Africa is substantially bigger than the gap between Latin America and the industrialized nations.

In fact, the proportion of the world's population living in abject poverty has declined since the 1980s. Most international organizations use an international absolute poverty line equivalent to about $1.50 a day per person in today's dollars, taking into account differences in the cost of living across countries. By this measure,

In the 1960s, a majority of South Koreans lived in poverty. Today, South Korea has a strong economy and a standard of living comparable to that of western Europe. Understanding the domestic and international factors that lead some countries to develop successfully and others to fail is one of the most compelling endeavors in the field of political economy.

while more than 40 percent of the developing world's population lived in absolute poverty in 1980, today the proportion is about 20 percent.[2] This improvement is largely the result of successful development in China and India. In 1981, fully 64 percent of China's people lived in absolute poverty; today, the percentage is under 10 percent. In India, the decline was a less remarkable but still impressive drop from 55 to 30 percent. Given that these two countries account for nearly 2.5 billion people—almost half the developing world's total population—this explains most of the progress.

Nonetheless, the stark fact remains that some 6 billion of the total world population of about 7 billion live in poor countries.[3] While not everyone in poor countries is poor, these nations have an average income per person of just one-quarter that of the rich countries (those in western Europe and North America, as well as Japan, Australia, and New Zealand). Most of the world's people are poor.

The continued poverty of much of the world's population leads us to ask why so many countries are poor. Equally important are questions of comparison: Why have the experiences of less developed countries differed so widely? Why have some countries developed successfully, while others have stagnated? Within these questions lie related issues about the relationship between developing countries and international politics: How has the international political economy affected the development of poor nations? Has it been a hindrance or a help to them? This chapter makes several points about the politics and economics of development.

CORE OF THE ANALYSIS

▶ Although everyone in poor countries prefers more development to less, individuals and groups within countries may have conflicting interests with respect to development policy. The pursuit of private interests by powerful groups can impede the adoption of measures that would spur economic growth.

▶ Domestic social and political institutions can have a major impact on how these conflicts of interest affect development. They can either empower or overcome special interest groups that stand in the way of development. They can either facilitate or impede the ability of actors to cooperate to promote government policies conducive to economic growth.

▶ At the international level, rich and poor nations generally have a common interest in accelerating the economic growth of the developing world. However, there have been many instances of rich countries supporting policies and institutions that disfavor less developed countries.

▶ Successful economic growth requires that a country overcome both the domestic obstacles posed by interests and institutions that are detrimental to development, and the international impediments created by conflicts of interest with wealthy nations, which can draw on superior reserves of economic and political power.

---

2. See Pranab Bardhan, *Globalization, Inequality, and Poverty* (Washington, DC: Inter-American Development Bank, 2006). The best source on the issue, from which most of these data are taken, is Branko Milanovic, *Worlds Apart: Global and International Inequality 1950–2000* (Princeton: Princeton University Press, 2005).

3. Observers use a variety of terms for these countries. During the Cold War, it was common to refer to them as *third world* countries, to distinguish them from the capitalist *first world* and the communist *second world*. Today, it is more common to use the label *less developed country* (LDC) or, more optimistically, *developing country*. Another convention is to refer to these countries collectively as *the South* because they tend to be located geographically to the south of the richer countries. We will use some of these terms interchangeably.

If Everyone Wants Development, Why Is It So Hard to Achieve?

Less developed countries (LDCs) want to develop, and few people would deny them the opportunity to do so. However, steps to improve a nation's developmental prospects sometimes threaten the interests of certain actors at home or abroad. Recognizing this fact, we can identify three prominent approaches that explain why such a universally accepted goal appears to be so difficult to attain. These approaches consider geography, domestic factors, such as a nation's political economy, and domestic institutions.

GEOGRAPHIC LOCATION

One view is that the geographical realities of some countries impede their growth. The fact that the world's tropical regions are generally poor, while its temperate regions are generally rich, suggests that geography and climate affect development, directly or indirectly. There is little doubt that such factors play some part in explaining patterns of development. Landlocked countries, regions with diseases that are difficult to control or cure, and areas that are very far from major markets for their goods are all at a developmental disadvantage—and this disadvantage was probably greater in an earlier era, when medical knowledge was limited and transportation and communications costs were much higher. By virtue of weather and disease, tropical environments in particular may be less conducive to urbanization and industrialization than temperate zones. Some scholars ascribe a substantial portion of the developmental problems of such tropical regions as sub-Saharan Africa, for example, to geography itself.[4]

But geographical determinism cannot be the whole story, as there is a great deal of variation among countries within the same regions. Indeed, if we compare LDCs with very similar geographical characteristics, we find that some have done extremely well while others have done very poorly. (See "What Shaped Our World?" on p. 335.) While the climate and geography of a nation shape its development, they do so by way of their impact on the people, social structures, politics, and policies of the nation.

Two other approaches dominate attempts to explain patterns of development. One focuses on domestic factors, another on domestic institutions. International factors are relevant as well, and we return to them below. However, the fact that there is so much variation among countries that are similarly situated, and that face similar international conditions, implies that domestic factors and institutions are crucially important.

---

4. For prominent statements on geography and development, see Jared Diamond, *Guns, Germs, and Steel* (New York: Norton, 1997); David Bloom and Jeffrey Sachs, "Geography, Demography, and Economic Growth in Africa," *Brookings Papers on Economic Activity* 2 (1998): 207–95; Jeffrey Sachs, Andrew Mellinger, an d John Gallup, "The Geography of Poverty and Wealth," *Scientific American*, March 2001.

Country Pairs

It is illuminating to compare countries that began their modern developmental experience under similar conditions, especially when such countries now diverge substantially. The divergences suggest that domestic factors play a key role in development paths, and they raise important questions about what leads one country to do so much better than another. Some exemplary pairs are described below.

1. *Zambia and Botswana.* These two southern African countries gained their independence from Great Britain in 1964 and 1966, respectively. Both countries are landlocked, and both have substantial mineral wealth. At independence, Zambia was much richer than Botswana, perhaps twice as rich.[a] The new Zambian government took over the country's copper mines from private owners, discriminated against the country's farmers, and focused most of its spending on providing benefits to its supporters. The new Botswanan government, on the other hand, encouraged private investment in the country's natural resources (mainly diamonds), supported agriculture and ranching, and spent heavily on such public goods as education. Today, Botswana is a thriving, democratic nation with a per capita GDP of about $6,000; Zambia is an economically, politically, and socially troubled country whose per capita GDP is about $600, one-tenth that of its neighbor.

2. *Burma (Myanmar) and Thailand.* At the time of its independence from Great Britain in 1948, Burma (currently, and controversially, called Myanmar by its rulers) was the wealthiest nation in Southeast Asia. It was a major exporter of rice and had substantial other natural resources. Its neighbor Thailand had not been a direct colony and was also relatively prosperous. Burma soon opted for an extremely closed economy with severe limits on foreign investment and trade, while Thailand chose the export-oriented path pioneered by countries in East Asia. The results were striking: Burma has stagnated and regressed, while Thailand has been one of the world's faster-growing newly industrializing countries. Today, per capita income in Thailand, at nearly $10,000 per year, is about six times that of Burma, estimated at $1,700 per year. Thailand's capital, Bangkok (pictured below), has become a significant international business hub.

3. *North Korea and South Korea.* After World War II, the former Japanese colony of Chosen (Korea) was divided between Soviet and American occupiers, a division that hardened after the Korean War (1950–1953). Communist North Korea (officially, the Democratic People's Republic of Korea) was for some time regarded as the economic powerhouse of the peninsula, having a more impressive industrial base. But by the 1970s, South Korea (officially, the Republic of Korea) was one of the fastest-growing countries in the world, while North Korea stagnated. North Korean economic performance worsened as it kept its system of self-sufficient centralized state planning, even as China and the Soviet Union moved toward developing markets at home and abroad. Over the 1990s, while South Korea "graduated" to developed status and joined the OECD (a club of rich nations), North Korea collapsed into famine and economic catastrophe. Today, North Korea's standard of living is widely believed to be one of the world's lowest, while South Korea's has surpassed that of some western European countries.

There are many reasons why one country in each of these pairs has done so much better than the other, most having to do with government policies and domestic politics. The principal purpose of this simple comparison is not to evaluate the sources of these different economic paths, but to demonstrate that countries with similar starting points, and facing similar international conditions, can go in very different directions. This itself is strong evidence that domestic factors are powerful—albeit not exclusive—determinants of national development. ■

---

a. Real gross domestic product per capita here and elsewhere in this section comes from Alan Heston, Robert Summers, and Bettina Aten, Penn World Table Version 6.1 (Center for International Comparisons at the University of Pennsylvania, CICUP, October 2002), http://pwt.econ.penn.edu/ (accessed 11/26/08); and from World Development Indicators, www.worldbank.org/data (accessed 11/26/08).

DOMESTIC FACTORS

Within developing nations, there are interests, interactions, and institutions that can speed or impede economic growth. While every country is different and every experience is unique, certain common features of national political economies can help explain why some nations have been more successful than others. (For a vivid illustration of the relative wealth of countries based on their economies, see "What Do We Know?" on p. 337.) At the outset, it is crucial to recognize that a government's policies have a powerful impact on economic growth because they can either encourage or retard it. In fact, almost all explanations of development and underdevelopment consider the results of the actions (or inactions) of governments.

A very important policy that governments can undertake to boost development is to provide public goods that contribute to economic growth and prosperity. One such public good is the economic **infrastructure**. This includes a physical infrastructure of roads, railroads, airports, utilities, ports, and the like, which are necessary to allow trade and exchange. It also includes such economic institutions as financial and monetary systems, which permit people to carry out payments and investments easily. A social infrastructure, too—public health and sanitation, education, urban planning—can encourage growth and development by allowing citizens to focus their efforts on economic activity in a productive way. In contrast, if the government does not build and maintain roads and schools, impedes normal banking operations, lets prices spiral out of control, and allows disease and social problems to persist, it is hard to imagine how the economy could develop.

Another crucial function for government is to ensure the security of property. After all, economic growth requires everyone from farmers to factory owners to invest in improving their ability to produce, and such improvements are unlikely to be made if property rights are not safe. Secure property rights—which people in developed countries take for granted—mean that a property owner can be confident that his or her material goods will not be seized arbitrarily. A commitment to protect private property is not necessarily something that benefits only the rich: in most poor societies, the principal property owners are farmers. For them to take advantage of new economic opportunities, they have to set aside time, energy, and money to improve the soil. Farmers have to put their livelihood on the line in order to plant coffee trees, clear woodland, or irrigate. How could they undertake such risky investments if they could not be sure that the benefits would come back to them? if marauders could steal their animals and torch their fields? if local government officials could extort any wealth they saw being earned? if the national government taxed away all their earnings?

Long-term economic growth requires a stable and reliable environment within which people can make economic plans for the future. A government that invests in education and public health, that creates an efficient economic infrastructure, and that ensures a stable monetary and financial system can do a great deal to facilitate economic growth. In all these instances, people need a credible commitment that the government will abide by its promises to provide such public goods. Governments that cannot or will not credibly promise to provide such public goods inhibit their citizens' ability to take advantage of economic opportunities.

infrastructure: Basic structures necessary for social activity, such as transportation and telecommunications networks, and power and water supply.

Relative Wealth

This map shows the countries of the world, adjusted for the size of their economies. If you compare this map, based on economic size, with a map based on physical geography or population, you will see how enormous the disparity is between rich and poor nations. The relative sizes of rich and poor nations are extraordinarily distorted, which illustrates the great inequality of incomes between the developed and developing world. The economy of the United States, with about 300 million people, is substantially larger than the combined economies of all the developing countries of Africa, Asia, and Latin America, whose combined population is well over 5 billion people. The Dutch economy is substantially bigger than the Russian economy. The economy of Germany is larger than that of China and India combined; Spain's is larger than all of Africa's; Italy's is larger than all of Latin America's. Overall, the developed countries account for less than one-sixth of the world's total population, but about four-fifths of its economy. As this map shows, the world's economic activity is heavily concentrated in just a handful of countries with a very small percentage of the world's population. ■

WORLD WEALTH, 2007

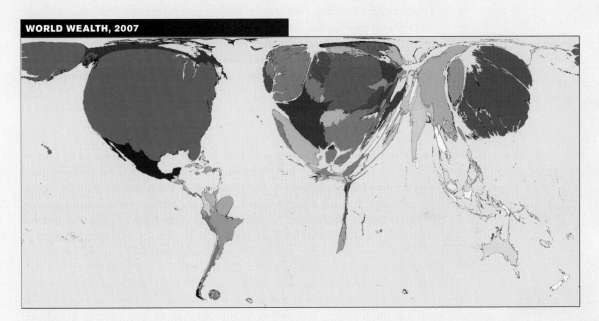

Source: www.worldmapper.org/display.php?selected=169 (accessed 12/8/08).

Why might a government not be willing or able to commit to creating a favorable environment for economic growth? After all, even the most selfish rulers presumably stand to benefit from a prosperous economy. And all societies have workers, farmers, and businesspeople with an interest in active and effective government policies to expand the range of economic opportunities.

Some countries' governments might simply lack the technical expertise to manage modern economic growth, in which case foreign assistance, in the form of both money and skills, may be needed. More often, unfortunately, the answer is not so easy.

In many societies, certain actors have interests that go against broad-based economic development. This is not to say that such actors consciously desire to limit growth, but that a pursuit of their own interests can ultimately harm the economy. (This is, of course, not a phenomenon specific to LDCs; every country has actors with an interest in manipulating the economy to benefit themselves, even at the cost of slowing economic growth.) In developing countries, such actors are often engaged in traditional economic sectors whose livelihood would be threatened by the growth of a more modern economy. For example, wealthy landowners may prefer that the property rights of poor farmers not be protected, so that the rich can encroach on the land being farmed by the poor. Owners of labor-intensive plantations or mines may have little reason to support urbanization, industrialization, or education, because these developments would draw workers away and raise labor costs. Powerful corporations that receive generous subsidies and protection want to maintain them, even if they are a burden on taxpayers and consumers. Bureaucrats who can extort bribes in return for favors have nothing to gain from a more open and efficient administration.

The dismal experience of sub-Saharan Africa since independence provides an example of how actors whose interests are at odds with the general social interest can impede economic growth. As Map 9.1 shows, many of the world's poorest countries are found in sub-Saharan Africa. Development policy in the region has largely served to benefit small groups and to harm the rest of society. For decades, governments systematically drained resources from the countryside in order to channel them into the cities, either by direct taxation of farmers, or by keeping farm prices artificially low, or by other means. These policies were often justified as a way of speeding urbanization and industrialization, and they may indeed have had that effect. But in societies that were 80 or 90 percent rural, this process amounted to impoverishing the masses to benefit a narrow urban elite. However, the urban elite was a politically important base of support for African governments. It included urban businessmen, government employees, and the military, on which many governments relied to stay in power. As a result, many African governments pursued economic policies that depleted the farm sector—which represented most of the population and most of the meaningful economic opportunities—in the interest of catering to inefficient urban enterprises and bureaucracies.[5]

Self-serving groups whose goals conflict with those of the rest of society can significantly impede development, but interests alone are insufficient to explain countries' different paths of development. After all, every country has powerful special interests, including groups who may be inimical to broader development,

---

5. Robert Bates, *Markets and States in Tropical Africa* (Berkeley: University of California Press, 1981), is the classic examination of this process.

but every country also has masses of farmers, workers, businesspeople, and others who stand to benefit from policies that promote economic growth. What ultimately determines the character of government policies toward development is not just the interests in play, but also their interactions: how politicians, social groups, and the public bargain, fight, cooperate, and negotiate their way toward an outcome.

In some societies, there may be particularly propitious conditions for actors to come together in pursuit of shared goals, while in others there may be endemic divisions that make this collaboration very difficult. Hostility and conflict among ethnic or regional groups can impede both political stability and effective national government policies, if intergroup rivalries overcome a concern for the common good. Because many LDCs have boundaries that were determined by colonial powers without regard to preexisting ethnic, religious, and racial features of the population, they can be very diverse, and competition among groups can complicate the making of economic policy in these countries.[6]

Generally speaking, as we saw in Chapter 2, the larger the group, the more difficult collective action is. This means that, as with trade policies analyzed in Chapter 6, broad social interests are less likely to be organized than narrower special interests. Thus, special interest groups have an advantage in influencing policy. Nonetheless, sometimes the existence of a powerful common national goal (such as national unification or resistance to an external threat) can lead groups to set aside their differences and focus together on developmental requirements. It has been suggested that South Korea and Taiwan were strongly motivated to grow rapidly in part because of their competition with North Korea and China, respectively. The economist Mancur Olson was optimistic that development could be spurred, and venal special interests denied, when societies were dominated by encompassing coalitions—that is, alliances that include enough of society to be concerned for broad social welfare.[7]

Whether important social actors interact in a cooperative manner to spur development also depends on domestic political institutions. These institutions affect the influence of those pressing for the public interest and for the goals of specific groups. More representative political institutions, for example, are likely to give more weight to broad public concerns about overall economic growth. Countries with more democratic political institutions appear to provide more public goods than do authoritarian political systems—more basic education, more public health, more equitable and efficient distributions of land.[8] In fact, part of the problem in postcolonial Africa has been the very undemocratic nature of most of the region's political systems, which allowed a narrow urban elite to use the government to exploit the masses of farmers and other rural dwellers.

6. For a survey, see Alberto Alesina and Eliana LaFerrara, "Ethnic Diversity and Economic Performance," *Journal of Economic Literature* 63 (September 2005): 762–800. This is not a problem only for poor countries, but it can be particularly troubling there.

7. Mancur Olson, *The Rise and Decline of Nations: Economic Growth, Stagflation, and Social Rigidities* (New Haven: Yale University Press, 1982).

8. See, for example, David Lake and Matthew Baum, "The Political Economy of Growth: Democracy and Human Capital," *American Journal of Political Science* 47, no. 2 (April 2003): 333–47; Nancy D. Lapp, *Landing Votes: Representation and Land Reform in Latin America* (New York: Palgrave/Macmillan, 2004); David Stasavage, "Democracy and Education Spending in Africa," *American Journal of Political Science* 49, no. 2 (2005): 343–58; David S. Brown and Wendy A. Hunter, "Democracy and Human Capital Formation: Education Spending in Latin America, 1980 to 1997," *Comparative Political Studies* 37, no. 7 (2004): 842–64.

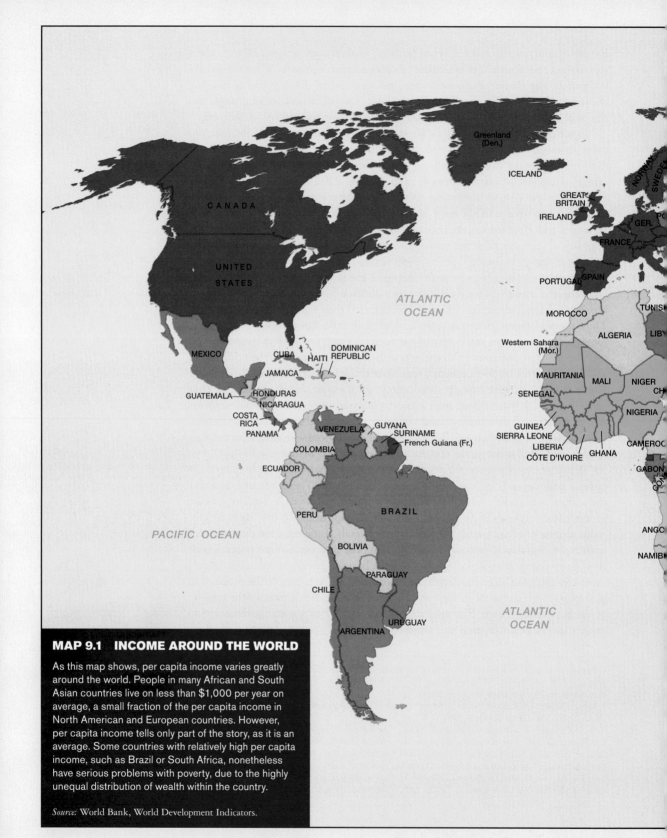

Greenland
(Den.)

ICELAND

CANADA

UNITED
STATES

ATLANTIC
OCEAN

MEXICO

CUBA
JAMAICA
HAITI
DOMINICAN
REPUBLIC

GUATEMALA HONDURAS
NICARAGUA
COSTA
RICA
PANAMA

VENEZUELA
COLOMBIA

GUYANA
SURINAME
French Guiana (Fr.)

ECUADOR

PERU

BRAZIL

PACIFIC OCEAN

BOLIVIA

PARAGUAY

CHILE

ATLANTIC
OCEAN

URUGUAY

ARGENTINA

NORWAY
SWEDEN

GREAT
BRITAIN
IRELAND
GER.
FRANCE

PORTUGAL SPAIN

MOROCCO

TUNIS

Western Sahara
(Mor.)

ALGERIA

LIB

MAURITANIA
MALI
NIGER
CH

SENEGAL

NIGERIA

GUINEA
SIERRA LEONE
LIBERIA
CÔTE D'IVOIRE
GHANA

CAMEROO

GABON

ANGO

NAMIB

MAP 9.1 INCOME AROUND THE WORLD

As this map shows, per capita income varies greatly
around the world. People in many African and South
Asian countries live on less than $1,000 per year on
average, a small fraction of the per capita income in
North American and European countries. However,
per capita income tells only part of the story, as it is an
average. Some countries with relatively high per capita
income, such as Brazil or South Africa, nonetheless
have serious problems with poverty, due to the highly
unequal distribution of wealth within the country.

Source: World Bank, World Development Indicators.

FINLAND

RUSSIAN FEDERATION

ARUS

RAINE

M.

KAZAKHSTAN

MONGOLIA

TURKEY

UZBEKISTAN
KYRGYZSTAN

SYRIA
TURKMENISTAN
TAJIKISTAN

N. KOREA

JAPAN

ISRAEL
IRAQ
AFGHANISTAN

Kashmir

CHINA

S. KOREA

IRAN

PAKISTAN

PACIFIC OCEAN

EGYPT

KUWAIT
SAUDI ARABIA

NEPAL

TAIWAN

OMAN

BANGLADESH

INDIA

MYANMAR
(BURMA)

Hong Kong

YEMEN

VIETNAM

Macau

SUDAN

THAILAND

PHILIPPINES

CAMBODIA

NTRAL
RICAN
P.

ETHIOPIA

SRI
LANKA

SOMALIA

UGANDA

KENYA

MALAYSIA

M.
EP.
OF
HE
NGO

TANZANIA

INDONESIA

PAPUA
NEW
GUINEA

MBIA

INDIAN
OCEAN

SAMOA

MADAGASCAR

EAST TIMOR

MBABWE
TS.

AUSTRALIA

MOZAMBIQUE

TH
ICA

NEW
ZEALAND

Per capita income, 2007

low, $935 or less

lower middle, $936 – $3,705

upper middle, $3,706 – $11,455

high, $11,456 or more

DOMESTIC INSTITUTIONS

How and why have certain societies developed institutions that are conducive to economic growth, while others have not? Of course, the interests that characterize a society, the interactions among them, and the institutions that develop within them are all interrelated. Nonetheless, some scholars emphasize how the resource endowments of societies give rise to sets of interests and institutions that may be more or less favorable to development. This view incorporates the geographical features of different regions of the world into a broader interpretation of developmental paths.

One instructive comparison is between North and South America. The two regions were colonized by Europeans at roughly the same time and got their independence within a few decades of each other; since then, however, they have diverged in important ways. Two economic historians, Stanley Engerman and Kenneth Sokoloff, have made an influential argument that the kinds of economic activities the regions undertook early in their history had a lasting impact on their subsequent social, political, and economic evolution.[9]

Many Latin American colonies and countries were drawn into the world economy on the basis of plantation agriculture (sugar, cotton) or labor-intensive mining (silver, gold). These economic activities created highly unequal societies made up of wealthy landowners or miners, on the one hand, and poorly paid workers or slaves, on the other. The great inequalities in society were reflected in undemocratic political institutions, which the wealthy used to hold on to power, and in the lack of government policies to improve education, public health, or the economic opportunities of the poor. Such biased institutions, and such a lack of developmentally oriented policies, retarded economic growth.

In most of North America, however, early economic activities created fewer inequalities. Small-scale wheat farming in the United States and Canada, for example, produced a class of independent family farmers and a society that was quite equal. This equality was reflected in democratic political institutions, as well as substantial government investments in infrastructure, education, and other economically important activities. Here, the developmentally oriented institutions and policies encouraged economic growth.

The experience of the American South underscores this point. In the southern United States, unlike in the North and Midwest, there were substantial slave plantation regions growing cotton and tobacco. Engerman and Sokoloff show that in the former plantation areas in the eighteenth and nineteenth centuries, inequalities were much greater than elsewhere in the United States; the right to vote was much more restricted (and, of course, these restrictions persisted for a century after slavery was abolished); and there was much less spending on education and other public works. The highly unequal nature of southern American society, Engerman and Sokoloff argue, created an enduring legacy that was reflected in the South's institutions and that held back its economic growth for many decades. The South's

---

9. A summary of their work is in Stanley Engerman and Kenneth Sokoloff, "History Lessons: Institutions, Factor Endowments, and Paths of Development in the New World," *Journal of Economic Perspectives* 14, no. 3 (2000): 217–32.

experience demonstrates how the domestic economic, political, and social interests and institutions created early in a region's economic history can have a long-lasting impact on its subsequent development.

This broader perspective helps explain the surprising fact that many regions that are extremely rich in natural resources are developmental disasters. The relationship between resource wealth and underdevelopment is strong enough to have prompted theories of a "resource curse" in which initial wealth gives rise to subsequent poverty. The idea is that the government of a country with a natural resource that can be easily and lucratively exploited has few reasons to encourage productive activities other than those associated with the resource, and that the effortless inflow of money to the government can provide a fertile ground for corrupt practices. In contrast, the government of a country with few natural resources, if it wants economic growth, has little choice but to undertake measures that will make the economy more productive. Recalling the comparison of Zambia and South Korea noted at the outset of this chapter, it may be that Zambia's copper wealth gave its rulers little incentive to increase the country's ability to produce anything other than raw materials by improving education, public health, and the economic infrastructure; by contrast, South Korea's lack of any major exportable raw materials forced its government to focus on improving the productive capacities of its people.[10] The broader point is that geographical and other inherent features of a country are important for subsequent development inasmuch as they have a substantial impact on the kinds of interests and institutions that arise on their basis.

Many countries that are rich in natural resources remain poor. Nigeria is one of the world's largest oil exporters, but the average Nigerian has hardly benefited from this natural wealth. Poor Nigerians frequently risk death to pilfer oil from pipelines.

In sum, to understand why countries have developed in a certain way, we need to understand people's interests and their ability or inability to cooperate, as well as the political institutions that determine how people's interests are translated into policy. Domestic factors, and especially national government policies, are crucial to understanding national developmental success or failure.

Nonetheless, there are many ways in which the international environment shapes the constraints and opportunities faced by developing countries—and not always in a positive way. Many people in the LDCs argue that international conditions have not been helpful to their prospects, and indeed that that the current poverty of much of the world is due to the structure of the international system.

10. See, for example, Michael Shafer, *Winners and Losers: How Sectors Shape the Developmental Prospects of States* (Ithaca: Cornell University Press, 1994); Halvor Mehlum, Karl Moene, and Ragnar Torvik, "Institutions and the Resource Curse," *Economic Journal* 116 (2006): 1–20; Macartan Humphreys, Jeffrey D. Sachs, and Joseph E. Stiglitz, eds., *Escaping the Resource Curse* (New York: Columbia University Press, 2007).

Are Rich Countries Responsible for the Problems of the Developing World?

There is evidence that interests, interactions, and institutions at the international level are responsible for at least some of the current problems of poor nations. While developed and developing countries have many interests in common, there are also many real and potential conflicts of interests among them.

Rich and poor nations have many shared interests. Economic growth in the developing world can create enormous opportunities for wealthy countries. As we saw in Chapters 6, 7, and 8, rich-country corporations can profit from investing in and selling to developing nations, while poor countries can benefit from the capital, technology, and expertise that such corporations bring. LDC exports provide cheap goods for industrial-country consumers while they make money for the exporters. Banks from the industrialized world are eager to make loans to developing countries, many of which are eager to borrow money because they are short of capital. The growth of poor countries' economies expands investment opportunities and markets for rich-country businesses. All these factors suggest why the relationship among rich and poor nations could be cooperative, and the scope for mutually beneficial exchange very large.

By the same token, all countries have a common interest in the successful management of international economic affairs. Developed and developing countries alike benefit from well-functioning international trading, financial, and monetary systems. Few, if any, nations stand to gain from a breakdown of the international economy or from the transmission of financial crises from one country to another. International collaboration to smooth the operation of the world economy, and to deal with problems that may arise, is generally in the interest of all countries. Indeed, most international economic organizations—including the International Monetary Fund, the World Bank, and the World Trade Organization—have both rich and poor nations as their members.

However, the interests of developed and developing countries may also clash. As we have seen in other areas of international politics, agreement over the desirability of cooperation coexists with disagreement over how to distribute the benefits of cooperation. A multinational mining company and an LDC government have a common interest in getting minerals out of the ground and to market, but they are likely to disagree about the division of the profits. Similarly, LDC companies and governments may appreciate being able to borrow from international banks, but they are likely to be less enthusiastic about paying back their debts—especially in hard times. The fact that rich countries' corporations can profit from low wages in the LDCs can give them little interest in encouraging development that will raise wages. Such a mix of interests in common and in conflict is central to the international political economy of development. It can be seen in many historical and contemporary examples.

DID COLONIALISM HAMPER DEVELOPMENT?

One aspect of the international order that is often invoked as an important determinant of development is the legacy of colonialism. As we discussed in Chapter 1, from the sixteenth through the twentieth centuries colonial rule was often justified as being in the interests of both the colonial powers and the colonized. Indeed, there are many instances of colonialism that encouraged broad-based economic growth in poor countries, for sometimes the interests of rulers and ruled were similar. Some colonial regimes supplied roads, railroads, ports, and other infrastructure both to facilitate their rule and to gain access to the colonies' resources; this infrastructure facilitated the economic and political development of the colonial society overall. After all, some of today's most developed nations—the United States, Canada, Australia, New Zealand—were longtime colonies.

Nonetheless, the interests of the colonizers and the colonized were frequently in conflict, so that the enduring impact of colonialism was often negative. Most imperial powers wanted to use their colonies for the mother country's benefit even if this was not beneficial to the colonial society. They often reserved economic advantages to their own citizens and restricted the access of colonial subjects to economic opportunity. And when the colonial rulers' interests were inconsistent with local development, it was the rulers' interests that prevailed. This situation led to interactions that subordinated colonial societies and economies to the needs of the empire.

Colonialism, indeed, institutionalized a relationship in which the interests of the colonies were secondary to those of the mother country. For example, colonial policy commonly directed colonial trade toward the mother country, restricted manufacturing in the colonies, and otherwise gave trading privileges to the colonial power. (This was true of British policy toward the 13 colonies in North America; see p. 9 of Chapter 1.) Such preferential policies were intended in part to benefit residents of the great power, in part to deny benefits to real or potential enemies in other empires. This approach can hardly have been beneficial for development, and it may have been highly detrimental.

There are many instances of colonial rule that was negligent at best, predatory at worst. One famous example is that of King Leopold of Belgium in the Congo (the former Belgian Congo, now known as the Democratic Republic of the Congo). When the European powers colonized Africa in the late nineteenth century, they permitted Leopold to turn the Congo into his own personal possession. For decades, Leopold exploited the indigenous people mercilessly, forcing them to gather ivory, rubber, and other raw materials and to turn them over to his own colonial government.[11]

Three scholars have analyzed how the form colonialism took had a systematic impact on subsequent development. Daron Acemoglu, Simon Johnson, and James Robinson suggest that the countries and regions of the colonial world can be divided into two types. The first includes countries where European settlers could live easily, without fear of high mortality due to tropical diseases or other threats. In these regions, settlers from the colonial powers, the scholars write, "went and settled in the colonies and set up institutions that enforced the rule of law and encouraged investment."[12] European settlers, in other words, went where they could

---

11. A classic analysis of the Congo's experience is Adam Hochschild, *King Leopold's Ghost* (Boston: Houghton Mifflin, 1998).
12. Daron Acemoglu, Simon Johnson, and James Robinson, "The Colonial Origins of Comparative Development," *American Economic Review* 91, no. 5 (December 2001): 1395.

This 1933 French illustration shows an idealized vision of colonialism, one in which the European settlers fostered development through education and efficient industry. In reality, however, the interests of colonial rulers were often at odds with local development, and the long-term effects of colonialism were frequently negative.

survive, and they established social, political, and economic institutions that were conducive to economic growth. These institutions persisted, and in such countries as Canada and Australia the result was successful development.

In other regions, where European settlers were much more likely to die of disease or other factors, the colonial powers engaged in predatory policies. There, the scholars say, the Europeans "set up extractive states with the intention of transferring resources rapidly to the metropole. These institutions were detrimental to investment and economic progress."[13] In other words, where large-scale European immigration and settlement were not feasible, the colonial powers simply exploited the region for their own benefit, establishing institutions that were not conducive to economic growth. These institutions, too, persisted and served to impede successful development.

To evaluate their argument, Acemoglu, Johnson, and Robinson looked at the death rates of early European settlers in colonial regions between the 1600s and the 1800s. There is little reason to think that these death rates would in themselves have a direct impact on modern economic growth, but in fact the settlers' mortality rates were strongly correlated with underdevelopment today. This is powerful evidence for the kind of effects the three scholars anticipated. It seems clear that different types of colonial experiences, and the different institutions put in place by colonial powers, have had enduring effects on development. Where the common interests of colonial powers and people in the colonies predominated, the impact of colonialism was favorable (or at least neutral). However, where the colonial powers' interests went against those of the local population—such as in extracting labor and resources from the colony by force—and the colonialists imposed their will, the impact of colonialism was detrimental.

While the lasting effects of colonialism explain some of the disparity between rich and poor nations, they cannot explain all of it. After all, most Latin American

13. Ibid

nations have been independent for nearly 200 years—longer than many developed countries have been in existence—and even most former colonies in Africa, Asia, and the Caribbean have been independent for at least 50 years. Some poor countries—such as China, Thailand, Iran, Liberia, and Ethiopia—have never been colonies[14] and yet have suffered from severe developmental problems. However, other international factors are often invoked as barriers to development as well.

IS THE INTERNATIONAL ECONOMY BIASED AGAINST LDCS?

Some analysts believe that general features of the international economy impede the development of poor nations. One prominent argument was made in the 1950s by Raúl Prebisch, an Argentine economist and for many years the head of the United Nations Economic Commission for Latin America (ECLA).[15] Prebisch accepted that in principle trade was good for both rich and poor countries. However, he noted that LDCs produced mostly raw materials and agricultural products, while rich countries produced mostly manufactured goods. He contended that this very fact meant that trade worked against the interests of the LDCs and in favor of the interests of the developed countries.

The problem, Prebisch said, was that the prices of the LDCs' products tended to decline over time relative to the prices of the industrialized countries' products. This occurred because LDCs sold mainly **primary products**—that is, agricultural goods and raw materials. And because markets for the LDCs' primary products were very competitive (there were millions of cocoa or coffee farmers), prices moved up and down very easily. However, markets for manufactured goods (automobiles, machinery) were controlled by a few large **oligopolistic** firms—that is, firms that could control their markets. Such firms could ensure that prices rose whenever possible and did not fall even in adverse market conditions.[16] The result was that the **terms of trade**—the relative movement of export and import prices—of countries that specialized in primary products deteriorated: they got less for what they sold, and they paid more for what they bought. Countries that specialized in producing raw materials and farm products for world markets, Prebisch and his supporters argued, were at a fundamental disadvantage.

Prebisch and his followers in ECLA concluded that the very structure of the world economy was biased against the developing world. In this view, the industrialized countries had an interest in maintaining a structure of international trade that was detrimental to the LDCs. Although many scholars were skeptical of the argument, it was very popular in the developing world. Indeed, it justified policies that many LDCs were pursuing—of protecting the home market and artificially spurring industrialization.

primary products: Raw materials and agricultural products, typically unprocessed or only slightly processed. The primary sectors are distinguished from secondary sectors (industry) and tertiary sectors (services).

oligopolistic: Characterizing an industry whose markets are dominated by a few firms.

terms of trade: The relationship between a country's export prices and its import prices.

---

14. However, parts of China were occupied by foreign powers, and Ethiopia was invaded and occupied by Italy for several years.
15. For a survey and analysis, see Joseph L. Love, "Raúl Prebisch and the Origins of the Doctrine of Unequal Exchange," *Latin American Research Review* 15 (1980): 45–72.
16. Prebisch also observed that manufacturing was usually unionized, so that wages were also less flexible, which contributed to the rigidity of industrial prices.

ARE INTERNATIONAL INSTITUTIONS BIASED AGAINST LDCS?

Even among those who accept that the world economy can benefit the LDCs, many scholars believe that international *political* factors are responsible for exacerbating the problems of development. They emphasize the relative powerlessness of developing nations in their interactions with richer countries. In this view, the principal obstacle facing LDCs is not global markets, but the character of the international order and of international institutions whose rules are written by rich nations in order to serve their own interests.

While all countries can benefit from international economic exchange, the greater power of rich countries to influence patterns of international trade and finance can certainly work against the interests of the LDCs. Indeed, rich countries often pursue their own interests in ways that harm prospects for development in poor countries. The problem is not that the industrialized nations purposefully or maliciously attempt to impoverish poor countries. Rather, it is that rich countries' policies to safeguard their own interests (or at least the interests powerful enough to matter to their governments) create problems for poor countries. Farm trade policy is a good example. As we saw in Chapter 6, almost all industrialized countries extensively subsidize and protect their farmers. This policy has the effect of restricting the opportunities of LDC farmers, many of whom would otherwise be able to undersell farmers in North America, Western Europe, and Japan. There is no intellectual or economic justification for these protectionist policies; they are simply the result of the interests of American, European, and Japanese farmers, which are in conflict with the interests of developing-country farmers.

American cotton policy illustrates the point. The U.S. government spends several billion dollars a year to subsidize American cotton farmers. This is lucrative for the recipients of the subsidies and politically attractive for American politicians. The subsidy program pays farmers extra to produce cotton, which increases American output of cotton beyond what it would otherwise be; it therefore raises the world supply of cotton and lowers its price. This in turn drives down the price received by cotton farmers in developing countries, who may be lower-cost producers than the American farmers but who do not have the luxury of expensive farm support programs. The upshot is that about 25,000 American cotton farmers get $3 or $4 billion a year in subsidies, while several million cotton farmers in Africa, Asia, and Latin America have their incomes cut by the resultant reduction in the world price of cotton.

The power disparity between rich and poor countries clearly works against the LDCs. The governments of the developing world have been almost entirely unsuccessful at getting their farmers greater access to the markets of the industrialized nations. Meanwhile, the governments of the rich countries have been quite successful in getting the LDCs to open their markets to manufacturers, multinational corporations, and international banks from the developed world. The weakness of the LDCs relative to the developed nations means that they often lose out in international interactions of this sort, to the ultimate detriment of their economic prospects.[17]

---

17. Joseph Stiglitz, *Making Globalization Work* (New York: Norton, 2006), discusses many such examples. The cotton example mentioned here is on pages 85–86.

The same pattern prevails within the major international economic institutions. While the LDCs participate in international economic institutions—most are members of the International Monetary Fund (IMF), the World Bank, and the World Trade Organization (WTO)—these institutions are dominated by the rich countries and biased against the interests of the poor nations.

We saw in Chapter 7 that many critics in the developing world regard the International Monetary Fund as a tool of the rich nations. Indeed, in the IMF voting is weighted by the financial and economic size of the member states, so that rich countries effectively control the institution (see Figure 9.1). In fact, the United States has enough votes to veto any proposal, as do the member states of the European Union. This means that the rich countries can bend IMF policies and procedures in their favor—for example, to deal lightly with their allies or harshly with their enemies—even when such action is not generally consistent with the IMF's own rules.

International trade agreements similarly reflect the interests of the rich and powerful. Initiatives of the developing countries are frequently ignored, even when they clearly would go in the direction of the WTO's purported goal, trade liberalization. Many developing-country exports face protectionist barriers in the industrialized nations, provided at the behest of affected industries that do not want to face such stiff competition. Perhaps most important is the attempt by the developing nations (and a few industrial countries that export farm products) to push for the WTO to encourage greater openness to farm products, especially on the part of the highly protectionist rich countries. Agricultural trade liberalization would open up important new opportunities to farmers in developing countries, many of whom are low-cost agricultural producers. But because the principal losers would be farmers in developed countries, the rich nations have adamantly resisted including trade in farm products on the agenda for liberalization.

The interests of developed- and developing-country governments clash in many arenas. The power disparities between rich and poor countries typically mean that interactions among them are decided in favor of the rich. Moreover,

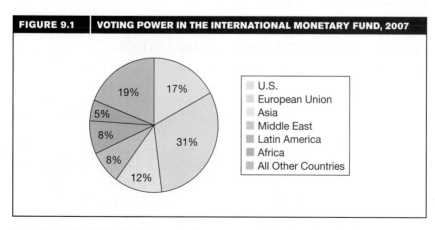

FIGURE 9.1   VOTING POWER IN THE INTERNATIONAL MONETARY FUND, 2007

17%
19%
5%
8%
8%
12%
31%

- U.S.
- European Union
- Asia
- Middle East
- Latin America
- Africa
- All Other Countries

Source: International Monetary Fund, www.imf.org/external/np/exr/ib/2007/041307.htm (accessed 3/19/09). IMF vote shares mentioned in Ch. 9, p. 16.

the international institutions that govern the international economy were largely created by rich and powerful countries, so their policies and decision rules reflect their own concerns. In all these ways, the alignment of interests, interactions, and institutions in the international order can limit the prospects for successful development of poor nations.

Development Policies and Development Politics

Over the past century, poor countries have experienced many changes in the domestic and international spheres that have affected their development. Before 1914, most developing regions—whether they were independent, as in Latin America, or colonial, as in most of the rest of the world—focused their efforts on primary products (agricultural goods and raw materials). They welcomed access to global markets and foreign capital, as they strove to develop their mineral wealth and their farmland. Many poor nations did quite well in the late nineteenth and early twentieth centuries, selling copper, coffee, cotton, and other primary goods to Europe and North America. In the process, they usually accepted general economic openness: relatively free trade, the gold standard, and inflows of foreign capital.

But after 1914, as the world economy experienced serious trouble, most developing regions turned inward. World War I, the troubled interwar years and the Great Depression of the 1930s, World War II, postwar reconstruction, and the start of the Cold War all kept the developed world preoccupied—and relatively uninterested in the developing regions. International investors were otherwise engaged at home; the foreign markets into which the LDCs had previously sold their products were stagnant, or heavily protected, or both. The developing regions, both independent and colonial, were forced to fend for themselves as their ties to the developed world began to dwindle.

IMPORT SUBSTITUTING INDUSTRIALIZATION

In the context of these international trends, beginning in the 1930s many developing countries adopted policies that encouraged industrial development so that domestic producers could supply goods that had previously been imported. Latin America led the way in practice as in theory, adopting measures to stimulate industry.

The initial turn inward may have been forced by international events, the dislocations of the two world wars, and the Great Depression, but eventually it became a more conscious strategy. The complex of policies became known as **import substituting industrialization** (ISI), due to the goal of substituting local products for imports. It was in this context that Raúl Prebisch and his followers argued that such enforced self-sufficiency was actually desirable and should be deepened.

import substituting industrialization (ISI): A set of policies, pursued by most developing countries from the 1930s through the 1980s, to reduce imports and encourage domestic manufacturing, often through trade barriers, subsidies to manufacturing, and state ownership of basic industries.

There were powerful domestic interests in favor of ISI. Most generally, developing-country governments wanted their economies to move away from primary (raw materials and agricultural) production and toward industry. This interest grew out of such theoretical conceptions as those of Prebisch, that accelerated industrialization would aid broader development; out of the belief that modern societies required a manufacturing base; out of a national security desire for indigenous industrial capacity; and out of other broad goals. At the same time, there were more specific interests in favor of the new policies. The previously predominant emphasis on primary production for export was associated with the political dominance of producers of these goods—copper miners, oilmen, plantation owners, ranchers. As foreign markets collapsed, these internationally oriented groups lost influence. They were supplanted by such pro-industrial groups as the urban business and middle classes and the industrial working class, who strongly supported ISI.

Import substitution policies meant that many LDCs attempted to produce most manufactured goods domestically. Starting in the 1950s, Brazil and Mexico developed their own automobile industries almost from scratch. Here, Brazilan workers assemble cars in a Volkswagen plant in São Paulo.

Both broad and narrower interests in ISI were also at play in the former colonies in Africa and Asia as they won their independence. Colonialism had been associated with selling primary products to the colonial power, but decolonization was associated with efforts to replace raw materials and agricultural production with urban manufacturing. And just as colonial societies were often dominated by colonial or local miners, oilmen, or farmers, postcolonial societies came to be dominated by such urban interest groups as businessmen, the middle classes, labor, and government employees. For these reasons, after 1945 almost all of the long-independent developing nations of Latin America and the newly independent ones of Africa, Asia, and the Caribbean reduced their economic ties with the rest of the world, protected and subsidized local manufacturing, and attempted to stimulate domestic industrial development. In important ways, these policies reflected the view that engagement with the world economy could be an impediment to national economic development.

For decades, most LDCs followed the broad outlines of import substitution, including:

- trade barriers to protect domestic manufacturers from foreign competition and encourage national industrial development,
- government incentives to industry, including tax credits, cheap loans, and other subsidies to draw investors into the modern industrial sector, and
- government provision of basic industrial services by public enterprises—electric power, telecommunications, transport, finance—to supplement or replace private provision that was seen as too expensive or too limited.

All over the third world, government policies encouraged the development of large state sectors behind high protectionist barriers. The result was rapid industrialization in many areas. Between 1950 and 1970, for example, Brazil and

A strategy of export-oriented industrialization led some developing countries to produce high-quality goods to be sold overseas. By the 1980s, this strategy had proved highly successful for countries like South Korea, and companies in these countries were able to produce increasingly sophisticated products for export. Here, a South Korean worker assembles radios in a Samsung electronics factory.

Mexico developed large automobile industries where none had previously existed, and by the 1970s the two countries were producing a million cars a year. By the 1970s, indeed, most of the larger developing countries pursuing ISI—India, Brazil, Mexico, Argentina—were largely self-sufficient in manufactured products.

However, ISI had weaknesses. The industries it encouraged were not efficient and had difficulty selling their goods abroad. After all, they had grown up in protected markets and were not originally expected to be competitive in international markets. Over time, as countries continued to need to earn money to pay for essential imports, the difficulties the new manufacturers encountered in exporting were worrisome.

As problems accumulated, the inward-looking self-sufficiency of ISI began to lose support. In part, the Prebisch-ECLA view declined for intellectual reasons: evidence accumulated that the argument might not be correct, or that economic ties with developed countries might not have as negative an impact as had been suggested. There were also pragmatic and political reasons why the LDCs turned toward global integration. Many producers came to believe that selling only to a small and poor home market restricted their potential. The insularity of protected markets left many manufacturers technically backward, making products of low quality—a fact that became increasingly worrisome with the rise of modern electronics and computing. The bias against producing for export meant that developing countries sold little in world markets. This meant they could not buy much abroad, which left them vulnerable to crises when, for example, oil prices skyrocketed in the 1970s. And the ISI bias against agriculture impoverished many farmers, leading to mass internal migrations that flooded the cities with the formerly rural poor. By the early 1980s, ISI was in trouble.

EXPORT-ORIENTED INDUSTRIALIZATION

There was also an alternative available, for a handful of countries in East Asia had tried something different. Beginning in the mid-1960s, South Korea, Taiwan, Singapore, and the British colony of Hong Kong had turned toward **export-oriented industrialization (EOI)**. These governments had encouraged their manufacturers to produce for foreign, especially American, consumers. They used many techniques to push exports: low-cost loans and tax breaks to exporters, and a very weak currency to make their products artificially cheap. While the rest of the third world turned industry inward in the 1960s and 1970s, the export-oriented countries pushed it outward. This meant relying on often volatile international markets, but it had the advantage of forcing national manufacturers to produce goods that met rigorous technological, quality, and price standards.

export-oriented industrialization (EOI): A set of policies, originally pursued starting in the late 1960s by several East Asian countries, to spur manufacturing for export, often through subsidies and incentives for export production.

By the late 1970s, the four East Asian economies were flooding world markets with toys, clothing, furniture, and other simple manufactures. South Korean exports skyrocketed from $385 million in 1970 to $15 billion in 1979, 90% of them manufactured goods. On this basis, South Korea's government pursued heavy industrial development by sponsoring modern steel mills, chemical factories, and a new auto industry. By the early 1980s, the country had the world's largest private shipyard and largest machinery factory.[18]

THE TURN TOWARD GLOBALIZATION

While the EOI model was pursued by a relatively small number of countries prior to the 1980s, only a decade later it became the dominant strategy throughout the developing world. The devastating debt crisis that hit the developing world in the early 1980s (see Chapter 7) dealt a fatal blow to ISI. For one thing, the ISI economies were particularly severely affected because they had so much trouble increasing exports and generating the money they needed to service their debts. But the East Asian EOI economies weathered the crisis with less trouble. Their businesses were used to selling abroad and could increase exports rapidly to service their debts. After a couple of difficult years, the so-called Asian Tigers resumed rapid growth. Meanwhile, the deep crisis in the ISI economies eventually drove them to turn toward export promotion themselves. By the late 1980s, almost all developing countries had abandoned ISI and opted to integrate their economies into global markets. The positive experience of EOI, and the negative experiences of ISI, seemed to point the way toward a new, globalized economic future for the developing world.

The debt crisis also left the LDCs vulnerable to pressure from the industrialized countries—and from such international institutions as the IMF and World Bank—to change their economic policies. In return for having their debts restructured, LDCs came under pressure to implement reforms favored by governments and institutions from the rich world. For both domestic and international reasons, then, over the course of the 1990s many LDCs adapted to the new interest in globalization. The economist John Williamson[19] dubbed the complex of policies associated with this transformation the **Washington Consensus**, which came to connote the general acceptance of market-oriented policies. Among the policies that were, in varying degrees, adopted by the LDCs were the following:

- *trade liberalization,* the removal of barriers to imports and exports in an attempt to make national producers more competitive on world markets
- *privatization,* the selling off of many government enterprises to private investors who would presumably run them more efficiently
- *fiscal and monetary policies* to avoid large deficits and high inflation
- *openness* to foreign investment and to international capital flows more generally

Washington Consensus:
An array of policy recommendations generally advocated by developed-country economists and policymakers starting in the 1980s, including trade liberalization, privatization, openness to foreign investment, and restrictive monetary and fiscal policies.

18. Jeff Frieden, "Third World Indebted Industrialization: International Finance and State Capitalism in Mexico, Brazil, Algeria, and South Korea," *International Organization* 35, no. 3 (Summer 1981): 426.
19. John Williamson, "What Washington Means by Policy Reform," in *Latin American Readjustment: How Much Has Happened,* ed. John Williamson (Washington, DC: Institute for International Economics, 1989).

These policies were also generally embraced by the governments of countries in eastern and central Europe and the former Soviet Union, as they made their way from Communist central planning toward market societies in the 1990s.

The shift away from economic nationalism toward economic openness had both international and domestic sources. As the rest of the world economy grew rapidly, and as globalization advanced elsewhere, it was hard for poor nations to continue to deny themselves access to the opportunities the world economy might make available. Powerful domestic actors in the developing world were increasingly interested in tapping into global markets, global capital, and global technologies. And economic integration seems to have worked relatively well. Countries such as China and India have grown very rapidly since they turned toward world markets, and they have been followed by dozens of other LDCs. Meanwhile, demands from the developed countries and the international institutions they dominated pushed even many reluctant LDCs in the direction of globalization. This move highlights the fact that many actors in the developing world resent the perceived bias of international economic institutions, and that many LDC governments have attempted to counter the power imbalance with the power of numbers.

ATTEMPTS TO REMEDY THE BIAS OF INTERNATIONAL INSTITUTIONS

Developing countries confronted their problems at the international level as well as through national policies. Beginning in the 1950s, many countries in Asia, Africa, and the Caribbean that gained their independence after World War II organized themselves into a Non-Aligned Movement and pledged to avoid alliances with either the American-led West or the Soviet-led East. The Non-Aligned Movement eventually gave rise to developing-country coalitions at the United Nations and in international institutions more generally. The UN variant was formed in 1964 with 77 members and has since been known as the **Group of 77** (although it currently has over 130 member countries). These developing country–based institutions attempt to use the collective power of numbers in the world political arena to reform the economic order in favor of the developing world.

The most systematic efforts along these lines came in the 1970s, when developing countries fought in the United Nations and elsewhere for what they called a **New International Economic Order**. Its purpose was to renegotiate the bargain that had constituted the international economic order, so that it would be more in line with the economic needs of poor nations. The proposals included curtailing the rights of foreign investors in developing countries, revising trade agreements to favor the products of the developing world, and enhancing the influence of LDC governments in international economic organizations. These efforts resulted in some UN resolutions and other initiatives, but little of a concrete nature was accomplished.

The LDCs were more successful at using their control over natural resources to strengthen their bargaining position with the rich nations. The most striking example came from the members of the Organization of Petroleum Exporting Countries (OPEC), a group of developing-country oil producers whose creation

Group of 77: A coalition of developing countries in the United Nations, formed in 1964 with 77 members; it has grown to over 130 members but maintains the original name.

New International Economic Order: A reorganization of the management of the international economy demanded by LDCs in the 1970s in order to make it more favorable to developing nations.

in 1960 had gone almost unnoticed. But in 1973, in the midst of a war between Israel and its Arab neighbors, OPEC's Arab members doubled the price of oil to more than $5 a barrel, then two months later doubled it again to nearly $12 a barrel. They did so by purposely restricting their supply of oil to world markets, a move that drove up world oil prices. As the price increases persisted, it was clear that a small group of developing countries had dramatically changed the terms on which they sold their goods. Tens of billions of dollars flowed into the coffers of developing-country governments, and for the first time a group of developing nations appeared to have the upper hand in economic dealings with the West. In the wake of this electrifying development, other third world commodity producers—of copper, coffee, iron ore, bauxite, and bananas—tried to emulate OPEC in creating international **commodity cartels**, organizations of producers who cooperate to restrict the supply and raise the price of their products.

Some of the other commodity cartels had an impact, but the oil sector was unique in the scale of its achievements. Oil producers were particularly successful for several reasons. There were few readily available substitutes for oil, so price increases did not reduce consumption very much. Also, just a few OPEC members controlled a very large share of the world's oil: Saudi Arabia, Kuwait, Qatar, and the United Arab Emirates together had nearly half the world's oil reserves. They did not need to sell oil quickly and could hold it off the market to keep prices high. An additional source of power was the solidarity of OPEC's Muslim members in and around the Middle East, who shared cultural and political ties.

OPEC was able to obtain enormous amounts of money for its members. Some of this income was shared with other developing countries, although many poor countries that did not have oil themselves were harmed by the oil shocks. In addition, oil states were able to leverage their resources into

commodity cartels:
Associations of producers of commodities (raw materials and agricultural products) that restrict world supply and thereby cause the price of the goods to rise.

LDCs may be able to use their control of natural resources as a source of power in their interactions with developed countries, by forming commodity cartels like OPEC. Here, OPEC ministers meet in Iran to discuss whether to increase the oil supply in the face of record high prices in 2005.

increased influence at the IMF and World Bank. For a while, it appeared that commodity cartels would have a more general effect on third world power, strengthening demands for a new economic order. But, by the early 1980s, LDC attempts to achieve far-reaching international reforms had largely failed. Some natural resource producers had gotten richer, but the underlying institutions of the international political economy had not fundamentally changed. The less developed countries still found themselves subject to international economic trends and constrained by international institutions, over which they had little or no control.

IS FOREIGN AID AN ANSWER?

Many people believe that problems of development could be substantially alleviated by increased foreign aid from the rich nations of the world. (See "Controversy," p. 357.) And there are certainly examples of places and projects where foreign aid has made a difference to the quality of life of people in poor nations. However, foreign aid is unlikely to play a major role in overcoming problems of underdevelopment, for at least two reasons.

First, the amounts of aid given are quite small and are unlikely to grow. In recent years, total foreign assistance has been about $100 billion a year. This may seem like a lot, but it averages out to less than $20 per person in the LDCs, and it is dwarfed by the amounts of private investments and loans that come into the developing world from abroad. Although the rich countries have often expressed support for increasing aid, few countries have followed through in practice. In 1970, the rich nations set a target of 0.7 percent of their GDP as aid, but the actual number today is about one-third of that target. There is very little popular support for foreign aid in most developed nations, and there seems to be little prospect that it will change.

Second, and perhaps more important, there is good reason to believe that even increased levels of aid would not go very far toward solving the basic problems of developing countries. LDC governments that act in the narrow interests of themselves or their supporters are likely to use the aid they receive for similarly narrow purposes. There is substantial evidence that much foreign aid is misused by recipient governments. By the same token, there is evidence that much foreign aid is given by developed-country governments for geopolitical and military reasons and not to alleviate poverty.

To be sure, humanitarian assistance can make a difference to the lives of people in the developing world. However, sustained economic development provides the best hope for achieving the broader goal of lifting poor countries out of poverty. Governments that are willing and able to pursue policies aimed at stimulating growth may use aid effectively, as a supplement to good policies. But aid alone, especially in the small amounts currently available, cannot go far toward satisfying the massive needs of impoverished people in developing countries.[20]

---

20. For two divergent views on aid, see William Easterly, *The White Man's Burden: Why the West's Efforts to Aid the Rest Have Done So Much Ill and So Little Good* (New York: Penguin, 2007); Jeffrey Sachs, *The End of Poverty: Economic Possibilities for Our Time* (New York: Penguin, 2006).

What Responsibility Do Rich Countries Have to the Global Poor?

In 1998, a severe famine hit southern Sudan. The region's farmers, who barely subsist at the best of times, found themselves facing a chronic shortage of food and water following a two-year drought. Widespread malnutrition, starvation, and disease resulted. As many as 70,000 people died, and more than that number were displaced into surrounding regions in a desperate search for food. Thanks to an international aid effort and improved weather conditions, the immediate crisis subsided. But famine warnings continued at regular intervals throughout the succeeding decade. Today, the Darfur region of western Sudan again risks suffering a famine that some observers claim could be at least as serious as that of 1998. This case is but one example of the many ways in which extreme poverty continues to cripple the lives of much of the world's population. Perhaps eventually we will see a world in which all countries enjoy a level of economic development sufficient to secure their citizens' basic needs, but that goal is currently distant. In the meantime, millions of people continue to suffer. What responsibility do citizens of the developed world have to assist them?

In 1972, in one of the best-known papers in ethics, the philosopher Peter Singer proposed a simple and startling answer to this question.[a] The argument depends on an analogy between two cases. In the first case, imagine you are walking past a shallow pond and see a child drowning. Should you jump into the pond and rescue the child? Clearly, Singer says, you should. Although your clothes will get wet, that fact is morally insignificant in comparison to the child's drowning. In the second case, imagine that people are starving overseas. Should you donate the money needed to help save them? Again, Singer claims, clearly you should, and for the same reason. Although you may have to sacrifice some luxuries, those things are morally insignificant in comparison to saving the starving people. And the same argument applies, Singer claims, to every starving person in the world. In practice, this means that you ought to give away

all resources beyond those necessary to support yourself and your dependents, until global poverty is eradicated.

This conclusion calls for radical redistribution. Opponents of this perspective assert that Singer's argument underestimates the role of conflicting interests, cooperation failures, and weak institutions in undermining the effectiveness of aid interventions. For example, consider that aid donations must pass through several hands before they reach their intended beneficiaries. And the interests of some of the intermediaries involved may not be well aligned with those of the poor. Famine in the Sudan, for instance, is not primarily caused by lack of rain. Throughout recent decades, as a tactic in an ongoing civil war, the Sudanese government and associated militias have intentionally impoverished the country's poorest civilians, sometimes by seizing and diverting aid supplies for military purposes. Those who do have the interests of the starving at heart—international aid organizations—often struggle to effectively cooperate with the communities they aim to serve. Their struggle is partly a function of geographical and cultural distance, and partly a function of weak domestic institutions in less developed countries. These common problems suggest that the private aid recommended by Singer may in many cases be ineffective or even counterproductive.

The debate over the effectiveness of foreign aid interventions continues among political scientists and economists. A second response to Singer's argument sidesteps these empirical disputes and questions Singer's moral premise more directly. It is commonly held that there are limits on the extent to which we are morally required to sacrifice our own interests for the sake of others, however desperate their situation may be. A moral requirement to save a drowning child, should we come across one, is unlikely to run up against these limits, since most of us will rarely if ever find ourselves in such a situation. A moral requirement to save every person suffering from severe deprivation, on the other hand, may well run up against these limits, given the sheer magnitude of global poverty. The extreme demand that this moral requirement makes may be enough to undermine it. Nonetheless, scenes like those we see today in Darfur make the question of how to respond to poverty and suffering hard to ignore. ▪

a. Peter Singer, "Famine, Affluence and Morality," *Philosophy and Public Affairs* 1, no. 1 (1972): 229–43.

GLOBALIZATION AND ITS DISCONTENTS

Over the past 20 years, developing countries have gradually committed themselves to more engagement with the global economy. In this context, their interests may be more in line with those of the developed nations. The LDCs have also tended to participate more fully in international economic institutions. This reflects a widespread acceptance of the desirability of economic integration and a broader belief that there is scope for some of the common interests of developed and developing nations to create opportunities that will speed economic growth and development in Africa, Asia, and Latin America.

But the turn toward globalization in the developing world has not been without difficulties and critics. One source of stress has been the series of financial and currency crises that have affected a score of developing countries (see Chapters 7 and 8). While such developing countries as Mexico, Thailand, and Argentina benefited from massive inflows of capital, they also suffered debilitating crises when these flows stopped. As developed countries had themselves discovered, integration into world markets has costs as well as benefits, creates losers as well as winners. The depth of the currency and financial crises led many observers to question whether the benefits of openness to international investment truly outweighed its costs.

The threat of crisis was heightened by the concern that the new economic openness was not delivering the kind and rate of economic growth many analysts had anticipated. Economic reform was, in the minds of many, justified by pointing to how rapidly such countries as South Korea had rushed to modernity, and at how relatively equitable their societies had become in the process. This justification was immensely attractive to people in developing countries whose economies had been stagnant, and in which the gap between rich and poor had been growing. But many developing countries grew only slowly or not at all, an outcome that disappointed those who had hoped to see tangible results of the economic reforms. Even more disturbing was that income appeared to be getting more unequally distributed in many of the reformed developing countries. Then there were true developmental disasters, countries that seemed to be sinking ever farther into destitution and, in some cases, social chaos.

While there have been success stories, the overall picture is still troubling. Many of the developing world's people still live in poverty. While the impoverished are a smaller share of LDC population than 25 years ago, due to population growth there has still been an increase of about 100 million people in the ranks of the poor. Meanwhile, many developing countries—including some of the fastest growers—have become more unequal as they have grown.

The sense of disappointment with the past 25 years of development policies and outcomes has led to a backlash against the economic reforms of the 1980s and 1990s. Some of this backlash has taken the form of electoral successes by politicians who have been very critical of current policies—such as Hugo Chávez in Venezuela, Evo Morales in Bolivia, and more broadly the government of the Islamic Republic of Iran. Even governments that remain fully committed to integration in the world economy have searched for ways to mitigate the social costs of this integration and to address the political discontent that has become common in much of the developing world.

Conclusion: Toward Global Development

At the human level, the most pressing issue today is how to improve the living standards of the billions of people in the developing world who live in or near poverty. This is why so many nongovernmental organizations (which we will discuss more in Chapter 10) focus on development issues. Most generally, finding an effective path toward the goal of broad-based economic development requires a clear understanding of how and why countries have failed or succeeded in developing. While scholars and others continue to debate the matter heatedly, the discussion above points to several components of a reasonable diagnosis of the sources of underdevelopment, and suggestions about what might be done to overcome them.

ADDRESSING INTERNATIONAL FACTORS

While developed and developing countries have many interests in common, there are also important areas in which their interests conflict. And interactions between developed and developing countries almost always favor developed countries. Industrialized nations are richer and more powerful than the LDCs and can usually get their way in bilateral and multilateral negotiations. Although scores of developing nations have been involved in international trade bargaining rounds, the outcomes of these interactions have been far more reflective of developed-country concerns than of developing-country preferences. International institutions tend to reflect inherent power relations among nations, which means that they favor developed over developing nations. The principal international economic organizations—the International Monetary Fund, the World Bank, the World Trade Organization—all have an implicit or explicit bias toward the interests of the rich nations. Sometimes the bias is formal, as when votes are weighted by economic size in the IMF; sometimes it is informal, based only on the greater wealth and power of the industrialized world. Either way, the policy bias of these international institutions can bend outcomes in ways that are not favorable to the developmental prospects of poor nations.

The developed countries are unlikely to cede influence over the outcome of international bargaining, or over international institutions, for purely humanitarian reasons. Yet there are common interests between rich and poor nations, and there may be scope for agreement on reforming international institutions to make them more responsive to the LDCs. Indeed, the IMF and World Bank have undertaken reform efforts to address some LDC criticisms of their activities. But there are many observers who believe that reform of international institutions has to go farther in order to have a substantial impact on development prospects.[21]

To the extent that these international factors impede LDC progress, their mitigation might speed it. And inasmuch as both the developed and the developing

---

21. Stiglitz, *Making Globalization Work*, is a prominent statement of the position that lays much of the blame on the structure of the international order and that presents proposals for global reform.

world can benefit from faster growth and more stability in the LDCs, there is scope for LDC and developed-country interests to emphasize shared goals over individual ones. However, a diagnosis of failures of development that rests too strongly on international constraints faces the reality that the same international conditions seem to allow for strikingly different national economic outcomes—for example, Burma and Thailand, Botswana and Zambia. While the external environment may not be as favorable as LDCs might like, it has permitted the emergence of some very striking success stories in addition to spectacular failures. This observation leads us back to the conclusion that domestic forces are probably the principal factors affecting economic growth and development.

ADDRESSING DOMESTIC FACTORS

As we have seen, interests within a poor country can stand in the way of its overall economic progress. Powerful groups may hamper the government's ability to improve education, social services, or the economic infrastructure. But even the most malevolent interests can only impede economic progress if they are successful in dominating society and politics. Where the impact of self-interested groups is countered by broad public pressure, the result is less likely to impede economic development. Where groups can cooperate to support the provision of public goods, rather than fighting over private benefits, all of society will be better off in the long run. Likewise, the political institutions of developing nations have a powerful impact on whether their citizens are able to overcome obstacles to development. A well-functioning electoral democracy, for example, can reduce the impact of venal private interest groups and can serve as a brake on the activities of corrupt public employees.

The conclusion that domestic features of LDCs are key to understanding their problems is guardedly optimistic. It is optimistic because it suggests that the future of the developing nations is in their own hands, rather than being hostage to geographical destiny or the nature of the international system. Indeed, a growing number of countries have succeeded in narrowing the development gap. But this optimism must be guarded. For where economic development has been held back for decades, even generations, by domestic interests, interactions, or institutions, it is likely to be difficult to change these conditions. Nonetheless, this would appear the most promising path forward in the continuing effort to reduce the enormous disparity between the world's rich minority and its poor majority.

Reviewing Interests, Interactions, and Institutions

INTERESTS	INTERACTIONS	INSTITUTIONS
Citizens share a common interest in national economic development. However, some groups may have interests that conflict with broader national development goals.	Actors within a developing society often collaborate, both among themselves and with government, to provide the conditions for economic growth. However, frequent conflicts among contending groups can impede successful development.	Such international institutions as the International Monetary Fund, the World Bank, and the World Trade Organization help order economic relations between developed and developing world.
Most countries agree on the desirability of economic development in the poor nations.	Developed and developing countries cooperate on many dimensions to organize and carry out trade, finance, and investment between North and South.	These institutions are heavily influenced by the rich and powerful developed nations, often to the detriment of the interests of the developing world.
There are substantial conflicts of interest among countries over how the international economy should be organized, and in particular how the benefits of international exchange should be divided among developed and developing countries.	There is frequent conflict between developed and developing countries over the division of the benefits of their trade, financial, investment and other economic relations.	There is frequent conflict over the "rules of the game" of the international economy, which are now largely written by and for the wealthy. There have been continuing demands from poor countries for a more equitable distribution of influence in international economic organizations.

Key Terms

less developed countries (LDCs), p. 334

infrastructure, p. 336

primary products, p. 347

oligopolistic, p. 347

terms of trade, p. 347

import substituting industrialization (ISI), p. 350

export-oriented industrialization (EOI), p. 352

Washington Consensus, p. 353

Group of 77, p. 354

New International Economic Order, p. 354

commodity cartels, p. 355

For Further Reading

Bates, Robert. *Markets and States in Tropical Africa.* Berkeley: University of California Press, 1981. Offers a classic analysis of how political factors can lead developing-country governments to pursue policies that impede economic growth.

Diamond, Jared. *Guns, Germs, and Steel.* New York: Norton, 1997. Makes a striking argument about the fundamental impact of geography on the development of nations and continents.

Milanovic, Branko. *Worlds Apart: Global and International Inequality, 1950–2000.* Princeton: Princeton University Press, 2005. Offers an impressive, and often startling, summary of the level of and trends in international inequality.

Rodrik, Dani. *One Economics, Many Recipes: Globalization, Institutions, and Economic Growth.* Princeton: Princeton University Press, 2007. Presents a prominent economist's ideas about how globalization can be made more compatible with the needs of developing countries.

Sachs, Jeffrey. *The End of Poverty: Economic Possibilities for Our Time.* New York: Penguin, 2006. Presents an optimistic argument by a leading public intellectual about the desirability, and the possibility, of lifting billions of people out of poverty.

Stiglitz, Joseph. *Making Globalization Work.* New York: Norton, 2006. Provides a critical look by the Nobel laureate and former World Bank chief economist at how the contemporary international economic order impedes economic growth and development, and what might be done about it.

FIND REVIEW AND STUDY MATERIALS ONLINE AT WWNORTON.COM/STUDYSPACE

Transnational Politics

The *Mayflower*, carrying settlers to the New World, took 66 days to cross the North Atlantic. You can now fly from London to Boston in just over seven hours. In the 1780s, a letter mailed from England took between eight months and a year to reach Australia; today, email blazes around the world in the blink of an eye. In 1930, a three-minute phone call from New York to London cost, in today's prices, approximately $250, in 1950 about $50, and today it is virtually free.

The same technologies that have spurred economic globalization, examined in the previous section, also permit individuals and groups to organize and interact globally in unprecedented ways. International political movements and groups have always existed. In the nineteenth century, for instance, abolitionists and suffragists in North America and Europe coordinated their campaigns to end slavery and gain women the right to vote, respectively. But today we are witnessing an explosion of transnational political actors. The Union of International Organizations has identified over 25,000 international nongovernmental organizations now operating around the globe. Some observers believe this growth in transnational organizations has the potential to transform the nature of world politics.

Given the high costs of communication and transportation in the past, for most of human history it was not inaccurate to believe that "all politics is local." For many, governments and their policies were distant abstractions, made manifest only in the tax collector or sheriff. What government did or did not do mattered little in daily life, except among the economic and political elite. And with the exception of war, the actions of foreign governments mattered even less to the average person. Today, governments have a much greater impact not only as a result of their larger size and responsibilities, but also because their policies often have consequences that reach beyond their territories and citizens. Government actions (and inaction) spill over and affect the welfare of actors in other countries. Ozone depletion, climate change, and other environmental threats are global challenges. Countries that act to reduce harmful emissions improve the welfare of everyone, and those that choose not to reduce them impose costs on us all. Human rights abuses by a government against its own citizens prompt moral outrage around the world, and individuals demand that their own governments do something to help the victims of these abuses. In our interdependent world, it is only a mild exaggeration to say that "all politics is global."

New transnational actors and new transnational issues combine to create a possibly new transnational politics. In the chapters in this section, we examine who these new actors are. What are their interests, and how and in what ways do they affect the interests of other actors? How do they interact with one another and with the other actors that populate the pages of this book, such as governments and businesses? Do they

In an increasingly interconnected world, transnational groups often play a prominent role in a range of international issues. Here, workers for Save the Children, a transnational network with organizations in dozens of countries, deliver food for refugees in Sudan.

modify or possibly even transform international institutions? And perhaps most important, do they contribute to international cooperation or, in the case of transnational terrorists, to international conflict?

We address these questions first in the case of transnational networks in Chapter 10, looking at both advocacy and terrorist networks. We then turn to two issue areas in which transnational problems call for transnational solutions. The movement for human rights is the subject of Chapter 11. The international environment and the politics of ozone depletion and global climate change are examined in Chapter 12.

Transnational Networks

By coordinating the efforts of organizations in over 90 countries, the International Campaign to Ban Landmines (ICBL) has succeeded in passing international laws to outlaw and remove deadly landmines in many countries. Here, runners in Nairobi, Kenya, participate in a road race as part of the ICBL's Mine Free World summit.

In a globalizing world, are transnational networks of private individuals and organizations transforming world politics?

I n 1997, the International Campaign to Ban Landmines (ICBL) and its coordinator, Jody Williams, were awarded the Nobel Peace Prize for their work in support of the Convention on the Prohibition of the Use, Stockpiling, Production and Transfer of Anti-Personnel Mines and on Their Destruction (known as the Ottawa Convention). The ICBL is a network of 1,400 nongovernmental organizations (NGOs) from over 90 countries working to outlaw and remove land mines, which are estimated to wound or kill approximately 15,000 to 20,000 people worldwide each year. The Norwegian Nobel Committee applauded the campaign for moving the ban from "a vision to a feasible reality" and acclaimed the organization as a model for international disarmament and peace. Signed by 122 countries, the Ottawa Convention prohibits land mines and mandates the clearing of existing mine fields. The convention entered into force in March 1999 and became binding under international law. Only 42 countries remain outside of the treaty entirely, including China, Egypt, Finland, India, Israel, Pakistan, Russia, and the United States. Since the successful adoption of the Ottawa Convention, the ICBL has continued to advocate universal ratification and full implementation of the agreement. In the ICBL, we see how a global network of committed activists can successfully mobilize public opinion and press governments to change policy and practice in ways that greatly improve the lives of countless individuals.

On September 11, 2001, Al Qaeda carried out the largest terrorist attack in history on the United States, destroying the World Trade Center in New York, damaging the Pentagon, crashing an airliner in Pennsylvania, and in total killing nearly 3,000 people. Emerging from the anti-Soviet resistance movement in Afghanistan in the 1980s,

Not all transnational groups are peaceful. Transnational terrorist networks, like Al Qaeda, use violence to try to bring about political change. In March 2004, a group affiliated with the Al Qaeda network detonated bombs on four commuter trains in Madrid, Spain, killing over 190 people and wounding many more.

Al Qaeda has now become a pan-Islamic network targeting regimes in the Middle East as well as Western governments. As a transnational network operating in at least 12 countries, it is responsible for multiple attacks. Following the 9/11 attacks, the United States launched a "global war on terror," invading Afghanistan in an attempt to destroy Al Qaeda and overthrowing the Taliban government with which it was allied. In spite of these efforts, Al Qaeda has proven remarkably difficult to identify and combat. Since 9/11, the network has carried out terrorist attacks against crowded commuter trains in Madrid, Spain, killing more than 190 and wounding over 1,400 people; against buses and subways in London, England, killing 52 and wounding over 700; and against multiple targets in Iraq, including foreign military forces, Iraqi police and military forces, and numerous civilian sites, with uncounted casualties. Like the ICBL, Al Qaeda is a transnational network of committed groups and individuals seeking to bring about political change. Unlike its peaceful counterpart, however, Al Qaeda has chosen to use violence in pursuit of its interests.

World politics have been conceived traditionally as an arena in which states are the dominant actors. Scholars have always recognized the existence of other potentially influential actors. As a leading international relations theorist and an advocate of a "state-centric" approach to studying world politics, the political scientist Kenneth Waltz writes: "states are not and never have been the only international actors. . . . The importance of nonstate actors and the extent of transnational activities are obvious."[1] Yet, analysts have long focused on states as the prime movers of world politics. In our age of transnational politics, when new connections are rapidly being forged between individuals and groups across national borders, this narrow focus is increasingly questioned.

Transnational networks are composed of sets of constituent actors engaged in voluntary, reciprocal interactions of communication and exchange across national borders.[2] The constituent actors may include: (1) international and domestic NGOs involved in research and advocacy, (2) local social movements, (3) foundations and other philanthropic organizations, (4) the media, and (5) churches, trade unions, and consumer and other civil

1. Kenneth N. Waltz, *Theory of International Politics* (Reading, MA: Addison-Wesley, 1979), 93–94.
2. On political networks, see Miles Kahler, ed., *Networked Politics: Agency, Power, and Governance* (Ithaca, NY: Cornell University Press, 2009).

organizations.[3] These actors are united by shared values and cooperate frequently in the exchange of information and services. Despite the sometimes large number of constituent actors, sustained cooperation is possible because of their common interests and repeated interactions, which allow for strategies of reciprocal punishment if temptations to defect arise. Although transnational networks may have central actors linked to many other actors or coordinating committees to set the agenda for the network, as voluntary and nonhierarchical entities, these networks lack a centralized authority that can mandate actions by their members. In the terms used in this book, we can think of transnational networks as actors composed of other actors united by shared interests in a dense web of cooperative interactions.

In this chapter, we focus on two kinds of transnational networks. Transnational advocacy networks (TANs), like the ICBL, aim to bring about political and social change through social mobilization, changes in social norms, and political pressure on governments. TANs have existed in different issue areas for centuries. Nonetheless, the number and scope of TANs have grown dramatically over the last few decades.

Transnational terrorist networks employ violence to bring about political change. Terrorists differ from TANs not necessarily in their aspirations, but in the way they interact with states and, obviously, in their choice of political strategy. Al Qaeda is perhaps the largest and certainly the most notorious of these groups. Although the exact numbers and structures of such clandestine networks remain unclear, they have seized a prominent place on the contemporary world stage and pose new threats to states and the existing international order.

Even if the reality of international politics has never quite fit the image of state-to-state diplomacy, the rapid growth of transnational networks in recent years is provoking a lively debate about the changing nature of world politics. On one side of this debate, some analysts claim that transnational networks are displacing states and creating new, more populist and dynamic forms of international politics. On the other side, other analysts assert that transnational networks exist only with the permission of states and remain under their control.

A focus on interests, interactions, and institutions can help us understand how transnational networks matter in world politics. In this chapter, we develop three major points.

CORE OF THE ANALYSIS

▶ Globalization is connecting people in new ways and mobilizing new actors with new interests across national borders in transnational networks. TANs seek to alter the interests of states by creating new knowledge or changing international norms by framing issues in ways that mobilize popular support. By contrast, terrorists have extreme interests that are not widely shared by others.

▶ Transnational networks interact with states in a variety of ways. TANs alter interactions between states by mobilizing social pressure for policy change, and they facilitate cooperation by providing information about international agreements and monitoring compliance. Terrorists use threats of violence to bargain with and extract concessions from states. Like war (see Chapter 3), acts of terrorist violence are caused by bargaining failures that arise from informational asymmetries and problems of credible commitment.

▶ The ability of transnational networks to bring about policy change is affected by domestic political institutions. Both TANs and terrorists can more effectively mobilize social pressures in democracies than in autocracies.

▶ Although transnational networks are exerting new pressures on states, the object of their political action continues to be state policy. This suggests that such networks are not displacing states as central actors or institutions of world politics.

3. Margaret E. Keck and Kathryn Sikkink, *Activists beyond Borders: Advocacy Networks in International Politics* (Ithaca, NY: Cornell University Press, 1998), 9. We exclude international organizations and governments from this list, although individuals in these organizations may interact with transnational networks. On public transnational networks, see Ann-Marie Slaughter, *A New World Order* (Princeton: Princeton University Press, 2004).

Do Transnational Advocacy Networks Make a Difference?

transnational advocacy network (TAN): A set of individuals and nongovernmental organizations acting in pursuit of a normative objective.

nongovernmental organizations (NGOs): Private organizations not directly affiliated with national governments and usually focusing on social, economic, and political change in a country or region.

Transnational advocacy networks (TANs) are, as the name implies, sets of activists comprising many individuals and **nongovernmental organizations (NGOs)** acting in pursuit of a normative objective, including (in the contemporary era) human rights, the environment, economic and social justice, democracy, women's rights, and abortion rights or, conversely, the right to life (see Figure 10.1). In fact, the number of TANs has grown dramatically over the past 50 years, with the most rapid increase occurring in the 1990s (see Figure 10.2). Nearly all the issues that mobilize individuals into politics within states now have an international counterpart. For example, the Planned Parenthood Federation of American, often on the front lines of the movement to make or keep abortion legal, has eight foreign affiliates and cooperates with hundreds of other organizations and countless individuals worldwide in the women's rights and legalized abortion movement. Heartbeat International, a network of pro-life pregnancy centers, has affiliates in 38 countries and works with many churches and other organizations to promote the right to life. Gaining momentum in the United States, the struggle over abortion has become an international political issue with transnational networks on both sides of the question coordinating action, sharing information and tactics, and mobilizing new members. TANs coordinate the activities of participants around the globe and initiate, lead, and actively direct collective action on issues of concern. TANs influence world politics in at least three fundamental ways.

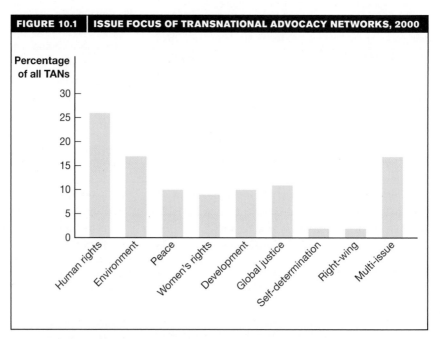

FIGURE 10.1 | ISSUE FOCUS OF TRANSNATIONAL ADVOCACY NETWORKS, 2000

Source: Jackie Smith, "Exploring Connections between Global Integration and Political Mobilization," *Journal of World System Research* 10, no. 1 (2004): 266, Table 2.

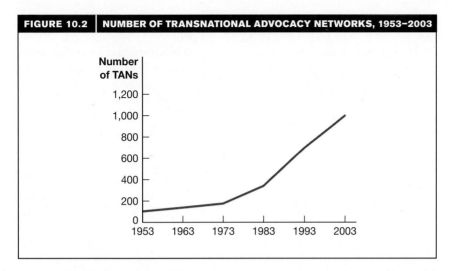

FIGURE 10.2 | NUMBER OF TRANSNATIONAL ADVOCACY NETWORKS, 1953–2003

Source: For 1953–1983, from Kathryn Sikkink and Jackie Smith, "Infrastructures for Change: Transnational Organizations, 1953–1993," in *Restructuring World Politics: Transnational Social Movements, Networks, and Norms,* ed. Sanjeev Khagram, James V. Riker, and Kathryn Sikkink, 30, Table 2.1 (Minneapolis: University of Minnesota Press, 2002). For 1993 and 2003 (estimated), from Jackie Smith, "Exploring Connections between Global Integration and Political Mobilization," *Journal of World System Research* 10, no. 1 (2004): 266, Table 2.

CHANGING MINDS, ALTERING INTERESTS

Much of the popular and scholarly attention to TANs stems from a belief in the power of ideas to alter perceived interests and to change behavior at the individual and state levels. TANs alter the way actors think about their interests, first, by bringing new knowledge to public attention. For example, as evidence of global warming has become increasingly clear, it has been brought to the attention of people around the globe by environmental TANs such as Greenpeace and former vice president Al Gore's Alliance for Climate Protection. By increasing public awareness, TANs have persuaded individuals to place a higher priority on stopping global warming. New public pressure, in turn, has helped to elevate the issue on the political agenda, even if action on policy remains halting and tentative. Responding to new public pressure, some politicians are beginning to place greater emphasis on protecting the environment.[4]

Yet, scientific or technical knowledge seldom translates directly into policy change. Expert consensus can call attention to new problems and point to possible solutions, but groups negatively affected by the proposed policy changes will also mobilize politically to influence government decisions. For example, the scientific community agreed for decades on the hazards of smoking before the tobacco industry lobby in the United States was finally defeated and policy altered. In many countries, government policy still favors smokers even in the face of nearly

---

4. Communities of technical experts who create and promote new knowledge are often called epistemic communities but are in practice similar to TANs. See Peter M. Haas, ed., *Knowledge, Power, and International Policy Coordination* (Columbia: University of South Carolina Press, 1997).

norms: Standards of behavior for actors with a given identity; norms define what actions are "right" or appropriate under particular circumstances.

universal scientific agreement on the harmful effects of smoking. Knowledge is power—but it alone may not be enough to set policy.

Perhaps more important, TANs also change how actors conceive of their interests by promoting new norms. **Norms** are standards of behavior for actors with a given identity; they define what actions are "right" or appropriate under particular circumstances. We share numerous norms in our daily lives, with some being so deeply internalized that we often fail to recognize their impact. For example, we all wear clothes in public and regard communities that have not adopted this practice as "primitive" and individuals who do not conform as "abnormal." In the United States, we do not eat certain foods like dogs, rodents, and insects, but these foods are part of a normal diet in some other cultures. In international relations, the laws of war, embodied in the Geneva Conventions, codify norms on the treatment of prisoners captured on the battlefield and civilians.[5] There appears today to exist a "nuclear taboo," or a norm that prohibits the first-use of nuclear weapons, as well as a prohibition on state-sanctioned assassinations of political leaders. This latter norm is evidenced by the nearly universal condemnation of Syria for its role in the killing of Lebanon's former prime minister, Rafik Hariri, in February 2005.

Norms are most easily observed when they are violated. Their presence is revealed both by the censure of others and, usually, by the justifications or excuses given by the offending party. For example, the strong norm against cannibalism in most societies can be appropriately broken under extraordinary circumstances. In 1972, the airplane carrying a college rugby team from Uruguay to a match in Chile crashed in the Andes mountains. Isolated and without significant supplies, the survivors eventually resorted to eating the flesh of their deceased teammates. Although the survivors later were broadly condemned in the press, many commentators observed that under the circumstances the survivors had had little choice. Even the Catholic Church later said that it would have been a greater sin to starve to death when an alternative, however odious, existed. Internationally, the strength of the norm on the treatment of prisoners of war was revealed relatively recently by former president George W. Bush's efforts to create a new category of detainee called "enemy combatants," which he claimed were exempt from the requirements of the Geneva Conventions—especially from the strictures on interrogations and imprisonment without trial. One can consider the creation of a new category as an attempt to excuse the violation of the norm by denying that it holds in the context of the war on terror. Nonetheless, the treatment of prisoners held by the U.S. government at Guantánamo Bay, Cuba, was criticized by many other countries, even some fighting alongside the United States in Iraq.[6] President Barack Obama moved quickly after taking office to terminate the category of enemy combatants and to close the prison at Guantánamo. In doing so, he sought to bring the United States into conformity with international norms.

---

5. There are six separate agreements that are collectively referred to as the Geneva Conventions. For a brief history and explanation, see www.genevaconventions.org.

6. In June 2006, the U.S. Supreme Court agreed with these critics, with the majority of the justices holding that as international law duly ratified by the United States, the Geneva Conventions clearly applied to the detainees and that therefore the U.S. government needed to respect those Conventions.

Norms affect behavior and, in turn, political outcomes by raising the costs of inappropriate actions and thereby making them less likely, and at an extreme by ruling out otherwise feasible alternatives. The norm against cannibalism was so strong that the Uruguayan rugby players resorted to eating the leather on the airplane seats, despite knowing that the chemicals used in its manufacture were harmful, before turning to the flesh of their deceased teammates. Although nuclear weapons could be used in military conflicts—and military planners certainly maintain a variety of options should the ultimate need arise—the nuclear taboo appears sufficiently strong that most states even in highly volatile crises do not expect disputes to be resolved in a nuclear holocaust. In most situations, nuclear weapons are simply not an option for states that possess them even when the potential target lacks the capacity to retaliate with an equally devastating counterattack. The norm creates a high cost—the potential outrage of the international community—for any state considering the use of nuclear weapons.[7]

The Norms Life Cycle

Of course, norms existed and spread throughout the world system prior to the recent growth in TANs. After all, not all norms are connected with TANs and their activities. But one important function of TANs is to encourage and support socially appropriate behavior and help spread norms across national borders. Martha Finnemore and Kathryn Sikkink, two leading scholars of norms in international relations, posit a three-stage **norms life cycle** that can help us understand how TANs shape norms and interests and, thus, political outcomes.[8]

In the first stage, norms entrepreneurs—individuals or groups with strong beliefs about desirable behavior—actively work to convince a critical mass of other individuals in other states to embrace their beliefs. The currently strong norm that medical personnel on the battlefield and wounded soldiers be treated as neutral noncombatants, for instance, is rooted in the crusade by Henry Dumont, a Swiss banker, who helped found the International Committee of the Red Cross. Similarly, the National Rifle Association (NRA) is working globally to promote the principle that owning a gun is a natural right. Although its charter prohibits the organization from funding groups in other countries, it is building a network of like-minded organizations around the world. Whether the NRA will succeed in establishing gun ownership as a right outside the United States is not clear, but its efforts already helped defeat a national gun control law in Brazil in October 2005.[9] It is during this first stage that most TANs develop as vehicles for the dissemination of new norms.

Norms entrepreneurs "frame issues to make them comprehensible to target audiences, to attract attention and encourage action, and to 'fit' with favorable institutional venues."[10] Perhaps most important, they find creative ways to connect the behavior they wish to encourage to other, preexisting norms; because

norms life cycle: A three-stage model of how norms diffuse within a population and achieve a "taken-for-granted" status.

---

7. See Nina Tannenwald, "The Nuclear Taboo: The United States and the Normative Basis of Nuclear Non-Use," *International Organization* 53, no. 3 (Summer 1999): 433–48.
8. Martha Finnemore and Kathryn Sikkink, "International Norm Dynamics and Political Change," *International Organization* 52, no. 4 (Autumn 1998): 887–917.
9. David Morton, "Gunning for the World," *Foreign Policy* (January/February 2006), 58–67.
10. Keck and Sikkink, *Activists beyond Borders,* 2–3.

TANs and other groups try to frame issues in a way that will win sympathy for their position. In the case of female circumcision, opponents have framed it as female genital *mutilation* (FGM) to emphasize the violence of the practice. Supporters of the tradition try to frame the controversy as a case of western values being forced on a local culture.

these norms are already widely accepted, audiences are likely to see the value in the desired behaviors or ends. Activists "win" by framing principles they want to promote so that they connect to principles that are already accepted in a community.

One effective frame is to redefine undesirable behaviors as perpetrating violence against innocent persons, which is nearly universally abhorred. The women's rights movement, for instance, failed to make progress for many years in the 1980s and 1990s because it was caught between three competing frames: one of discrimination, emphasizing the principle of gender equality articulated in the 1979 Convention on the Elimination of All Forms of Discrimination against Women; one of economic development and the need to improve the quality of life for women; and one of general human rights, claiming that civil and political rights for everyone could not be secured without protecting the rights of women as well, adopted at the 1993 World Conference on Human Rights. Seeking to build an integrated transnational movement, activists finally framed the issue as one of violence against women and made this approach the centerpiece of the United Nations Conference on Women in Beijing in 1995, successfully bridging the competing frames and rallying the women's rights network behind a unified message of opposition to all forms of violence against women.[11] In the case of female genital cutting, opponents framed the practice simply by changing the name from female circumcision (thereby breaking its association with the traditional practice of male circumcision, which does not produce the same long-term health problems) to female genital mutilation, which carries stronger connotations of violence against women. Traditionalists, in turn, attempted to frame the issue as one of local culture against western values imposed by colonial governors and Christian missionaries. By connecting the practice to the larger anticolonial struggle, they ensured some continuing support among local communities and, thus, continuing controversy.[12] Similarly, the NRA attempts to frame the issue of gun ownership by linking it to the concept of human rights, while advocates of gun control emphasize firearm safety and the threat to children.

During the second stage, once a new frame has taken hold, a "norms cascade" occurs as the number of adherents passes a tipping point beyond which the idea gains sufficient support that it becomes a nearly universal standard of behavior to which others can be held accountable. The tipping point is often hard to identify in advance; it is determined not only by the number of actors that adopt the new belief but also by those actors' leadership or visibility within the international community. Conformity to the new norm can then be established

11. Ibid., chap. 5.
12. Ibid., 67–71.

through coercion (such as economic sanctions in the case of human rights norms) or through socialization (a process akin to peer pressure in which, say, states adopt new behaviors because that is what "good" states do). The norm of national election monitoring appears to have recently crossed this threshold. Although the norm was essentially unknown before 1978, virtually all democratizing states now invite other governments or transnational NGOs to monitor their first elections. Indeed, the failure to invite external monitors is taken as an indication that the incumbent leader or party intends to steal the election by engaging in some form of fraud.[13]

In the third stage, norms are internalized or become so widely accepted that they acquire a "taken-for-granted" quality that makes conforming almost automatic. Indeed, even contemplating the violation of the deeply internalized norms against cannibalism or eating certain foods can make some people feel ill. Norms against slavery or violence against political prisoners, once the subjects of TAN activity, are now at least partially internalized within many countries, although violations still occur. Few norms governing relations between states have reached this final stage, although the rules of war embodied in the Geneva Conventions and the nuclear taboo may be close.

Once internalized, norms affect the way in which actors conceive of their interests. Prior to this stage, norms are enforced by the sanctions or moral disapproval of others. These forms of punishment raise the costs of engaging in behaviors that violate the norm, thereby affecting the choices actors make in particular interactions. But once a norm is internalized, certain actions are simply not considered because they are normatively prohibited (taboo) and others are favored as appropriate or correct. At this deepest level, internalized norms lead actors to reconceive their interests, to reorder how they evaluate alternative political outcomes and the appropriate means of achieving them.

PUTTING PRESSURE ON STATES

TANs exert leverage over states directly by calling attention to violations of widely held norms—a practice known as naming and shaming. States typically value their reputations as "good" countries that respect and comply with standards of appropriate behavior. A reputation as an honorable or norm-abiding country may have intrinsic value. It may also be valued because it facilitates cooperation with other countries. By calling attention to violations of norms, TANs mobilize the "court of world opinion" to castigate and shame states into altering abhorrent behavior. They also challenge and potentially damage the reputations of offending states. If countries violate norms frequently and are called to account repeatedly by TANs, they risk becoming international pariahs that other states will be reluctant to trust. Although naming and shaming might seem like a weak tool to leverage good compliance from otherwise strong states, over the long run it can severely weaken a state's reputation and put potentially profitable cooperation at risk.

---

13. Susan D. Hyde, "Catch Me If You Can: Why Leaders Invite International Election Monitors and Cheat in Front of Them," http://ssrn.com/abstract650262 (accessed 8/22/08).

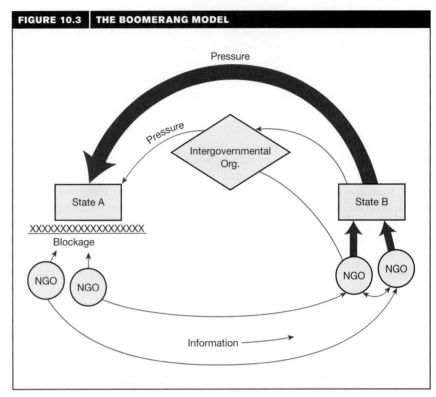

FIGURE 10.3 | THE BOOMERANG MODEL

Pressure

Pressure

Intergovernmental Org.

State A

XXXXXXXXXXXXXXXXXX

Blockage

NGO NGO

State B

NGO NGO

Information →

Note: This stylized depiction of the boomerang model shows how NGOs that are blocked from influence within their own state (State A) can appeal to other transnational NGOs, which press their states (State B) or an international organization to press State A to change its policy.

Source: Reproduced from Margaret E. Keck and Kathryn Sikkink, *Activists beyond Borders: Advocacy Networks in International Politics* (Ithaca, NY: Cornell University Press, 1998), 13.

boomerang model:
A process through which NGOs in one state are able to activate transnational linkages to bring pressure from other states on their own governments.

TANs can also affect the behavior of states and outcomes indirectly by invoking the coercive power of other states. In the **boomerang model** proposed by Margaret Keck and Kathryn Sikkink, NGOs in one state are able to activate transnational linkages to bring pressure from other states on their own governments (see Figure 10.3).[14] This process is most likely to be effective when NGOs are blocked from influencing their own governments, as is common in many nondemocratic regimes. Unable to appeal to their own governments, NGOs activate their transnational network and bring their plight to the attention of NGOs and individuals in other countries, who in turn press their governments or, perhaps, international organizations into action. These other governments then demand that the first state alter its behavior or remove the block on its own NGOs. In this way, foreign states are mobilized to try to influence the offending state. Reflecting the importance of domestic political institutions, the boomerang model is most likely to be activated by NGOs originating in nondemocratic regimes and directed at NGOs

14. Keck and Sikkink, *Activists beyond Borders,* 12–13.

in more democratic states, where governments are more sensitive to social demands pressed by their voters.

The anti-apartheid movement in South Africa is a good example of the boomerang model in action (see Chapter 11). Excluded from power and influence in the white-dominated government, black South Africans, their NGOs, and their allies in the society appealed to foreign TANs in their struggle. These advocacy networks mobilized opinion and voters in other countries—mostly in western democracies—whose governments placed sanctions on South Africa and eventually helped topple the apartheid regime. As this example suggests, the essence of the boomerang process involves domestic NGOs bringing greater pressure to bear on their government than they would be able to exert on their own. The process does not require any actor to alter its perceived interests; instead, the activation of transnational ties changes the nature of the political game in which the domestic actors are engaged and makes socially inappropriate behavior most costly.

FACILITATING COOPERATION

TANs can also affect behavior and outcomes by providing information to states both before a final agreement is reached, as endorsers, and afterwards, as monitors. In both cases, the information provided by TANs facilitates interstate cooperation that would otherwise fail. In this way, TANs provide important support for international cooperation.

TANs as Endorsers

International agreements can be quite complex. We assume that the negotiators themselves know and agree on the terms of any given treaty or executive agreement they sign, although many agreements contain ambiguous language to paper over differences between parties or do not consider all possible contingencies under which the agreement might hold. But members of the legislature that must ratify the agreement or implement its terms typically do not have a detailed understanding of its provisions. Furthermore, the voters who must reelect the executive who negotiated the deal, or the legislators who concurred, almost certainly do not know much about the agreement undertaken in their name.

Legislators and voters can learn whether to support or oppose an agreement from TANs that track the negotiations, study the final text, and endorse or reject its provisions. Legislators or voters need not know a great deal about the substance of the policy issue or the agreement, but they can make informed choices by taking cues from groups that (1) share their preferences or have some external incentive (such as penalties for lying) to truthfully reveal what they know, and (2) possess real knowledge about the agreement.[15] Thus, in considering whether to support a proposed environmental treaty, a legislator need not study the text closely but can notice whether representatives of a trustworthy TAN have endorsed the agreement and decide how to vote accordingly. Legislators who support tighter environmental

---

15. This discussion draws on Arthur Lupia and Mathew D. McCubbins, *The Democratic Dilemma: Can Citizens Learn What They Need to Know?* (New York: Cambridge University Press, 1998).

regulations will vote for treaties endorsed by, say, the Sierra Club, Greenpeace, and similar organizations; those who prefer less stringent regulations will vote against treaties endorsed by those same groups.

The endorsements by TANs provide an inexpensive informational shortcut that allows legislators or voters to make decisions (nearly) identical to those they would make if they were completely informed. TANs are often particularly effective endorsers precisely because they are perceived as principled actors with strongly held normative beliefs. When they speak for or against an issue on which they are perceived to possess expertise, their voices are typically quite loud and are heard clearly by legislators and voters.

By helping voters or legislators to make appropriate decisions on the basis of limited information, TANs enhance the prospects for cooperation between states. Whenever a domestic legislature must ratify an international agreement, the effect is to make cooperation between two countries less likely.[16] If the legislature is uncertain about the content and meaning of the agreement negotiated between the executive and the foreign state, it may mistakenly reject agreements that all three parties would prefer. Similar to the problem of bargaining in war (see Chapter 3), uncertainty makes bargaining inefficient and more likely to fail. TANs can reduce such uncertainty and improve the likelihood of cooperation by providing information to all the parties. In this way, TANs facilitate cooperation between states that would otherwise not occur.

TANs as Monitors

TANs can also monitor whether and how states comply with international agreements. By revealing information about compliance after an agreement is reached, TANs allow states to have greater confidence that future agreements will be honored.

Having reached an agreement, states acquire information about compliance in one of three ways. First, they can rely on the self-reports of others. Many international agreements depend on this mechanism, requiring states to report on their efforts to reduce atmospheric emissions, for instance. This mechanism is in fact relatively weak, as states that have incentives to cheat on agreements are also likely to have incentives to lie about their cheating. Self-reports are only useful when they can be verified by one of the other mechanisms.

Second, states can monitor one another's behavior directly. For example, the arms control agreements negotiated between the United States and the Soviet Union during the Cold War depended on direct monitoring. Yet, direct monitoring is often quite expensive, as each state must expend resources in collecting information about often hard-to-observe behaviors by others. Direct monitoring is sometimes likened to police patrols actively circulating on their "beats" looking for violations of the law.[17] Such direct monitoring can be inefficient, as monitors must be in the field even when violations are not occurring. It can also be imperfect, as monitors may be occupied or distracted elsewhere when violations do occur. Nonetheless, this practice is a common means of monitoring compliance in international relations.

---

16. See Helen Milner, *Interests, Institutions, and Information: Domestic Politics and International Relations* (Princeton: Princeton University Press, 1997).
17. See Mathew D. McCubbins and Thomas Schwartz, "Congressional Oversight Overlooked: Police Patrols versus Fire Alarms," *American Journal of Political Science* 28, no. 1 (February 1984): 165–79.

What Role Should TANs and MNCs Have in Upholding Labor Standards?

Nike is the largest athletic shoe company in the world, controlling over 33 percent of the industry's global market and employing 600,000 workers in 51 countries.[a] In recent decades, however, Nike's public image has sometimes been associated with scandal as well as success. One scandal broke on the morning of January 9, 2001, in the small Mexican town of Atlixco. At Kukdong International Mexico factory, a *maquiladora* manufacturing Nike college apparel for several large U.S. universities, over 850 striking workers seized control of the factory. The workers complained of appalling conditions, including worm-ridden cafeteria food, respiratory problems caused by lack of protective gear, physical and verbal abuse, forced overtime, wages of $30 for a 45-hour week, and violation of the right to unionize. International public outrage followed the revelations. Labor rights TANs, including the Worker Rights Consortium and the Fair Labor Association, lobbied university administrations to pressure Nike to intervene. As a result, several hundred fired workers were reinstated and allowed to organize in an independent union. More generally, Nike increased its efforts to implement independent factory inspections, made public its list of suppliers, and is now one of the industry leaders in developing corporate codes of social responsibility.

While some observers hear in this story a stirring tale of the power of transnational advocacy networks to promote global welfare, others interpret it more bleakly as illustrating some of the moral complexities involved in private political action across borders. International labor rights is an area where interactions among the holders of distinct interests, under the shadow of weak institutions, result in difficult choices. Are these choices ones that TANs are well placed to make?

Supporters of labor rights TANs argue that the case for advocating stricter labor standards in developing countries is extremely strong. After all, they say, decent working conditions

are a universal right possessed by everyone, regardless of nationality. While perhaps it was once solely a national responsibility to enforce those rights, this is no longer so. Through the global supply chains that deliver our new sneakers and college hoodies, we directly participate in, and benefit from, abuses like those the Kukdong workers suffered. However, this international connection also creates a new opportunity to help workers. We can use our influence as consumers and citizens to push for a fairer global economy.

Other observers argue that this approach is overly simplistic. Improved labor standards, they claim, may protect the interests of some workers, but only at the expense of the severely disadvantaged. The reason springs from the way in which labor protections interact with other features of the contemporary global economy. Multinational corporations (MNCs) like Nike subcontract to factories in developing countries like Mexico because those countries have a comparative advantage in cheap labor. Labor standards decrease that advantage by raising the cost of hiring workers. To stay competitive in industries with very tight margins, factories respond to increases in the cost of labor by employing fewer workers. Terminated employees become unemployed or move to even less attractive occupations. In the longer term, MNCs may abandon the host country entirely and shift production elsewhere, depriving that country of an important route to future economic growth. The result may be detrimental not only to a country's interest in escaping poverty, but also to its citizens' interest in collective autonomy: in making important social and economic decisions for themselves. These concerns reflect two ethical worries about TANs: their capacity to do inadvertent harm through ignorance of local economic and political circumstances, and their lack of accountability to those whom they attempt to help. The challenge that global labor activists face is one of finding a path that promotes the rights of all workers in a way that is sensitive to both national variation and national autonomy. Whether that path can be found depends on how well two important nonstate actors—TANs and MNCs—can cooperate with states to find it. ∎

a. Richard Locke, Fei Qin, and Alberto Brause, "Does Monitoring Improve Labor Standards? Lessons from Nike," *Industrial and Labor Relations Review* 61, no. 1 (2007): 3–13.

TANs may monitor compliance with international laws and call attention to violations. Greenpeace frequently monitors compliance with laws against whaling, pollution, and deforestation. Unlike many TANs, Greenpeace sometimes goes farther and confronts violators directly, in addition to reporting their actions.

Third, states can monitor indirectly by listening to the testimony of trustworthy third parties. Here, TANs can be useful in identifying and calling attention to violations of international agreements. Indirect monitoring is common in the human rights issue area, where organizations like Amnesty International and Human Rights Watch track practices globally and issue calls to their members and states when violations are observed. Similar practices are emerging in the issue area of the environment. Nearly 10,000 NGOs were officially permitted to participate in the 1992 Earth Summit, the largest-ever gathering of national leaders to discuss protecting the environment. Not only did these organizations conduct a parallel summit and make policy proposals to the interstate meeting, but through their participation they were accredited and legitimated as the watchdogs of the agreements made at the conference. With their new acceptance and prominence, this transnational environmental network has played an important role in calling international attention to poor environmental policies and practices worldwide. Indirect monitoring is similar to fire alarms: when problems arise, concerned parties pull the alarm and alert others who respond, but only when necessary. When trustworthy monitors are available, indirect monitoring is far less expensive to states and more efficient than the alternatives. By facilitating monitoring and reducing its costs, TANs help promote cooperation that states would otherwise be reluctant to endorse (see "Controversy," on p. 379).

In sum, TANs can make an important difference in international relations. By providing information and promoting new norms of behavior, TANs change individuals' and states' conceptions of their interests. In bringing pressure on states, TANs create new international interactions and help change state policy and practice. Finally, as endorsers and monitors, TANs facilitate cooperation between and among states. As we shall see again in the following chapters on human rights (Chapter 11) and the environment (Chapter 12), TANs play an important role on the international stage.

Why Do Some Transnational Networks Choose Violence?

The attacks by Al Qaeda on the United States on September 11, 2001, killed 2,982 people and disrupted the lives of tens of thousands more. After decades of steadily declining transnational terrorist attacks, this was by far the most lethal terrorist attack in modern history (see Figures 10.4 and 10.5). Indeed, of all the casualties suffered by Americans at the hands of transnational terrorists since 1968, when analysts first began to systematically document these trends, 97.5 percent occurred on that single fateful day.[18]

The United States responded vigorously. It stepped up homeland security efforts, which included imposing new security measures at airports and other public venues and hunting down and capturing suspected terrorists. It also responded with a global war on terror, invading and overthrowing the governments of both Afghanistan (for harboring Al Qaeda) and Iraq (in part because it was mistakenly believed to possess the potential to pass weapons of mass destruction to terrorists). The subsequent though less deadly attacks in Madrid, London, and elsewhere imply to many observers that we are now facing a worldwide struggle. Indeed, since 9/11, average fatalities per year from transnational terrorist networks have more than doubled from their pre-2001 levels. Yet, in the United States, the number of incidents and fatalities has fallen once again to near zero. It remains an open question whether the attacks on 9/11 were an anomaly from the more general pattern of declining incidents and fatalities, or whether the absence of attacks on Americans since 2001 reflects the success of the global war on terror.

The U.S. government defines **terrorism** as the use or threatened use of "premeditated, politically motivated violence against noncombatant targets by subnational groups or clandestine agents, usually intended to influence an audience."[19] In the absence of any political motivation, terrorism reduces to simple criminality. Terrorism is transnational, and properly the subject of international relations, when it crosses an international border by involving a perpetrator or victim from another country or when it aims to alter the behavior of a foreign government.[20]

How can we understand these incidents of hijacked airliners flying into skyscrapers and

> **terrorism:** The use or threatened use of violence "against noncombatant targets" by individuals or nonstate groups for political ends.

On July 8, 2005, terrorists attacked London subways and this bus during the morning rush hour. The suicide bombers who carried out the attacks appeared to be linked to the Al Qaeda network and left videotapes demanding that Britain withdraw troops from Iraq and Afghanistan.

---

18. All incident and fatality numbers for this chapter are derived from the MIPT Terrorism Knowledge Base, previously available at: www.tkb.org/Home.jsp. Data are current from June 21, 2007. Unfortunately, the dataset has been discontinued by the U.S. Department of Homeland Security.
19. United States Code, title 22, chapter 38, sec. 2656f(d). Any definition of terrorism is itself a political statement. *Terrorist* is a term of opprobrium intended to delegitimate the action and, in turn, the cause for which violence is used. Thus, who is and is not a terrorist is often contested. State-sponsored terrorism involves government funding or support of terrorists. State terrorism, which we do not consider here, involves the targeting of noncombatants by the government with the intent of influencing an audience.
20. Most terrorism, it should be noted, is purely domestic and does not cross national borders.

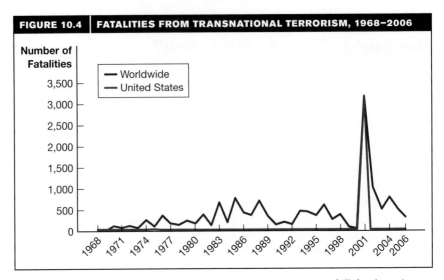

FIGURE 10.4 | FATALITIES FROM TRANSNATIONAL TERRORISM, 1968–2006

Note: From 1968 to 2000, approximately 271 people worldwide, on average, were killed each year in transnational terrorist attacks. The attacks on 9/11 in 2001 are unprecedented in the number of fatalities, as witnessed in the dramatic spike that year. Since 2001, deaths from terrorism have averaged 606 per year, more than double the overall pre-2001 rate. Deaths from transnational terrorism have been rare in the United States, averaging just two per year before 2001 and less than one in the years since.
Source: MIPT Terrorism Knowledge Base.

trains and buses destroyed by suicide bombers? The central puzzle about terrorism is why some transnational networks resort to violence—and especially violence against civilians—rather than use other, more peaceful strategies for influencing states. A common explanation is that terrorists are hate-filled, irrational extremists who win glory by taking the lives of others. This view is too simplistic. Rather, terrorism, like war, is a product of bargaining failures prompted by incomplete information or problems of credible commitment. As we shall see, violence arises from the terrorists' interactions with target states and other actors. Depending on the nature of the informational asymmetries they face, terrorists employ four different strategies: coercion, provocation, spoiling, and outbidding, each with a unique logic.

ARE TERRORISTS RATIONAL?

In popular discussions, it is often implied that terrorists are irrational. If so, this characterization would significantly challenge our ability to analyze their behavior within the analytic framework developed in this book. It is important to examine critically three reasons for this perception before turning to a positive explanation of terrorism.

First, groups that resort to violence often possess interests that are not widely shared, especially by the target audience. Describing terrorists as irrational may simply mean that terrorists rank alternative outcomes in ways that are "unreasonable," at least from the broader population's perspective. However, as we saw in Chapter 2, rationality refers to purposive behavior or the strategies by which individuals or groups pursue their interests; the term *rational* is not a statement about the substance

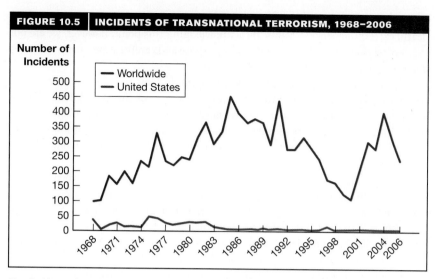

FIGURE 10.5 | **INCIDENTS OF TRANSNATIONAL TERRORISM, 1968–2006**

Note: Incidents of terrorist violence reached a peak in 1986 and declined steadily thereafter until 2001. Relatively few attacks have been directed against the United States, with the majority occurring in the 1970s in the form of airplane hijackings.
Source: MIPT Terrorism Knowledge Base.

of an individual or group's preferences. We may not agree with the preferences of terrorists and their supporters, but the fact that we disagree does not necessarily imply that the strategy they choose in pursuit of their interests is irrational. Indeed, there is substantial evidence that given their interests, terrorist networks choose targets, respond to risk, and adjust to counterterrorist efforts in quite purposeful or rational ways.[21] One common explanation for the expanding number of suicide attacks in recent years, for instance, is that as sites have become harder to destroy by more conventional methods, terrorists have upgraded from "dumb bombs" controlled by a timer, to "smart bombs" in the form of well-trained suicide bombers who can adapt to countermeasures and react to events on the scene.[22] Reflecting a highly rational calculus, terrorists appear to select targets according to how well they are defended, the chances of a successful attack, and the targets' political impact.

Second, a person's choice to become a terrorist—especially to become a suicide bomber—may entail costs larger than the gains to that individual and, thus, appears not to be an effective strategy for obtaining one's goals. It is true that we do not currently possess good explanations for why any particular individual chooses to become a terrorist or a suicide bomber. After all, the sacrifice of one's own life seems a high price to pay for any cause. However, we also lack complete explanations for why an individual man or woman may voluntarily choose to join a national military and go into battle to risk death for his or her country. For any

21. For an example of how terrorists rationally exploit cooperation failings between governments, see Todd Sandler, "Collective Action and Transnational Terrorism," *World Economy* 26, no. 6 (2003): 779–802.
22. Eli Berman and David Laitin, "Hard Targets: Theory and Evidence on Suicide Attacks" (Working Paper W11740, National Bureau of Economic Research, November 2005).

individual, such choices may be irrational in that the personal costs (the risk of death) exceed the personal gains. By acknowledging this point, however, we are not suggesting that a terrorist network lacks purpose and careful strategizing in how it deploys its forces, including suicide bombers.[23]

Third, terrorist attacks are sometimes random. In some cases, of course, it is clear why terrorists choose a certain target, as the selection of the World Trade Center and Pentagon as targets on 9/11 demonstrates. These sites were chosen because they represent the core of America's international power—business and the military. More generally, the most frequent targets of terrorists are businesses and diplomatic missions, which also serve as emblems of the target state's power (see "What Do We Know?" on p. 385). But certainly some terrorist attacks are random, as when a suicide bomber selects one crowded pizzeria rather than another. Random selection of targets and times, however, is often part of a terrorist's strategy. After all, one objective of terrorism is to strike fear into the target population. If terrorist attacks are systematic and predictable, the population will adjust accordingly and avoid likely targets when an attack is anticipated. By selecting random times and places, terrorists can make people feel unsafe everywhere and greatly magnify the threat they pose and the fear they instill. Sometimes, selecting targets randomly can be quite intentional.

THE STRATEGIC LOGIC OF TERRORISM

A key point in understanding terrorism is that terrorist networks are weak relative to their targets (usually, states) and, moreover, weak relative to the demands they make. This weakness influences the way they choose to interact with states and when bargaining failures occur.

Terrorism is an extreme form of asymmetrical warfare, or fighting between parties of highly unequal military capabilities. States are nearly always stronger politically and militarily than the terrorist networks they face. Whereas states have populations and economies they can tax for resources and standing militaries they can deploy, terrorist networks are often starved for resources, quite small in numbers, and poorly armed, especially in their formative stages when they are most vulnerable to government countermeasures. They must often resort to criminal activities such as drug running or bank robbery to acquire their initial funding, although some grow out of legitimate religious and service activities (such as Hamas) or depend on the personal wealth of their founder (such as Osama bin Ladin in the case of Al Qaeda; see "What Shaped Our World?" on p. 388).

Because terrorists lack the means to attack and defeat the target's military forces directly, they typically attack civilians, government embassies, and other official buildings. As the German military theorist Carl von Clausewitz (1780–1831) explained, the object of *war* is to defeat the other side's military so that the victor can impose its political will on the now-defenseless opponent. The object of *terrorism*, in contrast, is to bypass the other side's military (which would otherwise

---

23. Terrorist volunteers are often less educated and poor, while actual terrorists are well educated and generally more well off. For a screening model that explains this paradox, see Ethan Bueno de Mesquita, "The Quality of Terror," *American Journal of Political Science* 49, no. 3 (2005): 515–30.

Patterns of Terrorist Violence

A reader of North American newspapers might be forgiven for believing that terrorism is increasing, is directed largely toward the United States and its interests, is very deadly, and is always carried out by religious extremists. That reader would be wrong, because the pattern of violence is much more complex. Figures 10.4 and 10.5 in the text show that worldwide, incidents of terrorism had been falling dramatically until 9/11. In the United States, terrorist incidents peaked in the 1970s and have been very rare since the mid-1980s. Here, we elaborate further on these trends.

Since 1968, the most frequent sites of transnational terrorist attacks have been in the Middle East (including the Persian Gulf) and Western Europe, followed by Latin America and the Caribbean (see Figure A). Despite the current concern in the United States with terrorism, North America as a whole accounts for only 4 percent of all transnational terrorist attacks in the last 38 years (and only 0.3 percent in the years since 2000). The pattern looks different, however, if we examine fatalities; North America accounts for 23 percent of the total deaths from terrorism, but this high figure is almost entirely a product of the attacks on 9/11.

The image of terrorism seared into the minds of many is the collapse of the twin towers of the World Trade Center, which killed thousands. But most terrorist attacks kill far fewer people. Since 1968, the over 10,000 incidents of transnational terrorism worldwide have averaged 1.5 deaths—for a yearly average of 389 deaths. The modal, or most frequent, type of transnational terrorist attack produces no casualties at all.

In the United States, the 442 transnational terrorist attacks since 1968 have averaged 6.9 deaths per incident, which falls to less than 0.2 if we exclude the attacks of 9/11. Averaging 78 deaths per year (2 deaths per year, excluding the attacks of 9/11), transnational terrorism kills as many Americans as do bites by mammals other than dogs. Without minimizing the importance of lives lost to terrorism, we can say that one is far less likely to die in a terrorist attack than in virtually any category of accident tracked by the National Safety Council.[a]

The largest number of attacks—and the most deadly—are carried out by nationalist and separatist groups (see Figure B). Communist and socialist groups attack relatively frequently, but these incidents harm or kill comparatively few people. Religious groups account for only 15 percent of all attacks but for more than 50 percent of all deaths from terrorism worldwide. Other groups carry out attacks but produce no casualties, and there have been no recorded attacks or fatalities by transnational racist groups since 1968.

Finally, the most frequent targets of terrorism are diplomatic facilities and businesses, both relatively soft targets that are hard to defend and easy to attack. The largest numbers of fatalities have occurred in terrorist attacks on businesses and airports and airlines, followed by private citizens and property. Despite their obvious vulnerabilities, there have been no attacks on food and water supply systems or on telecommunications systems. ■

a. Nonterrorist deaths are for 2005 from the National Safety Council, available at www.nsc.org/research/odds.aspx (accessed 12/2/08).

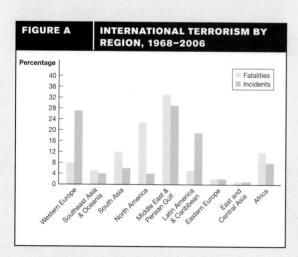

FIGURE A   INTERNATIONAL TERRORISM BY REGION, 1968–2006

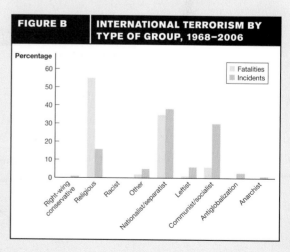

FIGURE B   INTERNATIONAL TERRORISM BY TYPE OF GROUP, 1968–2006

Source: MIPT Terrorism Knowledge Base, previously available at www.tkb.org/Home.jsp (accessed 6/21/07), but subsequently discontinued by the U.S. Department of Homeland Security.

result in certain defeat) and inflict pain and suffering on the target population so as to induce political change (see pp. 392–97).

Terrorists are also **extremists** in the sense that they are politically weak relative to their demands. Extremists may want to create a new utopia under their preferred laws and practices, but in reality they lack the capability to realize their aims in the foreseeable future. In other words, extremists possess interests that are not widely shared by others. In any population there is a range of individual interests over issues such as the most appropriate political system, the distribution of resources, proper religious beliefs, and so on. For most issues the range of interests is distributed in a bell-shaped curve, with most people being "moderate" and clustered in the middle of the distribution (see Figure 10.6). When we call someone "extreme," we typically mean that his or her interests are significantly different from those of the majority. In the curve illustrated in Figure 10.6, extremists exist in the "tails" of the distribution to either the left or the right of the moderate majority. In fact, what it means to be an extremist is relative: someone who is an extremist in one society might not be in a second (for example, moderates in Britain may have very different interests from moderates in Pakistan). But extremism implies that relatively few other individuals share their political preferences. Extremists, therefore, almost by definition are small networks of individuals who face a much larger majority that does not share their views and that will likely resist having those minority beliefs imposed on it. Unlike TANs, which can use framing to persuade others to accept their principled beliefs, extremists have difficulty in convincing others peacefully to share their interests. Their hope lies in using violence to coerce concessions or somehow alter the status quo in their favor.

Although they are unable to defeat the military power of the states they target, terrorists adopt organizational forms that make it difficult for traditional military force to defeat them. First, terrorists typically form networks of small, self-contained cells that are loosely connected to one another and, in some cases, to a central directorate (again, see "What Shaped Our World?" on p. 388). Unlike

extremists: Actors whose interests are not widely shared by others; individuals or groups that are politically weak relative to the demands they make.

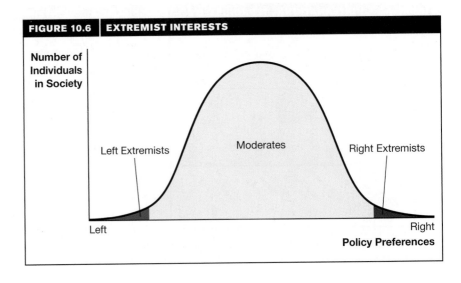

FIGURE 10.6 | **EXTREMIST INTERESTS**

Number of Individuals in Society

Left Extremists

Moderates

Right Extremists

Left

Right

Policy Preferences

states, which have internal hierarchies, and more like TANs, terrorists are organized in networks of individuals and groups that cooperate to achieve common aims. Yet, unlike TANs, which disseminate information widely in attempts to name and shame norm violators and to monitor international agreements, terrorists generally do not share information within the network; each cell is largely responsible for its own activities and acquires resources and information from other cells or the center only as necessary. This loose network insulates the individual cells and allows the organization to survive when penetrated or attacked. If the potential target state successfully infiltrates or destroys a cell, there is minimal impact on the rest of the network. Only if the central directorate is destroyed will the organization as a whole be damaged; but even then, as we have seen since the U.S. invasion of Afghanistan and the disruption of Al Qaeda's central node around bin Laden, the individual cells may still continue to function in some capacity.

Second, terrorists "hide" in sympathetic populations. In cases where the group is not too extreme, and thus has affiliated individuals who share (or at least do not oppose) their interests or in which the local population has been radicalized and now shares the extremists' beliefs, terrorists can live within a larger population that protects and supports them. This is the case for Palestinian extremists, who were once outliers but have gained support as the Palestinian community has become progressively more sympathetic to their cause. In other cases, terrorist groups can buy support from a corrupt, failed, or sympathetic state to gain refuge, as Al Qaeda did when, having been expelled from Saudi Arabia, it set up bases in Sudan and, after the Taliban seized power, subsequently returned to Afghanistan and helped support the strict Islamic government there. Hidden within larger populations, terrorists are difficult to identify. Attempts to eliminate them, in turn, are likely to cause collateral damage to the larger population, and thus raise the costs of any retaliatory or preemptive attack by the target state. Indeed, networks of loosely connected cells hidden in sympathetic populations make terrorist groups hard to eradicate.

WHY DO TERRORISTS USE VIOLENCE?

Like war, terrorism is a form of bargaining, and acts of terrorist violence are the result of bargaining failures. In the same way as states do, groups can use violence or threats of violence to raise costs to the other side in hopes of eliciting concessions. In this way, terrorism and threats of terrorism are a form of bargaining. Yet, if the target state knows the costs that terrorists can inflict on it, and the terrorists know that they are unlikely to defeat the state but can extract some concessions by threatening violence, why can the state and the terrorists not reach a compromise that reflects their relative bargaining positions? If such a bargain were possible, then the terrorists would be spared the costs of carrying out the attack and the state would not incur damage from the attack and subsequent widespread fear. One of the primary goals of Al Qaeda was for the United States to withdraw its troops from the Arabian peninsula, where they were perceived as defiling the holy land and the birthplace of Islam. The United States was resistant to withdrawing its troops, hoping to use bases in Saudi Arabia to project power in the Middle East. Yet, after the attacks on 9/11, within two years most American troops were

The Rise of Al Qaeda

Al Qaeda (which translates as "the base" or "the foundation") was forged in the anticommunist resistance to the Soviet Union's occupation of Afghanistan during the 1980s. Like many other Islamists, Osama bin Laden, a member of one of Saudi Arabia's wealthiest families, joined the mujahideen in Afghanistan, becoming the prime financier for an organization that recruited fighters from around the Muslim world. After the Soviet Union's withdrawal in 1989, bin Laden formed the Islamic Army, which eventually evolved into Al Qaeda, and returned home to Saudi Arabia. When Iraq invaded Kuwait and threatened Saudi Arabia in 1991, bin Laden offered the kingdom 12,000 Islamic fighters. Instead, the Saudi government invited in over 500,000 U.S. troops to defend the kingdom. Outraged that "infidels" would defend the holy sites in the birthplace of Islam, bin Laden grew critical of the Saudi monarchy and was eventually expelled for antigovernment activities. He then moved his activities to Sudan, where he was welcomed by the Islamist government in Khartoum.

In Sudan, bin Laden began to shift his focus from the "near-enemy," local governments viewed as anti-Islamist, to the "far-enemy," the United States. Al Qaeda's grievances against the West in general and the United States in particular focus on their support for Israel, their backing of anti-Islamist and dictatorial governments in the Middle East,

and their military bases in Saudi Arabia. During this period, Al Qaeda is suspected of staging its first attacks against American interests, including possible involvement in the killing of 18 American soldiers in Somalia (1993), the truck bombing of the World Trade Center (1993), and another truck bombing outside a U.S. military complex in Saudi Arabia (1996).

Under international pressure, bin Laden was expelled from Sudan in 1996. Returning to Afghanistan, he allied himself with the Taliban government, offering to help defeat the Northern Alliance, a coalition of groups then fighting the Islamist regime. On behalf of the World Islamic Front, in early 1998 bin Laden issued a fatwa (religious ruling) declaring jihad against Jews and Crusaders. Al Qaeda then attacked the U.S. embassies in Kenya and Tanzania (1998), provoking President Bill Clinton to retaliate by launching cruise missiles at Al Qaeda training camps in Afghanistan, placing a $25 million bounty on bin Laden for

information leading to his capture, and convincing the United Nations to impose economic sanctions on Afghanistan to force the Taliban to extradite bin Laden to the United States. Al Qaeda subsequently attacked the USS *Cole*, which was docked for resupply in Yemen (2000), and the World Trade Center, the Pentagon, and a third site—which was aborted—on September 11, 2001. The United States then invaded Afghanistan, deposed the Taliban regime, and searched for Al Qaeda's leadership, which escaped and is believed to be hiding in the mountainous border area between Afghanistan and Pakistan. Since 9/11, Al Qaeda has been associated with train bombings in Madrid (2004) and bus and subway bombings in London (2005).

Al Qaeda has been variously described as a social movement, an organization, and a network. In actuality, it contains elements of all three, but it is best characterized by its network structure that links together the other dimensions. At its core, Al Qaeda possesses a multinational group of professional terrorists under the leadership of bin Laden that directs political strategy, allocates resources, recruits followers, and directs the activities of other members. In many ways, this core resembles a hierarchical organization. Relations between the core and its followers, in turn, are more clearly networked, with regional groups and individual operatives receiving direction from the center but also possessing a measure of autonomy to conduct their own activities. More diffuse still is the substantially larger group of sympathizers—the movement—who identify with the political goals of the center and may occasionally supply resources, convey information, or assist in other ways.

After the U.S. invasion of Afghanistan and the overthrow of the Taliban government, Al Qaeda lost its state protector and has evolved, as far as we can tell, into an even more diffuse network. Unable to operate safely within the territory of a state, the core group of leaders appears to have dispersed. Even communication among the leaders, and between them and their followers, can be dangerous, as it exposes them to surveillance technologies. As a result, individual groups or cells within the organization now possess greater autonomy and may be able to carry out attacks at their own initiative. ■

Source: Miles Kahler, "Collective Action and Clandestine Networks: The Case of Al Qaeda," in *Networked Politics: Agency, Power, and Governance,* ed. Miles Kahler (Ithaca, NY: Cornell University Press, 2009).

redeployed to Qatar in the Persian Gulf. If the United States was ultimately willing to remove its forces, why could Al Qaeda and Washington not negotiate this deal in advance and without the loss of nearly 3,000 lives?

Terrorism is costly for both target and perpetrator, and it leaves both sides worse off than if they could agree to a bargain without resorting to violence. Indeed, the puzzle of terrorism parallels the puzzle of war, discussed in Chapter 3. As in war, relations between the target and the terrorists can break down and lead to costly conflict under certain conditions. We can identify three sources of potential bargaining failures that lead to terrorism.

Terrorism from Incomplete Information

Like states in conflict, terrorists have private information and incentives to misrepresent that information to targets. Precisely because terrorist networks are small, weak, and often shadowy organizations that hide within sympathetic populations or in fragile states, targets usually possess incomplete information about them. Often, the first time anyone learns of a new terrorist group is after it claims credit for an attack. Even when targets have intelligence sources within the terrorist group, they may acquire relatively little information: the cell that is infiltrated or monitored may know little about other cells. Terrorist networks, in turn, have incentives to misrepresent their capabilities and resolve. By exaggerating claims of strength and commitment, these networks seek to negotiate better deals from their targets; meanwhile the targets, knowing that the networks have incentives to exaggerate, discount their claims.

Perhaps most important, since their ability to carry out attacks against militarily more powerful targets typically hinges on the element of surprise, terrorists cannot reveal their true capabilities or strategies in advance without undermining their effectiveness. If Al Qaeda had announced before 9/11 that unless the U.S. government conceded to its demands it would fly hijacked airliners into the World Trade Center and the Pentagon, the United States would have quickly responded by grounding all airplanes (which it did immediately after the attacks) and surrounding New York and Washington, D.C., with constant air patrols. By tipping its hand in advance to demonstrate that indeed it could carry out attacks of an awesome nature and magnitude, Al Qaeda would have lost the ability to implement those very attacks on the United States. There are inherent limits on the information that terrorists and states are willing to share with one another. Thus, terrorists and states are essentially unable to arrive at agreements that both would prefer over actually fighting.

Terrorists also have difficulty making their threats credible. As discussed in Chapter 3, unless the target state believes that the challenger will actually carry out a threat, it has no incentive to make concessions. Since threats are easy to make and may sometimes produce concessions, but are costly to carry out, terrorist networks have incentives to bluff by threatening attacks they will not fulfill even if their demands are not met. Target states should not believe every threat made by every terrorist. Conversely, being secretive organizations, terrorist networks may not be able to signal the intensity of their commitments to the cause for which they will fight. Since they are weak relative to the target and often have extreme interests, terrorist networks may have few options short of actually attacking to demonstrate the high costs they are willing to bear to achieve their aims.[24] As we now know, the United States had numerous hints about the impending attacks on 9/11.[25] These warning signals were ignored in part because the separate agencies of the U.S. government were not able to put together the disparate pieces of the puzzle they had before them, and because officials saw other threats as more important. But the warning signs were also not assigned priority and were, in essence, disregarded as the normal blustering of terrorists.

Terrorism from Commitment Problems

Problems of credible commitment may be as difficult to resolve for terrorist networks as problems of asymmetric information.[26] As part of any agreement reached before or after an attack, the target will insist that the terrorist network promise not to employ violence in the future. The whole point of making concessions to terrorists is to reduce the threat and fear of future attacks. Without a commitment by the terrorist network not to attack, there is little to be gained in making any concessions or entering into any agreements. A lack of credibility may prevent the conclusion of agreements that both sides prefer. After an agreement has been reached, continuing attacks may convince the target that the terrorists are unwilling or unable to exert control, and the agreement may be abandoned.

In contemplating any agreement, the target must judge the trustworthiness of the terrorist leadership and its ability to exert control over potential defectors within its ranks. Given their organization as decentralized networks of loosely connected individuals and cells, however, centralized control is often difficult to achieve. Problems of credible commitment are central to war between states. With networks largely lacking internal hierarchy, such problems may be even more severe in the case of terrorism.

Terrorists can most credibly demonstrate their commitment to peace by publicly renouncing terror, disarming, and giving the target or some neutral third party full access to the network so as to alleviate any lingering informational asymmetries. This approach has been key to the still fragile peace between Catholics and Protestants in Northern Ireland, where the IRA has disavowed terrorism, disarmed, and joined the political process. Yet, if the terrorists disarm, how can they be certain that the target will honor its side of the agreement? After all, it was the fear of continuing attacks that gave terrorists power over the target in the first place. Once that ability is given up, the target no longer has any incentive to compromise with the terrorists. Credibly agreeing not to fight may be more difficult than credibly making threats in the first place. Indeed, the difficulties of committing to peace have been a source of continued fighting in many terrorist conflicts—including that between the Basque

---

24. Harvey E. Lapan and Todd Sandler, "Terrorism and Signaling," *European Journal of Political Economy* 9, no. 3 (1993): 383–97.

25. See the Final Report of the National Commission on Terrorist Attacks upon the United States, *The 9/11 Commission Report,* authorized ed. (New York: Norton, 2004), 254–77.

26. Ethan Bueno de Mesquita, "Conciliation, Counterterrorism, and Patterns of Terrorist Violence," *International Organization* 59, no. 1 (2005): 145–76; Navin Bapat, "State Bargaining with Transnational Terrorist Groups," *International Studies Quarterly* 50, no. 1 (2006): 213–29.

separatist group Euskadi Ta Azkatasuna (ETA) and Spain, where both sides now appear to want peace but still have difficulty in credibly committing to a plan for disarmament and regional autonomy.

Terrorism from Indivisibilities

Terrorism can also arise from disputed subjects that cannot be divided and, therefore, cannot be the object of bargaining. As in the case of war (see Chapter 3), scholars are often skeptical that many disputed subjects are truly indivisible. Although groups have incentives to claim that demands cannot be compromised and must be granted "all or nothing," few objects are such that they can never be divided in any way.

The most active terrorist groups (by number of incidents; again, see "What Do We Know?" on p. 385) fight to gain regional or national independence. Again, although terrorists' demands are frequently stated in absolutist terms, regional or national autonomy is actually highly divisible. Federal (by territory) or communal (by group) autonomy is a common solution to separatist conflicts; such arrangements may range from limited language and education rights to almost complete

Nationalist and separatist groups are responsible for the largest number of terrorist incidents. Some separatists in the republic of Chechnya have turned to terrorism in their fight for independence from the Russian Federation. This car packed with explosives was blown up by separatists in the Chechen capital of Grozny.

decentralization of all government powers. Groups and states can, in principle, divide government authority in a nearly infinite number of ways.[27]

It is often claimed, however, that religion and sacred sites associated with religions are indivisible. Religious terrorism accounts for only about 15 percent of all attacks but for over 50 percent of all injuries and deaths from terrorism, suggesting that religious conflicts are among the more violent types in which terrorists are active and, perhaps, lending credence to this view on the indivisibility of sacred sites. Nonetheless, religious rights and practices can be divided—not by individual, typically, as people tend to identify themselves with one faith, but by the way in which society accommodates differences. All religions can be allowed to practice freely (as in the United States), or there can be a dominant state-sanctioned religion with others permitted to practice openly (as in Great Britain with the Church of England), or there can be a state-sanctioned religion (or non-religion) with others tolerated or allowed to practice only in private (as in many countries under communist rule, where religion was officially suppressed but continued to be practiced in private), or there can be a single religion enforced by the state (as in Iran). In principle and practice, there is great variety in the separation between church and state. Similarly, religious sites can be shared in varying degrees. Religions have existed side by side with one another throughout

---

27. Autonomy agreements, however, often lack credibility. See David A. Lake and Donald Rothchild, "Territorial Decentralization and Civil War Settlements," in *Sustainable Peace: Power and Democracy after Civil Wars,* ed. Philip G. Roeder and Donald Rothchild, 125–30 (Ithaca, NY: Cornell University Press, 2005).

human history and have worked out satisfactory accommodations. Thus, indivisibilities are not likely to be major impediments to successful negotiations, either for states or for terrorist networks. Instead, problems of incomplete information and credible commitment are more likely to be the fundamental causes of terrorism.

HOW CAN TERRORISTS HOPE TO WIN?

When bargaining fails and a group turns to terrorism, there are four principal strategies by which it may use violence to pursue its interests.[28] These strategies are not exclusive, and any particular attack can involve elements of more than one. Each strategy, in turn, is defined by a particular form of incomplete information—in essence, each differs in terms of who is uncertain about what. Understanding these informational asymmetries and strategies helps us further grasp the strategic logic of terrorism. For simplicity, we will identify three generic actors interacting with one another: a target state or population, a terrorist organization, and the terrorist's "home" state or population. Not every actor will be involved in each strategy, but including them helps us explain their differences. Figure 10.7 summarizes the four strategies, which we discuss in detail below.

Coercion

coercion: A strategy that induces policy change by imposing or threatening to impose costs, usually pain or other harm, on the target.

Terrorists can attack or threaten to attack to coerce a target into making concessions. **Coercion** induces policy change by imposing costs—usually, civilian deaths and casualties—on the target. More specifically, it is the *threat* of imposed costs that matters. The target may change its policy or offer concessions to avoid the costs. But if a threat is carried out and the costs are realized—people are killed, buildings are destroyed—the target has no incentive to alter its behavior. At that point, only the threat of *future* attacks will lead it to change its policy. By threatening to inflict harm on the target, terrorists aim to intimidate potential victims into making concessions. Being unable to defeat the target's military and impose their own policy demands, terrorists often use the fear of future attacks to motivate individuals to press their own government to change its policy or even to change the governing party. By attacking apparently at random, moreover, terrorists aim to strike broad fear into all segments in society and mobilize maximum pressure on the government.

Since it is the fear of future attacks that may induce policy change, it follows that actual attacks occur only to make credible the threat of future violence. This is necessary, in turn, when the target is uncertain about the terrorists' capabilities or resolve. The terrorist group might threaten costs of a certain magnitude unless appropriate concessions are made, but the target knows that the group has incentives to bluff and exaggerate its capabilities or willingness to actually bear the costs

---

28. Andrew Kydd and Barbara Walter, "The Strategies of Terrorism," *International Security* 31, no. 1 (Summer 2006): 49–80. We combine their strategies of attrition and intimidation into a single strategy of coercion.

FIGURE 10.7 | **STRATEGIES OF TERRORISM**

Target

Terrorist

?

Home
Population

a. Coercion. Target is uncertain about Terrorist's capabilities or resolve (purple arrow). Terrorist attacks to make its demands credible (red arrow). Attack is a form of costly signaling. *Example:* Sunni and Shiite attacks on U.S. forces in Iraq.

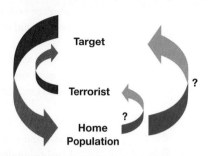

Target

Terrorist

?

Home
Population

?

?

b. Provocation. Home Population is uncertain about the interests of the Target and Terrorist (purple arrows). Terrorist attacks Target to provoke a response (small red arrow). Since it cannot identify Terrorist precisely, Target imposes collateral damage on Home (large red arrow). Home updates its beliefs about Target's interests and concludes that Target is greater threat than Terrorist. *Example:* Palestinian attacks on Israel.

Target

Terrorist

?

Home
Population

c. Spoiling. Target is uncertain about Home's ability or desire to honor agreement and restrain extremists (purple arrow). Terrorist attacks Target (red arrow), and Target updates its beliefs that Home cannot control Terrorist. Target is more likely to reject agreement as not credible. *Example:* Hamas attacks prior to Israeli elections in 1996 and 2001.

Target

Terrorist

?

Home
Population

d. Outbidding. Home is uncertain about Terrorist's interests and capabilities (purple arrow). Terrorist attacks Target to demonstrate capabilities and commitment to Home (red arrow). *Example:* Fatah and Hamas in West Bank and Gaza.

of carrying out the attack. To demonstrate its capabilities or resolve, the terrorist group must then attack the target to show that it can—and is willing to—carry out similar attacks in the future. In this way, attacks are a form of costly signaling intended to make credible the terrorists' threats of future violence unless their demands are met.

The costs to the terrorists of carrying out an attack are not only tangible (such as building bombs or recruiting suicide bombers), which tend not to be large, but also because an attack puts the group itself at risk. By attacking and then claiming credit for the violence, the network surfaces from within the population where it is hiding and risks calling forth the greater power of the state against itself. Bomb materials can often be traced, exposing its lines of supply. Specific individuals can be identified, allowing authorities to piece together links within the network and possibly undermine its operations. By demonstrating its capabilities, the network provokes a counterterror response against itself, which, if successful, may reduce its ability to carry out its threats of future violence. Thus, terrorist networks must balance the gain from making their threats credible against the risk of exposing themselves to counterattacks.

Nearly all terrorist attacks contain an element of coercion. Targets are almost always uncertain about the capabilities and resolve of terrorist networks, and networks must signal their ability and commitment through actual attacks. This type of signaling includes many small, demonstration attacks such as bomb scares, which are not designed to kill people or destroy property but to call attention to the network and signal that it has the ability to kill and destroy in the future if its demands are not met. In a form of pure signaling, the Basque separatist group ETA often gave warnings of its attacks so that people would not be killed. More spectacularly, Al Qaeda's attacks on 9/11 were almost certainly an attempt to coerce the United States into withdrawing its troops from the Arabian peninsula and perhaps ending its support for the Saudi regime. The simultaneous hijacking of four airliners and the destruction of the twin towers and the Pentagon were intended to demonstrate an ability to carry out great violence at the core of America's centers of power. The terrorist violence between Sunnis and Shiites in Iraq, often directed at heavily armed American troops, is also an attempt to demonstrate each group's capabilities and resolve as they struggle over the control of a future Iraqi state.

Coercive strategies of terrorism are most often directed at democracies. Reflecting the importance of domestic political institutions, governments in democracies are more responsive to the demands and views of their citizens. By targeting civilians and inducing fear in the population, terrorists hope to intimidate voters into pressing their governments to change policy in order to end the violence. Conversely, terrorism is used far less frequently against autocratic governments; when used in those environments, it is directed more at the political elite than at average citizens.[29]

Provocation

Terrorists may attack to provoke the target government into a disproportionate response that alienates moderates in the terrorists' home society or in other sympathetic audiences. Particularly dramatic and heinous attacks often leave the target government with little political choice but to respond with a vigorous counterstrike. After 9/11, there was significant domestic support—even pressure—for the administration of President George W. Bush to strike back forcefully against Al Qaeda. The Israeli government has long maintained a policy of at least "an eye for an eye," responding aggressively to all terrorist attacks on its soil or citizens. When terrorists are hiding within their home population, any counterstrike is likely to inflict collateral damage. If the target government is already

---

29. Robert Pape, "The Strategic Logic of Suicide Terrorism," *American Political Science Review* 97, no. 3 (2003): 343–61.

feared by the terrorists' home population as a threat to security, such a vigorous counterstrike can further radicalize that population and increase its support for the terrorists. Other audiences outside the terrorists' home society may also be alienated and possibly threatened by what are regarded as overly aggressive responses by the target. For example, Israel's counterstrikes against Palestinian militants cause many Arabs elsewhere in the Middle East to also oppose Israel. Following the terrorist attacks of 9/11, President Bush's reference to the forthcoming war on Afghanistan as a "crusade" was widely interpreted by Muslims in other countries as indicating hostility toward Islamic states everywhere.

Key to any strategy of **provocation** is the uncertainty of the terrorists' home population about the terrorists' and, more important, the target's interests.[30] The home population may worry that the terrorists themselves are extremists who pose a threat to their own security and safety. Although the terrorists may claim to be protecting the home population, that population may also be concerned about other dimensions of the terrorists' political agenda of which they disapprove. Simultaneously, however, the home population is uncertain about the target's interests and likely strategies. Many people in the Middle East, for instance, fear that the United States is an imperialist state aligned with Israel to impose its will on their countries. By attacking a target in the name of their shared interests, the terrorist network can provoke a disproportionate counterresponse and build support for its cause within its home population. In essence, the home population learns about how closely its interests are aligned with those of terrorists and the target. Disproportionate responses indicate to the home population that it has more to fear from the target than from the terrorist network. Members of the home population are then more likely to support the terrorists in their struggle with the now more threatening target. Through multiple applications of this strategy, terrorist networks can expand their base of support within their home populations and increase their political power over time.

Israel's retaliatory policy has had the effect, over time, of alienating moderate Palestinians and building support for more radical factions. Indeed, after years of skirmishing and occasional fighting, Israel's hard-line response to the (second) intifada, or "uprising," begun in 2000 finally led to the radical group Hamas (officially listed as a terrorist organization by the U.S. government) winning a majority in the parliament of the Palestinian Authority in January 2006. Similarly, although the invasion of Afghanistan and the overthrow of the Taliban regime by the United States after 9/11 were received with broad support, the American invasion of Iraq, widely seen internationally as unjustified, has served to persuade many people in foreign countries that the United States is now a significant threat to world peace. Indeed, with the exception of Germany, respondents in every country surveyed in 2006 by the Pew Global Attitudes Project identified the United States as a greater threat to world peace than either Iran or North Korea.[31]

provocation: A strategy of terrorist attacks intended to provoke the target government into making a disproportionate response that alienates moderates in the terrorists' home society or in other sympathetic audiences.

---

30. On provocation strategies, see Ethan Bueno de Mesquita and Eric S. Dickson, "The Propaganda of the Deed: Terrorism, Counterterrorism, and Mobilization," *American Journal of Political Science* 51, no. 2 (2007): 364–81.

31. The survey results are available at http://pewglobal.org/reports/display.php?PageID=824 (accessed 12/2/08).

Spoiling

Terrorists may also attack to sabotage, or spoil, a prospective peace between the target and the moderate leadership from their home society.[32] Target states are often uncertain whether an opponent, even if led by moderates, wants to settle the conflict and can control its extremists. Targets want to negotiate with trustworthy and capable moderates who want to and can make peace, but they do not want to negotiate with untrustworthy or incapable moderates who cannot or will not prevent further terrorist attacks. Unable to judge the sincerity or capability of the opponent's leadership, target governments watch for terrorist attacks to occur and break off negotiations when they do. By attacking, the terrorists can thus scuttle an agreement they oppose and hold out for terms they hope will be more favorable.

The purpose of the violence in **spoiling** is not to apply pressure on the target per se, but to play on doubts in the target state about whether the opponent can be trusted to implement a peace agreement and abide by it in the future. In this case, the target is uncertain about the home population's interests and capabilities, and whether it will be able to honor and enforce an agreement. When terrorists attack the target, the latter learns that the terrorists' home government either does not want to or cannot control its extremists, and thus it is more likely to reject agreements as not credible. Paradoxically, the effect of terrorist attacks on the target's willingness to make peace is greatest when the target initially believes the opponent's moderates are strong and able to restrain the terrorists. If the terrorists then attack, the target is more likely to conclude that the moderates are not sincere about making peace, as they apparently could—but chose not to—control the terrorists.

Spoiling is a problem in many peace negotiations. As the target and moderate elements of the home population get close to resolving their differences and signing a peace agreement, extremists attempt to halt progress by making renewed attacks. For example, repeated terrorist campaigns against Israel failed to scuttle the 1993 Oslo Peace Accords with the Palestinians. The Israeli Labor government, then in office, was more inclined than other parties to try to make peace, and it knew it was dealing with a fragmented coalition of Palestinians. Reflecting the paradox mentioned above, after the overwhelming victory of Yasir Arafat as president of the Palestinian National Authority in January 1996, Israel believed it was now dealing with a strong leader who could, if he so desired, control the extremists in his movement. When a new terrorist campaign erupted after the election, Israel concluded that Arafat was not sincerely interested in peace and that the Oslo agreement was doomed.

Outbidding

In poker, a player may raise the bet to convince others that she is holding a stronger hand. Likewise, when two or more terrorist networks or factions compete for support within their home populations, they may attack a target in an effort to outbid the other and demonstrate their capability for leadership and commitment to the

---

32. Andrew Kydd and Barbara F. Walter, "Sabotaging the Peace: The Politics of Extremist Violence," *International Organization* 56, no. 2 (2002): 263–96.

spoiling: A strategy of terrorist attacks intended to sabotage a prospective peace between the target and moderate leadership from the terrorists' home society.

cause for which they are fighting. In these cases, the purpose of the attack is not necessarily to coerce the target (although that may be a welcome by-product), but to cultivate support for the group within the home population. **Outbidding** arises when the home population is uncertain about which terrorist network is best able to represent and further its interests.

The rivalry between the Fatah and Hamas factions within the Palestinian movement has prompted each to attack Israel to demonstrate their credentials for leadership among a Palestinian population that is uncertain about which group to support. This rivalry has led to cycles of escalation wherein attacks by one network require attacks by the second so as not to be outdone by the first. Similarly, when Peru returned to democratic rule in 1980, the Shining Path group turned to violence to distinguish itself from rival groups that chose instead to participate in the electoral process. Outbidding appears to be driving many cases of suicide bombing, with the given network using a particularly heinous form of terrorism to demonstrate to its own people the depth of its commitment.[33]

The actors we call *target, terrorist,* and *home population* are convenient abstractions but obvious simplifications. Within any particular instance, these actors may need to be disaggregated further to reveal internal divisions. Likewise, the four strategies of terror are not exclusive. Terrorist networks can attack simultaneously to coerce a target into making concessions, provoke the target into a disproportionate response that radicalizes their home population, undermine prospective peace agreements, and build support for their faction over others within their home population. In any long-term struggle (such as that between Israel and the Palestinians, or between the Tamil Tigers and the government of Sri Lanka), all four strategies are likely to be employed at some point. We isolate the strategies here merely to highlight their different logics. Understanding the multiple strategies of terrorism, however, is important to designing effective counterterrorist responses.

> **outbidding:** A strategy of terrorist attacks designed to demonstrate a capability for leadership and commitment relative to another, similar terrorist group.

CAN TERRORISM BE PREVENTED?

Like the war on drugs, the war on poverty, or the war on crime, the global war on terror is likely to be a struggle without any clear end. As long as actors have different interests, and as long as individuals retain the ingenuity and ruthlessness that enabled 19 terrorists to use simple box cutters to transform airplanes into maneuverable kerosene-filled bombs, terrorism will remain a possibility. It is important to understand that problems of asymmetrical information and credible commitment will continue to lead terrorist networks to launch attacks simply to demonstrate that they can. Nonetheless, states can adopt certain counterterrorist strategies to make future attacks less likely and, perhaps, less destructive when they do occur. The same strategies also allow states to make smaller concessions to terrorists even when bargaining works and violence is avoided.

---

33. Mia M. Bloom, "Palestinian Suicide Bombing: Public Support, Market Share, and Outbidding," *Political Science Quarterly* 199, no. 1 (2004): 61–88.

Can Terrorism Be Deterred?

As discussed in Chapter 3, deterrence is a strategy to preserve the status quo by threatening challengers with unacceptable costs. Terrorism can in principle be deterred by potential targets threatening massive retaliation against terrorist networks should attacks occur. Although deterrence worked to avoid nuclear war between the superpowers during the Cold War, and although it may operate on a daily basis between states that might otherwise challenge one another if they thought the other would not fight back, many analysts are skeptical that in practice deterrence can work against terrorist networks—especially those armed with weapons of mass destruction.

Unlike states, terrorist networks do not possess a clearly identifiable location against which targets may respond. If terrorist networks believe they can escape retaliation by hiding in unknown locations, they are less likely to be deterred from attacking. This consideration is real. However, weapons materials can be traced, and nuclear and chemical weapons require large processing facilities that are hard to hide. Given today's advanced technological devices, it is quite likely that targets could, with time, identify who manufactured the weapons and where they originated. Thus, it is not the absence of a location against which to retaliate that undermines deterrence as much as two, more subtle, problems.

First, when terrorists use a strategy of provocation, retaliation by the target—especially massive retaliation with weapons of mass destruction—may simply play into their hands. Retaliating against a terrorist stronghold will likely kill a significant number of members of the home society, confirming for previously undecided moderates that the target really is a threat to their own security. Unless the retaliating target succeeds in eradicating the terrorist network, a cycle of attacks and counterattacks may over time serve only to increase political support for the terrorists.

Second, and closely related, the threat of retaliation by the potential target may not be credible. Since terrorists hide in larger populations, massive retaliation—especially with nuclear weapons—would likely kill many individuals who are unrelated to the terrorist network. Would the United States, for instance, be willing to annihilate hundreds of thousands of likely innocent people to destroy a terrorist cell operating in, say, Iraq? in a country allied with the United States in the global war on terror, such as Pakistan? or perhaps even in another advanced democratic country, like Germany? Nuclear deterrence in the Cold War, and especially extended deterrence in which the United States promised to launch a retaliatory attack against the civilian population should the Soviet Union invade West Berlin or Paris, always rested on threats that "left something to chance."[34] Although the United States might not have started another world war in response to a limited Soviet incursion in Europe, the risk that it might do so was sufficient to deter Russia. The risk that the United States or any other target would retaliate massively against terrorist attacks is not as likely or as clear. Knowing this, terrorists are less likely to be deterred than states—which are more likely to hold one another to account for uses of force. For both these reasons, deterrence may not be as robust against terrorism as it has been against interstate violence.

---

34. Thomas Schelling, *The Strategy of Conflict* (Cambridge, MA: Harvard University Press, 1960), 199–203.

Defensive measures against terrorists in Israel include a fortified wall between Israeli- and Palestinian-controlled territory, with numerous checkpoints manned by armed guards. These measures appear to have reduced the number of terrorist attacks in Israel, but they are expensive and inconvenient for everyone, not just the terrorists.

Defensive Measures

If deterrence against terrorism is at best imperfect, what else can states do to protect themselves against attacks and potentially defeat terrorists? First, states can employ defensive measures.[35] This has been a significant response in the United States since the attacks on 9/11. Airports now possess even more elaborate security procedures than those implemented after the rash of airplane hijackings in the early 1970s. American embassies abroad are being fortified. National monuments are protected by barrier defenses and, sometimes, armed guards. Border security forces and inspection regimes are being expanded. Numerous sites remain vulnerable, including the nation's shipping ports, but across the country homeland security efforts have been significantly increased. Similarly, after a campaign of suicide bombings, Israel has constructed a wall separating it from the West Bank, with dramatic results in reducing the number of attacks. Defensive measures work to reduce terrorism by raising the costs to groups of carrying out attacks. As it becomes more expensive to strike a target, whether in terms of resources deployed or time and effort consumed to evade security procedures, terrorism becomes less likely overall.

Defensive measures, however, are quite expensive. The U.S. Department of Homeland Security's budget for 2008, for instance, was over $47 billion and has been increasing at a rate of approximately 7 percent per year. Indirectly, such measures may impose even greater costs on society. Passengers must now arrive at airports earlier to clear security before boarding their planes, making air travel less

---

35. On the limits of defensive measures, see Robert Powell, "Defending against Terrorist Attacks with Limited Resources," *American Political Science Review* 101, no. 3 (2007): 527–41. On collective action problems in defensive responses, see Todd Sandler, "Collective versus Unilateral Responses to Terrorism," *Public Choice* 124, no. 1/2 (2005): 75–93.

efficient and more unpleasant than before. Trucks are subject to longer delays at the nation's borders. Measured by hours of productivity lost, these indirect costs may well dwarf the direct costs.

Defensive measures are also of limited effectiveness. Terrorists clearly substitute among sites based on the difficulty of penetrating defenses and the likely success of carrying out their attacks. As the United States stepped up its internal security measures after 9/11, Al Qaeda shifted its attacks to embassies abroad and American troops in Iraq. It is widely believed that Al Qaeda attacked three trains in Spain on March 11, 2004, because they were softer targets than airports. Given the many possible sites, it is prohibitively expensive to protect them all equally. But protecting some may only divert attacks onto the next less well-defended target.

Criminalization

States can criminalize terrorism and pursue specific individuals and groups for the attacks they have planned or carried out. Along with airport security measures, this was the primary response to the airplane hijackings that occurred in the late 1960s and early 1970s. By 1973, a series of international conventions on skyjackings were put into place through which states agreed not to harbor hijackers and to turn them over to appropriate authorities. Individual terrorists and groups were pursued and brought to justice in criminal proceedings. Combined with the use of metal detectors at airports, this strategy lead to a sharp decline in the number of airplane hijackings.

Criminalization is mostly reactive, seeking to arrest terrorists for attacks after they have been committed. By bringing individuals and groups to justice, states hope not only to disrupt terrorist groups but to deter others from carrying out attacks as well. For transnational terrorism, this strategy hinges on effective international cooperation. Nearly all countries would agree that airplane hijackings are odious and against their interests. Even the United States and Cuba, which cooperate in few other areas, have been able to work together effectively in capturing and prosecuting hijackers; the two nations signed a bilateral pact in 1973 in which they agreed to return immediately any planes, passengers, crew members, and hijackers to the country of origin. The growth of transnational networks may require the development of new international institutions to combat terrorism in the future.

Yet, countries do not always share such clearly compatible interests. States that sympathize with the goals pursued by terrorists and grant them safe haven, like the Taliban regime in Afghanistan, or states that are too weak internally to prevent terrorist groups from operating from within their territory, like Somalia, can effectively undermine the ability of other countries to capture indicted terrorists. The same forces of globalization that allow terrorists to attack anywhere around the world also permit terrorists to hide anywhere. To limit terrorism, states need to share intelligence and coordinate their counterattacks. To date, progress on this front has been slow, a problem deepened by international disagreements over the Iraq War and America's treatment of terrorist suspects. To expand efforts to track and prosecute terrorists will require greater compromise on policy differences with other states and increasingly effective institutions to secure compliance with anti-terrorist efforts.

Preemption

States can take the initiative and attempt to disrupt or destroy terrorists and their networks before they attack. This strategy of preemption was the most distinctive response of the Bush administration to the attacks of 9/11. In his National Security Strategy outlined in September 2002, President Bush placed emphasis, for the first time, on preempting attacks from terrorists and states that may possess weapons of mass destruction. By invading Afghanistan in retaliation for the attacks and in hopes of destroying Al Qaeda, the U.S. government has detained numerous "enemy combatants" captured in the region. It has also detained suspected terrorists around the globe and, in some cases, transferred the captives to countries known to use torture in interrogations. The U.S. government has also quietly expanded its intelligence gathering to identify terrorist networks and future attacks by monitoring phone calls, e-mails, and other communications into and out of the United States (and possibly within the United States) and by tracking international financial transactions. The war in Iraq was also justified by President Bush, in part, as a preemptive war on terror.

Preemption is costly in many ways. Surveillance is expensive relative to the number of attacks prevented. Like all police patrols, surveillance must be continuous—not just when attacks are under way—and comprehensive; otherwise, intelligence efforts are likely to be deployed elsewhere when actual attacks are being planned. Monitoring possible terrorist activities is akin to looking for the proverbial needle in the haystack, but in this case a potential terrorist attack is a well-hidden needle that we are not even sure exists. Moreover, surveillance is likely to infringe on the civil liberties of innocent civilians.

Preemption may also be perceived by foreign populations as a disproportionate response to threats, and it may in fact be perceived as threatening to those very populations. This is similar to the problem of deterring terrorism, but it is even more acute. By definition, preemptive action occurs before the threat is realized. Given that the target may have reasons to exaggerate possible threats and that prediction is always fallible, other states will be skeptical about its claims of impending danger. When the Bush administration expanded the war on terror from the invasion of Afghanistan, which many countries saw as a necessary and justified response to 9/11, to the invasion of Iraq, which was never linked to the attacks except rhetorically by the Bush administration, it signaled to countries worldwide that they were also at risk of preemptive attack if they were accused of harboring or associating with terrorists. Many foreign governments saw this move as a potential violation of their sovereignty and opposed the American invasion of Iraq partly for this reason. Targets must always balance the probability that they will make themselves safer in the short term by making preemptive attacks on potential terrorists against the risk that they will undermine their support within the terrorists' home population or internationally over the longer term.

Negotiation and Compromise

Finally, states can attempt to negotiate and compromise their differences with terrorist groups.[36] As explained above, bargaining failures are likely to be inevitable,

---

36. On bargaining, see Harvey F. Lapan and Todd Sandler, "To Bargain or Not To Bargain: That Is the Question," *American Economic Review* 78, no. 2 (1988): 16–21.

Although most states claim to have a policy of not negotiating with terrorist groups, they do sometimes hold talks or quietly make compromises behind the scenes. The Sri Lankan government has met with the Tamil Tiger separatist group, despite that group's use of terror tactics. Here, a representative of the Sri Lankan government (right) meets with the Tamil Tigers' chief negotiator.

and thus negotiations will not eliminate the problem of terrorism. Most states today maintain a policy of not negotiating with terrorists for fear of recognizing the legitimacy of their demands and tactics—and for fear of being charged with appeasement by domestic critics. In a world in which sovereign states are still the dominant actors, these same states have been reluctant to recognize nonstate groups—especially those that advocate violence—as their equals. Countries are also reluctant to negotiate with terrorists so as not to spur other groups making greater demands. Thus, few explicit negotiations occur between states and terrorists.

Nonetheless, states have compromised with terrorists and made important concessions, like the United States' withdrawal of troops from Saudi Arabia noted above. In the wake of suicide terrorist campaigns, American and French military forces withdrew from Lebanon in 1983, Israel made modest concessions to Hezbollah in 1983–1985 and to Hamas in 1994–1995 and again in 1997, and the Sri Lankan government entered negotiations with the Tamil Tigers between 1995 and 2002. Terrorists may never get everything they say they want (but actors rarely do in any bargain), and there have been at least an equal number of cases in which no concessions were made. But terrorism persists and may even be growing as a tactic because it works at least some of the time.[37]

Conclusion: Are Transnational Networks Changing the Nature of World Politics?

With this overview of the interests, interactions, and institutions of transnational networks, including terrorist groups, we can return to the puzzle that opened this chapter: are transnational networks transforming world politics? As we review this chapter's discussion, we must emphasize that there are two types of transnational networks: transnational advocacy networks, or TANs, which are law abiding; and terrorist networks, which are transnational but not law abiding. Both raise similar questions about the future of world politics.

On one side, traditionalists argue that states remain the dominant actors in world politics. Indeed, in their view, transnational networks exist only because states that

---

37. On the success of terrorist campaigns, see Robert A. Pape, "The Strategic Logic of Suicide Terrorism," *American Political Science Review* 97, no. 3 (August 2003): 351–55. For an alternative view, see Max Abrahms, "Why Terrorism Does not Work," *International Security* 31, no. 2 (Fall 2006): 42–78. For a selection effect that explains why concessions might appear not to work, see Ethan Bueno de Mesquita, "Conciliation, Counterterrorism, and Patterns of Terrorist Violence, *"International Organization* 59, no. 1 (2005): 145–76.

might otherwise regulate, control, and limit their interactions permit them to flourish. From this perspective, transnational advocacy networks reflect the interests and international prominence of liberal, democratic states that have active domestic civil societies and project these onto the global system. Were these states to weaken or choose otherwise, flourishing transnational advocacy networks might be undercut by less supportive governments.[38] Similarly, traditionalists see terrorists as dependent on safe havens within sympathetic states.

On the other side, globalists argue that transnational networks are emerging as a form of governance without government. In this view, political authority previously exercised by states is migrating to new transnational advocacy networks that are gradually assuming some of their responsibilities.[39] New private regulatory and standard-setting networks are replacing antiquated national regulatory bodies. Under the threat of consumer boycotts and naming and shaming, TANs are pressing corporations to change their production practices, such as ending the use of child labor or encouraging new "green" techniques. Likewise, globalists argue that to fight terrorist networks successfully will require that states become more "network-like" themselves.[40] For the globalists, transnational networks of all forms are rendering the state increasingly obsolete. This remains a lively debate in which scholars do not have settled answers.

Under globalization, new actors with new interests are mobilizing to effect international change. Transnational advocacy networks can, in some issue areas, bargain with other nonstate actors, especially corporations, to alter policy or to adopt corporate codes of social responsibility. This has been effective in certain cases, especially when the targets of network action are large firms that benefit from image-conscious brands (like Nike or Shell oil) for whom reputation matters. More commonly, these new TANs bring new pressures to bear on states themselves. TANs are pressing governments to act on issues that may not have been on their agendas even a few short years ago. Even if governments can ignore their own domestic societies, they cannot always ignore TANs. Not only can governments be named and shamed in the world press, but through the boomerang effect weak groups or those excluded from domestic politics can activate transnational linkages with foreign groups, who then press their own governments to put pressure on other governments perceived as violating norms of appropriate behavior. Thus, as a direct result of TAN activity, states are developing new interests and engaging in new interactions.

Transnational terrorists are also putting new pressures on governments and are challenging new targets worldwide. Traditional military-to-military warfare is being displaced or supplemented by terrorism. Although governments may

---

38. Among other traditionalists, see Robert Gilpin, *Global Political Economy* (Princeton: Princeton University Press, 2001), chap. 15; and Stephan D. Krasner, "Power Politics, Institutions, and Transnational Relations," in *Bringing Transnational Relations Back In: Non-State Actors, Domestic Structures and International Institutions,* ed. Thomas Risse-Kappen (New York: Cambridge University Press, 1995).
39. See David Held et al., *Global Transformations: Politics, Economics, and Culture* (Stanford, CA: Stanford University Press, 1999), especially chap. 1; and Walter Mattli, "Public and Private Governance in Setting International Standards," and Virginia Haufler, "Globalization and Industry Self-Regulation," both in *Governance in a Global Economy: Political Authority in Transition,* ed. Miles Kahler and David A. Lake (Princeton: Princeton University Press).
40. John Arquilla and David F. Ronfeldt, *Networks and Netwars: The Future of Terror, Crime, and Militancy* (Santa Monica, CA: Rand Corporation, 2001).

TANs have been instrumental in bringing attention to the atrocities suffered by Sudanese in the Darfur region. Groups like Amnesty International have rallied public support for action to protect basic human rights in Darfur, putting pressure on governments and intergovernmental organizations like the UN to intervene.

lack the ability to project military force over a great distance or to successfully attack foreign militaries, terrorists can wreak violence seemingly anywhere. The Al Qaeda attacks on New York and Washington, D.C., demonstrate that the oceanic moats that had long protected the United States from foreign attack are now easily bridged. In turn, governments cannot ignore demands made by potential terrorist networks regardless of where they may originate. Because terrorists can now "follow us home," as former president George W. Bush frequently asserted, Americans are engaged in disputes worldwide whether they want to be or not. Terrorism is also changing the interests of states and forcing them into interactions they would presumably avoid if they could.

The growth of transnational networks is also changing the pattern of interstate interaction. TANs make cooperation between countries more likely as endorsers and monitors of international agreements. They perform essential roles in supporting and observing compliance with both the international human rights and environmental regimes. Terrorist networks, in contrast, seek in part to undermine cooperation between states, explicitly so in the strategy of spoiling. Yet, combating terrorism is likely to require greater international cooperation over the long run, especially as states criminalize terror and need to coordinate their counterterror operations. Greater counterterror cooperation may require new institutions to create common rules and practices and to enforce the sharing of relevant information between states. As terrorism goes global, so must counterterrorism.

Transnational networks have clearly altered the interests and interactions of states. TANs have assumed some functions previously performed by governments, and they have enhanced the ability of states to perform other responsibilities. Although the traditionalists may be correct that states in principle have the authority to control transnational groups, it is not clear that they retain the ability or political will to do so. Precisely because TANs are often useful to states, it will become increasingly difficult for states to rein them in or restrict their activities. States themselves would lose valuable sources of support and information by constraining transnationalism. Although states clearly have stronger interests in suppressing actual or potential terrorists, traditionalists err in assuming that all states can control their territory and borders. Terrorists often find shelter in such states precisely because governments lack such control. Equally, it is difficult for states to identify and separate the "good" transnational networks they want to encourage from the "dark" networks they want to crush. Just as countries could greatly reduce terrorism by imposing domestic police states and curtailing the civil and political liberties of their populations, states could shut down all transnational networks by tightly regulating all transborder movements of people, information, and ideas—but this would come at a price that very few are willing to pay. Transnational networks are a political force that appears to be here to stay for the foreseeable future.

Globalists, however, may exaggerate the extent to which transnational networks can substitute for government. The areas of purely private authority remain limited, although they may grow in the future. Moreover, the TANs that are active in promoting social causes are voluntary associations that cannot legally bind their members, even less so others. Lacking the political authority attributed to states, they must rely on voluntary compliance from their targets, which is often uneven. Also, TANs benefit from the possibility of authoritative state regulation. Many private governance agreements either rely on state-provided legal systems to enforce their provisions or depend on the threat of state regulation to bring reluctant parties to the negotiating table. Even in ostensibly private governance, state authority often looms in the background.

More generally, although globalization and the growth of transnational networks have altered the way states act, they appear not to have displaced the central role of states on the world stage. Even though TANs are influencing interests, the norms advocated by TANs are still very much norms about appropriate *state* behavior. It is the human rights, environmental, economic, and political practices of *states* that TANs typically seek to change. Similarly, although TANs activate transnational linkages, they do so to mobilize foreign groups to urge their *states* to press the offending state to change its policy. Finally, although TANs facilitate cooperation, it is cooperation between *states* that is altered, and the information the TANs provide is about states to other states. In a similar way, terrorists typically attack with the object of altering state policy. Only in the case of outbidding is the purpose of the attack not directed at some state, at least in part; even then, the terrorist groups are usually competing for the vanguard position in some struggle within a state.

The state probably is not what it once was; indeed, it probably never dominated world politics to the extent traditionalists have assumed. Transnational networks have surely transformed world politics, but not as much as some theorists imply. Even as transnational networks have proliferated and grown in prominence, world politics remains very much an arena of states. The arena has changed such that states have different interests and interact in different ways, but states remain critical actors in international relations.

Reviewing Interests, Interactions, and Institutions

INTERESTS	INTERACTIONS	INSTITUTIONS
Globalization is connecting countries in new ways and mobilizing into politics new groups with different interests.	TANS exert new pressures on states by activating transnational linkages. The boomerang effect is one example.	Transnational groups are not displacing states as primary international actors, but they are altering states' policies and the environment in which they interact.
There are two types of transnational networks: transnational advocacy networks, or TANs, which are law abiding; and terrorist networks, which are transnational but not law abiding.	TANs facilitate cooperation by providing information about international agreements and compliance.	Coping with terrorism may require new forms of international cooperation and coordination.
TANs alter interests by creating new knowledge and changing international norms.	Terrorism is a bargaining failure rooted in problems of incomplete information and commitments that are not credible.	
Terrorists often have extreme interests that are not widely shared by others.	Terrorists pursue nonexclusive strategies: coercion, provocation, spoiling, and outbidding.	
	Potential targets can practice deterrence, adopt defensive measures, criminalize terrorist groups, preempt terrorist attacks, or negotiate and compromise with terrorists.	

Key Terms

transnational advocacy network (TAN), p. 370

nongovernmental organizations (NGOs), p. 370

norms, p. 372

norms life cycle, p. 373

boomerang model, p. 376

terrorism, p. 381

extremists, p. 386

coercion, p. 392

provocation, p. 395

spoiling, p. 396

outbidding, p. 397

For Further Reading

Bloom, Mia. *Dying to Kill: The Allure of Suicide Terror.* New York: Columbia University Press, 2005. Serves as one of two major studies on suicide terrorism (see also Pape, below).

Enders, Walter, and Todd Sandler. *The Political Economy of Terrorism.* New York: Cambridge University Press, 2006. Provides an excellent introduction to current research on terrorism.

Kahler, Miles, ed. *Networked Politics: Agency, Power and Governance.* Ithaca, NY: Cornell University Press, 2009. Offers applications to a variety of networks in international politics.

Keck, Margaret E., and Kathryn Sikkink. *Activists beyond Borders: Advocacy Networks in International Politics.* Ithaca, NY: Cornell University Press, 1998. Serves as a classic study of the growth and role of TANs.

Keohane, Robert O., and Joseph S. Nye. *Power and Interdependence,* 3rd ed. New York: Longman, 2000. Offers a classic statement of globalization's effects on transnational relations and world politics.

Khagram, Sanjeev, James V. Riker, and Kathryn Sikkink, eds. *Restructuring World Politics: Transnational Social Movements, Networks, and Norms.* Minneapolis: University of Minnesota Press, 2002. Presents interesting case studies of TANs in different issue areas.

Kydd, Andrew, and Barbara Walter. "The Strategies of Terrorism." *International Security* 31, no. 1 (Summer 2006): 49–80. Develops the four strategies of terrorism explained in this text.

Pape, Robert. *Dying to Win: The Strategic Logic of Suicide Terrorism.* New York: Random House, 2005. Serves as one of two major studies on suicide terrorism (see also Bloom, above).

Raustiala, Kal. "States, NGOs, and International Environmental Institutions." *International Studies Quarterly* 41, no. 4 (December 1997): 719–40. Explains the role of NGOs in monitoring compliance with international agreements.

Sageman, Marc. *Understanding Terrorist Networks.* Philadelphia: University of Pennsylvania Press, 2004. Explores the network structure of terrorist organizations.

Smith, Jackie. "Exploring Connections between Global Integration and Political Mobilization." *Journal of World-Systems Research* 10, no. 1 (Winter 2004): 255–85. Examines the link between globalization and the growth of transnational advocacy networks.

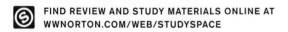 **FIND REVIEW AND STUDY MATERIALS ONLINE AT WWNORTON.COM/WEB/STUDYSPACE**

CHAPTER 11

Human Rights

Under apartheid, the South African government systematically denied the human rights of non-White citizens. By the 1980s, numerous countries had imposed economic sanctions on South Africa, often under pressure from local groups allied with the anti-apartheid movement in South Africa. These protesters demonstrated in Washington, D.C., to draw attention to rights abuses in South Africa and to demand that the U.S. government take action.

Why do states undertake costly actions to protect the human rights of people outside their borders? In light of the widespread support for the principle of human rights, why has the movement to protect those rights not been more successful?

For over 40 years, the White-dominated government of South Africa pursued a strict policy of racial segregation and inequality called apartheid. Distinguishing among Whites, Indians, Coloureds, and Africans or Blacks, this policy assigned everyone to a "homeland" within the territory of the state, regulated movement into the cities and employment, and created a pervasive system of racial discrimination designed to perpetuate the political and economic dominance of the White minority. Human rights abuses under apartheid were widespread. In addition to systematically denying the political, economic, social, and cultural rights of more than three-quarters of the country's population, the White government engaged in arbitrary arrests and detentions without trial, as well as torture and extrajudicial executions. The full extent of the abuses perpetrated by the "uniquely evil" regime were revealed only by the post-apartheid Truth and Reconciliation Commission.[1]

Transnational advocacy networks (TANs) worked closely with South African opposition groups to bring international pressure against the apartheid regime of the White-dominated government. In November 1962, the United Nations General Assembly adopted Resolution 1761 condemning apartheid and calling for all countries to terminate economic and military relations with South Africa. The country was excluded from the Organization of African Unity at the institution's founding in 1963 and was expelled from Olympic Games membership in 1968. The United Nations Security Council adopted a mandatory embargo on

What Are International Human Rights?
▶ Why Are Human Rights Controversial?
▶ Are Some Rights More Important Than Others?

Why Do Individuals and States Care about the Human Rights of Others?
▶ Why Do States Violate Human Rights?
▶ Why Do States Sign Human Rights Agreements?

Why Don't States Observe International Human Rights Law?
▶ Does International Human Rights Law Make a Difference?

What Can Lead to Better Protection of International Human Rights?
▶ When Do States Take Action on Human Rights?
▶ Will Protection of Human Rights Improve in the Future?

Conclusion: Why Protect Human Rights?

---

1. David Black, "The Long and Winding Road: International Norms and Domestic Political Change in South Africa," in *The Power of Human Rights: International Norms and Domestic Change,* ed. Thomas Risse, Stephen C. Ropp, and Kathryn Sikkink (New York: Cambridge University Press, 1999), 80.

weapons sales to the White regime in 1977. As domestic unrest flared in 1984 following constitutional reforms that gave political rights to Indians and Coloureds but not to Africans, the government began a brutal crackdown. To signal their displeasure with the widespread human rights abuses perpetrated by the White regime, by 1986 all of South Africa's major trading partners—including the United States—had adopted some form of economic sanctions. Often under pressure from student protests that forced universities to flex the power of their sometimes considerable endowments, some foreign firms eventually ended their investments in South Africa.[2]

Increasing internal dissent, both nonviolent and violent, combined with international censure to finally end apartheid in 1990 and start the peaceful transition to Black majority rule in 1994. Primary credit for the repeal of apartheid goes to the brave South African men, women, and children of all backgrounds who stood up against the racist regime. Nonetheless, the anti-apartheid struggle stands out for two larger effects on the global human rights movement. First, the national struggle played out on a global stage. Blocked at home from influencing the White regime, the Black majority appealed to allies abroad for support. By documenting and publicizing abuses, and by mobilizing activists worldwide, TANs helped bring about the end of the abhorrent but long-standing practice of systematic racial discrimination. The struggle against apartheid set a visible precedent for TAN activity and success in the broad area of human rights. Second, the anti-apartheid struggle demonstrated that states are, at times, willing to bear costs to express their disapproval of other governments and to support the victims of widespread human rights abuses. Not all states cooperated in the movement to repeal apartheid, and some were pushed into doing so only by vigorous pressure from activists. Nonetheless, opposing apartheid was an important turning point for states in using their influence to isolate and punish regimes that systematically abuse their own people.

Despite the concern expressed globally with South Africa's abuses and the eventual success in ending apartheid, the effort to promote human rights in other countries is highly uneven. Although nearly everyone supports human rights in principle, disagreement continues on what constitutes a human right and the priority that should be attached to their protection. Human rights violations in one country rarely affect the material welfare of other countries, the principal exception being when internal political conflict generates significant refugee flows. Moreover, noninterference by others in a state's internal affairs is a defining and often highly treasured principle of national sovereignty—a principle that the apartheid regime appealed to repeatedly in an effort to insulate itself from foreign scrutiny. By condemning the human rights abuses of others, states not only violate this norm of noninterference but risk opening themselves to foreign interference in their own affairs. Even the United States, which is constitutionally obligated to honor its own Bill of Rights, has come under fire for its continued use of the death penalty in criminal cases and its treatment of detainees in the war on terror—often from countries that it has condemned for violating other human rights. Why would any state undertake costly actions such as sanctioning South Africa with no immediate benefit to itself or its own citizens?

At the same time, the institution of international human rights law has proven to be of limited effectiveness. This is, of course, a situation of a glass being half full or half empty. As the example of South Africa makes clear, human rights practices around the globe are undoubtedly better than they would be without broad support for human rights, international rules governing how states treat their citizens, TANs "naming and shaming" abusers, and states occasionally punishing those violators with sanctions. Yet, human rights practices appear not to have changed dramatically over the last several decades despite greater TAN and state activity, few countries respect all human rights, and a significantly large number of countries violate many of these rights. Although there is important variation across different types of regimes, states that have

2. Audie Klotz, *Norms in International Relations: The Struggle against Apartheid* (Ithaca, NY: Cornell University Press, 1995).

Some human rights activists have argued that the U.S. government violated the rights of detainees held at Guantánamo Bay, Cuba. They were concerned about harsh interrogation methods and the lack of due process of law.

ratified international human rights agreements appear on average to fare no better in their human rights practices than those that have not ratified the agreements. Why isn't international human rights law more effective? This chapter develops three main points in addressing these puzzles.

CORE OF THE ANALYSIS

▶ International human rights law is an institution created by and largely reflecting the political norms of Western, liberal democracies. These norms remain controversial, are not shared equally by all countries, and have not yet been internalized in many societies and governments.

▶ Individuals and states have an interest in international human rights, and thus they undertake costly acts to punish states that violate the rights of their citizens. But these interests are rarely strong enough to compel states to pay high costs to protect vulnerable individuals and groups outside their own borders.

▶ States that violate human rights reason that in their interactions with other states they will likely not face serious consequences for their behavior and, therefore, can freely abuse individuals and groups. Unfortunately, these states are most likely correct. Although the institution of international human rights law does indeed promote improved practices, it appears to be of limited effectiveness in altering the actions of states.

What Are International Human Rights?

Human rights are rights that all individuals possess by virtue of being human, regardless of their status as citizens of particular states or members of a group or organization. These rights are, accordingly, universal and apply to all humans equally.

Human rights have a long philosophical tradition. The first systematic steps toward regulating how governments treat their citizens were undertaken in the United Nations Charter, adopted in 1945. Article 55 of the charter states that "based on respect for the principle of equal rights and self-determination of peoples, the United Nations shall promote . . . universal respect for, and observance of, human rights and fundamental freedoms for all without distinction as to race, sex, language, or religion."

Soon after the United Nations was founded, work began on an effort to clarify just what rights Article 55 embodied and what rights states would be expected to protect. The **Universal Declaration of Human Rights (UDHR)**, adopted by the United Nations General Assembly in 1948, is the product of those deliberations. Defined as a "common standard of achievement for all peoples" and broadly accepted as the foundation of modern human rights law, its 30 articles identify a diverse set of rights (see "What Shaped Our World?" on p. 413). Although it is not binding on states, the UDHR is today considered to be the authoritative standard of human rights.

René Cassin, one of the main authors of the UDHR, described the document as having four pillars supporting "dignity, liberty, equality, and brotherhood." Each of the pillars represents a different historical principle and philosophy of human rights. The first two articles of the UDHR stand for a timeless human dignity shared by all individuals regardless of race, religion, nationality, or sex. Articles 3–19 of the declaration define a first generation of civil liberties and other rights founded in a Western philosophical and legal tradition begun during the Enlightenment. Articles 20–26 focus on political, social, and economic equality, a second generation of rights that emerged during the Industrial Revolution and that is associated with socialist thought. Articles 27 and 28 address rights of communal and national solidarity, first developed in the late nineteenth century and championed by the states emerging from colonialism.[3] This last generation of rights, however, is far less developed in the UDHR than the first two.

The United Nations then began the much more difficult task of translating the UDHR into legally binding and internationally enforceable treaties. Unfolding over 18 years, the negotiations eventually produced two separate agreements: the **International Covenant on Civil and Political Rights (ICCPR)**, and the **International Covenant on Economic, Social, and Cultural Rights (ICESCR)**.[4] Although there was nearly universal agreement on the UDHR, the attempt to write binding international treaties protecting human rights got caught, like so many other attempts at cooperation, between the superpowers during the Cold War. The solution was to write two separate treaties: one focusing on the civil and

---

3. Micheline R. Ishay, *The History of Human Rights: From Ancient Times to the Globalization Era* (Berkeley: University of California Press, 2004), 3–4.
4. For more information on the Covenants and their texts, see www2.ohchr.org/english/law.

The Universal Declaration of Human Rights

The Universal Declaration of Human Rights (UDHR) was adopted by the General Assembly of the United Nations on December 10, 1948. It is strictly aspirational and seeks only to set a standard for human rights practices around the globe. It remains the definitive statement of human rights for all countries.

The origins of the UDHR lie in the Great Depression of the 1930s, the New Deal of U.S. president Franklin Delano Roosevelt, and World War II. In laying out his vision of a postwar peace, Roosevelt identified his famous four freedoms in a speech delivered on January 6, 1941, even before the United States entered the war:

In the future days, which we seek to make secure, we look forward to a world founded upon four essential human freedoms.

The first is freedom of speech and expression—everywhere in the world.

The second is freedom of every person to worship God in his own way—everywhere in the world.

The third is freedom from want, which, translated into world terms, means economic understandings which will secure to every nation a healthy peacetime life for its inhabitants—everywhere in the world.

The fourth is freedom from fear, which, translated into world terms, means a world-wide reduction of armaments to such a point and in such a thorough fashion that no nation will be in a position to commit an act of physical aggression against any neighbor—anywhere in the world.

This was a vision of a postwar order founded on respect for human rights as a bulwark against economic crisis and fascism.

Negotiations for the UDHR were extraordinarily rapid for an international compact of this sort. The United Nations at the time was composed mostly of countries allied during World War II and states from Latin America, all of whom (except for the Soviet Union and its clients, South Africa, and Saudi Arabia) were comfortable with the philosophy of fundamental individual rights that informed the agreement.[a] In turn, prior to the outbreak of the Cold War in the late 1940s, many citizens in the United States supported the notion of broad economic and social rights. Indeed, President Roosevelt himself had proposed an economic bill of rights within the United States in 1944. Building on this broad base of agreement, Eleanor Roosevelt, then chairwoman of the United Nations Human Rights Commission, used her stature and considerable leadership skills to facilitate quick agreement on a broad statement of rights.

---

a. These states abstained in voting on the UDHR; all the successor governments except Saudi Arabia have since publicly disavowed their abstentions.

Recognizing "the inherent dignity and . . . equal and inalienable rights of all members of the human family," the UDHR enumerates a variety of rights available to all "without distinction of any kind, such as race, colour, sex, language, religion, political or other opinion, national or social origin, property, birth or other status." The rights include:

- life, liberty, and the security of person (Art. 3)
- recognition everywhere as a person before the law (Art. 6)
- equal protection under the law (Art. 7)
- fair and public trials (Art. 10)
- the presumption of innocence until proven guilty (Art. 11)
- freedom of movement and residence (Art. 13)
- asylum from persecution (Art. 14)
- marriage, freely entered into, and procreation and family (Art. 16)
- property (Art. 17)
- employment, equal pay for equal work, and just remuneration necessary for an existence worthy of human dignity (Art. 23)
- form and join trade unions (Art. 23)
- rest and leisure, including reasonable limitation of working hours and periodic holidays with pay (Art. 24)
- an adequate standard of living (Art. 25)
- education, including compulsory free education in the elementary and fundamental stages (Art. 26)

The UDHR also recognizes as inherent rights the freedoms of:

- thought, conscience, and religion (Art. 18)
- opinion and expression (Art. 19)
- peaceful assembly and association (Art. 20).

In turn, the UDHR prohibits:

- slavery or servitude (Art. 4)
- arbitrary arrest, detention or exile (Art. 9)
- ex post application of law (Art. 11)
- arbitrary interference with privacy, home, or correspondence (Art. 12)
- arbitrary denials of nationality or the right to change one's nationality (Art. 15)

Placing responsibility on the international community, the UDHR declares that "Everyone is entitled to a social and international order in which the rights and freedoms set forth . . . can be fully realized" (Art. 28). Even today, the UDHR asserts an extraordinary range of goals toward which nearly all countries continue to strive. The UDHR, which is quite short, is worth reading in its entirety: see www.hrweb.org/legal/udhr.html. ■

political rights of liberty then favored by Western states, and one focusing on the economic, social, and cultural rights of equality and brotherhood supported by the then-communist states and others in the developing world. As formal treaties completed in 1966 and in force from 1976, the twin covenants are considered legally binding for all states that have ratified them.

The ICCPR details the basic rights of individuals and nations, defining in sometimes more specific terms the political and civil rights first claimed in the UDHR. Among the rights of individuals are life, liberty, and the freedom of movement, the presumption of innocence, equal standing before the law, legal recourse when rights have been violated, and privacy. In addition, all individuals are guaranteed freedom of thought, conscience, and religion, freedom of opinion and expression, and freedom of assembly and association. The Covenant forbids torture and inhumane or degrading punishment, slavery and involuntary servitude, and arbitrary arrest and detention. It also prohibits propaganda advocating war or hatred based on race, religion, national origin, or language. The treaty provides for the right of all people to choose freely whom they will marry and to found a family, and it requires that the duties and obligations of marriage and family be shared equally between partners. It guarantees the rights of children and prohibits discrimination based on race, sex, color, national origin, or language. It restricts the death penalty to the most serious of crimes, guarantees condemned people the right to appeal for commutation to a lesser penalty, and forbids the death penalty entirely for people under 18 years of age.

As of June 2008, 161 of the United Nations' 192 member countries were parties to the ICCPR. The United States ratified the treaty in 1992, but only after declaring that its provisions were "not self-executing"—meaning that although the agreement is binding as a matter of international law, its provisions would not automatically become domestic law without further legislation by the U.S. Congress. Human rights practices under the Covenant are monitored by the United Nations Human Rights Committee, a group of 18 experts who meet three times a year to consider periodic reports submitted by member states on their compliance with the treaty and interstate complaints of violations.

The parallel ICESCR specifies the basic economic, social, and cultural rights of individuals and nations, including the right to earn wages sufficient to support a minimum standard of living, equal pay for equal work, equal opportunity for advancement, the right to form trade unions and strike, paid or otherwise compensated maternity leave, free primary education and accessible schools at all levels, and copyright, patent, and trademark protection for intellectual property. The treaty forbids the exploitation of children and requires all countries to cooperate to end world hunger. Each nation that has ratified this covenant is required to submit annual reports on its progress in providing for these rights to the secretary-general of the United Nations. The ICESCR currently has 158 members. The United States signed the Covenant in 1977 under President Jimmy Carter but has never ratified it because of continuing opposition to provisions that would go substantially beyond existing domestic laws.

Together, the UDHR and the twin covenants are often referred to as the **International Bill of Rights**. Over time, additional rights have been added through supplementary conventions (see Table 11.1), including in certain cases the right of individual petition through which victims of human rights abuses can seek redress

International Bill of Rights:
Refers collectively to the UDHR, the ICCPR, and the ICESCR. Together, these three agreements form the core of the international human rights regime.

TABLE 11.1	UNITED NATIONS HUMAN RIGHTS AGREEMENTS	
Treaty	**Date Signed/In Force**	**Brief Description**
Universal Declaration of Human Rights (UDHR)	1948	Charter outlines basic human rights.
Convention on the Prevention and Punishment of the Crime of Genocide	1948/1951	Bans acts committed with the intent to destroy, in whole or part, a national, ethnic, racial, or religious group.
International Convention on the Elimination of All Forms of Racial Discrimination (ICERD)	1965/1969	Bans all racial discrimination, with particular attention to policies and practices of apartheid.
International Covenant on Economic, Social, and Cultural Rights (ICESCR)	1966/1976	Details the basic economic, social, and cultural rights of individuals and nations.
International Covenant on Civil and Political Rights (ICCPR)	1966/1976	Details the basic civil and political rights of individuals and nations.
Optional Protocol to the International Covenant on Civil and Political Rights (ICCPR-OP1)	1966/1976	Permits petitions from individuals for violations of Covenant.
Second Optional Protocol to the International Covenant on Civil and Political Rights, aiming at the abolition of the death penalty (ICCPR-OP2)	1989/1991	Commits state parties to abolish the death penalty.
Convention on the Elimination of All Forms of Discrimination against Women (CEDAW)	1979/1981	Bans discrimination against women, focusing on education, employment, health, marriage, and the family.
Optional Protocol to the Convention on the Elimination of Discrimination against Women (OP-CEDAW)	1999/2000	Permits petitions from individuals for violations of Convention.
Convention against Torture and Other Cruel, Inhuman or Degrading Treatment or Punishment (CAT)	1984/1987	Bans torture under all circumstances.
Optional Protocol to the Convention against Torture and Other Cruel, Inhuman or Degrading Treatment or Punishment (OP-CAT)	2002/2006	Establishes system of regular visits to monitor state practice.
Convention on the Rights of the Child (CRC)	1989/1990	Details the special rights of children.
Optional Protocol to the Convention on the Rights of the Child on the involvement of children in armed conflict (OP-CRC-AC)	2000/2002	Bans children under age eighteen and in the armed forces from participating in hostilities.
Optional Protocol to the Convention on the Rights of the Child on the sale of children, child prostitution, and child pornography (OP-CRC-SC)	2000/2002	Prohibits the sale of children, child prostitution, and child pornography.
International Convention on the Protection of the Rights of All Migrant Workers and Members of Their Families (ICRMW)	1990/2003	Details the special rights of workers outside their country of origin.
Convention on the Rights of Persons with Disabilities	2007/2008	Mandates equal status and treatment for individuals with disabilities.
Optional Protocol to the Convention on the Rights of Persons with Disabilities	2007/2008	Permits petitions from individuals for violations of the convention.
International Convention for the Protection of All Persons from Enforced Disappearance	2007/not yet in force	Prohibits arrest, detention, or abduction of individuals without acknowledgment by the state.

Note: For texts and updated membership information, consult www.ohchr.org/english/law.

directly from international courts. In short, the international community now possesses an extensive body of international human rights law, albeit one that remains controversial and possesses varying degrees of national support for different provisions.

WHY ARE HUMAN RIGHTS CONTROVERSIAL?

Because of differing legal traditions, domestic political regimes and institutions, and philosophies, states often have different interests in human rights. Even though human rights are by definition universal, states do not necessarily have the same interests in promoting the same rights to the same extent. States have interests in supporting rights that they already respect domestically and in fighting against new rights that they see as costly to protect. They also have an interest in preserving their own sovereignty. States may also have a strategic interest in promoting rights that their adversaries will deny or find costly to implement.

Many of the rights defined in the UDHR—especially many of the economic and social rights—are directly drawn from President Franklin D. Roosevelt's New Deal, adopted during the Great Depression of the 1930s. Through the 1950s, many people in the United States and other Western countries remained supporters of economic and social rights. As the New Deal lost popularity, however, support for enshrining many of its progressive policies into international law diminished. Human rights also became caught up in the Cold War competition of ideas. In public forums, Western states tended to emphasize first-generation civil and political rights already enshrined in their own systems, while the countries of the Soviet bloc and many countries in the developing world trumpeted their superior progress on second-generation economic, social, and cultural rights. This Cold War division and historical legacy continues to undermine support for the ICESCR in the United States today. Many conservatives in the United States, for instance, question whether economic, social, and cultural rights are actually rights at all since they pertain to particular classes or groups of people (for example, workers) rather than to all human beings.[5]

Critics of the rights specified in the UDHR point to their origin in a Western, liberal philosophical tradition that emphasizes first-generation individual rights over second- and third-generation collective rights. This is correct—to a point. The modern idea of human rights is rooted in a moral vision that sees all humans as equal and autonomous individuals. Political scientist Jack Donnelly observes that "it is a relatively simple matter to derive the full list of rights in the Universal Declaration from the political principle of equal concern and respect."[6] Although the rights founded in this tradition may now be accepted because of their status as international standards and law, the philosophical tradition itself is not universally shared. For example, in recent years some leaders—notably, Mahathir Mohamad, prime minister of Malaysia from 1981 to 2003—have led a campaign for "Asian values" that elevates the rights of families and communities and the goal of social and political stability over the rights of individuals. This differing philosophical tradition poses a direct challenge to the conception of human rights now enshrined in international law.

---

5. Jack Donnelly, *Universal Human Rights in Theory and Practice,* 2nd ed. (Ithaca, NY: Cornell University Press, 2003), 28.
6. Ibid., 45.

Human rights activists have denounced the Chinese government's discrimination against ethnic Tibetans. Just before the 2008 Summer Olympic Games in Beijing, protests broke out along the route of the torch relay, which passed through Tibet, and some supporters of Tibetans' rights went on to boycott the games. However, these actions appeared to have little effect on the government's policies toward Tibetans.

The debate over what rights individuals have continues, underscoring the point that rights are an institution that evolves over time. International human rights are not fixed or immutable but are a product of struggle, debate, and social interests. Although nearly everyone may agree that some human rights exist in principle, debate continues on exactly which rights humans possess.

This continuing debate also demonstrates that human rights have not been internalized as norms in all societies and governments. Although more deeply held in Western, democratic countries, few human rights have obtained the taken-for-granted quality in which violations are considered taboo or inappropriate except in the most dire circumstances. Freedom from torture is likely one of the most widely and deeply held human rights, but the recent and continuing debate in the United States on the treatment of terrorist suspects suggests that, even for some Americans, torture or practices that border on torture remain acceptable instruments of government policy. The power of the principle was evident in the careful attempt of the administration of President George W. Bush to deny it was engaging in torture, but practice suggests that the norm is ambiguous and fails to significantly constrain government behavior. The fact that human rights have not yet been internalized or, at best, are only weakly internalized implies that individuals and states still operate in the realm of purposeful and instrumental calculations whereby they act on human rights and enforce laws only when it is in their self-interest to do so.

ARE SOME RIGHTS MORE IMPORTANT THAN OTHERS?

Although the UDHR specifies a wide range of rights, it appears that (to paraphrase George Orwell's antitotalitarian tract *Animal Farm*) although all rights are equal, some are more equal than others. Although few if any human rights are internalized as norms, some rights in the UDHR and ICCPR do have a special status in international law and appear to have broader support than others.

In the ICCPR, Article 4 permits the suspension of some rights in cases of social or public emergency, but it simultaneously identifies a small number of other rights that cannot be suspended for any reason. These **nonderogable rights** include freedom from torture or cruel and degrading punishment, recognition as a person before the law, and freedom of thought, conscience, and religion.[7] Conversely, none of the rights identified in the ICESCR are nonderogable, and all can be limited by states acting under the law. Despite their special status, however, nonderogable rights are not automatically enforced more than other rights, as the continuing practice of torture in countries around the world makes clear.

In turn, many of these nonderogable rights have gained special support within human rights TANs. Amnesty International (AI), generally considered the world's leading human rights organization, identifies its core mission as protecting individuals from torture, cruel or inhuman or degrading punishment, and arbitrary arrest, detention, and exile, as well as defending the freedoms of thought, conscience, religion, opinion, and expression.[8] Individuals imprisoned solely for the peaceful expression of their beliefs are what AI calls **prisoners of conscience (POCs)**. This focus, overlapping to a considerable extent with the nonderogable rights of the ICCPR, is shared by many human rights organizations. In focusing on these more limited rights and publicizing violations of only these rights, AI has done much to shape notions of what human rights are today. To the extent that certain rights have become or moved toward becoming international norms, AI and the other major human rights organizations that make up the TAN have had much to do with shaping this process.[9]

Finally, by examining when states incur costly actions to punish human rights violations in other states, we can infer something about which rights are most important to them. Economic sanctions are a common tool that states use to punish violators of human rights. Since sanctions inflict costs on states that impose them, these states must weigh their interest in defending certain rights against their other priorities. Indeed, many violations of human rights go entirely unpunished, sometimes even unnoticed. In most cases, abuses are merely deplored by government officials, who simply issue a statement of disapproval. Actual sanctions against violators are relatively rare. But when states have taken steps to impose sanctions against human rights abusers, these steps have almost always been for unfair political detentions and torture and the suspension of peaceful political opposition.[10] For instance, the United States imposed sanctions on South Korea and Chile in 1973 for the detention and treatment of political prisoners, and on Paraguay, Guatemala, Argentina, Nicaragua, El Salvador, and Brazil in

nonderogable rights: Rights that cannot be suspended for any reason, including at times of public emergency.

prisoners of conscience (POCs): A label coined and used by the human rights organization Amnesty International to refer to individuals imprisoned solely because of the peaceful expression of their beliefs.

---

7. Specifically, Article 4 prohibits the suspension of Articles 6 (inherent right to life, referring to the death penalty), 7 (torture), 8 (paragraphs 1 and 2, on slavery and servitude), 11 (imprisonment from contractual obligation), 15 (ex post criminal offenses), 16 (recognition before the law), and 18 (freedom of thought, conscience, and religion).
8. Articles 5, 9, 18, and 19 of the UDHR.
9. See David A. Lake and Wendy Wong, "The Politics of Networks: Interests, Power, and Human Rights Norms," in *Networked Politics: Agency, Power, and Governance,* ed. Miles Kahler (Ithaca, NY: Cornell University Press, 2009).
10. Ibid., p. 148.

1977 for the same issues. Even in the case of South Africa, sanctions were not imposed against the country for its policy of apartheid in general, but only after the insurrection began and the South African government brutally repressed political opponents. States clearly act to enforce some rights more frequently than others. Through practice, the rights that states appear ready to defend are more narrow than the full panoply of the UDHR and may, in fact, be limited to the nonderogable rights identified in the ICCPR.

Overall, as an institution, international human rights remain a work in progress. Rights are themselves objects of political struggle, defining what is and is not acceptable government behavior toward its own citizens. Countries differ in their views on which rights they are bound to protect. They also differ on which rights they should seek to enforce when abused by others. Thus, we must examine not just human rights institutions themselves but also the interests and interactions of states to account for the politics of international human rights.

Why Do Individuals and States Care about the Human Rights of Others?

The body of international human rights law created since 1945 clearly suggests that individuals and states possess and exhibit an interest in the human rights of others around the globe. But the puzzle still remains. Why would individuals and states care about the way other states treat their citizens? Why is it in their interests to promote and potentially enforce laws governing the human rights practices of other states? In turn, as sovereign entities, why would states want to constrain the way they deal with their own people and open themselves to the scrutiny of others? In answering these questions, we begin by addressing why states violate human rights in the first place.

WHY DO STATES VIOLATE HUMAN RIGHTS?

States violate human rights for many reasons. Some violations arise from state incapacity. Many poor countries, for instance, may sincerely want but simply cannot afford to provide free primary schooling to everyone, as required under the ICESCR. Other governments may not be able to control their militaries or police sufficiently to stem human rights abuses. Recognizing varying capacities to implement standards, many human rights codified into international law are understood to be aspirations or goals toward which states should strive rather than strict rules to which they can and should be held accountable.

In other cases, however, states violate human rights in defense of their national security. Violent or potentially violent opposition to the state is illegal everywhere, and thus it counts as criminal, not political, behavior. AI specifically excludes as prisoners of conscience any individuals who use or advocate violence. Nelson Mandela, a leader of the anti-apartheid movement in South Africa, was originally designated a POC in 1962 after his arrest for organizing strikes to protest apartheid. Nonetheless, Mandela's status was revoked by AI after he was convicted of trying to overthrow the government violently in 1964. Yet, the dividing line between criminal and political activities is often ambiguous, and some states prosecute individuals as criminals for political actions that would be considered legal elsewhere. Even when actions are clearly criminal, however, prosecution and punishment may be abusive when individuals are not given due process under the law.

When under attack or perceived attack, states are sometimes tempted to violate the rights of groups or individuals they fear may be allied with a foreign power. Thus, the United States violated the civil and political rights of many of its own citizens in the infamous Red Scare of 1917–1920, following the Bolshevik revolution in Russia. During the first Red Scare, between 4,000 and 10,000 individuals were arrested, denied due process, and sometimes beaten during questioning. The United States also violated the rights of approximately 110,000 Japanese Americans who were interned in concentration camps following the attack on Pearl Harbor and the start of World War II, for which President Ronald Reagan apologized 40 years later and token compensation was eventually paid. And, in the second Red Scare of 1947–1957, the U.S. government blacklisted, jailed, and deported Americans suspected of following a Communist or other left-wing ideology. Today, following the terrorist attacks of September 11, 2001, the United States has been criticized for violating the human rights of citizens or residents accused of planning additional attacks or associating with terrorist organizations abroad.[11] Other countries have responded similarly to attacks on their own people or soil. Indeed, the existence of an interstate or civil war is strongly associated with increased human rights violations.[12] In justifying these violations, governments often claim that national security trumps the human rights of individuals.

Governments also violate the human rights of their citizens to preserve their own rule. This differs from the national security rationale just described. In these cases, the country is not under attack, but political opponents are abused in an effort to suppress internal dissent. To weaken and deter opponents, governments in essence declare war on their own citizens. One of the most egregious cases of such abuse occurred in Argentina following a military coup in March 1976. The three-man junta, led by General Jorge Rafael Videla, immediately began a seven-year campaign known as the Dirty War against suspected political dissidents and opponents of the military regime. Although some were publicly detained, many more individuals were "disappeared." While denying any official knowledge or involvement, the military eventually kidnapped, tortured, and killed nearly 10,000 perceived political opponents.[13] Many of the disappeared, we now know, were taken on death flights on which they were pushed from airplanes

---

11. The United States is also accused of violating international humanitarian law, specified in the Geneva Conventions, when it treats foreign detainees as "enemy combatants" supposedly outside international law. On the Geneva Conventions and laws of war, see James D. Morrow, "The Institutional Features of the Prisoners of War Treaties," *International Organization* 55, no. 4 (2001): 971–91.

12. Steven C. Poe and C. Neal Tate, "Repression of Human Rights to Personal Integrity in the 1980s: A Global Analysis," *American Political Science Review* 88, no. 4 (1994): 853–72; Matthew Krain, "State Sponsored Mass Murder: The Onset and Severity of Genocides and Politicides," *Journal of Conflict Resolution* 41, no. 3 (1997): 331–60.

13. The Argentine National Commission on the Disappeared provides an "official" figure of about 9,000 "disappeared" between 1976 and 1983. Internal documents from the Argentine security services suggest a figure of 22,000. Human rights organizations estimate that the total number of casualties of this Dirty War may be as high as 30,000.

Argentina's Dirty War, which began in 1976, provoked a strong response from a vast transnational human rights network. Here, the Mothers of the Plaza de Mayo in Argentina gather to protest abuses by the junta and to demand information on their "disappeared" children.

high above the Rio de la Plata or the Atlantic Ocean. As many as 500 newborns were taken from their imprisoned mothers and given to childless military families because, as General Ramón Camps (head of the Buenos Aires Provincial Police) later attempted to explain, "subversive parents will raise subversive children."[14] This was government-sponsored cruelty on a dramatic scale intended to crush and intimidate political opponents and keep the military regime in power. Like the case of apartheid in South Africa, the Dirty War in Argentina was critical in mobilizing the human rights TAN, and that network, in turn, was instrumental in bringing about political change in Argentina.

More generally, autocracies and unstable democracies are significantly more likely to violate the human rights of their citizens than established democracies, where political competition is respected and channeled through regular elections in which incumbent governments accept defeat and leave office.[15] Overt acts of torture (and possibly other human rights abuses as well) are most likely to occur in multiparty dictatorships. In single-party or personalist dictatorships, political opponents are sufficiently repressed that fewer acts of torture are necessary. These states might use torture if necessary, and broad civil liberties are typically denied, but opponents are deterred from challenging the government; thus, the regime does not often need to use violence against individuals to maintain its rule. In multiparty dictatorships, however, the political opposition usually remains visible and viable, and the government is tempted

---

14. On Camps, see www.terra.com.ar/canales/politica/134/134722.html. There have been 77 documented cases of kidnapped newborns.
15. Christian Davenport, "Multi-Dimensional Threat Perception and State Repression: An Inquiry into Why States Apply Negative Sanctions," *American Journal of Political Science* 39, no. 3 (1995): 683–713; Steven C. Poe, C. Neal Tate, and Linda Camp Keith, "Repression of the Human Right to Personal Integrity Revisited: A Global Cross-National Study Covering the Years 1976–1993," *International Studies Quarterly* 43 (1999): 291–313. Todd Landman, *Protecting Human Rights: A Comparative Study* (Washington, DC: Georgetown University Press, 2005), finds that more recently democratic states are more likely to engage in human rights abuses.

to use torture to suppress opponents to stay in power.[16] In all cases, the weaker or less legitimate the government, the more likely it is to abuse human rights.

There is no single explanation for why countries violate human rights. In turn, there is no single explanation for why individuals, groups, and states seek to protect human rights at home and abroad. Repressing human rights is a political strategy that states and governments employ to protect themselves from real and perceived threats. It should be no surprise, then, that protecting human rights is also a political strategy that a variety of political actors use for a variety of aims.

WHY DO STATES SIGN HUMAN RIGHTS AGREEMENTS?

Some states have an interest in imposing human rights law on themselves as a means of demonstrating their commitment to democracy and political liberalization. If some governments have an interest in repressing human rights to retain political power, liberal or liberalizing governments have an interest in promoting human rights as a means of committing themselves and their successors to political reforms.

Political scientist Andrew Moravcsik argues that democratizing states that sincerely seek to shed their autocratic and possibly abusive pasts sign human rights agreements in an attempt to lock in their new institutions and improved practices.[17] By committing to international agreements that may carry some cost if they are violated—even if that cost is only a loss of international reputation—new democratic leaders and coalitions attempt to make political backsliding more expensive and, thus, less likely. By obliging themselves to follow international human rights law, newly democratizing states aim to commit themselves credibly to political reform. This observation implies that the countries most eager to ratify human rights treaties should be newly democratic or democratizing states, a proposition for which Moravcsik and others find some support. In this conception, international human rights law is a tool that states use strategically to alter their own domestic political incentives.

This notion of using international human rights treaties to lock-in domestic political reforms also explains the weaker tendency and sometimes outright reluctance of established democracies to ratify human rights agreements. To the extent that human rights are already secured at home through constitutional protections and the rule of law, stable democracies have less need to bind themselves through international agreements.[18] Thus, with its own Bill of Rights and stable democratic institutions, the United States, for instance, needs international human rights treaties less than newly democratic states and therefore suffers the costs of international scrutiny without a corresponding domestic benefit. Increasingly, however, democracies are recognizing the contradiction inherent in advocating human rights for others while failing to ratify international human rights treaties themselves.

16. James Raymond Vreeland, "Political Institutions and Human Rights: Why Dictatorships Enter into the United Nations Convention Against Torture," *International Organization* 62, no. 1 (2008): 65–101.
17. Andrew Moravcsik, "The Origins of Human Rights Regimes: Democratic Delegation in Postwar Europe," *International Organization* 54, no. 2 (Spring 2000): 217–52.
18. These states will, however, also have lower costs for signing agreements that already accord with domestic practice. See Jay Goodliffe and Darren G. Hawkins, "Explaining Commitment: States and the Convention Against Torture," *Journal of Politics* 68, no. 2 (2006): 358–71.

Established democracies are now signing agreements they had previously rejected and shrinking the difference in treaty ratification between new and established democracies. The United States remains a visible exception to this trend, however, in its continuing reluctance to accept international human rights accords.

Finally, some states may sign international human rights treaties because they are induced to do so by contingent rewards provided by others, a form of linkage (see Chapter 2). Established democracies often provide inducements for new democracies to join such regimes. Inducements may include financial assistance or the promise of future membership in international organizations, such as NATO, that provide benefits on other dimensions. The European Union, for instance, has required countries applying for membership to sign and comply with a host of human rights treaties before being accepted. Turkey's human rights practices—especially its repression of the Kurds—have been one of the major stumbling blocks in its attempt to join the Union. By imposing human rights standards as a condition for assistance or membership in international organizations, other states hope to facilitate the lock-in of democracy in transitional governments—and to use the threat of expulsion to persuade states to live up to their promises once made.

As the example of the established democracies suggests, states also ratify international human rights treaties not to bind themselves but to constrain the human rights practices of others. They accept international oversight of their own affairs in order to secure their ability to scrutinize others. There are both altruistic and self-interested reasons why individuals and states seek to influence human rights in other countries.

Moral and Philosophical Motivations

Many individuals identify with a common humanity and feel personally affected by the welfare and treatment of others, including those in countries other than their own. As social animals, humans possess a degree of empathy that is weaker in some, stronger in others, but present in all. This is evident most dramatically in the international responses to natural disasters when individuals across the globe donate to relief efforts. The tsunami of December 2004, which wreaked havoc across Southeast Asia, for instance, generated billions of dollars in donations from governments and private individuals worldwide. When others suffer, we may hurt as well; this response can be a profound motivator of political action. Empathy produces support not only for victims of natural disasters but also for victims of human rights abuses. Indeed, human rights for all, and especially for the disadvantaged, is a cause that many individuals feel deeply about and are driven to try to protect by strong feelings of empathy.

Closer to home, our own human rights depend on state respect for the individual. It is our status as humans that creates and sustains our rights. It follows in the views of some philosophers and human rights advocates that we cannot secure these rights domestically unless we also seek to promote respect for rights abroad. If it is acceptable for some governments to abuse the rights of some people, what principled defense can we give if

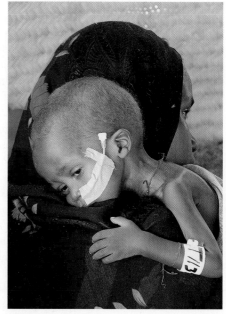

Many supporters of human rights abroad are motivated by compassion for the suffering of others. Images from Darfur of Sudanese citizens who have been persecuted and killed in a state-sponsored genocide have inspired people around the world to demand action by their own governments and the UN.

our own government wants to abuse our rights? In this view, human rights are only secure if they are universal not only in principle but also in practice.

Finally, as much if not more so than on other issues, we have been socialized to identify with universal human rights. Much of modern human rights law predates the growth of the transnational human rights movement. The UDHR, as we have seen, dates from 1948 and the twin covenants from 1966. AI, the first major human rights organization and the "grand-daddy" of the movement, however, was formed only in 1961. Human Rights Watch, which grew out of the Helsinki Accords, was founded in 1978. Nonetheless, these NGOs and the larger human rights advocacy network have played a critical role in educating the public about human rights and human rights practices, calling attention to human rights abuses, and eventually bringing pressure to bear on states. As discussed in Chapter 10, the human rights TAN has successfully framed the issue of international human rights in terms that resonate with the political freedoms and civil rights that already exist in established democracies. Given the wide acceptance of these principles within states, it is easier to persuade people to actively defend these rights abroad. The international human rights TAN has vigorously promoted concern with human rights among broad publics and has emphasized to many groups and individuals the extent to which human rights practices abroad affect our daily lives. It is in framing issues and socializing individuals to see their interests in different ways that TANs may have their greatest impact on the international politics of human rights.

Self-Interest Motivations

Even if we do not have altruistic interests in protecting the human rights of others, we do have self-interests in promoting peace and prosperity, which, in a globalizing world, cannot flourish at home without flourishing abroad. Modern human rights originated in the depths of the Great Depression and World War II. Reflecting on the causes of these twin disasters, President Roosevelt and others drew the conclusion that protecting human rights against fascism and other forms of totalitarianism was essential to the maintenance of international peace. By connecting human rights to the epic struggles against totalitarianism that defined much of the twentieth century, Roosevelt laid out the case that promoting human rights abroad was in the self-interest of both Americans and the citizens of other countries. This observation may be no less true today. As the *democratic peace* discussed in Chapter 4 shows clearly, there is an increasing recognition that democracy and the protection of political freedom can promote peace, economic interdependence, and growth that are of direct benefit to all countries.

More immediately, to the extent that suppressing human rights creates domestic political unrest and possible insurrection, such civil conflicts may spill into neighboring states either directly or indirectly. As a result, all states have an interest in preventing abuses in neighboring countries. The United States was forced to become involved in Haiti's internal political unrest in 1994 to stem the flow of people escaping by boat to southern Florida over treacherous waters. European countries sent troops into Bosnia to prevent political instability and ethnic violence in the former Yugoslavia from spilling over into the rest of the Balkans and possibly beyond. In an interdependent world, political instability and repression in one country can have direct consequences for others.

In addition to general self-interest motivations, particular interests within countries have promoted human rights law abroad for their own instrumental purposes. This is most evident in the labor movements within the United States and Europe, which now demand that human rights (and environmental) clauses be inserted into nearly all regional trade agreements (RTAs).[19] The North American Free Trade Agreement (NAFTA), for instance, includes extensive labor provisions that guarantee freedom of association and the right to organize, the right to bargain collectively and strike, freedom from discrimination, access to labor tribunals, and effective employment standards and minimum wage laws; it even establishes a trinational ministerial commission to monitor the labor provisions of the agreement.[20] Labor unions promote such clauses to level the political and, in turn, economic playing fields on which their own workers compete. To protect their ability to organize and strike for higher wages at home, unions want to ensure that workers in labor-abundant and low-wage countries have

Modern technology has helped bring human rights abuses to public attention around the world. Photos showing the abuse of detainees in the Abu Ghraib prison in Iraq were circulated widely and quickly on the Internet in 2004.

similar rights and, indeed, possess the broader political rights necessary to protect their ability to form effective trade unions. In this way, the economic self-interest of workers in developed states can dovetail with the interests of citizens in developing countries in more effective protections for human rights.

Labor demands for human rights clauses, however, may also disguise a form of trade protectionism. By inserting human rights clauses into RTAs, the unions may be making free trade pacts less appealing to foreign trading partners and, therefore, less likely to be approved. For example, the Mexican government strongly opposed the human rights clauses of the NAFTA. Moreover, human rights provisions open up the opportunity for subsequent claims that the trading partner is violating the terms of the agreement and that the trade concessions made by the home country should be withdrawn. For labor in the developed countries, human rights provisions in RTAs may be "poison pills" that are used to prevent further movements toward free trade.

Together, these various motivations for protecting human rights abroad suggest that interests are multiple and often quite complex. Each reason, however, prompts individuals or groups to press their governments to promote international human rights law. One person may be particularly motivated by a general concern for human well-being, another by a concern with protecting democracy at home, and a third by a hidden desire for trade protection, but all combine to bring pressure to bear on their governments to make international human rights a priority.

Such pressure on governments may be increasing. As TANs grow and succeed, as they have done in a more globalized world, they influence the views of more and more individuals. In turn, the same technology that facilitates the growth of TANs also brings the horror of human rights abuses to immediate public attention. The photos

19. Emilie M. Hafner-Burton, "Trading Human Rights: How Preferential Trade Agreements Influence Government Repression," *International Organization* 59, no. 3 (2005): 593–629.
20. Collectively, the labor provisions of the NAFTA are referred to as the North American Agreement on Labor Cooperation. On the purview and powers of the Commission for Labor Cooperation, see www.naalc.org.

from Abu Ghraib prison that showed American soldiers abusing detainees in Iraq flashed around the globe in moments. Although it has yet to generate any significant government action, the genocide unfolding in the Darfur region of Sudan is transported into our homes via television and the Internet. It is now much harder to ignore human rights abuses or to deny that we knew about the violations while they were occurring. This realization heightens awareness and may prompt individuals to demand that their governments be more aggressive in promoting international human rights.

Rarely would we expect governments to promote human rights abroad to the exclusion of all other interests they might be seeking in their relations with other states. Nonetheless, founded in the tragedy of World War II, supported by a growing transnational human rights movement, and accelerated by new technologies that bring abuses to the public's immediate attention, individuals and groups now increasingly recognize international human rights as part of their nations' interests and demand that their governments act accordingly.

Why Don't States Observe International Human Rights Law?

Given a by now extensive body of international law, broad agreement on the principle of human rights, and growing interests in promoting rights, do states actually protect human rights abroad? Is interest reflected in practice? Unfortunately, the answer appears to be no, or at least a qualified no. Although international human rights institutions are being developed, large-scale abuses continue to occur. The large swaths of dark colors in Maps 11.1 to 11.3 graphically illustrate the extent of the problem. While it can be difficult to measure such rights and some of the information in the maps may seem surprising, the data reflected in the maps are perhaps the best available and, on the whole, indicate that human rights practices have not improved significantly in recent decades. Indeed, disentangling the relationship between international human rights agreements and actual state practice is quite complex.

The most frequent and deadliest form of violence in the world today is by governments against their own citizens (including governments fighting civil wars). In violation of the ICCPR, governments continue to inflict violence against political dissidents. Defying the ICESCR, governments also violate the human rights of their citizens by misguided economic or social policies that lead to widespread suffering and deaths. For example, the Great Leap Forward in China (1958–1962) created a nationwide famine and left as many as 38 million people dead. R. J. Rummel, who coined the word *democide* to describe such government-sponsored killing, graphically writes:

> In total, during the first eighty-eight years of [the 20th] century, almost 170,000,000 men, women, and children have been shot, beaten, tortured, knifed, burned, starved, frozen, crushed, or worked to death; or buried alive, drowned, hung, bombed, or killed in any other of the myriad ways governments have inflicted death on unarmed, helpless citizens or foreigners. . . . This is as though our species has been devastated by a modern Black Plague.[21]

21. From www.hawaii.edu/powerkills/POWER.ART.HTM (accessed 11/12/07).

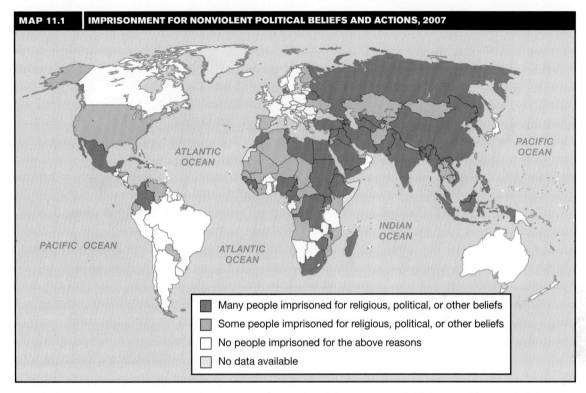

MAP 11.1 | IMPRISONMENT FOR NONVIOLENT POLITICAL BELIEFS AND ACTIONS, 2007

- Many people imprisoned for religious, political, or other beliefs
- Some people imprisoned for religious, political, or other beliefs
- No people imprisoned for the above reasons
- No data available

Note: The data presented in this map measure the incarceration in 2007 of people by government officials because of their speech; their nonviolent opposition to the government; their religious beliefs and practices; or their membership in a group, including an ethnic or racial group.
Source: David L. Cingranelli and David L. Richards, *The Cingranelli-Richards Human Rights Dataset*, www.humanrightsdata.org.

According to political philosopher Thomas Hobbes (1588–1679), states were created to lift humans out of the state of nature in which life was "solitary, poor, nasty, brutish, and short." This statement may be true; we do not know how dangerous life would be without states to provide a measure of social order and protection against other individuals—although failed states like Somalia suggest that life in the state of nature may be close to that envisioned by Hobbes. But today, governments around the world may themselves be the biggest threats to our human rights and, indeed, to our very lives.

Unfortunately, there are few systematic compilations of the human rights practices of states over an extended period. Rummel's data does show that the twentieth century appears to have been more violent and deadly than past centuries, but this may have more to do with the "improved" technology of state killing than with any change in state intent or practice. The modern Black Plague he describes, moreover, does not include human rights abuses that do not result in death, for which we have no data on long-term trends.

We do not know whether states today treat their citizens better than, worse than, or about the same as in the past. The best evidence indicates, however, that in the past 25 years human rights practices on average have remained the same or deteriorated over time. The two noteworthy exceptions are South America (which enjoyed a wave of democratization in the 1980s, supported in part by popular outrage at the

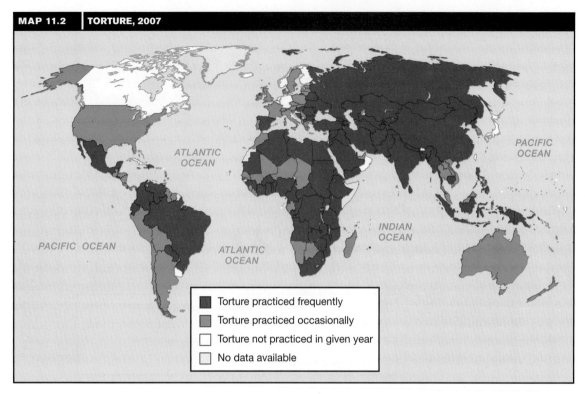

MAP 11.2 | **TORTURE, 2007**

PACIFIC OCEAN

ATLANTIC OCEAN

PACIFIC OCEAN

ATLANTIC OCEAN

INDIAN OCEAN

PACIFIC OCEAN

- ■ Torture practiced frequently
- ■ Torture practiced occasionally
- □ Torture not practiced in given year
- ▫ No data available

Note: The data presented in this map measure in 2007 the purposeful inflicting of extreme pain, whether mental or physical, by government officials or by private individuals at the instigation of government officials. Torture includes the use by police and prison guards of physical and other force that is cruel, inhuman, or degrading. This also includes deaths in custody due to negligence by government officials.
Source: David L. Cingranelli and David L. Richards, *The Cingranelli-Richards Human Rights Dataset*, www.humanrightsdata.org.

human rights abuses of the prior military regimes) and Central and Eastern Europe (which democratized in the 1990s after the fall of communism). For more on human rights around the world, see "What Do We Know?" on p. 430.

DOES INTERNATIONAL HUMAN RIGHTS LAW MAKE A DIFFERENCE?

Given the pattern discussed above, do international human rights institutions make a difference? Even if abuses continue to occur, do countries that ratify human rights treaties protect the rights of their citizens better than those that have not ratified the agreements? Do these human rights institutions constrain state behavior in significant ways?

Some recent research indicates, paradoxically, that ratification of human rights treaties is actually associated with worse rather than better human rights practice, once other factors (like income per capita and economic growth) that affect state practice are taken into account.[22] That is, ratifying various human rights

---

22. Oona Hathaway, "Do Human Rights Treaties Make a Difference?" *Yale Law Journal* 111, no. 8 (June 2002): 1935–2042; Eric Neumayer, "Do International Human Rights Treaties Improve Respect for Human Rights?" *Journal of Conflict Resolution* 49, no. 6 (2005): 925–53; Emilie M. Hafner-Burton and Kiyoteru Tsutsui, "Justice Lost! The Failure of International Human Rights Law to Matter Where Needed Most," *Journal of Peace Research* 44, no. 4 (2007): 407–25.

MAP 11.3 | WOMEN'S POLITICAL RIGHTS, 2007

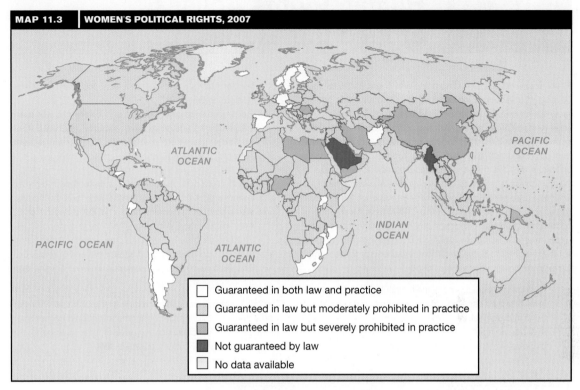

Guaranteed in both law and practice

Guaranteed in law but moderately prohibited in practice

Guaranteed in law but severely prohibited in practice

Not guaranteed by law

No data available

Note: The data presented in this map measure in 2007 women's political rights to vote, run for political office, hold elected and appointed government positions, join political parties, and petition government officials. Many countries in which rights are guaranteed in law but moderately prohibited in practice have only limited proportions of women (less than 30 percent) in elected or appointed government office. *Source*: David L. Cingranelli and David L. Richards, *The Cingranelli-Richards Human Rights Dataset,* www.humanrightsdata.org.

agreements is associated with greater violations of individual human rights, all else considered. Other research, however, finds that international human rights agreements exert a weak but nonetheless positive effect on human rights practices.[23] Either way, given our expectations that international institutions generally facilitate cooperation, the negative effect of human rights agreements on practice or the weak positive effect is surprising.

There are three possible explanations for this unexpected finding. First, reflecting the views of traditional skeptics, international human rights law just might not matter. After all, international law, like most international agreements, is dependent on self-help. In the absence of any third-party enforcers, international law places the burden of enforcement on the victims of the crime, who in the case of human rights law are the politically powerless individuals and groups who were abused in the first place. The burden of enforcement, therefore, rests on others who can speak and act on behalf of these victims. As we will see below, other states have a substantially weaker interest in penalizing violators

---

23. In *Protecting Human Rights,* p. 157, Landman uses a broader set of agreements and longer time period than other studies, as well as a nonrecursive model, and reports a positive effect of human rights agreements on practice. In a later survey of this debate, however, he concludes judiciously that no conclusive evidence exists; see Todd Landman, *Studying Human Rights* (New York: Routledge, 2006), 103.

Human Rights Abuses around the Globe

Political scientists David Cingranelli and David Richards have developed a variety of indices that track human rights abuses around the world. These indices have been combined into a database named CIRI after the first two letters of the researchers' surnames. Based on strict codings of the Amnesty International and U.S. Department of State annual reports on human rights violations, the CIRI database provides an essential tool in assessing human rights practices across countries and over time.[a]

The figure below displays trends by region for the Physical Integrity Index, a composite of the CIRI indices for the use of torture, extrajudicial killings, political imprisonments, and disappearances. The index varies from 0 (no government respect for these rights) to 8 (full government respect for these rights). Several important trends are evident:

- Human rights abuses continue to occur at about the same level as in past decades. On average, there is no noticeable trend at the global level. While some regions have improved their human rights practices, others have deteriorated. The global average is essentially constant.

- Western Europe and Oceania have the lowest reported rates of abuse.
- South America and Central and Eastern Europe are the only regions that have steadily improved their human rights record over the last 25 years. This trend reflects the democratization of both regions since the 1980s.
- North America experienced substantially improved human rights practices after the mid-1990s. This was also a product of democratization of countries in Central America and the Caribbean.
- South Asia has, on average, the worst human rights practices, followed by the Middle East and North Africa, East Asia, and sub-Saharan Africa. There is no long-term trend in any of these regions.

Overall, there has been less change in the practice of human rights than one might expect from the attention it has received in the press and, increasingly, by governments seeking to promote human rights in other countries. ■

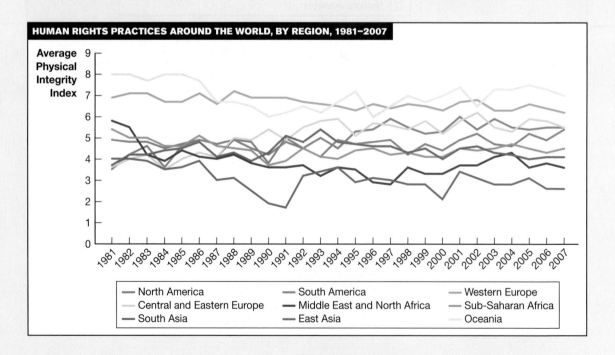

HUMAN RIGHTS PRACTICES AROUND THE WORLD, BY REGION, 1981–2007

Legend:
— North America
— Central and Eastern Europe
— South Asia
— South America
— Middle East and North Africa
— East Asia
— Western Europe
— Sub-Saharan Africa
— Oceania

a. David L. Cingranelli and David L. Richards, *The Cingranelli-Richards Human Rights Dataset,* Version 2008.03.12, www.humanrightsdata.org.
A second and similar set of indicators is the Political Terror Scale, available at www.unca.edu/politicalscience/images/Colloquium/faculty-staff/gibney.html.

of human rights; thus, international human rights law is, at best, sporadically enforced. Knowing this, states can choose to violate human rights with a degree of impunity.

Second, as described by international law professor Oona Hathaway, international law not only contains material costs and benefits but also offers an expressive value in which states seek to benefit by taking positions rather than by modifying their behavior.[24] By signing human rights agreements, Hathaway suggests, states may hope to give the appearance of conforming with civilized norms of behavior while continuing to engage in actual practices that violate human rights behind the scenes or out of the public eye. If other states condition rewards on clear, observable markers like signing treaties, and monitor or enforce rules on actual practices only occasionally, states may commit to human rights agreements in the hopes of gaining contingent benefits while at the same time evading closer scrutiny and criticism. In this explanation, states are being somewhat duplicitous by ratifying human rights agreements simply to mask their continuing patterns of abuse.

Third, our most developed explanation comes from political scientist James Vreeland, who finds that the countries most likely to violate human rights are also more likely to sign and ratify human rights agreements. Focusing on the Convention on Torture (CAT), Vreeland finds that democracies that do not practice torture sign and ratify the CAT at high rates. At the other extreme, multiparty dictatorships both sign the CAT and use torture, creating the apparent paradox. Multiparty dictatorships, he argues, are pressed by domestic political opponents, who have some influence, to ratify international conventions in hopes of changing the government's behavior over the long run. Since domestic opponents remain viable and their rule is unstable, they are also most likely to abuse human rights, including the use of torture against insurgents.[25] Putting these two trends together appears to explain why these types of countries sign human rights agreements and are also more likely to abuse those rights.

Because of these countervailing trends, it is very difficult to isolate the effect of international human rights agreements on state behavior—perhaps accounting for the inconsistent and confusing findings in the field. Joining human rights conventions might indeed be leading to better protections of human rights than otherwise; but at the same time, the effect on practice is being overwhelmed by the selection effect identified by Vreeland in the large, crossnational studies. Isolating the impact of agreements from the underlying incentives to join agreements is a difficult research problem for which further investigation is necessary.

Nonetheless, even if the effect of international human rights institutions is limited in the short term, they may exert a more beneficial effect on human rights practices in the long run.[26] Rather than just binding states, international human rights law also empowers social actors to advocate their own rights, sometimes leading to massive political change. For instance, the Helsinki Final Act of 1975, which established the applicability of human rights in all of Europe, served as the opening wedge that allowed human rights activists to mobilize within the communist bloc countries of Eastern Europe. The 35-country Conference on Security and Cooperation in

---

24. Hathaway, "Do Human Rights Treaties Make a Difference?"
25. Vreeland, "Political Institutions and Human Rights."
26. The statistical evidence on long-term effects is, at best, ambiguous as well. See Hafner-Burton and Tsutsui, "Justice Lost!"

Human rights TANs, including groups like Amnesty International, promote public awareness of human rights issues and may monitor states' compliance with international laws. In these ways, they pressure other states to take action against governments that violate human rights.

Europe was convened in 1972 to legitimate the territorial status quo left over from World War II and to expand economic contacts between East and West. Much against the wishes of the communist regimes, the countries of Western Europe insisted on the inclusion of human rights on the agenda. Trading concessions on other issues, the Western states were eventually able to gain the assent of their Eastern counterparts to the principle of "respect for human rights and other fundamental freedoms, including freedom of thought, conscience, religion or belief."[27] Although the communist countries first attempted to suppress publication and discussion of this principle, word spread and domestic groups began to agitate for their rights and made contact with their transnational counterparts in the West. In the bright lights of public awareness, the societal groups activated by the Helsinki accord were eventually able to mount effective challenges to the autocratic regimes that had long suppressed all dissent. Although many factors contributed to the fall of the communist regimes in Eastern Europe in 1989, the political freedom first created by the Helsinki agreement is broadly seen as a contributing cause of that political earthquake.[28]

In addition, international human rights law permits TANs to bring pressure to bear on governments to enforce human rights standards. Human rights TANs, of course, have no legal standing to issue mandatory sanctions or other punishments, but they do exert an important effect by naming and shaming violators of human rights.[29] Equally if not more important, by promoting public awareness and monitoring state human rights practices, TANs create political pressure that may eventually force states to act. TANs are not superseding the role of the state, but they do shape the political context in which states interact with their citizens and one another. Thus, even though international human rights law may not cause governments to change their behavior in the short run, it may lead to significant political change over time by legitimating and encouraging the mobilization of domestic political forces.

What Can Lead to Better Protection of International Human Rights?

Few human rights violators are actually punished. States do sanction one another for human rights abuses, as discussed, but such penalties remain rare. Although

27. Conference on Security and Cooperation in Europe, Final Act, Helsinki, August 1, 1975, Section 1, (a) VII, www.hri.org/docs/Helsinki.75.html (accessed 12/3/08).
28. Daniel C. Thomas, "The Helsinki Accords and Political Change in Eastern Europe," in *The Power of Human Rights: International Norms and Domestic Change,* ed. Thomas Risse, Stephen C. Ropp, and Kathryn Sikkink (New York: Cambridge University Press, 1999), 205–33.
29. The effectiveness of naming and shaming is open to debate. See Emilie M. Hafner-Burton, "Sticks and Stones: Naming and Shaming the Human Rights Enforcement Problem," *International Organization* 62, no. 4 (2008): 689–716.

states may be named and shamed by transnational human rights organizations, and some may modify their behavior to avoid public condemnation, most escape any significant costs for violating the rights of their citizens.

This combination of mostly empathetic interests in human rights practice abroad and few incentives to actually punish violators produces for most states an inconsistent human rights policy. Even the United States, a strong promoter of human rights, has often chosen not to act against abuses by states it supports— including the use of poison gas against his country's Kurdish minority in the late 1980s by Saddam Hussein, who was then being backed by the United States in his war against Iran, and widespread abuses by the military junta in Chile following an American-backed coup in 1973. At the same time, the United States did press human rights concerns against the White-majority regime in South Africa, contributing to the peaceful revolution that eventually led to Black-majority rule, and against China after the 1989 Tiananmen Square massacre, in which the government killed between 200 and 3,000 pro-democracy protestors.[30]

This inconsistent enforcement may explain the ineffectiveness of international human rights law. Facing opposition to their rule at home, states may be willing to take the small risk of international punishment to secure their tenure in office. That is, for some governments the temptation to ignore human rights law to secure their hold on power may be stronger than the fear of international penalties. With regime survival as a strong core interest and small punishments carried out only a small percentage of the time by the international community, few leaders may feel tightly constrained by international human rights institutions or the laws that they themselves have accepted as binding.

It is costly for states to enforce international human rights laws. Naming and shaming may anger a violator whose cooperation is needed on some other diplomatic issue. Pressing the human rights provisions of the Helsinki agreement, for instance, meant that European states gave up bargaining leverage on other issues they also cared about. Economic sanctions impose costs on the target state, but they also impose costs on exporters within the home state who lose a potential market for their goods. Businesses strongly resisted divesting from South Africa when it meant forgoing access to raw materials, cheap labor, and Africa's wealthiest consumers. If sanctions hurt the target state, they will also hurt the home state as well. (See "Controversy," p. 434.) Promoting human rights always carries a price. But states do, sometimes, act to punish human rights violations. When do they do so?

WHEN DO STATES TAKE ACTION ON HUMAN RIGHTS?

States are most likely to pay the costs of enforcing human rights law under three conditions. First, states act when faced with domestic pressure to "do something" to stop human rights abuses. Few governments have intrinsic interests in promoting international human rights, and most do so only in response to domestic political pressure. Governments normally weigh demands to stop abuses, however, against costs to

---

30. The Chinese government reports an estimate of 200 to 300 protesters killed; Chinese student associations cite a higher figure of 2,000 to 3,000 killed.

Should Economic Sanctions Be Imposed on Governments That Violate Human Rights?

Four days after Saddam Hussein's 1990 invasion of Kuwait, the United Nations Security Council passed a resolution imposing economic sanctions on Iraq, including a trade embargo on all exports to the country other than basic food and medical supplies.[a] Although in the ensuing Gulf War Iraqi troops were expelled from Kuwait within seven months, the sanctions continued for an additional twelve years. One initially popular justification for maintaining the policy was that restrictions on international trade and finance would sap Hussein's power and thereby end the human rights abuses that Hussein and his government had inflicted on the Iraqi population for over a decade. Within a matter of years, however, popular opinion turned decisively against the sanctions. The most dramatic evidence of the turnaround was the 1998 resignation of Denis Halliday, the humanitarian coordinator for Iraq, after a 34-year career with the UN. In explaining his departure, Halliday cited his concern that the sanctions program "satisfie[d] the definition of genocide."[b] Why did support for the sanctions on Iraq unravel?

Two significant barriers exist to the successful use of economic sanctions for humanitarian purposes. First, foreign nations generally impose sanctions aimed at ending human rights violations only if they perceive their interests in doing so to outweigh the costs involved. Second, sanctions, once imposed, only succeed if they are not subject to strategic manipulation by the target state. These two facts are the key to understanding why the sanctions on Iraq failed and, more generally, some of the moral complexities raised by international intervention to protect human rights.

The trade embargo initially seemed a perfect example of a case in which the balance of costs and benefits came out in favor of intervention. Hussein's government had engaged in systematic violations of its population's most basic rights, including acts of torture, rape, amputation, arbitrary imprisonment, and mass execution. These atrocities engaged the altruistic concern of the international community and also created geopolitical worries

about increased instability in the region. On the cost side, economic sanctions promised to be relatively inexpensive for the countries that imposed them. As it turned out, however, the sanctions imposed other costs that proved much more severe than many strategists had anticipated. The gravest impacts were on the basic interests of Iraqi civilians: the World Health Organization reported in March 1996 that sanctions-related deprivations had caused infant mortality to rise by a factor of six, equivalent to the deaths of hundreds of thousands of children under age five.[c] At the same time Iraqi industry, employment, and education collapsed; crime and violence escalated; and vital public infrastructure failed to be rebuilt after the war.

If the UN sanctions had succeeded in ousting Hussein's regime, perhaps the costs for Iraqi citizens might have been justified as the lesser of two evils. But a striking feature of the Iraq case was that the sanctions not only hurt civilians more than they hurt the targeted government officials, but also were strategically manipulated by Hussein to strengthen his regime. Hussein claimed his country to be a victim of the United Nations, presented the shortages that his government had itself induced as sanctions-related, and styled himself as the beneficent distributor of food aid. In the meantime, he used the rationing system to maintain a database on every citizen, and he enriched himself and his cronies with kickbacks he negotiated with corrupt foreigners through the UN's humanitarian program.

One conclusion that we can draw from the apparent failure of economic sanctions in the Iraq case is that such sanctions are always unjustifiable from a humanitarian standpoint. A more nuanced conclusion is that international sanctions may sometimes be justified, but only when they take into account the sorts of unintended effects exemplified in the Iraq case. Although opinions differ on how effectively outsiders can design and orchestrate sensitive sanctions of this kind, all parties can agree on one point: however compelling the universal protection of human rights is as a goal, measures aimed at securing it should not constitute a cure worse than the disease. ■

a. United Nations Security Council Resolution 661 Iraq/Kuwait (August 6, 1990).
b. Carlton Television, *Paying the Price: Killing the Children of Iraq,* broadcast on ITV, March 6, 2000.

c. World Health Organization, "The Health Conditions of the Population in Iraq since the Gulf Crisis," WHO/EHA/96.1 (March 1996).

business interests or other diplomatic initiatives. Domestic pressure often produces merely toothless condemnations of the abuse or loose and ineffective economic sanctions. Nonetheless, the more outrageous the abuse, the greater will be the domestic pressure on governments to act. In this way, the boomerang effect (described in Chapter 10) employed by TANs plays an important role in protecting human rights. Victims or other advocates in one country who are blocked from influencing their own states can bring their plight to the attention of concerned others in foreign countries who can then press their own governments into action against the offending regime. Domestic pressure also explains why democratic states are typically the most important promoters of international human rights. Not only are such rights more consistent with their own practice, but they are more susceptible to the demands of their citizens to undertake costly efforts to advance human rights abroad.

In turn, domestic demands for action are more likely the better informed are citizens about abuses in other countries. It is here, as monitors of practices around the globe, that human rights TANs may play their most important role. Almost by their very nature, human rights abuses are subterranean. They are typically perpetrated against individuals and groups that, though perhaps a potential threat to the regime, are nonetheless excluded from political power. Countries that violate human rights, in turn, are also likely to control access to the international media and other routes by which the abused might publicize their plight. It is through the links between domestic activists, who are often the victims of abuses, and transnational activists, who largely operate out of established democracies, that human rights violations are most often brought to light. AI's annual reports are an important vehicle for documenting state practice. Even though the U.S. Department of State also issues its own annual reports, many of the abuses in that document are first uncovered and brought to public attention by TANs. Without TANs, many more governments would be able to abuse their citizens, being confident that their odious practices would escape international scrutiny. This is one issue area where the networks of individuals and groups promoting new international norms, and pressing their governments to make greater efforts in pursuit of those goals, have had a significant effect on state practice.

Second, states are more likely to act against human rights violators when doing so serves larger geopolitical interests. Raising human rights issues as part of the Helsinki accords was applauded by many in the West as another way to bring pressure to bear on the Soviet Union and its allies for political and economic reform. Saddam Hussein's human rights record became an issue in the relations between Washington and Baghdad only after the Iraqi dictator invaded Kuwait in August 1991. His human rights violations later became one of several reasons given by President George W. Bush to remove Hussein from power in the Iraq War of 2003. Raising human rights concerns and demanding policy change in other states can be goals in themselves, but they may also be instruments in larger political and economic struggles.

Third, states are more likely to act when the gap between the principle of sovereignty and international human rights law can be bridged. Central to the concept of sovereignty is the principle of nonintervention, which is often jealously protected by precisely those states most likely to be sanctioned by the international community for their violations of human rights law. States are, therefore, reluctant to criticize one another, except when the principle of nonintervention can be reconciled with other principles. The anti-apartheid movement was broadly supported, for instance, because it was framed not as foreign intervention but as an anticolonial struggle; thus, it fell under the right to national self-determination guaranteed in the twin covenants. The postcolonial states in Africa are among the states most committed to the principle of nonintervention. Under many circumstances, they would have been reluctant to intervene in the affairs of South Africa for fear of legitimating external intervention in their own domestic politics. A key move in the anti-apartheid struggle was defining it as an anticolonial struggle against one of the last White-minority regimes on the continent.[31] So conceived, Black-majority-rule states not only could join the sanctions against South Africa but also could actively press Western states to join in the liberation struggle.

Countries do promote international human rights and punish violators, even if only in a weaker or more episodic way than some advocates desire. When faced with strong domestic pressures and lower costs, states do act to further human rights abroad. Yet, states are often inconsistent in their human rights policies. Human rights are seldom the only or even a principal motivation behind a state's foreign policy. The inconsistency of enforcement may make international human rights law comparatively ineffective and, thus, may explain why international human rights treaties appear to have only a weak effect on human rights practices.

WILL PROTECTION OF HUMAN RIGHTS IMPROVE IN THE FUTURE?

As with all international cooperation, efforts to promote more effective collaboration between and among states involves building better international institutions. There are at least four ongoing innovations in international human rights institutions that may have important implications for the future.

Individual Petition

One of the most important developments in international human rights law is the right of private or **individual petition** to a supranational court, found most prominently in the European Convention on Human Rights and Fundamental Freedoms (ECHR) adopted in 1950 by the Council of Europe and its now 47 member states.[32] Preceding it by 26 years, the ECHR recognizes many of the same rights ultimately in the ICCPR. It does not incorporate economic, social, or cultural rights into the corpus of rights it protects. Its most innovative features are the European Court of Human Rights and its right of individual petition.[33] The Court currently consists of 47 judges from the member states of the Council of Europe. It hears cases, offers

individual petition: A right that permits individuals to petition appropriate international legal bodies directly if they believe a state has violated their rights.

---

31. On the construction of a norm of self-determination, see Neta C. Crawford, *Argument and Change in World Politics: Ethics, Decolonization, and Humanitarian Intervention* (New York: Cambridge University Press, 2002). On the norm of racial equality in mobilizing support for the anti-apartheid movement, see Klotz, *Norms in International Relations*.

32. Rights of individual standing are also found in the Optional Protocols to the ICCPR and CEDAW (see Table 11.1) and in Article 14 of the ICERD and Article 22 of the CAT. In all cases, however, states must actively declare their willingness to allow the appropriate UN review committee to accept petitions from individuals. On the dynamics of state acceptance of the right of individual petition, see Heather Smith, "Explaining Ratification of Global Human Rights Instruments: Empirical Evidence of Regional Dynamics," paper presented at the annual meeting of the American Political Science Association, Philadelphia, PA, August 31–September 1, 2006.

33. On the Court, see www.echr.coe.int/ECHR.

decisions that are binding on members, and awards damages. Although there is no formal mechanism for ensuring compliance, responsibility for enforcing the decisions of the Court rests with the Council of Ministers of the Council of Europe. Enforcement is informally overseen by the European Union.

Since 1998, individuals in all member states have possessed the right to petition the Court for redress. Prior to this date, an optional protocol allowed individuals to petition the European Commission of Human Rights, which could then launch cases in the Court on their behalf. By adopting Protocol 11, all members are now required to allow individuals to petition the Court directly if they believe a state has violated their rights as specified in the ECHR. This provision is nearly unique in international law, in which states—not individuals—are normally the subjects. In the Court, individuals can now bring suit against their own governments for violations of internationally recognized human rights. In the year before the new provisions took effect, 5,891 petitions were filled with the Commission—a significantly large number. In 2001, the first full year under the new rules, 13,845 petitions were filed, representing an increase of approximately 138 percent. In 2007, the most recent year for which data are available, 41,700 applications were filed, of which 1,503 were ultimately decided by the Court.[34] Today, nearly all petitions before the Court are from private individuals and the success rate is over 50 percent, indicating that petitioners quite often win their cases against their own states. The ECHR is clearly having a profound effect on human rights practices in Europe, and especially in the newly democratizing states of Eastern Europe.

Without the right of individual petition, states act as gatekeepers, blocking international courts from hearing cases that they might lose. Some human rights activists advocate expanding the right of individual petition to other supranational courts as a check against human rights abuses. This move would open channels to international courts now blocked by states and would likely lead to greater attention to, if not better enforcement of, human rights violations.

Universal Jurisdiction

Universal jurisdiction is a new and controversial principle in which countries claim the right to prosecute perpetrators of crimes against humanity regardless of the citizenship of the individuals involved and the location where the crimes occurred. States normally exercise jurisdiction over crimes committed on their own territories, regardless of the perpetrator's nationality, and in some cases over crimes committed by their citizens in another state's territory (called extraterritoriality). More controversially, states may in some circumstances possess jurisdiction over crimes committed against their citizens by foreign nationals in foreign territories. For example, Spain attempted to extradite former Chilean dictator Augusto Pinochet from England, where he was undergoing medical treatment, on the grounds that some victims of the human rights abuses he had authorized were Spanish citizens. This case was never resolved,

---

34. On the Court's caseload, see www.coe.int/t/dc/files/themes/cedh/1–2248184-Survey_of_activities. pdf (pp. 62–63) (accessed 6/25/08). Although the courts themselves have different rules, procedures, and roles, for comparison the U.S. Supreme Court in 2006 (most recent year for which data are available) received 8,857 case filings, of which 74 were decided. See the annual report of the Supreme Court at www.supremecourtus.gov/publicinfo/year-end/2007year-endreport.pdf (accessed 6/25/08).

More than 100 states have accepted the jurisdiction of the International Criminal Court since it was established in 1998. However, as of 2009, only four cases had been referred to the ICC prosecutor.

as the British court found that Pinochet was not medically able to stand trial and he returned to Chile (where he was granted immunity under the constitution he wrote before leaving office). Similarly, the National Court in Madrid, Spain, referred to a special prosecutor for review and possible indictment six high-level officials in the administration of U.S. president George W. Bush, including Attorney General Alberto R. Gonzales, for providing the legal justification for torture carried out against five Spanish citizens at the American military base and detention center at Guantánamo Bay, Cuba.[35] This case is pending and may lead to further investigations against top-level officials in the administration. Universal jurisdiction is even more controversial because it claims to apply even when none of the victims of any crime are citizens of the prosecuting state. To the extent it is recognized, universal jurisdiction is expected to hold only for war crimes, genocide, torture, and other serious offenses under international human rights law. In September 2005, for instance, Hissène Habré, Chad's dictator, was indicted by a Belgian court for crimes against humanity, torture, war crimes, and other human rights violations. Arrested in Senegal following requests from Senegalese courts, he is now under house arrest and waiting for (an unlikely) extradition to Belgium.[36]

Universal jurisdiction is not a settled principle of international or even national law. The United States explicitly rejects the notion out of concern that its political leaders and military will be subject to politically motivated "show trials."[37] But by extending international human rights law inside the borders and against violators in another state, it has the potential of becoming another effective weapon against human rights abuses. By permitting the prosecution of violators who hide behind immunity, as in the case of Pinochet, or behind weak judicial institutions in their own countries, universal jurisdiction opens up the possibility that the assets of and even the abusers themselves may be seized as punishment for violating human rights. Whether universal jurisdiction becomes accepted international law remains to be seen. In the meantime, the debate over whether countries can prosecute foreign nationals for crimes against humanity has been superseded by the creation of a new international court for that very purpose.

35. Marlise Simons, "Spanish Court Weighs Inquiry on Torture for 6 Bush-Era Officials," *New York Times*, March 28, 2009. Available online at www.nytimes.com/2009/03/29/world/europe/29spain.html (accessed 4/9/09).

36. The two states that have been most active in asserting claims to universal jurisdiction are Belgium, which adopted a law of universal jurisdiction in 1993 that was subsequently revised as too broad, and Spain, where the Supreme Court declared that the "principle of universal jurisdiction prevails over the existence of national interests."

37. War crimes accusations have already been made against members of the Bush administration for actions taken in the so-called Global War on Terror. For a summary of one complaint made under Germany's universal jurisdiction law, and almost immediately thrown out by German courts, see http://ccrjustice.org/ourcases/current-cases/german-war-crimes-complaint-against-donald-rumsfeld%2C-et.-al.

The International Criminal Court

The **International Criminal Court** (ICC) was established in 1998 and came into force in July 2002 after receiving the necessary 60 ratifications of its founding treaty. Today, more than 100 states have accepted the jurisdiction of the ICC and thus have become "state parties." The ICC possesses jurisdiction only if the accused is a national of a state party, the crime took place on the territory of a state party, or the United Nations Security Council has referred the case to the prosecutor. Moreover, the ICC is a court of last resort, meaning that it cannot act if a national judicial authority has genuinely investigated or prosecuted a case—regardless of the outcome of that investigation or prosecution. The ICC can act only when a state cannot or will not act itself. To date, four cases have been referred to the ICC prosecutor: (1) in Uganda, the government referred a case against five senior commanders of the Lord's Resistance Army, a rebel group, for crimes against humanity and war crimes, including summary executions, torture and mutilation, recruitment of child soldiers, child sexual abuse, rape, forcible displacement, and looting and destruction of civilian property; (2) in the Democratic Republic of the Congo, the government similarly referred the commander of the Force de Résistance Patriotique en Ituri for crimes against humanity, including the command to "wipe out" the civilians of the village of Bogoro; (3) at the request of the government of the Central African Republic, the prosecutor is investigating armed individuals following a failed coup for massive rapes and other acts of sexual violence; and (4) the United Nations Security Council has accused the Sudanese Armed Forces and Janjaweed militia of genocide for their systematic attacks on Blacks in Darfur and, on March 4, 2009, the ICC ordered the arrest of President Omar Hassan al-Bashir for his "essential role" in the murder, rape, torture, pillage, and displacement of large numbers of civilians in the region.[38] In January 2009, the ICC began its first trial, against Thomas Lubanga, a Congolese warlord.[39]

The ICC remains highly controversial, especially in the United States. The treaty establishing the ICC was signed by President Bill Clinton shortly before leaving office, which permitted the United States to participate in further negotiations on the Court's rules of procedure. Almost immediately on taking office, President George W. Bush "unsigned" the treaty, a symbolic act with no legal effect since the United States would not be bound by the agreement unless it had already ratified it.

The U.S. government raises many objections to the ICC.[40] Foremost is the fear of frivolous and politically motivated prosecutions against political leaders or American military personnel for actions taken to protect the security of the United States or on peacekeeping or peacemaking missions abroad. Given what is often seen as the special role of the United States in maintaining international peace and security, and

> **International Criminal Court (ICC):** A court of last resort for human rights cases that possesses jurisdiction only if the accused is a national of a state party, the crime took place on the territory of a state party, or the United Nations Security Council has referred the case to the prosecutor.

---

38. Marlise Simons, "Court Issues Arrest Warrant for Sudan's Leader," *New York Times,* March 3, 2009. Available online at www.nytimes.com/2009/03/05/world/africa/05court.html (accessed 4/9/09). Sudan rejected the arrest warrant, and three weeks later Bashir safely attended an Arab League summit, where he was warmly embraced by the region's leaders.

39. Marlise Simons, "International Court Begins First Trial," *New York Times,* January 26, 2009. Available online at www.nytimes.com/2009/01/27/world/europe/27hague.html (accessed 4/9/09).

40. See statement by John R. Bolton, then Under Secretary for Arms Control and International Security, Department of State, and later U.S. Ambassador to the United Nations: www.state.gov/t/us/rm/25818.htm. For a review, see the Congressional Research Service's report at www.fas.org/sgp/crs/misc/RL31495.pdf (accessed 9/21/06).

After a warrant was issued by the ICC for his arrest, Sudanese president Omar Hassan al-Bashir led supporters in the capital of Khartoum in condemning the action, later telling cheering crowds that "we are not succumbing, we are not bending" to outside pressure.

real anti-Americanism in many countries, some skeptics of the ICC fear a string of political prosecutions in which leaders are prosecuted not for violations of law but merely for "show" or because others disagree with their policies. There is also concern that leaders would be constrained by fears of future politically motivated prosecutions. Although the United States could negate prosecution by the ICC by undertaking a genuine investigation or prosecution under its national laws, the statute is sufficiently ambiguous on what constitutes an adequate national-level inquiry that politically motivated prosecutions might still be possible.

The U.S. government also claims the ICC is insufficiently accountable and lacks oversight mechanisms for both the judges and prosecutors. Without the ability to remove activist judges, opponents are concerned that personnel at the ICC may escape political control and develop too much independence. In addition, international human rights case law and precedent are thin. Without adequate guidance from state parties on the intent of international law, the Court might not just interpret but essentially make international law itself. Finally, given its prosecutorial and judicial independence, critics claim that the ICC might clash with the more political and problem-solving approach of the United Nations Security Council. Where diplomacy must be flexible and aware of context, judicial proceedings that stress precedent, statutory interpretation, and equity across similar cases may conflict with the Security Council's charge to maintain peace and security.

Since the ICC entered into force in 2002, the United States has actively sought to undermine the Court and to exempt American nationals from its jurisdiction. Most important have been the Article 98 agreements urged—some might say, forced—on other countries by former president George W. Bush. Article 98 of the ICC exempts a country from handing over a foreign national to the Court if it is prohibited from doing so by a bilateral agreement with the national's country of origin. By June 2005, over 100 countries had signed bilateral agreements with the United States under threat of losing all foreign and military aid or the withdrawal of American peace-keeping forces. Despite sometimes significant aid cutoffs, other countries including Barbados, Brazil, Costa Rica, Peru, Venezuela, Ecuador, Saint Vincent and the Grenadines, and South Africa have refused to sign these agreements. Whether the ICC will survive the opposition of the world's most powerful state and grow into an effective institution to protect international human rights remains to be seen.

Harnessing Material Interests

A final source for optimism is the proliferation of regional trade agreements (RTAs) with human rights provisions. Indeed, nearly every country in the world now belongs to at least one RTA, and nearly all of them contain some provisions on human rights.

Some agreements are "soft," or merely declarative, and appear to have no effect on behavior. Increasingly, though, RTAs are starting to contain "hard" human rights provisions that bind states to international standards of behavior and threaten to withdraw trade and financial benefits if periodic reviews find substantial abuses of human rights. These hard provisions link concrete, material benefits of market access to a state's human rights practices. Unlike human rights agreements in general, and even soft RTAs, these hard provisions do have a significant if nonetheless substantively small effect on the level and extent of human rights violations.[41] Ironically, those protectionist groups looking to insulate themselves from import competition by including human rights provisions in free trade agreements may have devised effective weapons to protect human rights abroad—and their self-interest in seeing benefits revoked may make threats to use these weapons credible. Human rights advocates would do well to find other ways by which to harness often instrumental, material interests to the cause of promoting better human rights practices.

Conclusion: Why Protect Human Rights?

The puzzle of why states seek to protect the human rights of people outside their own borders is primarily explained by the interests of states. Whether because of concern for the well-being of others, an understanding of common humanity and the need to preserve democracy, or purely instrumental goals, individuals, groups, and thus states do have interests in promoting human rights abroad. TANs have been critical to the spread of international human rights norms in recent decades and in activating citizens to press their governments to act more forcefully to protect human rights. The fact that human rights are today an issue in international relations and that states concern themselves with human rights abroad is testament to the activities of the human rights TANs.

International human rights law is itself an institution. The at best mixed effectiveness of this institution in constraining abuses, in turn, follows from strategic interaction—or, perhaps more precisely, the lack of real and consistent enforcement. While states have interests and are willing to pay some cost to protect human rights within other countries, rarely are they willing to make human rights a priority. In short, although states are willing to pay some cost to promote human rights, they are not willing to pay significant costs or compromise substantially on other goals to secure the rights of others. As a result, states may publicly condemn abuse but impose few penalties on those who violate human rights. Knowing this, states abuse their citizens with little fear that they will be sanctioned. The fact that the human rights clauses of RTAs do improve practice, however, suggests that institutions that link behavior to real consequences can have important effects. Current issues in international human rights law focus largely on the breadth and depth of the law itself—individual petitions, universal jurisdiction, and the ICC. Given the modest effect of international human rights law on practice, perhaps human rights advocates would do better by focusing on designing more effective enforcement institutions.

---

41. Emilie M. Hafner-Burton, "Trading Human Rights: How Preferential Trade Agreements Influence Government Repression," *International Organization* 59, no. 3 (2005): 593–629.

Reviewing Interests, Interactions, and Institutions

INTERESTS	INTERACTIONS	INSTITUTIONS
States have different interests in promoting different sets of human rights. International human rights are subject to continuing debate.	Governments violate human rights due to incapacity, national security, or a desire to secure their own rule.	International human rights law is itself an institution.
Democratizing states have interests in signing human rights agreements to lock-in domestic political reforms.	States are inconsistent in enforcing international human rights law.	International human rights institutions are of limited effectiveness in controlling human rights abuses.
Other states have altruistic and self-interested incentives to promote human rights abroad.	Since violators are unlikely to face serious consequences, they can usually violate human rights with impunity if they choose to do so.	States that are most likely to abuse human rights may also be the ones most likely to sign international agreements.
Human rights TANs have influenced conceptions of human rights.	States are most likely to sanction human rights violators when subject to domestic pressure from concerned actors, when doing so serves geopolitical interests, or when it is not inconsistent with the principle of sovereignty.	TANs are important monitors of human rights practices around the globe.
Interests in international human rights are usually not sufficient to compel countries to pay high costs to protect individuals and groups outside their own borders.		Reforms including individual petition, universal jurisdiction, the International Criminal Court, and human rights provisions in economic agreements promise to improve the efficacy of international human rights institutions.

Key Terms

human rights, p. 412

Universal Declaration of Human Rights (UDHR), p. 412

International Covenant on Civil and Political Rights (ICCPR), p. 412

International Covenant on Economic, Social, and Cultural Rights (ICESCR), p. 412

International Bill of Rights, p. 414

nonderogable rights, p. 418

prisoners of conscience (POCs), p. 418

individual petition, p. 436

International Criminal Court (ICC), p. 439

For Further Reading

Angle, Stephen. *Human Rights in Chinese Thought: A Cross-Cultural Inquiry.* New York: Cambridge University Press, 2002. Examines conceptions of human rights from a non-Western perspective.

Clark, Ann Marie. *Diplomacy of Conscience: Amnesty International and Changing Human Rights Norms.* Princeton, NJ: Princeton University Press, 2001. Analyzes Amnesty's role in promoting human rights norms.

Donnelly, Jack. *Universal Human Rights in Theory and Practice,* 2nd ed. Ithaca NY: Cornell University Press, 2003. Presents a general overview of the philosophy and practice of international human rights law.

Forsythe, David. *Human Rights in International Relations.* New York: Columbia University Press, 2000. Offers an introduction to international human rights, with detailed analyses of international courts, regional human rights agreements, and other issues.

Ishay, Micheline R. *The History of Human Rights: From Ancient Times to the Globalization Era.* Berkeley: University of California Press, 2004. Serves as a comprehensive analysis of human rights philosophy and practice from ancient Greece to the present.

Landman, Todd. *Protecting Human Rights: A Comparative Study.* Washington, DC: Georgetown University Press, 2005. Presents a comprehensive empirical study of the international human rights regime and state practice.

Landman, Todd. *Studying Human Rights.* New York: Routledge, 2006. Addresses many of the methodological and empirical challenges of investigating human rights.

Risse, Thomas, Stephen C. Ropp, and Kathryn Sikkink, eds. *The Power of Human Rights: International Norms and Domestic Change.* New York: Cambridge University Press 1999. Analyzes how human rights norms have spread internationally.

Sikkink, Kathryn. "Human Rights, Principled Issue-Networks, and Sovereignty in Latin America." *International Organization* 47, no. 3 (1993): 411–41. Probes how sovereignty is being reshaped by international human rights law and advocacy.

Smith, Jackie, and Ron Pagnucco with George A. Lopez. "Globalizing Human Rights: The Work of Transnational Human Rights NGOs in the 1990s." *Human Rights Quarterly* 20, no. 2 (1998): 379–412. Describes patterns of human rights NGO formation and activity.

Waltz, Susan. "Universalizing Human Rights: The Role of Small States in the Construction of the Universal Declaration of Human Rights." *Human Rights Quarterly* 23, no. 1 (2001): 44–72. Reviews the development of the UDHR with an emphasis on the contributions of smaller countries.

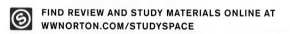

FIND REVIEW AND STUDY MATERIALS ONLINE AT WWNORTON.COM/STUDYSPACE

CHAPTER 12

The Global Environment

Although most people agree that stronger action should be taken to protect the environment, there is intense debate over who should bear the costs of such action. For example, the U.S. government has argued that agreements like the Kyoto Protocol would force Americans to bear an unfair portion of the costs. Here, a chemical plant in Michigan emits potentially harmful gases.

Nearly everyone wants a cleaner and healthier environment. Why, then, is it so hard to cooperate internationally to protect the environment?

Humans are changing the global climate. By emitting greater quantities of greenhouse gases, we are trapping more of the sun's energy within the earth's atmosphere and gradually warming the planet. Greenhouse gases are comprised of approximately 30 chemical compounds, the most important of which is carbon dioxide (CO_2) produced as a by-product of burning coal and oil. The Intergovernmental Panel on Climate Change (IPCC), sponsored by the World Meteorological Organization and the United Nations Environmental Program, currently estimates that global temperatures will rise on average between 3.5 and 8 degrees Fahrenheit by the year 2100.[1] Temperature changes in this range will melt glaciers and raise ocean levels, with devastating consequences for low-lying areas, including many Pacific islands, Bangladesh, and coastal cities in North America and Europe. A warmer climate will also melt the polar ice caps, alter weather patterns, create more extreme storms, expand deserts near the equator, modify crop yields and growing patterns, and spread tropical diseases to formerly temperate areas.

Despite considerable public attention, little progress has been made in reducing CO_2 emissions. The Kyoto Protocol to the Framework Convention on Climate Change (FCCC), signed in 1997 and entered into force in 2005, establishes targets for reducing emissions by 7 percent below 1990 levels for the United States, 8 percent for the European Union, and 6 percent for Japan and Canada. Some

Why Are Good Intentions Not Good Enough?
▶ Collective Action and the Environment
▶ Solving Collective Action Problems

Why Do Polluters Usually Win?
▶ Domestic Winners and Losers
▶ International Winners and Losers
▶ Bargaining over the Future Environment

How Can Institutions Promote International Environmental Cooperation?
▶ Setting Standards and Verifying Compliance
▶ Facilitating Decision-Making
▶ Resolving Disputes

Conclusion: Can Global Environmental Cooperation Succeed?

---

1. "IPCC, 2007: Summary for Policymakers," in *Climate Change 2007: The Physical Science Basis. Contribution of Working Group I to the Fourth Assessment Report of the Intergovernmental Panel on Climate Change,* ed. S. Solomon, D. Qin, M. Manning, Z. Chen, M. Marquis, K. B. Averyt, M. Tignor, and H. L. Miller (New York: Cambridge University Press, 2007), 13, Table SPM.3, http://ipcc-wgl.ucar.edu/wgl/Report/AR4WG1_Print_SPM.pdf (accessed 12/17/08).

countries may fail to meet their goals: Japan and Canada, for instance, are 30 and 29 percent above their target levels, respectively.[2] The United States has refused to ratify the protocol, and it does not apply to developing countries, which will add dramatically to the output of CO_2 in coming decades. In a summit of the world's richest countries in June 2007, the heads of state could only agree on a diplomatic process that might eventually lead to substantial cuts in greenhouse gases by the year 2050.

Global climate change will remain a key environmental challenge for decades, and other environmental problems will continue to grow. For example, within the last generation 20 percent of the world's tropical rainforest has been cleared for agriculture or logged for commercial uses. Human-induced change is causing an estimated 40,000 living species to become extinct each year, greatly reducing biodiversity. These mounting problems suggest a bleak future.

The news is not entirely bad, however. Ozone depletion caused by the release of chlorofluorocarbons (CFCs) into the atmosphere has been brought under control. The ozone layer is found in the lower stratosphere, approximately six to 30 miles above the earth. If it were compressed to the pressure of air at sea level, it would be only a few millimeters thick. Nonetheless, the ozone layer is essential to life on earth because it blocks harmful ultraviolet (UV) radiation from reaching the planet's surface. Within years of discovering that CFCs were harming the ozone layer, and within months of the discovery of an ozone "hole" over Antarctica, countries worldwide united to approve the Vienna Convention for the Protection of the Ozone Layer (1985) and, subsequently, the Montreal Protocol (1989), virtually eliminating the release of CFCs into the atmosphere. If climate change is an example of the failure to achieve effective international cooperation, ozone depletion is a sterling case of success.

There are other, equally notable examples of progress. The Long-Range Transboundary Air Pollution

Earth Day has been celebrated around the world since 1970, and protecting the global environment has become an increasingly high priority for people in many countries. This banner displayed in Guatemala City on Earth Day in 2008 declares, "Everything has a limit—including our planet!"

(LRTAP) Convention signed in November 1979 significantly reduced sulfur and, to a lesser extent, nitrogen oxide emissions, thereby mitigating the scourge of acid rain across Europe and North America. Similarly, many regional agreements have resulted in the cleanup of international rivers, lakes, and waterways. The Danube River, for instance, whose drainage basin includes 19 European countries, was once highly polluted. Since the signing of a regionwide convention in 1994, however, the river is now on the path to recovery. These cases of success suggest the possibilities of greater international environmental cooperation.

Why is such cooperation so difficult to achieve? Equally, why does it sometimes succeed despite these difficulties? One popular explanation for the relative lack of international environmental cooperation is ignorance. If populations and national leaders would only recognize or understand the problems, some observers believe, greater progress in improving the environment could occur. Transnational advocacy networks (or TANs, see Chapter 10) that act on behalf of environmental issues, and that comprise hundreds of environmental organizations and individual activists, have sought to make all of us more environmentally aware and have deepened our understanding of environmental problems. Much has been accomplished. Over recent decades,

2. "The Heat Is On: A Survey of Climate Change," *The Economist*, September 9, 2006, 17.

support for the environment has become broad-based. Ever since Rachel Carson's *Silent Spring* (1962) galvanized the environmental movement, citizens in most developed countries have become more environmentally conscious and have altered their daily behavior in myriad ways. As but one example of increasing awareness, approximately 20 million Americans participated in the first Earth Day, on April 22, 1970. Twenty years later, in 1990, this now-annual event had grown to over 200 million participants in 141 countries, making it the largest secular gathering in world history. More recently, Al Gore's much-discussed documentary, *An Inconvenient Truth,* winner of an Academy Award, has called broader attention to the issue of global climate change. For his leadership on this issue, the former vice president along with the IPCC was awarded the Nobel Peace Prize in 2007. Few people in developed countries now lack information about impending environmental degradation. Yet, recognizing the magnitude of the environmental problems we face is not enough to produce effective solutions. If this were the case, countries would have already taken more vigorous action to save the planet.

A second common explanation for the lack of progress points to the influential role of special interests in blocking environmental regulations. Clearly, there are certain groups that would lose from policies designed to improve the environment. Such groups are important actors in the analysis we develop in this chapter. But as the case of ozone depletion indicates, progress is sometimes possible despite the presence of highly motivated special interests. As the environmental movement has grown, citizens have pressed their governments to improve water quality, air quality, and other visible forms of environmental degradation. In the 1990s, "green" parties in Europe were important political forces, with their representatives holding office in coalition governments in Belgium, France, Finland,

Germany, and the Netherlands. Special interests matter, but we must examine more fully the cases in which they win out over the collective interest in a cleaner environment. Focusing mainly on the contrasting cases of ozone depletion and global climate change, this chapter develops four main points in explaining the difficulties of international environmental cooperation.

CORE OF THE ANALYSIS

▶ Despite widely shared interests in the quality of the environment, the interactions of individuals as well as countries suffer from problems of collective action. In the absence of any international authority that can mandate improved performance, the net result is less overall environmental cooperation than individuals and even countries themselves collectively desire.

▶ Small groups of actors, one of whom is substantially larger than the others and all of whom interact frequently on multiple issues, are most likely to cooperate effectively on issues relating to the international environment.

▶ Individuals, groups, and countries have conflicting interests over who bears the costs of mitigating harmful environmental practices. How environmental policies distribute these costs affects how likely actors are to cooperate successfully on issues relating to the environment.

▶ International institutions facilitate environmental cooperation primarily by enhancing information and verifying compliance. TANs and other nongovernmental organizations now play an essential role in monitoring compliance with environmental agreements. The clearer and more easily verified the standard, the more likely states are to cooperate successfully.

Why Are Good Intentions Not Good Enough?

Despite broad-based interests in environmental quality, cooperation is thwarted by interactions in which it is difficult to coordinate large numbers of individuals or, at the international level, moderately large numbers of states. We might personally care about the environment and want to improve the quality of the world we inhabit—that is, we have an interest in environmental cooperation—but our individual actions have little effect on the local or global ecosystem. For example, if everyone else is keeping their house warm at 70 degrees during the winter, your decision to lower your thermostat to 65 degrees will have a negligible effect on total energy usage and CO_2 emissions. You make a personal sacrifice to reduce pollution by keeping your house colder, while the benefits of your efforts, however small they may be, are not recouped by you alone but are broadly shared by others. Conversely, if everyone else is polluting less by setting their thermostats lower, your decision to keep your home at 70 degrees will also have negligible effects. Although you might use more energy and produce more emissions than others, your overconsumption also diffuses and imposes a very small cost on everyone. You may reap a personal benefit by staying warmer, but everyone bears the cost of your greater emissions.

Since we often benefit from others' efforts to preserve the environment while having only a marginal effect ourselves, we typically avoid changing our personal behaviors or incurring costs to reduce pollution. In short, even though we prefer a cleaner environment, we nonetheless seek to free ride on the efforts of others. Since everyone makes the same calculation, we interact within a Prisoner's Dilemma in which we individually defect and collectively produce a suboptimal outcome for society as a whole (also known as a Pareto suboptimal or inferior outcome; see Chapter 2 and the Special Topic appendix to Chapter 2). Thus, even though we may all have a shared interest in protecting the environment, our incentives to free ride usually win out and, through our interactions, we collectively degrade the ecosystem. Rather than sacrificing by living in cooler homes in the winter, we keep the thermostats turned up high—and hope for the best.

The same logic applies at the international level, except—as we shall see—for especially large countries. Most countries' efforts to conserve resources or limit pollution have only a small effect on the global environment. Since the costs of their pollution fall on others as well as themselves, they do not bear the full consequences of their decision to pollute. Similarly, if they sacrifice income by imposing tighter environmental controls on themselves, they create benefits for other countries that have not paid a similarly high price. Thus, countries seek to free ride on other countries, and the global environment suffers. Despite being the world's largest source of greenhouse gases, for instance, the United States is unwilling to constrain its own emissions in the absence of controls on all other countries. As former U.S. Secretary of Energy Samuel Bodman stated in rejecting unilateral limits on emissions, "We are a small contributor to the overall [problem], when you look at the rest of the world, so it's really got to be a global solution."[3] The Prisoner's Dilemma

---

3. Elisabeth Rosenthal and Andrew C. Revkin, "Science Panel Says Global Warming Is 'Unequivocal,'" *New York Times*, February 3, 2007.

that exists at the individual level is reproduced at the international level with the same consequences. The paradoxes of collective action are every bit as important for countries as for individuals.

COLLECTIVE ACTION AND THE ENVIRONMENT

The problem of collective action and our incentives to free ride on the environmental efforts of others arise because our choices produce **externalities**. An externality is created whenever a decision creates costs or benefits for stakeholders other than the actor making the decision. In other words, in an externality the decisionmaker does not bear all the costs or reap all the gains from its action. If a firm decides to dump waste into a river, others bear the costs of either using contaminated water or purifying it themselves. In this case, the firm has imposed a cost, or negative externality, on others. If a school club cleans a stretch of beach, not only do its members benefit from a litter-free and safer swimming area, but so do all others who might use the same spot. In this instance, the club has provided benefits, or created a positive externality, for others.

Externalities create a divergence between the individual costs or benefits of action and the broader costs or benefits to society as a whole. As a result, in the case of a negative externality, too much of the good is produced from the collective viewpoint. In the case of a positive externality, too little of the good is produced. Individuals are typically motivated to act only by their private costs and benefits, and they do not take into account the costs and benefits imposed on others. As a result, from the point of view of society at large, people individually decide to dump too much waste or fail to clean up enough beaches. When externalities exist, the independent decisions of individual actors lead to Pareto suboptimal results (see Figure 2.1 in Chapter 2). Through some form of cooperation, everyone's welfare can be improved and each individual, in principle, can be made better off.

Many environmental issues take the form of a more specific type of externality known as a *public good*. Public goods possess two characteristics that we encountered briefly in Chapter 2 when discussing problems of collaboration. First, once the public good is available for one person, others cannot be excluded from either suffering the cost or enjoying the benefit of that good. Technically, the good is **nonexcludable**. For example, **chlorofluorocarbons (CFCs)** emitted into the atmosphere destroy ozone molecules in the stratosphere, thinning the life-protecting **ozone layer** around the entire globe. No one can be excluded from the damage, and everyone suffers from higher levels of UV radiation reaching the earth's surface (see the Special Topic appendix to this chapter). Conversely, now that CFC production is greatly reduced and the ozone layer is beginning to repair itself, no one can be excluded from enjoying the benefits. In fact, CO_2 emissions have a similar effect in **global climate change**. Greater emissions harm everyone by raising global surface temperatures. Lower emissions, if they occur, will benefit everyone by eventually stopping or perhaps reversing the rise in temperatures.

Second, the use or consumption of the public good by one person does not diminish the quantity of the good available for use by others. Again, the good is technically said to be **nonrival in consumption**. In the case of ozone depletion, the greater UV radiation that reaches one person, and that increases his or her risk of skin cancer, does not diminish the greater quantity of UV radiation that might

externalities: Costs or benefits for stakeholders other than the actor undertaking an action. When an externality exists, the decisionmaker does not bear all the costs or reap all the gains from his or her action.

nonexcludable: Characterizing a public good: if the good is available to one actor to consume, then other actors cannot be prevented from consuming it as well.

chlorofluorocarbons (CFCs): Chemical compounds used in aerosols, insulating materials, refrigerator and air conditioner coolants, and other products. CFCs are widely banned today due to their damaging effect on the ozone layer.

ozone layer: Part of the lower stratosphere, approximately six to 30 miles above the earth, with relatively high concentrations of ozone (O_3), which blocks harmful ultraviolet (UV) radiation.

global climate change: Human-induced change in the environment, especially from the emissions of greenhouse gases, leading to higher temperatures around the globe.

nonrival in consumption: Characterizing a public good: one actor's consumption of the good does not diminish the quantity available for others to consume as well.

also harm a second person—or the billionth person. Similarly, the increase in temperature for one country from global warming does not reduce the temperature for other countries. All suffer from the warmer atmosphere and its consequences, including rising sea levels from melting glaciers. Conversely, one individual's enjoyment of lower UV levels or cooler temperatures does not diminish others' ability to enjoy the same environmental improvements. We all suffer, or not, together. It is these qualities of nonexcludability and nonrivalry that make ozone depletion and climate change—along with many other environmental issues—global problems.

Public goods arise partly from nature. Given the existence of a single atmosphere, we all suffer from a thinner ozone layer and a warmer climate. But the public aspect of goods is also partly a function of technology and, in turn, how much we are willing to pay to exclude ourselves from harm or others from benefits. By wearing UV-protected clothing or applying sunscreen, we can significantly reduce the effects of ozone depletion and the risk of contracting skin cancer. But these personal benefits are costly and do not protect others.

Public goods are also produced by social practice and law. For centuries, villages in Europe had a commons that was open to all the villagers' animals for grazing. One of the great social transformations of the late feudal period in Europe was the enclosure movement, through which the commons was divided into private plots—most of which ended up in the hands of the already rich landowners. Similarly, the **Kyoto Protocol**, adopted in 1997 and entered into force in 2005, creates a carbon trading system that, in essence, privatizes the public good that previously existed. Before Kyoto and continuing for those countries that remain outside the agreement, the environment is treated as a global commons, free for anyone to use even when that use produces emissions of harmful chemicals and other pollutants. Local or national governments may regulate the amount of toxic emissions that are allowed, but any actor meeting the national regulatory requirements essentially gains a right to pollute. Some countries simply choose not to regulate emissions. Under the provisions of the Kyoto Protocol, however, this right is overturned and the ability to pollute is restricted, at least for the advanced industrialized countries bound by the agreement.

Since 2005, Europe has used an Emissions Trading Scheme (ETS) that covers its five "dirtiest" industries and 13,000 factories and plants rated as particularly dirty. Each firm received tradable allowances for greenhouse gases up to the level of its existing emissions. Firms wanting to exceed those levels now have to purchase credits from other European firms or from developing countries with projects certified by the United Nations. Buying credits from another European firm simply shifts emissions from one company to another, with little effect on overall output.[4] Purchasing credits from developing countries actually reduces total emissions. In its first year, through this mechanism, consumers in developed countries invested $2.7 billion to cut developing-country greenhouse gases by the equivalent of 347 million tons

---

4. The ETS is what is known as a "cap and trade" system. Initial caps were set at existing emissions levels, meaning that firms did not have to restrict their emissions unless they wanted to sell the credits. In future years, caps will be gradually reduced, forcing firms to conserve or pay more for the limited credits. Current caps for most European industries covered by the ETS are now 7 percent below 2005 emissions levels and may increase to as much as 21 percent below 2005 by 2020. Nonetheless, in 2006, the first year of operation, firms covered by the ETS increased emissions by 0.4 percent, and in 2007 firms increased emissions by a further 0.7 percent. See James Kanter, "The Trouble with Carbon Markets," *New York Times*, June 20, 2008, sec. C.

of CO_2.[5] By design, the system creates incentives for businesses to reduce emissions by selling the credits they have not used themselves. Harnessing the profit motive to reduced emissions is key for reducing incentives to free ride. It is also expected to lead to more efficient allocations of resources as those industries or countries that face relatively high costs in reducing their emissions can instead buy carbon credits from others for whom reducing emissions is less costly. The key point, however, is that the global commons is now restricted and emissions can be bought and sold. The rules are designed to create a market in pollution credits that will correct previous incentives to free ride on others.

In addition to public goods, other types of externalities can create collective action problems. Many environmental issues, such as those related to open ocean fisheries, wildlife, and natural resources involve common pool resources. **Common pool resources** are nonexcludable but rival in consumption: it is difficult to exclude anyone from using the common pool, but one user's consumption reduces the amount available for others. In the case of common pool resources, the collective action problem that arises is **overexploitation**. Instead of failing to contribute, as in the case of public goods, actors are likely to overuse the resource.

Whaling provides a particularly clear example of overexploitation of a common pool resource.[6] It is difficult to exclude whalers from the open ocean or to effectively monitor their activities on the high seas. Nonetheless, any whale that is killed reduces the population of whales available for others to catch. Indeed, if too many whales are caught and the population becomes too small or geographically dispersed, there may be insufficient opportunities to reproduce and a whale species may "crash" or even become extinct. One whaler's decision to stop or, conversely, resume hunting will have only a small effect on the total whale population. As a result, his incentive is to catch as many whales as he can find. But if every whaler follows the same logic, the sum of their actions will deplete the whale population too rapidly.

To address this issue, the whaling industry created the International Whaling Commission (IWC) in 1946. In an attempt to limit annual catches to sustainable yields, each country was assigned an annual quota by the governing council. With the governing council composed almost entirely of representatives of whaling states, and with each member country lobbying to set its quota as high as possible, the IWC set the aggregate quota far above that which would allow the whale population to regenerate itself. As a result, the number of whales plummeted. Starting in the early 1960s, annual catches fell from approximately 15,000 to under 5,000 whales per year—not as a result of strict quotas, but owing to declining whale populations. Even though the industry recognized that its long-term health required lower quotas and rates of exploitation, the member states were unable to

Rapid industrialization in developing countries like China has come at a cost to the environment. This image shows a river in China's Sichuan Province that has been polluted by a paper mill.

common pool resources: Goods that are available to everyone, such as open ocean fisheries; it is difficult to exclude anyone from using the common pool, but one user's consumption reduces the amount available for others.

overexploitation: Consumption of a good at a rate that is collectively undesirable, even if it is efficient from the view of any single actor.

5. "The Heat Is On," 17–19.
6. M. J. Peterson, "Whalers, Cetologists, Environmentalists, and the International Management of Whaling," *International Organization* 46, no. 1 (Winter 1992): 147–86.

resist their incentives to catch as many whales as quickly as they could. Under pressure from environmentalists, the IWC finally enacted a complete ban on whaling in 1982, and it took effect in 1985. (See "What Shaped Our World?" on p. 453.)

In sum, externalities create a disjuncture between individual interests and collective welfare. The interactions of large numbers of individuals or countries can produce outcomes that are undesirable for society as a whole. Even though we all value the environment, our individual actions have a marginal impact and we free ride on the efforts of others. Problems of collective action apply among individuals and states. Choices that are reasonable for a single actor sometimes create collectively tragic results.

SOLVING COLLECTIVE ACTION PROBLEMS

Although they make environmental cooperation difficult, collective action problems need not thwart cooperation entirely. And although they create similar incentives for everyone to defect from cooperation, they may nonetheless vary in severity and ease of solution.

First, the magnitude of collective action problems varies by group size.[7] The larger the group of actors affected by an externality, the more likely they are to free ride on one another, as the contribution of each will be a proportionately smaller percentage of the total. The smaller the group, the more likely actors are to contribute to solving the problem. This helps explain why acid rain, a problem in the 1970s, was relatively easy to address. Acid rain is produced when sulfur dioxide and nitrogen oxide are emitted into the atmosphere, are subsequently absorbed by water droplets creating a mild solution of sulfuric and nitric acid, and then eventually fall to earth as precipitation. The highly acidic rain affects the chemical balance of soil, lakes, and streams. Indeed, acid rain killed many forests and both plant and aquatic life in lakes before being brought under control. Acid rain is primarily a localized phenomenon, however, falling mostly downwind of large, coal-burning industrial centers. Thus, emissions from the United States fell mostly on itself and Canada; British emissions, on Scandinavia; West European emissions, on Eastern Europe; and so forth. Although restricted to countries downwind of large polluters, the same problem occurs in many different regions. The limited number of countries in each acid rain region was a key factor in facilitating negotiations for the Convention on Long-Range Transboundary Air Pollution (LRTAP) and its optional protocol, completed in 1979 and now possessing 51 members from across several acid rain regions. Together, the member states have reduced sulfur emissions by more than 50 percent since 1983.[8] Small numbers do not guarantee success, however. In China alone, acid rain caused by burning high-sulfur coal remains an acute problem affecting over one-third of its territory.

Since they affect the largest possible population, global environmental problems such as ozone depletion and climate change are more difficult to solve. Nonetheless, the relatively smaller number of countries involved was one of the factors that

---

7. Mancur Olson, *The Logic of Collective Action: Public Goods and the Theory of Groups* (Cambridge, MA: Harvard University Press, 1965).

8. United Nations Economic Commission for Europe, *Twenty-Five Years of International Cooperation on the Convention on Long-Range Transboundary Air Pollution, 1979–2004* (Geneva, Switzerland: UNECE, 2004), www.unece.org/env/lrtap/ExecutiveBody/2004_lrtap_eng.pdf (accessed 12/17/08).

The Campaign to Save the Whales

Since 1982, the International Whaling Commission (IWC) has banned the killing of whales for commercial purposes. As noted in the text, whales are a common pool resource that, if unregulated, will be overexploited. Created in 1946 by countries with significant whaling industries to limit annual catches to sustainable levels, the IWC had the goal of maintaining the viability and profitability of a historic industry. But it failed. By the early 1960s, whale populations around the globe had crashed. Under pressure from environmentalists, however, a complete ban on commercial whaling was enacted in 1982. How the ban came about illustrates the role of transnational advocacy networks (TANs) in successfully manipulating institutional rules to preserve a valued part of the environment.

When environmentalists began a campaign to save the whales in the 1970s, the choice of animal was quite strategic. Although whales were not any more endangered than some other species of fish or marine life, as marine mammals (and apparently intelligent ones) they were perceived as especially sympathetic.

The whaling states on the IWC vigorously opposed a ban. While environmentalists made a normative argument against killing any marine mammals, whalers argued that they should be permitted to continue to hunt at lower, but sustainable, rates. Environmentalists finally launched a key strategy to exploit a loophole in the voting rules of the IWC.

The IWC voting rules give each member country one vote and allow any state that pays dues to join. Decisions are made by a supermajority of three-quarters of voting states. The membership of the IWC was intentionally left open to gain the participation of not only current whaling states but also any state that might develop a whaling industry in the future. Environmentalists shrewdly used this rule to stack the membership of the IWC by encouraging anti-whaling states to join. In becoming a member, for instance, Switzerland became the first landlocked country to join any international fishery organization. Environmental organizations also paid the membership dues for small, poor countries that did not previously belong. By 1982, the year the ban was adopted, environmentalists had succeeded in shifting the majority membership of the IWC away from those states backing the commercial exploitation of whales to those supporting a moratorium.

The ban remains controversial to this day. Reversing the strategy used so effectively by environmentalists to shape the composition of the IWC, Japan appears to be tying its growing foreign aid for smaller states to their support for its own efforts to overturn restrictions on commercial whaling. Indeed, in a famous interview with Australian ABC television in July 2001, in which he described minke whales as "cockroaches of the sea," Japanese Fisheries Agency official Maseyuku Komatsu said that offering aid was "a major tool" in obtaining backing for a return to commercial whaling. The most recent attempt (in June 2005) to overturn the ban on commercial whaling was defeated by just a handful of votes. At the 2006 meeting, a majority composed of pro-whaling states enacted a nonbinding resolution stating that the moratorium was no longer necessary and that the IWC should cease to be a whale protection organization. After losing two previous votes at that meeting, the majority tipped in favor of the pro-whaling coalition only after a representative from Togo showed up late and paid his country's membership dues of $10,000 in cash.[a]

Why was the ban effective? In part, the ban was enforceable because it created a clearly observable standard: no whaling was permitted. Any whale meat, whale ivory, or other physical evidence was presumed to result from illegal activities. Equally important, however, was U.S. domestic law. All nations have the right to regulate fishing in their exclusive economic zone (EEZ), which in most cases extends 200 nautical miles from their coastline. Because the U.S. EEZ is rich in fish and highly desirable to foreign fishing fleets, the U.S. government sells rights to fish in the EEZ to foreign countries. Environmentalists pushed legislation through the U.S. Congress requiring that fishing rights be denied to any country not in compliance with the IWC ban on whaling.

Today, Norway is the only country that continues to hunt whales on a commercial basis. Japan and, recently, Iceland have pursued scientific whaling programs, which are carefully monitored and sometimes disrupted by TANs like Greenpeace (see text). Whale populations have begun to recover. However, as several species have been removed from the endangered list, calls for resuming commercial whaling are arising. ▪

---

a. See the report on the 2006 meeting, "So long, thanks for all the fish," *Sydney Morning Herald*, June 21, 2006, www.smh.com.au/news/world/so-long-thanks-for-all-the-fish/2006/06/20/1150701555097.html.

Groups that interact repeatedly and frequently are more likely to cooperate. For example, Nepalese farmers, who form a community that is tightly linked in numerous ways, have been able to cooperate on irrigation. Their irrigation system is a common pool resource that they have successfully shared such that no one farmer is able to overexploit the water supply at the expense of others.

contributed to more effective collective action on ozone than on global climate change. In the case of ozone depletion, CFC production and usage was relatively concentrated in a few countries. In the late 1980s, the United States (22 percent), Japan (16 percent), and Russia (11 percent) accounted for just under half of the world's total emissions of CFCs. Just 12 countries accounted for 78 percent of all emissions. The benefits of reduced emissions would also be greatest in temperate countries, where the ozone holes would be most serious. In the case of climate change, the producers and consumers of fossil fuels that account for the majority of CO_2 emissions are very broadly dispersed. Fossil fuels are deeply integrated into the heart of nearly all industrialized and industrializing economies and are the primary sources of energy for most of the world today. Altering the usage of oil and coal will have profound effects extending throughout the economy of every nation. With the large number of countries involved in climate change, the problem of collective action is relatively more severe. Even within global environmental issues, group size matters.

Second, as we saw in Chapter 2, groups that interact repeatedly (iteration) or frequently on other issues (linkage) will be able to induce greater contributions from one another through strategies of reciprocal punishment in which contributors sanction noncontributors by withholding future cooperation. Empirically, tightly linked and enduring communities with very large numbers of actors have been found to cooperate successfully over long periods. In Nepal, for instance, irrigation networks—a common pool resource shared among hundreds of farmers—have endured for centuries because of the farmers' mutual dependence on each other.[9] Similarly, the resolution of the acid rain problem in North America and Europe was facilitated because the neighboring states interacted frequently on many dimensions (Canada and the United States are each other's largest trading partners, for instance) and expected to interact intensely into the foreseeable future. Downwind states whose lakes were slowly dying from acid rain thus expected to have plenty of opportunities to punish their upwind neighbors if the latter did not live up to the terms of the LRTAP Convention. Conversely, the diverse array of countries with widely varying patterns of interactions involved in global issues, including both ozone depletion and climate change, make cooperation more difficult.

Third, when public goods come bundled with private goods for which actors are willing to pay, cooperation is also facilitated. These are called joint products.[10] Rainforests absorb significant amounts of CO_2 and thus help reduce the

---

9. Elinor Ostrom and Roy Gardner, "Coping with Asymmetries in the Commons: Self-Governing Irrigation Systems Can Work," *Journal of Economic Perspectives* 7, no. 4 (Autumn 1992): 93–112; Elinor Ostrom, *Governing the Commons: The Evolution of Institutions for Collective Action* (New York: Cambridge University Press, 1990).

10. Also called selective incentives. See Todd Sandler, *Global Challenges: An Approach to Environmental, Political, and Economic Problems* (New York: Cambridge University Press, 1997), 45–46.

problem of global climate change, and they are home to many different species, thereby enhancing biodiversity. Saving acres in a rainforest to preserve a global carbon sink and promote biodiversity also provides erosion control to local landowners and opportunities for ecotourism; those landowners may pursue such measures for those private benefits. Similarly, the DuPont company saw an opportunity for increased profits as the pressure to ban CFCs began to increase in the 1980s. DuPont was a leading producer of CFCs, accounting for nearly 50 percent of all production in the United States and 25 percent of global production. But as the leading innovator of alternatives for CFCs as well, DuPont was also well positioned to gain from a ban.[11] In this case, the positive externality of eliminating the production of CFCs also provided a private profit for DuPont. A similar transition may occur for large energy companies as they diversify into alternative fuels, but none appear to have reached the critical point where the gains from wind, solar, or other energy sources appear sufficiently promising for them to strongly advocate greener technologies. For all joint products, the public good is provided as a by-product of efforts to obtain the private good. The larger the private benefits relative to the public good, the less free riding we will observe.

Finally, when actors vary in size (as states do) or in the intensity of their preferences for public goods, a privileged group may emerge (see Chapter 2). A privileged group is comprised of one or a small number of actors who receive sufficient benefits themselves from the public good that they are willing to bear the cost of providing that good for all. The benefits of reducing ozone depletion were sufficiently large to the United States, for example, that it was willing to bear the costs of banning CFCs unilaterally and leading the international fight against their use. The United States produced 30 percent of the world's CFCs, and the savings to it alone were sufficient to justify a major effort to limit CFC emissions. After some initial reluctance, the United States took a leadership position in the negotiations at Vienna and afterwards. (Table 12.1 identifies treaties enacted and in force since the Vienna Convention.)

Conversely, one of the major problems in global climate change has been the relatively smaller benefits and higher costs to the United States from controlling emissions of greenhouse gases and its corresponding unwillingness to take a vanguard role in this area. Even though the United States accounts for a large percentage of CO_2 emissions similar to its CFC production, it is unlikely to be affected by global warming as much as some other countries (other than in New Orleans, parts of Florida, or other low-lying coastal areas). To date, the United States has been a laggard rather than a leader in controlling CO_2 emissions. It has opposed the Kyoto Protocol largely because the amendment exempts most developing countries and, in the eyes of some critics, puts an unfair burden on American producers and consumers.

Collective action problems are not constant across environmental issues. In all public goods, some free riding will occur. Countries will always be tempted to

---

11. Karen Litfin, *Ozone Discourses: Science and Politics in Global Environmental Cooperation* (New York: Columbia University Press, 1994), 123–27.

TABLE 12.1	TREATIES CONTROLLING OZONE-DEPLETING SUBSTANCES	
Treaty	Date Enacted/ Date in Force	Notable Accomplishments
Vienna Convention for the Protection of the Ozone Layer	March 1985/ September 1988	Served as a framework convention that mandated states to study the harmful effects of CFC emissions on the ozone layer.
Montreal Protocol	September 1987/ January 1989	Implemented progressive cuts, rising to 50 percent of 1986 levels, in the consumption and production of five CFCs. Froze the production and consumption of three halons at current levels.
London Amendment	June 1990/ August 1992	Increased cuts for fifteen CFCs to 85 percent of 1986 levels and eventually eliminated them. Imposed increasing cuts on three halons, carbon tetrachloride, and methyl chloroform. Imposed nonbinding cuts on HCFCs.
Copenhagen Amendment	November 1992/ June 1994	Accelerated the phaseout of fifteen CFCs, three halons, carbon tetrachloride, and methyl chloroform. Entered HCFCs, HBFCs, and methyl bromide on the list of controlled substances.
Montreal Amendment	September 1997/ November 1999	Phased out methyl bromide. Increased the list of controlled depleters to ninety-four.
Beijing Amendment	December 1999/ February 2002	Controlled bromochloromethane. Developed better controls for ozone depleters.

Source: Todd Sandler, *Global Collective Action* (New York: Cambridge University Press, 2004), 216.

overexploit a common pool resource. Because no actor bears the full costs or benefits of its decisions, externalities will always be produced. Yet, as the contrasting outcomes in ozone depletion and global climate change suggest, some collective action problems can be solved.

Why Do Polluters Usually Win?

Political struggles over the environment often involve bargaining problems as well as collective action problems. These bargaining problems pit a majority favoring tighter regulations against a minority of special interests that, if not actually advocating environmental degradation, aim to block costly new regulations or to shift the costs of policy change onto others. Even though all may share an interest in the environment, any policy to improve environmental practices will create losers, who will have to curtail activities or practices that were previously permitted, and winners, who will enjoy the benefits of a greener world. This situation creates a problem of bargaining or redistribution in which one side's gains come at the expense of another side's losses. Why do those who stand to lose from tighter environmental restrictions often win? Why do those special interests that oppose environmental regulations tend to succeed in blocking greater controls? To answer these questions, we must examine two sets of winners and losers in international environmental policy.

DOMESTIC WINNERS AND LOSERS

Almost by definition, "dirty" industries that impose negative externalities on others enhance their profits by not paying the full (or social) costs of production, which include not only their immediate costs of production but also the negative externalities they impose on others. Industries that emit pollutants into the air or water benefit from lax environmental policies that do not require them to pay to clean up their production processes, but rather leave it to others to do so or live with dirty air or water. Similarly, clear-cutting of forests is usually cheaper than selectively harvesting trees in a way that limits deforestation and helps preserve biodiversity. The losses from deforestation, including greater erosion and possible flooding, and reduced biodiversity are costs to others that are incurred long after the lumber companies have moved on to new areas.

Even though they may extract or manufacture their products in ways that do not directly degrade the environment, industries that produce goods that harm the environment also have interests in looser environmental laws. The oil industry, which frequently promotes its clean production methods in glossy magazine ads, has fought attempts to require cleaner-burning fuels like ethanol that would, were they widely available, reduce the value of their reserves and force them to invest in new capacity to develop and distribute these alternatives. Likewise, the auto industry has opposed efforts to improve gasoline mileage or reduce emissions because the new technologies would raise the price of cars and, at least at the margin, reduce demand.

Competition at home and abroad constrains firms to reduce their costs of production as much as possible. The process of economic globalization heightens this constraint by bringing domestic firms into competition with foreign manufacturers, which may not face the same pressures for increased environmental regulations in their bases of production. By opposing new environmental regulations—and at an extreme, by lobbying to remove existing regulations as competition increases—firms lower their costs of production at the expense of the environment.[12] By producing at lower cost, however, not only do the firms benefit but so do consumers, who gain from cheaper prices for goods. Indeed, lax environmental regulations lower the cost of goods and, thus, give consumers an incentive to ignore environmental degradation as well.

Nearly every alternative policy for protecting the global environment creates losers and winners who press their governments to change policy in their preferred direction. Nonetheless, the balance of political power typically favors entrenched or vested interests. The industries and groups that would lose from tighter environmental regulations are relatively few, in comparison with the majority that

---

12. Firms may also use disputes over differing international environmental regulations to attempt to restrict international trade and competition. In such cases, concern over the environment can be a form of hidden protectionism. It is no coincidence that environmentalists and labor unions have joined forces against globalization in most developed countries.

gains from a greener environment, and they suffer direct and immediate costs. In this way, polluters are similar to protectionist industries (discussed in Chapter 6) that gain concentrated benefits from import restrictions and are more motivated to enter the political arena as a result. Oil markets are dominated by just a few major firms, for which the costs of environmental regulations are also highly concentrated. Automobile manufacturers claim that increased mileage standards will require costly new research and development and raise the price of cars, thereby reducing demand. These concentrated costs give the potential losers a stronger incentive to attempt to influence government policy. As an exception that tests the rule, CFC producers—especially DuPont, the industry leader—dug in their heels on reducing emissions until it became clear that new chemical alternatives would soon be available and might even increase profits. When the costs of change are not large, even politically powerful industries may yield to demands for tighter environmental regulations. Once regulated, moreover, firms may then lobby hard to create international agreements that level the playing field by regulating foreign firms as well.[13]

Conversely, the benefits of a cleaner environment are diffuse and the beneficiaries, as a result, suffer from collective action problems. Because the benefits are spread across many individuals or groups, few have strong interests in lobbying their governments to alter current practices. The intensity of the losers' interests in opposing stiffer regulations typically compensates for their smaller numbers relative to the majority.

Moreover, these industries and groups have employees and stockholders who are citizens and voters. Industries can mobilize those workers and stockholders to press their case on elected politicians. Oil companies, for example, have political influence because of the number of voters whose livelihoods, in one form or another, depend on that industry, including all related industries that use inexpensive fossil fuels. Alternative industries, such as wind or solar power firms, lack the same resources. Their future growth, and the workers and stockholders who might benefit directly from their growth, are mostly promises rather than real-life voters who can reward or punish politicians for the legislation they adopt today. Even though the industries may grow in the future, the number of companies, employees, and communities that depend on electricity generated from wind or solar power remains very small. Consequently, these industries exert comparatively little influence on current policy. There are, of course, exceptions. For example, American farmers have been a driving force behind efforts to add ethanol to traditional petroleum-based gasoline products as a way of creating a new market for corn and increasing its price.[14] But in general,

---

13. On domestic business interests, see Elizabeth R. DeSombre, *Domestic Sources of International Environmental Policy: Industry, Environmentalists, and U.S. Power* (Cambridge, MA: MIT Press, 2000).
14. Even here, however, the logic of winners and losers comes into play. Corn's net energy balance—the amount of energy it yields relative to the amount of energy required to produce it—is lower than sugar-based alternatives. Nonetheless, corn farmers have successfully lobbied for subsidies to promote corn-based ethanol. In turn, the United States is comparatively disadvantaged in producing sugar (see Chapter 6). High tariffs on imported sugar raise the price so that it is not cost effective to use it for thanol. The concentrated benefits of tariffs for American sugar producers and subsidies for corn growers are leading the United States toward an ethanol policy that will cost consumers more in the long run. But at pennies per gallon more for ethanol, few consumers will feel motivated to fight the more highly motivated interests in the sugar and corn lobbies.

prospective "greener" industries do not have political clout today. This situation creates an important bias toward the status quo and against policies aimed at improving the environment. With concentrated costs and a political system biased toward existing rather than future industries, domestic groups that would lose from tighter environmental regulations tend to have more political power and to win policy contests even in the face of majorities who prefer a cleaner environment.

INTERNATIONAL WINNERS AND LOSERS

Environmental issues also divide developed and developing countries. Historically, the largest polluters have been rich states in Europe and North America. Since 1950, nearly 70 percent of cumulative CO_2 emissions have been released by these countries. Even today, the United States uses far more energy per capita and emits far more pollutants per capita than any other country. With 4.6 percent of the world's population, the United States emits 23 percent of the world's CO_2. Worldwide, the average individual produces 4.0 metric tons of CO_2 each year. The average American emits 19.8 tons per year, more than in any other country (Japan, a state at a comparable level of economic development, averages 9.3 metric tons per person per year). The developed countries have by far the largest cumulative and ongoing impact on the environment.

The greatest source of new pollutants in the future will be the developing countries. As China industrializes, its CO_2 emissions—which doubled between 1980 and 2001 and now constitute about 14 percent of the world's total—will rise to almost 18 percent by 2025 (per capita, China emits only about 2.2 metric tons per person per year, about 11 percent of the level in the United States). China's level of increased emissions of greenhouse gases over the next 25 years will probably exceed that for all developed countries combined and will surpass by five times the reductions in emissions required under the Kyoto Protocol.[15] Heavily dependent on coal for energy, China already leads the world in sulfur oxide and is third in nitrogen oxide emissions. Aerial particulates from burning coal, overgrazing, and soil erosion already blow from China to Korea, Japan, the Pacific Islands, and within a week to the United States. China's current per capita output of these airborne pollutants remains far below the world average.[16] Yet, as China industrializes further, its emissions of these chemicals and particulates will increase dramatically.[17] Although China's large

Many international conferences, such as the UN Climate Change Conference, have brought together delegates from numerous countries to discuss the environment. However, states and other actors often disagree over how the costs of environmental protection should be distributed.

15. Keith Bradsher and David Barboza, "Pollution from Chinese Coal Casts Shadow around Globe," *New York Times*, June 11, 2006, sec. A.

16. Due to the comparatively high proportion of China's energy derived from coal, SO_S is the primary exception. In 2000, China released 2,700 metric tons of SO_S per square kilometer of territory, compared to a global average of 1,700 metric tons.

17. On China and the environment, see Jianguo Liu and Jared Diamond, "China's Environment in a Globalizing World," *Nature* 435 (June 30, 2005): 1179–86; Also, see www.eia.doe.gov/emeu/cabs/chinaenv.html.

population and growing economy put its environmental practices on the front pages of the world's newspapers, the same story could be told for virtually every other developing country. Development has always been a dirty business—and it still is.

In addition, some of the easiest steps to prevent further environmental degradation could be taken in the developing world (see Map 12.1). It is much less expensive to reduce emissions and pollutants in developing than developed countries. As a direct result of the environmental movement and government legislation, many of the sources of pollution that are easiest to correct have already been addressed in developed countries, whereas developing countries are just beginning the process of installing cleaner technologies. To reduce an extra ton of emissions from an already relatively clean European steel mill, for instance, is far more costly than to cut an equivalent ton from an Indian or Indonesian steel mill that has never used smokestack scrubbers. This is a key rationale behind the ETS adopted by the European Union that allows allows its firms, facing high costs to reduce further their emissions, to buy carbon credits from developing countries, where the costs of reducing an equivalent amount of CO_2 are much lower. Similarly, it is cheaper to maintain the earth's tropical rainforests in developing countries than it is to reforest areas in North America; and it is more effective to maintain biodiversity in these forests than to wait for nature to reproduce the variety that once existed in replanted North American forests.

There are strong ethical concerns created by the tension between development and the need to preserve the environment. By prodding developing countries to adopt a cleaner path to development, the already rich countries are essentially demanding that the world's poor increase their costs of production. This restriction will limit their ability to sell their goods in developed country markets, will slow their rates of economic growth, and will delay the time when they attain the present standard of living of citizens in the developed countries. Rich countries are asking poor countries to pay a price that the rich countries did not have to pay in their own climb to wealth—and to help solve a problem for which the rich developed countries are largely responsible. (See "Controversy," on p. 461.)

Research indicates that environmental quality falls with economic growth and industrialization and then begins to improve once national income per capita rises above approximately $16,000 per year.[18] (See "What Do We Know?" on p. 465.) Below that level of income, most citizens in most countries seem to be more concerned with improving their quality of daily life—educating their children, getting electricity to rural villages to power appliances, finding cheap modes of transportation to expand markets and job opportunities—than with improving the quality of the environment per se. For countries like China and India, with per capita annual incomes in 2008 of only approximately $5,400 and $2,600, respectively, the day when indigenous environmental movements are likely to arise and demand change from their governments is decades in the future. Until then, pressure to maintain environmental quality in most developing countries will continue to come from foreign environmental TANs and governments in developed countries.

---

18. Gene N. Grossman and Alan B. Krueger, "Economic Growth and the Environment," *Quarterly Journal of Economics* 110, no. 2 (1995): 353–77. Their figure of $8,000 (1985 dollars) is converted to current dollars in the text.

Who Should Bear the Costs of Addressing Global Climate Change?

Nepal's Sagarmatha National Park features an expanse of snowy ranges, ancient glaciers, deep gorges, and the ancient villages of the Sherpa people, as well as the homes of the rare snow leopard, musk deer, and red panda. Recently, however, things have started to warm up in Nepal. In a development scientists interpret as human-induced climate change, average air temperature has risen by double the global average in the Himalayan region over the past 30 years, and in the past decade two-thirds of the range's glaciers have retreated.[a] If these trends continue, the surrounding regions will be devastated first by floods as glaciers melt more rapidly, and then by water shortages affecting a full third of the world's population. Homes, livelihoods, and cultures will be destroyed; famine, disease, and conflict will rage; plants and animals will go extinct.

Everyone agrees that such outcomes would be tragic, affecting not just Nepal but also the rest of the world. Halting global climate change constitutes a global public good. As is common with such goods, however, a collective action problem arises over which countries ought to bear the burdens of mitigating the disaster. Effective international collaboration to address global climate change will require an international bargain over the distribution of those burdens. What sort of bargain would be fair?

A Nepalese might reason as follows. Developed countries have made by far the largest contributions to current greenhouse gas concentrations. Those countries also have a much higher standard of living than Nepal and its neighbors do, meaning that those countries are both better able to protect their populations from the effects of climate change and better able to absorb the costs of environmental preservation without imposing unbearable sacrifices on their citizens. Together, these twin facts—responsibility and capacity—suggest that the developed world ought to bear the costs of reducing future global CO_2 emissions.

An American might object that it is unfair for the United States to reduce its future emissions when developing countries—including some very large CO_2 emitters—are not being asked to make similar sacrifices. Nepal and its neighbors China and India would be free riding on U.S. efforts. The American might admit that the United States has been a major contributor but would likely emphasize that this was mostly at a time when no one knew of the environmental dangers. Moreover, she might add, the same U.S. economic activity that has contributed to the melting of the Himalayan glaciers has also resulted in important benefits for the Nepalese by contributing to the worldwide dispersion of a range of products and technologies.

The Nepalese might reply that the ability to buy a TV, say, is not of much use when one's house has been swept away by floods. He could also point out that asking Nepal to reduce its future emissions would increase its production costs, thereby stalling the progress of Nepal toward the level of economic development that industrialized countries have enjoyed for decades. Here the American might claim that at least the large polluters China and India ought to take up some of the burden, especially since a cleanup of their "dirty" industries would provide a more efficient means of reducing emissions than would additional efforts by the already-cleaner industries of the developed world.

Some observers suggest that the simplest and most politically acceptable option would be to wipe the slate clean and assign each person an equal right to a fixed amount of future emissions.[b] If these rights were tradeable, they would both benefit developing countries with initially low emissions and create incentives for reductions to occur where they could be achieved most inexpensively. Could this proposal serve as a fair and workable basis for future international collaboration? With the failure of the United States to agree to even the lesser obligations built into the Kyoto Protocol, that prospect currently seems unlikely. In the meantime, snow and ice will continue to melt in the Himalayas. ■

a. J. Thomas and S. Rai, "An Overview of Glaciers, Glacier Retreat, and Subsequent Impacts in Nepal, India and China" (Kathmandu, Nepal: WWF Nepal Program, 2005), http://assets.panda.org/downloads/himalayaglaciersreport2005.pdf (accessed 1/16/09).

b. Peter Singer, *One World: The Ethics of Globalization* (New Haven: Yale University Press, 2002), 35, 43–44.

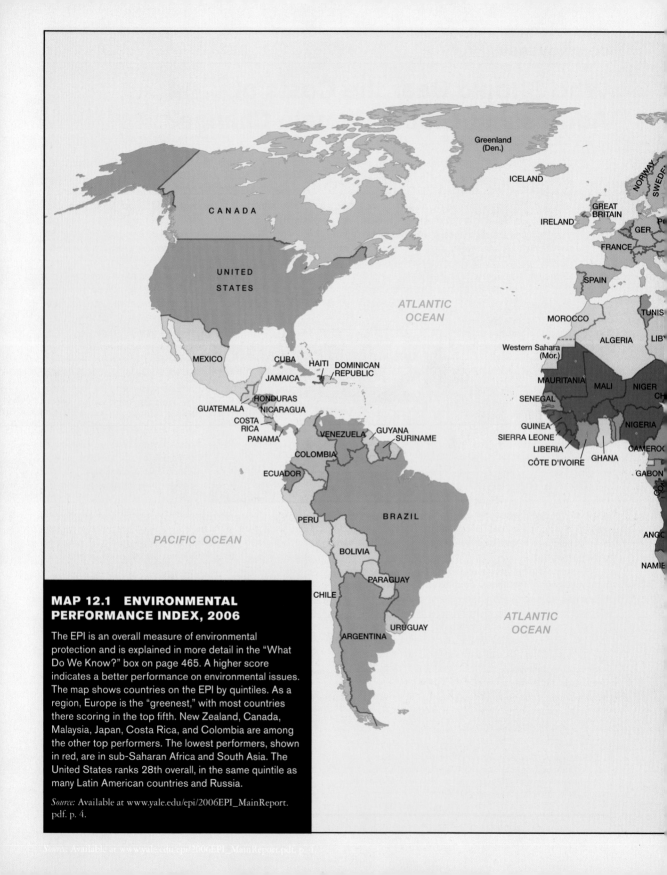

MAP 12.1 ENVIRONMENTAL PERFORMANCE INDEX, 2006

The EPI is an overall measure of environmental protection and is explained in more detail in the "What Do We Know?" box on page 465. A higher score indicates a better performance on environmental issues. The map shows countries on the EPI by quintiles. As a region, Europe is the "greenest," with most countries there scoring in the top fifth. New Zealand, Canada, Malaysia, Japan, Costa Rica, and Colombia are among the other top performers. The lowest performers, shown in red, are in sub-Saharan Africa and South Asia. The United States ranks 28th overall, in the same quintile as many Latin American countries and Russia.

Source: Available at www.yale.edu/epi/2006EPI_MainReport. pdf. p. 4.

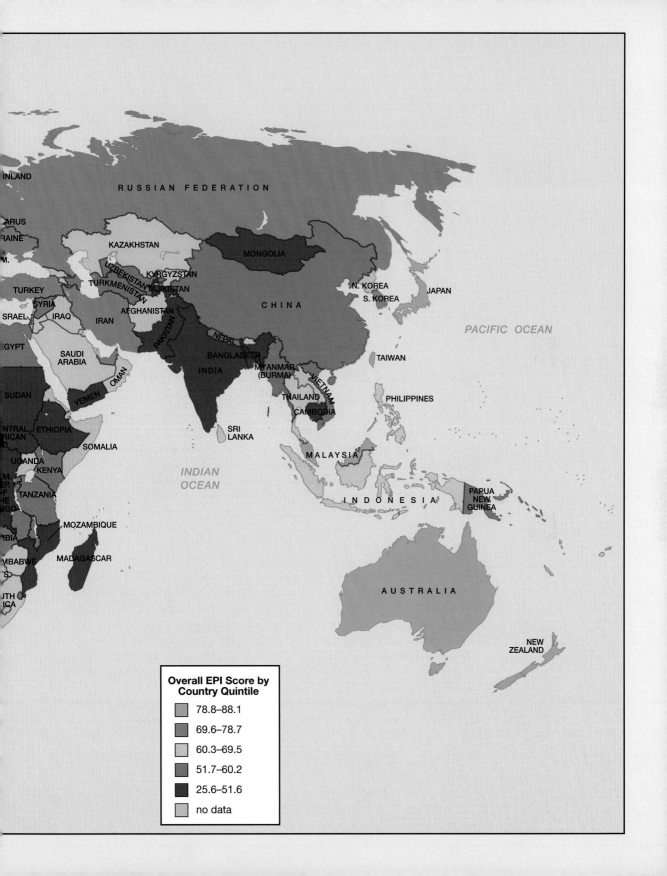

INLAND

RUSSIAN FEDERATION

ARUS

RAINE

M.

KAZAKHSTAN

MONGOLIA

TURKEY

UZBEKISTAN

KYRGYZSTAN

SYRIA

TURKMENISTAN

TAJIKISTAN

N. KOREA

JAPAN

ISRAEL

IRAQ

AFGHANISTAN

CHINA

S. KOREA

IRAN

EGYPT

PAKISTAN

NEPAL

SAUDI
ARABIA

OMAN

INDIA

BANGLADESH

MYANMAR
(BURMA)

VIETNAM

TAIWAN

PACIFIC OCEAN

SUDAN

YEMEN

THAILAND

CAMBODIA

PHILIPPINES

NTRAL
RICAN

ETHIOPIA

SRI
LANKA

SOMALIA

INDIAN
OCEAN

MALAYSIA

UGANDA

KENYA

M.
EP.
HE
NGO

TANZANIA

INDONESIA

PAPUA
NEW
GUINEA

BIA

MOZAMBIQUE

MBABWE
S

MADAGASCAR

JTH
ICA

AUSTRALIA

NEW
ZEALAND

**Overall EPI Score by
Country Quintile**

78.8–88.1

69.6–78.7

60.3–69.5

51.7–60.2

25.6–51.6

no data

Even recognizing that they have a disproportionate responsibility for cleaning up the environment, because of both their past practices and their relatively greater present wealth, some developed countries still want to link their efforts to greater contributions by developing countries. The main reason given by former American president George W. Bush for not ratifying the Kyoto Protocol is that it places an unreasonable burden on the United States while exempting developing countries, especially China, from reducing their emissions. There are, of course, specific interests within the United States that oppose the environmental accord because it would restrict their production or raise the price of their goods. They offer vigorous political support for calls for international equity, perhaps as a way to kill restrictions that they oppose for other reasons. By withholding its consent to the treaty, however, and by refusing to adhere to targets for limiting greenhouse gases, the United States claims to be seeking to extract greater commitments to the environment from developing countries. This negotiating position came under review following the election of President Barack Obama and the arrival of a new administration. Nonetheless, the hard bargaining between developed and developing countries over the costs of preserving the environment is currently blocking greater international cooperation.

BARGAINING OVER THE FUTURE ENVIRONMENT

Alternative policy solutions create gains and losses for different groups. Industries prefer that consumers or taxpayers pay to clean up their environmental waste, and developing countries prefer that developed countries restrict their pollutants more severely so that they (the developing countries) can industrialize at lower cost. Even though everyone may gain from cooperation, each actor prefers a different policy outcome. As shown in Figure 2.1 in Chapter 2, cooperation creates net gains through a movement toward the Pareto frontier, but actors will still bargain over where on the frontier a policy will settle. Cooperation and bargaining occur simultaneously. The political fight is not about the need for protecting the environment, but about who bears the costs of a cleaner environment.

Often, the political battle results in compromise. In the European ETS discussed previously, economists argued that the most efficient system would be to auction emissions credits equal to total output, thereby allocating the credits to those firms that needed them the most and generating income for the governments involved. Instead, at the insistence of firms, the credits were simply given free to existing companies based on current emissions levels. This move allowed the firms to pass higher costs along to consumers while at the same time selling their credits in the ETS. Great Britain's power-generation sector pocketed a net profit on emissions trading alone of $1.5 billion in 2005, the first year of operation. Other industries, initially excluded from the ETS but desiring the higher profits, are now clamoring for a similar trading system—and even firms in the United States are warming to the idea of a "cap and trade" system based on the same principles.[19] In this case, although firms are now capped in their emissions and must buy credits to offset any excess,

---

19. "The Heat Is On," 17–20.

Patterns of Environmental Performance

Environmental protections vary widely across countries, regions, and income levels. In 2006, the Center for Environmental Law and Policy at Yale University and the Center for International Earth Science Information Network at Columbia University issued the first composite environmental performance index (EPI) for 133 countries. It provides a common way to measure countries' performance on a range of important environmental issues (see Map 12.1).[a] The index was created from 16 indicators of environmental health, air quality, water resources, biodiversity and habitat, productive natural resources, and sustainable energy.

Environmental performance is closely associated with income. Richer countries nearly always perform better, and poorer countries perform worse. Countries with per capita incomes above $10,000 (in 2006 dollars) all have EPI scores above 65, whereas countries with per capita incomes of less than $1,000 all have scores below 60. Even within similar income categories, however, countries differ widely in their environmental performance. The figure at right depicts the relationship between gross domestic product (GDP) per capita (log scale) and the EPI.

In this figure, income is presented on a logarithmic scale of base 10, often used to display data that cover a large range of values. Unlike a linear scale, which increases in value through addition, a logarithmic scale increases in value through multiplication (by 10s). Note that 10,000 is ten times larger than 1,000, and 100,000 is ten times larger than 10,000. Countries above the solid blue line in the figure perform better than others at similar levels of income; countries below the line perform worse than their peers. Among high-income countries, New Zealand and the United Kingdom are high performers. In contrast, the United States, Norway, and Belgium are comparatively low performers. For middle-income countries, Colombia, Ecuador, and

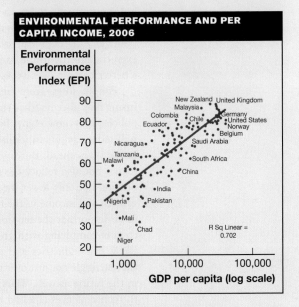

ENVIRONMENTAL PERFORMANCE AND PER CAPITA INCOME, 2006

Source: Pilot 2006 Environmental Performance Index, www.yale.edu/epi/2006EPI_MainReport.pdf, p. 26 (accessed 1/16/09).

Nicaragua stand out as unusually good stewards of the environment; but South Africa, China, and India are noteworthy low performers. The variation is greatest among the poorest countries. Malawi and Tanzania are high performers relative to others in this category; Niger and Chad are the lowest performers, both compared to poor countries and overall. ∎

Source: Daniel C. Esty, Marc A. Levy, Tanja Srebotnjak, Alexander de Sherbinin, Christine H. Kim, and Bridget Anderson, *Pilot 2006 Environmental Performance Index* (New Haven: Yale Center for Environmental Law & Policy, 2006), www.yale.edu/epi/2006EPI_MainReport.pdf (accessed 12/17/08).

a. The main report, as well as detailed data on each of the 16 indicators, is available at http://epi.yale.edu/Home (accessed 12/17/08).

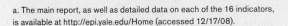

the net effect is to pay producers a hefty subsidy to reduce emissions in developing countries. Environmentalists got what they wanted—lower global emissions—but at a substantial cost to consumers in European countries.

Sometimes, however, the fight is sufficiently intense that it has blocked movements toward greater cooperation. Paradoxically, the more we care about the future and, in turn, about the future environment, the more that is at stake and the more intense this political fight will be. For the winners from environmental protection, a higher value on the future environment mobilizes supporters into the political arena to change policy. Because they care more about the future, they are willing to exert greater effort today in promoting policies to protect that environment. The longer into the future the winners look, in turn, the more likely they are to forgo agreement today in hopes of getting a better agreement that guarantees their preferred policies for a longer period. Each day that passes without significant political progress means that more CO_2 is accumulating in the atmosphere. But even though the immediate environment might suffer from a lack of cooperation, a better bargain over a longer period might make such a delay worthwhile.

For the losers from tighter environmental regulations, a higher value on the future may also mobilize them into the political arena to try to protect the favorable policies they now enjoy. Policies that greatly reduce CO_2 emissions, for instance, will reduce profits in industries that depend on fossil fuels not only today but also in the years ahead. Burning less fossil fuel will not only reduce profits for oil companies but also reduce the value of the oil reserves they own. Higher costs of production not only lower incomes in developing countries in the present but reduce growth and income in the future. The greater the value we place on the future, the more important the environment is to the winners—but the more important the costs of complying with greater regulations are to the losers as well.

When industries and environmentalists or rich and poor countries bargain, they struggle not just over the division of gains today but over the division of gains in the future as well. Thus, the greater the value we place on the future, the more the consequences of a bad bargain for either side are magnified. The result can be a political stalemate. Such a deadlock may be arising over global climate change. The future of the global environment is at stake, but so is the future of those industries and countries that are depend on fossil fuels. The stakes are high not just because of the present but also because any agreement is likely to affect both the environment and the affected industries and countries far into the future. Neither side is yet willing to compromise.

Coupled with the problem of bargaining over the future is the equally difficult problem of representing future generations in current decision-making. After all, no political system possesses a mechanism that represents the interests of future citizens to the present generation. Given the notoriously short attention spans of politicians, who are often driven only by the next election, who in any political system represents the interests of future citizens and voters? We know little about the interests of future generations. Although we can extrapolate from our current preferences, many factors can intervene. We do not know what the future rate of technological change will be, which may make various environmental problems easier or harder to solve than we expect. Assuming that wealth and incomes continue to rise, we do not know how future citizens may evaluate yet more consumption of physical goods, like cars, relative to consumption of intangible goods, like the scenic beauty of an unspoiled coastline or old-growth forest.

Even if we could estimate future interests, there is no one at present to advocate for those future generations in any systematic way. In bargaining between actors at a single moment in time, the winners and losers can choose to be actively involved, or not, in the political process. In bargaining between domestic groups, the winners and losers of alternative policies can fight for themselves, if they so choose.

But there is no realistic way of representing future generations in present political decisions. Environmental TANs often claim that they are representing future generations, but their political clout is still limited. Future generations neither vote now nor pay membership dues to TANs that can, in turn, press governments to change policy. TANs can make normative arguments on behalf of future generations, but this is at best an indirect and significantly weaker form of representation than if the future citizens' votes and voices could be heard today. As a consequence, we are bargaining with ourselves on behalf of future generations—and it is perhaps not surprising that we usually let ourselves win.

How Can Institutions Promote International Environmental Cooperation?

Within countries, governments play an important role in mitigating externalities. Producing public goods and regulating the use of common pool resources are fundamental roles for any government. States can command citizens to contribute to public goods and limit their exploitation of common pool resources, or they can impose legal penalties. Historically, and even in some developing countries today, governments demand that their citizens contribute a number of days of labor per year to build and repair roads, irrigation systems, and other public works. In all but the so-called failed states, governments tax citizens and use the revenue to provide a variety of public goods, including national defense, police and fire protection, public infrastructure, public health, education, and, of course, environmental protection. Governments also impose restrictions on automobile emissions, the dumping of toxic waste, oil drilling, and so on that aim to improve environmental quality and use scarce resources more efficiently. Government is not a perfect solution (as continuing environmental problems within countries demonstrate only too clearly), but its ability to allocate resources authoritatively helps mitigate collective action problems that would otherwise make environmental cooperation even more difficult.

National laws and policies are the primary means for implementing international environmental cooperation. Even if states create international institutions, most of their provisions are enforced authoritatively through national legislation and policy. For instance, the LRTAP Convention and its eight subsequent protocols, all designed to reduce acid rain, required participating states to reduce sulfur emissions by at least 30 percent, based on 1980 levels, and to reduce nitrogen oxide emissions to their 1987 levels. The treaty did not mandate how states would achieve these cuts. Instead, individual states implemented these targets through changes in national laws and regulations. Transnational environmental problems and solutions still require strong, effective national governments to transform aspirations into practice.

In international relations, in turn, there is no higher authority that can compel states to cooperate in mitigating externalities. On global environmental issues, states are limited to voluntary cooperation implemented by laws passed at the national level. Relative to externalities regulated by authoritative governments,

The effectiveness of environmental regulations may depend on how easy it is to verify compliance. A change in the rules related to dumping oil at sea made it much easier to check whether ship captains were adhering to the standard and increased compliance rates to over 98 percent.

Vienna Convention:
A framework convention adopted in 1985 to regulate activities, especially emissions of CFCs, that damage the ozone layer.

Montreal Protocol:
An international treaty, signed in 1989, that is designed to protect the ozone layer by phasing out the production of a number of CFCs and other chemical compounds.

international cooperation between sovereign states will always be more difficult and tenuous. States free ride on each other's efforts and overexploit their shared resources. Nonetheless, as we saw in Chapter 2, international institutions facilitate cooperation among states on the environment by setting standards and verifying compliance, with lesser roles for reducing decision-making costs and resolving disputes.

SETTING STANDARDS AND VERIFYING COMPLIANCE

International environmental institutions support cooperation by establishing clear standards of behavior to which states can be held accountable. Although each issue area and agreement has unique features and histories, countries often negotiate framework conventions that establish general principles to which all states can agree. The Convention on Biological Diversity, for instance, states that diversity is "a common concern of humankind" that all countries have a duty to protect; the document includes additional principles for the development and use of genetic resources. After establishing such frameworks, states proceed in some issue areas to negotiate more stringent environmental safeguards specifying limits on emissions, banning certain practices, or otherwise defining unacceptable behavior. The series of protocols and amendments subsequently attached to the **Vienna Convention** for the Protection of the Ozone Layer (enacted in 1985) illustrate this common trajectory. Beginning with a general framework, additional agreements—including the **Montreal Protocol** (in force in 1989)—specified progressively deeper cuts in emissions and increased the range of restricted chemicals and practices (see again Table 12.1).[20]

Restrictions on the intentional discharge of crude oil at sea demonstrate how the clarity and transparency of the standard matter in supporting cooperation.[21] After a tanker delivers its cargo of crude oil, an average of 300 tons remains onboard, stuck to the cargo tank walls. Before regulations were put into effect, ships would clean their tanks on the return voyage by pumping seawater into the tanks and discharging the slop back into the ocean. With many ships making multiple trips each year, oil tankers were intentionally discharging approximately 1 million tons of oil into the ocean annually. In the International Convention for the Prevention of Pollution of the Seas by Oil, adopted in 1954, countries first set standards that permitted tankers to continue cleaning tanks with seawater but mandated that discharges be no more than 100 parts oil per million parts seawater. The standard was subsequently tightened in 1969. Nonetheless, both the looser and the

20. A second pattern of negotiations and agreements is simply to establish a procedural regime with a commission that makes annual decisions about regulatory rules. The IWC is an example of this type of organization. On patterns of agreement formation, see Oran R. Young, *International Governance: Protecting the Environment in a Stateless Society* (Ithaca, NY: Cornell University Press, 1994), especially chap. 4.
21. This case is drawn from Ronald B. Mitchell, "Regime Design Matters: Intentional Oil Pollution and Treaty Compliance," *International Organization* 48, no. 3 (Summer 1994): 425–58.

tighter standards were widely ignored. Oil company surveys from the 1970s show that tankers owned by the oil companies themselves averaged discharges of three times the legal limit and that independently owned tankers averaged discharges of 30 times the legal limit.

In 1978, countries adopted new standards that required all tankers to use new but more expensive technologies that minimized discharges by preventing the oil and seawater from coming into contact or by using crude oil itself to wash the tanks. These new technologies were required for all tankers built after 1982, and all existing tankers had to be retrofitted by 1985. Despite the greater cost, compliance rates rose over to over 98 percent by 1991.

What explains the difference? Since cleaning the tanks with seawater usually took place on the open ocean, far from other observers, ship captains could act with impunity and ignore mandated discharge limits—and it appears that they usually did. The new technologies, in contrast, required the installation of clearly observable equipment on every ship. On entering port, it could be easily verified whether the tanker met with the new standard. The ease of verification forced tanker captains to alter their behavior, virtually ending the intentional discharge of crude oil into the ocean.

For similar reasons, complete bans are easier to verify than restrictions on emissions; this fact helps to account for the success of the Vienna Convention and subsequent amendments outlawing CFCs. With CFCs, as with the ban on whaling or endangered wildlife, any possession or trade in prohibited substances is sufficient evidence of noncompliance. Enforcement efforts can then focus on tracking down any sales of CFCs (or elephant ivory, rhinoceros horns, and other banned goods). Soon after the major cuts in CFCs went into effect, for instance, the black market grew to about 20 percent of prior consumption. In 1995, the illegal trade in CFCs in the Port of Miami and along the U.S.-Mexican border was second in value only to trade in illegal drugs, prompting a unilateral effort by the United States to block the smuggling. The important point is that the clear rules banning CFCs allowed this crackdown to occur. Restrictions on emissions, in turn, are harder to enforce, especially when many independent agents, such as firms, are potentially contributing to the problem. Evidence of some CO_2 in the atmosphere is not evidence of cheating. Only consistent monitoring of emissions over long periods can demonstrate that a country is failing to live up to its commitments on global warming—a much more daunting task.

In addition to official monitoring and reporting, environmental TANs have been central in verifying compliance with international environmental accords. Most environmental agreements depend on self-reporting of emissions. As we noted in Chapter 2, self-reporting is effective only when reports are subject to external verification. TANs often play the role of fire alarm, sounding the alert when governments violate agreements or fail to report accurately. By calling attention to failures to live up to the letter and, sometimes, the spirit of the agreements, TANs assist member states in identifying and bringing pressure on noncomplying governments. The by now dense network of committed environmental activists relieves governments from much of the responsibility for monitoring one another's performance, thereby facilitating and enhancing the prospects for successful cooperation.

As one example of TAN monitoring, as we saw earlier in the chapter, the International Whaling Commission instituted a complete ban on whaling in 1982. After phasing out its commercial operations, Japan continued to engage in scientific whaling, which aims to demonstrate that whale populations are robust enough to permit some commercial whaling. Much of the whale meat nonetheless ends up for sale in Japanese fish markets. Japan currently catches approximately 800 whales per year for self-declared scientific purposes, about the same as Norway's commercial catch (the only country to defy the ban completely) and all aboriginal whaling catches combined (which are exempt from the ban). Iceland also recently began a scientific whaling program. Although it is impossible to police the entire ocean, the limited scope of scientific whaling allows NGOs to track the whaling fleets and observe their operations, often filming the killing and cataloging each whale caught. Each season, ships from Greenpeace, an international environmental action group, shadow the Japanese and Icelandic fleets, sometimes attempting to disrupt their operations by harassing the factory ships and placing themselves between the hunters and their prey. Countries report their scientific whaling activities to the IWC every year. But as a result of these efforts by the NGOs, relatively accurate independent verification of these self-reports is possible.

FACILITATING DECISION-MAKING

Even though international environmental institutions do not, for the most part, have highly developed governing bodies or rules, they do facilitate decision-making between states. As the Vienna Convention has been modified and its provisions strengthened, it has developed a clear administrative structure. There are now rules for adjustments in controlled substances that do not require further national ratifications, and a supermajority requirement for adding new substances. The **Framework Convention on Climate Change (FCCC)** is perhaps more typical of other environmental agreements. Although it includes a Conference of the Parties (COP) for elaborating rules, it is primarily a forum for ongoing negotiations rather than a body with established procedures for reaching decisions.[22] Agreements frequently proceed by consensus decision-making and often contain clauses allowing countries to opt-in or opt-out of specific obligations. Yet, even framework agreements that are limited to unanimity can be important in setting a direction for future negotiations and creating a forum for continuing diplomacy. As suggested by the history of agreements on ozone-depleting substances summarized in Table 12.1, initial frameworks outlining the goals of environmental cooperation often generate substantive agreements and protocols. The initial agreement, in other words, provides a forum that channels progress within the issue area.

Framework Convention on Climate Change (FCCC): An international agreement enacted in 1992, and entered into force in 1994, that provided an overall framework for intergovernmental efforts on climate change.

---

22. Indeed, the COP's rules remain a source of contention, with disagreement over whether the conference can proceed with a two-thirds supermajority vote or whether all decisions must be unanimous. See Daniel Bodansky, "International Law and the Design of a Climate Change Regime," in *International Relations and Global Climate Change,* ed. Urs Luterbacher and Detlef F. Sprinz (Cambridge, MA: MIT Press, 2001), 212–13.

Environmental TANs also provide important policy input for international agreements, creating a nearly unique international public-private partnership on the environment that facilitates cooperation. At the United Nations Conference on Environment and Development in 1992—the so-called Earth Summit—that produced both the Convention on Biological Diversity and the FCCC, over 10,000 NGOs were accredited to participate. In a parallel conference, these organizations helped set the agenda, provided policy input, and brought pressure to bear on the negotiations. This role is now institutionalized in the FCCC, which allows any qualified organization to be admitted to meetings and negotiations unless at least one-third of the member states present object.[23] Many observers credit the success of the summit to the important role played by the TANs.

RESOLVING DISPUTES

International environmental agreements generally lack dispute resolution mechanisms. Few such agreements contain autonomous or independent procedures for resolving disputes; rather, most treaties depend on the good faith of countries themselves to work out disagreements within a multilateral setting. The Montreal Protocol to the Vienna Convention, however, was the first global environmental agreement to develop and use a noncompliance response system, located in its Implementation Committee. This mechanism remains focused on facilitating, not enforcing, compliance. During the 1990s, it became clear that several countries from the former Soviet Union (including Belarus, Russia, and Ukraine), as well as some developing countries, were not in full compliance with their emissions obligations. This led the Implementation Committee to urge and finally approve new phaseout plans, with additional financial resources from other industrialized countries, the Global Environmental Facility, and the World Bank facilitating compliance. In the Kyoto Protocol, which is often described as a model for dispute resolution for future environmental compacts, a Compliance Committee comprises a facilitative branch and an enforcement branch.[24] As its name suggests, the facilitative branch provides advice to the member states on how to implement the Protocol. The enforcement branch can find a state to be in violation of the agreement, but its sole sanction is to request the member state to make up the difference between its targeted and actual emissions, plus an additional 30 percent, in a future period or to suspend its participation in the carbon trading plan. Most environmental agreements simply refer the disputing parties to mediation or the International Court of Justice, options to which the states are entitled under international law anyway. Some environmental provisions are attached to Regional Trade Agreements and can be adjudicated under the specialized dispute settlement procedures they contain. This is an area for future progress in international environmental institutions.

---

23. Kal Raustiala, "Nonstate Actors in the Global Climate Regime," in *International Relations and Global Climate Change*, 96, 99.
24. See http://unfccc.int/kyoto_protocol/compliance/introduction/i tems/3024.php (accessed 12/17/08).

Conclusion: Can Global Environmental Cooperation Succeed?

We began this chapter asking why international environmental cooperation is so hard to achieve. To answer that puzzle and tie the threads of our analysis together, we can compare the relative success of international environmental cooperation on ozone depletion and the relative failure of states to make significant progress on global climate change. Both ozone depletion and global climate change became issues at around the same time. The first convention on ozone depletion was negotiated in 1985, the first on global climate change in 1992. What accounts for the difference in the two outcomes? How can the analytic tools of interests, interactions, and institutions help us understand why we find successful international cooperation in the first case, and only limited (at best) cooperation in the second?

At its root, the answer to our puzzle is quite simple. People's daily actions create significant externalities for the environment and one another. These externalities, in turn, produce severe problems of collective action. Every individual and every country would like to benefit from a cleaner environment but would also like others to bear the costs of protecting environmental quality. Both the stratospheric ozone layer and the quantity of greenhouse gases in the atmosphere are global public goods. Although everyone benefits from a thicker ozone layer and natural greenhouse gases, and everyone is harmed by CFC and CO_2 emissions, this may be precisely the problem. Since we all share the benefits of a healthy atmosphere and we all face private costs in changing our behavior, we all attempt to free ride on one another, hoping to reap the benefits of a greener environment without having to give up our current lifestyles.

In the case of ozone depletion, the gains from a ban far exceeded the costs of change. Although the cost of transitioning to new chemical alternatives was estimated to be $5.5 billion by 2010 and $27 billion by 2075, the Environmental Protection Agency calculated that the reduced skin cancers for Americans alone would save $6.5 trillion in medical costs over the same period.[25] In the case of climate change, however, there are large immediate and continuing costs for reducing CO_2 emissions, and only long-term benefits, the magnitude of which depend on the exact rise in global temperatures—which no one can predict precisely. Reflecting again the central role of fossil fuels in the modern economy, reducing CO_2 emissions by 50 percent—the level necessary to stabilize concentrations at current levels—will cost between 2 and 8 percent of world product (the sum of economic activity or GDP in all countries) in perpetuity. Failing to curb greenhouse gases, in contrast, will cost the United States, by one estimate, only about 0.25 percent of its annual GDP in the future. Other countries will bear higher costs, particularly those nearer the equator or with low-lying territories. Yet, in most economic estimates, the total costs of a warmer climate are typically less than 2 percent of global product. Pointing this out is not to advocate doing nothing. There may be advantages to a less polluted environment that are not captured in models of future economic income. These estimates, in turn, do not consider the

---

25. Litfin, *Ozone Discourses*, 128.

worst-case scenarios posited by some scientists. But given the balance between large immediate and continuing costs and only long-term benefits, it is not surprising that few politicians want to push hard for reducing the emission of greenhouse gases.

Although both issues involve collective action problems, cooperation in ozone depletion was easier to achieve due to the highly concentrated nature of the CFC industry—both in a relatively small number of firms and within a relatively small number of countries, with most production and usage occurring in just a handful of developed states. The smaller number of firms and countries involved lowered the costs of collective action and made effective cooperation possible. The United States enjoyed a preeminent position in the industry as both the largest producer and consumer of CFCs. Its leadership on the issue was decisive.

Environmental activists outside the 2007 UN Climate Conference in Bali, Indonesia, called for stricter limits on greenhouse gas emissions.

Second, the problem of collective action is compounded by the distributional consequences of alternative policy solutions, especially in the case of global climate change. Every policy creates winners and losers, but the benefits of eliminating CFCs were clear. In the case of climate change, in contrast, hydrocarbon fuels are the life blood of modern economies, and the interests who would lose from any significant change in policy are large and politically powerful. To date, these vested interests have played upon the basic incentive of all actors to free ride to block any policy change—and postpone the day of final reckoning.

Finally, international institutions have played a role in facilitating and codifying cooperation in both ozone depletion and global climate change. Negotiations have occurred within meetings of global leaders, and the agreements reached at these meetings have been institutionalized into conventions and subsequently amended in various protocols. Both began with conventions outlining broad principles of cooperation and then moved on to substantive cuts in subsequent protocols. Greater cooperation on ozone depletion has been helped by relatively clear rules reducing and, later, banning specific chemicals. The rules governing reductions in CO_2 and other greenhouse gases, in contrast, are less well articulated, perhaps because the underlying issues remain highly contested.

Success and failure are, of course, relative terms. The damage to the ozone layer from past emissions of CFCs will continue for another century. We may be witnessing the first signs of global warming in more severe storms and other more subtle changes in ecology, but its effects are certain to grow in the future. Many factors contributed to the relative success of the Vienna Convention and its subsequent amendments that helped to bring about the restrictions on CFC production. The case stands out for its clear lesson that countries can cooperate quickly and effectively when the prospective harm to the environment is sufficiently large, the costs of alternative practices are sufficiently small, and it is possible to design clear and verifiable standards. Although we continue to live with the consequences of our past emissions, the ability of countries to rally together to halt harmful practices and begin to reverse the damage to the ozone layer gives reason for cautious optimism for the future of our shared planet.

Reviewing Interests, Interactions, and Institutions

INTERESTS	INTERACTIONS	INSTITUTIONS
Individuals and countries possess common interests in protecting the environment.	Externalities create collective action problems. Public goods suffer from free riding. Common pool resources are overexploited.	International environmental institutions facilitate cooperation by setting clear standards and creating mechanisms to verify compliance.
TANs are critical in promoting international environmental awareness and advocating specific policies, thereby altering interests.	Groups and countries bargain over who will bear the costs of adjustment.	International environmental institutions create forums for decision-making but typically lack dispute resolution provisions.
Alternative policies to protect the environment impose costs on different groups within countries, and on rich versus poor countries.	The more we value the future, the greater the stakes for both winners and losers and the more difficult it is to reach agreement.	TANs play an important role as monitors of environmental agreements and practices.

Key Terms

externalities, p. 449
nonexcludable, p. 449
chlorofluorocarbons (CFCs), p. 449
ozone layer, p. 449
global climate change, p. 449
nonrival in consumption, p. 449
Kyoto Protocol, p. 450

common pool resources, p. 451
overexploitation, p. 451
Vienna Convention, p. 468
Montreal Protocol, p. 468
Framework Convention on Climate
    Change (FCCC), p. 470

For Further Reading

Gibson, Clark. *Politicians and Poachers: The Political Economy of Wildlife in Africa.* New York: Cambridge University Press, 1999. Examines the local politics of wildlife conservation in Africa.

Gibson, Clark, Margaret A. McKean, and Elinor Ostrom, eds. *People and Forests: Communities, Institutions, and Governance.* Cambridge, MA: MIT Press, 2000. Presents an in-depth analysis of local communities and forest preservation.

Gore, Albert. *Earth in the Balance: Ecology and the Human Spirit.* Boston: Houghton Mifflin, 2000. Offers a manifesto on preserving the environment.

Gore, Albert. *An Inconvenient Truth: The Planetary Emergency of Global Warming and What We Can Do about It.* Emmaus, PA: Rodale Press, 2006. The book version of the Academy Award–winning movie by the same title.

Litfin, Karen. *Ozone Discourses: Science and Politics in Global Environmental Cooperation.* New York: Columbia University Press, 1994. Presents a detailed study of the politics behind the Vienna Convention.

Luterbacher, Urs, and Detlef F. Sprinz, eds. *International Relations and Global Climate Change.* Cambridge, MA: MIT Press, 2001. Offers a theoretical survey of several different international environmental regimes and institutions.

Mitchell, Ronald B. *Intentional Oil Pollution at Sea: Environmental Policy and Treaty Compliance.* Cambridge, MA: MIT Press, 1994. Presents a detailed study of international institutional design and effectiveness.

Peterson, M. J. "Whalers, Cetologists, Environmentalists, and the International Management of Whaling." *International Organization* 46, no. 1 (Winter 1992): 147–86. Examines the origins of the "save the whales" campaign and the politics behind the ban on commercial whaling, with a focus on scientific expertise.

Raustiala, Kal. "States, NGOs, and International Environmental Institutions." *International Studies Quarterly* 41, no. 4 (December 1997): 719–40. Focuses on the role of global civil society in the negotiation and monitoring of international environmental agreements.

Sandler, Todd. *Global Challenges: An Approach to Environmental, Political, and Economic Problems.* New York: Cambridge University Press, 1997. Reviews many global environmental problems, with an emphasis on problems of collective action.

Sprinz, Detlef, and Tapani Vaahtoranta. "The Interest-Based Explanation of International Environmental Policy." *International Organization* 48, no. 1 (Winter 1994): 77–105. Focuses on domestic winners and losers from alternative international environmental institutions.

Victor, David. *Climate Change: Debating America's Policy Options.* New York: Council on Foreign Relations, 2004. Gives a timely review of the politics of global climate change from the perspective of U.S. foreign policy.

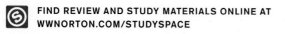

FIND REVIEW AND STUDY MATERIALS ONLINE AT WWNORTON.COM/STUDYSPACE

The Science of Ozone Depletion and Global Climate Change

Ozone depletion and climate change are global environmental problems because of complex chemical and physical processes that largely occur in the upper atmosphere. The effects of CFC or CO_2 emissions are not confined to the countries or even regions of origin. In fact, they spread rapidly if somewhat unevenly through the upper atmosphere and, thus, over the entire earth. This appendix briefly explains these chemical and physical processes as background to the political choices that are the subject of the chapter.

OZONE DEPLETION

Ozone is a highly toxic and naturally occurring form of oxygen. Unlike the familiar oxygen compound we breathe, which contains two atoms of oxygen, each molecule of ozone has three oxygen atoms. Scattered throughout the stratosphere, it soaks up dangerous ultraviolet (UV) radiation from the sun. Without the shield, UV radiation would kill virtually all life on the planet. The small amount of UV radiation that does get through to ground level is a primary cause of eye disease (cataracts) and also causes about 12,000 fatal skin cancers every year. It also harms phytoplankton, a microscopic plant that drifts on the surface of the ocean, is the base of the food chain, and collectively absorbs about half of the world's carbon dioxide emissions.

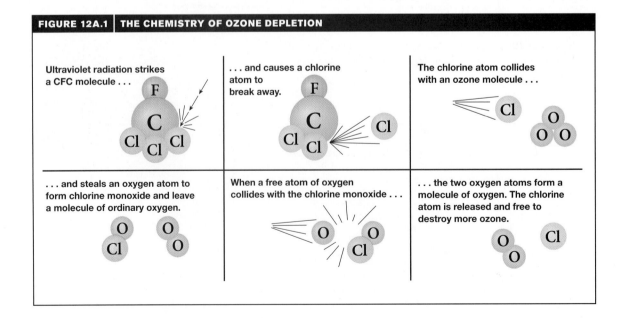

FIGURE 12A.1 | THE CHEMISTRY OF OZONE DEPLETION

Ultraviolet radiation strikes a CFC molecule . . .

. . . and causes a chlorine atom to break away.

The chlorine atom collides with an ozone molecule . . .

. . . and steals an oxygen atom to form chlorine monoxide and leave a molecule of ordinary oxygen.

When a free atom of oxygen collides with the chlorine monoxide . . .

. . . the two oxygen atoms form a molecule of oxygen. The chlorine atom is released and free to destroy more ozone.

As early as 1974, scientists began to suspect that chlorofluorocarbons (CFCs) could migrate to the stratosphere and break down under sunlight. This process was later confirmed. Halocarbons (known as halons) and bromide-based substances (like methyl bromide) were later recognized to have similar effects. Developed in 1930s, CFCs were used widely as propellants in aerosols, insulating materials, coolants in refrigerators and air conditioners, and artificial plastic foams for packing materials. CFCs take up to eight years to migrate to the stratosphere.

Once in the atmosphere, CFCs break down into chlorine (see Figure 12A.1), which forms stable reservoirs (pockets of condensed gas) over the poles during the long, cold winters; in spring, as the atmosphere warms, the now free chlorine begins to disperse more widely. When a chlorine atom collides with an ozone molecule, it steals an oxygen atom to form chlorine monoxide and leaves a molecule of ordinary oxygen (with two atoms of oxygen). These chemicals are not harmful in themselves, but ozone is destroyed in the process. When a free (single) atom of oxygen subsequently collides with the chlorine monoxide, the two oxygen atoms form a molecule of ordinary oxygen, releasing the chlorine atom once again. This single chlorine atom is then free to collide with and destroy more ozone. Through this iterative process, each CFC molecule can destroy up to 100,000 molecules of ozone.[a1]

In 1984, scientists first confirmed that an ozone hole was opening over the Antarctic. This is now an annual occurrence. The notion of "hole" is something of a misnomer. Rather, as the spreading chlorine moves through the atmosphere each spring, it reduces the amount of ozone in the atmosphere by about 60 percent in an area roughly the size of North America. This hole then drifts northward during the summer, reaching its maximum extent usually in October (see Figure 12A.2). As colder weather starts to reconcentrate chlorine over the poles, the remaining ozone disperses and "fills in" the hole. The consequence, however, is a thinning of the overall ozone layer. In 1990, scientists discovered a similar hole over the North Pole, but it is not as large because of warmer temperatures in the Artic.

Since the 1960s, when CFCs were first used widely, the ozone layer has thinned by about 5 percent. Every 1 percent loss of ozone lets in about 2 percent more UV radiation,

FIGURE 12A.2 OZONE HOLE ON SEPTEMBER 24, 2006
This image depicts the largest ozone hole ever observed: 11.4 million square miles. This severe hole resulted from high levels of ozone-depleting substances combined with record cold conditions in the Antarctic stratosphere. Satellite instruments measure the amount of ozone in the stratosphere, and the data is used to illustrate the size of the hole. The purple and blue areas are where there is the least amount of ozone; the green and yellow areas are where there is more ozone

Source: www.nasa.gov/images/content/160657main_OZONE_large. jpg (accessed 7/2/07).

a1. A good website for the basics of ozone depletion is www.nasa.gov/vision/earth/environment/ozone_ hole101.html. The animation is particularly good.

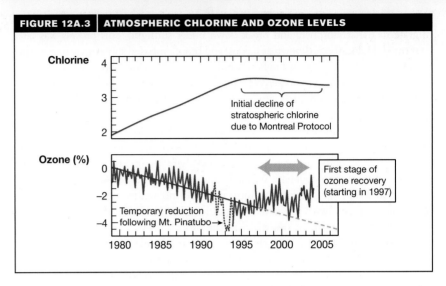

FIGURE 12A.3 | ATMOSPHERIC CHLORINE AND OZONE LEVELS

Note: NASA/NOAA satellite data show the rise in the stratospheric chlorine (top panel) and correspond-ing decline in ozone layer thickness. In 1997, after the passage of the Montreal Protocol, these trends began to reverse in a first stage of ozone recovery.

Source: www.nasa.gov/vision/earth/environment/ozone_recovering.html (accessed 7/2/07).

suggesting that UV exposure at ground level is now about 10 percent higher than in the 1960s. CFCs can also last up to 100 years, so even if their release were ended today their full effects would not be felt for up to a century. It is estimated that a total ban would take 50 years to return the ozone layer to 1970 levels. Atmospheric chlorine levels peaked in 1996 and have been slowly but steadily decreasing since (see Figure 12A.3), although as Figure 12A.2 suggests the ozone hole is still grow-ing to record size and the problem—although in principle being reversed—is still very serious.

GLOBAL CLIMATE CHANGE

The earth's atmosphere, composed of naturally occurring gases, acts as a blanket insulating the planet and, in turn, retaining heat. Solar radiation, emitted from the sun, passes through our atmosphere and is absorbed by the earth's surface, warm-ing it and the lower atmosphere (see Figure 12A.4). Some solar radiation is reflected back into space by the atmosphere and the earth itself. Infrared radiation, the por-tion of solar radiation that we cannot see but do feel as heat, is captured but also reflected by the earth's surface. One portion of the infrared radiation that reaches earth bounces back through the atmosphere into space. Another portion, however, is absorbed and diffused in all directions by the so-called greenhouse gases. By cap-turing infrared radiation, this greenhouse effect warms the earth's surface and the lower atmosphere and prevents the earth from freezing. The bulk of the atmosphere is naturally occurring oxygen and nitrogen, which do not trap infrared radiation. The greenhouse gases that do contribute to global warming are primarily carbon

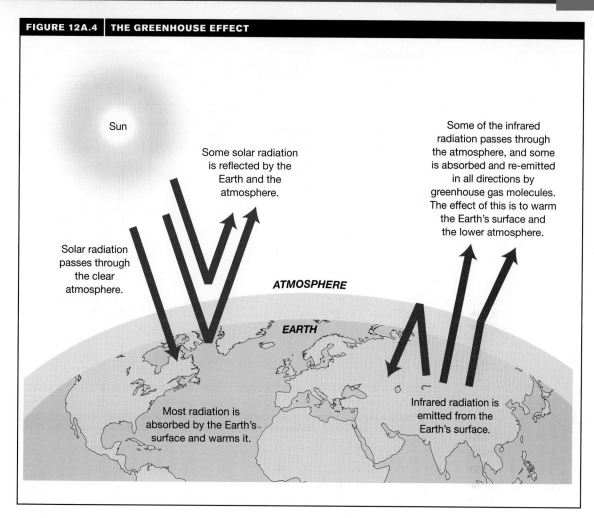

Source: www.combatclimatechange.ie/uploadedfiles/Climate_Change_Facts/greenhouse%20effect%20 from%20safeclimate%20site.jpg (accessed 1/16/09).

dioxide (CO_2) as well as water vapor, CFCs (see above), methane, nitrous oxide, and 25 others. As CO_2 and other greenhouse gases are added to the atmosphere, the greenhouse effect increases and surface temperatures of the earth rise (see Figure 12A.5).

Prior to the industrial revolution in the late eighteenth century, the earth was naturally balanced between processes that added CO_2 to the atmosphere and those that withdrew it. For 10,000 years, the amount of CO_2 changed relatively little. It is now growing exponentially (see Figure 12A.6). From a pre-industrial average of about 280 parts per million (ppm), CO_2 concentrations had risen to 379 ppm by 2005. At current rates of growth in emissions, CO_2 concentrations in the atmosphere will double over the next century to approximately 800 ppm. Anything

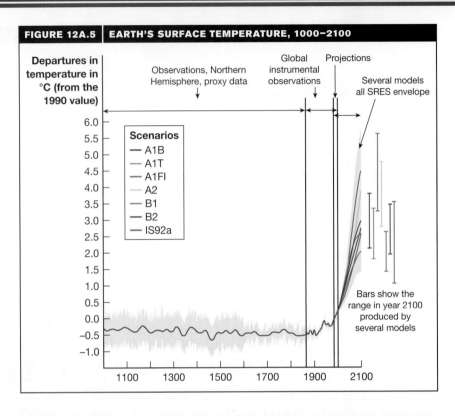

FIGURE 12A.5 | **EARTH'S SURFACE TEMPERATURE, 1000–2100**

Departures in temperature in °C (from the 1990 value)

Observations, Northern Hemisphere, proxy data

Global instrumental observations

Projections

Several models all SRES envelope

Scenarios
— A1B
— A1T
— A1FI
— A2
— B1
— B2
— IS92a

Bars show the range in year 2100 produced by several models

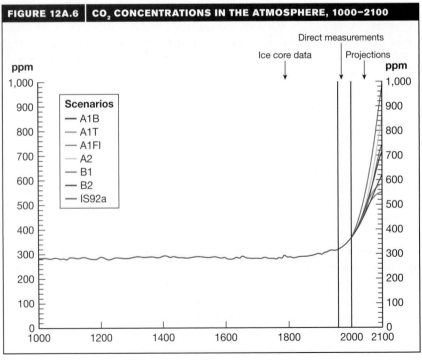

FIGURE 12A.6 | **CO₂ CONCENTRATIONS IN THE ATMOSPHERE, 1000–2100**

Direct measurements

Ice core data

Projections

ppm

ppm

Scenarios
— A1B
— A1T
— A1FI
— A2
— B1
— B2
— IS92a

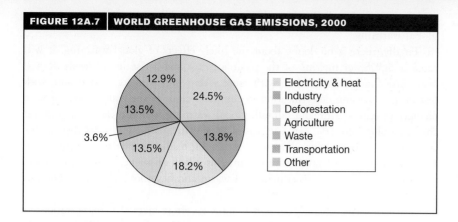

FIGURE 12A.7 | WORLD GREENHOUSE GAS EMISSIONS, 2000

12.9%
24.5%
13.5%
3.6%
13.8%
13.5%
18.2%

- Electricity & heat
- Industry
- Deforestation
- Agriculture
- Waste
- Transportation
- Other

much above 550 ppm makes scientists nervous.[a2] Since CO_2 emissions remain in the atmosphere for as long as 200 years, it will take a long time for concentrations to decline even if new restrictions are put in place.

Greenhouse gases are emitted from various sources (see Figure 12A.7). The single largest source of emissions is electricity and heat, largely from burning coal and natural gas. Transportation, which has received significant attention and prompted some drivers to switch to more fuel-efficient cars, accounts for only 13.5 percent of all emissions worldwide (but 27.4 percent in the United States). Deforestation, often through intentionally set fires to clear land for agriculture, accounts for a surprising 18.2 percent of all greenhouse gases, more than either industry or agriculture.

Global warming is sometimes described as controversial, or lacking a scientific consensus. Although there is some uncertainty, there any many more points that scientists agree on. The Intergovernmental Panel on Climate Change (IPCC), in its fourth report issued in early 2007, declared for the first time that global warming is "unequivocal" and that human activity is the main driver, "very likely" causing most of the recent rise in global temperatures.[a3]

There is no doubt in the scientific community that human activity has increased the quantity of greenhouse gases, especially CO_2, in the atmosphere. About 80 percent of this additional CO_2 comes from burning coal, oil, and natural gas, with the rest coming from a variety of other sources including tropical deforestation. About 55 percent of the additional CO_2 we release into the atmosphere is absorbed again by the oceans and increased plant growth. The rest is added to the atmosphere.

There is also no doubt that the increased greenhouse gases will alter the global climate. At a general level, as explained above, the mechanics of the atmosphere are very well understood. The greater the concentration of greenhouse gases, the more of the infrared radiation that will be retained and the larger will be the warming effect. Thus, human-made increases in greenhouse

a2. "The Heat Is On: A Survey of Climate Change," *The Economist*, September 9, 2006, p. 23.

a3. Elisabeth Rosenthal and Andrew C. Revkin, "Science Panel Says Global Warming Is 'Unequivocal,'" *New York Times*, February 3, 2007, A1.

gases will increase global temperatures—producing what is widely known as global warming.

Finally, there is no doubt about the likely effects of global warming. It will cause a significant melting of the polar ice caps and a rise in sea levels. It will also cause changes in weather, with more severe storms in some areas and, with less rain, increasing desertification in countries close to the equator. Along with changes in temperature and rainfall, global warming will also cause a significant shift in ecology, creating new patterns of agriculture and new paths of disease dissemination, with previously "tropical" diseases spreading outward from equatorial regions. Despite what is often represented as a lack of scientific consensus, there is really no doubt that the climate will warm and have noticeable effects on our daily lives.

What remains controversial is how large an effect increased concentrations of greenhouse gases will have on the climate over the long run. The IPCC currently estimates that global mean temperatures will rise between 3.6 and 8.1 degrees (Fahrenheit) by the year 2100. This is a broad range. The consequences of global warming will be determined by where in this range we actually end up. If the actual increase is toward the low end of the range, the effect will be significant but probably not catastrophic. If the increase is closer to the high end, the consequences will be quite severe. Current climate models could also prove to be way off—in either direction.

Scientists are uncertain about the magnitude of climate change for many reasons. After all, the earth's climate is an extremely complex system. There are four main sources of uncertainty. First, the earth is an evolving ecosystem that warms and cools itself over very long periods. Ice ages had come and gone of their own accord long before humans inhabited the planet. Second, although we are rapidly developing new sources of information and accumulating more data from indirect measures of temperature over longer periods, we lack a full history of the earth's temperature cycles and how they relate to past levels of greenhouse gases. To predict the future, it helps to understand the past.

Third, the global climate is what scientists sometimes call a "massively interactive" system. In fact, different processes can interact in unexpected ways. The IPCC's first estimates of global warming were off by a significant amount because it did not factor into the climate model the role of sulfate particles—some from burning fossil fuels—that reflect sunlight back into space and have a cooling effect. As the earth warms, more water evaporates and the resulting water vapor traps more heat. The polar ice caps reflect much of the sunlight that reaches them back into space; as the ice caps shrink, more of the sun's energy will be retained within the atmosphere. The ocean absorbs CO_2, with colder seas trapping more than warmer ones. As the ocean's temperature rises, less CO_2 will be absorbed and, in a potentially catastrophic turn, it may even release large quantities of CO_2 back into the atmosphere. Understanding these complex interactions precisely will take time.

Fourth as a massively interactive system, the global climate may be quite sensitive to small changes, forming what scientists call a nonlinear or "chaotic" system. For instance, forests recycle huge amounts of carbon, extracting it from the atmosphere and locking it away in plants and trees. Yet if trees and plants cannot adapt quickly enough to higher CO_2 levels in the atmosphere and die, for instance, they might release their stores of carbon into the atmosphere and greatly exacerbate the original problem that caused their demise. Moderate climate change might produce changes in ocean currents, perhaps resulting in a more southerly course for the Gulf Stream. This would likely have a profound influence on the climate of western Europe, produce a possible reduction of upper-level ocean cycling in the Southern Ocean, and possibly lead to rapid disintegration of part of the Antarctic ice sheet with dramatic consequences for the global sea level. In these examples, small changes in climate might have massively disproportionate effects.

Given such a complicated system, our ability to predict the global climate 100 years in the future is still imperfect. Yet we should be aware that this scientific uncertainty—not about the basic phenomenon of global warming, but about exactly how hot it's going to get—is used by groups with particular interests to shape the political debate and policy choices in ways they favor. Environmental groups are sometimes prone to catastrophic doomsday scenarios, emphasizing extreme predictions at the high end of the possible range of global warming and playing on our fears. Conversely, business groups sometimes exploit the uncertainty surrounding the magnitude of global warming to minimize its impact and to advocate delaying any change in policy while scientists do more research. It is important to separate what we do know from what we don't, and to avoid either worst- or best-case thinking. Human-induced climate change is real. It is coming. And its effects will be noticeable and possibly significant in some areas. It is only the question of how dramatic the changes will be that remains uncertain.

PART FIVE

Looking Ahead

CHAPTER 13

The Future of International Politics

China's rapid economic growth has led many observers to question whether its increasing power will eventually bring it into conflict with the United States. The city of Shanghai, shown here, has become a symbol of China's economic rise.

In the coming decades, the international system may experience the spread of weapons of mass destruction, the rise of a new superpower in Asia, a clash between forces propelling economic globalization and those resisting it, and demands for greater global governance. Can political science tell us what the future will hold?

I n 1963, U.S. president John F. Kennedy predicted that by 1975 some 20 to 25 countries might possess nuclear weapons, a prospect that he considered "the greatest possible danger and hazard" facing mankind.[1] His prediction was far off the mark. In 1975, only five states had these devastating weapons—the United States, the Soviet Union, Great Britain, France, and China—the same five that had them when Kennedy made his prediction. Almost a half-century later, only four new countries have joined the nuclear club: India, Pakistan, Israel, and North Korea.

In 1987, a best-selling book titled *The Rise and Fall of the Great Powers* received a good deal of attention for suggesting that America, like all great powers before it, faced a future of inevitable decline.[2] The ongoing military competition with the Soviet Union, combined with the impressive economic growth of Germany, Japan, and China, meant that the United States would be hard pressed to remain the predominant global leader. The book predicted that the main task facing American leaders over the next several decades would be managing the relative erosion of U.S. power. A few years later, the Soviet Union collapsed, and the United States emerged from the Cold War as the single most powerful country in the world. Its military dominance by the turn of the twenty-first century was unprecedented in modern history.

In 1992, another best-selling book, *The End of History and the Last Man,* argued that the end of the Cold War had ushered in the definitive triumph of Western liberalism and democracy and that

Can the Spread of WMD Be Stopped?
▶ What Do Theory and History Tell Us?
▶ Preventing the Spread of WMD

Will China and the United States Fight for Global Leadership?
▶ What Do Theory and History Tell Us?
▶ A Coming Showdown, or Peaceful Engagement?
▶ What Will the United States Do?

Will Economic Globalization Continue?
▶ What Do Theory and History Tell Us?
▶ Resistance to Globalization in the Developed World
▶ Resistance to Globalization in the Developing World
▶ Backlash and the International Trading System

Will Globalization Lead to Global Government?
▶ What Do Theory and History Tell Us?
▶ Coming Conflicts over Global Governance
▶ Who Will Set the Rules?

Conclusion: Can Our Common Interests Prevail?

---

1. "Text of President Kennedy's News Conference on Foreign and Domestic Affairs," *New York Times,* March 22, 1963.
2. Paul Kennedy, *The Rise and Fall of the Great Powers* (New York: Random House, 1987).

New challenges facing the international community have led some observers to argue that more governance is needed at the international level. The European Union represents a significant step in this direction, with the supranational institutions of the EU taking on some functions that used to be handled solely by the national governments of member countries. Here, the Czech prime minister Mirek Topolanek addresses a European Parliament meeting on the EU's coordinated response to the economic crisis that began in 2008.

the world had reached "the end point of mankind's ideological evolution."[3] The next year, on February 26, 1993, Islamic extremists detonated a bomb under the World Trade Center in New York, a prominent symbol of Western capitalism. Although the terrorists failed to topple the towers on that day, this attack augured the rise of a movement whose conflict with the West would come to define the first part of the twenty-first century: militant Islam.

We start this chapter on the future of international politics with these examples in order to emphasize that predicting the future is always a difficult business. The world is a complicated place, and unforeseen developments can thwart any attempt at prognostication. The temptation to extrapolate current trends and assume that they are permanent can easily lead one astray. With that in mind, the purpose of this chapter is not to lay out predictions about the future, but to use the tools developed in this book to think through the future implications of some current trends. Going forward, what developments are likely to have a major impact on

international politics? What might their impact be, and why? How might different policy choices influence the way events unfold?

Trying to answer these questions also gives us an opportunity to look back at history. Surveying the last several centuries of international politics, it is striking how much can change over time. There have been periods in which violent conflict was quite common, and other periods in which the world was relatively peaceful. There also have been dramatic changes over time in the level of international cooperation and the depth of economic interdependence. We have to understand this variation in order to predict how current trends and developments will play out. Hence, in thinking about the future, theory and history are our best guides.

As we have done throughout this book, we approach the topic of change over time by thinking in terms of interests, interactions, and institutions. Actors' interests change when the costs and benefits associated with different strategies and outcomes change. For example, advances in technology can lower the costs of certain activities—whether trading goods across oceans, or acquiring weapons capable of killing millions in the blink of eye, or networking with activists on opposite sides of the globe. In some cases, these changes will generate

3. Francis Fukuyama, *The End of History and the Last Man* (New York: Free Press, 1992), xi.

common interests, as actors find new opportunities for mutual gain and/or new shared challenges. In other cases, change will benefit some actors at the expense of others, leading to conflicts between winners and losers. As interests change, so does the relative frequency of different interactions. When common goals or common threats arise, the need for cooperation grows. When changes benefit some actors and hurt others, the potential for conflict increases, as the winners seek to exploit their gains and the losers fight back. Technological change and economic growth can also shift the relative bargaining power of actors. Those that adopt new technologies or benefit from rapid development grow stronger, and they may seek to rewrite previous bargains in their favor. Finally, changes in interests and interactions can create demand for new and different institutions. Actors may seek new rules to further cooperation or to contain violent conflict, and new ideas about politics can lead to the promotion of new forms of governance.

In this chapter, we use our framework to consider four issues that are high on the agenda of world politics today and will continue to be so in the coming decades: the spread of weapons of mass destruction (WMD), the rising economic and military power of China, economic globalization, and the demand for new types of governance in the international system. In each case, we consider how changes in underlying conditions like technology, economic resources, and ideas are driving a convergence or divergence in the interests of the relevant actors, how their interactions reflect these changes, and what role institutions might play in governing these interactions going forward.

CORE OF THE ANALYSIS

▶ The growing ease of producing nuclear, biological, and chemical weapons makes acquiring these weapons an inexpensive and effective way for some states and nonstate actors to pursue their interests. As a result, there will be growing conflict between actors who want WMD and those who would be harmed by proliferation. Whether the spread of WMD can be slowed depends on whether the latter actors can find a way—through cooperation, coercion, or institutions—to alter the interests of potential proliferators.

▶ The rise of China as a global power may lead to increased conflict between that country and the current world leader, the United States. Whether this dynamic will lead to war depends on the interests that prevail in both countries and on whether international and domestic institutions can make China a partner, rather than a rival, of the United States.

▶ Economic globalization creates winners and losers and increases the potential for political conflict within and among countries. Whether this conflict will disrupt the process of globalization depends on the winners' willingness and ability to compensate the losers so that all actors see some benefits.

▶ As globalization increases the scope of international cooperation, there will be greater demand for global institutions to govern these interactions. Although most people agree that stronger governance is desirable, there will be conflicts over the rules and decision-making procedures of any such institutions.

Can the Spread of WMD Be Stopped?

Throughout history, changes in military technologies have had dramatic effects on international politics. Key innovations such as the stirrup, the longbow, gunpowder, automatic firing mechanisms, the airplane, the tank, the aircraft carrier, the intercontinental ballistic missile, the nuclear bomb—all profoundly influenced the nature and costs of warfare. Moreover, the emergence and diffusion of these technologies have constituted a major factor in changing the distribution of military power worldwide. States that innovate and adopt new technologies often gain an edge in international competition; however, as technology and knowledge spread to others, that initial advantage can diminish.

In the contemporary world, the spread of nuclear, chemical, and biological weapons—collectively known as weapons of mass destruction (WMD)—has been a particularly pressing issue. Although President Kennedy was overly pessimistic in his predictions about nuclear weapons, the potential for their spread is very real. At the time of this writing, nine states are known to possess nuclear weapons (the United States, Russia, Great Britain, France, China, India, Pakistan, Israel, and North Korea), and at least one state (Iran) is strongly suspected of seeking these weapons. Moreover, about 20 states possess the technology and knowledge to produce nuclear weapons in a very short time frame if they chose to do so (see "What Shaped Our World?" on p. 498). Fewer states are known to have chemical and/or biological weapons—whose production and use are outlawed by international treaties—but a handful of states are suspected of having illicit stocks or programs under way to develop them.[4] In addition to the possibility that more states will acquire such weapons, there is a looming danger of their acquisition by terrorist groups, a development that would greatly increase the damage that these nonstate actors could inflict. Indeed, in December 2008, a U.S. commission charged with studying this threat concluded that it was more likely than not that a weapon of mass destruction would be detonated someplace in the world before the end of 2013.[5]

Given this risk, the proliferation of WMD is likely to be high on the agenda of world politics for decades to come. Advances in technology and the diffusion of scientific knowledge have made it easier to acquire these destructive devices. Some states and nonstate actors will increasingly see the possession of WMD as an inexpensive and effective way to advance their interests. As a result, the prospect of proliferation will likely generate conflictual interactions between those who want these weapons and those who want to stop their spread. What implications would the spread of such weapons have? What, if anything, can be done to stop their proliferation to states and nonstate actors such as terrorists?

---

4. See, for example, Joseph Cirincione, Jon Wolfstahl, and Miriam Rajkumar, *Deadly Arsenals: Nuclear, Biological, and Chemical Threats,* 2nd ed. (Washington, DC: Carnegie Endowment for International Peace, 2005).

5. Commission on the Prevention of Weapons of Mass Destruction Proliferation and Terrorism, *World at Risk* (New York: Vintage Books, 2008), www.preventwmd.org/report (accessed 12/10/08).

WHAT DO THEORY AND HISTORY TELL US?

Given the horrendous killing power of WMD, it may seem obvious that their spread is undesirable; however, the lessons of theory and history actually suggest otherwise. Particularly in the case of nuclear weapons, one can make a strong argument that their overwhelming destructive power has made them a force for peace. This argument hinges on the idea that nuclear war jeopardizes the overriding interest of most actors: survival. Whatever other interests states or individuals may have, those goals are meaningless if attaining them will lead to the actor's destruction.[6] Thus, a war involving nuclear weapons threatens to impose costs that far exceed the value of whatever good might be at stake in a dispute. The massive costs of nuclear war mean that the bargaining range of deals that both sides prefer to war generally includes any possible division of the good; a state should prefer any deal, even one in which it gets nothing, to starting a nuclear war. At the very least, the enormous destructive potential of any war between states with nuclear weapons should induce caution and greater willingness to compromise. In short, possession of highly destructive weapons should create a condition of mutual deterrence in which neither side would contemplate an attack on the other, forcing them resolve their disputes in other ways.

To work, mutual nuclear deterrence has very few requirements.[7] The first is that each side must possess a survivable second-strike force—that is, each state must possess enough weapons so that its arsenal could survive a first strike by the other state and still be formidable enough to wreak unacceptable levels of damage on the initiator. Why is this necessary? If one state's nuclear arsenal is relatively easy to destroy with a crippling first strike, then a commitment problem arises that could generate preemptive incentives on both sides. In the event of a crisis, the stronger state would be tempted to deliver a knockout blow that would deprive the other state of any ability to retaliate. In the absence of a credible commitment by the stronger state not to strike first, the vulnerable state would face a temptation to "use them or lose them"—to launch its weapons first in order to ensure that they are not destroyed on the ground. Only when both states have enough weapons to ride out a first strike and still deliver a crippling blow of their own would neither state have a destabilizing temptation to launch preemptively. In practice, this means each side must have not only a large number of weapons but also a means of protecting them, such as by hardening missile sites against attack or by making them mobile (on vehicles, airplanes, or submarines) so that they are hard to eliminate.

The second requirement for mutual deterrence to work is that the leaders be rational, at least in the very limited sense that they care about their survival. The deterrent effect of nuclear weapons depends on their inducing caution by making the costs of war loom large relative to the potential benefits. For this to happen, those whose fingers are on the trigger must value their own survival and the survival of their nation enough to consider war unacceptably costly. Also, the weapons must not be easily subject to accidental launch. Finally, mutual deterrence assumes that

---

6. Obviously, individuals who engage in suicide terrorism may have different priorities, as we saw in Chapter 10.
7. See Scott D. Sagan and Kenneth N. Waltz, *The Spread of Nuclear Weapons: A Debate Renewed,* 2nd ed. (New York: Norton, 2003), chap. 1.

in the event of an attack, each side can reliably verify where that attack originated. Deterrence hinges on the expectation that anyone who initiates an attack will face a devastating counterattack. Hence, it must be the case that the initiator expects the target to be able to identify it. If it were impossible to know where the attack originated, then a potential initiator might think it could escape retaliation.

What does the evidence suggest? Although the logic of mutual deterrence may seem overly optimistic, the historical track record is encouraging. There has never been a nuclear war. Indeed, the only actual use of nuclear weapons—the bombings of Hiroshima and Nagasaki, Japan, by the United States in 1945—occurred when a nuclear country attacked a nonnuclear one. This observation suggests that what is dangerous about nuclear weapons is not their spread per se but their *uneven* spread, which leaves haves and have-nots. Even conventional war between states possessing nuclear weapons is extremely rare; the only such case is the 1999 Kargil War between India and Pakistan (see in Chapter 4). This effect is most prominently evident in a phenomenon known as the Long Peace, a term that refers to the absence of war between the United States and the Soviet Union from 1945 to 1990.[8] It may seem odd to use this term to describe the Cold War, which was anything but peaceful to people in much of the world. Nonetheless, despite the deep ideological hostility between the two states and the fact that they supported one another's enemies around the globe, it is remarkable that the superpower rivals never fought each other directly. Although several factors contribute to this observation (including the role of the Cold War alliance system discussed in Chapter 5), the fact that both states had enormous nuclear arsenals induced a level of caution and pragmatism in their relationship that allowed them to avoid direct warfare and to make compromises when necessary.

If the logic and historical track record of nuclear deterrence is so solid, why are so many people worried about the proliferation of nuclear weapons, as well as other WMD? Why might some states have an interest in preventing the spread of these weapons? There are three main reasons. First, even if nuclear weapons may reduce the danger of war in some circumstances, they nonetheless influence the distribution of power among states. A state whose power increases—such as by acquiring a potent new weapon—may seek to revise the status quo in its favor. This development could harm the interests of other states, even if it never leads to war. For example, if Iran were to acquire nuclear weapons, its power and influence in the Middle East would increase, probably to the detriment of the United States, Israel, Saudi Arabia, and any other country that has disputes with Iran. Hence, states may have an interest in stopping the spread of WMD in order to protect other interests that would be jeopardized by the emergence of an enemy with such capabilities.

Second, the states that have recently obtained, or may soon obtain, these weapons may be unable to meet all of the requirements set out above. Unlike the United States and the Soviet Union during the Cold War, many of these states are relatively poor and domestically unstable. They may not have the resources to build and protect an adequate second-strike force, and they may not have the technology or resources to safeguard their weapons against theft or accidental launch.

---

8. See John Lewis Gaddis, "The Long Peace: Elements of Stability in the Postwar International System," *International Security* 10 (Spring 1986): 99–142.

The case of Pakistan, which acquired nuclear weapons in the late 1980s, illustrates some of these concerns.[9] For example, Pakistan's military has considerable independence from the civilian leadership, and evidence suggests that the military has handled its nuclear weapons in a risky manner during several crises with India, thereby raising the danger of unintentional use. Also, influential elements of the regime, particularly the intelligence services, have close ties to militant groups in the region, thereby raising concerns about a transfer of nuclear technology to extremists. Moreover, Pakistan seems to have exercised loose control over its nuclear scientists. A. Q. Khan, the "father" of Pakistan's bomb, is suspected of running a network that sold key technologies to Iran, Libya, and North Korea.[10] If new proliferators resemble Pakistan rather than a more stable state such as, say, Great Britain, then there is reason for concern.

In 2004, the Pakistani nuclear scientist A. Q. Khan confessed on state television that he had sold nuclear weapons technology to Iran, Libya, and North Korea. The disclosure highlighted concerns that less stable governments might handle WMD and related technology in a risky manner.

The third concern, and one that has come to fore since the 9/11 terrorist attacks, is that the spread of WMD may make it more likely that these weapons will fall into the hands of terrorist organizations. This could happen intentionally (such as if a hostile state were to give or sell a weapon to a terrorist) or unintentionally (through theft or the complicity of extremist elements within the state). There is reason to doubt whether the logic of deterrence could prevent the use of WMD by terrorist organizations in the same way it does with states. While terrorists may act in rational ways (as we discussed in Chapter 10), at least some have demonstrated their willingness to commit suicide for their cause, which suggests that the threat of retaliation may not dissuade them. Moreover, unlike states, terrorist networks do not constitute a geographically defined target, so it can be especially hard to identify the perpetrators and their base. For example, after the attack on a U.S. warship, the USS *Cole*, in October 2000, it took months for investigators to say with confidence that the attack was the work of Al Qaeda and had been orchestrated by its leaders in Afghanistan—a delay that prevented any response to the attack.[11] And even if the responsible organization can be found, it can be difficult to carry out retaliatory strikes without also killing innocent people, since terrorists embed themselves within civilian populations that may or may nor share their goals. While it might have been credible during the Cold War for the United States to threaten the Soviet Union with massive retaliation in the event its leaders ordered a nuclear strike, it is harder to make the same threat today against, say,

9. For a discussion of these concerns, see Sagan and Waltz, *The Spread of Nuclear Weapons,* chap. 3; and Scott D. Sagan, "How to Keep the Bomb from Iran," *Foreign Affairs* (September/October 2006).
10. The status of these allegations is unclear. Although the Pakistani government admitted Khan's involvement—and pardoned him after he confessed—Khan later retracted his confession.
11. *The 9/11 Commission Report: Final Report of the National Commission on Terrorist Attacks upon the United States* (New York: Norton, 2004), 195, 200–201.

Pakistan for the activities of a small number of terrorists operating within its borders. Hence, a terrorist organization may expect to be able to escape retaliation, and/or it may consider the risks of retaliation acceptable given terrorists' extreme preferences.

PREVENTING THE SPREAD OF WMD

How can the proliferation of WMD be prevented? The answer depends in part on whether one is trying to prevent the spread of these weapons to states or to nonstate actors such as terrorists. In general, there are two ways to prevent an actor from acquiring WMD: (1) by altering the actor's incentives so that abstention becomes a better course of action, or (2) by preventing the actor from getting the necessary technology and material, such as the fissile material required to fuel a nuclear explosion. These strategies are not mutually exclusive, but they are likely to meet different levels of success depending on the actor in question.

As we saw in Chapter 10, terrorists have extreme interests that make them particularly willing to kill and be killed for their cause. Efforts to alter a cost-benefit analysis are less likely to succeed with such actors. It is unclear what promises or threats would induce them to alter their behavior voluntarily. As a result, preventing terrorists from acquiring a WMD capability requires a focus on the denial of technology—that is, ensuring that they do not get their hands on highly enriched uranium or plutonium for nuclear weapons, or on chemical or biological agents that can be weaponized. Since nuclear and chemical facilities are large and obvious, most clandestine terrorist organizations cannot pursue this route to developing weapons; they are more likely to buy or steal the components that they need. The task of denial therefore primarily entails securing nuclear and laboratory facilities against theft and policing efforts to buy or sell these materials on the black market.

Preventing the spread of WMD to states may also entail denial of nuclear, biological, and chemical ingredients; but given the current diffusion of scientific knowledge and technology, most reasonably advanced states already have the resources to develop a WMD program. As a result, efforts to slow proliferation among states focus primarily on shaping their interests. States that contemplate developing or acquiring WMD do so because they believe there will be some benefit to having them: enhanced security from an outside threat, or greater prestige and influence regionally or globally. Strategies for preventing the spread of WMD must alter these incentives, either by increasing the costs of proliferation or by increasing the benefits of abstinence.

The main strategies that have been used to this end coincide with the three core concepts of our framework: finding alternative ways to address the security interests of potential proliferators, cooperating through international institutions to establish and enforce rules against proliferation, or engaging in a coercive interaction designed to forcibly disarm hostile states.

Guaranteeing the Security Interests of Potential Proliferators

One approach to preventing the spread of nuclear weapons is to address the underlying reason why a state may want such technology in the first place. The most common motive is fear of attack by another nuclear-armed state.[12] This is evident from the historical pattern of proliferation. The United States developed nuclear weapons in the midst of World War II amid a fear that Nazi Germany would acquire them first. With the onset of the Cold War, the Soviet Union responded with a nuclear program of its own, achieving a nuclear capability in 1949. This development sparked concerns in Great Britain and France, which then sought their own nuclear deterrent. In the early 1960s, a growing rift between the Soviet Union and China led the latter to seek its own nuclear arsenal, which it achieved in the mid-1960s. The Chinese bomb induced fear in neighboring India, which had already had several clashes with China over their disputed border. The Indian nuclear program produced a usable weapon in the 1980s, with the result that India's long-time enemy, Pakistan, embarked on a program of its own. Hence, the spread of nuclear weapons has been driven largely by security concerns, with each new proliferator sparking fears in its rivals and leading them to seek a bomb of their own.

It follows that proliferation can be halted by finding ways to address the security interests that lead states to proliferate. Indeed, the historical record suggests a number of cases in which this strategy has worked—cases in which states that faced stronger and/or nuclear-armed rivals, and had the technological and scientific ability to develop nuclear weapons, nonetheless abstained from doing so. For example, why did China's acquisition of nuclear weapons lead India to respond in kind, while other states in the region that also had reason to fear China (particularly Japan, Taiwan, and South Korea) did not? The answer lies in the fact that these states found other ways to redress their insecurity. In particular, all three had defensive alliances with the United States, which meant that even though they did not have a nuclear deterrent of their own, they were protected by the "nuclear umbrella" of the United States. There is evidence that the Soviet Union induced similar restraint in its ally Syria, which was tempted to develop nuclear weapons in response to Israel.[13] By extending security guarantees to friendly states, the superpowers helped to dampen those states' incentives to seek their own arsenals. Such guarantees do not always work—as the British and French nuclear programs attest—since they must be sufficiently credible that potential attackers are deterred. It may be that the Cold War was a unique period because the intense competition between the superpowers generated particularly strong incentives for them to defend their allies. Nonetheless, the general point remains: incentives to proliferate can be lessened if states find credible alternative ways to address their security interests.

International Institutions: The Nuclear Non-Proliferation Treaty

An alternative mechanism for preventing proliferation relies on an international institution to foster cooperation among states with a shared interest in this goal. The primary institutional mechanism for this purpose is embodied in the Nuclear

---

12. For a discussion of the motives behind nuclear proliferation, see Scott D. Sagan, "Why Do States Build Nuclear Weapons? Three Models in Search of a Bomb," *International Security* 21, no. 3 (Winter 1996/1997): 54–86.
13. Benjamin Frankel, "The Brooding Shadow: Systemic Incentives and Nuclear Weapons Proliferation," *Security Studies* (Spring/Summer 1993): 47–51.

In the early 1990s, IAEA inspectors found evidence that North Korea had diverted plutonium in violation of NPT rules, setting off a prolonged crisis that led to North Korea's withdrawal from the NPT in 2003. The IAEA, the United States, and other states in the region have sought to bring North Korea into compliance with nonproliferation standards. Here, a U.S. researcher inspects a fuel fabrication facility in North Korea in 2008.

Non-Proliferation Treaty (NPT). Signed in 1968, the NPT provides for two kinds of states: nuclear weapons states and non-nuclear weapons states. The former consisted of the five states that had already acquired nuclear weapons by the time the treaty was signed: the United States, the Soviet Union, Great Britain, France, and China. All other states can only sign on as non-nuclear powers. The treaty represents a deal between these two groups. The recognized nuclear states promise not to transfer their weapons to non-nuclear states, to make good-faith efforts to reduce and eventually eliminate their own nuclear stockpiles, and to assist the non-nuclear states in the development of peaceful, civilian nuclear energy programs. In return, the other states promise not to try to develop nuclear weapons and to submit their nuclear energy programs to inspections by an international body, the International Atomic Energy Agency (IAEA). These inspections ensure that non-nuclear states do not divert enriched uranium or plutonium from their reactors and use those fissile materials to build nuclear weapons. Thus, the NPT benefits the recognized nuclear powers by securing their monopoly on nuclear weapons, and it benefits the rest of the signatories by assisting their development of nuclear energy and by limiting their non-nuclear rivals' access to these weapons.

As with many international institutions, the strength of the NPT lies in setting out standards of acceptable behavior and providing mechanisms for monitoring compliance; it is weaker when it comes to enforcement, which is left to the states themselves. The IAEA enters into safeguard agreements with non-nuclear weapons states, in which the latter agree to a program of inspections designed to ensure that nuclear material is not diverted. IAEA inspections uncovered evidence of plutonium diversion by North Korea in the early 1990s, and they documented numerous instances of noncompliance by Iran going back several decades. Once cheating is discovered, the IAEA has no authority to impose sanctions. Instead, it must submit charges of noncompliance to the United Nations Security Council, which has the ability to authorize economic or military sanctions. As we saw in Chapter 5, however, the UN Security Council is not a neutral body; rather, it is dominated by five permanent members (the P5), each of which can veto any enforcement action it does not like. In the cases of both North Korea and Iran, effective sanctions have been blocked by veto threats from China and Russia. Hence, enforcement of the NPT requires consensus in the Security Council—something that is hard to obtain if the noncompliant state has backers within that body.

How well has the NPT fared in preventing the spread of nuclear weapons? The track record is mixed. From one perspective, the NPT regime has seen some notable successes. The number of signatories has grown from 61 in 1970 to 189 today, and although originally designed to last only 25 years, it was extended indefinitely in 1995. Among its new members are several that previously refused to sign and had active nuclear programs, such as South Africa, Brazil, and Argentina. In the cases of Brazil and Argentina, the IAEA played a central role in helping these two former rivals shed their nuclear programs in a transparent manner. The NPT regime also played a productive role in defusing a potential crisis caused by the breakup of the Soviet Union. With the dissolution of that country into 15 new states, a number of the new states were "born nuclear" due to the presence of Soviet-era weapons on their territory. Although there was general agreement that the largest of these states, Russia, would inherit the former Soviet Union's designation as a nuclear weapon state, the other three states—Ukraine, Belarus, and Kazakhstan—all came under pressure to give up their weapons and sign the NPT as non-nuclear weapon states. Because of long-standing fears of Russia, some policymakers in Ukraine thought that the arsenal they had inherited would serve as a useful deterrent against their larger, nuclear-armed neighbor. However, the other nuclear powers insisted that Ukraine could only join the NPT as a non-nuclear weapon state and that the alternative was to be ostracized by the international community, threatening the new state's standing and access to economic aid.[14] Ukraine signed the NPT as a non-nuclear power in 1994 and transferred all of its nuclear weapons to Russia by 1996. Belarus and Kazakhstan followed suit. In this example, the international institution performed exactly as one would hope: by setting a clear standard for acceptable behavior and raising the expected costs of noncompliance.

The NPT regime has also had notable failures, however. Several states have managed to cheat on their obligations and escape detection or punishment for some time. North Korea, Iraq, Libya, and Iran were all NPT signatories, and all managed to have active or nascent nuclear programs at some point after signing. As already noted, the IAEA detected noncompliance by North Korea and Iran, but efforts to sanction them through the UN Security Council have been hampered by disagreements among the P5. Libya had an active nuclear program for some time before it agreed to dismantle under a 2003 deal with the United States. Iraq's nuclear program went undetected for years and only came to light after the first Persian Gulf War in 1991. Another limitation of the NPT is that there is no mechanism to force states to sign or to prevent them from backing out after they have signed. Although instances of cheating by NPT members are rare, this is because many of the states that developed nuclear weapons after the treaty came into force—most notably, India, Pakistan, and Israel—refused to sign on in the first place. Moreover, Article 10 of the treaty permits states to withdraw from the NPT with only six months' notice, with no provision for penalties in this event. This is precisely what North Korea did in 2003, after being confronted with evidence that it had been illicitly enriching uranium. Hence, the NPT does not provide foolproof protection against determined proliferators.

Coercive Disarmament

What, then, can be done about states like North Korea, Iran, or Iraq under Saddam Hussein—states that have actively sought or, in the case of North Korea, actually acquired nuclear weapons? These states' actions show that they do not fear the international disapproval and possible economic sanctions that come with

---

14. Sagan, "Why Do States Build Nuclear Weapons?" 80–82.

The Proliferation of Nuclear Weapons

Like the proverbial glass that is both half full and half empty, the history of nuclear proliferation can be seen in either optimistic or pessimistic terms. On the one hand, the number of states that actually possess these weapons is relatively small—just nine out of the almost 200 countries in the world. Indeed, nuclear abstinence is much more common: there are states that have forsworn these weapons after possessing or actively seeking them, and there are many states that could produce them but have chosen not to. Moreover, the pace of nuclear proliferation has slowed. Whereas it took 20 years (1945–1965) for the first five nuclear powers to arise, only four new nuclear states have emerged in the more than 40 years since.

On the other hand, a pessimist would point out that the spread of nuclear and scientific knowledge means that there are more "latent" nuclear states today than ever before—that is, states that could develop nuclear weapons within a relatively short time.

The time required to realize a usable weapon has shortened as well, particularly if states with illicit programs assist one another. Moreover, environmental pressures may make the problem worse going forward. With concerns about climate change prompting countries to move away from fossil fuels, nuclear power has become an increasingly attractive source of energy. This means that there will be more demand for nuclear reactors as well as for the technologies that are part of the nuclear fuel cycle: centrifuges for enriching uranium, and reprocessing plants for extracting plutonium from spent fuel rods. While these technologies have legitimate and peaceful uses, they can also be employed to generate fissile material for a nuclear weapon. An increasing reliance on nuclear power would thus put greater demands on the IAEA, which is charged with making sure that nuclear fuel is not diverted in this way. All this means that we could relatively quickly find ourselves in a world with many more nuclear states. ■

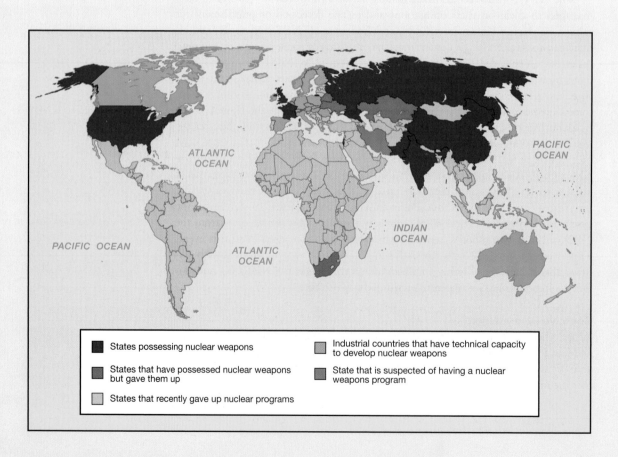

Legend:
- States possessing nuclear weapons
- States that have possessed nuclear weapons but gave them up
- States that recently gave up nuclear programs
- Industrial countries that have technical capacity to develop nuclear weapons
- State that is suspected of having a nuclear weapons program

being in noncompliance with the NPT. Nor do these states have strong protectors who can cover them with a nuclear umbrella. Moreover, these states' interests in nuclear weapons may be rooted in more than just insecurity that can be assuaged through security guarantees. For example, Iran has aspirations for regional influence, and nuclear weapons would be useful to this end.

The ultimate tool for stopping or reversing nuclear proliferation is coercive disarmament: the threat or use of military force. A state can issue a compellent threat against a would-be proliferator to dismantle its program or face attack. The United States issued veiled threats to this effect against North Korea during a 1994 crisis over that country's nuclear program, and it made such threats explicit during the crisis that led to the invasion of Iraq in 2003 (though it was later determined that Iraq had already halted its WMD programs). If threats alone are not enough to induce disarmament, the final option is to use military force to eliminate a foe's nuclear program altogether. A classic example of this strategy is Israel's attack on an Iraqi nuclear reactor in 1981. Without warning, Israeli planes entered Iraqi airspace and bombed a reactor at Osirak that had been part of Iraq's nascent nuclear program. Widely criticized at the time, the attack succeeded in setting back Iraq's program for at least a decade. More recently, in September 2007, Israeli planes launched a similar attack on an alleged nuclear site in Syria. Although there is uncertainty about exactly what the Israelis destroyed—and Syria denies that the site was part of a nuclear program—subsequent investigations by the IAEA found evidence consistent with undeclared nuclear activities.[15]

There are several major obstacles to the success of coercive disarmament. First, the threat of force alone is unlikely to work because disarmament generates a potentially dramatic power shift: the state that gives up its weapons makes itself weaker and, thus, vulnerable to further demands. To frame this point in the language of Chapter 3, coercive disarmament generates a commitment problem: the threatening state must credibly commit that if the target gives in to its demands and disarms, it will not exploit the target's weakness by making further demands. If such a commitment cannot be made credibly, then the target has good reason to resist the threat.

In actual cases that the United States has confronted, a credible commitment along these lines may be hard to achieve because of the underlying conflict of interests. As we noted in Chapter 3, the United States' conflicts with North Korea and Iran were not caused by those countries' nuclear programs. In fact, the causal arrow ran in the opposite direction: the United States had long-standing conflicts with those countries, and the conflicts contributed to those countries' desire to acquire nuclear weapons. Thus, it would not be unreasonable for Iran and North Korea to fear that if they gave in to U.S. demands to dismantle their weapons programs, they would essentially be making themselves more vulnerable to further demands. Indeed, one lesson these states may have drawn from the Iraq War is that a nuclear arsenal is useful for keeping the United States at bay. After all, it was Iraq, with no nuclear weapons, that was invaded; North Korea, with a small arsenal of such weapons, was not. To enhance the chances that threats of force will succeed, they have to be matched with some effort to reassure the target that its newfound weakness will

15. Director General, International Atomic Energy Agency, "Implementation of the NPT Safeguards Agreement in the Syrian Arab Republic," November 19, 2008, www.isis-online.org/publications/syria/IAEA_Report_Syria_19Nov2008.pdf (accessed 12/10/08).

not be exploited. Given the United States' underlying conflicts with these countries, it is not always obvious how to make such a commitment believable.

If threats alone do not work, then force may be the last resort, as in the case of the Israeli attack on the Osirak reactor and the American-led war on Iraq. A central difficulty with replicating the Israeli approach, besides the costs associated with using force, is that states have learned from this example. Proliferators have taken steps to harden and disperse their nuclear sites so that they are less vulnerable to attack. North Korea, for example, makes extensive use of tunnels and underground bunkers to hide and protect key elements of its nuclear program. As a result, it is hard to ensure that air attacks will succeed. The alternative approach of invading and occupying a country, as in the case of Iraq, increases the chances of verifiably eliminating a program, but the costs associated with such a venture are much higher.

What policymakers are left with in these tough cases is making a decision from among several alternatives, each of which has drawbacks. Military force is costly and of questionable effectiveness, particularly in the long term. Economic sanctions, to be effective, require effective international cooperation, which in many cases is lacking. The international community could, of course, let the state acquire nuclear weapons and rely on deterrence to render those weapons harmless. Deterrence has a good track record historically, but one cost of this approach is that each case of proliferation generates incentives for neighboring states to follow suit. The probable chain reaction increases the risks of accidents or of weapons falling into the wrong hands.

Alternatively, the United States and its allies may need to consider bargaining with states such as North Korea and Iran to address some of the underlying conflicts that led them to seek nuclear weapons in the first place. Such a deal would require these states to relinquish their weapons in exchange for economic aid, an end to diplomatic isolation, some kind of security guarantees, and probably substantive compromises on some of the regional issues that are the source of hostility. The United States and North Korea crafted such a deal in October 2007, and there have been some encouraging signs of progress, including North Korea's decision to dismantle the reactor that had produced plutonium for its weapons. However, this deal unraveled in the spring of 2009, when North Korea test-launched a long-range missile and then responded to international criticism by expelling IAEA inspectors and testing a nuclear device. At the time of this writing, it seems doubtful that North Korea will agree to give up its existing weapons and plutonium stocks. As this example suggests, the strategy of reaching a "grand bargain" with determined proliferators carries both promise and uncertainty. Whether a deal can be reached, whether it would be desirable to all sides, and whether everyone can be expected to live by it—or whether continued conflict and the threat of war are the only possible recourse—remain central questions.

Will China and the United States Fight for Global Leadership?

The proliferation of WMD is a relatively recent and small part of a much older and larger phenomenon in world politics: the ever-changing distribution of military power. If this book had been written in the sixteenth century, it would have focused on the foreign policy of the Habsburg Empire, an empire ruled from Spain that reaped enormous wealth from its overseas possessions in the New World. If this book had been written in the seventeenth century, many of its pages would have been devoted to the Dutch Republic, which officially won its independence from the Habsburgs in 1648, throwing that empire into fatal decline, and then went on to dominate international finance and commerce. An eighteenth-century version of this book would have detailed the exploits of France, which built an impressive empire in the first half of the century under Louis XIV and then plunged the entire European continent into war at the end of the century under Napoleon. A nineteenth-century version would have marveled at Great Britain's emergence as a world leader, as that country took advantage of its early industrialization to build an unparalleled navy and amass a global empire on which "the sun never

The Chinese economy has grown rapidly in recent decades, thanks in part to the export of manufactured goods like the McDonald's toys produced in this factory.

set." An early twentieth-century edition would have focused on the rising power and ambition of Germany, which propelled the world into the two costliest wars it has ever experienced. And had this book been written in 1985, it would have focused on the Cold War between the United States and the Soviet Union, a conflict that seemed like it would go on indefinitely—but which, we now know, ended five years later with the collapse of the Soviet Union.

The cast of major actors on the world stage is always in flux as states and empires rise and fall. The underlying mechanism usually revolves around technology and economic growth.[16] States that discover and adopt new technologies and economic models tend to experience rapid growth in resources and power, thereby extending their influence in world politics. As other states catch up or make their own innovations, previous leaders can be challenged and even usurped, allowing a new set of players to take center stage. This process not only changes the identity of the main actors in international politics but also creates dynamics that are themselves important. In some cases, a shift in the distribution of power can cause massive upheaval and war, as in the rise of Germany; in other cases, like the Cold War, challenges end with a whimper rather than a bang.

As we think about how this process will play out in the future, no development today seems more important than the rising economic and military power of China. Since 1979, when the Chinese government started enacting a series of economic reforms, the country's economy has grown tenfold. While long-term economic projections are fraught with uncertainty, some analysts have predicted that China will overtake the United States as the world's largest economy sometime in the first half of the twenty-first century (see Figure 13.1). Hence, while the U.S. economy is currently about six times larger than China's, the gap between the two is likely to close considerably over the next few decades.

---

16. See, for example, Kennedy, *The Rise and Fall of the Great Powers,* and Robert Gilpin, *War and Change in World Politics* (Cambridge: Cambridge University Press, 1981).

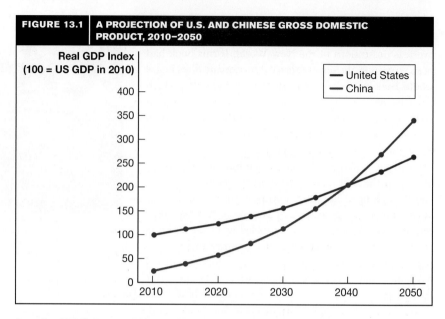

FIGURE 13.1 | **A PROJECTION OF U.S. AND CHINESE GROSS DOMESTIC PRODUCT, 2010–2050**

Source: Jim O'Neill, Dominic Wilson, and Roopa Purushothaman, "Dreaming with BRICs: The Path to 2050," *Global Economics Paper* 99 (October 2003), 20. Available at www2.goldmansachs.com/ideas/brics/book/99-dreaming.pdf (accessed 6/24/08).

China's growing wealth has translated into increased military power. Although figures on China's military spending are uncertain and controversial, it is estimated that the country's defense budget grew at an annual rate of 10–12 percent from 1996 to 2007.[17] China has long possessed the largest army in terms of personnel, but its increases in military spending have helped modernize the Chinese military with advanced technology. In the process, China has enhanced its power projection capabilities—that is, its ability to project military force beyond its borders—through investments in aircraft carriers and mid-air refueling technologies. Moreover, China also possesses a modest arsenal of nuclear weapons: around 100 missiles, all of which can hit targets throughout Asia and some of which can reach Europe and the United States.[18] To be sure, the United States will likely continue to be the world's dominant military power for some time. In recent years, U.S. defense spending has roughly equaled that of the rest of the world combined. The United States also enjoys a large technological lead, and its nuclear arsenal dwarfs China's many times over.[19] Nonetheless, it seems likely that the gap between these countries in relative military power will shrink in the coming decades.

17. United States Department of Defense, *Annual Report to Congress: Military Power of the People's Republic of China 2008,* 31–32. Available at www.defenselink.mil/pubs/pdfs/China_Military_Report_08.pdf (accessed 6/24/08).
18. Ibid., 24–26.
19. In January 2008, the United States was estimated to have about 5,400 nuclear warheads. The Strategic Offensive Reductions Treaty (SORT) requires the United States and Russia to reduce their arsenals to between 1,700 and 2,200 operationally deployed warheads each by 2012. See, for example, Robert S. Norris and Hans M. Kristensen, "U.S. Nuclear Forces, 2008," *Bulletin of Atomic Scientists* 64 (March/April 2008): 50–53.

What are the implications of China's rise? To answer this question, we need to identify how rising power affects the interests of the rising state and its interaction with the current world leader, the United States. We also need to examine the role that institutions, both international and domestic, might play in containing potential conflict between the two.

WHAT DO THEORY AND HISTORY TELL US?

Both theory and history tell us that the rise of a new major power is potentially dangerous because of its effect on states' interests and the bargaining interaction between them. We saw in Chapter 3 that a large shift in the relative military power of two states has several effects. As a state becomes more powerful, it expects to do better in the event of a war. As a result, it will be more willing to threaten force to change the status quo. Bargains that were acceptable when the state was relatively weak will no longer be satisfactory. Hence, a rising state has an interest in using its newfound power to renegotiate preexisting arrangements. Of course, this development alone does not make war inevitable, since the costs of war ensure that a bargaining range exists. It is possible that the demands of the rising state can be defused peacefully through negotiated changes that reflect the new power distribution. Nonetheless, opportunities for crises will increase, along with the attendant danger of war due to the information and commitment problems.

One such problem is particularly dangerous in this context: because the rising state cannot commit *not* to revise deals in the future, the declining state may have an incentive to wage preventive war. As we saw in Chapter 3, the declining state may decide that war now is preferable to some future bargain that favors the rising state. An anticipated decline creates a temporary window of opportunity to try to secure one's military advantage by fighting and defeating the rising challenger. Theory tells us, then, that a change in relative power influences both interests and interactions in a way that makes conflict more likely: the rising state acquires an interest in revising the status quo, and the declining state faces a strategic environment that encourages preventive war.

Does the historical record confirm this fear? The argument that rising power increases the danger of war can be traced to one of the earliest known scholars of war, the Greek historian Thucydides. Writing in the third century BC, Thucydides sought to explain the Peloponnesian Wars between two Greek city-states, Athens and Sparta. In his view, the wars arose because Sparta, which had once dominated the region, sought to contain the growing power and ambition of Athens, which was increasingly challenging Sparta's predominance. His often-quoted conclusion: "What made war inevitable was the growth of Athenian power and the fear which this caused in Sparta."[20] More recently, scholars have seen echoes of this logic in the wars that accompanied the rise of Germany in the early twentieth century.[21] As we discussed in Chapter 5, a key dynamic underlying both world wars was the growing

---

20. Thucydides, *History of the Peloponnesian War,* trans. Rex Warner (London: Penguin Books, 1954), 49.
21. For an argument that Thucydides' logic is central to understanding major wars in the modern era, see Robert Gilpin, "The Theory of Hegemonic War," *Journal of Interdisciplinary History* 18 (Spring 1988): 591–613.

ambition of Germany following its unification and rapid industrial and population growth in the late nineteenth century. Prior to World War I, this assertiveness manifested itself in a drive to acquire more territory, expand its colonial holdings, and wield influence in world politics commensurate with its power. The settlement that followed World War I—which stripped Germany of territory, colonies, and influence—only exacerbated the mismatch between what Germany possessed and what it believed it could possess, given its resources. Although Germany's fanatical, genocidal goals in World War II were largely due to Hitler's extreme ideology, this mismatch ensured that Germany would seek to revise the restrictive terms of the postwar settlement at some point.[22] Hence, the connection between rising power and an assertive foreign policy is borne out in the German case.

It is crucial, however, not to overgeneralize from this case, notwithstanding its obvious importance. There are also cases in which rising power did not lead to war. For example, the United States overtook Great Britain by most measures of power around the dawn of the twentieth century. The transition took place relatively peacefully, with Britain acquiescing to U.S. dominance in the Western Hemisphere in a series of crises over Venezuela and the Alaskan boundary with Canada. The handover of world leadership from Britain to the United States proceeded over the next several decades, aided by their common effort against Germany. By the 1950s, Britain was clearly a junior partner of its former colony. At that point, the United States faced a strong challenge from the Soviet Union, which built a massive conventional force and attained nuclear parity with the United States by the 1970s. Although the Cold War was a tense and dangerous time, this rivalry also ended without direct warfare between the two superpowers. The combination of American alliances (see Chapter 5) and nuclear weapons helped contain and deter the Soviet threat, and the Soviet Union eventually collapsed due to economic exhaustion. Finally, as the Cold War waned, there were concerns about an emerging struggle for power between the United States and either Germany, a powerhouse economy at the center of Europe, or Japan, whose dynamic economic growth in the 1980s led to warnings of a "coming war with Japan."[23] Neither of these predictions came true. Although the United States has in some ways accommodated the rising influence of these states, the process was peaceful and never gave rise to threats of military conflict.

Why does the interaction between a rising power and the current leader sometimes end peacefully? A large part of the answer lies in the states' interests: how severely their interests conflict, and how costly it is to use military power to force change. Consider Figure 13.2, which revisits the simple bargaining framework introduced in Chapter 3. As before, the horizontal line represents all possible divisions of the good in dispute, and the relative military power of the states involved is captured by a point on the line corresponding to the share that each state expects to obtain in the event of a war. Both parts of this figure illustrate a power shift in favor of State A. Initially, State B is the stronger state and the expected war outcome, p_1, is close to its ideal point. We then

---

22. This case is made famously by A. J. P. Taylor, *The Origins of the Second World War* (New York: Atheneum, 1961), especially p. 24.
23. See, for example, George Friedman and Meredith Lebard, *The Coming War with Japan* (New York: St. Martin's Press, 1991).

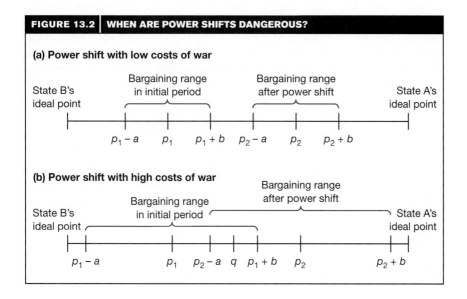

FIGURE 13.2 | WHEN ARE POWER SHIFTS DANGEROUS?

(a) Power shift with low costs of war

State B's ideal point

Bargaining range in initial period

Bargaining range after power shift

State A's ideal point

$p_1 - a$ p_1 $p_1 + b$ $p_2 - a$ p_2 $p_2 + b$

(b) Power shift with high costs of war

State B's ideal point

Bargaining range in initial period

Bargaining range after power shift

State A's ideal point

$p_1 - a$ p_1 $p_2 - a$ q $p_1 + b$ p_2 $p_2 + b$

assume that after a period of relative growth State A will be stronger, so that the war outcome after this power shift will be at p_2, closer to State A's ideal point. What is the difference between the two parts? In (a), the costs of war, a and b, are small relative to the shift in power, whereas in (b), the costs of war are large.

The situation in (a) is obviously quite dangerous, as we saw in Chapter 3. The declining State B expects to get more through war in the initial period ($p_1 + b$) than it expects to get from any deal that is in the bargaining range after the power shift—that is, any feasible bargain in the second period is farther from State B's ideal point than what it can achieve by fighting now. Hence, the danger of preventive war is quite real. This is not the case in (b), however. In this case, the bargaining range that will hold after the power shift includes deals that the declining State B prefers to fighting a war now. If the states were to reach a deal at, say, the point labeled q, then State A could credibly commit not to use force to revise the deal in the future: a deal at q gives State A more than it can expect to get through war even after it has grown stronger ($p_2 - a$). As a result, State B has no incentive to wage a preventive war in the initial period. The danger of war is much lower in (b) because the costs of war loom large relative to the shift in power. These costs make it harder for the rising State A to take advantage of its newfound power.

Recall that the costs of war in this model are measured relative to the value of whatever good is in dispute. Hence, the interaction between a rising and a declining state is more likely to look like that in (b) if either the material costs of war are very high or the value of the good in dispute is low. In short, a power shift is not particularly dangerous if war is too costly to contemplate or if the conflict of interests in the relationship is so small that there is little worth fighting over.

This logic helps explain the relatively peaceful power shifts mentioned above. The Cold War challenge by the Soviet Union coincided with an enormous increase in the costs of war due to the advent of nuclear weapons. As we just saw, war was avoided in large part because of the threat of mutually assured destruction in the event of a nuclear exchange. In the case of Germany and Japan in the late twentieth century, there was little threat of a military confrontation with the United States because of the common interests that bound them together—common interests stemming from a shared strategic threat during the Cold War, strong commercial and financial ties, shared democratic values, and a history of beneficial cooperation.

A COMING SHOWDOWN, OR PEACEFUL ENGAGEMENT?

We have, then, three kinds of historical precedents for thinking about the implication of China's rise: The rise of Germany in the first half of the twentieth century witnessed a series of major wars. The Soviet challenge during the Cold War was contained until the country collapsed. And the rise of Germany and Japan in the last decades of the twentieth century was peacefully accommodated. How, then, is the rise of China in the twenty-first century likely to play out?

The pessimistic view is that China's rise is inherently dangerous because there are large conflicts of interest between that communist nation and the United States.[24] In this view, China, unlike Japan, cannot be accommodated in an American-led international order that values capitalism and democracy, and it will instead seek to overturn that order and institute its own. Just as Germany sought mastery of Europe in the first half of the twentieth century, China will use its new power to seek mastery in Asia, pushing out American influence. If so, the United States will have to react with alarm, since it has strong economic interests in the region that would be jeopardized. In this view, the dangers of Chinese assertiveness and the preventive incentives of the United States loom large.

Supporters of this view argue that the best way to respond to this prospect is to contain China in the same way that the West contained the Soviet Union during the Cold War.[25] Such a policy would be designed to slow down China's rise and to deter war by increasing the costs. The containment strategy would have two main prongs. The first would be an effort to slow down China's amazing economic growth by denying it access to the large U.S. market. Since a good deal of China's growth is based on exports to the West, advocates of containment argue that allowing these exports to have free access to Western markets serves only to strengthen an inevitable adversary. The second prong of the containment strategy would be to strengthen and build alliances with China's neighbors in order to provide an effective counterweight to its growing power. This would mean maintaining U.S. military bases in the region, particularly in Japan, South Korea, and the Philippines, and building ties with other states that have reason to fear China's growing might, such as India and Vietnam. By adding the power of these countries to that of the United States, such alliances would blunt the impact of China's growth on the balance of military capabilities (that is, lower p_2) and increase the costs of war (that is, increase a). In short, the containment strategy would seek to prevent China from becoming more aggressive by slowing the rise of its power and making war less attractive.

---

24. See, for example, Aaron Friedberg, "The Struggle for Mastery in Asia," *Commentary* 110 (November 2000): 17–26.
25. See, for example, Gideon Rachman, "Containing China," *Washington Quarterly* 19 (Winter 1996): 1291–40.

China's growing wealth has translated into increased military power. These soldiers are marching to a defense technology exhibit in Beijing that focused on the development of high-tech weaponry. The implications of China's rise are as yet uncertain.

Against this pessimistic view is a more optimistic one that places faith in the role of institutions, both international and domestic, to mitigate the risk of war.[26] This argument holds that China's participation in international institutions, combined with a reform of its domestic institutions, could transform that country's interests so that it becomes a supporter, rather than a challenger, of the status quo. If so, then war can be avoided by eliminating conflicts worth fighting over. Supporters of this view promote a strategy of engagement that seeks to encourage positive institutional changes.

At the international level, the engagement strategy would involve promoting Chinese membership in a web of institutions dealing with security, trade, and finance. For example, supporters of engagement have pushed for China to be admitted into the World Trade Organization (WTO); for China to play a larger role in the Association of South East Asian Nations (ASEAN), which deals with regional security issues; and for China to have a larger say in the decisions of the International Monetary Fund (IMF) and World Bank. Such efforts seek to increase the benefits that China derives from the existing set of international institutions, and thereby diminish its incentives to upend that order. These reforms not only move the status quo in China's favor but also increase the costs of war relative to the benefits that can be won. The hope is that by enmeshing China in a web of existing institutions, that country's leaders will find a belligerent foreign policy—and the threat of exclusion from those institutions—to be too costly.[27]

---

26. See, for example, James Shinn, ed., *Weaving the Net: Conditional Engagement with China* (New York: Council on Foreign Relations, 1996); Audrey Cronin and Patrick Cronin, "The Realistic Engagement of China," *Washington Quarterly* 19 (Winter 1996): 141–70; Kenneth Lieberthal, "A New China Strategy," *Foreign Affairs* 74 (November/December 1995): 35–49.
27. For an argument that membership in security institutions can change the way China's foreign policy makers see their security interests, see Alastair Iain Johnston, *Social States: China in International Institutions, 1980–2000* (Princeton: Princeton University Press, 2008).

At the same time, advocates of engagement hope that economic growth will, over time, lead to change in China's domestic institutions toward greater political freedom and democracy. The underlying idea is that wealth and trade will give rise to a potent middle class of businesspeople and merchants who will demand greater political liberalization. A vibrant and politically active middle class is generally seen as a key ingredient in the emergence of democracy in Western Europe. Advocates of engagement argue that the same model can work in East Asia—where growing wealth led to democratization in Taiwan and South Korea. If so, then China's growing power can be rendered harmless through democracy, which will weaken the influence of the Chinese military and sensitize its leaders to the costs of military conflict. In this case, the rise of China could be as benign as the rise of the United States in the late nineteenth century or of Western Europe and Japan in the late twentieth century.

WHAT WILL THE UNITED STATES DO?

U.S. policy in the last decade has combined aspects of both strategies, although the engagement approach has been emphasized. The United States has maintained its bases in East Asia while pursuing closer relations with India and Vietnam. To date, however, there has been no effort to pursue defensive alliances equivalent to an East Asian NATO, and there is no serious talk of preventive war. At the same time, the United States has pushed for Chinese admission into the WTO, guaranteeing favorable treatment of Chinese exports, and has promoted China's active participation in a variety of regional and global organizations.

The adoption, so far, of an engagement policy reflects a number of international realities. Many East Asian countries profit from trade ties with China, and they are reluctant to jeopardize those ties by taking a more confrontational approach. Moreover, the enormous potential costs of a military conflict with China make preventive war an extremely unattractive, and hence unlikely, option. Although China's nuclear arsenal is currently rather small and vulnerable, it is developing more survivable capabilities, including submarine-launched ballistic missiles, that would give it a second-strike force. Thus, nuclear deterrence may play a role in U.S.-China relations similar to the role it played during the Cold War.

In addition to these international considerations, policy toward China is heavily influenced by the interaction of domestic interests within the United States. The impressive economic development of China has not only led to concerns about its military power; it has also led businesses in the United States and around the world to eagerly contemplate the prospects of selling into that enormous market. Imagine over 1 billion Chinese consumers wealthy enough to buy cellular phones or cars. The potential profits are enormous. As a result, American businesses have lobbied hard to improve relations between the two countries. For example, President Bill Clinton threatened in 1993 to revoke China's most-favored-nation trading status unless it made concrete improvements in its human rights record. When China refused to comply, American business interests pressured the Clinton administration to drop its threat.[28] The same

---

28. See David M. Lampton, "America's China Policy in the Age of the Finance Minister: Clinton Ends Linkage," *China Quarterly* 139 (September 1994): 597–621.

interests weighed in strongly in 1999 to push successfully for China's admission into the WTO. Hence, export-oriented businesses interested in the potential of the Chinese market have influenced policymakers' calculations on how much to confront or accommodate this rising power.

We should note that the word *potential* is an important qualifier here, since, to date, China has played a much larger role as an exporter of its own products (primarily low-cost clothes and toys) than as an importer of U.S. products. Indeed, the United States has consistently run an enormous trade deficit with China, on the order of $260 billion in 2008.[29] So far, it is Chinese workers, not Chinese consumers, who are driving that country's economic relations with the United States. As a result, American workers have not welcomed China's emergence in the world economy the way American exporters have. Trade unions representing American workers who compete with Chinese imports have been vocal in protesting that country's human rights record and its trading practices. Although these groups have not called for anything like a preventive war to restrain China's growth, they have opposed more accommodating policies, such as China's admission into the WTO, and they have found common cause with so-called China hawks in the U.S. government and military who advocate a tougher line, including military containment. While export-oriented businesses have so far been more influential, an increase in the power of these more hawkish groups would make it harder for the United States to peacefully accommodate China's rise. It is clear that U.S. policy toward China will be driven as much by the push and pull of domestic interests as by strategic considerations at the international level.

If the coalition supporting engagement continues to hold in the United States, then we will learn whether or not the adherents of this view are right. Growing membership in international institutions and/or liberalization of political institutions at home may turn China into a partner, rather than a rival, to the United States. It is also possible, of course, that domestic political reforms may never materialize and that China will find its newfound power too tempting not to wield aggressively in international bargaining. It is also possible that the interests in the United States supporting a harder line against China will become stronger in the face of economic and military competition. If so, increased conflict will be hard to avoid. In short, the implications of China's rise will depend a great deal on the interests that come to prevail in both countries.

Will Economic Globalization Continue?

China's impressive economic growth over the past few decades is part of a much larger process that has important consequences throughout the world: economic globalization. The term *globalization* refers to the spread of activities and ideas across the globe. As applied to economics, globalization involves increasing integration of national economies through the movement of goods, services, and money across borders. This process, in its most recent manifestation, took off in the last decades of the twentieth

---

29. U.S. Census Bureau, "Foreign Trade Statistics," www.census.gov/foreign-trade/statistics/highlights/top/top0812yr.html (accessed 4/8/09).

century owing to improvements in technology, particularly transportation, communication, and information technologies. The development of containerized shipping in the 1950s—with goods placed on ships in standardized containers that can be directly transferred to trucks or train cars—dramatically lowered the costs of international trade. Advances in telecommunications and computing, and particularly the advent of the Internet in the 1990s, have reduced the effects of distance, making it possible to transmit information anywhere in the world instantaneously.

Globalization has also occurred alongside changes in ideas about the proper relationship between the state and the economy. In the eighteenth century, the ideology of mercantilism saw economics as subordinate to state interests and led states to intervene extensively in economic relations with the goal of building and protecting their wealth. The twentieth century saw the rise of an extreme form of economic intervention known as central planning. The Soviet Union and other communist states sought to govern economic exchanges from the center, with production levels and prices determined not by supply and demand, but rather by the dictates of a government bureaucracy. These systems outlawed private ownership of the means of production, making them the property of the state. Both ideologies have given way to a liberal economic view that the state should respect private property and that economic exchanges should be determined by the choices of private actors—in short, that markets, rather than governments, should be the primary driver of economic outcomes. This view has been influential since the eighteenth century, but its influence relative to these alternatives has ebbed and flowed. The end of the Cold War, and the collapse of the Soviet model, ushered in a period in which the liberal economic view has been ascendant.

In concert with these changes, governments worldwide have lowered many of the barriers to trade and financial flows, as we saw in Chapters 6 and 7. This process has been aided by a series of global and regional trade agreements such as the World Trade Organization (WTO), the North American Free Trade Agreement (NAFTA), and the European Union. The result has been an explosion of world trade over the last 50 years and a dramatic increase in the flow of capital across borders. Figure 13.3 shows how the volume of world exports has grown dramatically since 1950, faster than the overall world GDP.

Although the steady upward slope of the lines in this figure suggests an inexorable trend, there are also strong forces pushing in the opposite direction. As we saw in Chapters 6 through 9, freer trade and capital flows create losers as well as winners, and the former have interests in slowing or reversing the process of globalization. The existence of an antiglobalization backlash was dramatically illustrated in November 1999, when delegates to a conference of the WTO met in Seattle to jump-start a new round of global trade talks. The delegates were greeted by throngs of demonstrators protesting the WTO and the process of globalization for which it stood. Protestors blocked streets and clashed with police in an effort to disrupt the meeting and have their voices heard. Inside the WTO meeting hall, the conflicts that arose among the delegates were more diplomatic and restrained, but no less severe. The meeting adjourned without an agreement on the important issues facing the world trade system. The so-called Battle of Seattle was the first of what are now routine public demonstrations that greet meetings of the WTO and other institutions associated with globalization, such as the World Bank and the IMF.

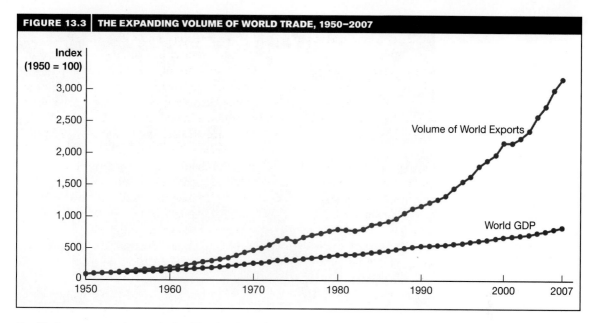

FIGURE 13.3 | THE EXPANDING VOLUME OF WORLD TRADE, 1950–2007

Note: The figure compares the growth of world trade and GDP by setting the values of both in 1950 equal to 100 and measuring subsequent years relative to that baseline. An index value of, say, 500 indicates that the quantity of interest is five times larger than it was in 1950. *Source:* World Trade Organization, *International Trade Statistics 2008* (Geneva: WTO, 2008), Table A1a.

Will globalization continue, pushed forward by the incessant march of technology? Or will the turbulence associated with these changes engender a political backlash that causes the process of globalization to grind to a halt? Thinking through these questions requires that we understand the interests generated by globalization, how the interaction between the winners and losers will play out, and the whether existing institutions can survive this conflict.

WHAT DO THEORY AND HISTORY TELL US?

Changes in technology influence the way economic actors pursue their interests, particularly their interest in maximizing income. Declining transportation and communication costs create strong incentives to overcome boundaries and increase the scope of markets so that they are global, rather than national or regional. When goods are costly to transport, it makes sense for production facilities to be located close to where the goods will be sold. As transportation costs decline, proximity to the consumer becomes less important. A company trying to decide where to build a production facility can use different criteria, such as how much it costs to pay workers and tax or regulatory policies. Improved transportation technologies thus allow companies to look around the world to find a location that will allow them to maximize profits.

This is true whether the company produces a physical good, such as a toy or an article of clothing, or a service, such as accounting or insurance. Indeed, the decline

Meetings of the WTO and IMF are now routinely accompanied by demonstrations against the perceived injustices of economic globalization. Globalization has created winners and losers, and their conflicting interests raise questions about the future of the world economy.

of communication costs brought about by the Internet has allowed many companies to move offshore many services that have traditionally been done domestically. For example, when you call customer support for your new computer, it is quite likely that you will be connected to someone in the Philippines. Some hospitals in the United States have even sent patients' X-rays to India to be read by radiologists there—radiologists who demand a much lower wage than do their American counterparts.[30] The ability to create a flawless digital scan of an X-ray and send it to the other side of the world instantaneously—unthinkable only a decade ago—makes this possible.

The economic interests created by these advancements make themselves heard in the political realm as well. As companies find it profitable to increase the scope of markets, they pressure governments to lower barriers to the movement of goods, services, and money across borders. A company that wants to locate in China but sell its wares to the United States will lobby the United States to allow free entrance of Chinese-made products. Otherwise, trade barriers may nullify the advantages of making the goods in China. Multinational companies also have an interest in ensuring that they can move their capital around the globe freely, so that profits made in one country can be moved to another or so that they can make direct investment decisions without having to worry about barriers. These companies also have an interest in strong protections for their property rights, so that they can open facilities in any country they like without having to fear that their property or profits will be seized. As we have seen, there

---

30. Frank Levy and Kyoung-Hee Yu, "Offshoring Radiology Services to India" (working paper MIT-IPC-06-005, Industrial Performance Center, Massachusetts Institute of Technology, September 2006).

are a number of reasons why these multinational companies wield substantial influence on government policy and, hence, why they are a potent force in pushing globalization forward.

History also tells us, however, that globalization is neither inevitable nor irreversible. People living in 1913 could look back at similarly impressive trends. In the preceding century, trade had grown from 2 percent of world income to 18 percent. International capital flows were also increasing impressively. Foreign-held assets grew from about 7 percent of world GDP in 1870 to 17.5 percent in 1913. And the movement of people was at a scale that dwarfs migration rates of today: between 1870 and 1910, about 10 percent of the world's population relocated permanently from one country to another; the comparable figure for the past three decades is no more than 2 percent.[31] World War I and the economic dislocations that followed brought this period of globalization crashing to a halt, and the period between the world wars saw the erection of new national barriers against the flow of goods and money. The war itself was not caused by globalization—though economic issues heightened the tensions among the European powers—but this case shows quite dramatically how political conflict can slow or even reverse seemingly inevitable economic processes.

Indeed, globalization in its contemporary form has generated no shortage of conflicts, both among and within states. Globalization generates conflict because it creates losers as well as winners. Among the winners are those economic actors that can take advantage of increased opportunities to move money and goods throughout the world—particularly, multinational companies and investors. Increased efficiency has also benefited consumers in the form of lower prices on imported goods. Who are the economic losers?

Recall from Chapter 6 that there are two different theories for thinking about who wins and who loses from trade liberalization. The Ricardo-Viner, or specific factors, model holds that trade interests are determined by the sector one works in: those in sectors that compete with imports want protection, while those in sectors that rely on exports want liberalization. The alternative theory, Stolper-Samuelson, holds that trade interests are determined by the factor of production—capital, labor, or land—that provides one's income. In this view, free trade benefits those factors that are relatively abundant in a country at the expense of those factors that are relatively scarce. In the developed world, where capital is relatively abundant and labor is scarce (particularly, unskilled labor), capital wins from free trade, while unskilled labor loses. In the developing world, where unskilled labor is abundant, holders of capital lose from free trade, while labor benefits. It is generally thought that while the predictions of Ricardo-Viner hold in the short term, long-run patterns of conflict follow the predictions of Stolper-Samuelson.[32] In other words, as globalization persists and deepens, conflicts will increasingly crystallize

---

31. These figures are from David Dollar and Aart Kraay, "Spreading the Wealth," *Foreign Affairs* 8, no. 1 (January/February 2002): 122–23; and Nicholas Crafts, "Globalisation and Economic Growth: A Historical Perspective," *World Economy* 27, no. 1 (January 2004): 46.
32. Michael Mussa, "Tariffs and the Distribution of Income: The Importance of Factor Specificity, Substitutability, and Intensity in the Short and Long Run," *Journal of Political Economy* 82 (November–December 1974): 1191–1203.

along class lines: capital versus labor, with the positions of each being determined by whether they are in the developing or developed world.

RESISTANCE TO GLOBALIZATION IN THE DEVELOPED WORLD

In developed countries, the group most negatively affected by globalization is workers—particularly, unskilled workers. As rich countries become more closely integrated with developing countries, workers in the former face increasing competition from unskilled workers in the latter. A company that makes toys or clothing can find workers willing to accept much lower wages in China or Vietnam than in the United States. As a result, production of labor-intensive goods has moved away from developed countries to the developing world, causing job losses in the former. For example, from 1970 to 2000, the textiles and clothing industries in the five richest developed countries shed over 4 million jobs, over 62 percent of their labor force.[33] Workers in affected sectors who have not lost their jobs have experienced stagnant or falling wages and have suffered from job insecurity.

Given this situation, it is not surprising that labor unions in rich countries have been at the forefront of a backlash against globalization. What may be surprising is how broadly based the opposition to globalization among labor unions has been. Consider, for example, what happened in 1999, when the United States approved a treaty admitting China into the WTO—thereby giving China permanent most-favored-nation trading status. Unions representing textile and clothing workers were in full-throated opposition to the pact, which would increase international competition for this beleaguered sector. They were joined by some apparently strange bedfellows.[34] For example, the Teamsters Union, which represents truckers, lobbied against the treaty. This stance was curious because at the same time one of the Teamsters' largest employers, United Parcel Service, was lobbying for a coveted new air route for landing cargo planes in China. One U.S. official summed up the contradiction: "It seems that the Teamsters want us to have more cargo flights to China, but no cargo." Even stranger was the opposition of the United Auto Workers. Prior to China's admission into the WTO, virtually no U.S.-made cars could be sold in China; after the treaty passed, U.S. automakers would have freer access to the Chinese market. Why would American autoworkers not be in favor of this? Stranger yet was the opposition of a major dockworkers' union, the International Longshore and Warehouse Union. These workers make their living loading and unloading ships that are engaged in international trade. One would think that expanding trade with China should be in their interests. And yet, opposition to the pact came not only from workers in sectors that directly compete with Chinese imports, but also from workers in sectors that thrive on exports and might, therefore, have been expected to support the deal.

---

33. OECD, "A New World Map in Textiles and Clothing: Adjusting to Change," Table 3.1, www.oecd.org/dataoecd/29/53/34042484.pdf (accessed 9/21/06).
34. The following is based on Thomas L. Friedman, "What's Going On with the American Labor Movement?" *New York Times,* May 9, 2000, sec. A.

This kind of class-based, rather than sector-based, opposition is exactly what the Stolper-Samuelson theorem predicts. The insecurities that globalization has created for workers in sectors that compete with imports is rippling outward and affecting the attitudes of workers in other sectors as well, generating political cleavages along class lines. Their fears are based on a number of concerns that include, but also go beyond, issues of job losses. One fear is that globalization is exacerbating inequality, with workers increasingly left behind. Indeed, there is evidence of increasing income inequality in many countries, although economists debate how much of this trend is due to international trade. After all, other developments over the last several decades, including the weakening of labor unions and the increasing importance of technology, account for some of gap. Regardless of the actual role of trade in exacerbating inequality, the perception of a strong effect is widespread and politically potent. (For more on this issue, see "What Do We Know?" on p. 516.)

In addition, there is a growing asymmetry between labor and investment capital that derives from the fact that capital can move around the globe in search of higher profits much more easily than workers can move around looking for jobs and better wages. Companies can threaten to close up shop and move, and this threat gives managers (who represent capital) bargaining leverage over workers to lower wage and benefit demands. It also leads to increased job insecurity. Unions have also expressed concerns about a "race to the bottom" in labor standards. In the developed world, unions fought hard for a number of protections that most people now take for granted: minimum wage laws, prohibitions on child labor, limits on the length of the work week, and worker safety regulations. These protections either do not exist or are much weaker in developing countries. Unions fear that the increased mobility of investment capital means that companies can move around the world looking for places with fewer worker protections. If countries compete for capital by weakening or resisting demands for these protections, hard-fought gains in labor standards could wither away.

Opposition to globalization does not come solely from its economic losers, however. Labor unions have been joined by an ally motivated by a noneconomic interest: groups concerned about protecting the environment.[35] The environmental case against globalization is driven by several concerns. The first is that the rapid growth of economic activity will hasten the degradation of the environment. Increasing industrial production in countries like China, Brazil, India, and Mexico threatens all manner of environmental harms, including increased pollution and greenhouse gas emissions and a hastening of deforestation and biodiversity loss. These concerns are particularly pronounced because of a second concern: developing countries often lack environmental regulations that limit destructive activities. Indeed, just as workers express fears of a race to the bottom in labor standards, environmentalists worry that the globalization of production will lead to a race to the bottom in environmental regulations. Finally, these groups fear that efforts to protect the environment will be sacrificed on the altar of free trade.

---

35. See, for example, Daniel C. Esty, *Greening the GATT: Trade, Environment, and the Future* (Washington, DC: Institute for International Economics, 1994).

Is Globalization Increasing Inequality?

One of the fears associated with economic globalization is that increasing exposure to trade and financial flows will widen the gap between rich and poor within countries. Rising inequality not only strikes many people as fundamentally unfair but also generates a risk of political and social conflict. To what extent has increased integration of the global economy contributed to inequality?

We know that income inequality within countries has generally increased at the same time that globalization has increased. The amount of inequality within a country is generally measured by using a number called a Gini coefficient, named after the Italian statistician Corrado Gini. The Gini coefficient ranges from 0 to 100, with a value of 0 indicating that everyone has the same income (that is, perfect equality) and a value of 100 indicating that all of the income is earned by one individual (that is, maximum inequality). Using this measure, the International Monetary Fund (IMF) estimates that average income inequality within countries has increased in almost every region of the world over the last two decades, with the exception of the states of the former Soviet Union and in sub-Saharan Africa. The figure here shows changes in the Gini coefficients for selected countries from 1985 to 2005. Although inequality has gone down in a few cases (for example, France and Brazil), the general pattern is in the other direction.

It might be tempting to conclude that because increased globalization has gone hand in hand with increased inequality, then globalization must cause inequality. The story is more complex than that, however, because other factors drive income inequality as well. Foremost is the growing importance of technology in virtually all sectors of the global economy. The dramatic advances in information and communications technology (ICT) that helped make globalization possible have also transformed the way people work and the skills they need to be productive. As these technologies have spread around the globe, they have boosted the productivity of people with the knowledge to use them and of owners of capital with the resources to invest in them. As a result, the demand for low-skilled labor has decreased, and the premium paid to highly skilled workers and owners of capital has increased. Hence, the growing use of ICT is a likely factor in the widening of the income gap.

How much of growing income inequality is due to trade and financial integration, and how much is due to technology? Economists at the IMF analyzed the data on income equality in order to tease out the different effects.[a] They examined how income inequality changes over time within countries in response to (1) how closely the country is integrated into global markets through trade and financial flows, and (2) how much of the country's capital stock consists of ICT.

The results show that the relative contributions of globalization and technology to income inequality depend on the country's level of development. Among developed countries, rising income inequality over the last two decades has been caused in roughly equal parts by both factors. In these countries, increasing economic globalization and the rising use of ICT have benefited both skilled workers and owners of capital; in contrast, both factors have hurt unskilled workers, who face increased job and wage competition from computers at home and from unskilled workers abroad. In developing countries, however, globalization and technology have had different effects. Trade and financial integration were estimated to cause a slight decrease in income inequality within developing countries, as unskilled workers benefited from their ability to export labor-intensive goods to the developed world. This effect was offset, however, by increasing income inequality due to the spread of ICT. Overall, then, the income gap in the developing world has increased—not because of economic globalization, but because of the increasing importance of the technologies that have made globalization possible. ■

CHANGE IN INCOME INEQUALITY IN SELECTED COUNTRIES, 1985–2005

Source: International Monetary Fund, *World Economic Outlook 2007: Globalization and Inequality* (Washington, DC: International Monetary Fund, 2007), Fig. 4.3. Data available at www.imf.org/external/pubs/ft/web/2007/02/index.htm#ch4fig (accessed 7/15/08).

a. International Monetary Fund, *World Economic Outlook 2007: Globalization and Inequality* (Washington, DC: International Monetary Fund, 2007), chap. 4. Available at www.imf.org/external/pubs/ft/weo/2007/02/index.htm (accessed 7/15/08).

This concern arose in the early 1990s when a body of the General Agreement of Tariffs and Trade (see Chapter 6) ruled against an American ban on imports of tuna caught in nets that kill dolphins. While environmentalists saw this ban as a reasonable way to protect dolphins, Mexico argued successfully that the ban violated GATT rules. The GATT's successor, the WTO, similarly ruled against U.S. clean-gas standards that affected imports from Brazil and Venezuela and a ban on the import of shrimp caught with nets that also kill sea turtles. These rulings galvanized the environmental movement to oppose unrestricted trade liberalization.

RESISTANCE TO GLOBALIZATION IN THE DEVELOPING WORLD

People in poorer countries have also experienced insecurity as a result of globalization. The Stolper-Samuelson theorem predicts that in the long run, trade liberalization will raise the incomes of unskilled workers in developing countries. And, indeed, despite the lamentable conditions for workers in much of the developing world, the opportunities created by access to rich markets have improved the lot of many, as we saw in Chapter 9. Nonetheless, there are several reasons why people in poor countries face globalization with fear and resistance.

One reason has to do with the relatively weak social safety nets that exist in developing countries. In the developed world, growing exposure to international trade after World War II coincided with the expansion of government assistance designed to protect workers from economic hard times. Unemployment benefits, poverty alleviation programs, government-subsidized health insurance, job retraining programs, minimum guaranteed pensions—all these policies had the effect of cushioning workers from the hard edges of international competition. People who lose their jobs due to foreign trade receive some assistance in making ends meet and in getting a new job. In poorer countries, however, these safety nets are generally not as strong, so workers face economic dislocations with greater insecurity.

Workers in the developing world may also have less access to institutions that give them clout in political and economic decision-making. Representative democracy, for example, is still more common in rich countries than in poor ones. As a result, workers in the latter have a harder time translating their numbers into political power to demand greater redistribution. Similarly, the right to form labor unions is not as strong in many developing states as it is the developed world. These institutions enable workers to pool their efforts and resources and to act collectively in pursuit of wage and benefit demands from employers. Even if globalization creates a larger pie of profits, weak or nonexistent unions make it harder for workers to get a larger slice of that pie.

Finally, increasing capital mobility has increased the volatility of poor economies, as large sums of foreign money can enter or leave at a moment's notice. As we saw in Chapters 7 and 9, countries that lose

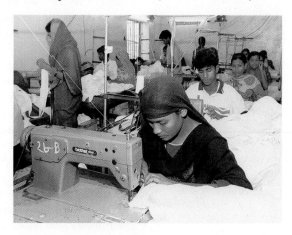

Although globalization has benefited many in the developing world, workers often have very limited rights and protections. Here, Bangladeshi children work in a factory that produces clothes for export.

the faith of international capital markets can suffer a devastating punishment. In a very short time, capital flight can cause inflation and unemployment to spike. And while international institutions like the IMF may come to a country's rescue, their assistance often requires that governments cut back spending and subsidies that benefit the poor. Given all this, it is easy to see why many people in the developing world do not perceive what economic theory tells us is their long-term interest in globalization.

BACKLASH AND THE INTERNATIONAL TRADING SYSTEM

Actors who see their interests as being harmed by globalization are at the forefront of a political backlash that has the potential to create conflict both within and among states. Just as those who stand to gain from globalization have pushed governments to lower barriers to trade and money flows, those who stand to lose have sought to influence policy in the other direction. The economic losers have an incentive to seek protection from foreign competition in the form of trade barriers or restrictions on capital flows. In addition, the increased insecurity caused by globalization generates a greater demand for social welfare programs designed to cushion workers from the shocks of competition. Workers and their representatives have demanded increased government spending to provide unemployment insurance, health insurance, and job retraining programs. Such redistribution would naturally come at the expense of the winners, who may or may not accommodate those demands.

Demands by those who stand to lose from globalization can also spill over into international tensions and jeopardize the institutions that govern world trade. To the extent that threatened groups are successful in raising trade barriers against foreign competition, they invite retaliation by other countries. For example, the United States has increasingly imposed trade restrictions on countries for allegedly dumping goods in the United States at artificially low costs. To consumers of those goods, these low costs are a boon. But to producers who have to compete with cheap imports, they are a threat. Producers who suspect they have been hurt by dumping can appeal to the U.S. government for sanctions against the alleged offender. The United States has used such antidumping measures with increasing frequency over the past decade, prompting other countries to cry foul. Since dumping is sometimes hard to prove, targets of antidumping sanctions claim that these measures are simply a guise for protectionism. As a result, the proper use and regulation of these sanctions has been an important, and divisive, issue in world trade talks.

Indeed, efforts to move forward on a new round of global trade talks have been thwarted ever since the 1999 Battle of Seattle mentioned earlier. The deadlock at the Seattle meeting presaged a series of similar failures, and even though the WTO launched the Doha Round of talks in 2001, negotiations have since broken down. Conflict between the rich and poor countries has been central to the talks' collapse. Among the key issues of contention have been the use of antidumping and related mechanisms (which rich states favor and poor states oppose) and whether trade rules should take into account labor or environmental standards (which environmentalists and labor unions in the developed world want and developing country governments have resisted).

Most significantly, however, rich and poor countries have also come into conflict over the pace and scope of trade liberalization. Since World War II, the most dramatic liberalization has taken place in the realm of manufactured goods, the primary producers of which are located in developed countries. Rich countries have also pushed hard to liberalize trade in services, such as banking, accounting, and communications—sectors in which their companies are very competitive. Poor countries, in contrast, have sought greater liberalization of the agricultural sector, since farming constitutes a significant portion of their economies. Liberalizing trade in agriculture would require rich countries to reduce or eliminate the very generous agricultural subsidies that they pay to their farmers. These subsidies account for about 25 percent of total farm receipts in developed countries, and over 50 percent in some countries, including Japan, South Korea, and Norway.[36] These government payments support farmers' incomes, allowing them to keep the prices of agricultural products artificially low. In the process, they deprive farmers in the developing world of much-needed income. Recent trade talks have stalled due to conflict between rich country governments, which are reluctant to alienate a politically powerful constituency, and poor country governments, which represent most of the world's farmers.

As we look forward, then, globalization generates two interrelated phenomena that have to be reconciled. On the one hand, increasing integration among national economies can produce enormous wealth. This is certainly true for the producers who can take advantage of their mobility to locate themselves in an efficient manner. There is also some evidence that it is true of countries as a whole: a study by the World Bank showed that countries that are most closely integrated in the global economy have on average grown faster than those that are less well integrated.[37] On the other hand, globalization has had negative impacts on the jobs, livelihoods, and economic security of many people. These people have understandably organized to slow the process of economic integration and to seek protection from the harms that global competition can cause.

The global economic crisis that started in 2008 gave additional impetus to such forces. Shrinking economies and rising unemployment increased the pressure on governments to protect jobs by erecting barriers to imports. Even if recent protectionist pressures are resisted, there is likely to be little appetite any time soon for further trade liberalization. In the longer run, the crisis has probably increased the bargaining power of those actors who seek an end to unrestrained capitalism. The fact that a banking crisis in the United States triggered a global economic downturn underscored the risks associated with close economic integration. It also strengthened the case for greater government regulation of financial institutions. Although there are still actors with a strong interest in globalization, the political support for liberalizing policies and the attractiveness of liberal economic ideas weakened. In the political conflict between globalization's winners and losers, recent events have most likely strengthened the hand of the latter.

Although there are reasons to be concerned about how these tensions will play out, economic theory tells us that conflict is not inevitable. As we noted in

---

36. See Organization for Economic Cooperation and Development, *Agricultural Policies in OECD Countries: Monitoring and Evaluation 2007* (Paris: OECD Publishing, 2007).
37. Dollar and Kraay, "Spreading the Wealth."

Chapter 6, while trade liberalization creates winners and losers, the overall benefits generally exceed the economic value of the jobs that may be put in jeopardy. Given this observation, globalization can in theory make everyone better off, but only if some of the gains to the winners are redistributed to compensate those who stand to lose.[38] Hence, pursuing a common interest in prosperity will require a bargain that shares the benefits and institutions of governance capable of upholding such a bargain. The prospects for the latter are where we now turn.

Will Globalization Lead to Global Government?

We live in a world in which companies, goods, and money freely move across national boundaries. As a result, people's economic livelihoods are increasingly influenced by the choices made by actors in other countries. Decisions made by consumers in Canada can influence whether a person in Vietnam has a job. Investment decisions made by a company executive in New York can determine whether a worker in Costa Rica will be able to feed his family. Decisions made by the Chinese government about how to set its exchange rate can influence how much consumers in Australia will pay for Chinese toys and whether a toy manufacturer in Germany can compete. And, as the recent financial crisis has shown, a collapse in the housing market in the United States can cause banks in other countries to fail.

While markets respect national boundaries less and less, the legal reach of governments still ends at their borders. Although states can try to influence one another's policies through threats and promises, the ability to impose taxes, regulate companies, manipulate the supply of money, or dole out welfare benefits to needy people is limited by their territorial reach. As we just saw, however, globalization creates demands for redistribution and regulation on a global scale. The increasing scope of markets from national to global raises the question of whether government will need to expand in scope as well, with national governments giving way to some form of global governance.

Demands for greater global governance may also arise from noneconomic motives. Just as money and goods flow across borders, so too do pollution and other kinds of harms. As we saw in Chapter 12, growing threats to the global environment have propelled a search for new agreements and institutions to promote international cooperation in this area. In addition, advances in communications and information technology mean that problems in one place can be immediately felt around the globe. The genocide in Darfur, the violent suppression of Buddhist monks protesting for democracy in Burma, the repression of women and homosexuals in Iran—news of such events travels instantly around the world through television and the Internet. The ease with which we can now learn about such events intersects with and reinforces some of the developments we saw in

---

38. See, for example, Kenneth Scheve and Matthew Slaughter, "A New Deal for Globalization," *Foreign Affairs* 86, no. 4 (July/August 2007): 34–47.

Chapters 10 and 11: stronger norms regarding human rights and growing activity by transnational advocacy networks to promote those norms and to publicize their violations. As a result, people know more and care more about how foreign governments treat their citizens. The principle of sovereignty—which holds that what governments do within their own boundaries is nobody else's business—is increasingly bumping up against this new reality.

Will globalization render obsolete the current international system, in which territorially defined sovereign states operate without an overarching political authority? Will we witness a transition from anarchy to global government? In considering these questions, we need to think about how the interests generated by globalization influence the demand for new institutions of governance. Who will want new rules, and what kinds of rules will they want? As we will see, globalization generates demands on all sides for new institutions, but it also generates disagreement about the form and content of those institutions.

WHAT DO THEORY AND HISTORY TELL US?

We have seen throughout this book that institutions set out rules of acceptable behavior, create mechanisms for joint decision-making, and provide ways to monitor and enforce compliance with the rules. Institutions are particularly valuable when actors have common interests but face collective action problems because there are incentives to cheat or free ride, when the number of participants is so large that the procedures for making joint decisions (for example, voting rules) have to be regularized, and when the actors interact so frequently that it makes sense to have standing rules rather than to renegotiate the rules every time. This theory tells us that as the potential benefits from cooperation grow, as the number of participants in an interaction grows, and as the frequency of interaction grows, so too grows the demand for institutions. Hence, as processes of globalization expand the depth, scope, and speed of cooperative interactions, it is reasonable to expect that institutions will follow.

The most dramatic example of economic integration driving an expansion of governance is the case of the European Union (EU). The emergence of the EU reflects the remarkable transformation of European relations during the twentieth century, from unprecedented violence to unprecedented cooperation. Wracked by warfare during the first half of the century, Europe is today a peaceful and prosperous continent, where former enemies like France and Germany have close political and economic relations. And the EU is a supranational governance structure unlike any the world has seen before.

The EU started as a relatively modest project when, in 1951, six countries agreed to form the European Coal and Steel Community (ECSC): France, West Germany, Italy, Belgium, the Netherlands, and Luxembourg. These countries were rebuilding after the devastation of World War II and facing a growing threat from the Soviet Union to the east and from communist movements at home. The ECSC created a common market for coal and steel, essentially pooling the production of these strategically important heavy industries. This project had several goals. Economically, it would help promote growth and improve living standards by eliminating restrictions on the movement of coal and steel within the boundaries of the community. Politically, it would cement the alliance among countries that had, only six years before, been deadly enemies.

From these humble beginnings, the project of European integration advanced impressively. As trade within the community grew, the members sought to expand the common market to include other goods. In 1957 came the European Economic Community, which created a customs union—that is, a union of states with low internal tariffs and a common external tariff when trading with the rest of the world. In 1992, this gave way to the European Union, which created a single market among its members, eliminating all barriers to trade. As a result of this process, the volume of intra-European trade has grown dramatically. Today, Europe is the most economically integrated region in the world. About three-quarters of European countries' merchandise exports are bought by other European countries; by comparison, about half of North American or Asian exports stay within their respective regions.[39] In the process, the number of members has grown from the original six to 27 in 2008, with more slated to join in coming years.

Trade integration also led to efforts to stabilize exchange rates (see Chapter 8). In the 1970s, European countries experimented with an exchange rate mechanism to the limit the fluctuation of currencies. When this mechanism broke down in the face of several crises, the demand for stable exchange rates led some EU members to the next logical step: eliminating national currencies altogether and issuing a common European currency, the euro. In 1999, 11 EU members adopted the euro and phased out their own currencies; by 2008, four additional countries had followed suit. Thus, a century that began with Germany and France fighting two major wars ended with those countries using the same money.

Institutional development in Europe has not been limited to the economic realm, as the EU has also created supranational governance structures. It has an executive branch, the European Commission, made up of representatives appointed by each member, and there is a European Parliament elected by voters throughout the region. By treaty, laws made by the EU supersede those made by national governments. To ensure compliance, there is a European Court of Justice, which adjudicates disputes arising from EU laws, and a European Court of Human Rights, which can rule on the human rights practices of member states. EU institutions also oversee several policies that redistribute wealth among countries. About one-third of the EU budget, which is funded by member states, is given to needy areas to support economic and social development. Another 40 percent of the EU budget funds a system of agricultural subsidies that support farm income. Hence, the EU does many things that used to fall under the purview of national governments.

COMING CONFLICTS OVER GLOBAL GOVERNANCE

If economic integration within Europe could bring about such robust regional institutions, it is natural to ask whether globalization could have the same effect on a larger scale. In fact, we have already seen an impressive growth in the number and scale of international organizations over the past 50 years. Figure 13.4 shows estimates for the number of intergovernmental organizations—defined as organizations that have

---

39. World Trade Organization, *World Trade Report 2007* (Geneva: WTO, 2007), Table I.4. Available at www.wto.org/english/res_e/statis_e/its2007_e/section1_e/i04.xls (accessed 1/11/07).

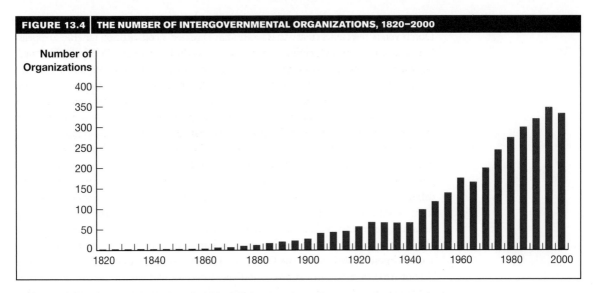

Source: Jon C. Pevehouse, Timothy Nordstrom, and Kevin Warnke, "The COW-2 International Organizations Dataset Version 2.0," *Conflict Management and Peace Science* 21, no. 2 (2004): 101–19.

representation of at least three member states—in existence from 1820 to 2000. The explosive growth of these organizations after World War II is particularly pronounced. While none of these organizations have robust governance roles like the EU, the trend toward increasing institutionalization of international relations is clear.

That said, it does not immediately follow that the experience of the EU at the regional level can be replicated at the global level. European countries have cultural, political, and economic similarities that make close integration among them practical. It is not clear that this model could be scaled up to include a much more heterogeneous set of states. At a more fundamental level, the effort to create global governance will inevitably generate conflict. Recall that while institutions facilitate mutually beneficial cooperation, they are rarely neutral in their distributional effects. The rules inevitably advantage some set of interests over others or empower certain actors over others. Hence, even if everyone agrees that the world needs more and bigger governance structures, they may disagree strongly about the form and content of those institutions.

Indeed, even in Europe, despite all the shared interests and common qualities, the process of building institutions has seen conflicts and reversals.[40] Interstate bargaining over the terms of governance has at times been intense, and despite the enormous benefits of closer economic integration, several states have opted out of some parts of the project. For example, in September 2000, Danish voters rejected joining the monetary union, electing to preserve their national currency in spite of Denmark's strong trade ties with the rest of the Continent. Other EU members, such as Britain and

---

40. For an analysis of interstate bargaining over European integration, see Andrew Moravcsik, *The Choice for Europe: Social Purpose and State Power from Messina to Maastricht* (Ithaca, NY: Cornell University Press, 1998).

Sweden, have likewise chosen not to adopt the euro. Similarly, in 2005, French and Dutch voters rejected a treaty that would have created a constitution for the European Union and streamlined its decision-making procedures. After a "period of reflection," European leaders cobbled together a new reform treaty that would expand the power of European institutions in some areas. But in 2008, Irish voters rejected this treaty. Since EU rules require that such treaties be approved by all member states, the Irish rejection left the process of institutional reform in doubt. Thus, even under the most favorable conditions, the creation of supranational institutions can hit rough waters.

Any effort to strengthen governance on the global level will similarly be rife with conflict. This is most clearly evident when thinking about institutions to govern economic globalization. The winners and losers of globalization have very different interests when it comes to defining the rules. Those actors that benefit from trade and finance have a strong interest in international rules that prevent national governments from erecting obstacles to crossborder flows. Exporters favor institutions that will lead to the elimination of trade barriers. They want rules, such as those enshrined in the GATT and WTO, that facilitate liberalization and delegitimize or even punish protectionism. International traders generally also prefer monetary rules that ensure the convertibility of currencies and lead to stable exchange rates between currencies. Likewise, actors that benefit from foreign investment want rules that lower or eliminate barriers to capital flows, so that money can move freely across borders in search of higher returns. They want institutions, like the IMF, that encourage countries to dismantle capital controls that make it harder for money to flow in and out at a moment's notice. Multinational companies want rules that protect their property rights, so that they can build factories wherever it makes the most economic sense without fear of having those assets seized by foreign governments. Hence, they want to extend the property protections that they enjoy in rich countries to cover poorer countries as well. These companies would also like to see international rules protecting rights to intellectual property. After all, U.S. copyright laws may protect a Hollywood film company from having its films pirated in the United States, but these do little good if the same laws do not extend to China, where large industries have grown up copying and selling Western media and software. In short, the winners of economic globalization have an interest in international institutions that will spread market-friendly policies around the world and limit the ability of national governments to slow this process.

Those actors that stand to lose from globalization also have an interest in greater global governance, but they want these institutions to enforce a very different set of rules. In place of a single-minded push for liberalization, they want rules that permit more opportunities for countries to impose trade barriers or capital controls in order to protect their economies during hard times. Those that worry about a race to the bottom in labor or environmental regulations want these standards harmonized—at a high level—around the world. The race-to-the-bottom logic rests on fact that each government sets its own rules, so governments can be compelled to lower their standards in the competition to attract investment. If, however, there were worldwide standards, this kind of competition could not take place. To this end, labor unions and environmental groups have sought to change the rules of the WTO to permit trade restrictions against countries that do not meet certain standards. Finally, those actors that worry about the distributional effects of globalization would prefer to see global governance structures, like those in the EU, that can engage in redistribution: taxing the rich to give to the poor. Such an institution could create rules about how much foreign aid rich states should give and could oversee the distribution of that aid to needy regions and people.

WHO WILL SET THE RULES?

In addition to conflict over the content of the rules, the extension of global governance can also generate conflicts over the decision-making procedures: that is, who has the ultimate say in making decisions? Which actors and interests have a seat at the table? As we have seen throughout this book, such decisions matter a great deal for the kinds of outcomes that institutions produce.

Most existing international organizations have two features that greatly limit the ability of some actors to influence decision-making. First, representation is at the level of the state—each member state government appoints a representative, generally with the expectation that this person will act on that government's behalf.[41] As a result, how well any given actor is represented in an international body depends on that actor's influence with its home government. Groups or individuals who have little power domestically will similarly have little voice within international institutions, unless some other actor is willing to take up their cause. For example, as antiglobalization groups often point out, weak labor unions and nondemocratic institutions in developing countries mean that those countries' governments do not necessarily represent the interests of their workers. In this view, developing countries resist the inclusion of labor standards in WTO rules because their governments are insensitive to workers' needs. The system of state-level representation replicates at the international level whatever inequalities in political influence exist at the domestic level.

Second, many important international organizations have decision rules that favor some countries over others. We have already seen this several times: the permanent member veto in the UN Security Council, and the weighted voting rules of the IMF and the World Bank. As a result, countries that are wealthy or militarily powerful tend to have disproportionate influence in these bodies.

It is not by sheer chance that existing economic institutions push policies that more closely resemble the wish list of the actors that benefit from globalization than the wish list of those that oppose it. As we have seen, the main beneficiaries of globalization have been exporting and financial interests in developed countries—groups that wield considerable political influence. These actors have had a large role in creating institutions whose rules encourage further liberalization and whose decision-making procedures enshrine their influence.

Future battles over global governance will no doubt involve challenges to these procedures. Indeed, it is now common to hear the criticism that existing international institutions suffer from a democratic deficit: their voting rules are undemocratic, and they represent governments, many of them undemocratic, rather than

---

41. In some institutions, such as international courts, national representatives are not supposed to advance the agenda of the government that appointed them, but rather adhere to some organizational norms. It is not clear how often this ideal works in practice.

people. This deficit is particularly striking given the overall trend toward greater democracy within countries (see Chapter 4). Not only does a majority of states have democratic institutions, but the ideal of democracy has widespread appeal, consistent with growing concerns about human rights discussed in Chapter 11.

Arguments to reform international institutions in a more democratic direction play off this normative ideal, but at the same time they serve a particular set of interests. Those actors that feel threatened by globalization see greater democracy at the international level as a way to bring a new set of actors to the table. One proposal along these lines is to expand the number of permanent member states on the UN Security Council, with seats (and perhaps vetoes) for India, Brazil, and other large developing countries. This move would bring a new set of voices into discussions of global security matters.

More expansively, some actors advocate for more truly democratic forms and processes of representation. For example, imagine what would happen if voting rules in institutions such as the IMF weighted countries by population rather than by wealth. Figure 13.5 explores this scenario. The panel on the left shows the shares of voting power held in the IMF under the institution's current rules. To save space, only the top 10 states by voting power are shown. The ranking

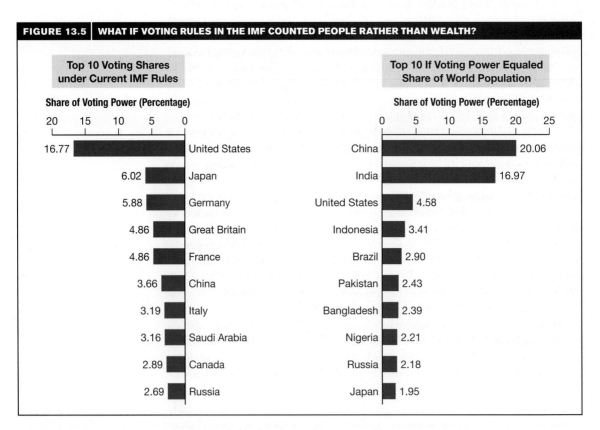

FIGURE 13.5 | WHAT IF VOTING RULES IN THE IMF COUNTED PEOPLE RATHER THAN WEALTH?

Top 10 Voting Shares under Current IMF Rules

Share of Voting Power (Percentage)

16.77	United States
6.02	Japan
5.88	Germany
4.86	Great Britain
4.86	France
3.66	China
3.19	Italy
3.16	Saudi Arabia
2.89	Canada
2.69	Russia

Top 10 If Voting Power Equaled Share of World Population

Share of Voting Power (Percentage)

China	20.06
India	16.97
United States	4.58
Indonesia	3.41
Brazil	2.90
Pakistan	2.43
Bangladesh	2.39
Nigeria	2.21
Russia	2.18
Japan	1.95

Source: IMF voting power from www.imf.org/external/np/sec/memdir/members.htm. Population figures from the World Bank at http://siteresources.worldbank.org/DATASTATISTICS/Resources/POP.pdf (accessed 7/1/08).

closely matches the ranking of these countries' GDPs, with the United States possessing by far the largest bloc of votes. The panel on the right shows what would happen if the rules were changed so that voting shares were determined by each country's share of world population. Under this hypothetical scenario, the world's developing countries would have a much larger say in the operations of the IMF. Such a reform would dramatically change the kinds of policies the IMF pursues, presumably leading to greater redistribution. Of course, the current voting rules reflect the fact that the developed countries provide the bulk of the money that the IMF relies on to stabilize financial markets. If the rules were changed in a way that diminished the developed countries' influence too much, they would keep their money and leave the institution impoverished. Any reform in the direction of greater democratization would have to be modest in order to give wealthy states an interest in participating.

Dealing with the problem of nondemocratic governments is another challenge. An international parliament elected by people throughout the world is probably impractical and undesirable. The U.S. House of Representatives, one of the larger legislatures in the world, has 435 members each representing a district with about 650,000 people. To keep the ratio of representatives to constituents about the same, an international parliament would need about 10,000 representatives. Moreover, supervising the elections, particularly in countries without democratic institutions, would be challenging if not impossible. A more modest reform would be to institutionalize a role for nongovernmental organizations (NGOs) that speak for the interests of unrepresented groups. In recent years, NGOs have been invited to attend international meetings, though as yet they do not have formal voting rights in international organizations.

Given the obstacles of altering international institutions built around states, it is not surprising that some recent reform efforts have sought to bypass these institutions altogether and develop new forms of governance. In recent years, transnational advocacy networks (TANs) have pressured industries into adopting codes of conduct that regulate companies' environmental, labor, and social policies.[42] Rather than relying on governments to enact such regulations, TANs have lobbied industries to regulate themselves. Lacking the same coercive or regulatory power of a government, these groups instead try to use publicity and the threat of consumer boycotts to encourage this process. For example, when international negotiations aimed at preserving rainforest failed in the early 1990s, two environmental groups, the World Wildlife Fund and Greenpeace, joined together to bargain directly with the timber industry and wood products manufacturers. The result was the Forest Stewardship Council (FSC), which brought together industries, NGOs, and indigenous peoples to establish strict guidelines aimed at ensuring that forests are managed in a sustainable manner. The FSC certifies those products that have been harvested according to the guidelines, and stores are encouraged to sell—and consumers are encouraged to buy—certified goods. Under

---

42. For a review of this development, see Virginia Haufler, "Globalization and Industry Self-Regulation," in *Governance in a Global Economy: Political Authority in Transition,* ed. Miles Kahler and David A. Lake (Princeton: Princeton University Press, 2003), 226–56.

The Forest Stewardship Council is a transnational institution that establishes guidelines related to the timber industry. Concerned that governments are not doing enough to preserve rainforests, the FSC works directly with the timber industry, NGOs, and indigenous peoples to protect forests. Here, a logging truck drives through a forest in Brazil.

pressure from environmentalists, major wood-products retailers like Home Depot and Ikea participate in the program.[43] The result is a transnational institution that articulates standards of behavior, provides mechanisms for monitoring compliance, and establishes rules for joint decision-making—but which does not have a single state in its membership. Similar codes of conduct now regulate a wide range of corporate behaviors.

As encouraging as such developments are, advocates of reforming global governance face an uphill battle. Current institutions and policies are the way they are because there were powerful actors who wanted them that way. It is hard to see why these actors would consent to a change in decision-making procedures that would dilute their influence. Institutions will change only if there is a change in interests of powerful actors and/or a change in the power of actors that alters the bargaining interaction between them. If those actors that benefit from globalization realize that their interests require some redistribution to the losers, then change may come from within. Alternatively, if the losers from globalization become better organized and politically powerful, they may be able to strike a better deal and create institutions more to their liking.

The danger, of course, is that this interaction will not play out peacefully. Those actors that feel they are losing out may decide to pursue their grievances through violence. In January 1994, there was a rebellion in the Mexican state of Chiapas by a group known as the Zapatista National Liberation Army. Although there were long-standing grievances about the treatment and welfare of the local population, the violence coincided with the signing of the North American Free Trade Agreement, which added economic insecurity to the mix. There are also those who see terrorism by militant Islamists as part of a "jihad vs. McWorld"—that is, a reaction against the globalization of Western capitalism and consumerism.[44] It is worth recalling that some of the longest and deadliest wars in recent decades have occurred not between states, but within them—that is, over issues of governance. Although international anarchy needs to be tamed by institutions to promote cooperation and contain conflict, a transition toward stronger global governance will not necessarily be peaceful—or successful.

Conclusion: Can Our Common Interests Prevail?

Every case considered in this chapter points toward a similar conclusion. Changes in technology, the distribution of resources, and ideas have the potential to create winners and losers. Economic growth and the acquisition of deadly military

---

43. Haufler, "Globalization and Industry Self-Regulation," 246–47.
44. Benjamin Barber, *Jihad vs. McWorld: How Globalism and Tribalism Are Reshaping the World* (New York: Ballantine Books, 1996).

technologies can make some states and actors more powerful and hence more threatening to others. The globalization of economic activity, driven by advances in transportation, communications, and information technology, has generated enormous wealth for some and insecurity for others. And the push for greater global governance will inevitably advantage some actors over others. The resulting clash of interests will color future interactions, leading to political, economic, and possibly military conflict. Those actors that stand to lose may lash out in the hopes of stopping the underlying changes, whether through preventive war or through efforts to disrupt global economic activity. Those actors that stand to win may try to exploit their gains through force and/or by cementing their political power in domestic and international institutions.

Set against this gloomy possibility is the recognition that change also generates common interests. The destructive potential of today's weapons means that the common interest in peace looms large relative to whatever gains could be won through war. As a result, states have an incentive to manage the rise of new powers and the spread of weapons of mass destruction in a peaceful manner. The wealth that can be created by globalization means that everyone can potentially gain, as long as the process is governed in a way that redistributes some of the gain to those actors that stand to lose. In short, the challenges posed by a changing world can be met if the winners recognize and act on a far-sighted interest in spreading the benefits.

Will this happen? The history of international relations warns us not to be overly optimistic. There are real hatreds in the world, and people do not always act on the basis of an enlightened self-interest. World politics will never be free of conflicting interests and hostile interactions, and institutions will never entirely eliminate these conflicts through rules and redistribution. And yet, we have also seen unmistakable signs of progress. Interstate war is not obsolete, but it is less frequent today than in the past. Although many people around the world still live in poverty, there have been tremendous advances in wealth and living standards. Democracy, considered a pernicious and destabilizing political form only two centuries ago, has spread to every continent, giving individuals greater say in the decisions that affect their lives. International cooperation to stop civil conflict and genocide, to protect human rights, and to safeguard the global environment has advanced significantly, even if these efforts fall short of the ideal.

We opened this book with the story of how a lone man prevented war between Arabs and Jews in 1921 by appealing to their shared interest in peace and prosperity. Although the peace of that day did not last forever, his efforts were still worthwhile. Progress is possible, even if perfection is not. Though conflicts will always remain, we have not yet exhausted all of the opportunities to recognize and act on humanity's common interests.

For Further Reading

Frieden, Jeffry A. *Global Capitalism: Its Fall and Rise in the Twentieth Century.* New York: Norton, 2006. Explains the development of the global economy over the last century.

Gilpin, Robert. *War and Change in World Politics.* Cambridge: Cambridge University Press, 1981. Develops a general theory of the rise and fall of global leaders and argues that this theory explains major wars over the last several centuries.

Goldberg, Pinelopi Koujianou, and Nina Pavcnik. "Distributional Effects of Globalization in Developing Countries." *Journal of Economic Literature* 45 (March 2007): 39–82. Reviews the theories and evidence on how globalization affects inequality in developing countries.

Johnston, Alastair Iain. *Social States: China in International Institutions, 1980–2000.* Princeton, NJ: Princeton University Press, 2008. Argues that China's increasing engagement with international institutions can change its foreign policy outlook in a way that leads to greater cooperation.

Kahler, Miles, and David A. Lake, eds. *Governance in a Global Economy: Political Authority in Transition.* Princeton, NJ: Princeton University Press, 2003. Surveys the main developments in global governance that are taking place in response to globalization.

Moravcsik, Andrew. *The Choice for Europe: Social Purpose and State Power from Messina to Maastricht.* Ithaca, NY: Cornell University Press, 1998. Examines the interests and bargaining interactions that brought about the institutions of the European Union.

Nye, Joseph S., Jr., and John D. Donahue, eds. *Governance in a Globalizing World.* Washington, DC: Brookings Institution Press, 2000. Examines how globalization affects governance institutions within and between states.

Rodrik, Dani. *Has Globalization Gone Too Far?* Washington, DC: Institute for International Economics, 1997. Provides a balanced account of the costs and benefits of economic globalization.

Sagan, Scott D. "Why Do States Build Nuclear Weapons? Three Models in Search of a Bomb." *International Security* 21, no. 3 (Winter 1996/1997): 54–86. Argues that security needs, domestic politics, and concerns about international status explain why some states try to acquire nuclear weapons while others do not.

Sagan, Scott D., and Kenneth N. Waltz. *The Spread of Nuclear Weapons: A Debate Renewed,* 2nd ed. New York: Norton, 2003. Presents a debate between two scholars over whether the spread of nuclear weapons is good or bad for the world.

Scheve, Kenneth, and Matthew Slaughter. "A New Deal for Globalization." *Foreign Affairs* 86, no. 4 (July/August 2007): 34–47. Argues that globalization can be made sustainable only if some of the income gains to the winners are redistributed to the economic losers.

Shirk, Susan. *China: Fragile Superpower.* New York: Oxford University Press, 2007. Examines how domestic politics within China will determine whether its rise as a global power takes place peacefully.

FIND REVIEW AND STUDY MATERIALS ONLINE AT WWNORTON.COM/STUDYSPACE

Glossary

absolute advantage The ability of a country or firm to produce more of a particular good or service than other countries or firms using the same amount of effort and resources.

accountability The ability to punish or reward leaders for the decisions they make, as when frequent fair elections enable voters to hold elected officials responsible for their actions by granting or withholding access to political office.

actors The basic unit for the analysis of international politics; can be individuals or groups of people with common interests.

adjustable peg A monetary system of fixed but adjustable rates. Governments are expected to keep their currencies fixed for extensive periods, but are permitted to adjust the exchange rate from time to time as economic conditions change.

agenda-setting power A "first mover" advantage that helps an actor to secure a more favorable bargain.

alliances Institutions that help their members cooperate militarily in the event of a war.

anarchy The absence of a central authority with the ability to make and enforce laws that bind all actors.

appreciate In terms of a currency, to increase in value in terms of other currencies.

audience costs Negative repercussions for failing to follow through on a threat or to honor a commitment.

balance of power A situation in which the military capabilities of two states or groups of states are roughly equal.

bandwagoning A strategy in which states join forces with the stronger side in a conflict.

Bank for International Settlements (BIS) One of the oldest international financial organizations, created in 1930. Its members include the world's principal central banks, and under its auspices they attempt to cooperate in the financial realm.

bargaining An interaction in which actors must choose outcomes that make one better off at the expense of another. Bargaining is redistributive: it involves allocating a fixed sum of value between different actors.

bargaining range The set of deals that both parties in a bargaining interaction prefer to the reversion outcome. When the reversion outcome is war, the bargaining range is the set of deals that both sides prefer to war.

bilateral investment treaty (BIT) An agreement between two countries about the conditions for private investment across borders. Most BITs include provisions to protect an investment from government discrimination or expropriation without compensation, as well as establishing mechanisms to resolve disputes.

boomerang model A process through which NGOs in one state are able to activate transnational linkages to bring pressure from other states on their own governments.

Bretton Woods monetary system The monetary order negotiated among the World War II allies in 1944, which lasted until the 1970s and which was based on a U.S. dollar tied to gold. Other currencies were fixed to the dollar but were permitted to adjust their exchange rates.

brinksmanship A strategy in which adversaries take actions that increase the risk of accidental war, with the hope that the other will "blink," or lose its nerve, first and make concessions.

bureaucracy The collection of organizations—including the military, the diplomatic corps, and the intelligence agencies—that carry out most tasks of governance within the state.

chlorofluorocarbons (CFCs) Chemical compounds used in aerosols, insulating materials, refrigerator and air conditioner coolants, and other products. CFCs are widely banned today due to their damaging effect on the ozone layer.

civil war A war in which the main participants are within the same state, such as the government and a rebel group.

coercion The threat or imposition of costs on other actors in order to change their behavior. Means of international coercion include military force, economic sanctions, and embargos.

coercive diplomacy The use of threats to influence the outcome of a bargaining interaction.

collaboration A type of cooperative interaction in which actors gain from working together but nonetheless have incentives to not comply with any agreement.

collective action problems Obstacles to cooperation that occur when actors have incentives to collaborate but each acts in anticipation that others will pay the costs of cooperation.

collective security organizations Broad-based institutions that promote peace and security among their members. Examples include the League of Nations and the United Nations.

commodity cartels Associations of producers of commodities (raw materials and agricultural products) that restrict world supply and thereby cause the price of the goods to rise.

common pool resources Goods that are available to everyone, such as open ocean fisheries; it is difficult to exclude anyone from using the common pool, but one user's consumption reduces the amount available for others.

comparative advantage The ability of a country or firm to produce a particular good or service more efficiently than other goods or services, such that its resources are most efficiently employed in this activity. The comparison is to the efficiency of other economic activities the actor might undertake, not to the efficiency of other countries or firms.

compellence An effort to change the status quo through the threat of force.

cooperation An interaction in which two or more actors adopt policies that make at least one actor better off relative to the status quo without making others worse off.

coordination A type of cooperative interaction in which actors benefit from all making the same choices and subsequently have no incentive to not comply.

credibility Believability. A credible threat is a threat that the recipient believes will be carried out. A credible commitment is a commitment or promise that the recipient believes will be honored.

crisis bargaining A bargaining interaction in which at least one actor threatens to use force in the event that its demands are not met.

decolonization The process of shedding colonial possessions, especially the rapid end of the European empires in Africa, Asia, and the Caribbean between the 1940s and the 1960s.

default To fail to make payments on a debt.

democracy A political system in which candidates compete for political office through frequent, fair elections in which a sizable portion of the adult population can vote.

democratic peace The observation that there are few, if any, clear cases of war between mature democratic states.

depreciate In terms of a currency, to decrease in value in terms of other currencies.

depression A severe downturn in the business cycle, typically associated with a major decline in economic activity, production, and investment; a severe contraction of credit; and sustained high unemployment.

deterrence An effort to preserve the status quo through the threat of force.

devalue To reduce the value of one currency in terms of other currencies.

diversionary incentive The incentive that state leaders have to start international crises in order to rally public support at home.

exchange rate The price at which one currency is exchanged for another.

export-oriented industrialization (EOI) A set of policies, originally pursued starting in the late 1960s by several East Asian countries, to spur manufacturing for export, often through subsidies and incentives for export production.

externalities Costs or benefits for stakeholders other than the actor undertaking an action. When an externality exists, the decisionmaker does not bear all the costs or reap all the gains from his or her action.

extremists Actors whose interests are not widely shared by others; individuals or groups that are politically weak relative to the demands they make.

first-strike advantage The situation that arises when military technology, military strategies, and/or geography give a significant advantage to whichever state attacks first in a war.

fixed exchange rate An exchange rate policy under which a government commits itself to keep its currency at or around a specific value in terms of another currency or a commodity, such as gold.

floating exchange rate An exchange rate policy under which a government permits its currency to be traded on the open market without direct government control or intervention.

foreign direct investment (FDI) Investment in a foreign country via the acquisition of a local facility or the establishment of a new facility. Direct investors maintain managerial control of the foreign operation.

Framework Convention on Climate Change (FCCC) An international agreement enacted in 1992, and entered into force in 1994, that provided an overall framework for intergovernmental efforts on climate change.

free ride To fail to contribute to a public good while benefiting from the contributions of others.

General Agreement on Tariffs and Trade (GATT) An international institution created in 1948 in which member countries committed to reduce barriers to trade and to provide similar trading conditions to all other members. In 1995, the GATT was replaced by the World Trade Organization (WTO).

genocide Intentional and systematic killing aimed at eliminating an identifiable group of people, such as an ethnic or religious group.

global climate change Human-induced change in the environment, especially from the emissions of greenhouse gases, leading to higher temperatures around the globe.

gold standard The monetary system that prevailed between about 1870 and 1914, in which countries tied their currencies to gold at a legally fixed price.

Group of 77 A coalition of developing countries in the United Nations, formed in 1964 with 77 members; it has grown to over 130 members but maintains the original name.

Heckscher-Ohlin trade theory The theory that a country will export goods that make intensive use of the factors of production in which it is well endowed. Thus, a labor-rich country will export goods that make intensive use of labor.

hegemony The predominance of one nation-state over others.

human rights The rights possessed by all individuals by virtue of being human, regardless of their status as citizens of particular states or members of a group or organization.

import substituting industrialization (ISI) A set of policies, pursued by most developing countries from the 1930s through the 1980s, to reduce imports and encourage domestic manufacturing, often through trade barriers, subsidies to manufacturing, and state ownership of basic industries.

incomplete information A situation in which parties in a strategic interaction lack information about other parties' interests and/or capabilities.

individual petition A right that permits individuals to petition appropriate international legal bodies directly if they believe a state has violated their rights.

indivisible good A good that cannot be divided without diminishing its value.

infrastructure Basic structures necessary for social activity, such as transportation and telecommunications networks, and power and water supply.

institutions Sets of rules, known and shared by the community, that structure political interactions in specific ways.

interactions The ways in which the choices of two or more actors combine to produce political outcomes.

interest groups Groups of individuals with common interests that organize to influence public policy in a manner that benefits their members.

interests What actors want to achieve through political action; their preferences over the outcomes that might result from their political choices.

International Bill of Rights Refers collectively to the UDHR, the ICCPR, and the ICESCR. Together, these three agreements form the core of the international human rights regime.

International Covenant on Civil and Political Rights (ICCPR) The agreement completed in 1966 and in force from 1976 that details the basic civil and political rights of individuals and nations.

International Covenant on Economic, Social, and Cultural Rights (ICESCR) The agreement completed in 1966 and in force from 1976 that specifies the basic economic, social, and cultural rights of individuals and nations.

International Criminal Court (ICC) A court of last resort for human rights cases that possesses jurisdiction only if the accused is a national of a state party, the crime took place on the territory of a state party, or the United Nations Security Council has referred the case to the prosecutor.

International Monetary Fund (IMF) A major international economic institution that was established in 1944 to manage international monetary relations and that has gradually reoriented itself to focus on the international financial system, especially debt and currency crises.

international monetary regime A formal or informal arrangement among governments to govern relations among their currencies, and which is shared by most countries in the world economy.

interstate war A war in which the main participants are states.

iteration Repeated interactions with the same partners.

Kyoto Protocol An amendment to the United Nations Framework Convention on Climate Change, adopted in 1997 and entered into force in 2005, that establishes specific targets for reducing emissions of carbon dioxide and five other greenhouse gases.

League of Nations A collective international security organization formed in the aftermath of World War I. The League was supplanted by the United Nations after World War II and was dissolved in 1946.

less developed countries (LDCs) Countries at a relatively low level of economic development.

linkage The linking of cooperation on one issue to interactions on a second issue.

mercantilism An economic doctrine based on a belief that military power and economic influence were complements; applied especially to colonial empires in the sixteenth through eighteenth centuries. Mercantilist policies favored the mother country over its colonies and over its competitors.

military-industrial complex An alliance between military leaders and the industries that benefit from international conflict, such as arms manufacturers.

monetary policy An important tool of national governments to influence broad macroeconomic conditions such as unemployment, inflation, and economic growth. Typically, governments alter their monetary policies by changing national interest rates or exchange rates.

Montreal Protocol An international treaty, signed in 1989, that is designed to protect the ozone layer by phasing out the production of a number of CFCs and other chemical compounds.

most favored nation (MFN) status A status established by most modern trade agreements guaranteeing that the signatories will extend to each other any favorable trading terms offered in agreements with third parties.

multinational corporation (MNC) An enterprise that operates in a number of countries, with production or service facilities outside its country of origin.

national interests Interests attributed to the state itself, usually security and power.

New International Economic Order A reorganization of the management of the international economy demanded by LDCs in the 1970s in order to make it more favorable to developing nations.

nonderogable rights Rights that cannot be suspended for any reason, including at times of public emergency.

nonexcludable Characterizing a public good; if the good is available to one actor to consume, then other actors cannot be prevented from consuming it as well.

nongovernmental organizations (NGOs) Private organizations not directly affiliated with national governments and usually focusing on social, economic, and political change in a country or region.

nonrival in consumption Characterizing a public good; one actor's consumption of the good does not diminish the quantity available for others to consume as well.

nontariff barriers to trade Obstacles to imports other than tariffs (trade taxes). Examples include restrictions on the number of products that can be imported (quantitative restrictions, or quotas); regulations that favor domestic over imported products; and other measures that discriminate against foreign goods or services.

norms Standards of behavior for actors with a given identity; norms define what actions are "right" or appropriate under particular circumstances.

norms life cycle A three-stage model of how norms diffuse within a population and achieve a "taken-for-granted" status.

North Atlantic Treaty Organization (NATO) An alliance formed in 1949 among the United States, Canada, and most of the states of Western Europe in response to the threat posed by the Soviet Union. The alliance requires the members to consider an attack on any one of them as an attack on all.

oligopolistic Characterizing an industry whose markets are dominated by a few firms.

outbidding A strategy of terrorist attacks designed to demonstrate a capability for leadership and commitment relative to another, similar terrorist group.

outside options The alternatives to bargaining with a specific actor.

overexploitation Consumption of a good at a rate that is collectively undesirable, even if it is efficient from the view of any single actor.

ozone layer Part of the lower stratosphere, approximately six to 30 miles above the earth, with relatively high concentrations of ozone (O_3), which blocks harmful ultraviolet (UV) radiation.

Pax Britannica "British Peace," a century-long period beginning with Napoleon's defeat at Waterloo in 1815 and ending with the outbreak of World War I in 1914 during which Britain's economic and diplomatic influence contributed to economic openness and relative peace.

peace-enforcement operation A military operation in which force is used to make and/or enforce peace among warring parties that have not agreed to end their fighting.

peacekeeping operation An operation in which troops and observers are deployed to monitor a cease-fire or peace agreement.

Peace of Westphalia The settlement that ended the Thirty Years' War in 1648; often said to have created the modern state system because it included a general recognition of the principles of sovereignty and nonintervention.

permanent five (P5) The five permanent members of the UN Security Council: the United States, Great Britain, France, the Soviet Union (now Russia), and China.

portfolio investment Investment in a foreign country via the purchase of stocks (equities), bonds, or other financial instruments. Portfolio investors do not exercise managerial control of the foreign operation.

power The ability of Actor A to get Actor B to do something that B would otherwise not do; the ability to get the other side to make concessions and to avoid having to make concessions oneself.

preemptive war A war fought with the anticipation that an attack by the other side is imminent.

preventive war A war fought with the intention of preventing an adversary from becoming stronger in the future. Preventive wars arise because states whose power is increasing cannot commit not to exploit that power in future bargaining interactions.

primary products Raw materials and agricultural products, typically unprocessed or only slightly processed. The primary sectors are distinguished from secondary sectors (industry) and tertiary sectors (services).

prisoners of conscience (POCs) A label coined and used by the human rights organization Amnesty International to refer to individuals imprisoned solely because of the peaceful expression of their beliefs.

protectionism The imposition of barriers to restrict imports. Commonly used protectionist devices include tariffs, quantitative restrictions (quotas), and other nontariff barriers.

provocation A strategy of terrorist attacks intended to provoke the target government into making a disproportionate response that alienates moderates in the terrorists' home society or in other sympathetic audiences.

public goods Individually and socially desirable goods that are nonexcludable and nonrival in consumption, such as national defense.

quantitative restrictions (quotas) Quantitative limits placed on the import of particular goods.

rally effect The tendency for people to become more supportive of their country's government in response to dramatic international events, such as crises or wars.

recession A sharp slowdown in the rate of economic growth and economic activity.

reciprocity In international trade relations, a mutual agreement to lower tariffs and other barriers to trade. Reciprocity involves an implicit or explicit arrangement for one government to exchange trade policy concessions with another.

resolve The willingness of an actor to endure costs in order to acquire some good.

Ricardo-Viner (specific-factors) model A model of trade relations that emphasizes the sector in which factors of production are employed, rather than the nature of the factor itself. This differentiates it from the Heckscher-Ohlin approach, for which the nature of the factor—labor, land, capital—is the principal consideration.

risk-return tradeoff In crisis bargaining, the tradeoff between trying to get a better deal and trying to avoid a war.

Security Council The main governing body of the United Nations; it has the authority to identify threats to international peace and security and to prescribe the organization's response, including military and/or economic sanctions.

sovereign lending Loans from private financial institutions in one country to sovereign governments in other countries.

sovereignty The expectation that states have legal and political supremacy—or ultimate authority—within their territorial boundaries.

spoiling A strategy of terrorist attacks intended to sabotage a prospective peace between the target and moderate leadership from the terrorists' home society.

state A central authority with the ability to make and enforce laws, rules, and decisions within a specified territory.

Stolper-Samuelson theorem The theory that protection benefits the scarce factor of production. This view flows from the Heckscher-Ohlin approach; if a country imports goods that make intensive use of its scarce factor, then limiting imports will help that factor. So in a labor-scarce country, labor benefits from protection and loses from trade liberalization.

tariff A tax imposed on imports; this raises the domestic price of the imported good and may be applied for the purpose of protecting domestic producers from foreign competition.

terms of trade The relationship between a country's export prices and its import prices.

terrorism The use or threatened use of violence "against noncombatant targets" by individuals or nonstate groups for political ends.

theory A logically consistent set of statements that explains a phenomenon of interest.

trade barrier Any government limitation on the international exchange of goods. Examples include tariffs, quantitative restrictions (quotas), import licenses, requirements that governments buy only domestically produced goods, and health and safety standards that discriminate against foreign goods.

transnational advocacy network (TAN) A set of individuals and nongovernmental organizations acting in pursuit of a normative objective.

Treaty of Versailles The peace treaty between the Allies and Germany that formally ended World War I on June 28, 1919.

United Nations (UN) A collective security organization founded in 1945 after World War II. With over 190 members, the UN includes all recognized states.

Universal Declaration of Human Rights (UDHR) Adopted by the United Nations General Assembly in 1948, this declaration defines a "common standard of achievement for all peoples" and forms the foundation of modern human rights law.

veto power The ability to prevent the passage of a measure through a unilateral act, such as a single negative vote.

Vienna Convention A framework convention adopted in 1985 to regulate activities, especially emissions of CFCs, that damage the ozone layer.

war An event involving the organized use of military force by at least two parties that satisfies some minimum threshold of severity.

Warsaw Pact A military alliance formed in 1955 to bring together the Soviet Union and its Cold War allies in Eastern Europe and elsewhere. It dissolved on March 31, 1991, as the Cold War ended.

Washington Consensus An array of policy recommendations generally advocated by developed-country economists and policymakers starting in the 1980s, including trade liberalization, privatization, openness to foreign investment, and restrictive monetary and fiscal policies.

World Bank An important international institution that provides loans at below-market interest rates to developing countries, typically to enable them to carry out development projects.

World Trade Organization (WTO) An institution created in 1995 to succeed the GATT and to govern international trade relations. The WTO encourages and polices the multilateral reduction of barriers to trade, and it oversees the resolution of trade disputes.

Credits

Index

Page numbers in *italics* refer to illustrations.

Hammarskjold, Dag, 211

Hariri, Rafik, 372

Hathaway, Oona, 428*n*, 431

Haufler, Virginia, 403*n*, 527*n*, 528*n*

Hawes, Michael Brewster, 273

Hawkins, Darren G., 422*n*

Heartbeat International, 370

Heckscher, Eli, 222

Heckscher-Ohlin trade theory, 222–24, *223*, 240
    foreign investment and, 265–66
    international migration and, 290

hegemonic stability, theory of, 242

hegemony, defined, 10

Hegre, Havard, 154*n*

Held, David, 403*n*

Helsinki Accords (1975), 424, 431, 432, 433, 435

Helwege, Ann, 262*n*

Henkin, Louis, 70*n*

Heston, Alan, 335*n*

Hezbollah, 402

Hiscox, Michael J., 232*n*, 236*n*

History of the Peloponnesian War (Thucydides), 80

Hitler, Adolf, 84, 99, *180*, 186, 504
    foreign policy and ideology of, 136
    rise of, 165–66

Hobbes, Thomas, 8, 427

Hobson, J. A., 143, 148, 151

Ho Chi Minh, 61

Hochschild, Adam, 345*n*

Holsti, Kalevi J., 86*n*

Holy Alliance, 12

Homeland Security Department, U.S., 399

Hong Kong, 279, 325, 352

host nation agreement, 196

House of Representatives, U.S., 68, 228, 235, 527
    agriculture committee of, 234

Hudson's Bay Company, 8

Hufbauer, Gary, 217*n*

Hull, Cordell, 224, 239*n*, 252

human capital, 289–90

human rights, 134, 178, 190, 247, 364, 365, 370, 375, *403*, 406, 409–42, *421*, 521, 529
    agreements on, *see* human rights agreements
    apartheid issue and, *408*, 409–10
    Asian values and, 416

boomerang effect and, 435
    CIRI database and, 430
    civil conflicts and, 424, 426
    criticism of, 416–17
    CSCE and, 431–32
    domestic pressure and, 433–35, 436
    economic sanctions and, 418–19, 437
    global abuses of, 430, *430*
    gun control issue and, 374
    ICC and, 438, 439–40
    inconsistent enforcement of, 423–33, 436, 441
    indirect monitoring and, 380
    individual petition principle and, 436–37
    institutions and, 442
    interactions and, 442
    interests and, 442
    labor movement and, 424–25
    MNCs and, 284
    NGOs and, 424
    nonderogable, 418
    nonintervention principle and, 435–36
    norms and, 417–18
    observing laws of, 426–32
    philosophic tradition of, 412, 416
    prisoners of conscience and, 418
    protection of, 432–41
    punishment for violations of, 432–33
    rates of abuse of, 430, *430*
    regional conflicts and, 424
    RTA's and, 425, 440–41
    sovereignty principle and, 435–36
    state-sponsored violations of, 426–27
    taking action on, 433–36
    TANs and, 421, 424, 432, *432*, 435, 441
    trade embargoes and, 434
    universal jurisdiction principle and, 437–38
    U.S.-China rivalry and, 508–9
    violations of, 419–22

human rights agreements, 422–31
    democracies and, 422–23, 424
    EU and, 423
    linkage and, 423
    moral and philosophical motives for, 423–24

ratification and violation of, 428–31
    self-interest and, 424–26

Human Rights Watch, 380, 424

Humphreys, Macartan, 343*n*

Hungary, 178
    1931 currency crisis in, 321
    Soviet invasion of, 27

Hunter, Wendy A., 339*n*

Hurd, Ian, 193*n*

Hussein, Saddam, 33, 34, *40*, 46, 48–49, 50, 51, 59, 60, 61, 65, 72–73, 90, 104, 109, 132, 178, 209, 210, 433, 497
    human rights record of, 434, 435
    onset of Iraq War and, 41–43
    onset of Persian Gulf War and, 94–95, *95*, 97–98, 99, 160

Huth, Paul K., 89

Hutus, 205

Hyde, Susan D., 375*n*

hyperinflation, 20–21, 22, 262

IBM, 284

Iceland, 32, 240, 453, 470

Ikea, 528

immigration, 14

imperialism, 263
    Hobson's theory of, 143, 148, 151

Import Substituting Industrialization (ISI), 350–52, *351*, 353
    definition of, 350

incomplete information, 96, 161
    in debtor-creditor interactions, 274–75
    financial relations and, 274
    onset of Gulf War and, 94–95, *95*
    Persian Gulf War and, 94–95, *95*, 98–99
    terrorism and, 382, 389–90, 392
    war and, 94–97, 104–5, 119, 124

Inconvenient Truth, An (film), 447

India, 29, 210, 227, 263, *337*, 460, 461, 465, 493, 506, 508, 515, 526
    economic growth, 332–33, 354
    ISI in, 352
    in Kargil War, 164, 492
    Kashmir conflict and, 87, 123, 164, 166
    migration from, 290
    nuclear weapons of, 487, 490, 495, 497
    Ottawa Convention and, 367

India (continued)
    protectionism in, 238
    trade specialization and, 223
    world trade and, 239
individual petition, principle of,
        436–37
indivisible good:
    compensation and, 118
    definition of, 111
    dividing, 117–18
    shared control and, 117–18
    war and, 111–15, 117–18, 119, 124
Indochina, 23
Indonesia, 29, *190, 223, 264, 271*
    debt crisis of 1997–1998 in, 275–76,
        278–80
    foreign investment in, 264
Industrial Revolution, 10, 412
inflation, 262, 302, 303, 316, 322, 518
Information and Communications
        Technology (ICT), 516, 520
infrared radiation, 478, 481
infrastructure, 345
    definition of, 336
Institutional Revolutionary Party
        (Partido Revolucionario
        Institucional) (PRI), Mexican,
        323
institutions, 3, 43, 62–72, 165, 251
    alliances and, 212
    anarchy and, 63–64
    bargaining interest and, 161
    cooperation and, 56–57, 63–67
    and costs of joint decision-making,
        66–67
    democracy and, 155
    development and, 361
    domestic politics and, 129, 132–34,
        167
    environment and, 467–71, 474
    of financial relations, 275–77, 293
    and following rules, 69–72
    human rights and, 442
    international, *see* alliances; collective
        security organizations
    and international environmental
        cooperation, 467–71
    international trade and, 239–48
    monetary relations and, 328
    policy bias and, 68–69, 70
    political, 235–37
    Prisoner's Dilemma and, 63

resolving disputes and, 67
in review, 73
standards of behavior and, 64–65
TAN's and, 406
trade and, 219, 253
verifying compliance and, 65–66
war and, 120
Intel, 284–85
interactions, 3, 48–50, 72
    actors and, 48–50, 75–76
    alliances and, 212
    bargaining and, 80–81
    best response strategy and, 49
    between host countries and MNCs,
        285–87
    and change in relative power, 503–4
    coercive, 60
    debtor-creditor, 272–75
    development and, 361
    domestic politics and, 132–34, 167
    environment and, 474
    financial relations and, 293
    game theory and, *see* game theory
    globalization and, 521
    hegemonic stability and, 242
    between host country and MNCs,
        284–85
    human rights and, 442
    iteration and, 57, 454
    monetary relations and, 328
    repeated, 243
    in review, 73
    strategic, 49, 242–44
    TANs and, 406
    trade and, 219, 239–44, 253
    war and, 120
    see also bargaining; cooperation
Inter-American Development Bank,
        268, 287
interest groups:
    definition of, 133–34
    small, 149–51
interest rates, 313, 316
    currency collapse and, 321–22
    currency value and, 301–2
    exchange rates and, 306
    value and, 301–2
interests, 3, 43, 72, 165
    actors and, 46–48
    alliances and, 212
    bargaining and, 179–80
    democracy and, 161–62

development and, 338–39, 361
domestic politics and, 130–34,
        167
economic policy and, 230–33
environment and, 474
financial relations and, 293
of host country in MNCs, 284–85
human rights and, 442
labor rights and, 379
monetary relations and, 328
national, 46–47, 130–32
organization of, 233–35
political institutions and, 235–37
protectionism and, 233–35
in review, 73
schools of, 45
TANs and, 371–73, 406
territorial, 90
trade and, 253
variety of, 44–45
war and, 120, 130–34
intergovernmental organizations,
        522–23, *523*
Intergovernmental Panel on Climate
        Change (IPCC), 445, 447, 481,
        482
Interim Force in Lebanon, U.N.,
        191
International Atomic Energy Agency
        (IAEA), 65, *65,* 70, 71, 116,
        496–97, *496,* 498, 499
International Bill of Rights, 414–16
International Campaign to Ban
        Landmines (ICBL), *366, 367,
        368, 369*
International Committee of the Red
        Cross, 373
International Convention for the
        Prevention of Pollution of the
        Seas by Oil, 467–68
International Court of Justice (ICJ),
        90*n,* 471
International Covenant on Civil and
        Political Rights (ICCPR),
        412–14, 419, 426
    article 4 of, 418
    article 6 of, 418*n*
    Optional Protocols of, 436*n*
International Covenant on Economic,
        Social, and Cultural Rights
        (ICESCR), 412–14, 416, 418,
        419, 426

International Criminal Court, *438,* 439, 441
    U.S. and, 439–40
International Institutions, *see* alliances; collective security organizations
International Longshore and Warehouse Union, 514
International Monetary Fund (IMF), 25, 63, *68,* 69, 214, 215, 262, *271,* 287, 288, 292, 325, 326, 344, 353, 510, *511,* 516, 518, 524
    and attitudes toward globalization, 272
    certification function of, 275
    China and, 507
    creation of, 275, 314–15
    criticism of, 277
    debt crises and, 262, 263, 269
    establishment of, 275, 314–15
    fairness question and, 277
    functions of, 315
    globalization and, 272
    Indonesian debt crisis and, 275–76
    international agreements and, 276
    LDCs and, 349, 359
    motivation of, 273
    national sovereignty issue and, 277
    oil states and, 355–56
    role of, 275–76, 280
    U.S. and political alignment of, 273
    voting power in, 349, *349*
    voting rules of, 525, 526–27, *526*
international monetary regimes, 309–10
International Telephone and Telegraph Company (ITT), 286
international trade, 238–52
    Bretton Woods system and, 314
    cooperation problem in, 239–42, 244, 247
    domestic policy and, 229
    dumping problem in, 241, 242
    expanding value of, *511*
    globalization and, 510, 518–20
    Heckscher-Ohlin theory and, 240
    information and negotiations in, 242–43
    international environment and, 238–39
    international institutions and, 244–48

    linking concerns in, 243–44
    national institutions and, 251–52
    openness and, 252
    policy changes in, 250–52
    Prisoner's Dilemma and, 241
    reciprocity in, 244–45
    regional trade agreements and, 239–40
    repeated interactions in, 243
    strategic interactions and, 239–44
    tariffs and, 240
    trade barriers policy and, 251–52
    trends and patterns in, 248–52
    winners and losers in, 229–30
International Trade Organization, 25*n*
International Whaling Commission (IWC), 451–52, 453, 468*n,* 470
Internet, *425,* 426, 510, 520
    globalization and, 510, 511–12
interstate war, defined, 86, 190
intra-firm trade, 224*n*
intra-industry trade, 224*n*
IRA, 390
Iran, 15, 27, 59, 73, 84, 88, 104, 347, *355,* 358, 391, 395, 493, *493,* 497, 520
    1979 Revolution in, 106–8
    nuclear program of, *94,* 106, 108, 492, 496, 497–99, 500
Iran-Iraq War (1980–1988), 84, 86–87, 94, 433
Iraq, 52, 56, 72, 103, 104, 111, 132, 151, 177
    impact of economic sanctions on, 434
    Kuwait invaded by, *see* Persian Gulf War
    nuclear program of, 497–99, 500
    Osirau reactor raid and, 499, 500
    U.S. bargaining with, 60, 61–62
    U.S. relations with, 44, 46, 60, 61–62
Iraq Survey Group, 59*n*
Iraq War (2003–), 34, 44, 81, 83–84, 96, 109, 122, 131, 142, 146, 177, 210, 400, 435
    actors in, 46
    bargaining in, 52
    bureaucracy debate and, 144
    coalition of the willing in, 42
    deaths in, 42

    inspectors problem and, 42–43, 62, 72–73
    insurgency in, 42
    national interests and, 47
    NATO and, 178
    oil interests and, 84, 147
    onset of, 41–43, 88, 90
    opposition to, 41–42, 49, 69, *126,* 178, 209, 395, 401
    Sunni-Shia conflict in, 123, 394
    U.N. and, 41–42, 43, 61, 70–71, 209
    U.S. invasion in, 147, 395
    WMDs and, 59, 66, 88, 178, 381
Ireland, 283, 308, 524
"iron triangle," 150*n*
irrendentism, 122–23
Ishay, Micheline R., 412*n*
Islam, 199, 387
Islamic extremists, 36, 488
isolationism, 21
Israel, 106, 108, 167, 177, *191,* 355, 388, 397, 402, 495
    AIPAC and, 147–48
    anti-terrorist retaliation policy of, 394–95, 399, *399*
    Basic Law of, 113, 115
    indivisibility of Jerusalem and, 113–14, 118
    Iran's nuclear program and, 492
    nuclear program of, 487, 490, 497
    Osirak reactor raid and, 499, 500
    Oslo Accords and, 396
    Ottawa Convention and, 367
    in Six Day War, 87, 111, 113
Italy, 15, 23, 174, 178, 186, 226, 290, 308, 316, 322, *337*
    in ECSC, 240, 521
    IMF and, 275
    in League Council, 194
    in Pact of Steel, 174, *180*
    rise of fascists in, 21
    trade barriers of, 251
    in Triple Alliance, 183–84, 185*n*
iteration:
    cooperation and, 57–58
    definition of, 57
    interactions and, 57, 454

James, Lacey, 49*n*
James, Patrick, 140*n*
Janjaweed militia, 439

Japan, 7, 11, 14, 15, 18, 22, 23, 25, 28,
35, 54, 57, 84, 107, 146, 160,
174, 186, 226, 231, 244, 245,
263, 271, 276, 302, 333, 454,
459, 487, 495, 504, 506
agricultural subsidies in, 519
Asian debt crisis and, 279
atomic bombing of, 23, 492
emissions target of, 445–46
EPI of, *462*
floating exchange rate of, *304*
in League Council, 194
MNCs restricted in, 286
in Russo-Japanese War, 18, 139
trade barriers of, 251
whaling industry and, 456, 470
Japanese-Americans, 420
Japanese Fisheries Agency, 453
Jerusalem, city of, 113–14, *114,* 118,
118
Jervis, Robert, 58*n*
Jews, 23, 113–14, 388
Johnson, Lyndon B., 142
Johnson, Simon, 345–46
Johnston, Alastair Iain, 507*n*
Jones, Owen Bennett, 164*n*
Jones, Seth G., 210*n*
Jordan, 87*n,* 111, 114, 177
Jupille, Joseph, 70*n,* 318*n*

Kahler, Miles, 368*n,* 403*n,* 418*n,* 527*n*
Kahn, Joseph, 270*n*
Kaltenthaler, Karl, 318*n*
Kant, Immanuel, 158–59, 160, 166–67
Kanter, James, 450*n*
Kargil War (1999), 164, 492
Karp, Jeffrey, 318*n*
Karsh, Efraim, 99*n*
Kashmir conflict, 87, 123, 164, 166
Kaunda, Kenneth, 331
Keck, Margaret E., 369*n,* 373*n,* 376
Keith, Linda Camp, 421*n*
Kennedy, John F., 27, *101,* 487, 490
Kennedy, Paul, 487*n,* 501*n*
Kenya, 29, *366*
1998 embassy bombing in, 388
Keohane, Robert O., 63*n,* 307*n*
Keynes, John Maynard, 218
protectionism as viewed by,
232–33
Khan, A. Q., 493

Khrushchev, Nikita, 27
Kim, Christine, 291*n*
Kim Il-Sung, 107
Kim Jong-Il, 107
Kindleberger, Charles P., 57*n*
Kirchner, Nestor, *243*
Klotz, Audie, 410*n,* 436*n*
Knorr, Klaus, 176*n*
Kobrin, Stephen J., 286*n*
Komatsu, Maseyuku, 453
Korea, People's Democratic Republic
of (North Korea), 24, 28, 88,
99–100, 171, 179, 198, 339, 395,
493
Agreed Framework and, 107
bargaining with, 107, 108
lack of transparency in, *160*
nuclear program of, 106, 487, 490,
493, 497–99, 500
South Korea compared with, 335
Korea, Republic of (South Korea), 28,
99–100, 106, 107, 148, 171, 172,
198, 211, 339, *352,* 358, 418,
459, 495, 506, 508
agricultural subsidies in, 519
EOI in, 352
financial crisis of 1997–1998 in,
279–80, 324, 325
globalization and, 249
North Korea compared with, 335
protectionism of, 249
U.S.'s alliance with, 174–75, *175*
Zambia compared with, 331–32,
332, 343
Korean War (1950–1953), 28, 67, 103,
104, 106, 179, 211, 335
onset of, 99–100, 171
public approval ratings and, 142
UN and, 171, 198
Kose, M. Ayhan, 262*n,* 265*n*
Kosovo, 34, 88, 178
Račak massacre in, 206
Kraay, Aart, 513*n,* 519*n*
Krain, Matthew, 420*n*
Krasner, Stephen D., 46*n,* 151*n,* 403*n*
Kristensen, Hans M., 502*n*
krona, Swedish, 318
krone, Danish, 318
Krueger, Alan B., 460*n*
Kubota, Keiko, 235*n*
Kukdong International Mexico, 379
Kurds, 423

Kuwait, 33, 41, 94–99, *95,* 103, 104,
160, 179, 199, 202, 203, 211,
355, 388, 434, 435
Kydd, Andrew, 392*n,* 396*n*
Kyoto Protocol (1997), *444,* 459
carbon trading system and, 450–51
Compliance Committee of, 471
U.S. opposition to, *444,* 446, 455,
461, 464

labor, labor unions, 229, 235, 316, 525
child, 403
globalization opposed by, 513–16,
517, 518, 524
human rights and, 424–25
interests and, 379
migration and, 288, 289–90
MNCs and, 283–84
protectionism and, 231–32
Stolper-Samuelson model and, 236
sweatshop, 284
trade and, 222–23
upholding standards of, 379
Labor Party, British, *58*
Lacina, Bethany Ann, 83*n*
LaFerrara, Eliana, 339*n*
Lafta, Riyadh, 42*n*
Laitin, David, 123*n,* 383*n*
Lake, David A., 44*n,* 46*n,* 68*n,* 165*n,*
180*n,* 228*n,* 242*n,* 339*n,* 391*n,*
403*n,* 418*n,* 527*n*
Lal, Rollie, 210*n*
Lalman, David, 162*n*
Lampton, David M., 508*n*
Landman, Todd, 421*n,* 429*n*
Lapan, Harvey E., 390*n,* 402*n*
Lapp, Nancy D., 339*n*
Latin America, 6, 22, 25, 37, 149, 323,
332, *337,* 346–47, 351, 358, 413,
427–28
debt crisis of 1982 in, *260,* 261–62,
268, 278
decolonization and, 28
electoral systems in, 235
human rights record of, 430
ISI in, 350
lost decade of, 262, 279
migration from, 288
North America compared with, 342
plantation agriculture of, 342
proposed currency union for, 327
terrorist incidents in, 385

Mohanty, Samarendu, 234*n*
Molotov-Ribbentrop Pact, (1939), 174, 180
monetary relations, 297–328
 and absence of international system, 308–9, 316, 327
 collaboration and, 311
 commodity standard and, 309–10
 conflicts of interest and, 307
 cooperation and conflict in, 310–11, 326–27
 exchange rates and, *see* exchange rates
 global nature of, 303
 gold standard and, 311–14
 institutions and, 328
 interactions and, 328
 interests and, 328
 international monetary regimes and, 309–10
 international order of, 308–9
 national order of, 308–9
 national paper currency standard and, 310
 Prisoner's Dilemma and, 311
 see also Bretton Woods System; currency; euro
monopolies, 7–8
Montreal Protocol (1989), 446, 468, 471
 implementation committee of, 471
Morales, Evo, 358
Moravcsik, Andrew, 422, 523*n*
Morocco, 18, 290
Morrow, James D., 160*n*, 420*n*
Morton, David, 373*n*
most favored nation status (MFN), 244–45, 508
 of China, 508, 514
Mozambique, 207
Mueller, John E., 138*n*
multinational corporations (MNCs), 282–87, 292, 348, 524
 and access to local markets, 283
 conflicts and, 285
 criticism of, 283–84
 debt crises and, 287
 environment and, 284
 expertise and, 284
 globalization and, 512–13
 host countries' interactions with, 285–87
 host countries' interests in, 284–85

human rights and, 284
labor standards and, 379
labor unions and, 283–84
local politics and, 286
motivation of, 282–83
national sovereignty and, 287
outsourcing and, 283–84
political considerations and, 286
resource location and, 283
restrictions on, 286–87
Mundell-Fleming conditions, 306*n*
Murray, Williamson, 49*n*
Musharraf, Pervez, 164
Mussa, Michael, 513*n*
Mussolini, Benito, 84
"mutually assured destruction", 116, 505–6
Myanmar (Burma), 335, 360, 520

Namibia, *82*
naming and shaming tactic, 375–76, 403, 410, 432, 433
Napoleon I, emperor of France, 10, 12, 501
Napoleonic Wars (1804–1815), 5, 10
National Commission on the Disappeared, Argentine, 420*n*
National Court, Spain, 438
national interests, 46–47, 130–32
nationalism, 15
 decolonization and, 28–29
national paper currency standard, 310
National Rifle Association (NRA), 373, 374
National Safety Council, 385
National Security Strategy (2002), U.S., 401
Nazis, 21
Nepal, 454, *454,* 461
Netherlands, 7, 10, 15, 146, 204–5, 308, 337, 447, 524
 in ECSC, 240, 521
Neumayer, Eric, 428*n*
New Deal, 413, 416
New International Economic Order, 30
 definition of, 354
New World, 7–8, 13, 15, 501
New Zealand, 23, 289, 332, 333, 345, *462,* 465
Nicaragua, 27, 418–19, 465
Niger, 465
Nigeria, *343*

Nike company, *283,* 379, 403
Nixon, Richard, 315
Nobel Peace Prize, 367, 447
Non-Aligned Movement, 354
nonderogable rights, 418
nonexcludable public goods, 56, 449–50
nongovernmental organizations (NGOs), 359, 364, 368, 370, 375, 471, 527
 boomerang model and, 376–77, *376*
 global governance and, 527, *528*
 human rights and, 424
 Ottawa Convention and, 367
nonintervention, principle of, 435–36
nonrival in consumption, 449–50
nonstate actors, 34, 368
norms, 372–75, 406
 behavior and, 373–74
 human rights and, 417–18
 internalization of, 375
 life cycle of, 373–75
 spread of, 373
norms cascade, 374–75
Norris, Robert S., 502*n*
North America, 11
 Latin America compared with, 342
North American Agreement on Labor Cooperation, 425*n*
North American Free Trade Agreement (NAFTA), 32, 37, 64, 67, 214, *216,* 219, 239, 242, 244, 322, 510, 528
 human rights provisions of, 425
 members of, 245
North Atlantic Treaty Organization (NATO), 30, 181, 186, 193, 211, 224, 423
 Afghan conflict and, 180
 article 5 of, 178
 Bosnia War and, 34, 178
 Cold War and, 24–25
 core provisions of, 186–88
 creation of, 24
 expansion of, 177–78, 187
 Iraq War and, 178
 in Kosovo intervention, 178, 206
 military integration and, 188
 9/11 attack and, 178
 U.S. and, 174–75, 188–89
Northern Ireland, 390
Norway, 32, 453, 465, 470, 519

Nuclear non-Proliferation Treaty (NPT) (1968), 495–97, *496*
  Article 10 of, 497
  noncompliance and, 497–99
  track record of, 496–97
nuclear weapons, 6, 71, 102, 106, 108, 115–16, 151, 398, 489
  in Cold War, 25–27, *55*, 505–6
  commitment problem and, 491
  Cuban missile crisis and, 27
  deterrence and, *see* deterrence
  first use of, 372
  Iran's program of, *94*, 106, 108, 492, 496, 497–99, 500
  Iraqi, 41
  JFK's prediction on, 487, 490
  nuclear taboo and, 372
  proliferation of, 498
  states in possession of, 490
  terrorism and, 373, 375
  in World War II, 23, 492
  see also weapons of mass destruction

Obama, Barack, 142, 372, 464
O'Brien, Richard, 248*n*
offensive alliances, 174–75, 177, 181*n*
O'Halloran, Sharyn, 236*n*
Ohlin, Bertil, 222
oil, 29–30, 41, 72, 86, 220, 283, 352, 354–55, 458
  ethanol and, 457
  Iraq War and, 84, 147
  price of, 131–32, *131*
  tanker cleaning controversy and, 468–69
  U.S. foreign policy and, 130–32, 153
Olson, Mancur, 57*n*, 339, 452*n*
Olympic Games, 409
  of 1980, 30
  of 2008, 172, *417*
Oneal, James, 149*n*
Open Skies Treaty (1992), 66
Oppenheimer, Peter, 232*n*
opportunity cost of production, 255–56
Organization for Cooperation and Security in Europe, 190
Organization for Economic Cooperation and Development (OECD), 331, 335
Organization of African Unity, 409
Organization of American States, 190
Organization of Petroleum Exporting

Countries (OPEC), 29, 354–55, *355*
  oil shocks of 1973–1974 and, 31
O'Rourke, Kevin, 290*n*
Orwell, George, 417
Oslo Peace Accords (1993), 396
Ostrom, Elinor, 454*n*
Ottawa Convention, 367
Ottoman Empire, 12, 18, 21, 84
  collapse of, 19–20
outbidding strategy, 396–97
outside options, 61
outsourcing, 283–84
ozone depletion, 364, 365, 446, 447, 452–54, 455, 472–73
  Antarctic ozone hole and, 446, 477, *477*
  CFCs and, 477–78
  chemistry of, *476*
  nonexcludability and, 450
  nonrivalry and, 450
  science of, 476–78, *476–78*
  treaties controlling, *456*
  UV radiation and, 476, 477–78

Pact of Steel (1939), 174, *180*
Pakistan, 210, 386, 398, 494
  in Kargil War, 164, 492
  Kashmir conflict and, 87, 123, 164, 166
  nuclear program of, 487, 490, 493, 495, 497
  Ottawa convention and, 367
Palestinian Authority, 395, 396
Palestinians, 118, 387
Panama, 308, 317
Pan Am flight 103 bombing (1988), 135
Pape, Robert A., 394*n*, 402*n*
Paraguay, *243*, 245, 418–19
Pareto, Vilfredo, 51
Pareto frontier, 51–52, *51*, 237, 448, 449, 464
Parliament, British, 13
Parliament, European, *488*, 522
Partido Revolucionario Institucional (PRI), Mexican, 323
Paulson, Cole, 90*n*
Pax Britannica, 10–15
  balance of power and, 12
  colonialism and, 14–15
  Concept of Europe and, 12
  free trade and, 12–13
  gold standard and, 14

Hundred Years' Peace and, 11–12
  mercantilism and, 12–13
peacekeeping operations, 125, *191*, 193, 196, 210
  in Bosnia conflict, 203–5
  cost of, 208
  host nations and, 196–97
  P5 and, 195–98
  in Rwanda, 205
  size of, *208*
  UN and, 196–98, 200–205, 208, 210
Peace of Westphalia (1648), 10
Pearl Harbor attack, 23, 160, 420
Peloponnesian Wars, 503
People's Liberation Army, Chinese, 171
perestroika, 31
Pérez, Carlos Andrés, 277
Permanent 5 (P5), 194, 199, 207, 209, 496, 497
  peacekeeping operations and, 195–98
Peronist Party, Argentine, 297
Persia (Iran), 15
Persian Gulf War (1991), 33, 41, 64, 67, 73, 103, 104, 131, 142, 179, 207, 209, 210, 211, 434, 497
  coalition in, 199, *202*
  credibility and, 97–99
  Hussein and onset of, 94–95, *95*, 97–98, 99, 160
  incomplete information and, 94–95, *95*, 98–99
  international support for, 199–202
  Kuwait invaded in, 33, 34, 36, 41, 94–95, 199, 202, 388
  Resolution 678 and, 199
  UN and, 33, 64–65, 198, 199–203, 434
Peru, 397, 440
peso, Argentine, 298, *298*, 306, 320, 321
peso, Mexican, 300, 308, 322, *323*
Peterson, M. J., 451*n*
Pew Global Attitudes Project, 395
Philippines, 29, 220, 234, 506, 512
  Asian financial crisis of 1997–1998 and, 278–79, 324, 325
Physical Integrity Index, 430
Pinochet, Augusto, 286, 437–38
Planned Parenthood, 370
Plehve, Vladimir, 139*n*

Russia, Imperial, 12, 18, 19, 84, 112,
  185
  financial crisis of 1890 in, 312
  France's anti-German alliance with,
    176–77, 184
  in prelude to World War I, 179
  Revolution of 1905 in, 141
  in Triple Entente, 184
Russia, postcommunist, 33, 35, 57, 206,
    284, 337, 454, 471, 490, 496,
    497
  Chechnya conflict of, 125, *391*
  globalization and, 36–37
  Iraq War opposed by, 41–42, 49,
    69, 209
  1998 debt crisis in, 274, 278, 280,
    324
  Ottawa Convention and, 367
  in Permanent 5, 194, 199
  Security Council seat of, 69
Russo-Japanese War (1904–1905), 18,
    139, 141
Rwanda, 34, *82,* 190, 205, 207, 209,
    211

Saar, 22
Sachs, Jeffrey D., 334*n,* 343*n,* 356*n*
safeguard agreements, 496
Sagan, Scott D., 164*n,* 491*n,* 493*n,*
    495*n,* 497*n*
Sagarmatha National Park, Nepal, 461
Sainteny, Jean, 61*n*
Saint Vincent and the Grenadines, 440
Salinas, Carlos, 271
Sambanis, Nicholas, 207*n*
Samsung, *352*
Sandler, Todd, 383*n,* 390*n,* 399*n,* 402*n,*
    454*n*
Sarkozy, Nicolas, *128*
Sartori, Anne, 103*n*
satellite technology, 116
Satyanath, Shanker, 124*n*
Saudi Arabia, 98, 113, 131–32, 167, 177,
    202, 355, 413
  Al Qaeda expelled from, 387
  Aramco and, 130
  Iran's nuclear program and, 492
  U.S.'s withdrawal of troops from,
    387–89, 402
Sawers, Larry, 9*n*
scapegoating, 138
Schelling, Thomas, 61, 102, 189, 398*n*

Scheve, Kenneth, 520*n*
Schlieffen Plan, 112, 184
Schroeder, Paul, 176*n*
Schultz, Kenneth A., 161*n*
Schwartz, Thomas, 378*n*
Schweller, Randall, 177*n*
secessionism, 122–23
Sechser, Todd S., 146*n*
second-strike force, 491–92, 508
selective incentives, 454*n*
self-reporting, 469
Senate, Argentine, 297
Senate, U.S., 21, 68, 235, 250
  Agriculture Committee of, 234
  dollar depreciation resolution of,
    307
Senegal, 236–37, 438
Serbia, 84, 88, 112, 184, 203, 206
Sergenti, Ernest, 124*n*
Serra Puche, Jaime, *323*
Seven Years' War (1756–1763), 10
Shafer, Michael, 343*n*
Shapiro, Catherine R., 138*n*
Shapiro, Jeremy, 178*n*
Sharif, Nawaz, 164
Shell oil, 403
Sherman, William, 84
Shiites, 42, 46, 123, 394
Shining Path, 397
Shinn, James, 507*n*
Siam, *see* Thailand
Siemens, 284
Sierra Club, 278
Sierra Leone, 207
Sigmund, Paul, 286*n*
Sikkink, Kathryn, 369*n,* 373, 376,
    409*n,* 432*n*
Silent Spring (Carson), 447
silver standard, 310, *312,* 313
Simons, Marlise, 438*n,* 439*n*
Singapore, 325, 352
Singer, J. David, 86*n*
Singer, Peter, 357, 461*n*
Single European Act (1986), 69, 240
Siverson, Randolph M., 58*n,* 160*n*
Six Day War (1967), 87, 111, 113
Skidelsky, Robert, 218*n,* 232*n*
Slaughter, Ann-Marie, 369*n*
Slaughter, Matthew, 520*n*
slavery, 128, 364, 375, 413, 414
  in American South, 342–43
Slovakia, 178

Slovenia, 178, 203
Small, Melvin, 86*n*
Smith, Adam, 15, 220, *220*
Smith, Alastair, 160*n*
Smith, Heather, 436*n*
Smith, Jackie, 370*n*
Snidal, Duncan, 54*n,* 70*n*
Snyder, Glenn H., 182*n*
Snyder, Jack, 154*n,* 185*n*
Softwood Lumber Agreement (1996),
    242–43
Sokoloff, Kenneth, 342
Solomon, king of Israel, 113, 114
Solomon, S., 445*n*
Somalia, 33–34, 388, 400, 427
Soros, George, 325
South Africa, 123, 263, 433, 440, 465
  anti-apartheid movement in, 377,
    408, 409–10, 419, 435–36
  nuclear program of, 496–97
Southern Common Market, *see*
    Mercosur
sovereign lending, 264
sovereignty, 10, 46, 521
Soviet Union, 5, 6, 7, 23, 32, 136, 163,
    171, 186, 188, 193, 195, *229,*
    335, 354, 398, 413, 435, 445–46,
    471, 495, 504, 516, 521
  Afghanistan invaded by, 28, 30, 97,
    130–31, 388
  collapse of, 33, 56*n,* 178, 199, 487,
    496, 501, 510
  Cuban missile crisis and, 27, *101*
  Czechoslovakia invaded by, 27
  decolonization and, 29
  Hungary invaded by, 27
  on Molotov-Ribbentrop pact, 174,
    177, 180
  NPT signed by, 496
  in Permanent 5, 194
  U.S.'s Cold War rivalry with, 6,
    23–30, 55, 64, 66, 88, 98, 102,
    116, 186, 198, 224, 378, 493,
    501, 504
  in World War II, 174
Spain, 7, 8–10, 15, 178, 332, *337,* 501
  Basque separatists and, 390–91,
    394
  Madrid train bombings in, 368,
    381, 388, 400
  Pinochet prosecution and, 437–38
Spanish Armada, 8

Sparta, city-state of, 503
specific factors approach *see* Ricardo-Viner model
speculators, 324–25
speech, freedom of, 155
spoiling strategy, 390, 404
Sprinz, Detlef F., 470n
Srebrenica massacre (1995), 204–5
Sri Lanka, 397, 401, 402
Stag Hunt game, 78–79, 79
Stalingrad, Battle of (1943), 23
Stam, Allan C., 60n
Stasavage, David, 339n
state, definition of, 46
State Department, U.S., 98, 144, 150, 430, 435
    national interests and, 47
State of the Union (1991), 103, 202
State of the Union (1994), 155
steam power, 13, 14
steel industry, 219, 227, 228
    protection of, 229–30, 231, 232, 233
Stein, Arthur A., 54n
Stein, Ernesto, 308n
Stiglitz, Joseph E., 324, 343n, 348n, 359n
Stolper-Samuelson theorem, 230–32, 513, 515, 517
    labor and, 236
strategic ambiguity, policy of, 182–83
Strategic Defense Initiative, 31
Strategic Offensive Reductions Treaty (SORT), 502n
strategy, definition of, 50
Stueck, William, 100n
submarine warfare, 18
Sudan, 195, 195, 205, 387, 388, 403, 423, 439
    famine in, 357
Sudetenland, 186
suffrage, 128, 364
sugar industry, 217, 231, 458n
    protection of, 218–19, 233–35
Suharto, 276–324
suicide attacks, 383, 384, 491n, 493
Summers, Robert, 335n
Sunnis, 42, 46, 123, 394
supply, 257, 301
    commodity cartels and, 355
Supreme Court, Spain, 438n
Supreme Court, U.S., 372n, 437n

SVR (Foreign Intelligence Service), Russian, 144
Swanger, Rachel M., 210n
sweatshop labor, 284
Sweden, 290, 316
    euro and, 317, 318, 523–24
Switzerland, 32, 453
Syria, 87, 106, 111, 192, 372
    nuclear program of, 107, 495, 499

Taiwan, 103, 182–83, 195n, 198, 279, 324, 325, 332, 339, 495, 508
    EOI in, 352–53
Taliban, 97, 123, 178, 368, 387, 388, 395, 400
Tamil Tigers, 397, 401, 402
Tannenwald, Nina, 373n
Tanzania, 388, 465
tariffs, 225, 239, 259, 458n
    deadweight loss and, 258–59
    protectionism and, 225–26, 228, 229
    trade and, 225–26, 228, 229, 240
Tate, C. Neal, 420n, 421n
Taylor, A. J. P., 504n
Taylor, A. M., 303n
Teamsters Union, 514
technology, 488–89
    bargaining and, 488–89
    globalization and, 509–10, 511, 516, 528–29
    military, 490
    WMD proliferation and, 494
Telefónica de España, 282, 283
Temple Mount, 114
terms of trade, 347
terrorism, 36, 84, 125, 151, 178, 365, 369, 381–405
    as asymmetrical warfare, 384
    bomb scares and, 394
    casualties of, 381, 382, 385
    and choice of violence, 381–82
    commitment problem and, 390–91
    compromise and, 402
    cooperation and, 404
    cost of, 389
    credible threats of, 389–90, 392, 393, 398
    criminalization of, 400
    defensive measures against, 399–400, 399

deterrence of, 398, 401, 493–94
element of surprise and, 389
extremists and, 386, 386
globalization and, 528
home population and, 395–97
incidents of, 383, 385
incomplete information and, 389–90, 392
indivisibilities and, 391–92
interstate interactions and, 404
Israeli retaliation policy and, 394–95, 399, 399
local population and, 387
monitoring, 401
negotiation and, 402
networks of, 386–87
nuclear, 373, 375
object of, 384–85
organizational forms of, 386–87, 390
outbidding strategy of, 396–97
preemption strategy and, 401
prevention of, 397
provocation strategy of, 394–95, 398
random targets of, 384, 385
rationality of, 382–84
religions, 391–92
separatist conflicts and, 391
spoiling strategy of, 396, 404
state-sponsored, 381n
strategic logic of, 384–87
strategies of, 392–97, 393
suicide tactic of, 383, 384, 491n, 493
U.S.'s global war on, 368, 381
violence and, 385, 387–89
WMDs and, 398, 490, 493
see also specific events
terrorist attacks of September 11, 2001, 72, 137, 178, 384, 385, 388, 394–95, 401, 404, 420
    Al Qaeda and, 367–68
    casualties in, 381
    UN response to, 207–9
    U.S. response to, 399–400
    warning signs of, 390
textile industry, 13, 514
Thacker, Strom, 273
Thailand, 15, 264, 347, 358, 360
    Burma compared with, 335